Index to Illustrations of the Natural World

Index to Illustrations of the Natural World

Where to Find Pictures of the Living Things of North America

Compiled by JOHN W. THOMPSON

Edited by NEDRA SLAUSON

GAYLORD PROFESSIONAL PUBLICATIONS

Gaylord Bros., Inc., Syracuse, New York 13201

1977

Library of Congress Cataloging in Publication Data

Thompson, John W   1891-
    Index to illustrations of the natural world.

    Includes bibliography: p.
        1. Zoology—North America—Pictorial works—Indexes.
2. Botany—North   America—Pictorial   works—Indexes.
3. Zoology—North America—Indexes.   4. Botany—North
America—Indexes.   I. Title.
Z7998.N67T45 [QL151] 016.57497′022′2 77-4143
ISBN 0-915794-12-8

© John W. Thompson and Lucille Thompson Munz 1977
First published 1977 as a Gaylord Professional Publication,
Gaylord Bros., Inc., Syracuse, New York.

Printed in the United States of America

Contents

Preface

When I first began collecting plants in the 1920's, I had great difficulty in locating descriptive material and illustrations that would enable me to identify them. There was at that time no book available that even began to cover the plants of the Pacific Northwest. So, when I started to correspond with other botanists about the name of a certain plant, and we thought we had discovered what it was, I would record it with name and supporting data on a file card. This index to plants grew so fast that I soon had files full of cards -- several thousands of them. I would add to each of the cards the titles of books that I and other people had found, which had pictures and other data about each plant.

When my teaching responsibilities changed from botany to zoology I was faced with the need to identify animals, reptiles and fishes. Consulting many textbooks and a great variety of reference resources, I began as I had with the plants, to record data on cards, building a file in which items could be found under both their common and their scientific names. I started to collect a large library of books and with each new one, on whatever form of life, I had an addition to my file of sources of good pictures and information. I now have a library of some 3,500 titles on plants, mammals and other forms of life, and many of them are rare editions.

As early as the early 1940's when I was teaching at Cleveland High School in Seattle, I found that pictures can be a very important aid to learning. I used some borrowed slides in a classroom presentation and it was so effective that I convinced the principal that he ought to buy a camera so that other faculty members could make their own slides for use in teaching. By the time I moved on to another school in the system to teach biology, I had a camera of my own and from then on I made slides for my own teaching and for my fellow teachers. From there I eventually branched out to make slides and sell them by mail to teachers around the world.

Never was I in a school where there was enough money to buy all the books I wanted, so my students and I would raise special varieties of plants and have a plant sale in the spring. They worked hard and they loved it, and they felt a special pride in the books they were able to earn for the school library -- books with wonderful pictures of the natural world like those indexed in this book. Young people can relate to the natural world so well if they can only be made aware of it, and pictures in a good book are a fine way to start.

I love all kinds of books myself. When I had to drop out of school as a young boy, after attending for only three months, I taught myself to read by sounding out the letters I had learned in borrowed copies of **Robinson Crusoe, Treasure Island** and **Mrs. Wiggs of the Cabbage Patch**. I kept at it until I could read them all the way through, and I vowed that the first money I earned would go to buy a book -- and it did!

I have always wanted to stimulate awareness in others. The living things of the natural world have been a major part of my life, and sharing them with others has been my greatest joy. Hiking and riding in the mountains on discovery trips with my own children or my students, collecting, pressing and mounting specimens, and photographing them -- all of this has made me keenly <u>aware</u>. Any fool can destroy, but there is wisdom and lasting satisfaction in recognizing, learning about and preserving all of the varieties of life the earth has given us.

And now my index, developed in card files for so long, has become a book. I hope it will lead others to some of the joys that I have known.

John W. Thompson

Seattle, Washington
March, 1977

Biographical Data

John W. Thompson

This book represents a lifetime of enthusiasm and effort by an extraordinary man, now well into his eighties, who has been a science teacher, botanist, natural historian and producer of science media. Eighteen Northwestern plants have been named in his honor. Some of these had never before been sighted in the region until he found them, while others, like Thompson's Clover -- a seven-leaflet species -- has never been found elsewhere in the world. A section of the Wenatchee National Forest was dedicated in 1974 as the Thompson Clover Research Native Area -- one of many honors Mr. Thompson has received.

A backwoods boy who went to work in logging camps and lumber mills when he was 15, John, encouraged by a mill supervisor who was impressed by his ability, entered public elementary school at 17. Because he had taught himself to read and figure, he was able to complete enough schooling in two years to pass the examination for a teacher's certificate. He taught in a one-room school while he continued his own studying evenings and summers. During this period he began field work in botany, collecting and drying specimens. At age 34 he qualified to enter Willamette University to earn his master's degree in botany.

For many years an outstanding teacher in Seattle's public schools, Mr. Thompson taught both botany and zoology. Forced into early retirement because of ill health, he built up his own herbarium and presented it to the University of Washington botany department. He served for a number of years as the collection's assistant curator. He built up also the business he continues to this day: making and distributing photographic slides to be used in science teaching. More than a million of his slides have been used in the study of natural history in schools across this country and throughout the world.

Mr. Thompson started more than 50 years ago to compile information for an index to illustrations of plants, birds and animals. His purpose was, in his own words, "to provide librarians with a resource so that anybody who comes in and wants to know what a killer whale, a killdeer or kinnikinnick looks like can quickly find several sources of pictures of them."

Lucille Thompson Munz

Lucille Thompson Munz has accompanied and assisted her father for more than 20 years on many field trips to photograph plants and wildlife. They have ranged over the entire state of Washington and have toured the other western states -- Oregon, Idaho, Montana, Utah, Nevada, Arizona, Colorado, California -- making the outstanding photographs that have given Mr. Thompson's slides a world-wide reputation for excellence. Mrs. Munz also takes an active role in the day-to-day conduct of the Thompson slide business, commuting between her father's home in Seattle and the Munz family home 60 miles to the northeast in the Cascade Mountains.

Nedra G. Slauson

Nedra Slauson is a free-lance librarian and publications specialist. Her undergraduate degree was in journalism and she has a master's degree from the University of Washington School of Librarianship. Associated with a Seattle communications/publications firm, Barbara Krohn and Associates, she has had many years of experience as a writer and editor, and is a community college librarian. An active outdoorswoman, Mrs. Slauson is a member of the Seattle Mountaineers; she was able to share Mr. Thompson's enthusiasm for his subject through every step of their collaboration.

Introduction

A primary consideration in designing a reference book is its scope: How broad should its coverage be for maximum value to the user? In a book which is, like this one, an index to other books, this means not only how many entries it will include, but also how many source books it will refer the user to. There are approximately 6,200 entries -- plants, birds and animals -- listed in **Index to Illustrations of the Natural World**; the pictures of them cited are to be found in a total of 178 books, including many multi-volume works.

Each entry was chosen for the Index on the basis of two principal criteria: its existence in or on the North American continent, either as a wild or an introduced species; and its place in the organizational pattern of nature. For example, the ring-necked pheasant, an introduced species extant on this continent although native to Asia is included, while the passenger pigeon, native to North America but extinct since 1914, is omitted. The second criterion means that only a few of the thousands of beetle species are included, because an attempt to cover every beetle species in North America would require a disproportionate amount of attention to a specialized area in entomology.

Most of the books referred to in this Index have been published since 1960, but some classic works published earlier have been included. Almost all the books have some illustrations in color, and the great majority of the recent titles are illustrated entirely in color. All forms of illustration are represented -- paintings, line drawings and photographs.

Books were selected on the basis of their authoritativeness in their fields -- whether biology, botany, herpetology, or other natural science -- and also on the quality and abundance of their illustrations. Reproduction of pictures in a few of the older titles is not up to today's best printing standards but citations to a few such titles have been included for some uncommon items to increase the user's chance of finding an illustration of his subject. No entry has been included in the Index for which fewer than two reasonably good citations could be found, and for most entries the Index user is referred to from 5 to 10 illustrations.

Availability of the books in most medium-sized and larger libraries was an important criterion in selection. Several fine books of very limited circulation were excluded because it was thought that the user's chance of locating a copy would probably require access to a large academic or research library. Some older works, long out of print in hard-cover, have been included among the sources because they are now available in soft-cover reprints.

Geographically, the scope of the Index is from the Arctic Circle to Central America and from the Atlantic to the Pacific, including Hawaii and the Caribbean. Migratory creatures such as birds are included if they are found in North America at least occasionally. Coastal ocean life and deep-water varieties of fish and other marine species are included among the entries.

Organization of the Index

Each item is entered by its common name in **boldface** type. The common name is followed by its scientific name (in parentheses). If an entry has more than one widely used common name, it is found under the name used by most of the books in the Bibliography, with "see" references from the other names. When one name applies to two or more categories of living things, each category is identified (in boldface type) after the common name. For example, **Periwinkle, Greater (plant)** (Vinca major) and **Periwinkle, Sitka (mollusk)** (Littorina sitkana).

For the user of the Index who has only an item's scientific name, there is a **Scientific Name Index** included in the back of the book, so that the common name may be identified. If several species of the same genus, or several genera, are known by the same common name, their citations may be grouped under a single entry. Items which have been reclassified, or whose classification is in dispute, may have more than one scientific name listed.

Each book title to which the Index user is referred has been given a three-letter code. For example, **Dictionary of Birds in Color** by Bruce Campbell, New York, Viking Press, 1974 has the designation CDB; while **Oxford Book of Trees** by A.R. Clapham, London, Oxford University Press, 1975 is coded in the entries as OBT. The coded title to which the reader is referred is followed by page number and/or color or black and white plate number in that book. The title of the book is identified by consulting the **Bibliography by Code Letters** (pp. 15 – 21) which lists all titles indexed in alphabetical order by code letters. This Bibliography is found immediately following this preface and is printed on heavy paper stock to withstand frequent use. Citations within each entry are in alphabetical order to facilitate the decoding process of identifying the books needed.

The following entry is given as an example:

> **Eagle, Bald** (Haliaeetus leucocephalus) AAB 105; ALE 7:376, 8:229;
> ANE 3:581-582, 587; BBC 1:cp 30; CFG cp 3; GBC 104 (cp 15); GPB 95;
> IWE 1:128-129; NGB 1:66; NGW 236, 238-243; PBA 22:cps 43, 49;
> PEB 67 (pl 20); PWB 75 (pl 18); RBB 77; WAB 69.

Analysis of the meaning of this entry is as follows:

The illustration in AAB (decoded: The Audubon Illustrated Handbook of American Birds. Edgar M. Reilly, Jr. Drawings by Albert Earl Gilbert. New York, McGraw Hill, 1968.) is on page 105.

ALE's (Grzimek's Animal Life Encyclopedia. Bernard Grzimek, editor in chief. 13 vols.
New York, Van Nostrand Reinhold, 1974.) Volume 7 has an illustration on page 376, while
Volume 8's illustration is on page 229.

Volume 3 of ANE (Audubon Nature Encyclopedia. 12 vols. Philadelphia, Curtis Publishing,
1964) has an illustration across all or part of pages 581 and 582, plus another on page 587.

In BBC, (Birds of Colorado, Alfred M. Bailey and Robert J. Niedrich. 2 vols. Denver Museum of
Natural History, 1965.) Volume 1, the illustration is found on an unnumbered page identified as
color plate 30.

NGW (Water, Prey and Game Birds of North America. Washington, D.C., The National Geographic
Society, 1965.) has an illustration on page 236 and additional pictures on consecutive pages from
238 through 243.

PBA, (Birds of America. T. Gilbert Pearson, editor-in-chief. 3 vols in 1. Garden City, N.Y.,
Garden City Books, 1936.) Volume 2, shows the bald eagle on color plates 43 and 49.

PEB's (Field Guide to the Birds (east of the Rockies). Roger Tory Peterson. 2nd ed. Boston,
Houghton Mifflin, 1947.) illustration is on page 67, black and white plate 20.

Abbreviations are: **color plate(s)** -- cp(s). (Note that cps 21, 23 means two color plates,
while cp 21, 27 means the item is illustrated on color plate 21 and also on p. 27); **black-and-white
plate(s)** -- pl(s); **species** -- sp.; **variation** -- var. Note also that when the genus name is used a second
time in the same entry it is abbreviated by its initial letter (i.e. Douglasia laevigate and D. nivalis).

Entries are arranged alphabetically word by word: thus **Garlic** (without a modifying adjective)
precedes **Garlic, Field or Crow**, and **Top Shell** precedes **Topminnow** and **Sugar Bowl** precedes
Sugarberry. A hyphenated word is considered one word, so **Lily, Zephyr** precedes **Lily-of-the-Nile**.
Names of items beginning with an abbreviation -- as in **St.-John's-wort**, are placed as if the abbreviated
word were spelled out.

In a book of this kind, composed as it is of detail, the potential for error is great. All possible
care has been taken to minimize the occurrence of mistakes: every entry's citations have been
checked and rechecked against the sources, and painstaking care has been taken in both composition
and proof-reading. The editor wishes to acknowledge gratefully the careful and interested assistance
of Christine Vilches and above all the dedicated help of Lucile Thompson Munz who, with her
father and myself, served as a full and able partner in the making of a book from Mr. Thompson's
remarkable life work.

Nedra G. Slauson

Seattle, Washington
March, 1977

Bibliography by Code Letters

AAB The Audubon Illustrated Handbook of American Birds. Edgar M. Reilly, Jr. Drawings by Albert Earl Gilbert. New York, McGraw-Hill, 1968.

AAS American Seashells. R. Tucker Abbott. Photos by Frederick M. Bayer. Princeton, N.J., D. Van Nostrand, 1960 (c1954).

ABW Birds of the World. Oliver L. Austin, Jr. New York, Golden Press, 1961.

AFP Illustrated Flora of the Pacific States: Washington. Oregon and California. Leroy Abrams and Roxana Stinchfield Ferris. 4 vols. Stanford, Calif., Stanford University Press, 1960.

AGF The Complete Guide to Garden Flowers. Herbert Askwith, editor. New York, A. S. Barnes, 1961.

ALE Grzimek's Animal Life Encyclopedia. Bernhard Grzimek, editor-in-chief. 13 vols. New York, Van Nostrand Reinhold, 1974.

AMB Finding the Birds in Western Mexico. Peter Alden. Tucson, University of Arizona Press, 1969.

ANE Audubon Nature Encyclopedia. 12 vols. Philadelphia, Curtis Publishing, 1964.

ASN Seashells of North America. R. Tucker Abbott. (Golden Field Guide series.) New York, Golden Press, 1968.

AWW Rand McNally Atlas of World Wildlife. Foreword by Sir Julian Huxley. New York, Rand McNally, 1973.

BAR Amphibians and Reptiles of Kentucky. Roger W. Barbour. (Kentucky Nature Studies: 2.) Lexington, University Press of Kentucky, 1971.

BAW Animals without Backbones. Ralph Buchsbaum. Rev. ed. Chicago, University of Chicago Press, 1948.

BBC Birds of Colorado. Alfred M. Bailey and Robert J. Niedrach. 2 vols. Denver Museum of Natural History, 1965.

BBE Birds of Europe. Bertel Bruun. Paintings by Arthur Singer. New York, Golden Press, 1971.

BBF An Illustrated Flora of the Northern United States, Canada and the British Possessions. Nathaniel Lord Britton and Addison Brown. 2d ed. 3 vols. New York Botanical Garden, 1936.

BBW Birds of Western North America. Laurence C. Binford. Paintings by Kenneth L. Carlson. New York, Macmillan, 1974.

BGM Field Guide to the Mammals. William Henry Burt. Illustrated by Richard Philip Grossenheider. 2d ed., rev. (Peterson Field Guide series.) Boston, Houghton Mifflin, 1964.

BHB Hawaiian Birdlife. Andrew J. Berger. Honolulu, University Press of Hawaii, 1972.

BIA A Field Guide to the Insects of America north of Mexico. Donald J. Borror and Richard E. White. (Peterson Field Guide series.) Boston, Houghton Mifflin Co., 1970.

BKT The Glory of the Tree. B. K. Boom and H. Kleijn. Garden City, N.Y., Doubleday, 1966.

BLA The Lower Animals: Living Invertebrates of the World. Ralph Buchsbaum and Lorus J. Milne, with Mildred Buchsbaum and Margery Milne. (World of Nature series.) Garden City, N.Y., Doubleday, 1962.

BMC The Mammals of Canada. A. W. F. Banfield. Toronto, Ont., University of Toronto Press, 1974.

BOW Owls of the World. John A. Burton, editor. New York, E. P. Dutton, 1973.

BRW The World of Reptiles and Amphibians. Maurice Burton. New York, Crown Publishers, 1973.

BTN   Trees of North America. C. Frank Brockman. (Golden Field Guide series.) New York, Golden Press, 1968.

BWI   Birds of the West Indies. James Bond. 2d ed. Boston, Houghton Mifflin, 1971.

CAW   Living Amphibians of the World. Doris M. Cochran. (World of Nature series.) Garden City, N.Y., Doubleday, 1961.

CDB   Dictionary of Birds in Color. Bruce Campbell. New York, Viking Press, 1974.

CFG   Complete Field Guide to American Wildlife (east, central and north). Henry Hill Collins, Jr. New York, Harper, 1959.

CFW   Fishes of the World. Allan Cooper. (Grosset All-Color Guide.) New York, Grosset and Dunlap, 1971.

CGF   A Field Guide to the Ferns and Their Related Families. Boughton Cobb. (Peterson Field Guide series.) Boston, Houghton Mifflin, 1963.

CGR   The New Field Book of Reptiles and Amphibians. Doris M. Cochran and Coleman J. Goin. New York, G. P. Putnam's Sons, 1970.

COA   Native Orchids of North America (north of Mexico). Donovan Stewart Correll. Waltham, Mass., Chronica Botanica, 1950.

CRA   Field Guide to Reptiles and Amphibians of the Eastern United States and Canada. Roger Conant. (Peterson Field Guide series.) Boston, Houghton Mifflin, 1958.

CSB   The Spider Book. John Henry Comstock. Garden City, N.Y., Doubleday, Page, 1920.

CWF   Wild Flowers of British Columbia. Lewis J. Clark. Sidney, B.C., Gray's Publishing, 1973.

DBM   Field Guide to the Birds of Mexico and Central America. L. Irby Davis. Illustrated by F. P. Bennett, Jr. Austin, University of Texas Press, 1972.

DEW   Plants of the World. H. C. D. deWit. 3 vols. New York, E. P. Dutton, 1966-1969.

DFP   Color Dictionary of Flowers and Plants for Home and Garden. Roy Hay and Patrick M. Synge. New York, Crown Publishers, 1969.

DPW   Pheasants of the World. Jean Delacour. Illustrated by J. C. Harrison. London, Country Life, 1965 (c1951, 1957).

DRW   Reptiles of the World. Raymond L. Ditmars. Rev. ed. New York, Macmillan, 1941 (c1933).

EGA   Annuals. James Underwood Crockett. (Time-Life Encyclopedia of Gardening.) New York, Time-Life Books, 1971.

EGB   Bulbs. James Underwood Crockett. (Time-Life Encyclopedia of Gardening.) New York, Time-Life Books, 1971.

EGE   Evergreens. James Underwood Crockett. (Time-Life Encyclopedia of Gardening.) New York, Time-Life Books, 1971.

EGP   Perennials. James Underwood Crockett. (Time-Life Encyclopedia of Gardening.) New York, Time-Life Books, 1972.

EGT   Trees. James Underwood Crockett. (Time-Life Encyclopedia of Gardening.) New York, Time-Life Books, 1972.

EWF   Wild Flowers of the World. Barbara Everard and Brian D. Morley. New York, G. P. Putnam's Sons, 1970.

FFK   Guide to the Wildflowers and Ferns of Kentucky. Mary E. Wharton and Roger W. Barbour. (Kentucky Nature Studies: 1.) Lexington, University Press of Kentucky, 1971.

FGF   Garden Flowers in Color. Daniel J. Foley. New York, Macmillan, 1959 (c1943).

FHP   Flowering House Plants. James Underwood Crockett. (Time-Life Encyclopedia of Gardening.) New York, Time-Life Books, 1971.

FNC Wild Flowers of North Carolina. William S. Justice and C. Ritchie Bell. Chapel Hill, University of North Carolina Press, 1968.

FWA Fascinating World of Animals. Pleasantville, N.Y., Reader's Digest Association, 1971.

GAS Animals of the Seashore. Muriel Lewin Guberlet. 3d ed., rev. Portland, Ore., Binfords and Mort, 1962.

GBB The Gardener's Bug Book. Cynthia Westcott. 3d ed. Garden City, N.Y., Doubleday, 1964.

GBC The Birds of Canada. W. Earl Godfrey. Ottawa, Ontario, National Museum of Canada (Bulletin 203), 1966.

GBI Birds: A Guide to the Most Familiar American Birds. Herbert S. Zim and Ira N. Gabrielson. (Golden Nature Guide series.) New York, Golden Press, 1956.

GFB Families of Birds. Oliver L. Austin, Jr. (Golden Science Guide series.) New York, Golden Press, 1971.

GGB Gamebirds: A Guide to North American Species and Their Habits. Alexander Sprunt IV and Herbert S. Zim. (Golden Nature Guide series.) New York, Golden Press, 1961.

GGF Fishes: A Guide to Familiar American Species. Herbert S. Zim and Hurst H. Shoemaker. (Golden Nature Guide series.) New York, Golden Press, 1956.

GGI Insects: A Guide to Familiar American Insects. Herbert S. Zim and Clarence Cottam. (Golden Nature Guide series.) New York, Golden Press, 1951.

GGM Mammals: A Guide to Familiar American Species. Herbert S. Zim and Donald F. Hoffmeister. (Golden Nature Guide series.) New York, Golden Press, 1955.

GGS Seashores: A Guide to Animals and Plants along the Beaches. Herbert S. Zim and Lester Ingle. (Golden Nature Guide series.) New York, Golden Press, 1955.

GGT Trees: A Guide to Familiar American Trees. Herbert S. Zim and Alexander C. Martin. (Golden Nature Guide series.) New York, Golden Press, 1956.

GIP Insect Pests: A Guide to More Than 350 Pests of Home, Garden, Field and Forest. George S. Fichter. (Golden Nature Guide series.) New York, Golden Press, 1966.

GMC Edible and Poisonous Mushrooms of Canada. J. Walton Groves. Ottawa, Ontario, Research Branch Canada Department of Agriculture, 1962.

GPB The Great Book of Birds. John Gooders. New York, Dial Press, 1975.

GPL Pond Life: A Guide to Common Plants and Animals of North American Ponds and Lakes. George K. Reid. (Golden Nature Guide series.) New York, Golden Press, 1967.

GRA Reptiles and Amphibians: A Guide to Familiar American Species. Herbert S. Zim and Hobart M. Smith. (Golden Nature Guide series.) New York, Golden Press, 1956.

GSP Spiders and Their Kin. Herbert W. Levi and Lorna R. Levi. (Golden Nature Guide series.) New York, Golden Press, 1968.

GSS Sea Shells of the World. R. Tucker Abbott. (Golden Nature Guide series.) New York, Golden Press, 1962.

GUS Seaweeds at Ebb Tide. Muriel Lewin Guberlet. Illustrated by Elizabeth L. Curtis. Seattle, University of Washington Press, 1956.

HBT Birds of Trinidad and Tobago. G. A. C. Herklots. London, Collins, 1961.

HFP Wild Flowers of the Pacific Coast. Leslie L. Haskin. 2d ed. Portland, Ore., Binfords and Mort, 1967.

HFW Living Fishes of the World. Earl S. Herald. Garden City, N.Y., Doubleday, 1961.

HMG Manual of the Grasses of the United States. A. S. Hitchcock. 2d ed. Washington, D. C., Government Printing Office, 1950.

HPF Pacific Fishes of Canada. J. L. Hart. Ottawa, Ontario, Fisheries Research Board of Canada (Bulletin 180), 1973.

HSC Shrubs in Colour. A. G. L. Hellyer. Garden City, N. Y., Doubleday, 1966.

HWF Wild Flowers. Homer D. House. New York, Macmillan, 1961.

HYF Wild Flower Book. Clarence J. Hylander. Illustrated by Edith Farrington Johnston. New York, Macmillan, 1954.

IWE International Wildlife Encyclopedia. Maurice Burton and Robert Burton, editors. 20 vols. New York, Marshall Cavendish, 1969.

JAW Animal Atlas of the World. E. L. Jordan, Maplewood, N. J., Hammond, 1969.

JSS Seashore Animals of the Pacific Coast. Myrtle Elizabeth Johnson and Harry James Snook. New York, Macmillan, 1935.

KGB A Field Guide to the Butterflies of North America, East of the Great Plains. Alexander B. Klots. (Peterson Field Guide series.) Boston, Houghton Mifflin, 1951.

KIA Insects of North America. Alexander B. Klots and Elsie B. Klots. (Animal Life of North America series.) New York, Doubleday, n.d.

KIW Living Insects of the World. Alexander B. Klots and Elsie B. Klots. Garden City, N.Y., Doubleday, 1965(?).

KMF Mushrooms and Other Fungi. H. Kleijn. Garden City, N.Y., Doubleday, 1962.

KSL Seashore Life of Puget Sound, the Strait of Georgia and the San Juan Archipelago. Eugene N. Kozloff. Seattle, University of Washington Press, 1973.

KWF The Ducks, Geese and Swans of North America. Francis H. Kortright. Washington, D. C., American Wildlife Institute, 1943.

LBI The Birds. Roger Tory Peterson and editors of Life. (Life Nature Library.) New York, Time, Inc., 1963.

LBW Living Birds of the World. E. Thomas Gilliard. Garden City, N. Y., Doubleday, 1958.

LCS Pocket Encyclopedia of Cacti and Other Succulents in Color. Edgar Lamb and Brian Lamb. New York, Macmillan, 1970.

LDE The Desert. A. Starker Leopold and editors of Life. (Life Nature Library.) New York, Time, Inc., 1961.

LEA Larousse Encyclopedia of Animal Life. New York, McGraw-Hill, 1967.

LFI The Fishes. F. D. Ommanney and editors of Life. (Life Nature Library.) New York, Time, Inc.,1964.

LFO The Forest. Peter Farb and editors of Life. (Life Nature Library.) New York, Time, Inc., 1961.

LFW Flowers of the World (in Full Color). Robert S. Lemmon and Charles L. Sherman. Garden City, N.Y., Hanover House, 1958.

LHM Collins Guide to Mushrooms and Toadstools. Morten Lange and F. Bayard Hora. London, Collins, 1963.

LIN The Insects. Peter Farb and editors of Life. (Life Nature Library.) New York, Time, Inc., 1962.

LMA The Mammals. Richard Carrington and editors of Life. (Life Nature Library.) New York, Time, Inc., 1963.

LMT The Mountains. Lorus J. Milne and Margery Milne and editors of Life. (Life Nature Library.) New York, Time, Inc., 1962.

LNA The Land and Wildlife of North America. Peter Farb and editors of Life. (Life Nature Library.) New York, Time, Inc., 1964.

LPL The Plants. Frits W. Went and editors of Life. (Life Nature Library.) New York, Time, Inc., 1963.

LRE The Reptiles. Archie Carr and editors of Life. (Life Nature Library.) New York, Time, Inc., 1963.

LSE The Sea. Leonard Engel and editors of Life. (Life Nature Library.) New York, Time, Inc., 1961.

LVS Vanishing Species. Introduction by Romain Gary. New York, Time-Life Books, 1974.

LWF Wildflowers of North America (in Full Color). Robert S. Lemmon and Charles C. Johnson. Garden City, N.Y., Hanover House, 1961.

MAR The World of Amphibians and Reptiles. Robert Mertens. New York, McGraw-Hill, 1960.

MBH Birds of Hawaii. George C. Munro. Rutland, Vt., Charles E. Tuttle, 1960.

MEP Exotic Plants. Julia F. Morton. Illustrated by Richard E. Younger. (Golden Nature Guide series.) New York, Golden Press, 1971.

MGB Garden Bulbs in Color. J. Horace McFarland, R. Marion Hatton, Daniel J. Foley. New York, Macmillan, 1945 (c1938).

MGS Field Guide to Shells of the Pacific Coast and Hawaii. Percy A. Morris. 2d ed. (Peterson Field Guide series.) Boston, Houghton Mifflin, 1966.

MOL Ocean Life. Norman Marshall and Olga Marshall. (Macmillan Color series.) New York, Macmillan, 1971.

MSM The Savory Wild Mushroom. Margaret McKenny; revised and enlarged by Daniel E. Stuntz. Seattle, University of Washington Press, 1971.

MTB Field Guide to the Trees of Britain and Northern Europe. Alan Mitchell. Boston, Houghton Mifflin, 1974.

MWF What Flower is That? Stirling Macoboy. New York, Crown Publishers, 1971.

NFP Non-Flowering Plants. Floyd S. Shuttleworth and Herbert S. Zim. (Golden Nature Guide series.) New York, Golden Press, 1967.

NGA Wild Animals of North America. Washington, D. C., The National Geographic Society, 1960.

NGB The Book of Birds. Gilbert Grosvenor and Alexander Wetmore, editors. 2 vols. Washington, D., C., The National Geographic Society, 1937.

NGF Wondrous World of Fishes. Washington, D.C., The National Geographic Society, 1965.

NGS Song and Garden Birds of North America. Washington, D.C., The National Geographic Society, 1964.

NGW Water, Prey, and Game Birds of North America. Washington, D.C., The National Geographic Society, 1965.

NHE Natural History of Europe. Harry Garms. London, Paul Hamlyn, 1967.

OBI Oxford Book of Insects. John Burton et al. Illustrated by Joyce Bee, Derek Whiteley and Peter Parks. Oxford (England) University Press, 1968.

OBT Oxford Book of Trees. A. R. Clapham. Illustrated by B. E. Nicholson. London, Oxford University Press, 1975.

OBV Oxford Book of Vertebrates. Marion Nixon. Illustrated by Derek Whiteley. Oxford (England) University Press, 1972.

OFP Oxford Book of Food Plants. S. G. Harrison, G. B. Masefield, Michael Wallis. Illustrated by B. E.

Nicholson. Oxford (England) University Press, 1969.

OGF Oxford Book of Garden Flowers. E. B. Anderson et al. Illustrated by B. E. Nicholson. Oxford (England) University Press, 1963.

OIB Oxford Book of Invertebrates. David Nichols, with John A. L. Cooke. Illustrated by Derek Whiteley. Oxford (England) University Press, 1971.

OMW Our Magnificent Wildlife: How to Enjoy and Preserve It. Pleasantville, N. Y., Reader's Digest Association, 1975.

ONP Oxford Book of Flowerless Plants. Frank H. Brightman. Illustrated by B. E. Nicholson. Oxford (England) University Press, 1966.

OOW Wildflowers of Western America. Robert T. Orr and Margaret C. Orr. New York, Alfred A. Knopf, 1974.

OWF Oxford Book of Wild Flowers. S. Ary and M. Gregory. Illustrated by B. E. Nicholson. Oxford (England) University Press, 1960.

PAK Parade of the Animal Kingdom. Robert Hegner, with Jane Z. Hegner. New York, Macmillan, 1937.

PBA Birds of America. T. Gilbert Pearson, editor-in-chief. 3 vols in 1. Garden City, N.Y., Garden City Books, 1936.

PEB Field Guide to the Birds (east of the Rockies). Roger Tory Peterson. 2d ed. Boston, Houghton Mifflin, 1947.

PEI Pictorial Encyclopedia of Insects. V. J. Stanek. London, Paul Hamlyn, 1969.

PFF Fieldbook of Natural History. E. Laurence Palmer and H. Seymour Fowler. 2d ed. New York, McGraw-Hill, 1975.

PFW Flowers of the World. Frances Perry. New York, Crown Publishers, 1972.

PMB Field Guide to Mexican Birds (and Adjacent Central America). Roger Tory Peterson and Edward L. Chalif. Boston, Houghton Mifflin, 1973.

PMF Field Guide to Wildflowers (northeastern and north-central North America). Roger Tory Peterson and Margaret McKenny. (Peterson Field Guide series.) Boston, Houghton Mifflin, 1968.

PMG The Mammal Guide: Mammals of North America north of Mexico. Ralph S. Palmer. Garden City, N.Y., Doubleday, 1954.

PRP Pasture and Range Plants. Bartlesville, Okla., Phillips Petroleum Co., 1963.

PRW The Reptile World. Clifford H. Pope. New York, Alfred A. Knopf, 1956.

PWB Field Guide to Western Birds. Roger Tory Peterson. 2d ed. Boston, Houghton Mifflin, 1961.

PWC Wildlife Crisis. H.R.H. Prince Philip, Duke of Edinburgh, and James Fisher. New York, Cowles, 1970.

RBA Birds of North America. Austin L. Rand. (Animal Life of North America series.) New York, Doubleday, n.d.

RBB Birds of North America. Chandler S. Robbins, Bertel Bruun and Herbert S. Zim. (Golden Field Guide series.) New York, Golden Press, 1966.

RCT Between Pacific Tides. Edward F. Ricketts and Jack Calvin. 3d ed., rev. Stanford, Calif., Stanford University Press, 1962.

RUS Wild Flowers of the United States. Harold William Rickett. 6 vols in 14 parts. New York, McGraw-Hill, 1966.

RWA Wild Flowers of America. H. W. Rickett. New York, Crown Publishers, 1953.

RWF The World of Flowers. Herbert Reisigl, editor. New York, Viking Press, 1964.

SAA Animals of the Arctic: The Ecology of the Far North. Bernard Stonehouse. New York, Holt, Rinehart and Winston, 1971.

SCI Common Insects of North America. Lester A. Swan and Charles S. Papp. New York, Harper and Row, 1972.

SFT Forest Trees of the Pacific Slope. George B. Sudworth. Washington, D. C., Government Printing Office, 1908.

SGB Complete Guide to Bulbs. Patrick M. Synge. New York, E. P. Dutton, 1961.

SIG The Insect Guide. Ralph B. Swain. Garden City, N. Y., Doubleday, 1948.

SIR Living Reptiles of the World. Karl P. Schmidt and Robert F. Inger. Garden City, N. Y., Doubleday, 1957.

SLP The Last Paradises: On the Track of Rare Animals. Eugen Schuhmacher. Garden City, N. Y., Doubleday, 1967.

SLS Last Survivors. Noel Simon and Paul Geroudet. New York, World Publishing, 1970.

SMG The Mushroom Hunter's Field Guide. Alexander H. Smith. Rev. ed. Ann Arbor, University of Michigan Press, 1963.

SMW Living Mammals of the World. Ivan T. Sanderson. (World of Nature series.) Garden City, N. Y., Doubleday, 1961.

SOS Secrets of the Seas. Pleasantville, N.Y., Reader's Digest Association, 1972.

SRA Field Guide to Western Reptiles and Amphibians. Robert C. Stebbins. (Peterson Field Guide series.) Boston, Houghton Mifflin, 1966.

TBC Birds of Canada. P. A. Taverner. Ottawa, Ontario, National Museum of Canada (Bulletin 72), 1934.

TGF Guide to Garden Flowers. Norman Taylor. Boston, Houghton Mifflin, 1958.

TGS Guide to Garden Shrubs and Trees. Norman Taylor. Boston, Houghton Mifflin, 1965.

TSK Trees and Shrubs of Kentucky and Surrounding Areas. Mary E. Wharton and Roger W. Barbour. Lexington, University Press of Kentucky, 1973.

VPN Vascular Plants of the Pacific Northwest. C. Leo Hitchcock et al. 5 vols. Seattle, University of Washington Press, 1969.

VWA Vanishing Wild Animals of the World. Richard Fitter. Paintings by John Leigh-Pemberton. London, Midland Bank, 1968.

WAB World Atlas of Birds. London, Mitchell Beazley Publishers, 1974.

WCS Cacti of the Southwest (Texas, New Mexico, Oklahoma, Arkansas, and Louisiana). Del Weniger. Austin, University of Texas Press, n.d.

WEA The World Encyclopedia of Animals. Maurice Burton, editor. New York, World Publishing, 1972.

WFA Handbook of Frogs and Toads of the United States and Canada. Albert Hazen Wright and Anna Allen Wright. 3d ed. Ithaca, N.Y., Comstock Publishing, 1949.

WFW Fishes of the World: An Illustrated Dictionary. Alwyne Wheeler. New York, Macmillan, 1975.

WID Wildlife in Danger. James Fisher, Noel Simon, Jack Vincent. New York, Viking Press, 1969.

WMW Mammals of the World. Ernest P. Walker et al. 2 vols. Baltimore, Johns Hopkins Press, 1964.

WWS Handbook of Snakes. Albert Hazen Wright and Anna Allen Wright. 2 vols. Ithaca, N. Y., Comstock Publishing, 1957.

WYG The World in Your Garden. Wendell H. Camp, Victor R. Boswell and John R. Magness. Illustrated by Else Bostelmann. Washington, D. C., The National Geographic Society, 1957.

Index to Illustrations of the Natural World

A

Alligator, American (Alligator mississippiensis) ALE 6:126, 131; ANE 1:27, 28; AWW 35; CGR cp 5e; CRA 31; DRW pl 1; GPL 136; GRA 114; IWE 1:29; LEA 288; LNA 92, 93; LRE 116, 117; LVS 166; OMW 178; PAK 315; SIR 45.

Allspice, Carolina (Calycanthus floridus) BBF 2:132; DEW 1:57 (cp 21); FNC 72; HSC 22; LFW 198 (cp 448); TGS 151. (C. fertilis) TSK 43, 209. (C. occidentalis) EWF cp 150a; PFW 60.

Almond (Prunus sp.) AGF 104; DEW 1:277 (cp 157); DFP 221 (cps 1762-1764); MWF 245 (cps 804, 805); OBT 180; OFP 27; PFF 205; PFW 262; TGS 198.

Aluminum Plant (Pilea cadieri) DFP 79 (cp 627); MWF 233 (cp 763); PFW 302.

Alumroot (Heuchua americana) FFK 166; HWF cp 89; PMF 377; RUS 2:261. (H. micrantha) AFP 2:380; CWF 206; RUS 4:271, 5:241; VPN 3:14.

Alyssum, Sweet (Lobularia maritima or Alyssum maritima) DFP 29 (cps 230, 231); EGA 133; FHP 132; MWF 189 (cps 600, 601); NHE 134; OGF 135; PFF 182; RUS 5:183; TGF 77. (A. alyssoides) RUS 6:253; TGF 98.

Amanita—See **Mushroom**; see also **Death Cap** and **Destroying Angel**.

Amaranth—See also **Pigweed**.

Amaranth, Globe (Gomphrena globosa) DFP 38 (cp 302); EGA 121; LFW 164 (cp 364); MWF 144 (cp 437); TGF 45.

Amaryllis—See also **Lily, Aztec**; **Lily, Belladonna**; and **Lily, Scarborough**.

Amaryllis (Hippeastrum hybrids) AGF 21; DEW 2:217 (cp 131); DFP 69 (cps 549-552); EGB 84, 119; FHP 125; LFW 66 (cp 154), 67 (cp 155); MEP 19; MGB 164-166; MWF 155 (cp 482); PFW 24.

Amaryllis, Hardy (Lycoris squamigera) AGF 126; EGB 128; LFW 67 (cp 156); TGF 13.

Amazon—See **Parrot**.

Amberjack (Seriola dorsalis) GGF 95; NGF 112. (S. zonata) ANE 1:30; CFG 487; GGF 94.

Amberjack, Greater (Seriola dumerili) CFG 487; GGF 94; NGF 109; OBV 31; WFW 329.

Amoeba Proteus (Chaos diffugens) GPL 76; IWE 1:35, 20:2694; LEA 23; PAK 8.

Amphioxus (Branchiostoma virginiae) ALE 3:428, 429; IWE 10:1278; LEA 203; NHE 160; OIB 177; PFF 501. (B. caribaeum) CFG 460.

Amphissa—See **Snail, Wrinkled**.

Amphiuma—See **Eel, Congo**.

Anchovy, Bay or Common (Anchoa mitchilli) CFG 521; GGF 41.

Anchovy, Pacific or Northern (Engraulis mordax) GGF 41; HPF 104; IWE 1:43. (E. encrasicolus) WFW 183.

Andromeda, Japanese (Pieris japonica) AGF 159; DFP 218 (cp 1738); EGE 140; LFW 113 (cp 250); MWF 233 (cp 762); PFW 107.

Anemone, Alpine (Anemone alpina) DEW 1:123; DFP 21 (cp 167); NHE 269.

Anemone, Blue (Anemone oregana) HFP 100; RUS 5:127, 6:159; VPN 2:331.

Anemone, Canada (Anemone canadensis) BBF 2:99; HWF cp 67; HYF cp 62; LWF 248 (cp 390); PMF 31; RUS 1:125, 4:141, 6:159.

Anemone, Daffodil (Anemone narcissiflora) DFP 121 (cp 966); NHE 269.

Anemone, Drummond's (Anemone drummondii) AFP 2:196; CWF 147; OOW cp 28; RUS 6:159; VPN 2:328.

Anemone, Greek (Anemone blanda) DFP 84 (cp 671); EGB 95; EWF cp 8d; OGF 9; PFW 252.

Anemone, Japanese (Anemone japonica) AGF 23; DFP 121 (cp 964); EGP 95; FGF 25; MWF 40 (cp 58); TGF 61.

Anemone, Poppy (Anemone coronaria) AGF 23; DFP 84 (cp 672); EGB 54, 95; EWF cp 27f; FGF 24; LFW 11 (cps 22, 23); MWF 40 (cp 57); NHE 199.

Anemone, Sea—See **Sea Anemone**.

Anemone, Western (Anemone occidentalis) AFP 2:193; CWF 158, 159; OOW cp 2; RUS 5:123, 127, 6:157; VPN 2:331.

Anemone, Wood (Anemone nemorosa) BBF 2:100; DFP 85 (cp 673); NHE 26; OWF 67; PFW 252. (A. multifida) RUS 6:159. (A. quinquefolia) AFP 2:196; ANE 1:59; BBF 2:100; FFK 110; FNC 67; HWF cp 68a; HYF cp 55; LWF 248 (cp 389); PFF 171; PMF 31; RUS 1:125, 2:177, 5:127.

Angel Wing, Common (Barnea costata or Cyrtopleura costata) AAS 461; ASN 259; CFG 592; GGS 109; PFF 425.

Angel Wing, False (Petricola pholadiformis) AAS pl 32z; ASN 239; CFG 593; GGS 109; MGS pl 22; NHE 167; OIB 89.

Angelfish, Queen (Angelichthys ciliaris or Holacanthus ciliaris) CFW 115; GGF 131; IWE 1:49; MOL 112; NGF 212; WFW cp 340, 213.

Angel's Trumpet (Datura sp.) AFP 3:679; DFP 62 (cp

Auklet, Whiskered (Aethia pygmaea) AAB 223; ALE 8:229; NGB 1:338; NGW 410; PWB 146 (pl 35); RBB 151.

Avens, Large-leaved (Geum macrophyllum) BBF 2:271; CWF 243; HFP 176; PMF 137; RUS 1:137, 4:165, 5:143, 6:175.

Avens, Mountain (Dryas octopetala or D. drummondii) BBF 2:273; CWF 242, 243; DFP 8 (cp 60); EWF cp 2e; NHE 266; OOW cp 1; OWF 81; RUS 5:147, 6:185; RWA cps 173-176.

Avens, Purple or Water (Geum rivale) BBF 2:272; EWF cp 16d; HWF cp 100; HYF cp 81; LWF 183; NHE 179; OWF 117; PMF 263; RUS 1:137, 4:165, 6:175. (G. triflorum) CWF 247; PMF 263.

Avens, Yellow (Geum aleppicum var. strictum) HWF cp 98a; PMF 137; RUS 1:137, 2:189, 4:165, 6:175.

Avocado (Avocado Pear) (Persea americana) DEW 1:90; OFP 115; WYG 208.

Avocet, American (Recurvirostra americana) AAB 181; ALE 8:170; ANE 1:147; BBW 121 (cp 26); GFB 72; LBW 95 (cp 61); NGB 1:286; NGW 346; PEB 90 (pl 25), 103 (cp 30); RBA 112; RBB 109; WEA 54.

Awlwort (Subularia aquatica) AFP 2:260; NHE 94; VPN 2:550.

Axolotl (Ambystoma mexicanum or Siredon mexicanum) ALE 5:295; IWE 1:111; LEA 275; WEA 55.

Azalea, Alpine (Loiseleuria procumbens) CWF 399; EWF cp 6b; NHE 266; TGS 39.

Azalea, Flame (Rhododendron calendarlaceum) BBF 2:678; FNC 132; HYF cp 138; PMF 209; RWA cp 258; TGS 391; TSK 63, 260.

Azalea Hybrids (Rhododendron sp.) AGF 31-35; DFP 222-229 (cp 1802-1831); EGE 144, 145; FGF 32-38; FHP 106; HSC 102; LFW 5 (cp 9), 6 (cp 10-12), 7 (cp 13); MWF 50 (cp 88-94); TGS 390, 391.

Azalea, Mountain or Early (Rhododendron roseum) PMF 229; RWA cp 257; TSK 62, 257.

Azalea, Pink (Rhododendron nudiflorum) BBF 2:678; FNC 133; HWF cp 154; HYF cp 130; LFW 218 (cp 492); LWF 266 (cp 421); PFF 272; PMF 229; RWA cp 256; TGS 301; TSK 62, 258.

Azalea, Western (Rhododendron occidentale) AFP 3:301; LWF 34 (cp 58); OOW cp 36; VPN 4:33.

Azalea, White (Rhododendron viscosa) BBF 2:679; FNC 134; TGS 391.

B

Baby Blue-eyes (Nemophila menziesii) AFP 3:483; DFP 44 (cp 349); EGA 139; HFP cp 4; LWF 42 (cp 71); MWF 209; OGF 133; OOW cp 283; PFW 141; RUS 4:471, 5:403; TGF 172; VPN 4:156.

Baby's-breath (Gypsophila elegans) DFP 38 (cp 303); EGA 122; MWF 145; OGF 131. (G. paniculata) AGF 36; DFP 145 (cps 1153, 1154); EGP 120; LFW 54 (cp 124); PFF 164.

Bachelor's-button—See **Cornflower.**

Backswimmer (Notonecta glauca) ALE 2:188; NHE 130; OBI 31. (N. undulata) GGI 48; GPL 104; IWE 1:120; KIA 63; SIG cp 37; PFF 454. (Corixa punctata) NHE 130; OBI 31; PFF 456. (C. interrupta) GGI 48; GPL 103; SIG cp 38.

Badger (Taxidea taxus) ANE 1:149; ALE 12:83; AWW 27; BGM 100 (cp 9); CFG 269 (cp 32); IWE 1:122; JAW 117; LEA 564; NGA 186; PFF 687; PMG cp 9; WMW 2:1210.

Bagworm (Thyridopteryx ephemeraeformis) GBB 86; GGI 101; GIP 94; SIG cp 72.

Baldpate—See **Widgeon, American.**

Balloon Flower (Platycodon grandiflorum) AGF 37; DFP 18 (cp 138); EGP 140; LFW 112 (cp 248); MWF 236 (cp 771); OGF 109; PFW 63.

Balloon Vine (Cardiospermum halicacabum) DEW 2:59 (cp 27); EGA 103.

Balloonfish—See **Porcupine Fish.**

Balsam, Garden (Impatiens balsamina) AGF 37; DFP 39 (cp 311); EGA 127; FGF 40; LFW 168 (cp 377); MWF 162 (cp 507); TGF 141.

Balsamroot (Balsamorhiza deltoidea) AFP 4:107; HFP 378; RUS 4:685, 5:553; VPN 5:104.

Bamboo, Heavenly or Sacred (Nandina domestica) AGF 127; EGE 136; MWF 207 (cp 665).

Bamboo, Japanese (Arundinaria japonica) AGF 38; HSC 14; PFF 340.

Banana (Musa paradisiaca or sapientum) MWF 204 (cp 656, 657); OFP 109; PFF 388; RWF 39; WYG 205.

Bananaquit (Coereba flaveola) ABW 286; ALE 9:371; BWI 176 (cp 7), 207; CDB 203 (cp 886); DBM cp 37; GFB 185; GPB 307; HBT 241 (cp 14); LBW cp 191; PMB cp 37; WAB 99. (C. bahamensis) AAB 388; PEB 227 (cp 60).

Band Shell, Tulip (Fasciolaria tulipa) GGS 133; GSS 85; PFF 413.

Baneberry, Common (Actaea spicata) HFP 112; NHE 26; OWF 67.

Baneberry, Red (Actaea rubra) CWF 150; HWF cp 62; HYF cp 64; RUS 1:115, 2:169, 4:137, 5:115, 6:147; VPN 2:326. (A. arguta) AFP 2:184; BBF 2:90; RWA cp 116.

Baneberry, White (Actaea pachypoda) FFK 152; FNC 63; HWF cp 63b; HYF cp 64; LWF 252 (cp 396); PFF 175; PMF 55; RUS 1:117, 2:169, 6:147. (A. alba) BBF 2:90.

Barbados Pride (Caesalpinia pulcherrima) DEW 1:282 (cp 172); MEP 52; MWF 65 (cp 145); PFW 159.

Barbara's Buttons (Marshallia grandiflora) BBF 3:503; PMF 307; RUS 1:503. (M. graminifolia) FNC 203; RUS 2:631.

Barberry, Creeping (Berberis repens) OOW cp 87; RUS 6:207. (Mahonia repens) AFP 2:220; DEW 1:115; RWA cp 139.

Barberry, European (Berberis vulgaris) DEW 1:114; NHE 267; MWF 56 (cp 115); OFP 191; OWF 191; PFF 178.

Barberry, Japanese (Berberis thunbergii) AGF 38; DEW 1:99 (cps 42, 43); DFP 183 (cp 1459); PFF 178; TGS 230.

Barber's-pole (Allotropa virgata) AFP 3:294; CWF 374; HFP cp 3; OOW cp 160; RUS 5:315; VPN 4:6.

Barley (Hordeum vulgare) HMG 273; PFF 356; PRP 72.

Barley, Foxtail or Wild (Hordeum jubatum) DFP 39 (cp 308); HMG 269; PFF 356.

Barley, Little (Hordeum pusillum) HMG 271; PRP 44.

Barnacle, Acorn or Rock (Balanus sp.) CFG 645; GAS 348, 350; GGS 68; IWE 2:144; JSS 266; KSL 129; NHE 171; OIB 129; PAK 101; PFF 428.

Barnacle, Deep-sea or Goose (Lepas anatifera) IWE 2:144; KSL 210; MOL 85; NHE 171; OIB 129. (L. hillii) JSS 263; NHE 171.

Barnacle, Goose (Mitella polymerus or Pollicipes polymerus) GAS 346; KSL 138; PAK 101.

Barnacle, Northern Goose (Lepas fascicularis) CFG cp 48; GGS 68; JSS 263; KSL cp 23.

Barracuda, Great (Sphyraena barracuda) ALE 5:138, 150; CFG 482; GGF 83; IWE 2:153; LFI 52-53; NGF 130-131; PFF 517; SOS 67, 333; WEA 62; WFW cp 396.

Barracuda, Pacific (Sphyraena argentea) GGF 83; HPF 314.

Barrenwort (Epimedium hybrids) AGF 39; NHE 268; TGF 91.

Bartonia (Bartonia virginica) BBF 3:16; PMF 165; RUS 1:313, 2:395.

Bartsia, Yellow (Parentucellia viscosa) CWF 482. (Odontites lutea) NHE 74.

Basil, Sweet (Ocimum basilicum) EGA 140; OFP 143.

Basil, Wild (Satureja vulgaris or Clinopodium vulgare) HWF cp 186b; HYF cp 171; NHE 35; OWF 147; PMF 281; RUS 1:375, 2:477, 4:567, 6:561.

Basilisk, Banded (Basiliscus vittatus) DRW pl 9, 10; SIR 113.

Basket Shell (Nassarius fossatus) AAS pl 20s; ASN 143; GGS 132; MGS pl 37; PFF 413. (N. mendicus) AAS 238; ASN 143; GAS 294; MGS pl 37. (N. obsoletus) AAS pl 23p; CFG 573; GGS 132; MGS pl 37; PFF 411. (N. vibex) AAS pl 23q; ASN 141; CFG 574; GGS 132.

Basket-of-Gold (Alyssum saxatile) AGF 20; DFP 1 (cp 3); MWF 39 (cp 51); NHE 217; OGF 41; TGF 77.

Basket-star (Gorgonocephalus sp.) ALE 3:389; BLA 267 (cp 134); CFG 631; GAS 162; GGS 61; IWE 2:157; JSS 224.

Bass, Calico—See **Crappie, Black.**

Bass, Channel or Red Drum (Sciaenops ocellata) CFG cp 42; GGF 121; NGF 125.

Bass, Large-mouthed Black (Micropterus salmoides) ALE 5:80; GGF 99; GPL 125; IWE 2:160; LFI 132-135; NGF 283; NHE 123; PFF 519; WFW 249.

Bass, Rock (Ambloplites rupestris) CFG cp 44; GGF 103; NGF 282; PFF 519.

Bass, Sea—See **Sea Bass.**

Bass, Small-mouthed Black (Micropterus dolomieu) CFG cp 44; CFW 105; GGF 99; NGF 283; NHE 123; PFF 519; WFW 249.

Bass, Spotted (Micropterus punctulatus) CFG 543; GGF 99.

Bass, Striped (Roccus saxatilis or Morowe saxatilis) ANE 1:153; ALE 5:79; CFG cp 42; CFW 102; GGF 8; HPF 280; NGF 122; PFF 521; WFW 313.

Bass, White (Roccus chrysops) ANE 1:152; CFG cp 43; GGF 106; NGF 281.

298; PMF 123, 233, 393; RUS 1:413, 2:522, 3:407.
(Leptamniam virginianum) HWF 263.

Beefsteak Plant (Perilla frutescens) DFP 45 (cp 357);
EGA 144; RUS 1:385, 2:487, 3:385, 6:561.

Beet (Beta vulgaris var.) OFP 161, 171; OWF 57; PFF
155; WYG 138.

Beet, Sugar (Beta vulgaris) OFP 15, 171; OWF 57;
PFF 155.

Beetle—see also **Weevil.**

Beetle, Asiatic Garden (Autoserica castanea) EGA 50;
GBB cp 9; GIP 65.

Beetle, Asparagus (Crioceris asparagi) GGB cp 4; GGI
125; PEI 225 (cp 24a); SIG cp 118a. (C. duodecimpunctata) GBB cp 4; PEI 225 (cp 24b).

Beetle, Banded Net-winged (Calopteron reticulatum)
KIA 107; SCI 368; SIG cp 96. (C. terminale) BIA
cp 5; SCI 369.

Beetle, Blister (Epicauta sp.) BIA cp 6; GBB cp 5;
GIP 75, 96; GGI 122; KIA 114; PFF 462.

Beetle, Carpet (Anthrenus scrophulariae) ALE 2:226;
BIA cp 5; GGI 150; GIP 31; LPL 176; NHE 261;
PFF 464.

Beetle, Checkered (Enoclerus sphegeus) SIG cp 99.
(Aulicus terrestricus) KIA 110. (Trichodes apivorus)
ALE 2:225.

Beetle, Click (many species) ALE 2:226; BIA 167;
GGI 114; IEW 4:453; KIA 113; PFF 462.

Beetle, Cockchafer (Melolontha melolontha) GIP 65;
IWE 4:468, 469; LEA 152; NHE 65; OBI 183; PEI
267.

Beetle, Colorado Potato (Leptinotarsa decemlineata)
ALE 11:321; GBB cp 4; GGI 122; GIP 75; IWE
4:489; KIA 131; LEA 161; NHE 260; SIG cp 118c;
OBI 187; PEI 209 (cp 22b); PFF 465; WEA 109.

Beetle, Confused Flour (Tribolium confusum) GIP
147; IWE 4:514; PFF 463; SIG cp 109b.

Beetle, Cucumber (Diabrotica sp.) EGA 50; GBB
cp 12; GGI 123; GIP 77; LPL 177; SIG cp 118b.

Beetle, Dried Fruit (Carpophilus hemipterus) GIP
153; SIG cp 103.

Beetle, Dung (Many genera and species) AWW 26; BIA
cp 7; GGI 130; OBI 181; SIG cp 114a-d.

Beetle, Elm Leaf (Galerucella xanthomelaena) GBB
cp 6; GIP 139; PFF 466.

Beetle, Fiery Searcher or Hunter (Calosoma scrutator)
IWE 7:965; SIG cp 89a. (C. sycophanta) ALE
2:264.

Beetle, Figeater or Green June (Cotinis nitida) ANE
1:190; GBB cp 11; GGI 129; SIG cp 114j.

Beetle, Flat-bark (Cucujus clavipes or C. cinnaberinus)
ALE 2:235; SIG cp 104b.

Beetle, Flea (Epitrix cucumeris) GBB cp 7; GIP 62.
(Psylliodes affinis) OBI 187. (Systena blanda)
GBB cp 7; GIP 62.

Beetle, Ground (Many genera and species) BIA cp 5;
OBI 167, 169; PEI 218; SCI 339-348; SIG cps 89a-d.

Beetle, Hide (Dermestes maculatus) GIP 31; OBI 177;
SIG cp 102.

Beetle, Hister (Hister abbreviatus) SCI 367; SIG
cp 95b.

Beetle, Japanese (Popilla japonica) EGA 50; EGP 50;
GBB cp 8; GGI 111; GIP 9, 13, 129; KIA 122-123;
LPL 176; PFF 465; SIG cp 114h.

Beetle, Ladybird (Adalia sp.) GGI 118, 119; IWE
10:1272; NHE 260; OBI 177; SIG cp 106. (Coccinella sp.) ALE 11:321, 2:258; BIA cp 6; IWE
10:1272; KIA 119; NHE 260; OBI 177. (Hippodamia convergens) GGI 118; PFF 464.

Beetle, Larder (Dermestes lardarius) ALE 2:226; GGI
153; GIP 31; NHE 261; OBI 177.

Beetle, May (or June) (Phyllophaga fusca) GBB cp 8;
GGI 128; SIG cp 114f. (P. rugosa) GIP 65; PFF
464.

Beetle, Mealworm (Tenebrio molitor) IWE 11:1450;
NHE 261; OBI 181.

Beetle, Mexican Bean (Epilachna varivestis) GBB cp 9;
GGI 121; GIP 76; LPL 176.

Beetle, Powder-post (Lyctus opaculus) BIA 191; SIG
cp 110.

Beetle, Predaceous Diving (Dysticus marginalis) ALE
2:216; GGI 127; GPL 105; IWE 5:643; NHE 127;
OBI 169; PFF 460; SIG cp 90; WEA 128.

Beetle, Rhinocerus (Xyloryctes satyrus) GBB cp 11;
GGI 130. (Dynastes tityus) SIG cp 114i.

Beetle, Rose Chafer (Macrodactylus subspinosus)
GBB cp 11; GGI 110; GIP 96; NHE 65; OBI 183;
SIG cp 114g.

Beetle, Rove (Many genera and species) ALE 2:225;
GGI 113; GIP 11; IWE 15:1994; OBI 172, 173;
PEI 197; SIG cp 94.

Beetle, Saw-toothed Grain (Oryzaephilus surinamensis)
GIP 148; SIG cp 104a.

Beetle, Sexton (Necrophorus marginatus) PFF 460;
SIG cp 93a. (N. vespillo) NHE 261; OBI 171.

Beetle, Snout—See **Weevil.**

Beetle, Soldier (Chauliognathus pennsylvanicus) ALE
2:225; SIG cp 98.

Beetle, Spider (Ptinus fur) OBI 179; SIG cp 113.

Beetle, Stag (Pseudolucanus capreolus) BIA 191; GGI 132; SIG cp 116. (Lucanus cervus) OBI 183. (Neolamprima adolphinae) PEI cp 27a.

Beetle, Summer Chafer (Amphimallon majalis) SCI 434. (A. solstitialis) NHE 65; OBI 183.

Beetle, Tenebrionid or Darkling (Alobates pennsylvanica) AWW 25; KIA 122. (Stenocara eburnea) AWW 78.

Beetle, Tiger (Amblycheila cylindriformis) GGI 109; LIN 48, 102; SIG cp 88. (Cicidela sp.) ALE 2:262; GGI 109; GPL 106; KIA 99; LEA 160; OBI 165; NHE 260; SIG cp 88.

Beetle, Water Scavenger (Hydrophilus triangularis) ALE 2:216; GGI 126; GPL 106; PFF 461; SIG cp 92a.

Beetle, Whirligig (Dineutes americanus) GPL 105; KIA 101; SIG cp 91; PFF 461. (Enhydrus sulcatus) ALE 2:216. (Orectochilus villosus) OBI 169.

Beetleweed—See **Galax.**

Beggar-ticks, Leafy-bracted (Bideus comosa) BBF 3:496; PMF 169; RUS 1:453, 2:565, 6:645.

Beggar-ticks, Sticktight (Bideus frondosa) AFP 4:129; BBF 3:497; PFF 323; PMF 169; RUS 1:453, 2:565, 3:435, 5:547.

Begonia (Begonia semperflorens) DFP 31 (cp 242); EGA 98; FHP 106; MWF 55 (cp 109); PFF 254; PFW 41. (B. tuberhybrida) DFP 53 (cps 419-424), 54 (cps 425-430); LFW 188, 189; MWF 55 (cp 110). (B. rex) PFF 254.

Belladonna—See **Nightshade, Deadly.**

Bellflower, Chilean—See **Chile Bells.**

Bellflower, Creeping (Campanula rapunculoides) HWF cp 215b; HYF cp 185; NHE 235; OWF 167; PMF 317, 341; RUS 1:347.

Bellflower, Italian (Campanula isophylla) DFP 55 (cp 440); FHP 110.

Bellflower, Peach-leaved or Willow (Campanula persicifolia) DFP 127 (cps 1014, 1015); EGP 103; LFW 21 (cps 40, 41); NHE 36; PFW 61; TGF 188.

Bellflower, Tall (Campanula americana) BBF 3:297; FFK 139; FNC 184; HYF cp 183; PMF 341; RUS 1:347, 2:443, 6:529.

Bellflower, Tussock (Campanula carpatica) DFP 3 (cp 23); MWF 71 (cp 168); PFW 62; TGF 188. See also **Harebell.**

Bells of Ireland (Moluccella laevis) AGF 45; DFP 44 (cp 346); LFW 95 (cp 219); EGA 137; MWF 202 (cp 649).

Bellwort, Large-flowered (Uvularia grandiflora) EWF cp 167a; FFK 50; FNC 35; HWF cp 20b; PFF 371; PFW 175; PMF 103; RUS 1:27, 2:27, 6:27.

Bellwort, Perfoliate (Uvularia perfoliata) FFK 50; HWF cp 22; PMF 103; RUS 1:27, 2:27; RWA cp 47.

Bellwort, Sessile-leaved (Uvularia sessilifolia) HWF cp 20a; HYF cp 22; LWF 227 (cp 362); PMF 103; RUS 1:27, 2:29.

Beluga—See **Whale, White.**

Bentbill, Northern or Gray-throated (Oncostoma cinereigulare) AWW 102; DBM cp 26; PMB cp 29.

Bent-grass (Agrostis sp.) AFP 1:149-155; HMG 337-340; NHE 195, 244, 292; PFF 352, 353; PRP 6, 7; VPN 1:464, 466, 470, 472, 474, 476, 480.

Bergamot, Purple (Monarda media) BBF 3:132; HWF cp 190a; PMF 217; RUS 2:471.

Bergamot, Wild (Monarda fistulosa) BBF 3:132; CWF 458; FFK 197; HWF cp 190a; HYF cp 168; PMF 217; RUS 1:369, 2:467, 3:371; VPN 4:267.

Bergenia (Bergenia cordifolia) EGP 101; MWF 56 (cp 116); PFW 272. (B. purpuracens) DFP 126 (cp 1460); EWF cp 99d.

Billbug (Calendra setiger) GGI 135; SIG cp 120c. (C. callosa) GIP 105. (Sphenophorus maidis) BIA 205; GIP 105; SCI 496.

Bindweed—See also **Morning Glory.**

Bindweed, Black (polygonum convolvulus) AFP 2:65; BBF 1:674; NHE 224; OWF 59; PFF 154.

Bindweed, Field or Small (Convolvulus arvensis) AFP 3:388; BBF 3:47; CWF 426; DEW 2:110 (cp 71); NHE 228; OWF 125; PMF 13, 255; RUS 1:345, 2:427, 3:333, 5:439, 6:521; VPN 4:88.

Bindweed, Great or Hedge (Convolvulus sepium) AFP 3:385; BBF 3:46; CWF 422; HWF cp 176; HYF cp 152; LWF 196 (cp 307); NHE 228; OWF 95; PMF 13, 255; RUS 1:345, 2:427, 3:333, 4:513, 5:435, 6:521; VPN 4:88.

Bindweed, Mallow-leaved (Convolvulus althaeoides) DFP 5 (cp 37); EWF cp 36d.

Bindweed, Sea (Convolvulus soldanella) AFP 3:385; CWF 198; GGS 144; NHE 136; RUS 4:513; VPN 4:88.

Bindweed, Upright or Low (Convolvulus spithamaeous) BBF 3:47; FFK 118; HWF cp 164b; PMF 13.

Birch, Black or Sweet or Cherry (Betula lenta) ANE 2:199, 201; BBF 1:609; BTN 105; PFF 137; TSK 432, 433.

Birch, Common (Betula pubescens) EWF cp 12d; NHE 69; OBT 13, 17.

9:381; ANE 2:278; BBC 2:cp 106; CFG cp 22; GBC
301 (cp 62); NGB 2:232; NGS 181, 303; PBA 2:247;
PEB 198 (cp 53); PWB 263 (cp 52); RBB 281; TBC
368 (cp 72a); WAB 62.

Black-eyed Susan—See also **Cone-flower** (Rudbeckia
hirta).

Black-eyed Susan (Thunbergia alata) DFP 48 (cp
383); EGA 156; FHP 148; MEP 147; MWF 283 (cp
936); PFW 295; RUS 2:447. (T. erecta) MEP 147;
MWF 283 (cp 937). (T. grandiflora) AGF 75; EWF
cp 122b; LFW 181 (cp 408); MEP 147; PFW 295.

Blackfish, Alaska (Dallia pectoralis) ALE 4:255; CFW
59; IWE 1:23; NGF 289; WFW 174.

Blackfish, Common—See **Whale, Pilot**.

Black-haw—See **Haw, Black**.

Blackthorn or Sloe (Prunus spinosa) NHE 20; OBT 28;
OFP 67; OWF 181.

Bladder-nut (Staphylea pinnata) DEW 2:58 (cp 26);
HSC 115; NHE 22. (S. colchica) TGS 150. (S. trifolia) BBF 2:493; PFF 238; TSK 74, 208.

Bladder-pod (Lesquerella ludoviciana) OOW cp 107.
(Physaria didymocarpa) RWA cp 149, 150; RUS
6:235. (Isomeris arboreus) AFP 2:325; LWF 20
(cp 31).

Bladderwort, Common or Greater (Utricularia vulgaris)
AFP 4:13; CWF 499; GPL 64; NHE 99; OWF 31;
PMF 123; RUS 1:415, 2:521, 3:407, 5:519, 6:613.

Bladderwort, Humped (Utricularia gibba) AFP 4:13;
PMF 123; RUS 2:523, 5:630.

Bladderwort, Purple (Utricularia purpurea) FNC 177;
HWF cp 183; PMF 231; RUS 1:415, 2:521.

Bladderwort, Swollen (Utricularia inflata) FNC 176;
LWF 47 (cp 79); PMF 123; RUS 1:415, 2:521,
3:407.

Blanketflower—See **Gaillardia**.

Blazing Star (Chamaelirium luteum) See **Devil's-bit**.

Blazing Star (Liatris sp.) DFP 155 (cps 1234, 1235);
EGP 128; EWF cp 165e; FFK 237; FNC 190, 191;
HYF cp 201, 227; LFW 206 (cp 463); LWF 204 (cp
322); MWF 184 (cp 581); PFF 312; PMF 225, 283;
PRP 141, 142; RUS 1:497, 499, 2:623, 3:495, 497,
4:733, 6:717; TGF 237; VPN 5:259.

Blazing Star (Mentzelia lindleyi or laevicaulis) ANE
6:1162; AFP 3:136; CWF 338; DFP 43 (cp 342);
EGA 135; LWF 137 (cp 218); OGF 133; OOW
cp 132; RUS 4:189, 5:161, 6:197; VPN 3:457.

Bleak (Alburnus alburnus) ALE 4:341; NHE 122;
OBV 99.

Bleeding-heart, Fringed (Dicentra eximia) DFP 139
(cp 1108); EGP 113; FNC 75; LWF 129 (cp 206);
PMF 291; RUS 1:183, 2:241.

Bleeding-heart, Garden (Dicentra spectabilis) AGF
47; DEW 1:140; EGP 113; LFW 48 (cp 111); MWF
111 (cp 315); OGF 37; PFF 182; PFW 119; TGF
141.

Bleeding-heart, Western (Dicentra formosa) AFP
2:236; CWF 182; DFP 139 (cp 1109); HFP 122;
OGF 119; OOW cp 153; RUS 5:203; VPN 2:431.

Blenny, Red-lip (Ophioblennius atlanticus) NGF 210;
WFW cp 271.

Blenny, Striped (Chasmodes bosquianus) CFG 502;
GGF 144.

Blewits (Lepista saeva) OFP 189; ONP 31. (L. nuda)
MSM 113, cp 18; ONP 135; SMG 160, 161.

Blindfish—See **Cavefish, Southern**.

Blood Flower (Asclepias curassavica) DEW 2:97 (cp
42); EGA 96; LFW 232 (cp 517); MEP 112; RUS
2:401, 3:291, 4:435.

Bloodleaf (Iresine herbstii) EGA 128; MWF 165 (cp
516); PFF 159.

Bloodroot (Sanguinaria canadensis) ANE 2:282; DFP
24 (cp 186); FFK 112; FNC 73; HWF cp 77; HYF
cp 69; LFO 17; OGF 49; PFF 180; PFW 223; PMF
23; RUS 1:126, 2:181, 3:111, 6:161; TGF 76.

Blue Lips—See **Blue-eyed-Mary** (Collinsia grandiflora).

Blue-bead—See **Clintonia, Yellow**.

Bluebell (Endymion non-scriptus) DFP 91 (cp 727);
EWF cp 24d; MWF 265 (cp 875); NHE 38; OWF
169; RUS 3:31.

Bluebell, California (Phacelia campanularia) DFP 45
(cp 360); EGA 145; OOW cp 261; PFW 141; RUS
4:481; TGF 172.

Bluebell, Mountain (Mertensia ciliata) OOW cp 230;
RUS 4:499, 5:427, 6:511.

Bluebell, Spanish (Scilla campanulata) AGF 218; FGF
242; MGB 278; MWF 265 (cp 876).

Bluebell, Virginia (Mertensia virginiana) AGF 48; DFP
159 (cp 1270); EWF 163f; FFK 136; HWF cp 181;
HYF cp 163; LFW 212 (cp 475); PFW 49; PMF 323;
RWA cp 314; RUS 1:331, 2:423; TGF 173.

Bluebells of Scotland—See **Harebell** (Campanula
rotundifolia).

Blueberry (Vaccinium sp.) See also **Deerberry**, or
Huckleberry.

Blueberry (Vaccinium sp.) CWF 410; DFP 242 (cps
1933-1936); FNC 140; HYF cp 137; NHE 70; OFP

83; RWA cp 283; TSK 78, 79, 142, 143, 263-265;
VPN 4:33; WYG 220.

Bluebird, Eastern (Sialia sialis) AAB 357; ALE 9:221,
270; ANE 2:284; BBC 2:627; CDB 166 (cp 700);
CFG cp 15; GBC 253 (cp 52); GBI 88; LBW 278
(cp 168); NGB 2:165; NGS 218; PBA 3:241; PEB
166 (cp 45); PWB 231 (cp 48); RBA 197; RBB 235;
TBC 328 (cp 58b).

Bluebird, Mountain (Sialia currucoides) BBC 2:631;
CFG cp 15; GBC 253 (cp 52); LBW 279 (cp 169);
NGB 2:165; NGS 220; PBA 3:245; PWB 231 (cp
48); RBB 235; TBC 330 (cp 59b).

Bluebird, Western (Sialia mexicana) ANE 2:285; BBC
2:629; GBC 253 (cp 52); NGB 2:165; NGS 219;
PWB 231 (cp 48); RBB 235; TBC 330 (cp 59a).

Blueblossom—See **Lilac, California.**

Bluebonnet (Lupinus subcarnosus) EGA 133; PFF
210; RUS 3:273. (L. texensis) OOW cp 263; RUS
3:267, 269.

Bluebuttons—See **Scabious, Field.**

Bluecurls (Trichostema dichotomum) FFK 226; HWF
cp 182b; HYF cp 171; PMF 349; RUS 1:385, 2:493,
3:385.

Blue-eyed Grass (Sisyrinchium idahoense or S. com-
pestre) APF 1:466; BBF 1:544; EWF cp 166p; HFP
56; RUS 4:61; 5:69, 6:63. (S. bellum) AFP 1:467;
OOW cp 271; RUS 4:61, 5:69, 6:63.

Blue-eyed Grass, Narrow-leaved (Sisyrinchium angustifolium) BBF 1:543; CWF 74; FFK 61; FNC 38;
HWF cp 28a; HYF cp 33; RUS 1:51, 2:79, 3:53,
6:63; RWA cp 63; VPN 1:823.

Blue-eyed-Mary (Collinsia grandiflora) AFP 3:777;
CWF 463; HFP 320; RUS 5:507, 6:587; VPN 4:330.
(C. verna or Omphalodes verna) BBF 1:188; FFK
200; HYF cp 182; PFW 51; PMF 345; RUS 1:403,
2:507, 6:585; RWA cp 337.

Bluefish (Pomatomus saltatrix) ANE 2:286; CFG
cp 42; CFW 106; GGF 96; IWE 2:244; NGF 131.

Bluegrass, Alpine (Poa alpina) AFP 1:204; BBF
1:254; HMG 127; NHE 291; VPN 1:654.

Bluegrass, Annual (Poa annua) AFP 1:198; BBF 1
1:253; HMG 106; NHE 244; VPN 1:654.

Bluegrass, Fowl (Poa palustris) AFP 1:204; HMG 125;
NHE 106; VPN 1:676.

Bluegrass, Kentucky (Poa pratensis) AFP 1:202; BBF
1:256; FFK 89; HMG 114; NHE 195; PRP 58; VPN
1:676.

Bluehead—See **Wrasse, Bluehead.**

Bluet, Mountain (Centaurea montana) DFP 128 (cp
1020); EGP 104; NHE 288; TGF 236.

Bluets (Houstonia caerulea) ANE 2:287; FFK 137;
FNC 178; HWF cp 209b; HYF cp 190; LWF 158
(cp 253); MWF 156 (cp 486); PMF 41, 337; RUS
1:351, 2:451; RWA cp 354; TGF 188.

Bluethroat (Luscinia svecica) ALE 9:279; AWW 93;
BBE 263; PWB 308; RBB 231.

Boa Constrictor (Constrictor constrictor) ALE 6:376,
386; IWE 2:250, LEA 319; SOS 209.

Boa, Rubber (Charina bottae) ALE 6:383; DRW
pl 36; GRA 73; LRE 163; PFF 539; SRA cp 30;
WWS 57.

Boar, Wild (Sus scrofa) ALE 13:91, 94, 163; AWW 88;
CFG 335; FWA 79; IWE 13:1752; JAW 163; NHE
53; OMW 171; PFF 719; WEA 288, 393.

Boat Shell—See **Slipper Shell.**

Bobcat (Lynx rufus) ALE 12:284, 298; ANE 2:288;
BGM 69 (cp 8); CFG cp 32; GGM 61; IWE 2:253-
255; LEA 570; LMA 31; NGA 202-203, 208, 211;
PAK 616; PMG cp 15.

Bobolink (Dolichonyx oryzivorus) AAB 435; ALE
9:381; ANE 2:521; BBC 2:cp 106; CFG cp 21;
GBC 300 (cp 61); GBI 104; GPL 151; NGB 2:219;
NGS 298, 299; PEB 199 (cp 54); PBA 2:241, 242;
PWB 267 (cp 54); RBB 279; TBC 366 (cp 71a);
WAB 59.

Bobwhite (Colinus virginianus) AAB 124; ALE 7:429;
ANE 2:291; BBC 1:cp 39; CDB 68 (cp 194); CFG
cp 5; GBC 136 (cp 23); GBI 50; GGB 117, 132, 133;
NGB 1:229; NGW 282-283; PBA 2:4; PEB 70 (cp
21); PMB cp 9; PWB 91 (cp 22); RBB 91.

Bobwhite, Masked (Colinus ridgwayi) DBM cp 6; LVS
210; NGB 1:229; WID 215.

Boisduvalia, Dense-flowered (Boisduvalia densiflora)
HFP 228; RUS 5:305, 6:359.

Boletus, Brown-yellow (Boletus luteus) KMF 70 (cp
16b); LHM 187; MSM cp 2; NHE 46; ONP 109.

Boletus, Edible (Boletus edulis) ANE 4:755; DEW
3:142 (cp 72); GMC 215 (cps 319, 320); KMF 103
(cp 24a); LHM 191; MSM 4, cp 1; NFP 48; NHE 46;
OFP 189; ONP 143; PFF 78; SMG 96, cp 61.

Boletus, Elegant (Suillus grevillei or Boletus elegans)
DEW 3:140 (cp 70); GMC 233 (cp 334); KMF 71
(cp 16a); LHM 187; ONP 109; SMG 78, cp 45.

Boletus, Lurid (Boletus luridus) LHM 193; NFP 48;
NHE 48; SMG 93.

Boletus, Rough-stemmed (Boletus scaber) LHM 195;
NHE 46; ONP 115; PFF 78.

BTN 217; DEW 2:58 (cp 24); EGT 91; MWF 28 (cp 13); PFF 242; TSK 110, 308-309; VPN 3:416.

Bracken—See **Fern, Brake or Bracken**.

Bramble—See **Blackberry** (Rubus fruticosus).

Brambling (Fringilla montifringilla) ALE 9:336, 392; AWW 103; CDB 209 (cp 923); FWA 55; LEA 461; NHE 255; WAB 105.

Brant, American (Branta bernicla) ALE 7:61, 284; BBC 1:142; CFG 34; GBC 60 (cp 7); GGB 24; NGB 1:106; NGW 148-149; NHE 145; PBA 1:cp 22; RBB 41; SAA 144; TBC 82 (cp 5a); WAB 101; WEA 81.

Brant, Black (Branta nigricans) AAB 59; BBW 53 (cp 9); CFG 34; GGB 25; NGB 1:106; NGW 148-9; PBA 1:cp 22; PWB 27; RBB 41; TBC 82 (cp 5a).

Brass Buttons (Cotula coronopifolia) CWF 543; NHE 136; RUS 4:731, 5:611, 631.

Breadfruit (Artocarpus communis) DEW 1:104 (cp 53); OFP 115. (A. altilis) PFF 148.

Breadroot—See **Turnip, Prairie**.

Brick-tuft (Hypholoma sublateritium) NFP 83; ONP 141; PFF 86.

Bridal Wreath—See **Spiraea** (Cultivated hybrids).

Bride's Bonnet—See **Queen's Cup**.

Brier, Sensitive—See **Sensitive-brier**.

Bristle-grass (Setaria sp.) AFP 1:118; BBF 1:164-166; HMG 719-726; NHE 243; OFP 13; PFF 349; PRP 60, 61; VPN 1:698.

Brittle-bush (Encelia farinosa) AFP 4:123; LWF 106 (cp 171); RUS 4:653.

Brittle-star (Ophiura lutkenii) GAS 160. (O. sarsi) CFG 633.

Brittle-star, Common (Ophiothrix fragilis) ALE 3:390, 405; BLA 265 (cp 131), 266 (cp 133); IWE 3:285, 286-287; MOL 88; NHE 161; OIB 185.

Brittle-star, Daisy (Ophiopholis aculeata) CFG 633; GAS 158; GGS 61; KSL cp 16.

Brittle-star, Green (Ophioderma brevispinum) CFG cp 48; GGS 61; PFF 405.

Brittle-star, Scaly (Amphiopholis squamata) CFG 633; GGS 61; KSL 240; OIB 181.

Broccoli (Brassica oleracea var. botrytis) LPL 175; PFF 186; WYG 128.

Brocket—See **Deer, Brocket**.

Brodiaea (Brodiaea sp.) AFP 1:400-409; CWF 63; DFP 85 (cp 677, 678); HFP 8, 10, 12, 14, cp 13, cp 16c, cp 20b; OGF 71; OOW cp 282; RUS 4:39, 5:57, 59, 61, 6:45, 49; RWA cp 43.

Brome, Awnless or Smooth (Bromus inermis) AFP 1:229; BBF 1:277; HMG 38; NHE 196; PFF 360; PRP 23.

Brome, Barren (Bromus sterilis) AFP 1:235; BBF 1:275; HMG 53; NHE 243.

Brome, Downy or Drooping (Bromus tectorum) AFP 1:234; BBF 1:274; EWF cp 25b; HMG 55; NHE 243.

Brome, Japanese (Bromus japonicus) AFP 1:236; HMG 51; PRP 24.

Brome, Rye (Bromus secalinus) AFP 1:234; BBF 1:278; HMG 48; NHE 243; PFF 359.

Brome, Upright (Bromus erectus) AFP 1:229; BBF 1:276; NHE 196.

Brooklime, American—See **Speedwell**.

Broom, Butcher's (Ruscus aculeatus) DFP 237 (cp 1890); EWF cp 41f; HSC 110.

Broom, Scotch (Cytisus scoparius) AFP 2:517; BBF 2:350; CWF 283; DFP 194 (cp 1548); EWF cp 10f; HSC 39; LFW 39 (cp 88); MWF 103 (cp 284); NHE 69; OBT 36; PMF 155; TGS 135.

Broom, Spanish (Spartium junceum) DEW 1:285 (cp 179); DFP 240 (cp 1914); HSC 114; MWF 270 (cp 897); NHE 246; TGS 135.

Broom, Yellow—See **Hedysarum, Yellow**.

Broomrape (Orobanche fasciculata) LWF 156 (cp 251); OOW cp 89; RUS 1:413, 3:407, 4:613, 5:517, 6:613. (O. ludoviciana) OOW cp 260.

Broomrape, Branched (Orobanche ramosa) EWF cp 38f; NHE 233; PMF 325.

Broomrape, Lesser (Orobanche minor) OWF 139; PMF 325.

Broomrape, Naked or One-flowered (Orobanche uniflora) CWF 495; HWF 259; LWF 157 (cp 252); PMF 233, 327; RUS 1:413, 2:523, 3:407, 4:613, 5:517, 6:613; RWA cp 349.

Broomweed (Gutierrezia dracunculoides) PRP 133. (G. lucida) RUS 4:681, 6:663. (G. microcephala) RUS 3:457, 4:681.

Browallia (Browallia speciosa major) DFP 55 (cp 435); EGA 100; FHP 108; TGF 205.

Browallia, Orange (Striptosolen jamesonii) DFP 82 (cp 653); FHP 147; MEP 132; MWF 276 (cp 915).

Brussels Sprouts (Brassica oleracea var. gemmifera) LPL 175; OFP 157; PFF 186; WYG 127.

Bryony (Bryonia dioica) DEW 1:253; NHE 235; OWF 5.

Bryozoan (Bugula sp.) CFG 625; GAS 114, 116; GGS 58; KSL 78; OIB 173. (Dendrobeama lichenoides)

GAS 122; KSL 80. (Membranipora sp.) GAS 118; KSL 79; OIB 173. (Phidolopora pacifica) GAS 120. (Plumatella sp.) ALE 3:243; IWE 11:1513; OIB 175; PFF 403.

Bubble Shell (Bulla striata) ALE 3:79; GGS 136; GSS 128.

Buccinum—See **Whelk**.

Buckbean (Menyanthes trifoliata) CWF 418; EWF cp 15a; HWF cp 169; NHE 97; OWF 95; PFW 188; PMF 7; RUS 1:315, 5:377, 6:451; RWA cp 305; TGF 157; VPN 4:80.

Buckbrush (Ceanothus sanguineus) AFP 3:69; CWF 315; HFP 208; VPN 3:419. (C. cuneatus) AFP 3:77; HFP 210; VPN 3:419.

Buckeye—See also **Horse-chestnut**.

Buckeye, California (Aesculus californica) AFP 3:60; BTN 221.

Buckeye, Ohio (Aesculus glabra) ANE 2:317; BBF 2:499; BTN 219; EGT 96; TSK 59, 298, 299.

Buckeye, Red (Aesculus pavia) BBF 2:500; BTN 219; FNC 113; RWA cp 217; TGS 150; TSK 60, 297.

Buckeye, Yellow (Aesculus octandra) BBF 2:499; BTN 219; DFP 181 (cp 1442); FNC 114; OBT 189; PFF 244; TSK 60, 300, 301. (A. flava) MTB 352 (cp 35).

Buckthorn, Carolina (Rhamnus caroliniana) BTN 223; TSK 99, 127, 284, 418.

Buckthorn, Cascara (Rhamnus purshiana) BTN 223; CWF 318; PFF 245.

Buckwheat (Eriogonum fasciculatum) RUS 4:97, 5:97, 5:109. (Fagopyrum esculentum) PFF 156. (F. sagittatum) PMF 71.

Buckwheat, Climbing False (Polygonum scandens) HWF cp 15b; PMF 381; RUS 1:97, 3:77, 6:97.

Budgerigar—See **Parakeet, Budgerigar**.

Buffalo—See **Bison, American**.

Buffalo Berry (Shepherdia canadensis) AFP 3:166; BBF 2:576; CWF 318, 330; RWA cp 236; VPN 3:462. (Solanum rostratum) PRP 155; RUS 1:341, 2:501, 3:319, 4:501, 5:433, 6:517.

Buffalofish, Big-mouth (Ictiobus cyprinellus) GGF 55; GPL 122.

Buffalofish, Small-mouth (Ictiobus bubalus) GGF 55; NGF 271.

Buffalograss (Buchloe dactyloides or Bulbilis dactyloides) BBF 1:231; HMG 546; PRP 25.

Bufflehead (Bucephala albeola) AAB 78; ALE 7:310; BBC 1:cp 21; CFG cp 1; GBC 93 (cp 12); GGB 69;

KWF 424 (cp 18), 430 (cp 21), 456 (cp 34); NGB 1:127; NGW 182; PBA 1:cp 10; PEB 23 (pl 8), 27 (pl 10), 38 (cp 13); PWB 35 (pl 8), 43 (pl 10), 58 (cp 13); RBB 55.

Bug, Ambush (Phymata pennsylvanica) GGI 46; SIG cp 27. (P. crassipes) ALE 2:187.

Bug, Assassin (3,000+ species) BIA 119; IWE 1:98, 99; KIA 71; KIW cp 20; SCI 120; SIG cp 28.

Bug, Bed—See **Bedbug**.

Bug, Bill—See **Billbug**.

Bug, Blood-sucking Conenose (Triatoma sanguisuga) BIA cp 3; GIP 44; SCI 122.

Bug, Boxelder (Leptocoris trivittatus) BIA cp 3; GIP 35; SCI 126.

Bug, Chinch (Blissus leucopterus) GBB cp 17; GGI 47; GIP 9, 102; LPL 176; PFF 452; SCI 123; SIG cp 25.

Bug, Damsel (Nabis ferus) BIA 121; OBI 25; PFF 452; SCI 118; SIG cp 29.

Bug, Electric Light or Giant Water (Lethocerus americanus) GGI 49; GPL 103; PFF 455; SIG cp 36.

Bug, June—See **Beetle, Summer Chafer**.

Bug, Lace (Corythucha sp.) GIP 90; SCI 123; SIG cp 26. (Stephanitis rhododendri) GBB cp 17; OBI 25. (S. pyrioides) GIP 90.

Bug, Lady—See **Beetle, Ladybird**.

Bug, May—See **Beetle, Cockchafer**.

Bug, Mealy (Pseudococcus sp.) BIA 139; EGE 151; GBB cp 27; GGI 41; GIP 87, 135; PEI 144 (cp 13); SCI 158, 161; SIG cp 47a. (Orthezia insignis) GIP 87. (Phenacoccus gossypii) GIP 87.

Bug, Milkweed (Lygaeus reclivatus) GGI 45. (Onocopeltus fasciatus) KIA 71; SCI 126.

Bug, Pill or Sow—See **Pill-bug**.

Bug, Squash (Anasa tristis) BIA cp 3; GBB cp 12; GGI 44; GIP 71; PFF 452; SCI 126; SIG cp 24.

Bug, Stink (Harlequin) (Murgantia histrionica) BIA cp 3; GGI 42; GIP 70; KIA 74; SCI 128.

Bug, Stink (Southern Green) (Nezara viridula) BIA cp 3; GIP 70; LPL 177; SCI 128; SIG cp 23c.

Bug, Tarnished Plant (Lygus lineolaris) GBB cp 5; GGI 47; GIP 15, 71; LPL 176; SCI 118; SIG cp 32a. (L. hesperus) GIP 101.

Bug, Toad (Gelastocoris oculatus) BIA 115; GPL 104; SCI 116; SIG cp 34.

Bugbane—See also **Snakeroot, Black**.

Bugbane (Cimicifuga elata) AFP 2:184; HFP 114; RUS 5:123; VPN 2:340.

Bugbane, False (Trautvetteria caroliniensis) CWF 171; FFK 168; RUS 1:121, 2:173, 6:155. (T. grandis) RUS 4:145, 5:123.

Bugle (Ajuga reptans) BBF 3:101; DFP 120 (cp 955); LFW 3 (cp 6); MWF 35 (cp 34); NHE 186; OWF 144, 145; PMF 351; RUS 1:377, 3:379; TGF 189.

Bugle, Pyramid (Ajuga pyramidalis) DFP 120 (cp 954); NHE 35.

Bugloss, Viper's (Echium vulgare) EWF cp 20f; FFK 226; FNC 160; HWF cp 661a; HYF cp 165; MWF 121 (cp 346); NHE 229; OWF 171; PMF 317; RUS 1:331, 2:419, 3:309, 4:483, 5:415, 6:495.

Bullfinch (Pyrrhula pyrrhula) ALE 9:336; BBE 279; CDB 210 (cp 928); FWA 68; IWE 3:302; LBW 381; NHE 255; WAB 113; WEA 85.

Bullfrog (Rana catesbiana) ALE 5:400; ANE 4:736; BAR cp 23; BRW 34-35; CAW 150, 151, 184; CFG cp 39; CGR cp 3d; CRA 287 (cp 40); FWA 281; GPL 133; GRA 133; IWE 3:304; LEA 279; PFF 529; SRA cp 12.

Bullhead, Black (Ictalurus melas) CFG cp 44; GGF 62; GPL 127; NGF 272.

Bullhead, Brown (Ameiurus nebulosus) CFG 543; GGF 62; GPL 127; LEA 216; NGF 273; NHE 124. (Ictalurus nebulosus) PFF 513.

Bullhead, Yellow (Ictalurus natalis) CFG 543; GGF 62; GPL 127; NGF 273.

Bulrush, Great (Scirpus acutus) AFP 1:274; VPN 1:372. (S. validus) FFK 85; PFF 362.

Bumblebee—See **Bee, Bumble.**

Bumelia, Buckthorn (Bumelia lycioides) BTN 246; TSK 70, 255, 371.

Bunchberry (Cornus canadensis) AFP 3:285; BBF 2:664; CWF 363, 366; DFP 5 (cp 39); HFP 242, cp 25; HWF cp 150; HYF cp 128; LWF 138 (cp 220), 139 (cp 221); OOW cp 65; PFW 93; PMF 5; RUS 1:257, 5:319; RWA cp 249, 250; TGF 125. (C. suecica) EWF cp 3e; NHE 74.

Bunchflower (Melanthium virginicum) FNC 31; HWF cp 10; PMF 65; RUS 1:41, 2:39, 3:29, 6:41.

Bunting, Indigo (Passerina cyanea) AAB 459; ALE 9:352; ANE 2:323; BBC 2:748, cp 111; CFG cp 23; GBC 316 (cp 63); NGB 2:247; NGS 332; PBA 3:71, cp 86; PEB 215 (cp 56); PWB 275 (cp 56); RBB 295.

Bunting, Lapland (Calcarius lapponicus) BBE 294; CDB 195 (cp 852); NHE 151; SAA 138. See also **Longspur, Lapland.**

Bunting, Lark (Calamospiza melanocorys) BBC

2:cp 117; CFG cp 16; GBC 333 (cp 66); NGB 2:269; NGS 356; PBA 3:77; PEB 226 (cp 59); PWB 267 (cp 54); RBB 312; TBC 392 (cp 81); WAB 57.

Bunting, Lazuli (Passerina amoena) AAB 460; ANE 2:324; BBC 2:750, 751, cp 111; CDB 199 (cp 870); CFG cp 23; GBC 316 (cp 63); NGB 2:247; NGS 333; PBA 3:72, 73; PWB 275 (cp 56); RBB 295; TBC 38 (cp 77).

Bunting, McKay's Snow (Plectrophenax hyberboreus) NGB 2:296; NGS 375; PWB 308; RBB 325.

Bunting, Painted (Passerina ciris) AAB 458; ALE 9:352; BBC 2:cp 111; CDB 200 (cp 871); CFG cp 27; NGB 2:250; NGS 334; PBA 3:74; PEB 215 (cp 56); PWB 275 (cp 56); RBB 295; WAB 59.

Bunting, Snow (Eastern) (Plectrophenax nivalis) ALE 9:342; ANE 2:326; BBC 2:cp 124; CDB 198 (cp 864); CFG cp 26; GBC 364 (cp 69); IWE 3:314; NGB 2:296; NGS 375; NHE 151; PBA 3:20, cp 80; PEB 226 (cp 59); PWB 308; RBB 325; SAA 138; TBC 410 (cp 87).

Bunting, Varied (Passerina versicolor) NGB 2:247; NGS 333; PMB cp 46; PWB 275 (cp 56); RBB 295.

Burbot (Lota lota) CFG 529; GGF 70; WFW 187.

Burdock, Downy or Woolly (Arctium tomentosum) BBF 3:547; LWF 214 (cp 339); NHE 239; PMF 301.

Burdock, Great (Arctium lappa) AFP 4:509; BBF 3:547; NHE 239; OWF 155; PFF 330; PMF 301.

Burdock, Lesser (Arctium minus) AFP 4:509; BBF 3:548; CWF 518; NHE 239; PMF 301; RUS 2:611, 4:721, 5:599, 6:709.

Bur-Marigold, Nodding (Bidens cernua) AFP 4:127; BBF 3:495; CWF 531; FFK 251; HWF cp 262; NHE 100; OWF 33; PMF 187.

Burnet, Canadian (Sanguisorba canadensis) DFP 171 (cp 1364); FNC 91; HWF cp 94b; HYF cp 85; PMF 61; RUS 1:131, 2:187; RWA cp 144.

Burnet, Great (Sanguisorba officinalis) DEW 1:277 (cp 159); NHE 179; OWF 157; PMF 263.

Burnet, Sitka (Sanguisorba sitchensis) CWF 271; RUS 5:147, 6:185.

Burning Bush (Dictamnus alba) AGF 114; DEW 2:39; DFP 139 (cp 1111); EGP 114; EWF cp 35d; LFW 49 (cp 115); NHE 31; PFW 269; TGF 109.

Burning Bush (Euonymous atropurpurea) See **Wahoo, Eastern.**

Bur-reed (Sparganium sp.) AFP 1:81-83; BBF 1:70-74; GPL 47; NHE 107; PMF 385; RUS 1:95, 2:137, 4:79, 6:89.

Butterfly, Clouded Sulphur (Eurymus philodice) GGI 77; PFF 480.

Butterfly, Clouded Yellow (Colias croceus) ALE 2:311, 11:320; NHE 203; OBI 57. (C. hyale) NHE 203; OBI 57.

Butterfly Flower (Schizanthus hybrids) EGA 153; MWF 264 (cp 873); PFW 283; TGF 205.

Butterfly, Gray Hairstreak (Strymon melinus) GGI 74; KGB 129 (cp 16); SIG cp 87d.

Butterfly, Monarch (Danaus plexippus) ALE 2:314; AWW 19-20; BIA cp 9; GGI 60; IWE 11:1487, 1489; KIA 10, 11, 179; LEA 122; PAK 196, 197; PEI 473; SIG cp 84. (D. aglea) ALE 2:328.

Butterfly, Morpho (Morpho sp.) ALE 2:327, 360; 8:359; AWW 39-40; IWE 11:1508; OMW 22; PEI 442-445.

Butterfly, Orange-tip (Anthocharis cardamines) NHE 203; OBI 55; OMW 227.

Butterfly, Painted Lady (Vanessa cardui) ALE 2:353; GGI 71; NHE 204; OBI 47.

Butterfly, Peacock (Automeris memusae) AWW 51. (Nymphalis io) ALE 2:312; NHE 203; OBI 49.

Butterfly, Pearl Crescent (Phyciodes tharos) PFF 482; SIG cp 86d.

Butterfly, Pearl-bordered Fritillary (Argynnis euphrosyne or A. selene) IWE 6:823; OBI 45. (Clossiana selene) IWE 6:823.

Butterfly, Purple Emperor (Apatura iris) ALE 2:312-313, 353; IWE 14:1869; NHE 63; OBI 47; PEI 464; WEA 225. (A. ilia) PEI 466.

Butterfly, Question Mark (Polygonia interrogationis) GGI 69; KIA 174; SIG cp 86c.

Butterfly, Red Admiral (Vanessa atalanta) ALE 2:327, 353; BIA cp 9; GGI 70; KGB 113 (cp 14); NHE 203; OBI 49; SIG cp 86a.

Butterfly, Swallow-tail (Papilio sp.) ALE 2:354, 327; AWW 98; GGI 78-79; IWE 17:2323; KIA 164; KGB 193 (cp 24); NHE 204; OBI 55; PEI 491; PFF 479; SIG cp 82.

Butterfly, Viceroy (Limenitis archippus) BIA cp 9; GGI 61; PFF 484.

Butterfly, White Admiral (Limenitis arthemis) KGB 128 (cp 15); PFF 483. (L. camilla) OBI 47; PEI 467.

Butterflyfish, Blue-stripe (Chaetodon fremblii) NGF 334; WFW cp 318.

Butterflyfish, Long-nose (Forcipiger longirostris) NGF 335; SOS 69; WFW cp 334.

Butternut (Juglans cinerea) BBF 1:579; BTN 93; GGT 137; OFP 29; PFF 133; TSK 100, 336, 337.

Butterweed (Senecio websteri or S. neowebsteri) AFP 4:443; RUS 5:539; VPN 5:302. (S. glabellus) FFK 250.

Butterwort (Pinguicula vulgaris) AFP 4:11; BBF 3:226; CWF 498; NHE 75; OWF 139; PMF 319; RUS 1:413, 5:519, 6:613; RWA cp 347.

Buttonbush (Cephalanthus occidentalis) BBF 3:255; BTN 269; FNC 177; GPL 73; HWF cp 210; TGS 359; TSK 70, 117, 215.

Buttonweed (Diodia virginiana) FFK 172; PRP 125; RUS 2:453, 3:349.

Buttonwood—See **Sycamore, American.**

Buzzard—See **Vulture, Turkey.**

By-the-wind-sailor (Velella mutica or vellela) ALE 1:198, 271; CFG cp 47; LEA 43; MOL 59; NHE 174; OIB 11; WEA 89. (V. lata) GAS 40; JSS 76

C

Cabbage (Brassica oleracea var. capitata) EGA 99; LPL 175; NHE 215; OFP 157; PFF 185; WYG 124.

Cabbage, Chinese (Brassica pekinensis or B. chinensis) OFP 155; WYG 167.

Cabbage, Field (Brassica campestris) AFP 2:277; BBF 2:193; OWF 11; RUS 2:219, 4:207, 5:173; VPN 2:463.

Cabbage, Skunk—See **Skunk Cabbage.**

Cabbage Tree (Cordyline australis) DFP 191 (cp 1522); MTB 385 (cp 40); MWF 93 (cp 248); OBT 200.

Cabbageworm, Imported (Pieris rapae) GBB cp 26; GGI 76; GIP 13, 80; PFF 480; SIG cp 83a.

Cabezon (Scorpaenichthys marmoratus) GGF 125; HPF 540; NGF 207; WFW 326.

Cacao (Theobroma cacao) DEW 1:216 (cps 123-125); EWF cp 176a; OFP 113; PFF 252.

Cachalot—See **Whale, Sperm.**

Cacique, Yellow-rumped (Cacicus cela) ALE 9:381; CDB 206 (cp 908); GPB 313; IWE 12:1632.

Cacomistle—See **Ringtail.**

Cactus, Barrel (Echinocactus grusonii) DFP 65 (cp

Caterpillar, Tent (Malacosoma disstria and M. americana) BIA cp 11; GBB cp 18; GGI 97; GIP 143; KIA 143; PFF 472, 473; SIG cp 79.

Caterpillar, Woolly Bear (Isia isabella) BIA cp 11; GBB cp 20; GGI 83; GIP 83; PFF 478.

Caterpillar, Yellow-necked (Datana ministra) BIA cp 11; KIA 158-159; KIW 178; SCI 284; SIG cp 75.

Catfish—See also **Bullhead.**

Catfish, Blue (Ictalurus furcatus) CFG 543; GGF 61; NGF 273.

Catfish, Channel (Ictalurus punctatus) ALE 4:256; ANE 2:390; CFG cp 44; GGF 60; GPL 127; NGF 273.

Catfish, Electric (Malapterus electricus) CFW 74; IWE 6:704; WFW cp 158.

Catfish, Flathead (Pylodictis olivaris) CFG 543; GGF 61; NGF 272; WFW cp 304.

Catfish, Sea (Galeichthys felis) CFG 474; CFW 74; GGF 63.

Catnip or Catmint (Nepeta cataria) AFP 3:629; BBF 3:113; FFK 208; NHE 230; PMF 79, 351; RUS 1:377, 2:481, 3:377, 4:563, 5:469, 6:559. (N. mussinii) AGF 63; LFW 103 (cp 230); MWF 211 (cp 680); TGF 189.

Cat's-ear (Hypochoeris radicata) AFP 4:587; BBF 3:309; NHE 190; OWF 37; PMF 171; RUS 1:511, 2:639, 4:737, 5:617, 6:721.

Cat's-ear (Calochortus sp.) See **Lily, Mariposa.**

Cat's-foot—See **Pussy-toes.**

Cat-tail, Broad-leaved (Typha latifolia) ANE 3:393; AFP 1:80; BBF 1:68; EWF cp 23a; FFK 83; GPL 46; HWF 36; HYF cp 1; LWF 166 (cp 262); NHE 108; PMF 389; RUS 1:89, 2:133, 3:67, 4:75, 5:83, 6:85.

Cat-tail, Narrow-leaved (Typha angustifolia) AFP 1:80; BBF 1:69; FNC 3; GPL 46; NHE 108; PMF 389; RUS 1:89, 4:75, 5:83, 6:85.

Cattle, Brahman (Bos indicus) ALE 13:345; IWE 20:2682-2683; JAW 185; PFF 726; WMW 2:1428.

Cattle, Domestic (Bos taurus) ALE 13:346, 351; IWE 3:399-402; LEA 604-605; PFF 727-729; WEA 98; WMW 2:1427, 1428, 1430.

Cattleya—See **Orchid** (Cattleya sp.).

Cauliflower—See **Broccoli.**

Cavefish, Southern (Typhlichthys subterraneus) AWW 95; CFG 556; NGF 289.

Cedar, Alaska Yellow (Chamaecyparis nootkatensis) AFP 1:74; BTN 57; OBT 129; SFT 169.

Cedar, Atlantic or Atlas (Cedrus atlantica) BTN 37; DEW 1:54 (cp 12); DFP 251 (cp 2003); EGE 91; MTB 93 (cp 8); MWF 77 (cp 189); OBT 120.

Cedar, Deodar (Cedrus deodara) BTN 37; EGE 91; MTB 93 (cp 8); MWF 77 (cp 190); OBT 120; TGS 23.

Cedar, Incense (Libocedrus decurrens) AFP 1:71; BTN 55; DEW 1:44; DFP 253 (cp 2024); EGE 100; NFP 151; OBT 104, 128; PFF 126; SFT 149; TGS 23.

Cedar, Japanese (Cryptomeria japonica) BTN 51; DEW 1:55 (cp 16); DFP 252 (cp 2011); EGE 94; MTB 84 (cp 5); OBT 101, 124.

Cedar, Lebanon (Cedrus libani) BTN 37; EGE 92; MTB 93 (cp 8); OBT 100, 120.

Cedar, Northern White (Thuja occidentalis) ANE 1:113; BTN 55; EGE 108; GGT 39; MTB 65 (cp 4), 80; OBT 128; PFF 126; TGS 23.

Cedar, Pencil or Red (Juniperus virginiana) ANE 3:401; BTN 65; GGT 38; PFF 124; TSK 145, 148.

Cedar, Port Orford (Chamaecyparis lawsoniana) AFP 1:74; BTN 57; DFP 251 (cps 2004-2008); MTB 64 (cp 3); MWF 81 (cp 203); OBT 104, 113; SFT 173, 174.

Cedar, Western Red or Giant (Thuja plicata) AFP 1:71; ANE 1:114; BTN 55; DFP 256 (cps 2046-2047); EGE 109; MTB 65 (cp 4), 81; OBT 104, 113; SFT 155, 156.

Cedar, White (Chamaecyparis thyoides) ANE 3:400; BTN 57; GPL 71; NFP 151; PFF 125.

Celandine (Celandine majus) DEW 1:138; LWF 255 (cp 402); NHE 214; OWF 7; PFF 180; PMF 131.

Celery (Apium graveolens) NHE 135; OFP 149; OWF 47; PFF 267; RUS 3:191, 4:291, 5:267, 6:319; WYG 134.

Celery, Wild (Vallisneria americana) GPL 59; PFF 340; RUS 2:43.

Celeryworm (Papilio polyxenes) GBB cp 19; GGI 79; GIP 83.

Centaury (Centaurium umbellatum) AFP 3:353; PMF 265; RUS 5:375, 6:451.

Centipede, Giant (Scolopendra morsitans) FWA 235; PEI cp 5a.

Centipede, House (Scutigera coleoptrata) GIP 36; OIB 149; PFF 441; SIG xxii.

Century Plant—See **Agave.**

Ceramium (Ceramium fastigiatum) GGS 34; NFP 17. (C. pacificum) GUS 135. (C. rubrum) DEW 3:83; GGS 34; NHE 141; ONP 15; PFF 63.

Cereus, Night-flowering—See Cactus, Night-flowering Cereus.

Ceriman (Monstera deliciosa) MEP 12; MWF 202 (cp 651); OFP 97.

Cerith (Cerithium sp.) GGS 122; GSS 39.

Cero (Scomberomorus regalis) CFG 492; NGF 117; WFW 324.

Cestrum, Orange (Cestrum aurantiacum) DFP 56 (cp 444); MWF 79 (cp 198). (C. fasciculatum) DFP 56 (cp 445); MWF 79 (cp 199); PFW 283. (C. parqui) EWF cp 183c.

Chachalaca (Ortalis vetula) AAB 115; ANE 3:406; CDB 65 (cp 180); GPB 111; NGB 1:225; NGW 263; PMB cp 6; PWB 80; RBA 80; RBB 82. (O. poliocephala) DBM cp 9.

Chachalaca, Rufous-bellied or Wagler (Ortalis wagleri) AMB 34 (cp 2); DBM cp 9.

Chachalaca, Rufous-vented (Ortalis ruficauda) CDB 65 (cp 179); GFB 51; WAB 80.

Chachalaca, White-bellied (Ortalis leucogaster) DBM cp 9; PMB cp 6.

Chaenactis (Chaenactis douglasii) APF 4:241; CWF 534; RUS 4:731, 5:615, 6:717; VPN 5:125. (C. thompsoni) APF 4:239; VPN 5:125.

Chaffinch (Fringilla coelebs) ALE 9:392, 13:163; BBE 278; CDB 209 (cp 922); GFB 191; GPB 315; IWE 3:406-407; NHE 61.

Chameleon, American—See Anole, Green.

Chameleon Plant—See Yesterday, Today and Tomorrow.

Chamomile, Corn or Field (Anthemis arvensis) BBF 3:517; CWF 519; NHE 236; OWF 99; RUS 1:485, 2:603, 5:527.

Chamomile, German (Matricaria chamomilla) PFF 325; PMF 93; TGF 252.

Chamomile, Yellow (Anthemis cotula) APF 4:389; BBF 3:516; HYF cp 219; NHE 236; PFF 326; PMF 93; RUS 2:603, 3:481, 4:707, 5:577, 6:693. (A. tinctoria) AFP 4:389; BBF 3:517; DFP 121 (cp 968), 122 (cp 969, 970); EGP 96; LFW 13 (cp 27); MWF 42 (cp 62); NHE 236; TGF 252.

Chanterelle, Vermilion (Cantharellus cinnabarinus) FWA 65; GMC 25 (cp 47); NFP 76.

Chanterelle, Yellow (Cantharellus cibarius) ANE 4:755; GMC 25 (cp 46); LHM 59; MSM 21, cp 3; NFP 76; NHE 45; OFP 189; ONP 123; PFF 84; SMG 130, 131.

Chaparral—See Buckbrush.

Chard, Swiss (Beta vulgaris var. cicla) OFP 161; WYG 138.

Charlock—See Mustard, Field.

Charlock, Jointed—See Radish, Wild.

Chaste Tree (Vitex agnus castus) LFW 104 (cp 232, 234); NHE 109; TGS 327.

Chat, Gray-throated (Granatellus sallaei) DBM cp 44; PMB cp 37.

Chat, Ground—See Ground-chat.

Chat, Palm—See Palm Chat.

Chat, Red-breasted (Granatellus venustus) AMB 89 (cp 7); DBM cp 44; PMB cp 37.

Chat, Yellow-breasted (Icteria virens) AAB 424; ANE 3:407; CDB 204 (cp 895); CFG cp 18; GBC 284 (cp 59); GPB 309; NGB 2:185; NGS 287; PBA 3:162; PEB 183 (cp 48); PWB 262 (cp 51); RBA 217; RBB 271.

Chatterbox—See Helleborine, Giant.

Cheat—See Brome, Downy.

Checkerberry—See Wintergreen, Creeping.

Checkerbloom (Sidalcea malvaeflora) OOW cp 210; RUS 4:175, 5:151; TGF 124.

Checkered Lily—See Mission Bells.

Cheeses (Malva neglecta) NHE 220; PMF 33, 259, 327; RUS 1:149, 2:203, 3:123, 4:185, 5:147, 6:193.

Chenille Plant (Acalypha hispida) DFP 51 (cp 401); FHP 102; MEP 71; MWF 28 (cp 10); PFW 117.

Cherry, Bird or Pin (Prunus padus) DFP 220 (cp 1758); NHE 21; OBT 29. (P. pennsylvanica) BBF 2:328; BTN 167.

Cherry, Bitter (Prunus emarginata) BTN 169; CWF 258; OOW cp 25, 26.

Cherry, Black (Wild) (Prunus serotina) ANE 3:408; BTN 167; FNC 97; LFW 117 (cp 262); TSK 71, 135.

Cherry, Choke (Prunus virginiana) BTN 167; CWF 258; PRP 165; TSK 72, 129. (P. demissa) HFP 156.

Cherry, Cornelian (Cornus mas) DFP 191 (cp 1528); NHE 23; OBT 149; PFW 93.

Cherry, Flowering (Prunus serrulata) AGF 104; DFP 221 (cps 1762, 1763, 1764); EGT 136, 137; LFW 81 (cp 187), 112 (cp 249); MWF 245 (cps 804, 805); PFF 206; PFW 262; TGS 198.

Cherry, Ground (Physalis crassifolia) OOW cp 115; RUS 3:321, 4:507. (Quincula lobata) OOW cp 277; RUS 3:321, 4:507.

Cherry, Jerusalem (Solanum pseudocapsicum) FHP 145; MWF 268 (cp 890).

Cherry, Laurel—See **Laurel, Cherry.**

Cherry, Sargent's (Prunus sargentii) DFP 220 (cp 1760); EGT 136; OBT 176.

Cherry, Sour (Prunus cerasus) BBF 2:327; NHE 21; OFP 65; WYG 189.

Cherry, Spring (Prunus subhirtella) DFP 221 (cp 1765); EGT 137; MWF 245 (cp 806); OBT 176; PFW 263; TGS 198.

Cherry, Sweet (Prunus avium) BBF 2:327; DFP 220 (cp 1753); MTB 305 (cp 28); NHE 21; OBT 20, 24, 176; OFP 65; WYG 189.

Chestnut, American (Castanea dentata) ANE 3:408; BBF 1:615; BTN 117; DEW 1:185; FNC 51; GGT 82; TSK 104, 442, 443.

Chestnut, Cape (Calodendron capense) EWF cp 77e; MWF 68 (cp 158).

Chestnut, Horse—See **Horse-chestnut.**

Chestnut, Sweet or Spanish (Castanea sativa) BTN 117; DEW 1:185; FWA 65; MTB 208 (cp 19), 223; NHE 294; OBT 25; OFP 21, 25; TGS 87.

Chia (Salvia columbariae) AFP 3:640; RUS 4:549, 5:457, 6:551.

Chicalote (Argemone platyceras) AFP 2:231; LWF 68 (cp 109); OOW cp 52.

Chickadee, Black-capped (Parus atricapillus) AAB 318; ANE 3:415; BBC 2:cp 84; CDB 185 (cp 802); CFG 184; FWA 55; GBC 233 (cp 48); GBI 78; NGB 2:139; NGS 154; NHE 116; PEB 163 (cp 44); PWB 214 (cp 45); RBB 215; TBC 312 (cp 51).

Chicadee, Boreal or Brown-capped (Parus hudsonicus) AAB 320; CFG cp 28; GBC 233 (cp 48); NGB 2:139; NGS 157; PEB 163 (cp 44); PWB 214 (cp 45); RBB 215.

Chickadee, Carolina (Parus carolinensis) NGS 155; PEB 163 (cp 44); RBB 215.

Chickadee, Chestnut-backed (Parus rufescens) GBC 233 (cp 48); NGB 2:139; NGS 157; PWB 214 (cp 45); RBB 215; TBC 312 (cp 51); WAB 40.

Chickadee, Gray-headed (Parus cinctus) ALE 9:307; AWW 107; BBE 222; GBC 233 (cp 48); NGS 156; NHE 62; PWB 214 (cp 45); RBB 215.

Chickadee, Mexican (Parus sclateri) PWB 214 (cp 45); RBB 215.

Chickadee, Mountain (Parus gambeli) AAB 319; BBC 2:575, cp 84; GBC 233 (cp 48); NGB 2:139; NGS 156; PBA 3:212; PWB 214 (cp 45); RBB 215.

Chickaree—See **Squirrel, Douglas** and **Squirrel, Red.**

Chicken (Gallus domesticus) ALE 8:58, 59; IWE 4:423; PFF 585-589.

Chicken, Prairie—See **Prairie Chicken.**

Chicken-of-the-Woods—See **Mushroom, Chicken.**

Chickweed, Common (Stellaria media) AFP 2:140; BBF 2:43; NHE 225; OWF 75; PMF 37; RUS 1:193, 2:247, 3:169, 4:249, 5:219, 6:263.

Chickweed, Field (Cerastium arvense) AFP 2:144; BBF 2:49; CWF 138; HFP 92; HWF cp 63a; NHE 184; OOW cp 66; PMF 37; RUS 1:193, 2:247, 4:249, 5:223, 6:267.

Chickweed, Long-leaved (Stellaria longifolia) AFP 2:140; RUS 6:267.

Chickweed, Mouse-ear (Cerastium vulgatum) AFP 2:141; BBF 2:48; OWF 75; PMF 37; RUS 1:193, 2:247, 3:169, 4:249, 5:219, 6:267.

Chickweed, Star (Stellaria pubera) BBF 2:43; FFK 108; FNC 57; HWF cp 49; PMF 37; RUS 1:193, 2:247.

Chicory (Cichorium intybus) AFP 4:553; BBF 3:20; CWF 542; EWF cp 22d; FFK 241; FNC 186; HWF cp 230; LWF 216 (cp 343); NHE 239; OFP 151; OWF 179; PMF 93, 363; RUS 1:505, 2:637, 5:629, 6:735.

Chicory, Desert (Rafinesquia neomexicana) AFP 4:575; LWF 108 (cp 175); OOW cp 56; RUS 3:513, 4:751.

Chigger (Trombicula sp.) GIP 45; GSP 135; PFF 440.

Chile Bells (Lapageria rosea) MEP 16; PFW 229.

Chimera—See also **Rabbitfish.**

Chimera (Chimaera affinis) GGF 29; IWE 4:427; SOS 114.

Chiming Bells—See **Bluebell, Mountain.**

Chinaberry (Melia azedarach) BTN 201; EGT 127; MEP 66; MWF 199 (cp 642); TGS 294.

Chinese Hat Plant (Holmskioldia sanguinea) LFW 168 (cp 378); MEP 122; MWF 156 (cp 483).

Chinese Hat Shell—See **Snail, Chinese Hat.**

Chinese Houses (Collinsia hetrophylla) DEW 2:166 (cp 88); EGA 109; RUS 4:589, 5:505. (C. bicolor) DFP 34 (cp 271); OOW (cp 258); TGF 220.

Chinese Lantern (Physalis alkekengi or francheti) AGF 65; DFP 165 (cp 1318); EGP 139; LFW 112 (cp 247); MWF 232 (cp 759); NHE 232; PFW 284.

Chinquapin, Allegheny (Castanea pumila) BTN 117; FNC 52; PFF 140; TSK 104, 114, 444, 445.

Chinquapin, Golden-leaved (Castanopsis chrysophylla) AFP 1:515; SFT 274, 275; VPN 2:86.

Chipmunk, Eastern (Tamias strictus) ANE 3:433; BGM 116 (cp 11); BMC 71 (cp 10); CFG cp 30;

Cinquefoil, Mountain Meadow (Potentilla diversifolia) CWF 255; RUS 4:159, 5:137, 6:171.

Cinquefoil, Norwegian (Potentilla norvegica) NHE 92; PMF 149; RUS 1:133, 2:187, 3:115, 4:159, 5:137, 6:169.

Cinquefoil, Rough-fruited or Sulphur (Potentilla recta) BBF 2:254; DFP 167 (cp 1330); FFK 97; HWF cp 95; HYF cp 86; LWF 182 (cp 286); NHE 71; PMF 135; RUS 1:131, 2:187, 3:115.

Cinquefoil, Shrubby (Potentilla fruticosa) AFP 2:437; CWF 255; DFP 219 (cps 1745-1750); HSC 94; HWF cp 96b; HYF cp 87; LWF 132 (cp 210); OGF 161; OWF 17; PMF 135; RUS 1:133, 2:187, 4:163, 5:137, 6:169; RWA cp 170; TGS 294; VPN 3:143.

Cinquefoil, Sticky (Potentilla glandulosa) CWF 246; OOW cp 137; RUS 4:163, 5:139, 6:171.

Cinquefoil, Tall (Potentilla arguta) PMF 45; RUS 4:163, 6:171.

Cinquefoil, Three-toothed (Potentilla tridentata) PMF 29; RUS 1:133, 2:189.

Cisco (Coregonus artedii) GGF 49; NGF 266.

Clam, Amethyst Gem (Gemma gemma) AAS 418; ASN 237; GGS 100; PFF 423.

Clam, Atlantic Jackknife or Razor (Ensis directus) AAS pl 30k; ASN 253; CFG cp 46; GGS 105; GSS 154; PFF 425. (Tagelus gibbus) BLA 193.

Clam, Atlantic Razor (Siliqua costata) AAS pl 30f; ASN 253; CFG cp 46.

Clam, Atlantic Surf (Spisula solidissima) AAS pl 32p; ASN 255; CFG 572; GGS 106.

Clam, Basket (Corbula contracta) ALE 3:177; CFG 595. (C. luteola) MGS pl 23.

Clam, Bent-nose (Macoma nasuta) AAS 431; GAS 218; GGS 103; JSS 447, 449; KSL 220; MGS pl 21; PFF 423.

Clam, Butter or Washington (Saxidomus nuttalli) AAS pl 31l; ASN 237; MGS pl 19; PFF 423. (S. giganteus) ASN 237; GAS 214; KSL 226.

Clam, Dwarf Surf (Mulinia lateralis) AAS pl 32o; CFG 594; GGS 107.

Clam, Green Razor (Solen viridis) AAS pl 30n; ASN 253; CFG cp 46; GGS 105.

Clam, Horse or Gaper (Schizothaerus nuttalli or Tresus nuttalli) AAS pl 31z; ASN 255; GAS 230; JSS 463; MGS pl 24; PFF 425. (Mya truncata) GAS 232; MGS pl 25; NHE 168.

Clam, Littleneck (Protothaca staminea) AAS pls 31m, 31n; ASN 235; GAS 216; GGS 98; JSS 447; KSL 224; MGS pl 18; PFF 423.

Clam, Nut (Acila and Nucula sp.) AAS 334, 337, 338; ASN 191; CFG 595; GGS 83; IWE 12:1596; MGS pl 9; NHE 165.

Clam, Pacific Jackknife (Solen sicarius) AAS pl 29v; ASN 253; GAS 226; JSS 459; MGS pl 23.

Clam, Pacific Razor (Siliqua patula) AAS pl 29y; ASN 253; BLA 192; GAS 228; JSS 459; KSL 204; MGS pls 1, 23; PFF 425.

Clam, Pismo (Tivela stultorum) AAS pl 31h; ASN 235; GGS 101; MGS cp 1, pl 17; PFF 423.

Clam, Purplish Razor (Tagelus divisus) AAS pl 30g; ASN 251; CFG 594.

Clam, Quahog (Mercenaria mercenaria) AAS pl 32h; ASN 231; CFG 592; GGS 96; GSS 15, 146; OIB 75. (M. campechiensis) AAS pl 32g; GGS 96. (Arctica islandica) AAS pl 32f; CFG 592; NHE 166.

Clam, Rock-boring (Botula californiensis or Adula californiensis) AAS pl 29h; ASN 201; MGS pl 11.

Clam, Rough File (Lima scabra) GSS 133; MOL 71.

Clam, Soft-shell (Mya arenaria) AAS pl 32x; ALE 3:177; ASN 257; GGS 108; KSL 227; MGS pl 25; OIB 81; PFF 425.

Clam, Spoon (Periploma sp.) AAS pls 28v, 28w, 28x; ASN 263; CFG 594, 595; MGS pl 27.

Clam, Stout Razor (Tagelus plebeius) AAS pl 30d; ASN 251; CFG cp 46; GGS 105.

Clam, Wedge—See **Coquina.**

Clam, White Sand (Macoma secta) AAS 431; ASN 245; GAS 220; GGS 103; JSS 449, 452; MGS pl 21.

Clam, Yoldia—See **Yoldia.**

Clarkia (Clarkia amoena) CWF 339; EWF cp 156c; OOW cp 211; RUS 5:303. (C. pulchella) CWF 339; EGA 107; RUS 6:355. (C. rubicunda) OOW cp 213; RUS 4:335, 5:303. (C. elegans) AGF 72; DFP 34 (cp 269); EGA 107; MWF 86 (cp 224); PFW 204; TGF 124.

Clary—See **Sage.**

Cleavers—See also **Bedstraw.**

Cleavers (Galium aparine) NHE 100; PFF 301; PMF 41; RUS 1:355, 2:453, 3:353, 4:523, 5:445, 6:533.

Clematis, Blue (Clematis columbiana) CWF 166; RUS 6:153; RWA cp 129, cp 130.

Clematis, Leather-flower (Clematis viorna) FFK 125; FNC 64; HYF cp 63; PMF 231; RUS 1:117, 2:171; RWA cp 131.

Clematis, Showy (Clematis jackmanii) FGF 73; HSC 30; LFW 34 (cp 81, 82), 35 (cp 84); PFW 254; TGF 7; TGS 70.

Clematis, Virgin's Bower (Clematis virginiana) FFK 111; FNC 64; HWF cp 73; HYF cp 62; PMF 77; RUS 1:117, 2:171. (C. ligusticifolia) CWF 163; HFP 96; RUS 4:145, 5:129, 6:153. (C. verticillaris) HYF cp 63; PMF 339.

Cliffrose (Cowania stansburiana) LWF 71 (cp 115). (C. mexicana) BTN 181.

Clingfish (Gobiesox meandricus) HPF 210; KSL 200; LFI 139.

Clintonia—See also **Queen's Cup.**

Clintonia, Red (Clintonia andrewsiana) AFP 1:453; LWF 226 (cp 360); RUS 5:47.

Clintonia, White (Clintonia umbellatum) BBF 1:515; FFK 52; FNC 22; PMF 67; RUS 1:33, 2:45.

Clintonia, Yellow (Clintonia borealis) ANE 3:455; BBF 1:514; FNC 22; HWF cp 17; HYF cp 13; LWF 226 (cps 358, 359); PMF 103, 371; RUS 1:33, 2:47; RWA cp 48.

Clitocybe, Sweet-scented (Clitocybe odora) GMC 109 (cp 168); LHM 95; MSM 61; NFP 62; ONP 131.

Clockvine—See **Black-eyed Susan.**

Clotbur (Xanthium echinatum) HWF cp 213b; PMF 385. (X. strumorium) NHE 238; PFF 319.

Clover, Alsike (Trifolium hybridum) AFP 2:528; BBF 2:357; HYF cp 93; OWF 115; PMF 81, 247; PRP 104; RUS 1:265, 2:339, 4:369, 5:331, 6:383.

Clover, Bush—See **Bush-clover.**

Clover, Crimson (Trifolium incarnatum) AFP 2:532; BBF 2:355; PMF 247; PRP 105; RUS 1:265, 2:241, 3:251, 5:331, 6:379.

Clover, Hare's-foot or Rabbit's-foot (Trifolium arvense) AFP 2:529; BBF 2:355; CWF 303; EWF cp 10c; HWF cp 108a; HYF cp 95; NHE 212; OWF 115; PMF 247; RUS 1:265, 2:341, 3:249, 5:333.

Clover, Hop (Trifolium agrarium) BBF 2:354; HWF cp 93; LWF 185 (cp 291); PMF 151; RUS 5:329, 6:377. (T. campestre) NHE 180; OWF 21; RUS 1:267, 2:341, 3:249, 4:367, 6:377. (T. procumbens) PRP 107.

Clover, Japanese (Lespedeza striata) BBF 2:408; PFF 218; PRP 86. (L. stipulacea) FFK 190; RUS 2:353, 3:259, 6:393.

Clover, Lesser Yellow (Trifolium dubium) AFP 2:525; BBF 2:354; NHE 180; PMF 151; RUS 2:343, 3:249, 4:367, 5:329.

Clover, Owl's (Orthocarpus purpurascens) OOW cp 264; RUS 4:609, 5:493. (O. tenuifolius) LWF 153 (cp 245); RUS 6:573; RWA cp 343.

Clover, Prairie—See **Prairie-clover.**

Clover, Red (Trifolium pratense) BBF 2:355; FFK 183; LWF 185 (cp 290); NHE 180; OWF 115; PMF 247; PRP 106; RUS 1:265, 2:341, 3:249, 4:367, 5:333, 6:383.

Clover, Strawberry (Trifolium fragiferum) NHE 180; OWF 115; PRP 102.

Clover, Thompson's (Trifolium thompsoni) AFP 2:529; RUS 6:379; VPN 3:371.

Clover, White (Trifolium repens) AFP 2:528; ANE 3:458; BBF 2:358; NHE 180; OWF 83; PMF 81; PRP 108; RUS 1:265, 2:341, 3:249, 4:369, 5:331, 6:383.

Clover, White Sweet (Melilotus alba) AFP 2:517; BBF 2:352; HWF cp 99; NHE 212; PMF 81; PRP 111; RUS 1:267, 2:347, 3:251, 4:369, 5:335, 6:385.

Clover, Yellow Sweet (Melilotus officinalis) AFP 2:525; BBF 2:353; NHE 212; OWF 23; PMF 151; PRP 111; RUS 1:267, 2:347, 3:251, 4:371, 6:385. (M. indicus) RUS 5:335.

Clover, Zigzag (Trifolium medium) BBF 2:356; DEW 1:312; NHE 179; OWF 115.

Clubmoss (Lycopodium sp.) AFP 1:43-45; BBF 1:43-48; DEW 3:257, 258; FFK 44, 45; NFP 122-124; NHE 80; ONP 57; PFF 108.

Clubmoss, Little (Selaginella sp.) AFP 1:46-50; NFP 125, 126; PFF 109.

Cluster-lily—See **Brodiaea.**

Coachwhip (Masticophis flagellum) ALE 6:420; BAR cp 48; CFG cp 36; CRA 190 (cp 23); GRA 86; PFF 542; SRA cp 30; WWS 1:432.

Coalfish (Gadus virens) IWE 4:458; OBV 39.

Coati, White-nosed (Nasua narica) ALE 12:94; BGM 100 (cp 9); FWA 224; GGM 37; IWE 4:460, 461; NGA 169; PMG cp 35.

Cobia (Rachycentron canadum) CFG 484; CFW 106; NGF 133; WFW cp 305.

Cobra Plant—See **Pitcher Plant, California.**

Cockle, Dwarf or Little (Cerastoderma pinnulatum) AAS pl 30c; ASN 229; CFG 595.

Cockle, Great Heart or Giant Atlantic (Dinocardium robustum) AAS pl 32a; ASN 229; CFG cp 46; GGS 95; PFF 421.

Cockle, Heart or Nuttall's (Clinocardium nuttalli) AAS pl 31b; ASN 229; GGS 95; KSL 223; MGS pl 16; PFF 421. (Cerastoderma corbis) GAS 212.

Cockle, Iceland (Clinocardium ciliatum) AAS pl 32e; ASN 229; CFG 593; GGS 95; MGS pl 16.

Cockle, Morton's (Laevicardium mortoni) AAS pl 391;
ASN 227; CFG 594; PFF 421.

Cocklebur—See **Clotbur.**

Cockroach, American (Periplaneta americana) GGI
23; GIP 29; IWE 4:474, 475; KIA 20; LEA 132; OBI
11; PFF 443; SIG pl 4.

Cockroach, Common or Oriental (Blatta orientalis)
BIA cp 2; GIP 29; OBI 11.

Cockroach, German (Blattella germanica) ALE 2:126;
ANE 3:468; GGI 153; GIP 28; LPL 176; PFF 443.

Cockscomb (fish) (Anoplarchus purpurescens) HFP
329; KSL cp 23. (A. insignis) HFP 328.

Cockscomb (plant) (Celosia cristata) AGF 75; FGF 76;
MWF 77 (cp 193). (C. argentea) DFP 33 (cps 257,
258); EGA 103; MWF 77 (cp 192).

Cockscomb (tree) (Erythrina crista-galli) DEW 1:287
(cp 184); DFP 199 (cp 1592); MWF 126 (cp 366);
PFW 165.

Cocoa—See **Cacao.**

Codfish (Gadus morhua) ALE 4:431; CFW 94; GGF
71; IWE 4:477; LEA 250; MOL 106; NGF 198; NHE
152; OBV 35; WFW cp 192. (G. callarias) ANE
3:469; CFG cp 41. (G. macrocephalus) HPF 222.

Coffee (Coffee arabica) DEW 2:107 (cp 64, 65); EWF
cp 60d; FHP 113; OFP 111.

Coffee Bean (Trivia sp.) AAS pl 20; ASN 107; GGS
125; MGS pl 35; PFF 413.

Coffee-tree, Kentucky (Gymno cladus dioica) BBF
2:340; BTN 187; EGT 118; TGS 135; TSK 326, 327.

Cohosh, Black—See **Snakeroot, Black.**

Cohosh, Blue (Caulophyllum thalictroides) FFK 276;
FNC 68; HWF cp 75; PMF 367, 391; PFF 178.

Colchicum (Colchicum autumnale) AGF 168; DFP 86
(cp 686); EGA 103; MGB 189; MWF 90 (cp 237);
NHE 191; OWF 163; SGB 61 (cp 4); TGF 12. (C.
speciosum) DFP 86 (cp 688), 87 (cps 689, 690);
OGF 183.

Coleus (Coleus blumei) AGF 75; DFP 60 (cp 478);
EGA 108; MWF 91 (cps 239, 240); OGF 125; PFF
288; PFW 153; TGF 205. (C. thyrsoideus) DFP 60
(cp 479); MWF 91 (cp 242); PFW 152. (C. frederici)
EWF cp 63a.

Colic-root (Aletris farinosa) BBF 1:511; FFK 55; FNC
30; HWF cp 16; PMF 65; RUS 1:41, 2:47, 3:31. (A.
aurea) BBF 1:511; RUS 2:47, 3:31.

Collomia, Large-flowered (Collomia grandiflora) AFP
3:406; CWF 435; RUS 4:457, 5:395, 6:465.

Collybia, Buttery (Collybia butyracea) LHM 101; NFP
66; ONP 133; SMG 163, cp 114.

Collybia, Oak-loving (Collybia dryophila) GMC 135
(cps 225, 226); LHM 101; MSM 106; SMG 164,
cp 115.

Collybia, Rooting (Collybia radicata) NFP 65; PFF
82.

Collybia, Spotted (Collybia maculata) GMC 135 (cp
224); KMF 67 (cp 15b); LHM 101; ONP 103.

Coltsfoot (Tussilago farfara) BBF 3:531; HYF cp 204;
LWF 49 (cp 82); NHE 101; OWF 41; PMF 111; RUS
1:447.

Coltsfoot, Sweet (Petasites palmatus) BBF 3:531;
CWF 555; OOW cp 6. (P. sagittata) AFP 4:455;
BBF 3:532. (P. speciosa) HFP 386.

Columbine, Blue (Aquilegia coerulea) OOW cp 232;
PFF 173; RUS 4:131, 6:149, 151.

Columbine, Common (Aquilegia vulgaris) AGF 78;
BBF 2:93; EWF cp 8f; MWF 44 (cp 68); NHE 26.

Columbine, Eastern (Aquilegia canadensis) ANE
3:471; BBF 2:92; FFK 121; FNC 61; HWF cp 65;
HYF cp 58; PFF 173; PMF 217; RUS 1:117, 2:169,
3:103, 6:153; RWA cp 111.

Columbine, Western (Aquilegia formosa) AFP 2:184;
CWF 162; HFP 110; OOW cp 150; RUS 4:133,
5:115, 6:149.

Columbine, Yellow or Golden (Aquilegia flavescens)
AFP 2:184; CWF 162; RUS 6:149; RWA cp 112.
(A. chrysantha) OOW cp 78; RUS 6:149; TGF 141.

Colus—See **Whelk.**

Combfish (Zaniolepis latipinnis) HPF 471; WFW
cp 365.

Comb-jelly (Mnemiopsis sp.) CFG 622; GGS 3.
(Pleurobrachia sp.) ALE 1:271; CFG 622; GAS 62;
GGS 53; KSL 69; NHE 174; OIB 17.

Comfrey, Common (Symphytum officinale) DFP 175
(cp 1393); NHE 186; OWF 131; PMF 145, 293, 335;
RUS 1:337, 2:423, 5:427, 6:517. (S. peregrinum)
OGF 17.

Comfrey, Wild (Cynoglossum virginianum) FFK 147;
HWF cp 162; PMF 335; RUS 1:337, 2:423, 3:309,
6:499.

Compass-plant (Silphium laciniatum) HYF cp 205;
PFF 318; PMF 185; PRP 152; RUS 1:465, 2:579,
3:451.

Conch, Crown (Melongena corona) ASN 137; GSS 84.
(M. melongena) GSS 84. (M. patula) MGS pl 59.

Conch, Fighting (Florida) (Strombus alatus) ASN 105;
GGS 120; GSS 42; PFF 411.

Conch, Fighting (West Indian) (Strombus pugilis) ASN
105; GGS 121; GSS 42; WEA 109.

Conch, Queen (Strombus gigas) ALE 3:55; ASN 105; GGS 121; GSS 42; IWE 4:509.

Condor, California (Gymnogyps californianus) AAB 91; ALE 7:334; ANE 3:473-475; BBW cp 13; GPB 23; LBI 87; NGB 1:145; NGW 208, 214-215; OMW 79; PBA 2:55; PFF 573; PWB 75; RBB 65; WAB 27, 53; WID 194 (cp 18).

Cone Shell (Conus sp.) GGS 135; GSS 188, 119; IWE 4:512, 513.

Cone-flower (Rudbeckia hirta) AFP 4:117; BBF 3:470; CWF 55; DFP 46 (cp 368); FFK 256; FNC 200; HWF cp 254; HYF cp 218; LWF 208 (cp 331); MWF 258 (cp 855); PFF 320; PMF 113; PRP 148; RUS 1:459, 2:577, 3:457.

Cone-flower, Clasping-leaf (Rudbeckia amplexicaulis) EWF cp 165c; RUS 2:579, 3:457.

Cone-flower, Green-headed (Rudbeckia laciniata) DFP 169 (cp 1353); FFK 256; HWF cp 255; OGF 147; OOW cp 118; PFF 320; PFW 83; PMF 115; RUS 1:461, 2:577, 3:457, 4:685, 6:667; TGF 285.

Cone-flower, Orange (Rudbeckia fulgida) DFP 169 (cp 1352); EGP 21, 144; PFW 83; PMF 189; RUS 2:577.

Cone-flower, Prairie (Ratibida pinnata or columnaris) FFK 196; HYF cp 200; OOW cp 117; PMF 115; PRP 147; RUS 1:461, 2:575, 3:457, 4:685, 6:663.

Cone-flower, Purple (Echinacea purpurea) AGF 79; BBF 3:475; DFP 170 (cp 1354, 1355); EGP 115; FFK 261; HYF cp 221; MWF 120 (cp 343); OGF 123; PFF 320; PFW 83; PMF 309; RUS 1:483, 2:603, 3:481 (E. pallida); TGF 268.

Cone-flower, Thin-leaved (Rudbeckia triloba) FFK 255; HWF cp 253; LWF 221 (cp 496); PMF 113; RUS 1:461, 2:577.

Cone-plant (Hemitomes congestum) AFP 3:300; CWF 375; RUS 5:315; VPN 4:15.

Cony—See **Pika**.

Cookacheea—See **Whip-poor-will, Ridgway's**.

Coon—See **Raccoon**.

Coontie (Zamia floridana) NFP 149; PFF 111.

Coot, American (Fulica americana) AAB 143; ANE 3:478; BBC 1:cp 44; GBC 136 (cp 23); GGB 96, 97; GPL 146; IWE 4:516-517; NGB 1:289; NGW 311; PBA 1:214; PEB 71 (cp 22); PWB 99 (cp 24); RBA 95; RBB 105.

Cooter—See **Turtle, Cooter or Slider**.

Copepod (Various sp.) ALE 1:443; GGS 16; GPL 90; IWE 4:518-519; KSL 81, 82; LEA 162, 163; MOL 60, 77; OBV 21; OIB 127, 135, 141; PFF 428.

Copper Bush (Cladothamnus pyrolaeflorus) AFP 3:300; CWF 378; VPN 4:15.

Copperhead (Agkistrodon contortrix or Ancistrodon contortrix) BAR cp 63; CFG cp 35; CGF cp 16c; CRA 238 (cp 29); GRA 109; LEA 329; LFO 29, 146; MAR 186; PFF 547; PRW pl 140; SIR 250 (cp 132).

Coquette, Tufted (Lophornis ornata) ALE 8:453; HBT 145 (cp 6).

Coquina (Donax variabilis) AAS pl 30r; ASN 249; CFG 595; GSS 153; PFF 423. (D. fossor) ASN 249; GGS 104.

Coral Beads (Cocculus carolinus) FNC 69; TSK 123, 195.

Coral Bells (Heuchera sanguinea) AGF 79; DFP 147 (cp 1172, 1173); EGP 123; FGF 81; LFW 202 (cp 460); MWF 153 (cp 472); PFW 273; RUS 4:267; TGF 93.

Coral, Brain (Diplora labyrithiformis) GGS 51. (Meandrina meandrites) WEA 80.

Coral, Orange-red or Cup (Balanophyllia elegans) GAS 52; GGS 50; JSS 98 (cp 3); KSL cp 5; OMW 139; RCT 109 (pl 6).

Coral Plant (Russelia equisetiformis) FHP 142; LFW 264 (cps 589, 590); MEP 133. (R. juncea) MWF 260 (cp 858). (Jatropha multifida) MEP 72.

Coral, Red or Precious (Corallium rubrum) GGS 51; IWE 16:2198-2199; NHE 175.

Coral Shell—See **Snail, Coral**.

Coral Spot (Nectaria cinnabarina) ONP 145; PFF 71.

Coral, Star (Favia fragum) GGS 51. (Astrangia danae) CFG cp 47; GGS 50.

Coral Vine (Antigonon leptopus) AGF 80; LFW 231 (cp 516); MEP 35; MWF 43 (cp 65); PFW 236.

Coral-bean (Erythrina herbacea) BTN 193; RUS 2:347. (E. indica) MWF 126 (cp 367).

Coralberry (Symphoricarpos orbiculatus) AGF 80; TSK 127, 212.

Coralline (Corallina sp.) DEW 3:60 (cp 33); GGS 35; GUS 91; KSL 157; NHE 141; ONP 15; PFF 61.

Coral-root, Crested (Hexalectris spicata) FFK 92; RUS 1:73, 2:99, 3:59, 4:75.

Coral-root, Northern (Corallorhiza trifida) BBF 1:574; COA 334; EWF cp 7a; NHE 41; OWF 45; RUS 1:73, 4:75, 6:75.

Coral-root Spotted (Corallorhiza maculata) BBF 1:575; COA 327; CWF 86; HWF cp 73; HYF cp 38; OOW cp 7; PMF 243, 393; RUS 1:73, 2:99, 3:59, 4:75, 5:79, 6:75.

Cowbird, Giant (Scaphidura oryzivora) ALE 9:381; DBM cp 38; PMB cp 39.

Cowbird, Glossy or Shiny (Molothrus bonariensis) ALE 9:381; BWI 214; DBM cp 38.

Cowfish (Lactophrys quadricornis) CFG 511; CFW 150; GGF 136; NGF 213.

Cow-parsnip (Heracleum lanatum) BBF 2:635; CWF 354; HFP 232; OOW cp 67; RUS 1:223, 2:285, 4:295, 5:271, 6:321. (H. maximum) PMF 51.

Cowpea (Vigna sinensis) PFF 220; WYG 163. (V. luteola) RUS 2:333, 3:245. (V. unguiculata) OFP 45.

Cowry, Atlantic (Cypraea cinerea and C. spurca) AAS cp 6a, 6c; ASN 111; GGS 125; GSS 52.

Cowry, Carnelian or Orange-banded (Cypraea carneola) GSS 58; MGS pl 68.

Cowry, Chestnut (Cypraea spadicea) AAS cp 6b; ASN 111; GGS 124, 125; GSS 52; PFF 413.

Cowry, Hump-backed or Mourning (Cypraea mauriti-ana) GSS 58; MGS pl 68.

Cowry, Isabel's (Cypraea isabella) GSS 58; MGS pl 68.

Cowry, Measled (Cypraea zebra) AAS cp 6d; ASN 111; 111; GGS 125; GSS 52.

Cowry, Money (Cypraea moneta) GSS 61; MGS pl 68.

Cowry, Tiger (Cypraea tigris) ALE 3:55, 72; BLA 96 (cp 58); GSS 51, 57; IWE 4:544; MGS pl 68; MOL 68.

Cowslip (Caltha palustris) See **Marsh-marigold.**

Cowslip (Primula officinalis or P. veris) DEW 1:229; NHE 33; OWF 27.

Cowslip, Cape—See **Cape Cowslip.**

Cowslip, Virginia—See **Bluebell, Virginia.**

Cow-wheat (Melampyrum lineare) HWF cp 165a; PMF 125; RUS 1:403, 2:507.

Coyote (Canis latrans) ALE 12:206, 232; ANE 3:494, 495; BGM 68 (cp 7); BMC 230 (cp 22); CFG cp 32; FWA 125; GGM 52, 56; IWE 4:546-547, 548-549; JAW 95; LMA 92; NGA 132; PMG cp 12; SAA 127, 128-129, 143; WEA 130.

Coyote-mint (Monardella villosa) AFP 3:653; RUS 4:557, 5:461.

Coypu—See **Nutria.**

Crab, Black-clawed (Lophopanopeus bellus) GAS 402; JSS 388; KSL cp 20.

Crab, Blue (Callinectes sapidus) ANE 3:521, 522; CFG cp 48; GGS 74; PAK 107.

Crab, Box (Lopholithodes foraminatus) GAS 412; JSS 338, 346.

Crab, Butterfly or Sitka (Cryptolithodes sitchensis) JSS 338; KSL cp 22.

Crab, Dungeness (Cancer magister) BLA 212 (cp 96); GAS 404; GGS 76; JSS 380; KSL 253; NGF 192-193.

Crab, Fiddler (Uca sp.) ALE 1:476; ANE 3:497; BAW 274 (8); BLA 215 (cp 100); CFG 655; GGS 77; IWE 6:752; PFF 432.

Crab, Ghost or Sand (Ocypode quadratus) ALE 1:476; CFG cp 48; FWA 297; GGS 77; SOS 20, 21; WEA 164. (O. arenaria) BLA 214 (cp 99).

Crab, Green or Shore (Carcinus maenas) AWW 164; BLA 212 (cp 95); CFG 653; GGS 74; IWE 16:2127, 2128; LEA 166, 176; NHE 170; OIB 125.

Crab, Hairy (Cancer oregonensis) GAS 408; JSS 382; KSL cp 21.

Crab, Hermit (Pagurus sp.) BLA 217 (cp 104); CFG cp 48; GAS 380, 384; GGS 73; IWE 8:1055, 1056; KSL 134; PAK 108.

Crab, Horseshoe or King (Limulus polyphemus) ALE 1:393; ANE 5:890; BAW 274 (9); BLA 242; CFG 643; GGS 79; IWE 9:1228; LEA 185; MOL 76; PAK 112; SOS 23; WEA 198.

Crab, Kelp (Pugettia productus) GAS 394; GGS 78; JSS 366; KSL 194. (P. gracilis) GAS 392.

Crab, Lady (Ovalipes ocellatus) CFG cp 48; GGS 75.

Crab, Mole or Sand (Emerita analoga) GGS 72; JSS 338, 342. (E. talpoida) BLA 240; CFG cp 48.

Crab, Pea (Pinnotheres pisum) NHE 170; OIB 125; WEA 280.

Crab, Porcelain (Petrolisthes eriomerus) GAS 388; JSS 350; KSL 142.

Crab, Red (Cancer productus) GAS 406; JSS 359, 375; KSL 253.

Crab, Rock (Cancer irroratus) CFG cp 48; GGS 76; (C. pagurus) ALE 1:473.

Crab, Shore (Hemigrapsus nudus) AWW 37; GAS 390; JSS 356, 396; KSL 140, cp 20. (H. oregonensis) JSS 362, 396; KSL 141.

Crab, Spider (Libinia emarginata) CFG 652; GGS 78; PAK 109. (Oregonia gracilis) KSL 195. (Steno-rhynchus seticornus) WEA 117.

Crab-apple—See **Apple, Crab.**

Crabgrass—See **Grass, Crab**

Crake, Corn (Crex crex) ALE 8:83; BBE 104; CDB 74 (cp 224); GFB 63; IWE 4:532; NHE 201; RBB 103.

Crake, Spotted (Porzana porzana) ALE 8:97, 11:257;

GFB 70; GGB 102; NGB 1:271; NGW 332; PBA
1:cp 38; PEB 103 (cp 30); PWB 103 (cp 26); RBB
115.

Curlew, Mexican Stone—See **Thick-knee, Double-striped.**

Currant, Common or Garden (Ribes sativum) AFP
2:393; OFP 81; PFF 193; VPN 3:82; WYG 223.

Currant, Golden (Ribes aureum) AFP 2:394; HSC
103; TGS 230; VPN 3:68.

Currant, Red Flowering (Ribes sanguineum) AFP
2:397; CWF 234; DEW 1:279 (cp 162); DFP 230
(cp 1833); EWF cp 151c; HFP 136; HSC 103; MWF
254 (cp 837); OGF 25; PFW 134; TGS 230; VPN
3:82.

Currant, Sticky (Ribes viscosissimum) AFP 2:393;
CWF 235; VPN 3:88.

Cusk (Brosme brosme) ALE 4:431; CFG 478, 508;
NGF 200; NHE 154.

Custard-apple (Annona cherimolia) MWF 42 (cp 61);
OFP 97.

Cutlass-fish (Trichiurus lepturus) CFG 497; GGF 1;
WFW cp 355.

Cutworm (Various genera and species) GBB cp 23;
GIP 64; LPL 176; OBI 71; PFF 477.

Cyclamen (Cyclamen europaeum) AGF 84; DEW
1:230; MGB 198; PFW 240. (C. neapolitanum) DFP

91 (cp 721); MWF 100 (cp 275); OGF 177. (C. persicum) DFP 61 (cp 486), 91 (cp 722); EWF cp 48g;
FHP 116; LFW 39 (cps 91, 92); MWF 100 (cp 276);
PFW 239.

Cynthia—See **Dandelion, Goat or Dwarf.**

Cypress, Alaska—See **Cedar, Alaska Yellow.**

Cypress, Arizona (Cupressus arizonica and C. glabra)
BTN 59; DFP 252 (cp 2013); MTB 64 (cp 3); NFP
151.

Cypress, Bald or Swamp (Taxodium distichum) ANE
3:528; BBF 1:64; BTN 53; DEW 1:38, 39; DFP 256
(cp 2041); EGE 107; GGI 40; GPL 69; MTB 85 (cp
6); MWF 280 (cp 927); OBT 101, 125; TGS 22; TSK
354, 355.

Cypress, Flowering—See **Tamarisk.**

Cypress, Gowen (Cupressus goveniana) AFP 1:73;
BTN 59; MTB 72.

Cypress, Lawson—See **Cedar, Port Orford.**

Cypress, Monterey (Cupressus macrocarpa) AFP 1:72;
BTN 59; MTB 64 (cp 3); OBT 104, 129.

Cypress, Sawara (Chamaecyparis pisifera) EGE 94;
MTB 64 (cp 3), 66; OBT 129.

Cypress, Summer (Kochia scoparia) DFP 40 (cp 314);
EGA 128; PFF 157.

Cypress Vine (Quamoclit pennata) AGF 84; DEW
2:109 (cp 70); EGA 149; RUS 1:345, 2:433, 3:333.

D

Dab, Long Rough—See **Plaice, American.**

Dace, Redside (Clinostomus elongatus) CFG 539; GGI
58; NGF 269.

Dace, Southern Redbelly (Chrosomus erythrogaster)
CFG cp 44; GGF 59; NGF 268.

Daddy-long-legs (Tipula oleracea) ALE 2:394; ANE
3:529; NHE 206. (T. maxima) OBI 123. (Liobunum vittatum) GIP 37; PFF 433. (Nephrotoma
crocata) IWE 5:601-603.

Daffodil—See **Narcissus.**

Daffodil, Winter—See **Crocus, Autumn** (Sternbergia
lutea).

Daggerfish (Anotopterus pharao) HPF 177; WFW 115.

Dagger-pod (Phoenicaulis cheiranthoides) AFP 2:289;
RUS 5:189; VPN 2:531.

Dahlia (Dahlia hybrids) AGF 89-91; DFP 35 (cp 280),
36 (cp 281), 133 (cps 1060-1064), 134-136; EGA
113; FGF 90-92; LFW 194 (cp 437), 196-197 (cps

438-447); MGB 199-210; MWF 104-105 (cps 286-290); OGF 167; TGF 253.

Dahoon (Ilex cassine) BBF 2:487; BTN 207.

Daisy, African (Arctotis sp.) AGF 18; DFP 30 (cps
238, 239); EWF cp 83b; MWF 45 (cp 73); OGF 139;
TGF 269.

Daisy, African (Dimorphotheca aurantica) See **Marigold, Cape.**

Daisy, Blue (Felicia amelloides) EGA 118; EGP 117;
FHP 121; MWF 133 (cp 392); TGF 252. (F. angustifolia) MWF 133 (cp 393).

Daisy, Crown (Chrysanthemum coronarium) DFP 34
(cp 265); EGA 106; OFP 155.

Daisy, Cut-leaved (Erigeron compositus) AFP 4:355;
CWF 550; RUS 4:697, 5:587, 6:679; VPN 5:176.

Daisy, Desert (Melampodium leucanthemum) LWF
107 (cp 172); RUS 3:463, 4:659.

Daisy, Easter—See **Easter-daisy.**

Daisy, English or Lawn (Bellis perennis) AFP 4:305; AGF 100; BBF 3:402; CWF 531; DFP 31 (cp 243); EGA 98; EGP 100; EWF cp 22c; FGF 102; MWF 55 (cp 112); NHE 190; OGF 33; OWF 99; TGF 253.

Daisy, Livingstone (Mesembryanthemum criniflorum or Dorotheanthus bellidiformis) DFP 43 (cp 343); EGA 136; MWF 116 (cp 331); PFW 18.

Daisy, Michaelmas (Aster novaebelgii) BBF 3:421; DFP 124 (cps 986-991); EGP 99; FNC 195; LWF 56 (cp 94); OGF 179; PFW 80; PMF 357; RUS 1:471, 2:589; TGF 253.

Daisy, Ox-eye (Chrysanthemum leucanthemum) AFP 4:395; ANE 3:530; BBF 3:518; CWF 534; FFK 261; FNC 205; HWF cp 218; LWF 213 (cp 338); NHE 190; OWF 99; PMF 93; RUS 1:485, 2:603, 3:479, 4:703, 5:579, 6:689.

Daisy, Painted (Chrysanthemum coccineum) AGF 175; DFP 168 (cps 1341-1343); EGP 106; FGF 224; LFW 26 (cps 51, 52); OGF 123; TGF 252.

Daisy, Panamint (Enceliopsis covillei) AFP 4:123. (E. argophylla) OOW cp 112.

Daisy, Seaside (Erigeron glaucus) APF 4:351; GGS 145; HFP 368; LWF 56 (cp 93); OOW cp 278; RUS 4:699, 5:589.

Daisy, Shasta (Chrysanthemum maximum or C. shastense) AGF 220; DFP 132 (cp 1049); EGP 107; FGF 243; LFW 26 (cps 53, 54); TGF 252.

Daisy, Swan River (Brachycome iberidifolia) DFP 31 (cp 244); EGA 98; EWF cp 140b.

Daisy, Tahoka (Machaeranthera tanacetifolia) BBF 3:435; EGA 97; RUS 3:469, 4:695, 6:673; TGF 268.

Daisy, Transvaal (Gerbera jamesonii) AGF 115; EGP 119; LFW 19; MEP 153; MWF 141 (cps 428, 429); TGF 269.

Daisy, White (Aphanostephus skirrobasis) BBF 3:401; EGA 95; HWF cp 194; RUS 2:607, 3:479, 4:707, 6:689.

Daisy-bush (Olearia sp.) DFP 215 (cps 1714, 1715); HSC 82.

Damselfish, Blue-green (Chromis caeruleus) IWE 5:606; NGF 334; SOS 58. (C. cyanea) HFW cp 63; MOL 119. (C. chromis) WFW cp 157.

Damselfish, Three-striped or Black and White (Dascyllus aruanus) ALE 5:133; NGF 334; SOS 332; WFW cp 389.

Damselfish, Yellow-tail (Microspathodon chrysurus) ALE 5:133; SOS 48.

Damselfly (Enallagma sp.) BIA cp 1, 75; GPL 99; OBI 3; SAA 109; SCI cp 6h; SIG cp 49. See also **Dragonfly**.

Damselfly, Ruby-spot (Hetaerina americana) BIA 75; SCI 176; SIG cp 50.

Dandelion, Common (Taraxacum officinale) AFP 4:611; BBF 3:315; FFK 241; FNC 189; HYF cp 225; LWF 52 (cp 86); NHE 190; OFP 11; OOW cp 133; OWF 41; PMF 111, 171; RUS 1:511, 2:639, 3:507, 4:747, 5:623, 6:729.

Dandelion, Goat or Dwarf (Krigia biflora) FFK 242; HYF cp 225; LWF 217 (cp 345); PMF 111; RUS 1:515, 2:641, 3:511, 4:741, 6:729. (K. montana) FNC 188; RUS 3:507. (K. virginica) PMF 171.

Dandelion, Mountain—See **Mountain-dandelion**.

Dandelion, Tall (Leontodon autumnalis) BBF 3:310; NHE 190; OWF 37; PMF 171; RUS 1:511. (L. nudicaulis) CWF 550.

Daphne (Daphne mezereum) DFP 195 (cp 1554); EWF cp 18g; HSC 42; NHE 267; OGF 3; TGS 247.

Daphne, Sweet (Daphne odora) DFP 195 (cp 1555); FHP 117; MWF 106 (cps 291, 292); OGF 27; PFW 296; TGS 247.

Darter, Johnny (Etheostoma nigrum) CFW 104; GGF 97; GPL 125; NGF 279; PFF 521.

Date—See **Palm, Date**.

Dayflower (Commelia communis) FFK 63; FNC 14; HWF cp 66; HYF cp 8; PMF 315; RUS 1:61, 2:57, 3:53, 6:67. (C. erecta) LWF 167 (cp 263); RUS 1:61, 2:57, 3:53, 4:61, 6:67.

Daylily (Hemerocallis sp.) AGF 92, 93; DFP 146 (cps 1167, 1168), 147 (cps 1169-1171); EGP 63-67, 122; FFK 49; FGF 133; HWF cp 12; HYF cp 21; MWF 153 (cps 469, 470); PMF 207; RUS 2:55, 3:27; TGF 29.

Dead Man's Finger (fungus) (Xylaria sp.) NFP 39; PFF 73.

Dead Men's Fingers (coral) (Alcyonium sp.) ALE 1:240, 271; IWE 5:620; NHE 175; OIB 19.

Dead Men's Fingers (sponge) (Haliclona oculata) CFG 615; GGS 43; LSE 17; NHE 176.

Dead-nettle, Henbit (Lamium amplexicaule) BBF 3:121; FFK 206; FNC 162; NHE 231; OWF 149; PMF 281; RUS 1:385, 2:491, 3:385, 4:561, 5:465, 6:561.

Dead-nettle, Purple or Red (Lamium purpureum) AFP 3:630; BBF 3:121; NHE 231; OWF 149; PMF 281; RUS 1:383, 2:491, 3:385, 5:465.

Dead-nettle, Spotted (Lamium maculatum) AFP
3:630; BBF 3:122; DFP 154 (cp 1231); NHE 231;
PFW 151; RUS 1:385.

Dead-nettle, White (Lamium album) BBF 3:122; EWF
cp 20d; NHE 231; OWF 97; PMF 79; RUS 1:365.

Death Cap (Amanita phalloides) ANE 1:29; DEW
3:137 (cp 63); KMF 10 (cp 1a); LHM 117; MSM 28;
NFP 52; NHE 47; ONP 119.

Deer, Black-tailed (Odocoileus hemionus columbianus)
ALE 13:221; ANE 3:533; GGM 131; NGA 80; PAK
574.

Deer, Brocket (Mazama americana) ALE 13:223; IWE
16:2212; WMW 2:1398.

Deer, Fallow (Dama dama) ALE 13:210; IWE 6:730-
733; NHE 52; OBV 147; WMW 2:1387.

Deer, Florida Key (Odocoileus virginianus clavium)
ALE 13:220; ANE 3:537; NGA 77.

Deer Grass—See **Meadow-beauty, Virginia.**

Deer, Mule (Odocoileus hemionus) ANE 3:539, 540;
BGM 224 (cp 23); BMC 358 (cp 36); CFG 338; GGM
130-131; IWE 11:1530-1532; JAW 175; NGA 78-79,
80; PMG cp 40.

Deer, Red—See **Elk, American.**

Deer, White-tailed or Virginia (Odocoileus virginianus)
ALE 13:220; ANE 3:534, 541; BGM 224 (cp 23);
BMC 358 (cp 37); CFG 338; FWA 71; GGM 132,
133; JAW 174; LFO 24; NGA 75, 76; NHE 53; PAK
572; PMG cp 40; WMW 2:1393.

Deerberry (Vaccinium stamineum) HYF cp 139; RWA
cp 282; TSK 77, 261.

Deer-brush (Ceanothus integerrimus) AFP 3:72; OOW
cp 31; VPN 3:419.

Deer-fly—See **Fly, Deer.**

Deer-foot—See **Vanilla-leaf.**

Deermouse—See **Mouse, Deer.**

Deer's-tongue (Frasera speciosa) LWF 144 (cp 230);
VPN 4:70. (Swertia radiata) AFP 3:364.

Delphinium—See **Larkspur.**

Deodar—See **Cedar, Deodar.**

Desert Calico (Langloisia matthewsii) AFP 3:459;
LWF 103; RUS 4:443, 6:475.

Desert Candle—See also **Lily, Foxtail.**

Desert Candle (Caulanthus or Streptanthus inflatus)
OOW cp 262; RUS 4:231, 5:201.

Desert Star (Monoptilon bellioides) AFP 4:305; OOW
cp 51; RUS 4:703, 6:689.

Desert-willow (Chilopsis linearis) BTN 265; OOW
cp 201.

Destroying Angel (Amanita virosa or A. verna) ANE
4:754; GMC 52, 193 (cp 291); LHM 117; MSM 27;
NFP 52; NHE 47; ONP 131; PFF 81; SMG 175, 176.

Deutzia (Deutzia sp.) AGF 97; DEW 1:292; DFP 196
(cps 1562-1565); EWF cp 99e; FGF 97; HSC 43;
LFW 44 (cps 102, 103); MWF 109 (cps 308, 309);
OGF 59; PFW 229; TGS 182.

Devil Ray or Devilfish—See **Manta, Atlantic.**

Devilfish—See **Octopus.**

Devil's Fig—See **Poppy, Prickly.**

Devil's Paint Brush—See **Hawkweed, Orange.**

Devil's Walking-stick—See **Hercules'-club.**

Devil's-bit (Chamaelirium luteum) BBF 1:489; FFK
55; FNC 28; PMF 65; RUS 1:37, 2:39.

Devil's-breeches (Kohleria bogotensis) EWF cp 185e;
MEP 141.

Devil's-claw (Proboscidea sp.) See **Unicorn-plant.**

Devil's-claw (Phyteuma sp.) See **Rampion.**

Devil's-club (Oplopanax horridum) AFP 3:219; CWF
342; RWA cp 245; VPN 3:507.

Dewberry (Rubus caesius) NHE 20; OFP 79; OWF 79.

Dewdrop (Dalibardia repens) FNC 90; HWF cp 97b;
PMF 33; RUS 1:141, 2:195.

Diatom (Various genera and species) DEW 3:50 (cp
4); GGS 16; KSL 107; LPL 20-21; LSE 104, 119;
MOL 49; PFF 59; SOS 36.

Dickcissel (Spiza americana) ANE 3:554; BBC
2:cp 112; CFG cp 27; GBC 316 (cp 63); HBT cp 16;
NGB 2:250; NGS 335; PBA 3:76; PEB 215 (cp 56);
PWB 267 (cp 54); RBA 243; RBB 303.

Dill (Anethum graveolens) AFP 3:251; BBF 2:634;
OFP 139, 147.

Dipper (Cinclus mexicanus) AAB 335; ANE 3:557;
AWW 31; BBC 2:586, 588, cp 86; CDB 159 (cp
663); GBC 236 (cp 49); NGB 2:150; NGS 168-169;
PBA 3:173; PWB 219; RBB 219.

Dittany (Cunila origanoides) FFK 205; PMF 281;
RUS 1:365, 6:549.

Dock—See also **Sorrel.**

Dock, Broad or Bitter (Rumex obtusifolius) NHE 224;
OWF 59; PFF 152; PMF 381.

Dock, Curly (Rumex crispus) NHE 183; OWF 59;
PFF 151; PMF 381.

Dock, Golden (Rumex maritimus) CWF 115; NHE 96.

Dock, Water (Rumex aquaticus) NHE 96. (R. orbiculatus) PMF 381. (R. verticillatus) FFK 276.

Dodder (Cuscuta gronovii) HWF cp 170b; PFF 284;
PMF 43; RUS 1:525, 2:435, 3:339, 4:517, 6:529.
(C. rostrata) FNC 154.

Dodder, Salt-marsh (Cuscuta salina) AFP 3:395; CWF 414; KSL 259; RUS 4:517, 5:435, 6:529; VPN 4:94.

Dodder, Thyme (Cuscuta epithymum) AFP 3:395; NHE 228; OWF 125; VPN 4:94.

Dog (Canis familiaris) ALE 12:230-231; FWA 360; IWE 5:645-649; LEA 550-551; PFF 691.

Dog, Prairie—See **Prairie Dog.**

Dogbane, Blue (Amsonia tabernaemontana) BBF 3:20; 3:20; FFK 145; FNC 150; PMF 325; RUS 1:319, 2:401, 3:285, 6:453. (A. ciliata) HYF cp 147; RUS 2:401, 3:285.

Dogbane, Common or Hemp (Apocynum cannabinum) AFP 3:371; FFK 175; FNC 150; PMF 71; PRP 169; RUS 1:315, 2:399, 3:287, 4:431, 5:379, 6:453; VPN 4:80.

Dogbane, Spreading (Apocynum androsaemifolium) AFP 3:371; CWF 391; FFK 175; FNC 151; HFP 278; HWF cp 170a; HYF cp 147; OOW cp 171; PFF 282; PMF 293; RUS 1:315, 2:399, 3:287, 4:431, 5:377, 6:453; VPN 4:80.

Dog-fennel—See **Chamomile, Yellow.**

Dogfish, Freshwater—See **Bowfin.**

Dogfish, Spiny (Squalus acanthias) ALE 4:104; CFG 465; CFW 7, 8, 31; GGF 22; HPF 44; NHE 159; OBV 7; WFW cp 337.

Dogwinkle, Atlantic (Thais lapillus or Nucella lapillus) AAS pl 25g; ALE 3:56; ASN 129; CFG 573; GGS 128; NHE 163; OIB 43; PFF 411.

Dogwinkle, Emarginate (Thais emarginata) AAS 215; ASN 129; GAS 282; GGS 128; KSL 130; MGS pl 37; RCT 185 (pl 28).

Dogwinkle, Frilled (Thais lamellosa or Nucella lamellosa) AAS 215; ASN 129; BLA 94 (cp 54); GAS 280; GSS 14, 79; JSS 521; KSL 132; MGS cp 4, pl 37; PFF 411.

Dogwood, Alternate-leaf (Cornus alternifolia) BTN 237; TSK 93, 144, 256.

Dogwood, Dwarf—See **Bunchberry.**

Dogwood, Flowering (Cornus florida var.) AGF 71, 98; ANE 3:561, 562; BBF 2:664; BTN 237; DFP 191 (cp 1526); EGT 41, 106; FGF 98, 99; FNC 128; LFW 190, 191 (cps 429-431); MWF 94 (cp 252); OBT 149; RWA cps 247, 248; TGS 151; TSK 94, 123, 322-323.

Dogwood, Kousa or Oriental (Cornus kousa) DFP 191 (cp 1527); EGT 43, 107; LFW 191 (cp 431); PFW 90.

Dogwood, Mountain or Pacific (Cornus nuttallii) AFP 3:285; BTN 239; CWF 367; EGT 107; EWF cp 155c; HFP 240; OOW cp 29; VPN 3:591.

Dogwood, Western (Cornus stolonifera) AFP 3:285; BBF 2:662; BTN 237; CWF 370; GPL 72; HFP 244; RWA cp 246; TSK 219; VPN 3:591.

Dollar-a-dozen—See **Lucina, Cross-hatched.**

Dolly Varden—See **Trout, Dolly Varden.**

Dolphin (fish) (Coryphaena hippurus) ALE 5:102; CFG cp 42; CFW 107; GGF 91; IWE 5:652; LSE 26-27; NGF 108; NHE 155. (C. equiselis) MOL 94.

Dolphin, Bottle-nosed (Tursiops truncatus or T. gilli) ALE 11:480, 499, 500; BGM 253; CFG 312; FWA 317; GGM 153; IWE 2:272-275; JAW 88; NGA 393; NHE 143; OBV 185; PMG 335; SOS 181, 184; WEA 131; WMW 2:1116.

Dolphin, Common (Delphinus delphis) ALE 11:480; BGM 253; CFG 312; GGM 153; IWE 4:492-495; NGA 392; NHE 143; OBV 183; PMG 335; SOS 177, 181; WMW 2:1114.

Dolphin, Right Whale (Lissodelphis borealis) ALE 11:480; BGM 253; PMG 335.

Dolphin, Risso's (Grampus griseus or Gramphidelphis griseus) ALE 11:480; BGM 253; CFG 312; OBV 185; PMG 335; WMW 2:1115.

Dolphin, Rough-toothed (Steno bredanensis) ALE 11:480; WMW 2:1109.

Dolphin, White-beaked (Lagenorhynchus albirostris) BGM 253; CFG 312; OBV 185.

Dolphin, White-sided (Atlantic) (Lagenorhynchus acutus) ALE 11:480, 497; CFG 312; OBV 185; PMG 335.

Dolphin, White-sided or Striped (Pacific) (Lagenorhynchus obliquidens) BGM 253; FWA 317; NGF 164-165; WEA 131; WMW 2:1106, 1107, 1117.

Doodlebug—See **Ant-lion.**

Doris—See **Nudibranch.**

Dory, American John (Zenopsis ocellata) GGF 151; WFW cp 366.

Dory, John (Zeus faber) ALE 5:36; CFW 101; IWE 9:1199, 1200.

Dosinia (Dosinia discus) AAS pl 38o; ASN 237; CFG 593; GGS 100. (D. elegans) PFF 423. (D. ponderosa) MGS pl 47.

Dotterel (Eudromius morinellus) ALE 8:160, 169; BBE 113; CDB 81 (cp 263); GPB 11; IWE 5:662; LBW 162; NHE 147; RBB 111; SAA 91.

Douglasia (Douglasia laevigata) AFP 3:339; CWF 426; RUS 5:369; VPN 4:48. (D. nivalis) AFP 3:339; RUS 6:437; VPN 4:52.

Duck Foot—See **Pelican's Foot, American.**

Duck, Hawaiian (Anas wyvilliana) BHB cp 24; PWB 322; WID cp 17b.

Duck, Harlequin (Histrionicus histrionicus) AAB 80; ALE 7:309; BBC 1:cp 19, cp 22; CDB 52 (cp 11); CFG cp 10; GBC 96 (cp 13); GGB 71; KWF 430 (cp 21), 434 (cp 23), 458 (cp 35); NGB 1:127; NGW 183; PBA 1:cp 19; PEB 23 (pl 8), 27 (pl 10), 35 (pl 12); PWB 43 (pl 10), 51 (pl 12); RBB 55; SAA 92; TBC 102 (cp 11a).

Duck, Laysan (Anas laysanensis) AAB 66; BHB 76 (cp 25), 82; IWE 17:2380; MBH 45; OMW 255; WID 192 (cp 17c).

Duck, Masked (Oxyura dominica) AAB 87; BWI 52; GGB 57; KWF 450 (cp 31); PWB 35 (pl 8), 58 (cp 13); RBB 61.

Duck, Mexican (Anas diazi) BBC 1:cp 13; GGB 38; NGW 165; PWB 34 (pl 7), 59 (cp 14); RBB 45.

Duck, Mottled (Anas fulvigula maculosa) BBC 1:cp 1:cp 13; GGB 39; NGW 165; KWF 404 (cp 8), 454 (cp 33); PEB 39 (cp 14); RBB 45.

Duck, Muscovy (Cairina moschata) ALE 7:318; CDB 51 (cp 107); DBM cp 9; IWE 11:1539, 1540; LEA 378.

Duck, Redhead (Aythya americana) AAB 74; ALE 7:307; ANE 3:570; BBC 1:cps 17, 19; CFG 49-51; GBC 92 (cp 11); GFB 43; GGB 58, 59; GPL 145; KWF 420 (cp 16), 422 (cp 17); NGB 1:123; NGW 174, 178; PBA 1:cp 16; PEB 23 (pl 8), 27 (pl 10), 34 (pl 11); PFF 569; PWB 35 (pl 8), 43 (pl 10), 50 (pl 11); RBA 56; RBB 53.

Duck, Ring-necked (Aythya collaris) AAB 75; ANE 3:571; BBC 1:cp 19, cp 20; BBE 59; CFG 49, 50, 51; GBC 92 (cp 11); GGB 62, 63; GPB 82; KWF 424 (cp 18), 430 (cp 21), 456 (cp 34); NGB 1:123; NGW 178; PBA 1:cp 17; PEB 23 (pl 8), 27 (pl 10), 34 (pl 11); PFF 569; PWB 35 (pl 8), 43 (pl 10), 50 (pl 11); RBB 53.

Duck, Ruddy (Oxyura jamaicensis) AAB 86; ALE 7:320; BBC 1:cp 17, cp 19; BWI 51; CFG cp 1; GBC

93 (cp 12); GFB 43; GGB 56; GPL 145; KWF 448 (cp 30), 458 (cp 35); NGB 1:125; NGW 186; PBA 1:cp 10; PEB 23 (pl 8), 27 (pl 10), 38 (cp 13); PWB 35 (pl 8), 43 (pl 10), 58 (cp 13); RBB 61.

Duck, Tree—See **Tree-duck.**

Duck, Tufted (Aythya fuligula) ALE 7:61, 255, 308; BBE 59; CDB 50 (cp 101); GPB 82; IWE 13:1799; NHE 111; RBB 53.

Duck, Whistling—See **Tree-duck.**

Duck, Wood (Aix sponsa) AAB 84; ALE 7:317; ANE 3:571, 573; BBC 1:cp 16, cp 18; CFG cp 2, 41, 42; GBC 77 (cp 10); GGB 55; GPL 144; IWE 19:2639-2641; KWF 416 (cp 14), 418 (cp 15), 454 (cp 33); NGB 1:99; NGW 170; PBA 1:cp 14; PEB 22 (pl 7), 26 (pl 9), 38 (cp 13); PWB 34 (pl 7), 42 (pl 9), 58 (cp 13); RBA 53; RBB 51; TBC 94 (cp 9a).

Duckweed (Lemna sp.) AFP 1:347, 348; BBF 1:447, 448; CWF 4; FNC 12; GPL 57; NHE 107; PFF 366, 367.

Dulse—See **Sea Kale.**

Dulse, Pepper (Laurencia pinnatifida) NHE 141; ONP 7.

Dunlin (Erolia alpina or Calidris alpina) AAB 173; ALE 7:255; BBC 1:cp 52; CDB 85 (cp 277); CFG cp 9, 100; GBC 140 (cp 25); NGB 1:278; NGW 339; NHE 148; PBA 1:cps 33, 34; PEB 99 (pl 28), 102 (cp 29), 119 (pl 32); PFF 599; PWB 102 (cp 25), 115 (pl 30), 119 (cp 32); RBA 109; SAA 91.

Dusty Miller (Cineraria maritima or Senecio cineraria) DFP 34 (cp 267); EGA 153; MWF 266 (cp 881); PFW 88; TGF 236. (Artemisia stelleriana) PMF 167; TGF 237. (Centaurea rutifolia) EGP 104.

Dutchman's-breeches (Dicentra cucullaria) AFP 2:236; ANE 3:580; FFK 217; FNC 76; HWF cp 78; LFW 193 (cp 435); LWF 255 (cp 403); PFW 119; PMF 73; RUS 1:183, 2:241, 5:203, 6:211; RWA cp 147.

Dutchman's-pipe (Aristolochia durior) AGF 99; HSC 14; HYF cp 44; PMF 241, 389; RUS 2:137; TGS 70; TSK 68. (A. californica) OOW cp 193.

E

Eagle, Bald (Haliaeetus leucocephalus) AAB 105; ALE 7:376, 8:229; ANE 3:581-582, 587; BBC 1:cp 30; CFG cp 3; GBC 104 (cp 15); GPB 95; IWE 1:128-129; NGB 1:166; NGW 236, 238-243; PBA 2:cps 43, 49; PEB 67 (pl 20); PWB 75 (pl 18); RBB 77; WAB 69.

Eagle, Golden (Aquila chrysaetos) AAB 104; ALE 7:327, 375; ANE 3:583, 591; BBC 1:cp 30; BBE 73; CDB 55 (cp 135); CFG cp 3; GBC 104 (cp 15); GFB 47; GPB 94; NGB 1:164; NGW 246-247; PBA

2:cp 49; PEB 67 (pl 20); PFF 576; PWB 75 (pl 18);
RBB 77; WAB 122.

Eagle, Harpy (Harpia harpyja) ALE 7:366; DBM cp 4;
IWE 8:1025-1026; PMB cp 4; WAB 85.

Eagle, White-tailed or Gray Sea (Haliaeetus albicilla)
ALE 7:376, 385; ANE 3:584; BBE 73; CDB 58 (cp
150); CFG cp 10; NHE 147; WAB 12.

Earthball—See **Puffball, Thick-skinned.**

Earthstar (Geastrum triplex) KMF 127 (cp 30c); NFP
88; ONP 155; PFF 88. (G. rufescens) DEW 3:144
(cp 76).

Earthworm (Lumbricus sp.) BAW 237; IWE 5:679,
681; NHE 207; OIB 113; PAK 65; WEA 138.

Earwig (Forficula auricularia) ALE 2:115; GGI 29;
GIP 34; IWE 5:682-683; NHE 264; OBI 9; SIG
cp 14; WEA 139.

Earworm, Corn (Heliothis zea) GBB cp 13; GGI 94;
GIP 109; IWE 2:256; LPL 177; PAK 211; SIG
cp 74d.

Easter-daisy (Townsendia exscapa) RUS 4:703; 6:687.

Edelweiss (Leontopodium alpinum) DFP 13 (cp 98);
NHE 285; PFW 84; RWF 22; TGF 45.

Eel, American (Anguilla rostrata or A. bostoniensis)
CFG 475; CFW 76; GGF 52; GPL 126; LFI 155;
NGF 291; PAK 262; PFF 509; SOS 134-135.

Eel, California Moray (Gymnothorax mordax) HFW
46 (cp 28); NGF 336.

Eel, Conger (Conger conger) ALE 4:167; CFW 76;
GGF 53; IWE 4:515; NHE 153; OBV 85; WEA 110;
WFW cp 163. (C. oceanicus) CFG 75.

Eel, Congo (Amphiuma means) BAR cp 8; CRA 266
(pl 35); IWE 1:40; GRA 139.

Eel, Moray (Muraena sp.) ALE 4:168, 175; CFW 77;
IWE 11:1506-1507; LSE 143; NGF 43; NHE 153;
OBV 85; SOS 79, 332; WFW cp 19, 24.

Eel, Mud—See **Siren, Lesser or Mud.**

Eel, Snipe (Nemichthys scolopaceus) ALE 4:176;
CFW 79; FWA 303; HPF 90; LSE 29.

Eelgrass (Zostera marina) ANE 4:602; GGS 142; KSL
243; NHE 137; VPN 1:180.

Eggplant (Solanum melongena) OFP 127; PFF 292;
PFW 284; WYG 160.

Egret, Cattle (Ardeola ibis or Bubulcus ibis) AAB 41;
ALE 7:197; ANE 4:603, 606; BHB cp 51; BWI 33;
CDB 43 (cp 56); CFG cp 6; GBC 44 (cp 5); NGW
110; PWB 23 (pl 4); RBA 33; RBB 93; SLP 243.

Egret, Common or Great (Casmerodius albus or
Egretta alba) ALE 7:186, 195; ANE 4:607; BWI 35;

CDB 43 (cp 58); CFG cp 6; GBC 44 (cp 5); GGS
153; GPL 147; NGB 1:79; NGW 106-107; PEB 86
(cp 23); PWB 23 (pl 4); RBA 37; RBB 93; SLP 38.

Egret, Reddish (Dichromanassa rufescens) ANE
4:609; BBC 1:cp 4; BWI 34; GGS 153; NGB 1:79;
NGW 109; PEB 86 (cp 23); RBA 34; RBB 93, 95.

Egret, Snowy (Leucophoyx thula) AAB 42; ANE
4:611, 612; BBC 1:cp 6; BWI 35; CDB 44 (cp 60);
CFG cp 6; GBC 45 (cp 6); NGB 1:79; NGW 108;
PEB 86 (cp 23); PWB 23 (pl 4); RBA 34; RBB 93.

Egyptian Paper Plant (Cyperus papyrus) DFP 62 (cp
492); MWF 102 (cp 281); PFF 361.

Eider, Common or American (Somateria mollissima)
ALE 7:309, 8:187, 229; BBC 1:cp 22; BBE 66;
CFG cp 10; GBC 96 (cp 13); GGB 78, 79; KWF 436
(cp 24), 446 (cp 29), 456 (cp 34); NGB 1:112; NGW
184; PBA 1:cp 19; PEB 23 (pl 8), 35 (pl 12); PWB
35 (pl 8), 51 (pl 12); RBB 57. (S. var. nigra) KWF
436 (cp 24), 456 (cp 34); NGB 1:114.

Eider, King (Somateria spectabilis) ALE 7:309,
11:151; BBE 66; CFG cp 10; GBC 96 (cp 13); GGB
81; KWF 438 (cp 25), 446 (cp 29), 456 (cp 34);
NGB 1:112; NGW 184; NHE 146; PBA 1:cp 19;
PEB 23 (pl 8), 35 (pl 12); PWB 35 (pl 8), 51 (pl 12);
RBB 57; SAA 92.

Eider, Spectacled (Lampronetta fischeri) AAB 82;
ALE 7:307, 8:229; GBC 78; GGB 82; KWF 438 (cp
25), 446 (cp 34); NGB 1:114; NGW 184; PBA
1:145; PWB 51 (pl 12); RBB 57; SAA 92.

Eider, Steller's (Polysticta stelleri) AAB 81; ALE
7:309, 8:229; BBE 66; CDB 54 (cp 126); GBC 75;
GGB 80; GPB 81; KWF 434 (cp 23), 456 (cp 34);
NGB 1:114; NGW 184; NHE 145; PWB 51 (pl 12);
RBB 57; SAA 92.

Elaeagnus—See **Oleaster.**

Elaenia, Caribbean (Elaenia martinica) BWI 156; DBM
cp 30; PMB cp 28.

Elaenia, Greenish (Myiopagis viridicata) AMB 63 (cp
4); DBM cp 30; PMB cp 28.

Elaenia, Yellow-bellied (Elaenia flavogaster) ALE
9:143; DBM cp 30; HBT cp 12.

Elder, American or Black-berried (Sambucus canadensis) BBF 3:268; BTN 267; FNC 183; LWF 203
(cp 321); MWF 261 (cp 864); PFF 306; TSK 89,
133.

Elder, Blue (Sambucus cerulea or S. glauca) AFP
4:45; CWF 503; HFP 340; VPN 4:466.

Elder, Box—See **Box-elder.**

PMF 91; RUS 1:487, 4:713, 5:591, 6:701; RWA
cp 384; TGF 45.

Everlasting, Plantain-leaved (Antennaria plantaginifolia) BBF 3:451; FFK 233; HYF cp 214; PFF 317;
PMF 91; RUS 1:495, 2:607.

Everlasting, Rosy (Antennaria rosea) AFP 4:481;
CWF 518; RUS 5:595, 6:697; RWA cp 385.

Everlasting, Sweet (Gnaphalium obtusifolium) FFK
233; FNC 194; HYF cp 214; PMF 91; RUS 1:487,
2:607, 3:485.

F

Fairy Bell, Hooker's (Disporum hookeri) AFP 1:456;
CWF 27; RUS 5:27, 6:27.

Fairy Bell, Large-flowered (Disporum smithii) AFP
1:455; CWF 26; LWF 227 (cp 361); RUS 5:27.

Fairy Lantern—See also **Lily, Mariposa.**

Fairy Lantern (Calochortus albus) AFP 1:432; OOW
cp 32; RUS 4:25, 5:33, (C. pulchellus) AFP 1:432;
EWF cp 167f; LWF 232 (cp 368).

Fairy Ring (Marasmius oreades) GMC 135 (cps 231,
232); LHM 115; MSM 108, cp 17; NFP 67; OFP 189;
ONP 35; SMG 155.

Fairy-slipper (Calypso bulbosa) AFP 1:482; COA 280;
CWF 79, 82, 83; HFP 66; HWF cp 43a; HYF cp 35;
LWF 244 (cp 384); OOW cp 235; PMF 215; RUS
1:67, 4:73, 5:75, 77, 6:73; RWA cp 87.

Fairy-wand—See **Devil's-bit.**

Falcon, Aplomado (Falco femoralis) AAB 113; NGW
258; PMB cp 3; PWB 74 (pl 17); RBB 79.

Falcon, Laughing (Herpetotheres cachinnans) ALE
7:403; AMB 17 (cp 1); DBM cp 4; PMB cp 3.

Falcon, Orange-breasted (Falco deiroleucus) ALE
7:417; DBM cp 5; PMB cp 3.

Falcon, Peregrine (Falco peregrinus) AAB 112; ALE
7:417; ANE 4:638, 639; BBC 1:cp 32; BBE 86; CDB
62 (cp 169); CFG cp 4; FWA 61; GBC 109 (cp 18),
125 (pl 20); NGW 257; PEB 55 (cp 16), 66 (pl 19);
PFF 578; PWB 67 (cp 16), 74 (pl 17); RBB 79; WAB
17, 35.

Falcon, Prairie (Falco mexicanus) AAB 111; ALE
7:404; ANE 4:640; AWW 18, 27; CFG cp 4; FWA
125; GBC 109 (cp 18), 125 (pl 20); LNA 158-159;
NGW 256; PWB 74 (pl 17); RBB 79; WAB 57.

False Hellebore—See **Hellebore, False.**

False Miterwort—See **Foamflower.**

Fameflower (Talinum teretifolium) FNC 56; PMF
265; RUS 1:235, 2:297.

Fanwort (Cabomba caroliniana) GPL 61; PFF 168;
RUS 3:99. (C. piauhiensis) DEW 1:63 (cps 34, 35).

Farewell-to-spring (Clarkia sp.) See **Clarkia.**

Farkleberry (Vaccinium arboreum) BTN 242; HYF
cp 133; TSK 77, 261. (Batodendron arboreum)
BBF 2:698.

Fat Hen—See **Goosefoot, White.**

Fatsia (Fatsia japonica or Aralia japonica) DFP 202
(cp 1610); EGE 125; HSC 54; MWF 132 (cp 390);
TGS 246.

Featherbells (Stenanthium gramineum) FNC 32; PMF
65; RUS 1:45, 2:37.

Felwort, Marsh (Swertia perennis) LWF 145 (cp 231);
NHE 185; RUS 4:423, 5:377, 6:449.

Fennel (Foeniculum vulgare) DFP 143 (cp 1137);
EWF cp 17c; OFP 139; OWF 47; PFF 266; RUS
3:185, 4:287, 5:263, 6:315.

Fer-de-lance (Bothrops atrox) IWE 6:748-749; PFF
547.

Fern, Beech (Dryopteris phegopteris or Thelypteris
phegopteris) AFP 1:14; BBF 1:23; NFP 140; NHE
43. (Phegopteris hexagonoptera) FFK 37. (T. hexagonoptera) CGF 81.

Fern, Bird's-nest (Asplenium nidus-avis) DEW 3:268
(cp 147), 269 (cp 150); DFP 52 (cp 412).

Fern, Bladder or Brittle (Cystopteris fragilis or Filix
fragilis) AFP 1:7; ANE 4:652; BBF 1:15; CGF 159;
FFK 36; NFP 141; NHE 245; ONP 73; PFF 103.
(C. montana) BBF 1:15; NHE 293; VPN 1:72.

Fern, Boston (Nephrolepis exaltata) MWF 211 (cp
682); NFP 142.

Fern, Brake or Bracken (Pteridium aquilinum) AFP
1:23; ANE 4:655; BBF 1:32; NFP 134; NHE 43;
ONP 185; PFF 98. (P. latiusculum) FFK 42.

Fern, Chain (Woodwardia virginica) BBF 1:24; GPL
45; NFP 142; PFF 105.

Fern, Christmas (Polystichum acrostichoides) ANE
4:652, 655; BBF 1:16; CGF 127; FFK 29; NFP 140;
PFF 100.

Fern, Cinnamon (Osmunda cinnamomea) ANE 4:651,
652; BBF 1:7; CGF 173; FFK 27; GPL 45; NFP
129; PFF 106.

Fern, Cliff-brake (Pellaea sp.) AFP 1:29-31; FFK 35; NFP 135.

Fern, Climbing (Lygodium palmatum) ANE 4:652; BBF 1:9; FFK 28; NFP 130.

Fern, Deer (Blechum spicant or Struthiopteris spicant) AFP 2:21; DEW 3:267 (cp 146); NHE 43; ONP 189.

Fern, Filmy (Trichomanes radicans and T. krausii) NFP 130. (T. boschianum) FFK 30. (Hymenophyllum tunbridgense) NHE 293; ONP 61.

Fern, Grape (Botrychium sp.) AFP 1:3-5; ANE 4:652; BBF 1:3-6; CGF 185-193; FFK 25; GPL 44; NFP 128; NHE 198.

Fern, Hart's-tongue (Phyllitis scolopendrium) BBF 1:25; DEW 3:267 (cps 144, 145); NFP 143; NHE 43; ONP 191.

Fern, Hay-scented (Dennstaedtia punctilobula) BBF 1:14; CGF 117; FFK 41; NFP 141; PFF 103.

Fern, Holly (Polystichum lonchitis) AFP 1:9; ANE 4:652; BBF 1:16; NFP 140; ONP 55.

Fern, Interrupted (Osmunda claytoniana) ANE 4:652; BBF 1:8; CGF 171; FFK 28; NFP 129; PFF 105.

Fern, Lady (Athyrium filix-femina) AFP 1:19; BBF 1:30; CGF 111; FFK 40; NFP 137; NHE 43; ONP 189; PFF 99.

Fern, Lip—See **Lip-fern.**

Fern, Maidenhair (Adiantum pedatum) AFP 1:24; BBF 1:31; CGF 141; FFK 37; NHE 293; PFF 98.

Fern, Male (Dryopteris filix-mas) AFP 1:16; ANE 4:653; BBF 1:21; DEW 3:266 (cp 141), 286; NFP 138; NHE 43; ONP 185.

Fern, Marsh (Thelypteris palustris) GPL 44; NFP 139; NHE 109; PFF 102.

Fern, Mosquito or Water (Azolla caroliniana) BBF 1:38; GPL 43; NFP 146; NHE 108. (A. filiculoides) AFP 1:35; DEW 272 (cp 157); ONP 97; VPN 1:102.

Fern, New York (Dryopteris noveboracensis or Thelypteris noveboracensis) ANE 4:653; BBF 1:18; CGF 87; FFK 38; NFP 139; PFF 102.

Fern, Oak (Dryopteris dryopteris or Gymnocarpium dryopteris) AFP 1:13; ANE 4:653; BBF 1:23; NFP 143; NHE 43; ONP 55; PFF 98.

Fern, Ostrich (Matteuccia struthiopteris) BBF 1:11; CGF 119; NHE 43; PFF 104. (M. pennsylvanica) NFP 143. (Pteris pennsylvanica) GPL 45.

Fern, Resurrection (Polypodium polypodioides) CGF 133; NFP 132.

Fern, Rockcap (Polypodium virginianum) FFK 29; NFP 132; PFF 97.

Fern, Royal (Osmunda regalis) ANE 4:652; BBF 1:7; CGF 169; DEW 3:264 (cp 135); FFK 27; GPL 45; NFP 129; NHE 80; ONP 95.

Fern, Sensitive (Onoclea sensibilis) BBF 1:11; CGF 121; DEW 3:287; FFK 26; NFP 145; PFF 104.

Fern, Shield (Crested) (Dryopteris cristata) BBF 1:19; CGF 75; NFP 138; NHE 80; ONP 95; PFF 101. (D. intermedia) ANE 4:653; BBF 1:22; GPL 44.

Fern, Shield (Prickly) (Polystichum braunii) BBF 1:17; DEW 3:265 (cp 138). (P. scopulinum) AFP 1:11; BBF 1:17. (P. aculeatum) NHE 293.

Fern, Silver Stripe—See **Spleenwort, Silvery.**

Fern, Staghorn (Platycerium bifurcatum) DEW 3:269 (cp 149); MWF 236 (cp 770).

Fern, Sword (Polystichum munitum) AFP 1:10; VPN 1:92. (P. andersonii) AFP 1:12; VPN 1:98.

Fern, Venus-hair (Adiantum capillus-veneris) AFP 1:24; BBF 1:31; MWF 32 (cp 23); NFP 135; NHE 293; ONP 1.

Fern, Walking (Camptosorus rhizophyllus) ANE 4:653, 655; BBF 1:26; CGF 109; FFK 34; NFP 145; PFF 100.

Fern, Water (Salvinia natans) BBF 1:38; DEW 3:272 (cp 156); NHE 108.

Fern, Water-clover (Marsilea quadrifolia) DEW 3:271 (cp 155); GPL 43; NFP 146; NHE 108; PFF 106.

Fern, Whiskbroom (Psilotum nudum) LPL 25; NFP 119; PFF 110.

Fern, Wood (Marginal) (Dryopteris marginalis) BBF 1:20; CGF 65; FFK 42; NFP 138.

Fern, Wood (Spinulose) (Dryopteris spinulosa) ANE 4:653; BBF 1:21; CGF 69; FFK 41; PFF 101.

Fern, Wood (Spreading) (Dryopteris dilatata) AFP 1:17; BBF 1:21; NHE 80; ONP 187.

Ferret, Black-footed (Mustela nigripes) ALE 12:55; BGM 53 (cp 6); BMC 294 (cp 31); CFG 326; GGM 44; NGA 184; PMG cp 10; VWA cp 37; WID 76; WMW 2:1193.

Fescue, Meadow (Festuca elatior or F. pratensis) HMG 68; NHE 195; PFF 358.

Fescue, Sheep (Festuca ovina) DFP 142 (cp 1134); HMG 74; NHE 244.

Fescue, Tall (Festuca arundinacea) NHE 195; PRP 41.

Fetterbush (Lyonia lucida) FNC 137; HYF cp 134. (Leucothoe axillaris or L. catesbaei) FNC 137; HSC 77; TGS 407.

Feverfew (Chrysanthemum parthenium) DFP 168 (cp 1340); EGA 106; LFW 36 (cp 85); MWF 84 (cp

215); OWF 99; PMF 93; RUS 1:485, 5:579.
(Matricaria eximia) DFP 43 (cps 339, 340).

Fiddle-neck (Amsinckia intermedia) AFP 3:608; CWF
446; HFP cp 9, 298; OOW cp 124; RUS 4:495,
5:425, 6:509; VPN 4:179.

Fieldfare (Turdus pilaris) ALE 9:290; BBE 272; GPB
270; NHE 60.

Field-madder, Blue (Sherardia arvensis) AFP 4:25;
BBF 3:266; NHE 234; OWF 139; PMF 337; RUS
3:353, 4:523, 5:441.

Fig, Common (Ficus carica) BTN 147; DEW 1:160;
EGT 113; NHE 294; OBT 200; OFP 95; PFF 149;
WYG 196.

Fig Marigold (Mesembryanthemum chilense) AFP
2:120; RUS 4:147, 5:163. (M. edule) ANE 5:891;
RUS 4:147, 5:165.

Fig Shell (Ficus communis) GGS 123; GSS 70; PFF
411.

Fig, Weeping (Ficus benjamina) BTN 147; DFP 66 (cp
528); EGT 126; MWF 133 (cp 394).

Figwort, Cape (Phygelius capensis) DFP 217 (cp
1736); EWF cp 81a; HSC 90; MEP 133; OGF 169;
PFW 278.

Filbert—See also **Hazelnut**.

Filbert (Corylus avellana) DFP 192 (cp 1533); NHE
23; OBT 32; OFP 27; OWF 189.

Filbert, Giant (Corylus maxima) BTN 111; EWF
cp 12c; OBT 152; OFP 27.

Filbert, Western (Corylus californica or C. cornuta)
AFP 1:510; CWF 103; PFF 136; VPN 2:86. (C.
americana) TSK 102, 274.

Finch, Black Rosy (Leucosticte atrata) AAB 467; BBC
2:cp 113; PWB 274 (cp 55); RBB 299.

Finch, Brown-capped Rosy (Leucosticte australis)
BBC 2:cp 113; NGS 339; PWB 274 (cp 55); RBB
299.

Finch, Cassin's (Carpodacus cassinii) AAB 464; BBC
2:cp 112; GBC 332 (cp 65); NGB 2:252; NGS 338;
PWB 274 (cp 55); RBB 297; WAB 40.

Finch, Gray-crowned Rosy (Leucosticte tephrocotis)
ALE 9:392; BBC 2:cp 113; CFG cp 26; GBC 364
(cp 69); NGB 2:254; NGS 339; PWB 274 (cp 55);
RBB 299.

Finch, House (Carpodacus mexicanus) AAB 465; ALE
9:391; ANE 4:660; BBC 2:cp 112; BHB 227 (cp 58);
CDB 208 (cp 920); CFG cp 23; GBC 332 (cp 65);
NGB 2:252; NGS 336, 337; PBA 3:7; PFF 666; PWB
274 (cp 55); RBB 297.

Finch, Laysan (Psittirostra cantans) AWW 173; BHB
154 (cp 47); OMW 255; PWB 310 (cp 59); WAB
217.

Finch, Nutmeg or Spice—See **Ricebird**.

Finch, Purple (Eastern) (Carpodacus purpureus) AAB
464; ANE 4:662; BBC 2:cp 112; CFG cp 23; GBC
332 (cp 65); NGB 2:252; NGS 336, 337; PBA
3:cp 76; PEB 214 (cp 55); PFF 666; PWB 274 (cp
55); RBB 297.

Finch, Rufous-capped (Atlapetes pileatus) DBM
cp 47; PMB cp 45.

Finch, Yellow—See **Yellow-finch**.

Finfoot, American—See **Sungrebe**.

Fir, Alpine (Abies lasiocarpa) AFP 1:66; BTN 49;
RWA cp 1; SFT 108, 109; VPN 1:118.

Fir, Balsam (Abies balsamea) ANE 4:664; BBF 1:63;
BTN 47; GGT 33; PFF 121. (A. fraseri) BBF 1:63;
BTN 47.

Fir, Bristlecone (Abies bracteata or A. venusta) AFP
1:68; BTN 49; SFT 122, 123, 124.

Fir, Douglas (Abies menziesii, Pseudotsuga menziesii
or P. taxifolia) AFP 1:64; ANE 3:566; BTN 45;
EGE 105; GGT 31; MTB 145 (cp 12); NHE 18; OBT
100, 109; PFF 122; RWA cp 4; SFT 100; TGS 38.

Fir, Grand (Abies grandis) AFP 1:66; BTN 47; MTB
92 (cp 7); OBT 108; SFT 112, 113, 114; VPN
1:116.

Fir, Lovely or Silver (Abies amabilis) AFP 1:65; BTN
47; SFT 126, 127; VPN 1:114.

Fir, Noble (Abies procera or A. nobilis) AFP 1:68;
BTN 49; MTB 92 (cp 7); OBT 100, 108; SFT 129,
130; VPN 1:118.

Fir, Red (California) (Abies magnifica) AFP 1:67;
BTN 49; SFT 133, 134.

Fir, White (Abies concolor) AFP 1:67; BTN 49; EGE
90; GGT 32; PFF 121; SFT 117, 118; TGS 23; VPN
1:116.

Firebush (Embothrium coccineum) DFP 197 (cp
1572); HSC 47; MEP 32; OBT 80.

Firecracker Flower (Brodiaea ida-maia) AFP 1:410;
DFP 85 (cp 677); LWF 117 (cp 186); OOW cp 215;
RUS 5:61.

Firecracker Vine (Manettia bivolor or M. inflata) FHP
133; MWF 196 (cp 630).

Firefly (Photinus pyralis) BIA cp 5; GGI 116, 117;
IWE 6:763; KIA 103, 105; KIW cp 38; SIG cp 97a.

Firethorn (Pyracantha sp.) AGF 46, 102; DFP 222
(cps 1769, 1770); EGE 141; FGF 223; HSC 94; OGF

187; MEP 47; MWF 247 (cps 814-816); PFF 199; TGS 279.

Fireweed—See also **Willow-herb**.

Fireweed, Broad-leaved (Epilobium latifolium) AFP 3:172; BBF 2:590; CWF 350; PMF 271; RUS 4:337, 5:307, 6:361; RWA cp 243.

Fireweed, Common or Great (Epilobium angustifolium) AFP 3:172; ANE 4:667; BBF 2:590; CWF 338; DEW 2:50 (cp 5); EWF cp 4f; FNC 125; HFP 222; HWF cp 144b; HYF cp 119; OOW cp 159; OWF 111; PFF 262; PMF 225; TSK 125.

Fireweed (Pilewort) (Erechites hieracifolia) PFF 329; PMF 89; RUS 1:503, 2:627, 5:611.

Fireweed, Yellow (Epilobium luteum) CWF 339; RUS 5:311; RWA cp 244.

Firewheel Tree (Stenocarpus sinuatus) MEP 34; MWF 273 (cp 906).

Fisher (Martes pennanti) BGM 52 (cp 5); BMC 294 (cp 30); CFG 326; NGA 181; PFF 684; PMG cp 9; WMW 2:1196.

Five-spot (Nemophila maculata) AFP 3:486; EWF cp 163b; LWF 148 (cp 236); RUS 4:471, 5:403.

Flag—See also **Iris**.

Flag, Blue (Wild Iris) (Iris versicolor) ANE 2:286; BBF 1:537; DFP 151 (cp 1205); GPL 64; HWF cp 26; HYF cp 32; LWF 170 (cp 268); PFF 386; PMF 315; RUS 1:49; RWA cp 64.

Flag, Southern Blue (Iris virginica) FFK 61; LWF 10 (cp 14); RUS 1:49, 2:73, 3:53.

Flag, Sweet (Acorus calamus) BBF 1:446; FFK 84; GPL 56; HWF 43; HYF cp 1; NHE 107; PFF 366; PMF 117, 369; RUS 1:523, 3:67, 6:85.

Flag, Yellow (Iris pseudacorus) BBF 1:540; CWF 67; DFP 150 (cp 1198); EGP 126; NHE 104; OWF 29; PMF 101; RUS 1:49, 2:73, 5:69, 6:59; VPN 1:820.

Flamboyant Tree—See **Poinciana, Royal**.

Flame Vine (Pyrostegia venusta) EWF cp 180b; LFW 251 (cp 558). (P. ignea) MEP 137; MWF 248 (cp 817).

Flame Vine, Mexican (Senecio confusus) FHP 144; MEP 152.

Flamingo, American (Phoenicopterus ruber) AAB 53; ALE 7:238; ANE 4:684, 687; BWI 42; CDB 49 (cp 91); GFB 39; NGB 1:88; NGW 130, 132-133, 135; PBA 1:170, 171; PEB 86 (cp 23); PFF 558; RBA 41; RBB 99.

Flamingo Flower (Anthurium scherzeranum) FHP 105; MEP 12; MWF 42 (cp 64); PFW 34. See also **Lily, Flamingo**.

Flax, Blue (Linum lewisii) LWF 134 (cp 213); OOW cp 229; RUS 3:173, 4:271, 6:295. (L. perenne) AGF 103.

Flax, Common (Linum usitatissimum) LFW 90 (cp 210); PFF 223; PMF 327; RUS 1:211, 2:269, 3:173, 4:271, 5:231, 6:275.

Flax, Scarlet (Linum grandiflorum) DFP 42 (cp 329); EGA 132; OGF 133.

Flax, Yellow (Linum flavum) AGF 103; NHE 221. (L. virginianum) FFK 176; PMF 165; RUS 2:269, 3:177.

Flea, Cat (Ctenocephalides felis) GIP 50; SCI 656.

Flea, Chigoe (Tunga penetrans) ALE 2:404; GIP 51; SCI 660.

Flea, Dog (Ctenocephalides canis) BIA 309; GGI 151; PEI 531; PFF 494; SCI 656; SIG pl 175; WEA 151.

Flea, Human (Pulex irritans) ALE 2:404; GIP 50; OBI 19; PEI 530; PFF 494; SCI 656.

Flea, Rat (Xenopsylla cheopsis) ALE 2:531; GIP 50; KIA 60; PFF 494; SCI 656.

Flea, Sand (Beach Hopper) (Orchestia traskiana) ALE 1:496; GAS 354; KSL 211.

Flea, Sand (Long-horned) (Talorchestia longicornis) CFG 648; GGS 69.

Flea, Water—See **Water-flea**.

Fleabane, Annual (Erigeron annuus) NHE 189; PFF 316; PMF 95; RUS 1:481, 2:601, 3:473.

Fleabane, Common or Daisy (Erigeron philadelphicus) CWF 547; FFK 263; HWF cp 239b; HYF cp 220; PMF 309; RUS 1:481, 2:597, 3:473, 5:591, 6:679. (E. ramosus) PRP 127.

Fleabane, Salt Marsh (Pluchea purpurascens) PMF 285, 299; RUS 1:503, 2:625, 3:499, 4:727, 5:599, 6:713. (P. camphorata) HWF cp 249b.

Fleahopper, Garden (Halticus bracteatus) GBB cp 7; SIG cp 32b.

Flicker, Gilded (Colaptes chrysoides) CDB 136 (cp 543); NGB 2:70; NGS 85; PWB 167 (cp 40); RBB 181.

Flicker, Red-shafted (Colaptes cafer) ALE 9:108; ANE 4:693; BBC 2:cp 71; CFG cp 12; GBC 220 (cp 43); IWE 6:784; NGB 2:68; NGS 19, 82, 83; PFF 621; PWB 167 (cp 40); RBB 181.

Flicker, Yellow-shafted (Colaptes auratus) AAB 270; ALE 9:108; ANE 4:694; BBC 2:cp 71; CDB 136 (cp 542); CFG cp 12; GBC 220 (cp 43); GFB 116; IWE 6:783; NGB 2:68; NGS 84; PBA 2:cp 64; PEB 154 (cp 41); PFF 619; PWB 167 (cp 40); RBA 167; RBB 181; TBC 274 (cp 37b).

Forget-me-not, Alpine (Myosotis alpestris) DFP 44 (cp 347); EWF cp 5d; MWF 205 (cp 662); NHE 281; OOW cp 221; RWA cp 318.

Forget-me-not, Chinese (Cynoglossum sp.) AGF 65; DFP 133 (cp 1059); EGA 112; TGF 133.

Forget-me-not, Common or Field (Myosotis arvensis) AFP 3:543; NHE 229; OWF 173.

Forget-me-not, Smaller (Myosotis laxa) AFP 3:543; CWF 451; PMF 335; RUS 1:333, 2:423, 5:423.

Forget-me-not, Spring (Myosotis verna) PMF 56; RUS 2:423, 3:309, 6:509.

Forget-me-not, True (Water) (Myosotis scorpioides) AFP 3:539; AGF 108; EGP 133; EWF cp 20b; FFK 157; HWF cp 182; HYF cp 164; LFW 94 (cp 217); PMF 335; RUS 1:331, 333, 2:423, 5:423, 6:507, 509; TGF 173.

Forget-me-not, Woodland (Cultivated) (Myosotis sylvatica) AFP 3:543; DEW 2:163 (cp 83); EGA 138; OWF 173; PFF 286; PFW 49; RUS 5:423, 6:507; TFG 173.

Forsythia (Forsythia suspensa) AGF 109; DFP 203 (cps 1611, 1612); FGF 111; LWF 52 (cp 120); MWF 134 (cp 399); PFW 198; TGS 342.

Four O'Clock (Mirabilis jalapa) DFP 44 (cp 345); EGA 137; EGP 133; FGF 112; MEP 36; MWF 201 (cp 647); PFW 194; RUS 3:79, 4:103, 5:101.

Four O'Clock, Giant (Mirabilis multiflora) OOW cp 209; RUS 3:83, 4:107, 6:117.

Four O'Clock, Wild (Mirabilis nyctaginea) HYF cp 46; PFF 160; PMF 293; RUS 1:101, 2:144, 3:83, 4:107; 6:117.

Four-eyed Fish (Anableps sp.) ALE 4:456-457; CFW 87; HFW 144; IWE 6:813; NGF 44.

Fowl, Jungle (Gallus gallus) ABW 97; ALE 8:57, 13:285; BHB 77 (cp 27); CDB 69 (cp 201); IWE 4:426, 9:1201; WAB 165; WEA 211.

Fox, Arctic or White (Alopex lagopus) ALE 11:151; AWW 103; BGM 68 (cp 7); BMC 231 (cp 25); FWA 28; IWE 1:80, 81; JAW 97; NGA 137; NHE 82; PMG cp 13; SAA 130; WMW 2:1153.

Fox, Gray (Urocyon cinereo argentatus) ANE 4:723, 724; BGM 68 (cp 7); CFG cp 32; GGM 55; IWE 7:951, 952; JAW 100; LFO 29; NGA 136; PAK 606; PMG cp 13; WMW 2:1158.

Fox, Kit or Swift (Vulpes macrotis or V. velox) ANE 4:726; AWW 18, 29; BGM 68 (cp 7); GGM 53; LDE 85; NGA 135; OMW 202; PMG cp 13.

Fox, Red (Vulpes fulva or V. vulpes) ANE 4:730; AWW 89; BGM 68 (cp 7); CFG cp 32; GGM 54; JAW 98; LEA 554; NGA 133; OBV 167; PAK 604; PMG cp 13; SAA 32, 131; WMW 2:1155.

Foxglove (Digitalis purpurea) AFP 3:794; AGF 110; BBF 3:204; DEW 2:164, 165; DFP 37 (cps 289, 290); EGA 115; EGP 114; LFW 48, 49 (cps 112-114); MWF 114 (cp 323); NHE 35; OOW cp 218; OWF 123; PFF 297; PFW 276; RUS 4:603, 5:495; TGF 221.

Foxglove, Mullein (Dasistoma macrophylla) FFK 214; RUS 1:411, 2:515, 3:395.

Foxtail—See **Grass, Foxtail**.

Frangipani (Plumeria acutifolia) LFW 252 (cp 560); MWF 237 (cp 775); PFW 29.

Frangipani, Red (Plumeria rubra) DEW 2:103 (cp 56); EWF cp 180c; LFW 252 (cp 561); MWF 237 (cp 776); PFW 29.

Franklinia (Franklinia or Gordonia alatamaha) BTN 231; EGT 114; FGF 126; RWA cp 224; TGS 231.

Fremontia (Fremontia californica) AFP 3:113; DFP 248 (cp 1977); LWF 137 (cp 217); PFW 288. (F. mexicana) AFP 3:113; RWA cp 223.

Frigatebird, Great (Fregata minor) ABW 48; ALE 7:177, 178; AWW 173; BHB 54 (cp 15); GPB 64; PWB 319; SOS 349.

Frigatebird, Lesser (Fregata ariel) GFB 33; GPB 64; LEA 368.

Frigatebird, Magnificent (Fregata magnificens) AAB 35; ABW 48; ALE 7:177; CDB 41 (cp 53); FWA 261; GPB 64; NGB 1:56; NGW 94, 95; PEB 17; PWB 16; RBB 33; SOS 161, 228; WAB 24, 98; WEA 155.

Fringe Cup (Tellima grandiflora) AFP 2:376; CWF 222; HFP cp 26d; OOW cp 157; RUS 5:251, 255, 6:283; VPN 3:61.

Fringe Tree (Chionanthus virginica) AGF 111; BTN 253; EGT 42, 105; FNC 145; PFF 281; RWA cp 294; TGS 374; TSK 57, 140. (C. retusa) MWF 82 (cp 206).

Fritillary, Kamchatka (Fritillaria camtschatcensis) AFP 1:432; CWF 39; RUS 5:27.

Fritillary, Purple (Fritillaria atropurpurea) AFP 1:424; BBF 1:505; RUS 4:47, 5:29, 6:25; VPN 1:792.

Fritillary, Snake's Head (Fritillaria meleagris) DFP 299 (cp 739); EGB 115; LFW 53 (cp 123); NHE 192; OWF 163; PFW 171; TGF 28.

Frog, Barking or Robber (Eleutherodactylus angusti) ALE 5:449; CRA 271 (cp 38); GRA 130; SRA cp 10; WFA 369.

Frog, Bull—See **Bullfrog.**

Frog, Chorus (Pseudacris sp.) ALE 5:440; BAR cp 32;
CAW 117, cp 61; CFG cp 40; CGR 114, 116, cp 5c;
CRA 271 (cp 38); GPL 135; GRA 119, 124, 125;
SRA cp 13; WFA 233, 239, 249, 259, 265, 273.

Frog, Crawfish or Gopher (Rana areolata var.) BAR
cp 25; CFG cp 39; CGR 86; CRA 287 (cp 40); GRA
132; WFA 15, 403.

Frog, Cricket (Acris crepitans and A. gryllus) ANE
4:736, 737; BAR cp 28; CAW cp 57; CGR cp 5b;
CRA 271 (cp 38); GPL 135; GRA 129; SRA cp 13;
WFA 15, 221.

Frog, Green or Bronze (Rana clamitans) ANE 4:735,
737; AWW 32; BAR cp 23; CAW 193; CFG cp 39;
CGR cp 3e; CRA 287 (cp 40); GPL 133; GRA 133;
PFF 529; WFA 453.

Frog, Greenhouse (Eleutherodactylus ricordi planirostris) CGR cp 5d; CRA 271 (cp 38); IWE 7:945;
WFA 369.

Frog, Leopard or Meadow (Rana pipiens) ALE 5:400;
ANE 4:737; AWW 35; BAR cp 24; CAW cp 63; CFG
cp 39; CRA 287 (cp 40); GPL 129, 133; GRA 116;
IWE 11:1448; PFF 530; SRA cp 12; WFA 484, 493,
501, 510, 511, 515.

Frog, Mink (Rana septentrionalis) ANE 4:737; CFG
448; CGR 76; CRA 287 (cp 40); WFA 534.

Frog, Narrow-mouthed (Gastrophryne carolinensis)
BAR cp 26; CGR cp 4c; CRA 286 (pl 39); GRA 136.

Frog, Pickerel (Rana palustris) ANE 4:737; BAR
cp 24; CAW cp 66; CFG cp 39; CGR 84; CRA 287
(cp 40); GPL 133; GRA 134; PFF 530; WFA 477.

Frog, Red-legged (Rana aurora) CGR 80; GRA 132;
SRA cp 11, cp 12; WFA 415.

Frog, Spotted (Rana pretiosa) CGR 80; GRA 135;
SRA cp 11; WFA 528.

Frog, Tailed (Ascaphus truei) ALE 5:351; CAW cp 21;
CGR cp 3b; SRA cp 13; WFA 110. See also **Toad,
Bell.**

Frog, Tree—See **Treefrog.**

Frog, Wood (Rana sylvatica) ANE 4:737, 739; BAR
cp 25; CAW 159, cp 65; CFG cp 39; CGR cp 3f;
CRA 287 (cp 40); GRA 119, 135; PFF 530; SRA
cp 12; WEA 156; WFA 534, 545.

Frogbit (Hydrocharis morsus-ranae) EWF cp 23c; NHE
102; OWF 103.

Frogfish (Historio historio) CFW 15, 155; GGF 148;
MOL 92; NGF 30; SOS 89; WEA 318.

Frostweed—See also **Sunrose.**

Frostweed (Helianthemum canadense) HWF cp 131b;
PMF 143; RUS 1:155, 2:215.

Fruit-fly—See **Fly, Fruit.**

Fuchsia Hybrids AGF 112; DFP 67 (cps 534-536), 68
(cps 537-539); FGF 115; LFW 199 (cp 450); PFW
201, 202.

Fulmar (Fulmarus glacialis) AAB 12; ABW 31; ALE
7:61, 147, 8:229; BBE 20; CDB 37 (cp 28); CFG
19; GBC 28 (cp 3); GPB 46; IWE 6:833-835; LBW
36 (cp 9); NGB 1:43; NGW 58; RBB 23; SAA 74,
75; WEA 157.

Fume Root, Pink—See **Corydalis, Pale or Pink.**

Fumewort—See **Corydalis.**

Fumitory, Common (Fumaria officinalis) NHE 214;
OWF 137; PMF 290.

Fungus, Artist's or Shelf (Ganoderma applanatum)
KMF 55; NFP 24, 50; ONP 125; PFF 80; SMG 67.

Fungus, Beefsteak (Fistulina hepatica) ANE 4:755;
LHM 75; ONP 129; PFF 80; SMG 68.

Fungus, Bird's-nest (Crucibulum vulgare) KMF 107
(cp 25b); NFP 89; PFF 87. (C. levis) SMG 53, cp 25.

Fungus, Calocera (Calocera viscosa) DEW 3:132 (cp
51); KMF 83 (cp 19c); NFP 45; ONP 149.

Fungus, Carbon (Daldinia concentrica) LHM 47; NFP
39; ONP 147.

Fungus, Cone-like or Pine-cone (Strobilomyces floccopus or S. strolibaceus) GMC 235 (cp 348); LHM
195; NFP 48; PFF 78; SMG 108.

Fungus, Coral (Clavaria botrytis) GMC 252 (cp 361);
MSM 183, cp 28; NHE 47; PFF 77; SMG 115. (C.
stricta) GMC 235 (cp 349); NFP 46; SMG 112.

Fungus, Dryad's Saddle (Polyporus squamosus) GMC
253 (cps 356, 357); KMF 15 (cp 2); LHM 75; ONP
129.

Fungus, Early Cup (Peziza vesiculosa) DEW 3:130 (cp
46); KMF 135; LHM 37; ONP 41.

Fungus, Orange Cup (Aleuria aurantia or Peziza aurantia) DEW 3:130 (cp 45); KMF 135; LHM 35; MSM
193, cp 32; NFP 37; ONP 151.

Fungus, Scarlet Cup (Sarcoscypha coccinea or Peziza
coccinea) ANE 4:754; GMC 273 (cp 382); LHM 35;
ONP 151; PFF 70; SMG 21, cp 1. (P. repanda) GMC
273 (cp 381); LHM 37; ONP 151. (Plectania coccinea) NFP 37.

Funkia—See **Lily, Plantain.**

Furze—See **Gorse.**

G

Gadwall (Anas strepera) AAB 67; ALE 7:255, 305; BBC 1:cp 14, cp 18; CFG cp 2, 39, 41, 42; GBC 76 (cp 9); GGB 40, 41; KWF 408 (cp 10), 410 (cp 11), 454 (cp 33); NGB 1:101; NGW 169; NHE 113; PBA 1:cp 12; PEB 22 (pl 7), 26 (pl 9), 39 (cp 14); PWB 34 (pl 7), 59 (cp 14); RBA 51; RBB 47; SAA 145.

Gaillardia or Indian Blanket (Gaillardia pulchella or G. aristata) AFP 4:207; BBF 3:512; CWF 547; DFP 37 (cp 296), 143 (cp 1138, 1139); EGA 120; EGP 118; EWF cp 165e; FNC 203; OGF 147; RUS 2:573, 3:451, 4:673, 6:659; RWA cp 372; TGF 269; VPN 5:205.

Galax (Galax aphylla) BBF 2:707; FFK 154; FNC 142; HYF cp 141; PMF 63; RUS 1:297.

Gall, Oak-apple (Biorhiza pallida) ALE 2:438; ANE 4:760; OBI 149.

Gallinule, Common (Florida) (Gallinula chloropus) AAB 142; ABW 109; BBC 1:cp 44; BBE 106; CDB 74 (cp 227); CFG cp 5; GBC 136 (cp 23); GGB 95; GPL 146; IWE 11:1498-1499; NGW 310; PBA 1:cp 27; PEB 71 (cp 22); PWB 99 (cp 24); RBB 105.

Gallinule, Purple (Porphyrula martinica) ABW 108; ALE 8:84; ANE 4:763; BBC 1:cp 44; CDB 75 (cp 232); CFG cp 5; FWA 256; GGB 95; GPB 131; HBT cp 1; LBW cp 47; NGB 1:289; NGW 309; PBA 1:cp 27; PEB 71 (cp 22); RBB 105.

Gall-of-the-earth (Prenanthes trifoliata) HWF cp 226; PMF 74; RUS 1:509, 2:639.

Gamagrass, Eastern (Tripsacum dactyloides) BBF 1:111; HMG 791; PRP 71.

Gambusia—See **Mosquito-fish.**

Gannet (Sula bassana) AAB 30; ABW 47; ALE 7:61, 177; ANE 4:764, 765; BBE 29; CDB 39 (cp 42); GBC 29 (cp 4); GFB 32; GPB 54, 55; IWE 7:843, 844; NGB 1:52; NGW 74-79; PBA 1:cp 9; RBA 25; RBB 33; SAA 72; SLP 52, 53.

Gar, Alligator (Lepisosteus spatula) ALE 4:157; CFG 518.

Gar, Long-nosed (Lepisosteus osseus) ANE 4:766; CFG 518; CFW 41; GGF 33; GPL 128; HFW 71; NGF 249; WFW cp 18.

Gar, Spotted (Lepisosteus productus) CFG 518; NGF 249.

Gardenia (Gardenia jasminoides) AGF 114; EGE 71, 127; FHP 122; MEP 148; MWF 138 (cp 415); TGS 359. (G. spatulifolia) EWF cp 79g; PFW 266.

Garibaldi (Hypsypops rubicunda) ALE 5:132; CFW 121; HFW 163 (cps 65, 66); IWE 5:604; NGF 204.

Garland Flower (Daphne cneorum) AGF 92; DFP 6 (cp 47); EGE 121; HSC 42; NHE 267; PFW 296; TGS 247.

Garlic (Allium sativum) AFP 169; PFF 372; WYG 154.

Garlic, False (Nothoscordum bivalve) BBF 1:50; FFK 54; RUS 1:33, 3:27, 6:53.

Garlic, Field or Crow (Allium vineale) BBF 1:499; NHE 191; OWF 163; PMF 297; RUS 1:33, 2:43, 6:53.

Garlic, Golden (Allium moly) DFP 83 (cp 644); EGB 92; EWF cp 24e; PFW 19.

Garlic, Wild—See **Onion, Wild** (Allium canadense).

Gas-plant—See **Burning Bush** (Dictamnus alba).

Gaura, Biennial (Gaura biennis) HWF cp 148; PMF 71; RUS 1:247, 2:311, 6:359. (G. coccinea) RUS 3:225, 4:331, 6:359.

Gay Wings—See **Milkwort, Fringed.**

Gayfeather—See **Blazing Star.**

Gazania (Gazania hybrids) DFP 38 (cp 297); EGA 120; EGP 118; EWF cp 83g; FHP 122; MEP 152; MWF 139 (cps 418-420); PFW 87; TGF 269.

Gecko, Banded (Coleonyx variegatus) ALE 6:169; CGR cp 8a; CRA 111 (cp 14); GRA 47; LRE 26-27; PFF 536; PRW pl 156-158; SRA cp 29; SIR 74.

Gecko, Leaf-toed (Phyllodactylus xanti) CGR 177; SRA cp 29. (P. tuberculatus) GRA 46.

Geiger Tree (Cordia sebestena) BTN 260; MEP 119; PFW 48.

Gentian, Blue (Gentiana calycosa) AFP 361; LWF 145 (cp 232); RUS 5:371, 6:447; RWA cp 300; VPN 4:70.

Gentian, Catchfly (Eustoma exaltatum) AFP 3:357; RUS 2:295, 3:285, 4:429.

Gentian, Closed (Gentiana andrewsii) ANE 4:768; HWF cp 168; HYF cp 157; LWF 268 (cp 425); PMF 321; RUS 1:309, 2:387, 6:447; TGF 157.

Gentian, Fringed (Gentiana crinata) FNC 147; HWF cp 167; HYF cp 157; LWF 38 (cp 65); PFF 282; PMF 321; RUS 1:305, 2:387; RWA cp 297.

Gentian, Horse—See **Horse Gentian.**

Gentian, Marsh (Gentiana pneumonthe) NHE 185; OWF 177.

Gentian, Prairie (Eustoma grandiflorum) OOW cp 272; RUS 3:285, 4:429, 6:455.

Gentian, Rose (Gentiana amarella) AFP 3:361; RUS 1:305, 4:429, 5:375, 6:445; RWA cp 296; VPN 4:70.

Gentian, Soapwort (Gentiana saponaria) FFK 128; FNC 149; PMF 321; RUS 1:311, 2:391, 3:283; RWA cp 299.

Gentian, Spring (Gentiana verna) DFP 10 (cp 76, 77); NHE 280; OWF 177; PFW 121.

Gentian, Stiff (Gentiana quinquefolia) FNC 148; HYF cp 158; PMF 321; RUS 1:309, 2:391.

Gentian, Western Fringed (Gentiana thermalis) LWF 146 (cp 233); OOW cp 225; RUS 4:427, 6:445.

Gentian, Willow (Gentiana asclepiadea) DFP 143 (cp 1142); NHE 185; OGF 111; PFW 121.

Gentian, Yellow (Gentiana lutea) NHE 279; PFW 122.

Geoduck (Panope generosa) ASN 257; GAS 236; JSS 467; KSL 223; MGS pl 24; PFF 425.

Geranium, Bicknell's (Geranium bicknellii) AFP 3:6; RUS 1:237, 5:291, 6:345; VPN 3:382.

Geranium, Common (Pelargonium hortorum) AGF 115; DFP 75-77 (cps 598-612); FHP 138; LFW 56, 57 (cps 129, 131, 134, 135, 136); PFF 226; TGF 141.

Geranium, Ivy-leaved (Pelargonium peltatum) DFP 77, 78 (cps 613-617); LFW 56 (cp 130); MWF 224 (cp 730); PFW 125.

Geranium, Martha Washington (Pelargonium domesticum) DFP 74, 75 (cps 587-597); LWF 56, 57 (cps 132, 137); MWF 224 (cp 729); PFW 126.

Geranium, Sticky (Geranium viscosissimum) AFP 3:6; CWF 311; RUS 5:291, 6:345; RWA cp 208; VPN 3:386.

Geranium, Strawberry (Saxifraga sarmentosa or S. stolonifera) FHP 142; PFF 192.

Geranium, Wild—See **Cranesbill, Spotted or Wild.**

Geranium, Zonal (Pelargonium zonale) MWF 244 (cp 731); PFF 226; PFW 124, 125.

Gerardia, Purple (Agalinus or Gerardia purpurea) BBF 3:210; FFK 227; FNC 172; HWF cp 203; HYF cp 182; PMF 221, 269; RUS 1:399, 2:505, 6:587.

Gerardia, Slender (Agalinus tenuifolia) BBF 3:221; HWF cp 204; PMF 269; RUS 1:399, 2:507, 3:401, 6:587.

Gerbera—See **Daisy, Transvaal.**

Germander (Teucrium canadense) FFK 227; FNC 161; PMF 279; RUS 1:377, 2:481, 3:377, 4:567, 6:559. (T. chamaedrys) TGF 204.

Gherkin, Sea—See **Sea Cucumber.**

Giant Bird's Nest—See **Pine Drops.**

Giant-hyssop (Agastache scrophulariaefolia) BBF 3:112; PMF 279; RUS 1:381, 2:483.

Giant-hyssop, Yellow (Agastache nepetoides) BBF 3:111; FFK 208; PMF 127; RUS 1:381, 2:483.

Gila Monster (Heloderma suspectum) ALE 6:312, 341; ANE 4:774; CGR cp 10b; FWA 158; GRA 69; IWE 7:882-883; LRE 90; LVS 175; MAR 127 (pl 52); PFF 538; PRW pl 215-216; SIR cp 54; SRA pl 17; WEA 166.

Gilia, Blue (Gilia capitata) EGA 121; HFP 284; RUS 5:391, 6:465; TGF 172; VPN 4:106.

Gilia, Scarlet (Gilia aggregator or Ipomopsis aggregator) AFP 3:459; ANE 4:775; BBF 3:60; CWF 427; DEW 2:112; LFW 147 (cp 234); OOW cps 144, 155; RUS 3:301, 4:447, 5:395, 6:477; VPN 4:106.

Gill-over-the-ground—See **Ground Ivy.**

Ginger (Zingiber officinale) OFP 135; PFF 389.

Ginger, Hartweg's Wild (Asarum hartwegi) AFP 1:535; RUS 5:87.

Ginger, Lemmon's Wild (Asarum lemmoni) AFP 1:536; RUS 5:87.

Ginger, Shuttleworth's Wild (Hexastylis shuttleworthii) BBF 1:643; FNC 54; RUS 1:95, 2:137.

Ginger, Virginia Wild (Hexastylis virginianum) BBF 1:644; RUS 1:95.

Ginger, Western Wild (Asarum caudatum) AFP 1:535; CWF 111; EWF cp 150b; HFP 82; OOW cp 287; PFW 36; RUS 5:87, 6:89; VPN 2:105.

Ginger, Wild (Asarum canadense) BBF 1:642; FFK 275; FNC 53; HWF cp 46; HYF cp 44; LWF 246 (cp 386); PFF 151; PMF 241, 389; RUS 1:95, 2:141, 6:89; RWA cp 99.

Ginkgo Tree—See **Maidenhair Tree.**

Ginseng (Panax quinquefolium) FFK 164; FNC 125; PMF 366; RUS 1:215, 2:273, 6:297.

Ginseng, Dwarf (Panax trifolium) FFK 164; FNC

Godwit, Hudsonian (Limosa haemastica) BBC 1:cp 54; CFG cp 27; GBC 157 (cp 28); NGB 1:272; NGW 343; PBA 1:cp 38; PEB 90 (pl 25), 103 (cp 30); PWB 103 (cp 26), 106 (pl 27); RBB 115; WID 242.

Godwit, Marbled (Limosa fedoa) AAB 177; ANE 4:783; BBC 1:cp 54; CFG cp 8; GBC (cp 28); GFB 71; GGB 103; NGB 1:272; NGW 342; PBA 1:cp 38; PEB 90 (pl 25), 103 (cp 30); PWB 103 (cp 26), 106 (pl 27); RBB 115.

Gold Dust Tree—See **Laurel, Spotted.**

Gold Flower (Hypericum moserianum) EGP 124; HSC 70; PFW 134, 135; TGS 150.

Golden Alexanders—See **Alexanders, Golden.**

Golden Bells—See **Forsythia.**

Golden Chain Tree (Laburnum sp.) AGF 123; BKT cp 142; DFP 209 (cp 1669); EGT 41, 121; FGF 151; LFW 81 (cp 188); MWF 176 (cp 551); NHE 21; OBT 184; PFW 162; TGS 135.

Golden Club (Orantium aquaticum) BBF 1:445; DEW 2:288 (cp 174); FNC 9; HYF cp 6; LWF 2 (cp 25); PFF 366; PMF 117; RUS 1:89, 2:133; RWA cp 19.

Golden Cup (Hunnemannia) See **Poppy, Mexican Tulip.**

Golden Cup (Hypericum patulum) DFP 208 (cp 1657); EGE 68, 128; HSC 70; LFW 128 (cp 289).

Golden Pert—See **Hedge-hyssop, Golden.**

Golden Rain Tree (Koelreuteria paniculata) BKT cp 155; EGT 44, 121; MEP 74; MTB 337 (cp 34); 3; PFF 243; PFW 270; TGS 294.

Golden Shower (Cassia fistula) EGT 102; EWF cp 112a; MEP 54; MWF 74 (cp 181); PFW 161.

Golden-eye, American (Bucephala clangula) ALE 7:255, 308, 385; BBC 1:cp 19, cp 21; CFG 49, 50, 51; GBC 93 (cp 12); GGB 21, 66, 67; KWF 428 (cp 20), 430 (cp 21), 456 (cp 34); NGB 1:127; NGW 172, 180-181; PBA 1:18; PEB 23 (pl 8), 27 (pl 10), 34 (pl 11); PWB 35 (pl 8), 43 (pl 10); RBB 55; SAA 92; TBC 98 (cp 10b).

Golden-eye, Barrow's (Bucephala islandica) AAB 77; ALE 7:307; BBC 1:cp 19, cp 21; CDB 51 (cp 106); CFG cp 10, 55; GBC 93 (cp 12); GGB 68; KWF 428 (cp 20), 430 (cp 21); NGB 1:127; NGW 180; PBA 1:139; PEB 34 (pl 11); RBB 55; TBC 98 (cp 10b).

Goldenrod, Alpine (Solidago cutleri) BBF 3:385; PMF 201; RUS 1:439.

Goldenrod, Blue-stemmed (Solidago caesia) BBF 3:382; FFK 247; HWF cp 235a; HYF cp 213; RUS 1:437, 2:543.

Goldenrod, Bog (Solidago uliginosa) BBF 3:387; PMF 195; RUS 1:435.

Goldenrod, Broad-leaved or Zigzag (Solidago flexicaulis) BBF 3:383; FFK 248; HWF cp 236; PMF 197; RUS 1:437, 2:543.

Goldenrod, California (Solidago californica) AFP 4:293; ANE 4:783; RUS 4:627, 5:531.

Goldenrod, Canada (Solidago canadensis) AFP 4:293; BBF 3:393; CWF 559; DFP 173 (cps 1381-1384); HWF cp 238; HYF cp 207; MWF 268 (cp 891); PFF 313; PMF 191; RUS 1:431, 2:541, 5:529, 6:621; RWA cp 382; VPN 5:308.

Goldenrod, Downy (Solidago puberula) BBF 3:386; HWF cp 237b; PMF 201; RUS 1:437, 2:543.

Goldenrod, Dwarf (Solidago decumbens) AFP 4:297; CWF 559; RUS 4:623, 6:621.

Goldenrod, Early (Solidago juncea) BBF 3:393; FFK 245; HYF cp 207; LWF 205 (cp 325); PMF 193; RUS 1:435, 2:543.

Goldenrod, Elm-leaved (Solidago ulmifolia) BBF 3:391; FFK 246; PMF 197; RUS 1:431, 2:541.

Goldenrod, Erect or Slender (Solidago erecta) BBF 3:384; FFK 249; PMF 201; RUS 2:547.

Goldenrod, Fragrant or Grass-leaved (Solidago graminifolia) FFK 249; HWF cp 234; HYF cp 208; PMF 203; RUS 1:439, 2:547, 6:629.

Goldenrod, Gray (Solidago nemoralis) FNC 197; LWF 205 (cp 326); PMF 195; RUS 1:431, 2:541, 3:417, 6:625; VPN 5:312.

Goldenrod, Hairy (Solidago hispida) BBF 3:384; PMF 201; RUS 1:439, 2:545.

Goldenrod, Hard-leaved or Stiff (Solidago rigida) BBF 3:397; PMF 203; PRP 156; RUS 1:439, 2:547, 3:421, 6:621.

Goldenrod, Large-leaved (Solidago macrophylla) BBF 3:385; PMF 199.

Goldenrod, Late (Solidago gigantea) PFF 313; PMF 191; RUS 1:431, 2:541, 3:417; VPN 5:308.

Goldenrod, Pine-barren (Solidago fistulosa) BBF 3:390; PMF 195; RUS 2:543.

Goldenrod, Rough-leaved (Solidago patula) BBF 3:391; PMF 197; RUS 1:435, 2:545.

Goldenrod, Rough-stemmed (Solidago rugosa) BBF 3:390; FFK 246; PMF 193; RUS 1:435, 2:545.

Goldenrod, Seaside (Solidago sempervirens) BBF 3:389; GGS 143; HWF cp 235b; HYF cp 208; PMF 199; RUS 1:435.

Goldenrod, Sharp or Cut-leaved (Solidago arguta) BBF 3:393; PMF 193; RUS 2:551.

Goldenrod, Showy (Solidago speciosa) BBF 3:387; FFK 249; HYF cp 216; PMF 199; RUS 1:437, 2:545; 3:417.

Goldenrod, Slender Fragrant (Solidago tenuifolia) FNC 198; HWF cp 232b; PMF 203; RUS 1:443, 2:547.

Goldenrod, Stout (Solidago squarrosa) BBF 3:382; PMF 199; RUS 1:437, 2:545.

Goldenrod, Sweet (Solidago odora) BBF 3:389; PMF 191; RUS 1:525, 2:543.

Goldenrod, Tall (Solidago altissima) BBF 3:395; FFK 244; FNC 197; PMF 191; RUS 1:431, 2:541, 3:425.

Goldenrod, Wandlike (Solidago stricta) BBF 3:386; PMF 201; RUS 2:547.

Goldenrod, White or Silverrod (Solidago bicolor) BBF 3:383; FNC 196; HWF cp 237a; HYF cp 213; PFF 313; PMF 59; RUS 1:435, 2:545.

Goldenseal (Hydrastis canadensis) FFK 274; HWF 101; RUS 1:127, 2:181, 6:161.

Golden-stars (Bloomeria crocea) AFP 1:398; RUS 4:37, 5:55.

Goldentail, Blue-throated (Hylocharis eliciae) DBM cp 16; PMB cp 19.

Goldfinch, American (Spinus tristis) ALE 9:391; ANE 4:786; BBC 2:cp 114; CDB 210 (cp 932); CFG cp 26; GBC 317 (cp 64); GBI 115; NGB 2:254; NGS 343; PBA 3:cps 78, 79; PEB 214 (cp 55); PWB 274 (cp 55); RBA 240; RBB 301.

Goldfinch, Arkansas or Lesser (Spinus psaltria) BBC 2:cp 114; CFG cp 26; NGB 2:256; NGS 344; PWB 274 (cp 55); RBB 301.

Goldfinch, Lawrence's (Spinus laurencei) NGB 2:256; NGS 344; PWB 274 (cp 55); RBB 301.

Goldfish (Carassius auratus) ALE 4:334, 335; CFG 533; GPL 123; HFW 42 (cp 21), 120; IWE 7:917; NGF 246-247; OBV 113; WEA 171.

Goldstar (Chrysogonum virginianum) DFP 132 (cp 1050); FNC 198; HYF cp 196; LFW 192 (cp 434); PMF 113; RUS 1:459, 2:583; RWA cp 371; TGF 284.

Goldstars (Crocidium multicaule) AFP 4:455; CWF 535; RUS 5:543, 6:637; VPN 5:157.

Goldthread (Coptis groenlandica) PFF 172; PMF 31; RUS 1:127, 2:179. (C. trifoliata) HWF cp 60a; LWF 250 (cp 394).

Good King Henry (Chenopodium bonus-henricus) NHE 227; OFP 191; OWF 55.

Gooney-bird—See **Albatross.**

Goosander—See **Merganser, Common or American.**

Goose, Barnacle (Branta leucopsis) ABW 66; ALE 7:284, 385; BBE 45; CDB 51 (cp 104); KWF 394 (cp 3); NGB 1:106; NGW 145; NHE 145; PEB 18 (pl 5); RBB 41; SAA 144.

Goose, Bean (Anser fabalis) ALE 7:281, 385; BBE 50; NHE 112; SAA 144.

Goose, Blue (Chen caerulescens) AAB 62; ALE 7:283; BBC 1:cp 12; GGB 30, 31; KWF 396 (cp 4), 452 (cp 32); NGB 1:108; NGW 150, 151; PBA 1:cp 21; PEB 18 (pl 5), 19 (pl 6); PWB 26 (pl 5), 27 (pl 6); RBB 43; SAA 144.

Goose, Brent—See **Brant.**

Goose, Canada (Branta canadensis) AAB 58; ABW 66; ALE 7:284, 8:229, 11:151; BBC 1:cp 11; BBE 45; CDB 51 (cp 103); GBC 60 (cp 7); GGB 20, 22, 23; GPB 86; IWE 3:356, 357; KWF 392 (cp 2), 452 (cp 32); NGB 1:104; NGW 138, 139, 146-147; PBA 1:cp 22; PEB 18 (pl 5), 19 (pl 6); PWB 26 (pl 5), 27 (pl 6); RBA 49; RBB 41; TBC 76 (cp 4b); WEA 163.

Goose, Emperor (Philacte canagica) ABW 66; ALE 7:283, 8:229, 11:151; GGB 32; KWF 394 (cp 3), 452 (cp 32); NGB 1:106; NGW 153; PWB 26 (pl 5), 27 (pl 6); RBB 41.

Goose, Hawaiian (Branta sandvicensis) AAB 60; ALE 7:284; BHB 58 (cp 23); CDB 51 (cp 105); IWE 8:1042, 1043; LBW 80; LVS 198; NGW 204, 205; OMW 237; SLP 104, 105; SOS 232; WAB 217; WID 192 (cp 17a).

Goose, Ross (Chen rossii) AAB 63; ALE 7:283; BBC 1:cp 12; GBC 61 (cp 8); GGB 18, 28; KWF 398 (cp 5), 452 (cp 32); NGB 1:108; NGW 152; PWB 26 (pl 5); RBB 43; SAA 144.

Goose, Snow (Chen hyperborea) AAB 62; ABW 66; ALE 7:283, 11:151; BBC 1:cp 12; BBE 50; GGB 28, 29; GBC 61 (cp 8); KWF 398 (cp 5), 452 (cp 32); NGW 151; PBA 1:155; PEB 18 (pl 5), 19 (pl 6); PWB 26 (pl 5), 27 (pl 6); RBB 43; SAA 144; TBC 82 (cp 5b).

Goose, White-fronted (Anser albifrons) AAB 61; ABW 64; ALE 7:281, 385; BBC 1:cp 11; BBE 48; GBC 60 (cp 7); GGB 27, 30; KWF 396 (cp 4), 452 (cp 32); NGB 1:108; NGW 150; PBA 1:cp 21; PEB 18 (pl 5), 19 (pl 6); PWB 26 (pl 5), 27 (pl 6); RBB 43; SAA 144; TBC 82 (cp 5b).

Gooseberry, American (Ribes divaricatum) CWF 230; OFP 81; WYG 223.

Goosefoot, Many-sided (Chenopodium polyspermum) AFP 2:69; BBF 2:11; EWF cp 14e; NHE 227.

Goosefoot, Maple-leaved or Sowbane (Chenopodium hybridum) AFP 2:69; BBF 2:13; NHE 227; PMF 379; VPN 2:200.

Goosefoot, Nettle-leaved (Chenopodium murale) AFP 2:69; BBF 2:13; NHE 227; VPN 2:203.

Goosefoot, Oak-leaved (Chenopodium glaucum) AFP 2:73; BBF 2:10; NHE 227; VPN 2:200.

Goosefoot, Red (Chenopodium rubrum) AFP 2:73; BBF 2:13; NHE 227; OWF 55; PMF 311; VPN 2:203.

Goosefoot, Sticky or Feather Geranium (Chenopodium botrys) AFP 2:73; BBF 2:14; NHE 227; PMF 379; VPN 2:197.

Goosefoot, Stinking (Chenopodium vulvaria) BBF 2:11; NHE 227; OWF 55.

Goosefoot, White or Pigweed (Chenopodium album) AFP 2:69; BBF 2:10; DEW 1:203; NHE 228; OWF 55; VPN 2:197.

Gopher, Eastern or Plains Pocket (Geomys sp.) ALE 11:297; BGM 148 (cp 13); GGM 88; NGA 262; PAK 550; PFF 709; PMG cp 23; SMW 118; WMW 2:730, 732.

Gopher, Mexican or Plateau Pocket (Cratogeomys castanops) BGM 148 (cp 13); GGM 88; PMG cp 23.

Gopher, Western Pocket (Thomomys sp.) ANE 4:792; BGM 148 (cp 13); GGM 88; PMG cp 23; WMW 2:733.

Gorse (Ulex europaeus) AFP 2:516; BBF 2:349; CWF 307; DFP 368 (cp 1931); MWF 290 (cp 957); NHE 69; OBT 36; OGF 23; OWF 19; PFF 214; PMF 155; TGS 135; VPN 3:375.

Goshawk (Accipiter gentilis) ALE 7:332, 335; ANE 1:2; BBC 1:cp 26; BBE 79; CFG cp 28; GBC 105 (cp 16), 125 (pl 20); IWE 7:925, 926; NGB 1:154; NGW 225; PEB 55 (cp 16), 66 (pl 19); PFF 574; PWB 67 (cp 16), 74 (pl 17); RBB 69, 80.

Goshawk, Mexican—See **Hawk, Gray.**

Gourami, Kissing (Helostoma temmincki) ALE 5:220, 229; HFW 244; IWE 9:1241; NGF 239; WFW cp 461.

Gourd (Cucurbita pepo) AGF 124; EGA 122; OFP 123; WYG 118-119. (C. pepo ovifera) MWF 98 (cp 269); PFF 307.

Gourd, Wild (Cucurbita foetidissima) AFP 4:67; EWF cp 159d; OOW cp 119; RUS 3:353, 4:531, 5:452, 6:539.

Gout Plant or Guatemala Rhubarb (Jatropha podagrica) LFW 255 (cp 567); MEP 73; PFW 116.

Grackle, Boat-tailed (Cassidix mexicanus) AAB 446; ABW 290; ALE 9:381; CFG cp 22; DBM cp 38; IWE 7:930; LBW 374; NGB 2:230; NGS 312; PEB 198 (cp 53); PWB 263 (cp 52); RBB 283.

Grackle, Common (Quiscalus quiscula) AAB 447; ALE 9:381; ANE 5:792, 793; BBC 2:cp 108; CDB 207 (cp 913); CFG cp 27; GBC 301 (cp 62); IWE 7:928-929, 930; NGB 2:230; NGS 312, 313; PEB 198 (cp 53); PWB 263 (cp 52); RBB 283.

Grama, Blue (Bouteloua gracilis) AFP 1:179; HMG 541; PRP 20; VPN 1:498.

Grama, Hairy (Bouteloua hirsuta) AFP 1:179; BBF 1:227; HMG 540; PRP 21.

Grama, Sideoats (Bouteloua curtipendula) AFP 1:177; HMG 534; PRP 19; VPN 1:496.

Grampus—See **Dolphin, Risso's,** and **Whale, Killer.**

Grape (Vitis) DFP 250 (cps 1995-1997); GPL 73; NHE 23; OFP 91, 93; PFF 246; TSK 109, 202; WYG 190.

Grape Hyacinth (Muscaria botryoides) AGF 124; DFP 103 (cps 823-825); FHP 133; LFW 68 (cp 158); MGB 267; MWF 204 (cp 658); NHE 241; OGF 9; PFW 317; RUS 1:45, 2:47; SGB cp 24; TGF 13.

Grape, Oregon—See **Oregon Grape.**

Grape, Ornamental (Ampelopsis brevipedunculata) MWF 40 (cp 55); PFW 307; TGS 71.

Grapefruit (Citrus paradisi) OFP 87; PFF 228; WYG 202.

Grass, Barnyard (Echinochloa crusgalli) AFP 1:117; BBF 1:133; FNC 6; HMG 713; NHE 243; PFF 348; PRP 34.

Grass, Bent—See **Bent-grass.**

Grass, Bermuda (Cynodon dactylon) HMG 504; NHE 244; PFF 354; PRP 30; VPN 1:540.

Grass, Big Bluestem (Andropogon gerardi) HMG 758; PFF 347; PRP 9.

Grass, Blue—See **Bluegrass.**

Grass, Bottle-brush (Hystrix patula) FFK 88; PFF 357.

Grass, Cord (Spartina pectinata) GPL 52; HMG 510; PRP 64; VPN 1:708.

Grass, Couch—See **Quackgrass.**

Grass, Crab (Digitaria sanguinalis) HMG 577; NHE 243; PFF 347; PRP 32.

Grass, Dallis (Paspalum dilatatum) AFP 1:111; BBF 1:132; HMG 616; PRP 52.

Grass, Feather (Stipa pennata) DFP 147 (cp 1390); NHE 245.

Grass, Fountain (Pennisetum ruppellii) DFP 335 (cp 356); EGA 143.

Gromwell, Western (Lithospermum ruderale) AFP 3:549; CWF 447; RUS 5:425, 6:511.

Grosbeak, Black-headed (Pheucticus melanocephalus) ANE 5:813; BBC 2:cp 110; CDB 209 (cp 927); CFG cp 23; GBC 316 (cp 63); LBW 364 (cp 210); NGB 2:247; NGS 331; PFF 664; PWB 275 (cp 56); RBB 293; TBC 380 (cp 77a).

Grosbeak, Blue (Guiraca caerulea) ABW 296; ALE 9:352; CFG cp 23; NGB 2:245; NGS 331; PEB 215 (cp 56); PWB 275 (cp 56); RBA 233; RBB 293.

Grosbeak, Blue-black (Cyanocompsa cyanoides) DBM cp 45; PMB cp 46.

Grosbeak, Evening (Hesperiphona vespertina) AAB 463; ALE 9:392; ANE 5:814; CDB 209 (cp 925); CFG cp 28; GBC 317 (cp 64); NGB 2:250; NGS 335; PBA 3:cp 79; PEB 214 (cp 55); PFF 666; PWB 274 (cp 55); RBA 237; RBB 293; TBC 384 (cp 78a).

Grosbeak, Pine (Pinicola enucleator) ALE 9:382; ANE 5:815; BBE 285; CFG cp 28; NGB 2:252; NGS 338; PBA 3:cp 76; PEB 214 (cp 55); PWB 274 (cp 55); RBB 297; TBC 386 (cp 79a).

Grosbeak, Rose-breasted (Pheucticus ludovicianus) ANE 5:816; CFG cp 23; GBC 316 (cp 63); IWE 7:963; NGB 2:245; NGS 330; PBA 3:cp 85; PEB 215 (cp 56); PFF 664; PWB 275 (cp 56); RBB 293; TBC 378 (cp 76b).

Grosbeak, Yellow (Pheucticus chrysopeplus) ALE 9:352; AMB 105 (cp 9); DBM cp 45; PMB cp 45.

Ground Hog—See **Woodchuck.**

Ground Ivy (Glecoma hederacea) AFP 3:629; BBF 3:114; CWF 447; FFK 206; NHE 230; OWF 145; PFF 206; PMF 349; RUS 1:383, 2:487, 5:475, 6:561.

Ground Squirrel—See **Squirrel.**

Ground-chat (Chamaethlypis poliocephala) DBM cp 43; PMB cp 38.

Ground-cherry, Clammy (Physalis heterophylla) HWF cp 193; PFF 294; PMF 145; RUS 1:517, 2:439, 3:321, 4:503, 6:519.

Ground-cone, Vancouver (Boschniakia hookeri) AFP 4:10; CWF 494; RUS 5:519; VPN 4:428.

Ground-dove—See **Dove, Ground.**

Groundnut—See also **Ginseng, Dwarf.**

Groundnut (Apios americana) ANE 5:817; BBF 2:418; EWF cp 153b; FFK 186; HWF cp 117; HYF cp 92; LWF 187 (cp 294); PMF 252, 390; RUS 1:261, 2:329, 4:363, 6:377.

Groundsel, Common (Senecio vulgaris) AFP 4:453; BBF 3:539; NHE 237; OWF 43; PMF 167; RUS 1:447, 2:553, 3:421, 4:635, 5:537.

Groundsel, Golden—See **Ragwort, Golden.**

Groundsel-tree (Baccharis halimifolia) BBF 3:445; FNC 194; PMF 88; TGS 327.

Grouper, Black (Mycteroperca bonaci) GGF 110; NGF 119.

Grouper, Nassau (Epinephelus striatus) MOL 113; NGF 119; SOS 71.

Grouper, Red (Epinephelus morio) ALE 5:79; ANE 5:820; CFG 484; GGF 110; NGF 119.

Grouper, Yellow-fin (Mycteroperca venenosa) GGF 110; LSE 125.

Grouse, Blue or Sooty (Dendragapus obscurus) AAB 116; ALE 7:445; BBC 1:cp 34; CDB 66 (cp 182); FWA 46; GBC 129 (cp 22); GGB 127; GPB 115; NGB 1:236; NGW 269; PWB 90 (cp 21); RBB 85.

Grouse Flower (Synthyris reniformis) AFP 3:799; RUS 5:481; VPN 4:418. (S. rotundifolia) HFP 322; TGF 221.

Grouse, Ruffed (Bonasa umbellus) AAB 120; ABW 88; ALE 7:445; ANE 5:822, 824; BBC 1:cp 35; CFG cp 5; GBC 128 (cp 21); GGB 118, 119; NGB 1:234; NGW 270-271; PBA 2:cp 41; PEB 70 (cp 21); PWB 90 (cp 21); RBA 80; RBB 85; TBC 152 (cp 18b).

Grouse, Sage (Sage Hen) (Centrocercus urophasianus) ABW 88; ANE 5:826, 827; BBC 1:cp 38; CFG cp 5; FWA 123; GBC 128 (cp 21); GGB 120, 121; IWE 7:970, 971; NGB 1:242; NGW 277; PWB 90 (cp 21); RBB 85.

Grouse, Sharp-tailed (Pedioecetes phasianellus) BBC 1:cp 37; CDB 67 (cp 187); CFG cp 28; GBC 128 (cp 21); GGB 122, 123; NGB 1:242; NGW 277; PEB 70 (cp 21); PWB 90 (cp 21); RBB 85; TBC 160 (cp 19a).

Grouse, Spruce (Canachites canadensis) AAB 119; ABW 89; ALE 7:445; BBC 1:cp 35; CFG cp 28; FWA 46; GBC 129 (cp 22); GGB 116, 128; GPB 115; NGB 1:238; NGW 268; PEB 70 (cp 21); PWB 90 (cp 21); RBA 84; RBB 85.

Grouseberry (Vaccinium scoparium) AFP 3:330; CWF 414; RUS 6:481.

Grunion (Leuresthes tenuis and L. sardina) CFW 21; GGF 82; IWE 7:972, 973; SOS 22.

Grunt, Blue-striped (Haemulon sciurus) GGF 115; HFW 191, 193; NGF 127.

Grunt, White (Haemulon plumieri) GGF 115; HFW 170 (cp 79); NGF 147, 158, 162.

H

ABW 51; ALE 7:198; ANE 5:867; BBC cp 7; BBE 38; BHB 58 (cp 22); CFG cp 6; GBC 44 (cp 5); LBW 42 (cp 18); NGB 1:84; NGW 111; PBA 1:cp 24; PEB 87 (cp 24); PWB 23 (pl 4); RBB 97; TBC 60 (cp 3b); WEA 259.

Heron, Boat-billed (Cochlearius cochlearius) ABW 55; ALE 7:198; CDB 43 (cp 57); DBM cp 2; GPB 69; LBW 69; PMB cp 1.

Heron, Great Blue (Ardea herodias) AAB 39; ABW 50; ANE 5:862, 864; CFG cp 6; FWA 289; GBC 44 (cp 5); GGS 153; LBW 40 (cp 16); NGB 1:77; NGW 103; PEB 86 (cp 23); PWB 23 (pl 4); RBB 95; TBC 60 (cp 3a).

Heron, Great White (Ardea occidentalis) AAB 38; ANE 5:868; NGB 1:77; NGW 102; PEB 86 (cp 23); RBB 93.

Heron, Green (Butorides virescens) ABW 50; ANE 5:866; BBC 1:cp 7; CFG cp 6; FWA 289; GBC 44 (cp 5); HBT cp 1; NGB 1:82; NGW 104; PBA 1:cp 23; PEB 87 (cp 24); PWB 23 (pl 4); RBB 95.

Heron, Little Blue (Florida caerulea) AAB 49; ABW 51; ALE 7:197; ANE 5:865; BBC 1:cp 7; CDB 44 (cp 61); CFG cp 6; GBC 45 (cp 6); GGS 153; LBW 43 (cp 21); NGB 1:82; NGW 105; PEB 86 (cp 23); PWB 23 (pl 4); RBB 95.

Heron, Louisiana (Hydranassa tricolor) BBC 1:105; CDB 44 (cp 62); CFG cp 6; FWA 289; NGB 1:82; NGW 110; PEB 86 (cp 23); PWB 23 (pl 4); RBA 33; RBB 95.

Heron, Yellow-crowned Night (Nyctanassa violacea) ABW 51; ANE 5:867; BBC 1:cp 7; CDB 44 (cp 63); CFG cp 6; GBC 44 (cp 5); IWE 12:1571; NGB 1:84; NGW 112; PEB 87 (cp 24); RBB 97.

Herring, Lake—See **Cisco.**

Herring, Sea (Clupea harengus) ALE 4:197; CFG 521; CFW 44; GGF 40; HFW 74; IWE 8:1063; NGF 195; NHE 152; OBV 21; WFW 160. (C. harengus pallasi) HPF 96.

Hesperochiron (Hesperochiron pumilus) AFP 3:530; RUS 4:471, 5:403, 6:491.

Hibiscus (Hibiscus rosa-sinensis) DEW 1:220 (cp 134); DFP 69 (cp 548); EGE 71, 128; FGF 136; FHP 125; LFW 166 (cp 369), 167 (cps 370-374); MEP 78; MWF 154 (cp 476), 155 (cp 478); PFW 183.

Hibiscus, Fringed (Hibiscus schizopetolus) DEW 1:221 (cp 137); EWF cp 57b; MEP 78; MWF 154 (cp 479); PFW 183.

Hibiscus Tree (Hibiscus tiliaceus) MEP 79; MWF 155 (cp 481).

Hickory, Bitternut (Carya cordiformis) BBF 1:580; BTN 99; GGT 131, 134; MTB 198; PFF 136; TSK 342, 343. (C. leiodermis) BTN 101.

Hickory, Mockernut (Carya tomentosa) BTN 97; DEW 1:191; GGT 130, 133; PFF 135; TSK 345.

Hickory, Pignut (Carya glabra) BBF 1:583; BTN 99; OBT 193; PFF 135; TSK 350, 351.

Hickory, Shagbark (Carya ovata) ANE 5:877; BBF 1:581; BTN 97; GGT 130, 132; MTB 199; PFF 134; TSK 100, 346, 347.

Hickory, Shellbark (Carya laciniosa) BBF 1:582; BTN 97; MTB 200; PFF 134; TSK 100.

Hickory, Water (Carya aquatica) BBF 1:581; BTN 99; TSK 344.

Hind, Rock (Epinephelus adscensionis) NGF 120; WFW 185.

Hobblebush (Viburnum alnifolium) BBF 3:269; EWF cp 155a; FNC 181.

Hog, Domestic (Sus scrofa domestica) ALE 13:91, 94; FWA 360; IWE 13:1752; PFF 719.

Hog-fennel (Lomatium martindalei) CWF 351; RUS 5:255. (L. macrocarpum) AFP 3:262; RUS 5:255, 6:305; VPN 2:561.

Hog-fennel (Oxypolis rigidior) See **Cowbane.**

Hogfish (Lachnolaimus maximus) GGF 130; MOL 112; WFW cp 408.

Hognose, Eastern (Heterodon platyrhinos) BAR cp 46; CGR cp 12f; CRA 191 (cp 24); GRA 81; IWE 8:1084; LRE 164; PFF 541; SIR 213; WWS 1:305.

Hognose, Western (Heterodon nasicus) CRA 191 (cp 24); GRA 81; SRA cp 34; WWS 1:301.

Hog-peanut (Amphicarpa bracteata or Falcata comosa) BBF 2:419; FFK 181; HWF cp 118a; PFF 219; PMF 251; RUS 1:259, 2:329, 6:377.

Hog-potato (Hoffmanseggia densiflora) AFP 2:480; RUS 3:209, 4:305, 5:281, 6:333. (H. jamesii) RUS 3:205, 4:305, 6:337.

Hogsucker, Northern (Hypentelium nigricans) CFG 533; GGF 56; NGF 271.

Hogweed (Heracleum sphondylium) NHE 182; OWF 87.

Holly, American (Ilex opaca) AGF 131; ANE 5:878; BBF 2:486; BTN 207; EGE 130; FGF 137; FNC 111; PFF 237; RWA cp 212; TGS 199; TSK 95, 124.

EWF cp 19a; GGT 153; MTB 337 (cp 34); NHE 294; OWF 189; PFF 258. (A. carnea) EGT 41, 95.

Horse-fly—See **Fly, Horse**.

Horsemint (Monarda punctata) BBF 3:133; FNC 165; OOW cp 212; PMF 127; RUS 1:369, 2:471, 3:371, 4:545, 6:549; RWA cp 322.

Horsemint, European (Mentha longifolia) BBF 3:150; NHE 98; OWF 143; PMF 351.

Horsemint, Nettle-leaved (Agastache urticifolia) AFP 3:625; RUS 4:563, 5:467, 6:559; VPN 4:252.

Horse-nettle (Solanum carolinense) AFP 3:679; BBF 3:165; FNC 166; PMF 325; PRP 153; RUS 1:341, 2:439, 3:319, 4:501, 5:431, 6:517.

Horseradish (Armoracia rusticana) AFP 2:279; BBF 2:163; DEW 1:144; OFP 135; PFF 188; PMF 83.

Horsetail, Field or Common (Equisetum arvense) BBF 1:39; FFK 43; LWF 2 (cp 1); NFP 120; NHE 109; ONP 191; PFF 107; PRP 168; VPN 1:42.

Horsetail, Giant (Equisetum telmatiae) AFP 1:39; NFP 119; NHE 43; ONP 191; VPN 1:46.

Horsetail, Marsh (Equisetum palustre) AFP 1:40; BBF 1:40; DEW 3:260 (cps 126, 127); NFP 121; NHE 109; ONP 95; VPN 1:44.

Horsetail, Rough (Equisetum hyemale) AFP 1:42; BBF 1:41; FFK 43; NFP 119; NHE 43; PFF 107; VPN 1:44.

Horsetail, Water (Equisetum fluviatile) BBF 1:41; GPL 42; NFP 121; NHE 109; ONP 95; VPN 1:44.

Horsetail, Wood (Equisetum sylvaticum) BBF 1:40; DEW 3:260, 261 (cps 124, 125, 128); NFP 121; NHE 43.

Horse-weed (Erigeron canadensis or Conyza canadensis) AFP 4:385; CWF 543; PFF 316; PMF 89, 377; RUS 1:483, 2:597, 3:473.

Hottentot-fig (Mesembryanthemum edule) ANE 5:891; RUS 4:147, 5:165.

Hound's-tongue (Cynoglossum officinale) AFP 3:539; BBF 3:76; CWF 434; NHE 229; OWF 105; PMF 293; RUS 2:423, 5:425, 6:499; VPN 4:201.

Hound's-tongue, Western (Cynoglossum grande) AFP 3:539; CWF 446; HFP 294, cp 14; LWF 150 (cp 240); OOW cp 247; RUS 4:487, 5:425; VPN 4:201.

Housefly—See **Fly, House**.

Houseleek (Sempervivum tectorum) EWF cp 16b; NHE 270; PFW 96; TGF 92. (S. arachnoideum) DEW 1:280 (cp 164); DFP 26 (cp 205); NHE 270; OGF 91.

Huckleberry, Blue or Mountain (Vaccinium membranaceum) APN 3:328; CWF 410; VPN 4:33.

Huckleberry, Box (Gaylussacia brachycera) BBF 2:696; TSK 76. (G. dumosa) HWF cp 157b.

Huckleberry, Evergreen (Vaccinium ovatum) AFP 3:326; CWF 410; HFP 254; VPN 4:36.

Huckleberry, False (Menziesia ferruginea) AFP 3:301; CWF 387; VPN 4:19. (M. glabella) RWA cp 261.

Huckleberry, Red (Vaccinium parvifolium) AFP 3:329; CWF 403; VPN 4:36.

Hummingbird—See also **Emerald, Goldentail, Mango, Sabre-wing, Violet-ear, Wood-nymph**.

Hummingbird, Allen's (Selasphorus sasin) ANE 5:893; CDB 132 (cp 476); NGB 2:35; NGS 66; PWB 166 (cp 39); RBB 175.

Hummingbird, Anna's (Calypte anna) AAB 262; ALE 8:453; ANE 5:897; CDB 121 (cp 467); NGB 2:33; NGS 64; PWB 166 (cp 39); RBA 155; RBB 173.

Hummingbird, Azure-crowned (Amazilia cyanocephala) DBM cp 17; PMB cp 18.

Hummingbird, Bee (Calypte helenae) ABW 171; BWI 80 (cp 3); GFB 118.

Hummingbird, Berylline (Amazilia beryllina) AMB 63 (cp 4); DBM cp 17; PMB cp 18.

Hummingbird, Black-chinned (Archilochus alexandri) BBC 2:cp 70; GBC 105 (cp 42); GPB 204; NGB 2:33; NGS 63; PWB 166 (cp 39); RBB 175.

Hummingbird, Blue-tailed (Amazilia cyanura) DBM cp 17; PMB cp 18.

Hummingbird, Broad-billed (Cynanthus latirostris) CDB 122 (cp 471); NGB 2:37; NGS 71; PMB cps 19, 20; PWB 166 (cp 39); RBB 177.

Hummingbird, Broad-tailed (Selasporus platycercus) AAB 263; ALE 8:453; ANE 5:893; BBC 2:cp 70; CFG cp 14; GPB 205; NGB 2:35; NGS 65; PWB 166 (cp 39); RBB 173; WEA 202.

Hummingbird, Bumblebee or Heloise (Atthis heloisa) DBM cp 15; PMB cp 19.

Hummingbird, Cinnamon (Amazilia rutila) AMB 63 (cp 4); DBM cp 17; PMB cp 20.

Hummingbird, Costa's (Calypte costae) CDB 121 (cp 468); NGB 2:33; NGS 65; PWB 166 (cp 39); RBA 153; RBB 175.

Hummingbird, Dusky (Cynanthus sordidus) DBM cp 16; PMB cp 20.

Hummingbird, Lucifer (Calothorax lucifer) FWA 226; NGB 2:37; NGS 63; PMB cps 19, 20; PWB 166 (cp 39); RBB 177.

Hummingbird, Rieffer's or Rufous-tailed (Amazilia tzacatl) DBM cp 17; NGB 2:39; NGS 69; PMB cp 18.

I

India Rubber Plant (Ficus elastica) BTN 147; DFP 67 (cps 529, 530); MWF 133 (cp 395); PFF 149.

Indian Apple (Datura wrightii) RUS 2:443, 3:323, 4:507, 5:433, 6:521.

Indian Bean Tree—See **Catalpa, Southern.**

Indian Blanket—See **Gaillardia.**

Indian Consumption Plant (Lomatium nudicaule) CWF 355; RUS 4:283, 5:255, 6:305.

Indian Cup—See **Cup-plant.**

Indian Hemp—See **Dogbane, Common.**

Indian Paintbrush, Common Red (Castilleja miniata) AFP 3:839; CWF 459, 463; OOW cps 173, 174; RUS 4:607, 5:491, 6:577; RWA cp 344; RWF 111; VPN 4:314.

Indian Paintbrush, Golden (Castilleja levisecta) CWF 462; RUS 5:485. (C. sessiliflora) BBF 3:216; RUS 1:397, 3:395, 4:603, 6:575; VPN 4:325.

Indian Paintbrush or Painted Cup (Castilleja coccinea) BBF 3:214; DEW 2:167 (cp 90); FNC 172; HYF cp 175; LWF 200 (cp 314); PMF 231; RUS 1:397, 2:503, 6:579.

Indian Physic (Gillenia stipulata or G. trifoliata) FFK 115; FNC 92; PFF 196; PMF 29.

Indian Pipe (Monotropa uniflora) AFP 3:294; BBF 2:674; CWF 379; FFK 279; FNC 130; HFP 246, cp 29; HWF 199, cp 152b; HYF cp 136; LWF 264 (cp 419); OOW cp 20; PFF 271; PMF 21, 233; RUS 1:253, 2:315, 5:315, 6:367; RWA cp 278; VPN 4:19.

Indian Plum—See **Oso-berry.**

Indian Poke—See **Hellebore, False.**

Indian Shot—See **Canna.**

Indian Tobacco (Lobelia inflata) BBF 3:303; FFK 195; HWF cp 222a; PMF 343; RUS 1:421, 2:525.

Indian Turnip—See **Jack-in-the-pulpit.**

Indian Warrior (Pedicularis densiflora) AFP 3:801; LWF 269 (cp 429); OOW cp 147; RUS 4:599, 5:483.

Indiangrass (Sorghastrum nutans) BBF 1:120; HMG 776; PRP 62.

Indian-mallow—See **Velvet-leaf.**

Indian-plaintain, Pale (Cacalia atriplicifolia) BBF 3:537; FFK 234; PMF 89; RUS 1:503, 2:627, 6:713. (C. tuberosa) BBF 3:537; PMF 89; RUS 2:627, 3:499, 6:713.

Indigo (Indigofera sp.) HSC 70; MWF 163 (cp 511); RUS 2:361, 3:271, 6:401.

Indigo, Blue False (Baptisia australis) DFP 126 (cp 1001); EGP 100; FFK 180; FNC 99; HYF cp 98; OGF 77; PMF 353; PRP 78; RUS 1:265, 2:339; TGF 140.

Indigo, False (Amorpha fruiticosa) BBF 2:365; FNC 100; HYF cp 91; PFF 215; RUS 1:277, 2:361; TGS 150; TSK 73, 244.

Indigo, Nodding False (Baptisia leucophaea) FFK 180; RUS 1:261, 2:337, 3:267, 6:397.

Indigo, White False (Baptisia leucantha) BBF 2:346; RUS 1:261, 2:339, 3:263.

Indigo, Wild False (Baptisia tinctoria) BBF 2:345; HWF cp 107a; HYF cp 98; PFF 215; PMF 151; RUS 1:261, 2:337.

Inky-cap—See **Mushroom, Inky-cap.**

Innocence—See **Chinese Houses.**

Inside-out Flower (Vancouveria hexandra) AFP 2:222; OOW cp 17; RUS 5:207; VPN 2:418. (V. chrysantha) AFP 2:222; RUS 5:207.

Ipecac, American—See **Indian Physic.**

Ipecac, Carolina (Euphorbia ipecacuanhae) FNC 108; RUS 2:149.

Iris—See also **Flag.**

Iris (Iris hartwegi) AFP 1:463; RUS 4:59, 5:67. (I. hexagona) HYF cp 31; RUS 2:73, 3:53. (I. reticulata) DFP 98 (cps 780-783); OGF 11; PFW 142.

Iris, Bearded (Cultivated) (Iris germanica) DFP 151 (cps 1206-1208), 152 (cps 1209-1216), 153 (cps 1217-1221); EGP 60, 61, 62, 126; FGF 146; LFW 76 (cps 171, 174, 175), 77 (cps 177, 178); MGB 246, 247, 249; OGF 47; PFF 385; PFW 143; TGF 28.

Iris, Clackamas (Iris tenuis) AFP 1:463; HFP cp 20d; RUS 5:65; VPN 1:823.

Iris, Copper or Red (Iris fulva) EWF cp 166c; HYF cp 31; LWF 171 (cp 269); PMF 231; RUS 2:71.

Iris, Crested (Iris cristata) AGF 145; BBF 1:540; FFK 60; FGF 144; FNC 39; LFW 202 (cp 457); MGB 248; PMF 315; RUS 1:49, 2:71, 6:73; RWA cp 66.

Iris, Dutch Bulbous (Iris xiphium) AGF 144, 145; DFP 98 (cps 784-790); FGF 147; MGB 253.

Iris, Dwarf (Iris verna) DFP 12 (cp 95); FFK 60; FNC 38; PMF 315; RUS 1:49, 2:73; RWA cp 65.

Iris, Golden (Iris innominata) DFP 149 (cp 1190); LWF 119 (cp 189); RUS 5:69.

Iris, Ground (Iris macrosiphon) OOW cp 12, 76; RUS 5:67.

Iris, Japanese (Iris kaempferi) DFP 149 (cps 1192, 1193); FGF 145; LFW 78 (cps 181-183), 202 (cp 458); MGB 250; MWF 166 (cp 517); PFW 145; TGF 28. (I. japonica) AGF 144, 195; DFP 149 (cp 1191); EGP 126; MGB 251.

J

189; ABW 128; CDB 91 (cp 316); CFG cp 10; GBC 188 (cp 35); NGB 1:305; NGW 375; PBA 1:cp 4; PEB 7 (pl 2); PWB 22 (pl 3); RBB 131; SAA 82, 84.

Jaeger, Parasitic (Stercorarius parasiticus) AAB 188; ABW 128; ALE 8:229; BBC 1:cp 57; BBE 139; CFG cp 10; GBC 188 (cp 35); NGB 1:305; NGW 374; PBA 1:cp 4; PEB 7 (pl 2); PWB 22 (pl 3); RBB 131.

Jaeger, Pomarine (Stercorarius pomarinus) ABW 129; BBC 1:cp 57; CFG cp 10; GBC 188 (cp 35); NGB 1:305; NGW 374; PBA 1:cp 4; PEB 7 (pl 2); PWB 22 (pl 3); RBB 131.

Jaguar (Felis onca or Panthera onca) ALE 12:324, 339; BGM 69 (cp 8); FWA 225; GGM 58, 62; IWE 9:1183-1186; JAW 133; LEA 573; LVS 89; NGA 214, 215; PFF 696; PMG cp 14; WEA 209; WMW 2:1278.

Jaguarundi—See **Cat, Jaguarundi.**

Jasmine, Blue (Clematis crispa) RWA cp 128; RUS 2:171, 3:107.

Jasmine, Common (Jasminum officinale) OGF 165; PFW 199; TGS 39. (J. nudiflorum) AGF 149; DFP 208 (cp 1664); MWF 170 (cp 534); PFW 199; TGS 327.

Jasmine, Confederate (Trachelospermum jasmanoides) FHP 148; HSC 119; MEP 107; MWF 286 (cp 944); PFW 29; TGS 70.

Jasmine, Crape (Ervatamia coronaria) FHP 119; MWF 125 (cp 363).

Jasmine, Madagascar—See **Stephanotis.**

Jasmine, Night-blooming (Cestrum nocturnum) FHP 111; MEP 126; MWF 79 (cp 200).

Jasmine, Primrose (Jasminum mesnyi) EGE 132; MEP 105; MWF 170 (cp 533). (J. polyanthum) DFP 248 (cp 1978); EWF cp 95d; FHP 128; MWF 170 (cp 535).

Javelina—See **Peccary.**

Jawfish (Opisthognathus aurifrons) LFI 107; WFW cp 415. (O. macrognathus) NGF 214.

Jay, Azure-hooded (Cyanolyca cucullata) DBM cp 32; PMB cp 31.

Jay, Blue (Cyanocitta cristata) AAB 307; ABW 225; ANE 6:996; CFG cp 27; GBC 232 (cp 47); GBI 76; NGB 2:117; NGS 37, 40-41, 139; PBA 2:cp 70; PEB 199 (cp 54); PFF 629; PWB 199 (cp 44); RBA 183; RBB 209; TBC 304 (cp 48b); WAB 77.

Jay, Canada or Gray (Perisoreus canadensis) AAB 306; CFG cp 28; GBC 232 (cp 47); NGB 2:126; NGS 140; PBA 2:cp 71; PEB 199 (cp 54); PFF 629; PWB 199 (cp 44); RBB 211; TBC 304 (cp 48a).

Jay, Dwarf (Cyanolyca nana) DBM cp 32; PMB cp 31.

Jay, Green (Cyanocorax yncas) AAB 309; CDB 223 (cp 1003); LBW 230 (cp 137); NGB 2:122; NGS 143; PMB cp 30; PWB 199 (cp 44); RBB 211.

Jay, Magpie (Calocitta formosa) AMB 77 (cp 6); DBM cp 32; PMB cp 30.

Jay, Mexican or Arizona (Aphelocoma ultramarina) AAB 309; CDB 222 (cp 994); NGB 2:122; NGS 141; PMB cp 31; PWB 199 (cp 44); RBB 209.

Jay, Pinon (Pinyon) (Gymnorhinus cyanocephalus) AAB 315; ALE 9:497; BBC 2:cp 83; CFG cp 21; LBW 232 (cp 141); NGB 2:124; NGS 150; PWB 199 (cp 44); RBB 209; WAB 46.

Jay, Purplish-backed (Beechey's) (Cissilopha beechei) AMB 77 (cp 6); DBM cp 32; PMB cp 31.

Jay, San Blas (Cissilopha san-blasiana) AMB 77 (cp 6); DBM cp 32; PMB cp 31.

Jay, Scrub or Florida (Aphelocoma coerulescens) ANE 6:998; CDB 221 (cp 993); DBM cp 32; LBW 231 (cp 139); NGB 2:119; NGS 143; PEB 227 (cp 60); PFF 630; PMB cp 31; PWB 199 (cp 44); RBB 209; WAB 45.

Jay, Steller's (Cyanocitta stelleri) AAB 308; ANE 6:999; CDB 223 (cp 1002); GBC 232 (cp 47); GBI 18; GPB 339; NGB 2:117; NGS 8, 46, 141; PFF 630; PMB cp 31; PWB 199 (cp 44); RBA 185; RBB 209; WAB 41.

Jay, Tufted (Cyanocorax dickeyi) AMB 77 (cp 6); DBM cp 32; PMB cp 30.

Jay, Unicolored (Aphelocoma unicolor) ALE 9:497; DBM cp 32; PMB cp 31.

Jay, Woodhouse's (Aphelocoma coerulescens woodhousei) BBC 2:cp 81; NGB 2:119.

Jellyfish (Cassiopeia sp.) ALE 1:198; IWE 9:1193; LEA 47; MOL 53.

Jellyfish, Freshwater (Craspedacusta sowerbyi) GPL 79; OIB 7.

Jellyfish, Luminous (Pelagia sp.) IWE 9:1193; JSS 80 (cp 2); MOL 52; NHE 174; OIB 13.

Jellyfish, Moon (Aurelia aurita) ALE 1:183; CFG cp 47; GAS 44; GGS 45; IWE 9:1195; JSS 82; LEA 46; NHE 174; OIB 13; PFF 397; RCT 338; SOS 91.

Jellyfish, Pink or Sun or Sea Blubber (Cyanea capillata) CFG cp 47; GAS 42; GGS 45; IWE 9:1193; NHE 174; OIB 13.

Jellyfish, Red-eyed (Polyorchis penicillatus) GAS 36; JSS 67; RCT 338.

Jellyfish, Stalked (Haliclystus sp.) GAS 46; KSL 247;

K

Kalanchoe (Kalanchoe blossfeldiana) FHP 129; MWF 172 (cp 540); PFW 95.

Kale, Curly (Collards) (Brassica oleracea) OFP 157; PFF 186; WYG 123.

Katydid, Common True (Pterophylla camellifolia) ANE 5:806, 945; BIA 81; GGI 18; SCI 76.

Katydid, Fork-tailed Bush (Scudderia sp.) BIA cp 2; GGI 18; IWE 9:1217; PFF 444; SCI 73; SIG pl 9a.

Kelp, Bladder or Ribbon (Nereocystis leutkeana) GGS 29; GUS 59; KSL 154; PFF 57.

Kelp, Fan (Laminaria digitata) GGS 28; NHE 140; PFF 56.

Kelp, Perennial (Macrocystis sp.) GGS 29; GUS 63; PFF 57.

Kelp, Pompon (Pterygophora californica) GUS 65; KSL 151.

Kelp, Sea Palm (Postelsia palmaeformis) GGS 29; GUS 61; LSE 99; SOS 13.

Kelp, Seersucker (Costaria costata) GUS 53; KSL 110.

Kelp, Wing (Alaria sp.) DEW 3:57 (cp 26); GUS 67; KSL 152.

Kestrel, American—See **Hawk, Sparrow.**

Killdeer (Charadrius vociferus) AAB 185; ABW 120; ALE 8:169; ANE 6:1015; BBC 1:cp 46; BBE 112; CDB 81 (cp 262); CFG cp 7; GBC 137 (cp 24); GPL 150; IWE 9:1223, 1224; NGB 1:267; NGS 318; PBA 1:cp 39; PWB 102 (cp 25), 107 (pl 28); RBB 113; TBC 174 (cp 21b).

Killifish, Banded (Fundulus diaphanus) CFG 556; GGF 66; GPL 126; PFF 512. (F. majalis) CFG 481. (F. parvipinnis) NGF 287.

King Devil (Hieracium pratense) FNC 187; PMF 175; RUS 1:513, 2:641. (H. florentium) HWF cp 223.

King of the Alps (Eritrichium nanum) DFP 9 (cp 66); LWF 151 (cp 242); NHE 281.

King Protea (Protea cynaroides) MEP 33; MWF 242 (cp 795); PFW 244; RWF 57.

Kingbird, Cassin's (Tyrannus vociferans) AAB 285; BBC 2:cp 77; NGB 2:90; NGS 104; PMB cp 27; PWB 182 (cp 41); RBB 193.

Kingbird, Eastern (Tyrannus tyrannus) AAB 283; ABW 208; CDB 145 (cp 585); GBC 221 (cp 44); NGB 2:90; NGS 103; PBA 2:cp 67; PEB 155 (cp 42); PFF 624; PWB 182 (cp 41); RBB 193; TBC 288 (cp 42a).

Kingbird, Gray (Tyrannus dominicensis) AAB 284; HBT 208 (cp 11); NGS 105; PEB 227 (cp 60); RBB 193.

Kingbird, Thick-billed (Tyrannus crassirostris) PMB cp 27; PWB 182 (cp 41); RBB 193.

Kingbird, Tropical or Olive-backed (Tyrannus melancholicus) CDB 144 (cp 584); DBM cp 28; HBT 208 (cp 11); NGS 104; PMB cp 27; PWB 182 (cp 41); RBB 193. (T. melancholicus couchi) NGB 2:90; NGS 104.

Kingbird, Western or Arkansas (Tyrannus verticalis) BBC 2:cp 77; CDB 145 (cp 586); DBM cp 28; GBC 221 (cp 44); GPL 151; NGB 2:90; NGS 104; PEB 155 (cp 42); PFF 624; PMB cp 27; PWB 182 (cp 41); RBB 193; TBC 288 (cp 42b).

Kingfish (Menticirrhus saxatilis) CFG cp 41; NGF 124. (M. americanus) GGF 122.

Kingfisher, Belted (Megaceryle alcyon) AAB 268; ABW 176; ANE 6:1018; BBC 2:cp 71; CFG cp 21; GBC 192 (cp 37); GBI 61; GPL 150; NGB 2:87; NGS 72-75; PBA 2:cp 58; PEB 199 (cp 54); PFF 619; PWB 199 (cp 44); RBB 179; TBC 274 (cp 37a).

Kingfisher, Green or Texas (Chloroceryle americana) AAB 269; HBT 112 (cp 3); NGB 2:87; NGS 76; PMB cp 22; PWB 199 (cp 44); RBB 179.

Kingfisher, Pygmy (Chloroceryle aenea) DBM cp 3; HBT 112 (cp 3); PMB cp 22.

Kingfisher, Ringed (Ceryle torquata or Megaceryle torquata) BWI 49 (cp 2); DBM cp 3; PMB cp 22; RBB 179.

Kinglet, Golden-crowned (Regulus satrapa) AAB 389; ANE 6:1020; BBC 2:cp 93; CDB 175 (cp 748); CFG cp 14; GBC 256 (cp 53); GBI 91; NGB 2:152; NGS 226; PBA 3:cp 104; PEB 163 (cp 44); PWB 246 (cp 49); RBB 237.

Kinglet, Ruby-crowned (Regulus calendula) AAB 363; ALE 9:259; CDB 175 (cp 746); CFG cp 14; GBC 256 (cp 53); GBI 90; NGB 2:152; NGS 226; PBA 3:cp 104; PEB 163 (cp 44); PWB 246 (cp 49); RBB 237.

Kingsnake, California Mountain (Lampropeltis zonata) ALE 6:444; SRA cp 31; WWS 1:408, 412.

Kingsnake, Common (Lampropeltis getula var.) ALE 6:406; BAR cp 52; BRW 114, 115; CGR 301; CRA 159 (pl 20); FWA 160; GRA 98, 99; IWE 9:1237;

LEA opp. 305; LRE 63; PFF 543; SIR 190, 206 (cps 111, 112), 207 (cp 113); SRA cp 31; WWS 1:377, 381, 387, 395.

Kingsnake, Scarlet—See **Snake, Milk.**

Kinnikinnick—See **Bearberry.**

Kiskadee—See **Flycatcher, Derby or Kiskadee.**

Kite, Everglades or Snail (Rostrhamus sociabilis) AAB 95; ABW 76; ALE 7:346; ANE 6:1022; IWE 6:727; LVS 245; NGB 1:151; NGW 224; PEB 58 (pl 17); PMB cp 5; RBB 67; WAB 69; WID 202.

Kite, Hook-billed (Chondrohierax uncinatus) DBM cp 5; PMB cp 2.

Kite, Mississippi (Ictinia mississippiensis) AAB 95; ANE 6:1025; BBC 1:cp 25; CFG cp 27; NGB 1:149; NGW 224; PEB 66 (pl 19); PMB cp 2; PWB 74 (pl 17); RBB 67.

Kite, Plumbeous (Ictinia plumbea) ALE 7:346; DBM cp 5; PMB cp 2.

Kite, Swallow-tailed (Elanoides forficatus) AAB 94; ABW 76; ALE 7:346; ANE 6:1027; BBC 1:cp 25; GFB 46; GPL 150; NGB 1:149; NGW 222; PBA 2:61; PEB 66 (pl 19); RBB 67; WAB 69.

Kite, White-tailed (Elanus leucurus) AAB 93; ANE 6:1028; GFB 46; NGB 1:149; NGW 223; PBA 2:62; PEB 66 (pl 19); PWB 74 (pl 17); RBB 67.

Kittiwake, Black-legged (Rissa tridactyla) AAB 200; ALE 7:61, 8:207, 229; BBC 1:cp 58; CDB 93 (cp 333); GPB 162; LBW 131 (cp 67); NGB 1:307; NGW 389; PBA 1:cp 6; PEB 122 (pl 33), 123 (pl 34); PWB 138 (pl 33), 139 (pl 34); RBB 137; SAA 76, 77, 80-81; WEA 180.

Kittiwake, Red-legged (Rissa brevirostris) ALE 8:229; PWB 138 (pl 33); RBB 137.

Knapweed, American (Centaurea americana) HYF cp 226; PMF 307; RUS 2:637, 3:489, 4:725.

Knapweed, Brown (Centaurea jacea) AFP 4:545; LWF 216 (cp 342); NHE 240; PMF 307; RUS 1:507, 5:603; VPN 5:120.

Knapweed, Spotted (Centaurea maculosa) AFP 4:543; CWF 531; FFK 240; HYF cp 226; NHE 240; PMF 93, 307; RUS 1:507, 2:633, 4:725, 5:603; VPN 5:120.

Knot (Calidris canutus) ABW 121; ALE 11:151; BBC 1:cp 47; BBE 125; CDB 85 (cp 278); CFG cp 8; GBC 140 (cp 25), 168 (pl 31); NGB 1:276; NGW 337; PBA 1:cps 33, 34; PEB 98 (pl 27), 118 (cp 31), 119 (cp 32); PWB 114 (pl 29), 118 (cp 31), 119 (cp 32); RBB 123; SAA 91.

Knotgrass—See **Knotweed, Prostrate.**

Knotweed, Beach (Polygonum paronychia) AFP 2:57; CWF 115; RUS 5:101.

Knotweed, Mountain Meadow (Polygonum bistortoides) AFP 2:64; CWF 122; RUS 4:99, 5:97, 6:91.

Knotweed, Prostrate (Polygonum aviculare) AFP 2:57; BBF 1:661; NHE 224; OWF 127; PFF 153; PMF 387; RUS 4:99, 5:101.

Knotweed, Virginia (Polygonum virginianum) BBF 1:665; PMF 61; RUS 1:101, 2:143.

Kohlrabi (Brassica caulorapa) OFP 159; PFF 187; WYG 126.

Koloa—See **Duck, Hawaiian.**

Kudzu Vine (Pueraria lobata or P. thunbergiana) EGA 148; PFF 219; PRP 99; RUS 2:365.

Kumquat (Fortunella margarita) FHP 121; MWF 135 (cp 400); OFP 89; PFF 230.

L

Labrador Tea (Ledum groenlandicum) AFP 3:300; BBF 2:677; CWF 399; HFP 264; HWF cp 155a; HYF cp 134; PFF 272; PMF 3; RWA cp 251; TGS 406; VPN 4:20. (L. glandulosum) OOW cp 5.

Laburnum—See **Golden Chain Tree.**

Laceflower, Blue (Didiscus syn. trachymene caeruleus) AGF 48; DFP 36 (cp 288); EGA 158; TGF 125.

Lacepod (Thysanocarpus curvipes) CWF cp 194; OOW cp 60; RUS 4:239, 5:183, 6:251.

Lacewing, Brown (Boriomyia fidelis) GGI 53; SIG cp 54. (Hemerobius sp.) ALE 2:301; BIA 145; SCI 185.

Lacewing, Golden-eye or Green (Chrysopa sp.) ALE 2:292; ANE 6:1033; BIA 145; GGI 53; KIA 90, 91; PEI 293; PFF 447; SCI 185; SIG cp 55.

Ladder Shell—See **Wentletrap.**

Ladies'-tresses, Creeping—See **Rattlesnake-plantain, Creeping.**

Ladies'-tresses, Hooded (Spiranthes romanzoffiana) CWF 103; HFP 74, cp 20a; PMF 19; RUS 1:81, 4:69, 5:75, 6:81; VPN 1:856.

Ladies'-tresses, Nodding (Spiranthes cernua) BBF 1:565; FFK 65; FNC 48; HYF cp 38; LWF 14 (cp 19); PMF 19; RUS 1:81, 2:111, 3:63, 4:65, 6:81; RWA cp 85.

Ladies'-tresses, Slender (Spiranthes gracilis) BBF 1:566; FNC 48; PMF 19; RUS 1:83, 2:11, 3:63, 6:81; RWA cp 85.

Ladies'-tresses, Spring or Early (Spiranthes vernalis) BBF 1:565; FFK 65; PMF 19; RUS 2:113, 3:63, 4:69.

Ladies'-tresses, Wide-leaved (Spiranthes lucida) HWF cp 42a; PMF 19; RUS 6:81.

Ladybug—See **Beetle, Ladybird.**

Lady-fish—See **Bonefish.**

Lady's-fingers—See **Vetch, Kidney.**

Lady's-mantle (Alchemilla vulgaris) DEW 1:299; NHE 179; OWF 49; RUS 1:131. (A. major) OGF 35. (A. mollis) DFP 120 (cp 956).

Lady's-slipper, California (Cypripedium californicum) AFP 1:470; RUS 5:73.

Lady's-slipper, Clustered (Cypripedium fasciculatum) AFP 1:471; RUS 5:73; VPN 1:834.

Lady's-slipper, Mountain (Cypripedium montanum) AFP 1:471; CWF 87; HFP cp 1; OOW cp 21; RUS 5:73, 6:69; RWA cp 70; VPN 1:836.

Lady's-slipper, Pink (Cypripedium acaule) ANE 6:1185; BBF 1:550; FFK 67; FNC 39; HWF cp 33, 69; HYF cp 34; LFO 18; LNA 107; LWF 238 (cp 375); PFF 391; PMF 15, 213; RUS 1:63, 2:93; RWA cps 71, 72.

Lady's-slipper, Ram's-head (Cypripedium arietinum) BBF 1:548; HWF cp 32b, 67; LWF 236 (cp 373); PMF 213; RUS 1:67; RWA cp 67.

Lady's-slipper, Showy (Cypripedium reginae) BBF 1:549; FNC 40; HWF cp 30; HYF cp 36; LWF 239 (cp 377); PFF 391; PFW 206; PMF 15, 213; RUS 1:67, 2:93; RWA cp 69.

Lady's-slipper, Small White (Cypripedium candidum) BBF 1:549; HWF cp 29; HYF cp 42; LWF 238 (cp 376); PMF 15; RUS 1:67.

Lady's-slipper, Sparrow's-egg (Cypripedium passerinum) BBF 1:549; CWF 78; PMF 15; VPN 1:836.

Lady's-slipper, Yellow (Cypripedium calceolus var. pubescens) CWF 90; DEW 2:279 (cp 157); DFP 6 (cp 44); FFK 66; FNC 40; HWF cp 31; HYF cp 37; LWF 237 (cp 374); NHE 40; OOW cp 75; PMF 105; RUS 1:67, 2:93, 3:59, 4:65, 6:69; RWA cp 68; RWF 30; TGF 44; VPN 1:834.

Lady's-thumb (Polygonum persicaria) DEW 1:162 (cp 76); HWF cp 47b; HYF cp 45; NHE 224; OWF 127; PFF 154; PMF 277; RUS 1:95, 2:141, 3:77, 4:99.

Lambkill—See **Laurel, Sheep.**

Lamb's Quarters—See **Goosefoot, White.**

Lamprey, Sea (Petromyzon marinus) ALE 4:41; CFG 460; CFW 6, 26; GGF 19; GPL 120; HFW 14-15; LFI 144-145; NGF 39; NHE 159; OBV 1; PFF 503; WEA 218.

Lampshell (Terebratulina sp.) CFG 627; GAS 126; GGS 59; IWE 10:1277; OIB 171. (Terebratalia transversa) GAS 124; JSS 155; KSL 177; RCT 278.

Lancelet—See **Amphioxus.**

Land Caltrops—See **Caltrops, Land.**

Lantana (Lantana camara) AGF 148; DEW 2:472 (cp 102); EGA 129; HYF cp 167; LFW 254 (cps 564-566); LWF 44 (cp 73); MWF 179 (cp 563); PFF 287; TGF 189.

Lanternfish (Myctophum affine) GGF 51. (Protomyctophum thompsoni) HPF 196.

Larch, American (Larix laricina) ANE 6:1035; BTN 37; GPL 71; MTB 128 (cp 9); PFF 120.

Larch, Golden (Pseudolarix amabilis) EGE 105; MTB 128 (cp 9); TGS 22.

Larch, Western (Larix occidentalis) AFP 1:60; BTN 37; RWA cp 5; SFT 68.

Lark, Horned or Shore (Eremophila alpestris) AAB 300; ABW 215; BBE 198; CDB 148 (cp 601); CFG cp 26; GBC 237 (cp 50); GBI 70; GFB 136; NGS 119; PEB 226 (cp 59); PFF 626; PWB 267 (cp 54); RBB 205; WAB 130.

Lark, Meadow—See **Meadowlark.**

Lark, Sky—See **Skylark.**

Larkspur, Blue (Delphinium carolinianum) BBF 2:95; RUS 2:163, 3:103.

Larkspur, Candle (Delphinium elatum) EGP 111; MWF 107 (cp 298); NHE 268.

Larkspur, Dwarf (Delphinium tricorne) BBF 2:96; FFK 225; FNC 61; HYF cp 64; PMF 319; RUS 1:109, 2:161, 6:139.

Larkspur Hybrids (Delphinium sp.) AGF 95, 96, 149, 181; DFP 36 (cp 282), 136 (cps 1084-1088), 137 (cps 1089-1091); EGA 109; EGP 111; FGF 95, 96, 152, 153; LFW 40 (cps 93-95), 42 (cps 96, 97), 43 (cps 98, 99); MWF 107 (cps 297-299); OGF 81, 85, 87; PFF 174; PFW 249; TGF 141.

Larkspur, Menzies' (Delphinium menziesii) AFP 2:185; CWF 166; LWF 125 (cp 198); VPN 2:358.

Larkspur, Parry's (Delphinium parryi) AFP 2:192; ANE 6:1039; RUS 4:129.

Larkspur, Plains (Delphinium virescens) BBF 2:95; PRP 124; RUS 1:109, 2:163, 3:103, 4:127, 6:139.

cp 32; SAA 32, 118. (D. hudsonius) CFG 296; IWE 10:1302; SAA 118; WMW 2:830.

Lemming, Norwegian (Lemmus lemmus) ALE 11:300; FWA 29; IWE 10:1301; NHE 296; SAA 118; WEA 221.

Lemon (Citrus limonia) MWF 86 (cp 222); OFP 85; PFF 228; WYG 201.

Lenten or Winter Rose (Helleborus orientalis) DFP 146 (cp 1166); MWF 152 (cp 487); PFW 250. (H. atrorubens) OGF 5; PFW 250.

Lentil (Lens culinaris) NHE 212; OFP 43; PFF 221.

Leopard, American—See **Jaguar.**

Leopard's-bane (Doronicum pardalianches) AGF 152; FGF 100; LFW 51 (cp 119); MWF 116 (cp 330); NHE 286. (D. caucasian) DFP 140 (cp 1113); EGP 115. (D. plantagineum) TGF 284.

Lettuce, Blue (Lactuca pulchella) BBF 3:320; HYF cp 195; PMF 363; RUS 5:627, 6:731. (L. biennis) CWF 554; RUS 5:627, 6:731.

Lettuce, Garden (Lactuca sativa) OFP 151; PFF 333; WYG 149.

Lettuce, Prickly or Wild (Lactuca scariola or L. serriola) AFP 4:594; BBF 3:318; NHE 240; PFF 334; PMF 173; RUS 2:639, 5:627, 6:733.

Lettuce, Smooth White (Prenanthes racemosa) PMF 293; RUS 1:509, 6:735.

Lettuce, Tall White (Prenanthes altissima) FFK 243; PMF 75; RUS 1:509, 2:637.

Lewisia, Alpine or Dwarf (Lewisia pygmaea) AFP 2:136; RUS 4:313, 5:289, 6:343, 345; VPN 2:237.

Lewisia, Kellogg's (Lewisia kelloggii) AFP 2:140; RUS 5:289, 6:343.

Lewisia, Nevada (Lewisia nevadensis) AFP 2:136; RUS 4:313, 5:289; VPN 2:237.

Lewisia, Opposite-leaved (Lewisia oppositifolia) AFP 2:136; RUS 5:289. (L. leana) AFP 2:136; RUS 5:287.

Lewisia Rediviva or Lewisia Tweedyi—See **Bitterroot.**

Lewisia, Three-leaved (Lewisia triphylla) AFP 2:132; RUS 5:289; VPN 2:237.

Lichen (Cladonia cristatella) NFP 99; PFF 74. (C. bellidiflora) FWA 42; ONP 69. (C. coccifera) DEW 3:193 (cp 78); NHE 44; ONP 85. (C. gracilis) NFP 95, 99; ONP 51.

Lichen, Beard (Usnea strigosa) NFP 98. (U. barbata) PFF 74.

Licorice (Glycyrrhiza lepidota) RUS 1:519, 3:255, 4:373, 5:361, 6:389. (G. glabra) OFP 135.

Licorice, White Wild (Galium circaezans) PMF 41; RUS 2:453, 3:353, 6:533.

Lignum Vitae (Guaiacum officinale) BTN 197; EWF cp 178e; MEP 64.

Lilac, California or Blueblossom (Ceanothus thyrsiflorus) AFP 3:67; BTN 225; DFP 188 (cp 1504); EGE 188; MEP 75; MWF 76 (cp 188); PFW 257; TGS 231.

Lilac, Common (Syringa vulgaris) AGF 152-154; DFP 241 (cps 1922-1926); FGF 158, 159; HSC 118; LWF 82 (cps 189, 190); MWF 278 (cp 920); OBT 196; PFF 281; PFW 200; TGS 374.

Lily, African (Agapanthus africanus) DFP 120 (cp 953); EGB 91; FHP 103; MEP 15; MWF 32 (cp 26); OGF 175; PFW 20; TGF 13.

Lily, Alp (Lloydia serotina) AFP 1:430; EWF cp 7d; NHE 290; RUS 4:25, 5:27, 6:29; VPN 1:799.

Lily, Amazon (Eucharis grandiflora) DFP 66 (cp 525); EGB 113; FHP 120; MEP 21; PFW 26.

Lily, Atamasco (Zephranthes atamasco) AGF 102; FNC 37; HYF cp 28; LWF 229 (cp 364); MGB 292; PMF 11, 255; RUS 2:65; RWA cp 60.

Lily, Avalanche (Erythronium montanum) AFP 1:428; CWF 27; HFP cp 14a; OOW cp 18; RUS 5:43, 45; RWA cp 30; VPN 1:789.

Lily, Aztec (Sprekelia formosissima) AGF 36; DFP 111 (cp 883); EGB 140; FHP 146; MEP 21; MWF 272 (cp 903); PFW 26.

Lily, Belladonna (Amaryllis belladonna) DEW 2:219 (cp 134); DFP 84 (cp 670); EGB 94; EWF cp 86c; MGB 167; MWF 39 (cp 54); OGF 175; PFW 24; SGB cp 2.

Lily, Bengal (Crinum powellii or C. bulbispermum) DFP 87 (cp 693); EGB 106; FHP 114; OGF 175; PFW 24; SGB cp 5.

Lily, Blood (Haemanthus sp.) DFP 68 (cp 542); EGB 119; EWF cp 86d; FHP 124; MEP 19; MWF 146 (cps 445, 446); PFW 25.

Lily, Calla—See **Calla Lily.**

Lily, Canada (Lilium canadense) ANE 6:1059; DFP 101 (cp 802); FFK 48; FGF 163; FNC 34; HWF cp 14; HYF cp 23; LWF 169 (cp 267); MGB 113; PFF 373; PMF 103, 207, 255; RUS 1:25, 2:24; RWA cp 32.

Lily, Candlestick (Lilium umbellatum) AGF 158; RUS 4:25; RWA cp 35. (L. dauricum) FGF 165.

Lily, Checker—See **Mission Bells.**

Lily, Climbing—See **Lily, Glory.**

Lobelia, Water (Lobelia dortmanna) BBF 3:300; CWF 510; GPL 65; NHE 100; PMF 343; RUS 1:415, 5:523.

Loblolly-bay—See **Bay, Loblolly.**

Lobster (Homarus americanus) ANE 3:523; CFG 650; FWA 306; GGS 71; PAK 105; PFF 430.

Lobster, Spiny (Panulirus interruptus or Palinurus interruptus) JSS 316; NGF 209; PAK 106; RCT 143; SOS 126. (Panulirus argus) GGS 71.

Locoweed—See also **Larkspur, Tall Rocky Mountain.**

Locoweed (Oxytropis splendens) BBF 2:390; CWF 306; RUS 4:411, 6:413; RWA cp 200; VPN 3:347. (O. besseyi) LWF 133 (cp 212); RUS 6:413; VPN 3:341.

Locoweed, Scarlet (Astragalus coccineus) AFP 2:581; EWF cp 153c; OOW cp 183; RUS 4:407.

Locust, Black (tree) (Robinia pseudo-acacia) AFP 2:561; ANE 6:1074; BBF 2:375; BKT cps 140, 141, 143, 144; BTN 193; EGT 142; FNC 101; MTB 324 (cp 29); MWF 255 (cp 839); NHE 212; OBT 185; PFF 216; TGS 135; TSK 58, 332, 333.

Locust, Bristly (tree) (Robinia hispida) BBF 2:375; DFP 230 (cp 1836); EWF cp 153a; FNC 101; HSC 103; TSK 58, 243.

Locust, Carolina (insect) (Dissosteira carolina) GGI 26; SCI 73.

Locust, Honey (tree) (Gleditsia triacantha) BBF 2:339; BKT cp 52; BTN 189; EGT 117; PFF 208; TGS 135; TSK 328, 329.

Locust, Migratory—See **Grasshopper, Short-horned.**

Locust, Seventeen-year (insect) (Magicicada septemdecim) ANE 3:445, 446, 448; BIA pl 4; GGI 36; IWE 4:443, LFO 141; LIN 74, 75; PAK 171; PFF 456; SCI 133; SIG cp 40; WEA 103.

Locust, Water (tree) (Gleditsia aquatica) BTN 189; TSK 330.

Loggerhead—See **Turtle, Loggerhead.**

Loments, Yellow—See **Hedysarum, Yellow.**

London Plane Tree—See **Plane Tree, London.**

London Pride (Saxifraga umbrosa primuloides) DFP 25 (cp 200); OGF 49; TGF 93.

Longspur, Chestnut-collared (Calcarius ornatus) AAB 492; BBC 2:cp 124; CFG cp 26; GBC 364 (cp 69); GFB 190; NGB 2:294; NGS 374; PWB 267 (cp 54); RBB 325; TBC 408 (cp 86); WAB 54.

Longspur, Lapland (Calcarius lapponicus lapponicus) AAB 502; ALE 9:342; ANE 6:1076; BBC 2:cp 124; CFG cp 26; GBC 364 (cp 69); NGB 2:296; NGS 373; PBA 3:22; PWB 267 (cp 54); RBB 325; TBC 408 (cp 86).

Longspur, McCown's (Rhynchophanes mccownii) BBC 2:cp 124; CFG cp 26; GBC 364 (cp 69); NGB 2:294; NGS 374; PEB 226 (cp 59); PWB 267 (cp 54); RBB 325.

Longspur, Smith's (Calcarius pictus) AAB 503; CFG cp 26; GBC 364 (cp 69); NGB 2:296; NGS 375; PWB 267 (cp 54); RBB 325.

Lookdown (Selene vomer) ALE 5:101; CFG 487; GGF 93; NGF 213.

Loon, Arctic or Black-throated (Gavia arctica) AAB 2; ABW 25; ALE 7:116; BBE 15; BBW cp 1; CDB 35 (cp 14); CFG 19; GBC 12 (cp 1); GFB 21; GPB 40; IWE 5:642; NGW 41; PBA 1:cp 2; PWB 6 (pl 1); RBB 19; SAA 90; WAB 36.

Loon, Common (Gavia immer) AAB 1; ABW 25; ALE 7:116, 11:151; ANE 6:1081; BBC 1:cp 1; BBE 14, 16; CDB 35 (cp 15); CFG 19; GBC 12 (cp 1); GBI 21; IWE 5:641; NGB 1:30; NGW 39, 40; PBA 1:cp 2; PEB 6 (pl 1); PFF 551; PWB 6 (pl 1); RBA 13; RBB 19; SAA 90; TBC 38 (cp 1a).

Loon, Pacific (Gavia arctica pacifica) NGB 1:28; PEB 6 (pl 1). (Columbus articus) LBW 34 (cp 3).

Loon, Red-throated (Gavia stellata) ABW 25; ALE 7:61, 117; BBC 1:cp 1; BBE 15; CDB 35 (cp 16); CFG cp 1; GBC 12 (cp 1); NGB 1:28; NGW 41; PBA 1:cp 2; PEB 6 (pl 1); PFF 552; PWB 6 (pl 1); RBB 19; SAA 90.

Loon, Yellow-billed (Gavia adamsi) AAB 2; BBC 1:cp 1; BBE 16; GBC 12 (cp 1); NHE 144; RBB 19.

Loosestrife—See also **Moneywort** and **Swamp Candles.**

Loosestrife, False (Ludwigia palustris) EWF cp 16g; GPL 67; NHE 93; PMF 311; RUS 2:313, 3:227, 4:335, 5:307.

Loosestrife, Fringed (Lysimachia or Steironema ciliatum) BBF 2:713; FFK 104; FNC 143; HWF cp 162; HYF cp 143; PFF 278; PMF 141; RUS 1:303, 2:384, 6:441.

Loosestrife, Garden (Lysimachia vulgaris) BBF 2:71; NHE 97; OWF 27; RUS 1:301.

Loosestrife, Hyssop-leaved (Lythrum hyssopifolia) AFP 3:166; BBF 2:580; NHE 93; PMF 289; RUS 5:295.

Loosestrife, Lance-leaved (Lysimachia or Steironema lanceolatum) BBF 2:714; FFK 104; PMF 141; RUS 1:303, 2:385, 6:441.

Loosestrife, Large Yellow (Lysimachia punctata) BBF 2:711; DFP 158 (cp 1257); OGF 113; RUS 1:303.

Loosestrife, Purple or Spiked (Lythrum salicaria or L. lanceolatum) AFP 3:166; AGF 162; BBF 2:581; DFP 158 (cp 1258); EGP 131; FFK 277; HWF cp 143b; HYF cp 114; LWF 33 (cp 55); MWF 192 (cp 613); NHE 93; OWF 123; PFW 178; PMF 225, 289; RUS 1:237, 5:295; TGF 124.

Loosestrife, Slender (Lythrum virgatum) DFP 158 (cp 1258); PMF 289.

Loosestrife, Swamp (Decodon verticillatus) GPL 67; HWF cp 143; HYF cp 113; PMF 289; RUS 1:237, 2:301; TSK 53, 214.

Loosestrife, Tufted (Lysimachia or Naumburgia thrysiflora) BBF 2:715; CWF 426; HWF cp 163; NHE 97; OWF 26; RUS 1:305, 6:441.

Loosestrife, Whorled (Lysimachia or Steironema quadrifolia) BBF 2:711; FFK 103; FNC 144; HWF cp 160b; HYF cp 144; LWF 193 (cp 303); PFF 278; PMF 141; RUS 1:303, 2:385.

Loosestrife, Wing-angled (Lythrum alatum) BBF 2:581; DEW 2:50 (cp 2); HYF cp 115; PMF 289; RUS 1:237, 6:347.

Lopseed (Phryma leptostachya) FFK 210; HWF cp 208; PFF 300; RUS 1:413, 2:533, 3:417, 6:613.

Loquat (Eriobotrya japonica) DEW 1:295; DFP 199 (cp 1591); EGE 122; MWF 124 (cp 359); OFP 105.

Lord, Irish—See **Irishlord.**

Lotus—See also **Trefoil.**

Lotus, American (Nelumbo lutea) BBF 2:77; EWF cp 151d; FFK 106; GPL 61; HWF cp 55; HYF cp 53; LFW 83 (cp 192); PFF 168; PMF 101; RUS 1:105, 2:159, 3:99, 6:131.

Lotus, Sacred (Nelumbo nucifera) DEW 1:101 (cp 49), 129; OFP 33; PFW 193; RUS 1:105, 2:161.

Louse, Book (Liposcelis divinatorius) ALE 2:157; GIP 35; IWE 2:268; SIG cp 19. (Trogium pulsatorium) ALE 1:157; OBI 19.

Louse, Chicken or Shaft (Menopon gallinae) OBI 19; PFF 450; SCI 97. (Cuclotogaster heterographus) GIP 52; SCI 97.

Louse, Crab (Phtherius pubis) ALE 2:157; BIA 109; GGI 32; GIP 43; IWE 10:1350; KIW 58; SCI 101.

Louse, Dog (Linognathus setosus) IWE 10:1350. (Trichodectes canis) ALE 2:157; PEI 91.

Louse, Fish (Lironeca ovalis) CFG 648. (Argulus foliaceus) ALE 1:443; IWE 6:770; OIB 141.

Louse, Head or Body (Pediculus humanus var.) ALE 2:157; BIA 109; GGI 32; GIP 43; IWE 10:1351; OBI 19; PEI 94; PFF 451; SCI 100.

Louse, Hog (Haematopinus adventicius) SIG cp 21. (H. suis) ALE 2:157; GIP 53; IWE 10:1350; PEI 95, 96 (cp 11b); PFF 451.

Louse, Pigeon (Columbicola columbae) ALE 2:157; OBI 19; SCI 97; SIG cp 20.

Louse, Sheep-biting (Bovicola ovis) GIP 53; SCI 98.

Louse, Water or Wood—See **Sowbug, Water.**

Lousewort, Bracted or Fern-leaved (Pedicularis bracteosa) AFP 3:801; CWF 483; LWF 155 (cp 247); RUS 6:583; RWA cp 340.

Lousewort, Common (Pedicularis canadensis) BBF 3:221; FFK 192; FNC 173; HWF cp 205; HYF cp 175; LWF 269 (cp 428); PFF 298; PMF 125, 269; RUS 1:395, 2:503, 3:393, 6:585.

Lousewort, Swamp (Pedicularis lanceolata) BBF 3:221; HWF cp 206a; PMF 125; RUS 1:395, 2:503. (P. racemosa) AFP 3:812; CWF cp 486; RUS 6:583.

Love-in-a-mist (Nigella damascena) AGF 160; DEW 1:118; DFP 44 (cp 352), 45 (cp 353); EGA 140; EWF cp 27b; MWF 214 (cp 691); NHE 199; OGF 131; TGF 61.

Love-lies-bleeding (Amaranthus caudatus) AGF 160; DFP 263 (cp 232); EGA 93; LFW 158 (cp 348); OGF 129; PFW 22; TFG 29.

Lucerne—See **Alfalfa.**

Lucina, Cross-hatched (Divaricella quadrisulcata) AAS pl 30m; ASN 221; CFG 594.

Lucina, Tiger (Codakia orbicularis) ASN 223; GGS 94.

Lugworm (Arenicola claperedii or A. cristata) FWA 292; GAS 90; GGS 57; IWE 10:1353.

Luina (Luina hypoleuca) AFP 4:459; RUS 5:611; VPN 5:259. (L. nordosima) AFP 4:459; RUS 5:611, 6:713; VPN 5:259. (L. stricta) AFP 4:459; RUS 5:611; VPN 5:259.

Lumpsucker, Atlantic (Cyclopterus lumpus) ALE 5:66; GGF 127; HFW 253; IWE 10:1355; MOL 106; NHE 157; OBV 233; WEA 81; WFW 170.

Lumpsucker, Pacific Spiny (Eumicrotremus orbis) HPF 577; WFW 188.

Lungwort, Alpine (Mertensia alpina) OOW cp 222; RUS 4:499, 6:513; VPN 4:226. (M. longiflora) AFP 3:547; RUS 6:513; VPN 4:228.

Lungwort, Oregon (Mertensia bella) AFP 3:547; RUS 5:427, 6:511; VPN 4:226.

Lungwort, Sea (Mertensia maritima) BBF 3:83; OWF 171; PMF 335.

Lungwort, Tall (Mertensia paniculata) AFP 3:547;
BBF 3:83; CWF 451; RUS 5:427, 6:511; RWA
cp 315; VPN 4:228.

Lungwort, Tree (Lobaria pulmonaria) NHE 44; ONP
167. (L. oregana) NFP 98.

Lupine (Lupinus densiflorus) AFP 2:488; CWF 302;
RUS 4:389, 5:339. (L. caudatus) AFP 2:501; RUS
6:401; VPN 3:309. (L. latifolius) OOW cp 236; RUS
4:391, 5:341, 343, 6:401; VPN 3:314. (L. pusillus)
AFP 2:492; BBF 2:349; RUS 6:407; VPN 3:326.

Lupine, Dwarf (Lupinus nanus) AFP 2:493; RUS
4:391, 6:403.

Lupine, False (Thermopsis macrophylla) AFP 2:488;
OOW cp 90; RUS 4:381, 5:333.

Lupine Hybrids (Lupinus sp.) AGF 161; DFP 42 (cp
334), 156 (cps 1246-1248); EGA 133; EGP 130;
FGF 174; LFW 208 (cps 467-469), 209 (cp 470);
MWF 191 (cps 609, 610); OGF 77; PFW 163; TGF
140.

Lupine, Large-leaved (Lupinus polyphyllus) AFP
2:516; CWF 302; HFP 188; RUS 5:348, 6:407; VPN
3:324.

Lupine, Pursh's (Lupinus sericeus) AFP 2:508; BBF
2:349; CWF 290; RUS 6:407; VPN 3:329.

Lupine, Silvery (Lupinus argentus) OOW cp 253; PRP
90; RUS 6:401; VPN 3:307.

Lupine, Tree (Lupinus arboreus) AFP 2:512; CWF
294; HSC 75; LWF 26 (cp 43); OGF 77; RUS 4:387,
5:335; VPN 3:303.

Lupine, Wild or Common (Lupinus perennis) BBF
2:348; HWF cp 106; HYF cp 94; PFF 210; PMF
317; RUS 1:261, 2:335, 6:405; RWA cp 193.

Lynx (Lynx canadensis) AWW 31; BGM 69 (cp 8);
IWE 10:1360; JAW 126; NGA 210; PFF 694; PMG
cp 15; SAA 137; WMW 2:1270.

Lyonsia, Glassy (Lyonsia hyalina) AAS pl 28u; ASN
263; CFG 595.

Lyonsia, Sanded (Lyonsia arenosa) ASN 263; CFG
607; MGS pl 27.

M

Macaw, Blue-and-yellow (Ara ararauna) ABW 149;
ALE 8:336; DBM cp 7; IWE 10:1369, 1370; WAB
79, 83.

Macaw, Military (Ara militaris) ABW 149; ALE 8:336;
AMB 71 (cp 5); DBM cp 7; PMB cp 13.

Macaw, Red-and-blue (Ara chloroptera) ALE 8:336,
359; DBM cp 7; IWE 10:1372.

Macaw, Scarlet (Ara macao) ABW 149; ALE 8:336;
DBM cp 7; IWE 10:1369; PMB cp 13.

Mackerel, Atlantic or Common (Scomber scombrus)
ALE 5:191; ANE 6:1085; CFG cp 41; CFW 135;
GGF 84; IWE 10:1374; NGF 113; NHE 155; OBV
25; PFF 517; WFW cp 451.

Mackerel, Chub (Scomber colias) CFG 492; GGF 84;
OBV 25.

Mackerel, Horse—See **Scad.**

Mackerel, Jack—See **Jack Mackerel.**

Mackerel, King (Scomberomorus cavalla) CFG 492;
GGF 85.

Mackerel, Pacific (Scomber japonicus) ALE 5:191;
GGF 85; HPF 374; NGF 112; WFW 323.

Mackerel, Painted—See **Cero.**

Mackerel, Spanish (Scomberomorus maculatus) CFG
492; CFW 135; GGF 84; MOL 95.

Macoma Shell (Apolymetis intastriata) AAS pl 32y;
GSS 150. (Psammotreta intastriata) ASN 245.
(Macoma sp.) ASN 245; GGS 103; MGS pl 21; PFF
423.

Madder, Field—See **Field-madder.**

Madder, Wild—See **Bedstraw, Hedge.**

Madia—See **Tarweed.**

Madtom (Noturus sp.) GGF 61; GPL 127; NGF 273;
WFW 266. (Schilbeodes sp.) CFG 543.

Maggot, Fly (Rhagoletis pomonella) GBB cp 25; GIP
130; PFF 493. (Hylemya sp.) GBB cp 26; GIP 11,
84; SCI 633. (Meromyza americana) GIP 116.

Magnolia—See also **Cucumber Tree** and **Lily Tree.**

Magnolia, Big-leaf (Magnolia macrophylla) BBF 2:81;
BTN 153; TGS 279; TSK 42, 115.

Magnolia, Fraser's (Magnolia fraseri) BBF 2:81; BTN
153; FNC 71; TSK 42, 116, 358.

Magnolia, Saucer (Magnolia soulangeana) AGF 163;
DFP 212 (cps 1691, 1692, 1693); EGT 125; LFW
210 (cp 471); MWF 193 (cp 618); OBT 145; OGF
25; PFW 180; TGS 278.

Magnolia, Southern (Magnolia grandiflora) AGF 164;
ANE 6:1086; BTN 151; DFP 211 (cp 1684); EGE
71, 135; FNC 71; GGT 49; MEP 39; MWF 139 (cp
616); PFW 179; RWA cps 133, 134; TGS 278.

Magnolia, Star (Magnolia stellata) AGF 163; DFP 212 (cp 1694); EWF cp 90b; HSC 79; MWF 193 (cp 619); OBT 145; PFW 181; TGS 278.

Magnolia, Umbrella (Magnolia tripetala) BBF 2:82; BTN 153; TSK 42, 115, 360.

Magpie, Black-billed (Pica pica) AAB 310; ABW 225; ALE 9:497, 501, 11:321; ANE 6:1087; BBC 2:cp 83; BBE 213; CDB 224 (cp 1007); CFG cp 21; GBC 232 (cp 47); GFB 141; IWE 10:1375; NGB 2:115; NGS 134, 144; PFF 630; PWB 199 (cp 44); RBB 211.

Magpie, Yellow-billed (Pica nuttallii) AAB 311; NGB 2:115; NGS 145; PWB 199 (cp 44); RBB 211.

Maidenhair Tree (Ginkgo biloba) ANE 4:776; BKT cps 2-4; BTN 65; DEW 1:26, 50; DFP 252 (cp 2014); EGT 39, 70, 117; MTB 48 (cp 1); OBT 105, 133; PFF 112; TGS 22.

Malacothrix, Sow-thistle (Malacothrix xonchoides) AFP 4:579; RUS 4:743, 6:729.

Mallard (Anas platyrhynchos) AAB 65; ALE 7:293, 306; ANE 3:570; BBC 1:cp 13, cp 18; CDB 50 (cp 97); CFG cp 2, 39, 41, 42; GBC 76 (cp 9); GGB 21, 35; GPB 79; GPL 144; KWF 400 (cp 6), 404 (cp 8), 454 (cp 33); PBA 1:cp 12; PEB 22 (pl 7), 26 (pl 9), 39 (cp 14); PFF 565; PWB 34 (pl 7); RBA 49; RBB 45; SAA 145; TBC 86 (cp 6a).

Mallow, Carolina (Modiola caroliniana) AFP 3:85; BBF 2:523; RUS 2:205, 3:131, 4:185, 5:159.

Mallow, Common (Malva sylvestris) AFP 3:111; EWF cp 18b; NHE 220; OWF 131; PMF 259; RUS 1:147, 3:123, 6:193. (M. neglecta) PFF 248.

Mallow, Desert (Sphaeralcea ambigua) AFP 3:89; RUS 4:183, 6:193.

Mallow, Dwarf—See **Cheeses.**

Mallow, Globe (Sphaeralcea coccinea) OOW cp 205; RUS 1:149, 3:129, 4:183, 6:197. (S. davidsonii) RWA cp 220.

Mallow, Five-spot (Malvastrum rotundifolium) HYF cp 110; OOW cp 198; RUS 4:185.

Mallow, Jew's (Kerria japonica) AGF 148; DFP 209 (cp 1667); HSC 71; LFW 64 (cp 152); MWF 173 (cp 545); PFW 262; TGS 230.

Mallow, Marsh (Althaea officinalis) BBF 2:514; HWF cp 127; NHE 94; PFF 249; PMF 259.

Mallow, Musk (Malva moschata) AFP 3:108; BBF 2:515; HWF cp 128; HYF cp 110; LWF 189 (cp 296); MWF 195 (cp 627); NHE 220; OWF 131; PFF 248; PMF 219, 259; RUS 1:149, 2:203, 5:151.

Mallow, Poppy (Callirhoe involucrata) BBF 2:518; EGP 102; HYF cp 108; LWF 189 (cp 297); OOW cp 207; RUS 1:147, 3:121, 4:171, 6:185.

Mallow, Prickly (Sida spinosa) BBF 2:520; PFF 251; PMF 165; RUS 1:149, 2:205, 3:123, 6:187.

Mallow, Rose (Hibiscus palustris) LFW 63 (cp 149); LWF 31 (cp 52); PMF 5, 219; RUS 1:145, 2:197; TGF 124. (H. coccineus) LFW 64 (cp 153); MWF 154 (cp 474); RUS 2:199; TGF 124.

Mallow, Swamp Rose (Hibiscus moscheutos) BBF 2:524; EGP 123; FNC 116; HWF cp 129; HYF cp 109; PMF 259; RUS 1:147, 2:201; RWA cp 221; TGF 126 (cp 124).

Mallow Tree (Lavatera trimestris) DEW 1:258; EGA 131; EWF cp 35f; FGF 155; PFW 185. (L. arborea) DFP 209 (cp 1672). (L. assurgentiflora) LWF 30 (cp 51).

Maltese Cross (Lychnis chalcedonica) DFP 157 (cp 1249); EGP 131; LFW 92 (cp 213); PMF 223; RUS 1:191; TGF 71.

Manakin, Long-tailed (Chiroxiphia linearis) CDB 145 (cp 587); DBM cp 26; GFB 127; IWE 10:1389; PMB cp 26; WEA 241.

Manakin, Red-capped or Yellow-thighed (Pipra mentalis) ABW 206; DBM cp 26; LBW 266; PMB cp 26.

Manakin, Thrush-like (Schiffornis turdinus) DBM cp 27; PMB cp 26.

Manatee (Trichechus manatus) ALE 12:510, 520; ANE 6:1122; FWA 292; GGM 143; IWE 10:1390, 1391; JAW 153; LVS 109; NGA 364-365; OMW 79; PFF 739; PMG 324; SLP 101; SOS 166.

Mandarin (Streptopus) See **Twisted-stalk.**

Mandarin, Nodding or Spotted (Disporum maculatum) FFK 56; FNC 24; RUS 2:27.

Mandarin, Yellow (Disporum lanuginosum) FFK 57; PMF 371; RUS 1:27, 2:27.

Mandrake—See **Mayapple.**

Manefish (Caristius macropus) HPF 291; WFW 145.

Mango (plant) (Mangifera indica) DEW 2:52 (cp 10), 53 (cps 12, 13); EWF cp 120d; LFW 160 (cp 358); MWF 197 (cp 631); OFP 101; PFF 237; WYG 207.

Mango, Black-throated (bird) (Anthracothorax nigricollis) ALE 8:453; DBM cp 14; HBT 145 (cp 6).

Man-o'-war Bird—See **Frigatebird, Magnificent.**

Man-o'-war Fish (Nomeus gronovii) ALE 5:101; LEA 257; MOL 58; WFW 264.

Manta, Atlantic (Manta birostris) ALE 4:118, 127; CFG 469; CFW 32; GGF 25; IWE 5:627; NGF 103-105; SOS 102-103, 333; WFW 244.

Mantid, Carolina (Stagmomantis carolina) GGI 24; SCI 71; SIG pl 6.

Mantis, Praying (Mantis religiosa) ALE 2:125, 140; EGP 53; GGI 25; IWE 11:1403, 1404; NHE 208; PFF 443; SCI 70.

Manzanita, Bristly (Arctostaphylos columbiana) AFP 3:320; CWF 378; HFP 262; VPN 4:56. (A. manzanita) PFF 275.

Maple, Big-leaf or Oregon (Acer macrophyllum) AFP 3:57; ANE 6:1128; BTN 215; GGT 117, 124; MTB 336 (cp 33); PFF 240; SFT 387; VPN 3:416.

Maple, Black (Acer nigrum) BBF 2:496; BTN 211; GGT 116, 120; TSK 311.

Maple, Dwarf (Acer glabrum) AFP 3:57; BBF 2:497; BTN 217; GGT 117, 125; SFT 393, 394, 395; VPN 3:413.

Maple, Field (Acer campestre) BTN 217; DFP 179 (cp 1430); MTB 332 (cp 31); NHE 22; OBT 21, 25.

Maple, Flowering (Abutilon sp.) DFP 179 (cp 1427, 1428); EGA 90; EWF cps 177a, f; FHP 102; HSC 10; LFW 265 (cp 592); MEP 77; MWF 27 (cp 5); PFF 249; PFW 184.

Maple, Japanese (Acer palmatum) BTN 217; DFP 180 (cps 1434-1436); EGT 38, 92; HSC 10; MTB 336 (cp 33); MWF 29 (cp 14); OBT 188; TGS 151. (A. japonicum) BTN 217; DFP 179 (cp 1432).

Maple, Mountain (Acer spicatum) BBF 2:497; BTN 215; FNC 113; GGT 116, 123; PFF 240; TSK 74, 230.

Maple, Norway (Acer platanoides) ANE 6:1127; BTN 217; DFP 180 (cp 1438); EGT 92, 93; EWF cp 19b; GGT 117, 118; MTB 332 (cp 31); NHE 22; OBT 188; PFF 239; TGS 151.

Maple, Paperback (Acer griseum) DFP 179 (cp 1431); EGT 91; MTB 325 (cp 30); OBT 188.

Maple, Planetree—See **Maple, Sycamore.**

Maple, Red (Acer rubrum) ANE 6:1130; BBF 2:495; BTN 213; DEW 2:55 (cp 18); DFP 180 (cp 1440); EGT 93; GGT 117, 121; GPL 70; MTB 332 (cp 31); PFF 242; RWA cp 215; TSK 27, 98, 117, 314, 315.

Maple, Rocky Mountain—See **Maple, Dwarf.**

Maple, Silver (Acer saccharinum) ANE 6:1129; BBF 2:494; BTN 213; EGT 94; GGT 116, 122; MTB 332 (cp 31); PFF 241; TSK 312, 313.

Maple, Striped (Acer pensylvanicum) BBF 2:497; BTN 215; DFP 180 (cp 1437); PFF 241; TSK 316.

Maple, Sugar (Acer saccharum) ANE 6:1132; BBF 2:496; BTN 211; EGT 94, 95; GGT 116, 119; MTB 336 (cp 33); OFP 17; PFF 242; TSK 25, 110, 310.

Maple, Sycamore (Acer pseudoplatanus) BTN 217; DFP 180 (cp 1439); EWF cp 19c; GGT 126, 127; MTB 333 (cp 32); NHE 22; OBT 21, 25; PFF 241; TGS 151.

Maple, Vine (Acer circinatum) AFP 3:60; BTN 215; EGT 90; PFF 240; SFT 390, 391; VPN 3:413.

Mare's-tail (Hippuris vulgaris) AFP 3:214; BBF 2:612; GPL 65; NHE 93; OWF 53.

Margarite, Puppet (Margarites pupillus) AAS 108; ASN 69; GAS 318; MGS pl 32; PFF 409.

Margay—See **Cat, Margay.**

Marguerite, Golden—See also **Chamomile, Yellow** (Anthemis tinctoria).

Marguerite, Golden (Chrysanthemum frutescens) AGF 123; MWF 84 (cp 210).

Marigold, African (Tagetes erecta) AGF 164, 165; DFP 48 (cp 378, 379); EGA 155; FGF 178, 179; LWF 223 (cp 500, 501); MWF 279 (cp 922); TGF 253.

Marigold, Cape (Dimorphotheca aurantiaca) AGF 61; DFP 37 (cp 291); EGA 115; FGF 57; MWF 114 (cp 324); TGF 269.

Marigold, Corn (Chrysanthemum segetum) AFP 4:395; BBF 3:519; DFP 34 (cp 266); EGA 106; EWF cp 39b; NHE 237; OWF 39; RUS 5:579.

Marigold, Desert (Baileya multiradiata) AFP 4:197; LWF 108 (cp 174); RUS 3:461, 4:673.

Marigold, Fig—See **Hottentot-fig.**

Marigold, French (Tagetes patula) AGF 166; DFP 48 (cps 380, 381); EGA 155; FGF 181; LFW 222 (cps 498, 499, 500); MWF 279 (cp 924); OGF 143; PFF 324.

Marigold, Marsh—See **Marsh-marigold.**

Marigold, Pot (Calendula officinalis) AGF 56; DFP 31 (cp 248), 32 (cps 249, 250); EGA 101; FGF 46, 47; LFW 18 (cp 35); MWF 66 (cp 150); PFF 325; TGF 269; WYG 50.

Marijuana—See **Hemp, Soft.**

Mariposa—See **Lily, Mariposa.**

Marjoram (Origanum vulgare) DFP 162 (cp 1293); NHE 186; OFP 141; OWF 147; RUS 1:375, 5:467; TGF 204.

Marlin, Blue (Makaira ampla) ALE 5:192; CFG 492; CFW 133; GGF 88; SOS 98. (M. nigricans) MOL 95.

Marlin, Striped (Makaira audax) GGF 88; HFW 233, 234; NGF 128.

Marlin, White (Makaira albidus or Tetrapturus albidus)

BBF 3:30; CWF 426; HFP 276, cp 12a; LWF 195 (cp 306); RUS 3:291, 4:435, 5:379, 6:455; RWA cp 306; VPN 4:88.

Milkweed, Swamp (Asclepias incarnata) BBF 3:26; FFK 130; FNC 151; HWF cp 172; HYF cp 151; PMF 295; RUS 1:319, 2:401, 3:291, 4:435, 6:459.

Milkweed, White (Asclepias variegata) BBF 3:29; FFK 117; FNC 153; HYF cp 148; PMF 55; RUS 1:321, 2:403, 3:293.

Milkweed, Whorled (Asclepias verticillata) BBF 3:32; PMF 55; RUS 1:319, 2:405, 3:295, 6:455.

Milkwort, Cross-leaved or Marsh (Polygala cruciata) BBF 2:448; HWF cp 123b; HYF cp 103; PMF 245, 367; RUS 1:423, 2:531, 3:413.

Milkwort, Field (Polygala sanguinea) FFK 230; HYF cp 104; PFF 230; PMF 245; RUS 1:423, 2:527, 3:413, 6:615.

Milkwort, Fringed (Polygola pauciflora) BBF 2:452; FNC 105; HWF cp 125b; HYF cp 103; LWF 259 (cp 410); PFF 231; PMF 215, 245; RUS 1:423, 2:527; RWA cp 210.

Milkwort, Sea (Glaux maritima) AFP 3:333; BBF 2:716; NHE 136; OWF 125; PMF 43; VPN 4:52.

Milkwort, Short-leaved (Polygala brevifolia) BBF 2:448; PMF 245; RUS 1:425, 2:531.

Milkwort, Whorled (Polygala verticillata) BBF 2:448; PMF 63, 245, 367; RUS 2:531, 3:411, 6:615.

Milkwort, Yellow (Polygala lutea) BBF 2:447; FNC 106; HWF cp 123a; HYF cp 103; PMF 209; RUS 1:425, 2:531; RWA cp 209.

Milky Cap, Delicious (Lactarius deliciosus) ANE 4:755; GMC 27 (cps 57, 58); LHM 213; MSM 94, cp 13; NFP 65; NHE 45; ONP 105; PFF 84; SMG 235.

Milky Cap, Pitted (Lactarius scrobiculatus) GMC 45 (cp 74); MSM 99, cp 14.

Milky Cap, Velvet (Lactarius vellereus) GMC 47 (cp 85); LHM 207; ONP 131; SMG 243. (L. lignyotus) GMC 27 (cp 63); NFP 73.

Millet, Foxtail—See **Bristle-grass.**

Mimosa, Prairie (Desmanthus illinoensis) FFK 155; PRP 82; RUS 2:317, 3:199, 4:301, 6:333.

Miner's-lettuce (Montia perfoliata) AFP 2:128; CWF 134; HFP 88; RUS 4:309, 5:281, 6:339; VPN 2:244. (M. cordifolia) AFP 2:128; CWF 138; RUS 5:281, 6:339; VPN 2:241. (M. sibirica) AFP 2:132; CWF 134; RUS 5:281, 6:339; VPN 2:248. (M. parvifolia) AFP 2:125; CWF 138; RUS 5:285, 6:339; RWA cp 105; VPN 2:244.

Mink (Mustela vison) ALE 11:105, 12:41, 55; ANE 6:1183; BGM 53 (cp 6); CFG cp 32; FWA 58; GGM 38, 43; GPL 152; IWE 11:1467-1470; JAW 112; NGA 183; OBV 169; PFF 686; PMG cp 10; SAA 133; WEA 249.

Minnow, Blunt-nosed (Pimephales notatus) CFG 539; NGF 268; PFF 513.

Minnow, Sheepshead or Variegated (Cypriodon variegatus) CFG 480; GGF 66.

Minnow, Top—See **Topminnow.**

Mint, Apple-scented (Mentha rotundifolia) NHE 98; RUS 3:375, 4:553, 5:461.

Mint, Field or Wild (Mentha arvensis) CWF 450; NHE 231; OWF 143; PMF 79, 349; RUS 1:371, 3:375, 4:553, 5:461, 6:551. (M. canadensis) HWF cp 191a.

Mint, Water (Mentha aquatica) NHE 98; OWF 143; PMF 349.

Mission Bells (Fritillaria lanceolata) AFP 1:423; AGF 63; CWF 39, 43; HFP cp 26a; LWF 230 (cp 365); OOW cp 231; RUS 4:47, 5:29, 6:27.

Mist Flower (Eupatorium coelestinum) BBF 3:362; EGP 117; FGF 106; FFK 236; FNC 193; PMF 325; RUS 1:495, 2:613, 3:493; TGF 237.

Mistletoe (Phoradendron flavescens) PFF 150; RWA cp 98; TSK 146; VPN 2:99. (P. californicum) PFF 151. (P. villosum) HFP 78.

Mistletoe, Western Dwarf (Arceuthobium campylopodium) AFP 1:529; CWF cp 110; VPN 2:99.

Mistmaidens (Romanzoffia stichensis) AFP 3:530; CWF 439; HFP 290; RUS 5:415, 6:493; RWA cp 313; VPN 4:179. (R. suksdorfii) RUS 5:413, VPN 179. (R. unalaschcensis) CWF 447.

Mite, Chicken (Dermanyssus gallinae) GIP 55; OIB 147; PFF 439.

Mite, Cyclamen (Steneotarsonemus pallidus) GBB cp 29; GIP 90; OIB 153.

Mite, Follicle (Demodex sp.) GIP 55; OIB 145.

Mite, Itch (Sarcoptes scabiei) GIP 45, 54; OIB 145; PEI 15; PFF 439.

Mite, Spider (Tetranychus telarius) GBB cp 27; GIP 85; EGA 50; EGE 150; EGP 51; LPL 176.

Miter Shell (Mitra sp.) AAS cp 13, pl 26; ASN 151; GSS 94; MGS pls 8, 40, 60, 70; MOL 67.

Mitrewort (Mitella diphylla) FFK 153; HWF cp 90b; HYF cp 76; PFF 192; PMF 69; RUS 1:205, 2:259, 261. (M. calescens) HFP 150; RUS 6:285. (M. trifida) CWF 211; RUS 5:239, 6:285.

Mitrewort, False—See also **Foamflower.**

Mitrewort, False (Tiarella laciniata) CWF 213. (T. unifoliata) AFP 373; RUS 5:251.

Mocassin, Mexican (Agkistrodon bilineatus or Ancistrodon bilineatus) DRW pls 64, 66; SIR 251 (cp 134).

Mocassin, Water (Agkistrodon piscivorus or Ancistrodon piscivorus) AWW 35; BAR cp 62; CFG cp 35; CRA cp 29; DRW pls 64, 65; GPL 142; GRA 109; LFO 146; PFF 546; PRW pl 139; SIR 251 (cp 135), 265; WWS 2:917, 922.

Moccasin-flower—See **Lady's-slipper, Pink.**

Mock Orange (Philadelphus lewisii) AFP 2:386; ANE 6:1189; CWF 235; HFP 138; OOW cp 24; VPN 2:88. (P. hirsutus) FNC 83; TSK 43. (P. coronarius) BBF 2:232; DFP 216 (cp 1728); PFF 193; PFW 228; TGS 151.

Mockernut—See **Hickory, Mockernut.**

Mockingbird (Mimus polyglottos) AAB 343; ABW 249; ALE 9:221; ANE 6:1187, 1188; BHB 227 (cp 58); CDB 160 (cp 670); CFG cp 15; GBC 237 (cp 50); GFB 159; IWE 11:1478; NGB 2:167; NGS 201; PBA 3:cp 101; PEB 167 (cp 46); PFF 638; PWB 230 (cp 47); RBB 227. (M. polyglottos leucopterus) BBC 2:cp 88.

Mold, Bread (Rhizopus stolonifer) NFP 33; PFF 67.

Mold, Green (Penicillium digitatum) DEW 3:144 (cp 77); NFP 24; PFF 68.

Mold, Water (Saprolegnia sp.) GPL 38; NFP 24, 33; PFF 67.

Mole, Eastern (Scalopus aquaticus) ANE 6:1190; BGM 20 (cp 1); CFG cp 31; PFF 678; PMG cp 4; (S. latimanus) GGM 19.

Mole, Hairy-tailed (Parascalops breweri) ALE 10:190; BGM 20 (cp 1); CFG cp 31; GGM 18; PFF 679; PMG cp 4; WMW 1:174.

Mole, Oregon or Townsend's (Scapanus townsendii) ALE 10:190; BGM 20 (cp 1); NGA 324; PMG cp 4; WMW 1:175.

Mole, Shrew—See **Shrew-mole.**

Mole, Star-nosed (Condylura cristata) ALE 10:190; ANE 6:1192; BGM 20 (cp 1); CFG cp 31; FWA 73; GGM 18; GPL 154; IWE 11:1482; JAW 34; NGA 320, 321, 324; PMG cp 4.

Monarch-of-the-veldt (Venidium fatuosum) EGA 160; TGF 268.

Monardella, Mountain (Monardella odoratissima) AFP 3:653; RUS 4:557, 5:461, 6:553; VPN 4:267.

Money Plant—See **Honesty.**

Moneywort (Lysimachia nummularia) DEW 2:286 (cp 169); DFP 14 (cp 109); FFK 103; HWF cp 164a; HYF cp 145; NHE 186; OWF 27; PFF 278; PFW 243; PMF 141; RUS 1:301, 2:385, 5:371, 6:445.

Monkey Puzzle Tree (Araucaria imbricata) BKT cp 15; BTN 65; DEW 1:41; MTB 48 (cp 1); NFP 152; OBT 105, 133; TGS 23.

Monkey, Spider (Ateles sp.) ALE 10:340; AWW 48; JAW 44; OMW 116; SMW 84 (cp 43); WMW 1:435.

Monkey-flower, Bush (Mimulus aurantiacus) AFP 3:716; OOW cp 98; RUS 4:591, 5:497.

Monkey-flower, Common (Mimulus guttatus) AFP 3:713; CWF 474; HFP 326, cp 12d; OOW cp 136; OWF 25; RUS 1:399, 4:593, 5:497, 6:591; RWA cp 324; VPN 4:345.

Monkey-flower, Little (Mimulus alsinoides) AFP 3:703; CWF 475; RUS 5:499; VPN 4:341.

Monkey-flower, Musk (Mimulus moschatus) AFP 3:697; BBF 3:191; CWF 475; LWF 156 (cp 250); RUS 1:397, 2:505, 5:497, 6:593; VPN 4:348.

Monkey-flower, Pink (Mimulus lewisii) AFP 3:696; CWF 475; HFP 328; LWF 156 (cp 249); OOW cp 168; RUS 5:499, 6:591; RWA cp 326; VPN 4:348.

Monkey-flower, Primrose (Mimulus primoloides) AFP 3:697; DFP 14 (cp 110); RUS 4:593, 5:499, 6:591.

Monkey-flower, Square-stemmed (Mimulus ringens) BBF 3:190; FFK 201; FNC 167; HWF cp 191b; HYF cp 180; PFF 297; PMF 345; RUS 1:397, 2:505, 3:401, 6:593.

Monkshood, Columbia (Aconitum columbianum) AFP 2:192; CWF 150; LWF 126 (cp 120); RUS 4:133, 5:105, 6:139; VPN 2:323.

Monkshood, Common (Aconitum napellus) AGF 170; DEW 1:120; DFP 119 (cp 952); FGF 185; NHE 268.

Monkshood, Wild (Aconitum uncinatum) BBF 2:97; FNC 62; PFF 174; PMF 319; RUS 1:109, 2:163.

Montbretia (Tritonia crocata or T. crocosmaefolia) AGF 171; EGB 106; FGF 186; LFW 94 (cp 218); MWF 287 (cp 949); OGF 117; TGF 29.

Moon Shell, Atlantic—See **Natica, Atlantic.**

Moon Snail, Atlantic or Shark-eye (Polinices duplicatus) AAS cp 5k, pl 22h; ASN 113; CFG cp 45; GGS 117; GSS 15, 49; PFF 409.

Moon Snail, Common Northern (Lunatia heros) AAS 73; ASN 115; CFG 572; GGS 117; GSS 49.

Moon Snail, Iceland (Amauropsis islandica) AAS pl 22r; ASN 115; CFG 574.

Moon Snail, Lewis' (Polinices lewisii) AAS pl 24n;

Moth, Imperial (Eacles imperialis) GGI 93; PFF 470.

Moth, Indian-meal (Plodia interpunctella) GIP 149; OBI 117; PEI 330; PFF 470; SCI 311; SIG cp 71.

Moth, Io (Automeris io) ALE 2:359; GGI 90; KIA 154; KIW 166 (cp 72); LIN 25; PEI cp 37b; PFF 471; SCI 269.

Moth, Luna (Actias luna or Tropaea luna) ALE 2:327; GGI 91; KIA 147; KIW 165 (cp 70), 169 (cp 77); PAK 206; PFF 471; SCI 267; SIG cp 80b.

Moth, Polyphemus (Telea polyphemus or Antheraea polyphemus) GGI 89; KIA 147; KIW 166 (cp 71); SCI 267; WEA 224.

Moth, Promethea (Callosamia promethea) GGI 88; PFF 471.

Moth, Silk (Calosaturnia mendocino) KIW 168 (cp 76). (Philosamia cynthia) GGI 86.

Moth, Sphinx or Hawk (Protoparce quinquemaculata) GGI 84, 85; KIA 149; PAK 202; SIG cp 77.

Moth, Spruce Budworm (Archips fumiferana) GIP 142; LPL 176; SIG cp 67a.

Moth, Tiger (Isia isabella) KIA 166; KIW 174 (cp 87).

Moth, Tussock (Hemerocampa leucostigma) GGI 95; GIP 143; SIG cp 76. (Halisidota sp.) SCI 271.

Moth, Yucca (Tegeticula alba or T. yuccasella) AWW 28; IWE 20:2668-2669; KIA 137; KIW 147; OMW 132; PAK 213; SCI 327.

Mother-in-law's Tongue (Sansevieria trifasciata) DEW 2:211 (cp 118); DFP 81 (cp 643); MWF 262 (cp 865).

Motherwort, Common (Leonurus cardiaca) NHE 230; PFF 289; PMF 281; RUS 1:385, 2:491, 3:385, 4:567, 5:471.

Motmot, Blue-crowned (Momotus momota) ALE 9:32, 48; CDB 127 (cp 496); DBM cp 19; GFB 104; HBT 112 (cp 3); IWE 11:1516; LBW 244; PMB cp 22; WAB 96; WEA 253.

Motmot, Blue-throated (Aspatha gularis) ALE 9:48; DBM cp 19; PMB cp 22.

Motmot, Keel-billed (Electron carinatum) DBM cp 19; PMB cp 22.

Motmot, Russet-crowned (Momotus mexicanus) AMB 71 (cp 5); DBM cp 19; PMB cp 22.

Motmot, Tody (Hylomanes momotula) DBM cp 19; GFB 104; PMB cp 22.

Mountain Lion—See **Cougar**.

Mountain Pride (Penstemon newberryi) AFP 3:767; DFP 16 (cp 128); OGF 67; OOW cp 145; RUS 5:511.

Mountain-ash, American (Sorbus americana) BBF 2:287; BTN 165; FNC 95.

Mountain-ash, European (Sorbus aucuparia) AGF 172; BTN 165; DEW 1:295; DFP 239 (cp 1905); EGT 144; MTB 288 (cp 25); MWF 270 (cp 894); NHE 19; OBT 20, 24; PFF 197; TGS 317; VPN 3:191.

Mountain-ash, Sitka (Sorbus sitchensis) AFP 2:472; CWF 279; VPN 3:191.

Mountain-ash, Western (Sorbus scopulina) BBF 2:287; CWF 271; RWA cp 189; VPN 3:191.

Mountain-dandelion (Agoseris aurantiaca) AFP 4:565; OOW cp 83; RUS 4:743, 5:621, 6:729. (A. villosa) RWA cp 400.

Mountain-dandelion, Pale (Agoseris glauca) AFP 4:563; BBF 3:323; OOW cp 82; RUS 4:743, 5:621, 6:729; VPN 5:28.

Mountain-mint, Hairy (Pycnanthemum pilosum) PMF 79; RUS 6:561. (P. flexuosum) FFK 209; RUS 2:477, 3:377. (P. muticum) FNC 165; PMF 79; RUS 2:475.

Mountain-mint, Hoary (Pycnanthemum incanum) HWF cp 183a; PMF 79; RUS 1:371, 2:477. (P. pycnanthemoides) FFK 209; RUS 2:475.

Mourner, Brown—See **Manakin, Thrush-like**.

Mourner, Rufous (Rhytipterna holerythra) DBM cp 27; PMB cp 26.

Mouse, Beach or Oldfield (Peromyscus polionotus) BGM 165 (cp 16); NGA 281; PMG cp 30.

Mouse, Brush (Peromyscus boylei) BGM 165 (cp 16); CFG 296.

Mouse, Cactus (Peromyscus eremicus) BGM 165 (cp 16); GGM 97.

Mouse, Deer (Peromyscus maniculatus) ALE 11:297; BGM 165 (cp 16); BMC 134 (cp 15); CFG cp 31; GGM 98; IWE 5:623-625; LMA 154; PMG cp 30.

Mouse, Field or Meadow (Microtus pennsylvanicus) ALE 11:300; BGM 180 (cp 17); BMC 134 (cp 15); CFG cp 31; GGM 104; GPL 154; NGA 275; PFF 710; PMG cp 32; SAA 119.

Mouse, Grasshopper (Onychomys leucogaster) AWW 19; BGM 164 (cp 15); BMC 134 (cp 15); CFG cp 31; NGA 283; PMG cp 31.

Mouse, Harvest (Reithrodontomys sp.) BGM 164 (cp 15); CFG cp 31; GGM 96; NGA 283; PMG cp 31; WEA 187.

Mouse, House (Mus musculus) ALE 11:371; BGM 165 (cp 15); CFG 296; IWE 9:1127, 1129; JAW 82;

NGA 272; OBV 135; PFF 712; PMG cp 30; WEA
199.

Mouse, Jumping (Zapus hudsonius) ALE 11:399;
BGM 148 (cp 13); BMC 167 (cp 20); CFG cp 31;
NGA 278; PMG cp 33. (Z. princeps) BMC 134 (cp
15). (Napaeozapus insignis) ALE 11:399; BGM 148
(cp 13).

Mouse, Pine (Pitymys pinetorum) BGM 180 (cp 17);
GGM 105; NGA 278; PMG cp 33. (Microtus pinetorum) CFG 296.

Mouse, Pinon or Pinyon (Peromyscus truei) ALE
11:297; BGM 165 (cp 16); CFG 296; NGA 280;
PMG cp 30.

Mouse, Pocket (Perognathus sp.) ALE 11:297; BGM
148 (cp 13); CFG cp 31; GGM 90, 91; NGA 284;
PMG cp 31. (Liomys irroratus) ALE 11:297; BGM
148 (cp 13).

Mouse, Pygmy (Baiomys taylori) ALE 11:297; BGM
164 (cp 15).

Mouse, Red Tree (Phenacomys longicaudus) BGM 180
(cp 17); NGA 277; PMG pl 33.

Mouse, Red-backed—See **Vole, Boreal Red-backed.**

Mouse, Sea—See **Sea Mouse.**

Mouse, White-footed (Peromyscus leucopus) AWW 19;
BGM 165 (cp 16); BMC 135 (cp 16); CFG cp 31;
GGM 98; NGA 280; PFF 710; PMG cp 30.

Mousetail (Myosurus minimus) AFP 2:197; BBF
2:103; EWF cp 8g; NHE 210; OWF 5; RUS 1:117,
3:103, 4:133, 5:115, 6:149; VPN 2:375.

Mouton—See **Peony, Tree.**

Mud-dauber—See **Wasp, Mud-dauber.**

Mudpuppy (Necturus maculosus) ALE 5:251; BAR
cp 21; CAW 45; CGR cp 2c; CRA 266 (pl 35); GRA
138; GPL 130; IWE 11:1525; PFF 523.

Mugwort, Breckland (Artemisia campestris) AFP
4:413; NHE 238; VPN 5:61. (A. lactiflora) AGF 26;
DFP 123 (cp 977). (A. suksdorfi) AFP 4:407; CWF
530; VPN 5:72.

Mugwort, Common (Artemisia vulgaris) BBF 3:527;
NHE 238; OWF 61; PMF 375; TGF 237; VPN 5:72.

Mulberry, Black (Morus nigra) BKT cp 96; BTN 145;
DEW 1:158; MTB 256 (cp 23); MWF 203 (cp 654);
OBT 161; OFP 95.

Mulberry, Paper (Broussonetia papyrifera) BTN 145;
EGT 101; PFF 148; TGS 134; TSK 486.

Mulberry, Red (Morus rubra) BBF 1:631; BTN 145;
GGT 114, 115; PFF 149; TSK 103, 118, 382, 383.

Mulberry, White (Morus alba) BBF 1:631; BKT cp 95;

BTN 145; EGT 128; GGT 114, 115; MTB 256 (cp
23); PFF 148; TGS 87; TSK 118, 485.

Mule (Equus asinus x cabellus) ALE 12:551; IWE
1:95, 96-97; PFF 736.

Mule-ears (Wyethia glabra) AFP 4:103; LWF 163 (cp
261); RUS 4:653, 5:551. (W. helanthiodes) AFP
4:105; RUS 5:551, 6:645; VPN 5:335. (W. mollis)
AFP 4:105; OOW cp 85; RUS 5:551.

Mullein, Common (Verbascum thapsus) AFP 3:740;
BBF 3:173; CWF 494; FNC 168; HYF cp 177; LWF
20 (cp 316); NHE 233; OOW cp 125; OWF 29; PFF
295; PMF 107; RUS 1:391, 2:493, 3:389, 4:567,
5:475, 6:565.

Mullein, Moth (Verbascum blattaria) AFP 3:733; BBF
3:174; EGP 149; FFK 214; HWF cp 195b; HYF
cp 174; NHE 98; PMF 59, 107, 143; RUS 1:391,
2:493, 3:389, 4:571, 5:475, 6:565.

Mullein, White (Verbascum lychnitis) BBF 3:174;
HWF cp 195a; NHE 233; PMF 59. (V. nigrum) NHE
233; OGF 113. (V. thapsiforme) DEW 2:169 (cp
95); NHE 233.

Mullet, Striped (Mugil cephalus) CFG 483; CFW 142;
GGF 81; NGF 202; WFW 255.

Mummichog (Fundulus heteroclitus) CFG 481; GGF
66; WFW 192.

Murex Shell (Murex sp.) AAS cp 10, pl 24; ASN 123;
GGS 126, 127; GSS 71, 72, 76; MGS pl 57.

Murre, Common (Uria aalge) AAB 216; ABW 139;
ALE 7:61, 8:208; AWW 37, 151; BBE 156; CDB 96
(cp 346); CFG cp 10; FWA 258; GBC 189 (cp 36);
GFB 83; IWE 7:978, 980; NGW 404; PEB 11 (pl 4);
PFF 607; PWB 142; RBB 149; SAA 85; SOS 159.

Murre, Thick-billed (Uria lomvia) AAB 217; ABW
138; ALE 8:229; BBE 156; CFG cp 10; GBC 189
(cp 36); NGW 405; PBA 1:cp 3; PEB 11 (pl 4); PWB
142; RBB 149; SAA 84.

Murrelet, Ancient (Synthliboramphus antiquum) ABW
139; GBC 189 (cp 36); NGB 1:340; NGW 408; PWB
146 (pl 35); RBB 153.

Murrelet, Kittlitz's (Brachyramphus brevirostre) NGB
1:340; NGW 407; PWB 146 (pl 35); RBB 153; SAA
89.

Murrelet, Marbled (Brachyramphus marmoratum)
AAB 221; ALE 8:211; BBW 141 (cp 31); GBC 189
(cp 36); NGB 1:340; NGW 407; PWB 146 (pl 35);
RBB 153; TBC 236 (cp 29b).

Murrelet, Xantus' (Endomychura hypoleuca) NGB
1:344; NGW 407; PWB 146 (pl 35); RBB 153.

Mushroom—See also specific names (i.e., **Boletus, Morel. Puffball**, etc.).

Mushroom, Apricot Jelly (Phlogiotus helvelloides) GMC 255 (cp 367); MSM cp 31.

Mushroom, Black-stemmed (Marasmius androsaceus) LHM 115; NFP 67; ONP 47.

Mushroom, Brick-top (Naematoloma sublateritium) GMC 235 (cp 342); SMG 219. (N. capnoides) GMC 195 (cp 298); MSM 150, cp 24; SMG 220, cp 162.

Mushroom, Caesar's or Orange (Amanita caesarea) GMC 48; NFP 54; PFF 81. (A. calyptroderma) SMG 174.

Mushroom, Cauliflower (Sparassis crispa) KMF 79 (cp 18a); LHM 57; NHE 47. (S. radicata) MSM 180; SMG 110.

Mushroom, Chicken (Polyporus sulphureus or Lateiporus sulphureus) ANE 4:755; GMC 253 (cp 355); KMF 39 (cp 8c); MSM 170, cp 27; NFP 49; PFF 79; SMG 63.

Mushroom, Fairy Ring (Marasmius oreades) GMC 135 (cps 231, 232); LHM 115; MSM 108; NFP 67; OFP 189; PFF 85; SMG 155, cp 108.

Mushroom, Field or Meadow (Agaricus campestris) GMC 193 (cp 286); KMF 115 (cp 27c); LHM 133; MSM cp 22; NFP 81; OFP 189; ONP 31; PFF 87; SMG 190.

Mushroom, Fly (Amanita muscaria) ANE 4:754; GMC 50; KMF 86 (cp 20); LHM 117; MSM 30, cp 4; NFP 53; NHE 48; ONP 113; SMG 177, 178, cp 124.

Mushroom, Glistening Inky-cap (Coprinus micaceus) GMC 213 (cp 305); LHM 141; MSM 157; NFP 84; PFF 86; SMG 226 (cp 166).

Mushroom, Gypsy (Pholiota caperata or Rozites caperata) GMC 175 (cps 269, 270); MSM 119, cp 19; NFP 80; SMG 214.

Mushroom, Hedgehog (Hydnum repandum) GMC 253 (cp 359); KMF 26 (cp 5c); LHM 61; MSM cp 28; NFP 47; NHE 46; ONP 153; PFF 77.

Mushroom, Inky-cap (Coprinus atramentarius) GMC 278; LHM 137; MSM 156, cp 26; NFP 84; ONP 35; PFF 85; SMG 223, cp 164.

Mushroom, Lemon-yellow (Amanita citrina) GMC 69; LHM 119; NHE 47; ONP 119; SMG 181, cp 127.

Mushroom, Milky Cap—See **Milky Cap**.

Mushroom, Oyster (Pleurotus ostreatus) LHM 107; MSM 79; NFP 70; OFP 189; ONP 125; PFF 83; SMG 152, 153. (P. serotinus) GMC 51 (cp 112); MSM 81, cp 15.

Mushroom, Panther (Amanita pantherina) ANE 4:757; KMF 10 (cp 1b); LHM 119; MSM 30, cp 5; NFP 53; NHE 48; SMG 180.

Mushroom, Panus (Panus stipticus) NFP 71; PFF 85.

Mushroom, Parasol (Lepiota procera) GMC 92; KMF 111 (cps 26a, 26b); NFP 58; NHE 45; PFF 81. (L. rhacodes) MSM 42, cp 6; NFP 58; NHE 45; OFP 189.

Mushroom, Shaggy-mane (Coprinus comatus) ANE 4:755; DEW 3:138 (cp 64); GMC 195 (cp 301), 279; KMF 114 (cp 27a); LHM 137; MSM 155, cp 26; NFP 84; ONP 35; PFF 86; SMG 224, 225, cp 165.

Mushroom, Sponge—See **Morel**.

Mushroom, White Jelly (Pseudohydnum gelatinosum) DEW 3:154; GMC 255 (cp 366); MSM cp 31.

Muskellunge (Esox masquinongy) ALE 4:265; ANE 8:1476-1477; CFG cp 43; GGF 65; GPL 126; HFW 104; NGF 274; PFF 509; WFW 187.

Muskmelon or Cantaloupe (Cucumis melo) OFP 119; PFF 309; WYG 150.

Muskox (Ovibus moschatus) ALE 11:151, 13:469; ANE 7:1247; BGM 217 (cp 22); BMC 390 (cp 44); CFG 338; FWA 31; IWE 12:1544, 1545; JAW 203; NGA 104, 105; PFF 724; PMG cp 39; SAA 110, 111; SLP 54; SOS 214.

Muskrat (Ondatra zibethica) ALE 11:257; ANE 7:1249, 1251; BGM 196 (cp 19); BMC 103 (cp 14); GGM 110; GPL 153; IWE 12:1546; JAW 80; NGA 279; OBV 131; PFF 711; PMG cp 26; SAA 120; WMW 2:840.

Mussel, Blue or Edible (Mytilus edulis) AAS cp 35m; ALE 3:140; ASN 199; CFG cp 46; GAS 206; GGS 85; GSS 133; IWE 12:1548-1551; KSL 139; MGS pl 10; OIB 73; PFF 418; SOS 19.

Mussel, California or Surf (Mytilus californianus) AAS pl 29p; ASN 199; GAS 208; KSL 136; RCT 179.

Mussel, Hooked (Brachidontes recurvus) AAS cp 35n; ASN 201; CFG 593; GGS 85; PFF 421.

Mussel, Horse (Modiolus modiolus) AAS 80; CFG 592; GGS 85; MGS pl 11; OIB 73. (M. rectus) KSL 228; MGS pl 11; PFF 421. (M. capax) ASN 199; MGS pl 11.

Mussel, Ribbed (Atlantic) (Modiolus demissus) AAS pl 28h; CFG 593; GGS 85; GSS 133; MGS pl 11. (Geukensia demissa) PFF 421.

Mustard, Black (Brassica nigra) AFP 2:273; BBF 2:193; NHE 215; OFP 133; OWF 9; PFF 185; PMF 161; RUS 1:161, 2:219, 3:155, 4:207, 5:173, 6:225; VPN 2:463.

Mustard, Field (Brassica arvensis or B. kaber) AFP 2:273; OWF 9; PFF 184; PMF 161; RUS 3:155, 4:207, 5:173, 6:225; VPN 2:463.

Mustard, Garlic (Alliaria officinalis) BBF 2:170; FFK 149; NHE 30; PMF 87; RUS 1:177; VPN 2:440.

Mustard, Hare's-ear (Conringia orientalis) AFP 2:324; BBF 2:175; NHE 216; PMF 159.

Mustard, Hedge (Sisymbrium officinale) AFP 2:268; BBF 2:174; NHE 219; OWF 9; PMF 159; RUS 5:179, 6:225.

Mustard, Tumble (Sisymbrium altissimum) AFP 2:268; BBF 2:174; NHE 218; PFF 187; PMF 159; RUS 6:227.

Mustard, White (Brassica alba or B. hirta) PFF 184; PMF 161; RUS 6:222, 225. (Sinapis alba) AFP 2:273; BBF 2:191; DEW 1:145; NHE 215; OFP 133, 153; OWF 9.

Muttonbird—See **Shearwater, Sooty.**

Muttonfish—See **Snapper, Mutton.**

Mycena, Capped or Helmet (Mycena galericulata) GMC 176; KMF 23 (cp 4c); LHM 109; NFP 68; ONP 133; PFF 83. (M. epipterygia) ANE 4:758.

Myotis, Little Brown—See **Bat, Little Brown.**

Myrtle, Common (Myrtus communis) EGE 136; HSC 79; MWF 206 (cp 664); NHE 246; OGF 103; PFW 191.

Myrtle, Crape—See **Crape Myrtle.**

N

Naked Boys—See **Colchium.**

Nama (Nama hispidum) AFP 3:524; LWF 100 (cp 157); RUS 3:305, 4:467, 6:495.

Nannyberry (Viburnum lentago) BBF 3:273; BTN 267; PFF 305; TSK 91, 222.

Narcissus (Narcissus sp.) AGF 85-88; DEW 2:220 (cp 136); DFP 104-108 (cps 829-864); EWF cp 42d; FGF 190-196; LFW 96 (cp 221), 98 (cps 222-225), 99 (cp 226); MGB 62-92; MWF 208 (cps 667-672), 209 (cps 673, 674); NHE 192, 290; OGF 11, 19; OWF 29; PFF 383, 384; PFW 23; SGB cps 25-27; TGF 12, 18.

Narwhal (Monodon monceros) ALE 11:480; ANE 7:1253; BGM 247; CFG 308; GGM 145; IWE 12:1554-1555; NGA 391; NHE 143; PMG 337; SOS 176; WMW 2:1104.

Nassa—See **Basket Shell.**

Nasturtium—See also **Cress, Water.**

Nasturtium (Tropaeolum majus) AGF 173; DFP 49 (cps 387, 388); EGA 159; FGF 197; FHP 149; LFW 246, 247; MWF 288 (cp 950); PFF 224; PFW 299; RUS 5:517; TGF 141.

Natica, Arctic (Natica clausa) ASN 115; CFG cp 45; GGS 117; MGS pl 35.

Natica, Atlantic (Natica canrena) ASN 115; GGS 117; GSS 50; PFF 409.

Natica, Miniature (Natica pusilla) ASN 115; CFG 575.

Nautilus, Paper—See **Paper Nautilus.**

Necklace Weed—See **Baneberry, White.**

Nectarine (Prunus persica nectarina) OFP 73; WYG 180.

Nemesia (Nemesia strumosa) DFP 44 (cp 348); EGA 138; EWF cp 81c; MWF 209 (cp 676); OGF 143; TGF 220.

Nene—See **Goose, Hawaiian.**

Neptune, New England (Neptunea decemcostata) AAS pl 23s; ASN 135; CFG cp 45; GGS 130; GSS 15, 81.

Neptune, Tabled—See **Whelk, Tabled.**

Nerve Plant (Fittonia verschaffeltii) DFP 67 (cp 533); MWF 134 (cp 398); PFW 13.

Nettle, Dead—See **Dead-nettle.**

Nettle, False (Boehmeria cylindrica) BBF 1:637; HWF cp 45; PMF 383.

Nettle, Hedge—See **Hedge-nettle.**

Nettle, Stinging—See also **Tread Softly.**

Nettle, Stinging (Urtica dioica) BBF 1:635; CWF 342; DEW 1:180; NHE 223; OFP 191; OWF 65; PFF 150; PMF 383. (U. gracilis) BBF 1:635; PMF 383. (U. lyalli) AFP 1:525; CWF 342.

Newt, California (Taricha torosa) ALE 5:306; CAW 31; CGR 18; GRA 143; MAR 12 (cp 1); SRA cp 1.

Newt, Red-bellied (Taricha rivularis) CAW 32; SRA cp 1.

Newt, Red-spotted (Diemictylus viridescens) CAW 29, 30, cp 5; CFG cp 37; CRA 270 (cp 37); IWE 12:1565; PFF 523. (Notophthalmus viridescens) BAR cps 6, 7; GRA 143; CGR cp 2b.

Nighthawk, Common (Chordeiles minor) AAB 256; ABW 164; ALE 8:425; ANE 7:1341, 1342; BBC 1:cp 68; CDB 120 (cp 462); GBC 204 (cp 41); GFB 97; GPB 197; NGB 2:46; NGW 452; PEB 135 (cp

38); PFF 618; PWB 151 (cp 38); RBB 169. (C. virginianus) PBA 2:cp 65.

Nighthawk, Lesser or Texas (Chordeiles acutipennis) NGB 2:46; NGW 453; LBW 179 (cp 100); PWB 151 (cp 38); RBB 169. (C. acutipennis texensis) BBC 1:cp 68.

Nightingale-thrush, Black-headed (Catharus mexicanus) DBM cp 36; PMB cp 35.

Nightingale-thrush, Russet (Catharus occidentalis) AMB 89 (cp 7); DBM cp 36; PMB cp 35.

Nightjar, Buff-collared—See **Whip-poor-will, Ridgway's**.

Night-light (Noctiluca miliaris or N. scintillans) GAS 4; IWE 12:1585-1587; OIB 3; SOS 37.

Nightshade, Alpine Enchanter's (Circaea alpina) BBF 2:611; CWF 339; NHE 29; PMF 69; RUS 1:241, 2:307, 4:319, 5:307, 6:463.

Nightshade, Bitter (Solanum dulcamara) AGF 47; CW CWF 451; HWF cp 194a; HYF cp 173; NHE 98; OWF 131; PMF 325; RUS 1:341, 2:437, 5:431, 6:517.

Nightshade, Black (Solanum nigrum) AFP 3:675; BBF 3:164; HFP 312; NHE 232; OWF 95; PMF 73; PRP 154. (S. verbascifolium) BTN 262.

Nightshade, Common Enchanter's (Circaea lutetiana) NHE 29; OWF 95; RUS 1:241, 2:307, 3:217. (C. quadrisulcata) FFK 151; PMF 69.

Nightshade, Deadly (Atropa belladonna) NHE 232; OWF 131; PFF 293.

Nimblewill (Muhlenbergia schreberi) BBF 1:184; HMG 398; PRP 46.

Ninebark (Physocarpus capitatus) AFP 2:407; CWF 246. (P. opulifolius) FNC 94; PFF 195; TGS 231; TSK 71, 295.

Nipplewort (Lapsana communis) AFP 4:613; BBF 3:306; CWF 555; NHE 239; OWF 41; PMF 173; RUS 1:505, 5:629.

Noddy—See **Tern, Noddy**.

None So Pretty—See **Catchfly, Sweet William**.

Nudibranch, Brown or Plumed (Aeolis papillosa) AAS cp 15g; GGS 137. (Acanthodoris brunnea) GAS 258.

Nudibranch, Bushy-backed (Dendronotus frondosus) ALE 3:113; ASN 179; BLA 162 (cp 63); GGS 137; KSL cp 8.

Nudibranch, Carpenter's (Triopha carpenteri) AAS cp 16k; ASN 181; AWW 37; BLA 165 (cp 67); JSS 496 (cp 10); KSL cp 11; LSE 22; RCT 109 (pl 6).

Nudibranch, Giant (Dendronotus giganteus) GAS 260; JSS 500.

Nudibranch, Opalescent (Hermissenda crassicornis) BLA 162 (cp 62), 163 (cp 64); GAS 264; JSS frontispiece; KSL cp 8; RCT 144.

Nudibranch, Red (Rostanga pulchra) AAS cp 16g; GAS 250; JSS 484 (cp 8); RCT 107 (pl 5).

Nudibranch, Ringed (Diaulula sandiegensis) AAS cp 16d; GAS 252; JSS 493; KSL cp 10; RCT 109 (pl 6).

Nudibranch, Yellow (Cadlina marginata) GAS 256; JSS 449 (cp 9); RCT 128.

Nutcracker, Clark's (Nucifraga columbiana) AAB 316; ABW 225; ALE 9:497; ANE 7:1344; BBC 2:cp 83; CDB 224 (cp 1006); CFG cp 21; GBC 232 (cp 47); GFB 141; IWE 12:1592; NGB 2:124; NGS 151; PFF 632; PWB 199 (cp 44); RBA 180; RBB 211; WAB 35.

Nuthatch, Brown-headed (Sitta pusilla) AAB 329; BWI 164; CFG cp 14; NGB 2:143; NGS 165; PBA 3:204; PEB 163 (cp 44); RBB 221.

Nuthatch, Pygmy (Sitta pygmaea) ABW 238; ALE 9:319; BBC 2:cp 85; LBW 285 (cp 180); NGB 2:143; NGS 165; PBA 3:205; PWB 214 (cp 45); RBB 221.

Nuthatch, Red-breasted (Sitta canadensis) AAB 328; ABW 238; ALE 9:319; BBC 2:cp 85; CDB 186 (cp 810); CFG cp 14; GBC 233 (cp 48); GFB 150; NGB 2:143; NGS 164; PBA 3:cp 103; PEB 163 (cp 44); PFF 634; PWB 214 (cp 45); RBB 221.

Nuthatch, White-breasted (Sitta carolinensis) AAB 327; ABW 238; ALE 9:319; CFG cp 14; GBC 233 (cp 48); GBI 77; IWE 12:1594; NGB 2:143; NGS 163, 164; PBA 3:cp 103; PEB 163 (cp 44); PFF 633; PWB 214 (cp 45); RBA 189; RBB 221.

Nutmeg Bush (Iboza riparis) MEP 125; MWF 161 (cp 503).

Nutmeg, California (tree) (Torreya californica) BTN 20; MTB 49 (cp 2); OBT 105, 133; PFF 113.

Nutmeg, Common (mollusk) (Cancellaria reticulata) ASN 155; GSS 106; PFF 414.

Nutmeg, Helmet-shaped (mollusk) (Cancellaria cassidiformis) GSS 106; MGS pl 61.

Nutria (Myocastor coypus) ALE 11:438; AWW 52; BGM 196 (cp 19); CFG 301; GGM 116; GPL 153; IWE 4:550, 551; LEA 523; NHE 110; OBV 131; PFF 713; WEA 115.

O

Oak, Black (Quercus velutina) BBF 1:619; BTN 127; GGT 98; PFF 144; TSK 472, 473.

Oak, Bur (Quercus macrocarpa) BBF 1:623; BTN 121; GGT 88; PFF 141; TSK 462, 463.

Oak, Chestnut-leaved (Quercus castaneifolia) DEW 1:183; MTB 240 (cp 21); OBT 157.

Oak, Cork (Quercus suber) BKT cp 71; DEW 1:106 (cp 58), 183; MTB 209 (cp 20); NHE 42; PFF 142.

Oak, Gambel's (Quercus gambelii) BTN 123; GGT 94; PRP 166.

Oak, Garry's (Quercus garryana) AFP 1:518; BTN 123; SFT 284; VPN 2:89.

Oak, Kellogg's (Quercus kelloggi) AFP 1:517; BTN 131; EGT 140; VPN 2:89.

Oak, Live (California) (Quercus agrifolia) AFP 1:518; BTN 135; GGT 95; PFF 142; SFT 304-306.

Oak, Live (Eastern) (Quercus virginiana) BBF 1:625; BKT cp 77; BTN 135; EGE 142; EGT 142; GGT 93; PFF 142.

Oak, Pin (Quercus palustris) BBF 1:617; BTN 127; EGT 141; GGT 101; MWF 249 (cp 819); PFF 143; TGS 86; TSK 470, 471.

Oak, Red (Quercus rubra) BBF 1:617; BKT cps 73, 75; BTN 127; GGT 99; OBT 157; PFF 143.

Oak, Scarlet (Quercus coccinea) BBF 1:619; BTN 127; GGT 102; MTB 209 (cp 20); OBT 157; PFF 143; TSK 468, 469.

Oak, Shingle (Quercus imbricaria) BBF 1:622; BTN 133; GGT 105; PFF 144.

Oak, Water (Quercus nigra) BTN 133; EGT 141; GGT 104; GPL 69; TSK 477.

Oak, White (Quercus alba) BBF 1:622; BTN 121; EGT 139; GGT 86; PFF 140; TGS 86; TSK 456, 457.

Oak, Willow (Quercus phellos) BBF 1:621; BTN 133; EGT 141; GGT 106; MTB 240 (cp 21).

Oar-fish (Regalecus glesne) CFW 96; IWE 12:1599; WFW 308.

Oat (Avena sativa) AFP 1:171; BBF 1:218; HMG 301; OFP 5; PFF 353; PRP 72; VPN 1:496.

Oat, Wild (Avena fatua) AFP 1:171; BBF 1:218; HMG 301; NHE 244; PFF 354; VPN 1:494.

Oat-grass, Tall (Arrhenatherum elatius) AFP 1:172; BBF 1:220; HMG 304; NHE 195; PRP 18; VPN 1:494.

Oat-grass, Yellow (Trisetum flavescens) BBF 1:216; EWF cp 25d; HMG 291; NHE 196; VPN 1:722.

Obedient Plant—See **Dragonhead, False.**

Ocean Spray (Holodiscus discolor) AFP 2:415; CWF 243, 246; HFP 164; PFW 261; VPN 3:118.

Ocelot (Felis pardalis or Panthera pardalis) ALE 8:359, 12:300, 323; BGM 69 (cp 8); FWA 225; IWE 12:1603; JAW 130; LVS 73; NGA 216; PAK 614; PFF 696; PMG cp 14; WEA 262.

Oconee Bells (Shortia galacifolia) FNC 141; RUS 2:381; RWA cp 287; TGF 156.

Ocotilla (Fouquieria splendens) AFP 3:477; DEW 1:176 (cp 106); EWF cp 160b; LWF 76 (cp 123); OOW cp 199; RWA cp 310.

Octopus, Common (Octopus vulgaris) ALE 3:198, 223; ASN 265; BLA 170 (cp 77); GGS 138; IWE 12:1605; NHE 162; OIB 93; RCT 139 (pl 21); WEA 263. (O. bairdii) PFF 426. (Paroctopus apollyon) GAS 342; SOS 63.

Octopus, Two-spotted (Octopus bimaculatus) GGS 139. (Polypus bimaculatus) JSS 577, 578.

Odostome (Odostomia sp.) AAS 289; ASN 175; MGS pl 33.

Oeoe—See **Petrel, Harcourt's Storm.**

Oilbird (Steatornis caripensis) ABW 157; ALE 8:425; CDB 119 (cp 454); DBM cp 13; FWA 227; GFB 94; GPB 194; HBT 131; IWE 12:1609; LBW 214; WAB 82.

Okra (Hibiscus esculentus) OFP 165; WYG 147.

Old-squaw (Clangula hyemalis) AAB 79; ALE 7:309; BBC 1:cp 21; CDB 52 (cp 112); CFG 49, 50, 51; GBC 96 (cp 13); GGB 70; KWF 432 (cp 22), 456 (cp 34); NGB 1:112; NGW 183; NHE 146; PBA 1:cp 20; PEB 23 (pl 8), 27 (pl 10), 35 (pl 12); PFF 577; PWB 35 (pl 8), 43 (pl 10), 51 (pl 12); RBB 59; SAA 92.

Oleander (Nerium oleander) AGF 174; DFP 214 (cp 1710); EGE 75, 137; EWF cp 36b; LFW 178 (cp 400); MEP 110; MWF 213 (cp 688); NHE 109; PFW 30; TGS 359.

Oleaster (Elaeagnus pungens) DFP 197 (cps 1570, 1571); EGE 121; HSC 48; PFW 104.

Olive (Olea europaea) DFP 215 (cp 1713); EGE 137; NHE 294; OFP 23; PFW 200; WYG 195.

Olive, Russian (Elaeagnus angustifolia) AGF 217; EGT 111; NHE 134; TGS 278; VPN 3:462.

Olive Shell, Beatic Dwarf (Olivella baetica) AAS pl 20q; GAS 270; GGS 134; MGS pl 40.

Olive Shell, Lettered (Oliva sayana) AAS pl 12a; ASN 149; GGS 134; GSS 89; PFF 414.

Olive Shell, Purple Dwarf (Olivella biplicata) AAS pl 12i; ASN 149; GGS 134; GSS 14; KSL 205; MGS pl 40; PFF 414; RCT 283 (pl 36).

Olive Shell, Tent (Oliva porphyria) GSS 18, 88; MGS pls 6, 60.

Olive, Sweet (Osmanthus fragrans) FHP 136; MWF 219 (cp 709); TGS 327.

Omao—See **Thrush, Hawaiian.**

Onion, Common (Allium cepa) OFP 167; PFF 371; WYG 154. (A. fistulosum) NHE 241; OFP 167; WYG 154.

Onion, Hooker's (Allium acuminatum) AFP 1:390; CWF 7; HFP 16, cp 10c; RUS 4:35, 5:53, 6:51; VPN 1:743. (A. crenulatum) AFP 1:387; RUS 5:49; VPN 1:748.

Onion, Narrow-leaved (Allium amplestens) AFP 1:394; HFP 18; RUS 4:35, 5:53, 6:51. (A. falcifolium) OOW cp 281.

Onion, Nodding (Allium cernuum) AFP 1:382; BBF 1:498; CWF 6; DFP 83 (cp 660); FFK 58; FNC 36; LFW 8 (cp 16); PMF 297; RUS 1:31, 2:45, 3:25, 4:35, 6:51; RWA cp 44; VPN 1:748.

Onion, Wild (Allium canadense) BBF 1:499; FFK 58; PFF 372; PMF 297; RUS 1:33, 2:43, 45; 3:27, 6:53. (A. stellatum) BBF 1:498; HYF cp 11; PMF 297; RUS 1:31, 3:25.

Oo, Kauai (Moho braccatus) ALE 9:320; BHB 97 (cp 35); WID 299 (cp 27c).

Opah (Lampris regius or L. guttata) ALE 5:36; HPF 269; IWE 12:1614; NGF 215; OBV 41.

Opaleye (Girella nigricans) GGF 117; NGF 209; WFW 197.

Opossum (Didelphis marsupialis or D. virginiana) ALE 10:62; ANE 7:1388, 1390; BGM 196 (cp 19); BMC 3; FWA 79; GGM 17; IWE 12:1617; JAW 20; LEA 482; LFO 23; NGA 313-315; PFF 677; PMG cp 35; SMW 34 (cp 4); WMW 1:24.

Opossum, Water (Chironectes minimus) ALE 10:62; FWA 284; WMW 1:25.

Opuntia, Fragile—See **Prickly-pear, Brittle or Fragile.**

Orache, Common (Atriplex patula) AFP 2:80; CWF 122; NHE 227; OWF 55; PMF 379. (A. hortensis) AFP 2:80; EGA 97; OFP 161; VPN 2:190.

Orache, Halberd-leaved (Atriplex hastata) AFP 2:80; BBF 2:18; NHE 227. (A. littoralis) NHE 136; OWF 55.

Orange, Chinese or Japanese (Poncirus trifoliata) DFP 218 (cps 1742, 1743); HSC 91; PFW 269; TGS 326.

Orange, Mock—See **Mock Orange.**

Orange, Osage (Maclura pomifera) BTN 149; DEW 1:159; EGT 123; PFF 147; TGS 87.

Orange, Seville or Sour (Citrus aurantium) BKT cp 150; EWF cp 119c; MWF 86 (cp 220); OFP 85; PFF 229; WYG 199.

Orange, Sweet (Citrus sinensis) DEW 2:57 (cp 23); EGE 119; OFP 85; PFF 229; PFW 268; WYG 199.

Orange-plume—See **Orchid, Orange- or Yellow-fringed.**

Orchard-grass (Dactylis glomerata) AFP 1:195; BBF 1:251; HMG 185; NHE 195; PFF 360; PRP 31; VPN 1:544.

Orchid—See also **Adder's Mouth, Epidendrum,** and **Pogonia.**

Orchid (Cattleya sp.) AGF 174; DFP 56 (cp 442); EGB 55; LFW 260 (cps 573, 574), 261 (cp 584); MEP 30; MWF 76 (cp 187); PFF 390; PFW 205, 209.

Orchid, Butterfly (Epidendrum tampense) COA 304; HYF cp 39; RUS 2:127; RWA cp 89.

Orchid, Clamshell (Epidendrum cochleatum) COA 290; FHP 58; RUS 2:127.

Orchid, Cymbidium (Cymbidium hybrids) DFP 61 (cps 487, 488); 62 (cps 489-491); FHP 55; MEP 30; MWF 100 (cps 277, 278), 101 (cp 279).

Orchid, Dollar (Epidendrum boothianum) COA 288; RUS 2:127. (E. o'brienianum) MWF 122 (cp 351).

Orchid, Large Round-leaved (Habenaria orbiculata) COA 94; CWF 98; HWF cp 35, 73; LWF 240 (cp 378); PMF 17; RUS 1:79, 2:109, 5:75, 6:79; VPN 1:847.

Orchid, Orange- or Yellow-fringed (Habenaria ciliaris) COA 63; FFK 72; FNC 44; HWF cp 37b; HYF cp 41; LWF 12 (cp 16); PMF 121, 209; RUS 1:79, 2:107, 3:61; RWA cp 75.

Orchid, Pansy (Miltonia hybrids) DFP 70 (cps 558, 559); MWF 201 (cp 646); PFW 213.

Orchid, Peacock (Acidanthera bicolor) AGF 178; DEW 2:223 (cp 140); DFP 83 (cp 657); OGF 117.

Orchid, Phantom (Cephalanthera austinae) AFP 1:478; COA 135; HFP 64, cp 16d; RUS 5:79; VPN 1:836.

Orchid, Poor Man's—See **Butterfly Flower.**

Orchid, Purple-fringed (Habenaria psycodes) COA 98,

99; FFK 71; FNC 42; HYF cp 40; LWF 241 (cp 379); PMF 243; RWA cp 77. (H. fimbriata) HWF cp 39a; PFF 390; PMF 225, 243; RUS 1:75, 2:105.

Orchid, Ragged-fringed (Habenaria lacera) COA 84; FNC 41; HWF cp 39b; HYF cp 40; PMF 121, 373; RUS 1:75, 2:109, 3:61, 6:79; RWA cp 76.

Orchid, Rosebud—See **Pogonia, Spreading**.

Orchid, Small Green (Habenaria clavellata) COA 66; PMF 17; RUS 1:79, 2:109.

Orchid, Spider (Brassia caudata) COA 358; FHP 57; RUS 2:121.

Orchid, Stream—See **Helleborine, Giant**.

Orchid, Tall White Bog (Habenaria dilatata) COA 70; CWF 87; LWF 174 (cp 274); OOW cp 10; PMF 17; RUS 1:79, 4:69, 5:75. (H. leucostachys) COA 70; CWF 98; VPN 1:844.

Orchid, Three-birds—See **Pogonia, Nodding**.

Orchid Tree (Bauhinia sp.) EGE 113; MEP 50; MFW 54 (cps 103-106); PFW 158, 159.

Orchid, White-fringed (Habenaria blephariglottis) COA 58; FNC 43; HWF cp 38; PMF 17; RUS 1:79, 2:107, 3:61.

Orchis, Round-leaved (Orchis rotundifolia) BBF 1:551; COA 45; CWF 102; HWF 70; PMF 15, 243; RUS 6:75; RWA cp 74; VPN 1:856.

Orchis, Showy (Orchis spectabilis) COA 47; FFK 68; FNC 41; HWF cp 34; HYF cp 38; LWF 243 (cp 383); PFF 392; PMF 213; RUS 1:75, 2:105; RWA cp 73; TGF 44.

Oregon Grape (Berberis aquifolium or Mahonia aquifolium) AFP 2:220; CWF 170; DFP 212 (cp 169); EGE 135; HFP 116; HSC 78; PFF 179; VPN 2:416. (B. nervosa) AFP 2:220; CWF 175; VPN 2:416. (B. repens) OOW cp 87.

Oregon Sunshine—See **Sunflower, Woolly**.

Oriole, Baltimore (Icterus galbula) AAB 443; ALE 9:381; ANE 8:1392, 1394; BBC 2:cp 107; CDB 207 (cp 910); CFG cp 21; GBC 300 (cp 61); GBI 108; NGB 2:226; NGS 307; PBA 2:259; PEB 199 (cp 54); PFF 660; PMB cp 40; PWB 266 (cp 53); RBA 228; RBB 287; TBC 370 (cp 73a).

Oriole, Black-headed (Icterus graduacauda) GFB 186; NGS 308; PMF cp 40; PWB 266 (cp 53); RBB 285.

Oriole, Bullock's (Icterus bullockii) ANE 8:1395; BBC 2:cp 107; CFG cp 21; GBC 300 (cp 61); LBW 356 (cp 194); NGB 2:228; NGS 310; PBA 2:263; PFF 660; PMB cp 41; PWB 266 (cp 53); RBB 287; TBC 370 (cp 73b).

Oriole, Hooded (Icterus cucullatus) AAB 441; NGB 2:228; NGS 309; PMB cp 41; PWB 266 (cp 53); RBB 287.

Oriole, Lichtenstein's (Icterus gularis) DBM cp 39; PMB cp 41; PWB 266 (cp 53); RBB 287.

Oriole, Orange (Icterus auratus) DBM cp 39; PMB cp 40.

Oriole, Orchard (Icterus spurious) AAB 440; ANE 8:1396, 1398; BBC 2:cp 107; CFG cp 27; GBC 300 (cp 61); NGB 2:226; NGS 308; PBA 2:cp 75; PEB 199 (cp 54); PMB cp 41; PWB 266 (cp 53); RBB 285.

Oriole, Scott's (Icterus parisorum) AAB 442; AWW 28; NGB 2:228; NGS 310; PBA 2:255; PMB cp 40; PWB 266 (cp 53); RBB 285.

Oriole, Spot-breasted (Icterus pectoralis) ABW 288; ALE 9:381; DBM cp 39; NGS 309; PMB cp 41; RBB 287.

Oriole, Yellow-backed (Icterus chrysater) DBM cp 39; PMB cp 40.

Oriole, Yellow-tailed (Icterus mesomelas) DBM cp 39; PMB cp 41.

Oropendola, Chestnut-headed (Zarhynchus wagleri) ABW 288; ALE 9:381; DBM cp 38; PMB cp 39.

Oropendola, Montezuma (Gymnostinops montezuma) ABW 288; ALE 9:381; DBM cp 38; PMB cp 39; WAB 97.

Orpine—See **Live-forever** (Sedum).

Osier, Red—See **Dogwood, Western**.

Oso-berry (Osmaronia cerasiformis) AFP 2:468; CWF 254; HFP 158; HSC 82; VPN 3:127.

Osprey (Pandion halietus) AAB 107; ABW 82; ALE 7:398; AWW 31, 106; BBC 1:cp 31; BBE 84; CDB 60 (cp 160); CFG cp 3; GBC 105 (cp 16), 125 (pl 20); GBI 47; GFB 48; GPB 98; LBW 111; NGB 1:169; NGW 249, 250; PBA 2:cp 43; PFF 577; RBA 75; RBB 77; WAB 17, 18, 219.

Ostrich-plume—See **Hydroid, Ostrich-plume**.

Oswego Tea—See **Bee-balm**.

Otter, River (Lutra canadensis) ALE 11:257; BGM 52 (cp 5); BMC 341; CFG cp 32; GGM 47; GPL 152; JAW 120; NGA 187; PFF 688; PMG cp 8; SAA 132; SLP 100; WMW 2:1215.

Otter, Sea (Enhydra lutris) ALE 8:229, 12:93; BGM 52 (cp 5); BMC 344; GGM 46; IWE 15:2076-2077; JAW 121; NGA 188-189; OMW 260, 261; PFF 689; PMG cp 8; SOS 164, 165; VWA cp 38; WMW 2:1222. (E. lutris nereis) AWW 187; LVS 105; WID 78.

Our Lord's Candle (Yucca whipplei) LWF 62 (cp 101); MEP 17; RUS 4:49.

Ouzel, Water—See **Dipper.**

Ovenbird (Seiurus aurocapillus) AAB 421; ALE 9:371; AWW 25; CDB 205 (cp 899); CFG cp 18; GBC 284 (cp 59); GBI 99; LBW 354 (cp 190); NGB 2:185; NGS 282; PBA 3:cp 92; PEB 183 (cp 48); PFF 654; PWB 247 (cp 50); RBB 271; TBC 360 (cp 68).

Ovenbird, Least—See **Xenops, Plain (Little).**

Owl, Barn (Tyto alba) AAB 240; ABW 156; ALE 8:380, 393-396; BBC 1:cp 66; BBE 176; BOW 23; CDB 113 (cp 429); CFG cp 12; GBC 193 (cp 38); GFB 92; IWE 2:149, 150, 152; LBW 144 (cp 95); NGB 2:11; NGW 446, 447; PBA 2:cp 53; PEB 150 (cp 39); PFF 613; RBB 163; WAB 219.

Owl, Barred (Strix varia) AAB 246; ABW 157; ALE 8:380; BBC 1:cp 67; BOW 124; CDB 118 (cp 452); CFG cp 12; GBC 200 (cp 39); NGB 2:15; NGW 443; PBA 2:cp 54; PEB 150 (cp 39); PFF 616; RBB 163; TBC 266 (cp 34a).

Owl, Bearded Screech (Otus barbarus) BOW 96; DBM cp 11.

Owl, Black-and-white (Ciccaba nigrolineata) BOW 121; DBM cp 11; PMB cp 16.

Owl, Boreal (Aegolius funereus) AAB 250; ALE 8:380, 396; BBE 170; BOW 170, 171; CDB 114 (cp 432); CFG cp 28; GBC 201 (cp 40); NGB 2:18; NGW 445; PEB 151 (cp 40); RBB 165.

Owl, Burrowing (Speotyto cunicularia) ABW 155; ALE 8:380; AWW 29; BBC 1:cp 66; BBW cp 38; BOW 167, 168; CDB 117 (cp 449); CFG cp 12; GBC 201 (cp 40); IWE 3:318, 319; NGB 2:20; NGW 441; PEB 151 (cp 40); PFF 615; PWB 161; RBB 165; TBC 262 (cp 33b); WAB 56.

Owl, Cooper Screech (Otus cooperi) BOW 97; DBM cp 11.

Owl, Elf (Micrathene whitneyi) AAB 245; ABW 156; ALE 8:380; AWW 18; BBW cp 37; BOW 169; CDB 116 (cp 443); NGB 2:22; NGW 441; PBA 2:121; PFF 615; PMB cp 16; PWB 161; RBB 167; WAB 48.

Owl, Ferruginous Pygmy (Glaucidium brasilianum) AAB 245; ABW 157; BOW 177; DBM cp 11; NGB 2:22; PMB cp 16; PWB 161; RBB 167.

Owl, Flammulated Screech (Otus flammeolus) BBC 1:cp 65; BOW 105; NGB 2:18; NGW 436; RBB 167.

Owl, Great Gray (Strix nebulosa) AAB 247; ALE 8:380, 393; BBE 172; BOW 129; CDB 118 (cp 451); CFG cp 28; FWA 40; GBC 200 (cp 39); GPB 188;

LBW 212; NGB 2:13; PBA 2:cp 54; PEB 151 (cp 40); PFF 616; RBB 163; WAB 35, 105.

Owl, Great Horned (Bubo virginianus) AAB 243; ABW 156; ALE 8:380; BOW 77; CDB 116 (cp 441); CFG cp 12; GBC 193 (cp 38); LBI 70-71; LBW 213; LNA 110; NGB 2:9; NGW 437; PBA 2:cp 57; PEB 150 (cp 39); PFF 614; RBA 143; RBB 161; TBC 258 (cp 32a); WAB 76.

Owl, Hawk (Surnia ulula) ALE 8:380; BBE 176; BOW 162, 163; CDB 118 (cp 453); CFG cp 28; GBC 201 (cp 40); NGA 274; NGW 438; PEB 151 (cp 40); PFF 615; RBB 165; TBC 258 (cp 32b). (S. ulula caparoch) NGB 2:20; PBA 2:cp 55.

Owl, Long-eared (Asio otus) AAB 248; ALE 8:379; BBC 1:cp 67; BBE 175; BOW 139, 140; CDB 115 (cp 435); CFG cp 12; FWA 60; GBC 193 (cp 38); NGB 2:11; NGW 444; PBA 2:cp 53; PEB 150 (cp 39); PFF 616; RBB 161; TBC 266 (cp 34b).

Owl, Mottled Wood (Ciccaba virgata) BOW 120; DBM cp 11; PMB cp 16.

Owl, Pacific Screech—See **Owl, Cooper Screech.**

Owl, Pygmy (Glaucidium gnoma) BBC 1:cp 65; BBW cp 36; BOW 176; GBC 201 (cp 40); NGB 2:22; NGW 441; PWB 161; RBB 167.

Owl, Richardson's—See **Owl, Boreal.**

Owl, Santa Barbara Screech—See **Owl, Bearded Screech.**

Owl, Saw-whet (Aegolius acadicus) AAB 287; ALE 8:380, 395; BBC 1:cp 65; BOW 172-173; CDB 113 (cp 431); CFG cp 28; FWA 60; GBC 201 (cp 40); LBW 142-143 (cp 93); NGB 2:18; NGW 445; PBA 2:cp 55; PEB 151 (cp 40); PFF 617; RBA 147; RBB 165.

Owl, Screech (Otus asio) AAB 242; ABW 157; AWW 25; BOW 102, 103; CDB 117 (cp 446); CFG cp 12; GBC 193 (cp 38); GPB 189; LBW 142 (cp 91); NGB 2:24; NGW 434, 435; PBA 2:cp 56; PEB 150 (cp 39); PFF 614; RBB 161, 167.

Owl, Short-eared (Asio flammeus) AAB 249; ALE 8:380, 11:105; AWW 86; BBC 1:cp 67; BBE 175; BOW 144; CDB 114 (cp 434); CFG cp 12; GBC 200 (cp 39); LBI 56, 134; LBW 211; NGB 2:11; NGW 444; PBA 2:cp 56; PEB 150 (cp 39); PFF 617; RBB 161. (A. flammeus sandwichensis) BHB 96 (cp 33).

Owl, Snowy (Nyctea scandiaca) AAB 244; ABW 156; ALE 11:151; AWW 103; BBC 1:cp 66; BBE 172, 174; BOW 91, 93; CDB 116 (cp 445); FWA 33; GBC 193 (cp 38); GPB 186-187; IWE 16:2194; NGB 2:13;

NGW 439; PBA 2:cp 54; PEB 151 (cp 40); PFF 614; RBB 163; SLP 56; WAB 37.

Owl, Spectacled (Pulsatrix perspicillata) ABW 156; ALE 8:380; BOW 117, 118; DBM cp 11; LBI 18; PMB cp 16; WAB 91.

Owl, Spotted (Strix occidentalis) BBC 1:cp 67; BBW cp 39; BOW 126; GBC 200 (cp 39); NGW 443; RBB 163.

Owl, Striped (Rhinoptynx clamator) BOW 138; DBM cp 11; PMB cp 16.

Owl, Tengmalm's—See **Owl, Boreal.**

Owl, Unspotted Saw-whet (Aegolius ridgwayi) BOW 174; DBM cp 11; PMB cp 16.

Ox-eye (Heliopsis helianthoides) BBF 3:467; FFK 258; FNC 199; HWF cp 252; HYF cp 219; PFF 319; PMF 182; RUS 1:463, 2:585, 4:687, 6:667; TGF 285.

Ox-eye Daisy—See **Daisy, Ox-eye.**

Oyster, Atlantic Thorny (Spondylus americanus) ASN 213; GSS 138.

Oyster, Coon (Ostrea frons) AAS pl 28d; ASN 215.

Oyster, Eastern or Virginia (Crassostrea virginica) AAS pl 28a; ASN 215; CFG 572; GGS 89; PFF 418.

Oyster, Flat Tree (Isognomon alatus) AAS pl 35b; ASN 203; GSS 132.

Oyster, Japanese or Giant Pacific (Ostrea gigas or Crassostrea gigas) AAS pl 29g; ALE 3:141; ASN 215; GAS 196; IWE 12:1657; KSL 228.

Oyster, Native Pacific (Olympia) (Ostrea lurida) AAS pl 29f; ASN 215; GAS 194; GGS 89; JSS 419; MGS pl 9; RCT 280.

Oyster, Pacific Pearl (Pteria nebulosa) GGS 91; MGS pl 64.

Oyster, Pearl (Pinctada mertensi) GSS 131. (P. radiata) AAS pl 35c; ASN 203.

Oyster Plant (Tragopogon) See **Salsify.**

Oyster, Rock (Pododesmus macroschisma) AAS pl 29d; ASN 213; GAS 204; JSS 426; KSL 94; RCT 278.

Oyster-catcher, American (Haematopus palliatus) AAB 145; ABW 121; ANE 8:1432; CFG cp 7; GGS 148; NGB 1:265; NGW 315; PEB 90 (pl 25), 103 (cp 30); RBA 97; RBB 109.

Oyster-catcher, Black (Haematopus bachmani) BBW cp 22; GBC 160 (cp 29); NGB 1:265; NGW 314; PWB 103 (cp 26), 106 (pl 27); RBB 109.

P

Packrat—See **Rat, Wood.**

Paddle-fish (Polyodon spathula) ALE 4:146; CFG cp 44; CFW 38; GGF 32; IWE 12:1670; NGF 252; WFW cp 16.

Pagoda Tree (Sophora japonica) BKT cp 138; EGT 43, 144; OGT 185; TGS 150.

Paintbrush, Indian—See **Indian Paintbrush.**

Painted Cup—See **Indian Paintbrush.**

Painted Tongue (Salipiglossus sinuata) AGF 217; DFP 47 (cp 369); EGA 62, 151; EWF cp 183c; FGF 238; OGF 129; PFW 285.

Palm Chat (Dulus dominicus) ALE 9:196; BWI 145 (cp 6); GFB 171; IWE 12:1677; WAB 99.

Palm, Coconut (Cocos nucifera) BTN 73; EWF cp 191b; MEP 10; OFP 19; PFF 363.

Palm, Date (Phoenix dactylifera) BTN 73; DEW 2:282 (cps 162-164); MWF 231 (cp 755); OFP 107; PFF 363; RWF 49; WYG 193.

Palm, Desert (Washingtonia filifera) AFP 1:345; BTN 71; EWF cp 191j.

Palm, Sago (Cyas revoluta) BTN 21; DEW 1:18; LFW 160 (cp 356); MWF 100 (cp 274); NFP 149; OFP 185; PFF 111.

Palmetto, Cabbage (Sabal palmetto) BTN 69; GGT 128; GPL 71; PFF 364.

Palo Verde, Blue (Cercidium floridum) AFP 2:477; ANE 8:1440; BTN 191; LWF 73 (cps 117, 118). (C. microphyllum) AFP 2:477; BTN 191.

Pandora Shell (Pandora gouldiana) AAS 470; ASN 263; GGS 92; PFF 421. (P. bilirata) MGS pl 27.

Pansy, Field (Viola rafinesquii) FFK 221; FNC 121; HYF (cp 115); RUS 1:293, 2:379, 3:231, 4:355; RWA cp 231.

Pansy, Wild Yellow—See **Violet, California Golden.**

Papaw or Pawpaw (Asimina triloba) BBF 2:83; BTN 155; EGT 99; FNC 72; PFF 177; RWA cp 138; TGS 246; TSK 43, 120, 255, 361.

Papaya (Carica papaya) BTN 221; DEW 1:250; MWF 73 (cp 176); OFP 115; WYG 208.

Paper Nautilus, Brown (Argonauta hians) AAS 481; ASN 267; CFG 610; GSS 156.

Paper Nautilus, Common (Argonauta argo) AAS

cp 1c, pl 26y; ALE 3:198; ASN 267; GSS 156; IWE 1:82; MOL 72; NHE 162; PAK 95.

Paper-bag Bush—See **Sage, Bladder.**

Parakeet, Aztec or Olive-throated (Aratinga astec) DBM cp 7; PMB cp 14.

Parakeet, Barred (Bolborhynchus lineata or B. lineola) ALE 8:335; DBM cp 8; PMB cp 14.

Parakeet, Budgerigar (Melopsittacus undulatus) ABW 147; ALE 8:310; IWE 3:297-299; LBW 137 (cp 82); PFP 611.

Parakeet, Carolina (Conuropsis carolinensis) AAB 234; ALE 8:335; LBI 171; NGB 2:81; PBA 2:123.

Parakeet, Green (Aratinga holochlora) AMB 71 (cp 5); DBM cp 7; PMB cp 14.

Parakeet, Orange-chinned (Brotogeris jugularis) DBM cp 8; PMB cp 14.

Parakeet, Orange-fronted (Aratinga canicularis) AMB 71 (cp 5); DBM cp 7; PMB cp 14.

Paramecium (Paramecium sp.) ALE 1:108; GPL 76; PFF 394.

Parrot, Lilac-crowned (Amazona finschi) AMB 71 (cp 5); DBM cp 8; PMB cp 13.

Parrot, Puerto Rican (Amazona vittata) AWW 45; BWI 32 (cp 1); LVS 221; WID 257.

Parrot, Red-crowned or Green-cheeked (Amazona viridigenalis) DBM cp 8; PMB cp 13; WEA 279.

Parrot, St. Lucia (Amazona versicolor) AWW 45; BWI 32 (cp 1); WAB 27; WID 258.

Parrot, St. Vincent (Amazona guildingii) AWW 45; BWI 32 (cp 1); LVS 222; WID 258.

Parrot, Thick-billed (Rhynchopsitta pachyrhyncha) AAB 235; DBM cp 7; LVS 222; NGB 2:81; NGW 423; PMB cp 13; RBB 179.

Parrot, White-crowned (Pionus senilis) ALE 8:326; DBM cp 8; PMB cp 14.

Parrot, White-fronted (Amazona albifrons) AMB 71 (cp 5); DBM cp 8; PMB cp 13.

Parrot, Yellow-billed (Amazona collaria) AWW 45; BWI 32 (cp 1).

Parrot, Yellow-headed Amazon (Amazona ochrocephala) DBM cp 8; PMB cp 13; WAB 17.

Parsley (Petroselinum sativum or P. crispum) OFP 147; PFF 266; WYG 135.

Parsley, Water (Oenanthe sarmentosa) CWF 362; RUS 4:291, 5:271.

Parsnip (Pastinaca sativa) AFP 3:245; BBF 2:634; FFK 158; NHE 222; OFP 175; OWF 13; PFF 267; PMF 163; RUS 1:219, 2:279, 3:185, 4:287, 5:263; VPN 3:577; WYG 136.

Parsnip, Cow—See **Cow-parsnip.**

Partridge, Bearded (Dendrotyx barbatus) DBM cp 6; PMB cp 8.

Partridge, Chukar or Rock—See **Chukar.**

Partridge, Gray or Hungarian (Perdix perdix) ALE 7:467-469, 481, 11:321; BBC 1:cp 40; BBE 96; CDB 70 (cp 205); CFG cp 5; GBC 136 (cp 23); GGB 117, 148, 149; IWE 13:1710; NGB 1:227; NGW 291; PEB 70 (cp 21); PFF 581; PWB 91 (cp 22); RBB 91.

Partridge, Highland or Ruby-crowned (Dendrotyx leucophrys) CDB 68 (cp 197); DBM cp 6; PMB cp 8.

Partridge, Red-legged (Alectoris rufa) ABW 91; BBC 1:cp 40; BBE 97; CDB 68 (cp 191); FWA 81; IWE 13:1710; LBW 83 (cp 38).

Partridge-berry (Mitchella repens) BBF 3:255; FFK 120; FNC 178; HWF cp 211b; HYF cp 191; LWF 271 (cp 432); PFF 302; PMF 41, 237; RUS 1:353, 2:447, 3:349; RWA cp 355; TGF 188.

Partridge-foot (Luetkea pectinata) AFP 2:413; CWF 247; RUS 5:145, 6:185.

Partridge-pea (Cassia fasciculata) FFK 211; FNC 98; HYF cp 96; PMF 106, 152; RUS 1:209, 2:319, 3:209, 4:305, 6:337; RWA cp 191. (Chamaecrista fasciculata) BBF 2:337; HWF cp 105b; PRP 79.

Pasque Flower (Anemone pulsatilla or A. patens) BBF 2:102; CWF 151; DEW 1:97 (cp 38); EWF cp 8e; HYF cp 56; LFW 13 (cp 26); LWF 117 (cp 278); NHE 71; OGF 35; OOW cps 268, 269; OWF 139; PFF 171; PMF 23, 327; RUS 1:125, 3:105, 4:141, 5:127, 6:157; TGF 61.

Passion Flower—See also **Maypops.**

Passion Flower (Passiflora caerulea) AGF 177; DFP 249 (cp 1986); HSC 86; OGF 165; PFW 225; RWF 95. (P. alato-caerula) FHP 137; LFW 256 (cp 568); MWF 222 (cp 724).

Patience Plant or Patient Lucy (Impatiens sultanii) DFP 69 (cp 552); EGA 127; FHP 127; LFW 168 (cp 379); MWF 163 (cp 509).

Paulownia, Royal (Paulownia tomentosa) BTN 265; DFP 216 (cps 1722, 1723); EGT 131; EWF cp 103b; MTB 384 (cp 39); OBT 197; PFW 280; TGS 358; TSK 66, 320-321.

Pauraque (Nyctidromus albicollis) ALE 8:425; DBM cp 10; NGW 451; PMB cp 15; PWB 151 (cp 38); RBB 169. (N. albicollis merrilli) NGB 2:48.

Pawpaw—See **Papaw.**

Pintail, Bahama or White-cheeked—See **Duck, Bahama.**

Pinxter Flower—See **Azalea, Pink.**

Pipefish (Syngnathus sp.) CFG 479; GGF 80; HFW 83 (cp 36); HPF 278; IWE 13:1772; MOL 92; NGF 219; WFW 344.

Pipewort (Eriocaulon compressum) BBF 1:454; FNC 13. (E. septangulare) BBF 1:454; HWF cp 6a.

Pipistrel—See **Bat, Pipistrel.**

Pipit, American or Water (Anthus spinoletta) AAB 368; ABW 264; ALE 9:184, 189; BBC 2:cp 93; BBE 202; CFG cp 24; GBC 237 (cp 50); LBW 287 (cp 185); NGB 2:176; NGS 231; PEB 226 (cp 59); PWB 267 (cp 54); RBA 205; RBB 239; WAB 52.

Pipit, Sprague's (Anthus spraguei) AAB 369; BBC 2:cp 93; CFG cp 24; GBC 237 (cp 50); NGB 2:176; NGS 230; PEB 226 (cp 59); PWB 267 (cp 54); RBB 239.

Pipsissewa (Chimaphila umbellata) AFP 3:294; BBF 2:672; CWF 390; HFP 248; HWF cp 152a; HYF cp 140; NHE 34; PFF 271; PMF 27, 235; RUS 1:251, 2:317, 4:339, 5:313, 6:367; RWA cp 273; VPN 4:10.

Pipsissewa, Spotted—See **Wintergreen, Spotted.**

Pitcher-plant (Sarracenia purpurea) BBF 2:202; EWF cp 158c; FNC 80; GPL 65; HWF cp 83; HYF cp 73; LWF 22 (cp 36), 180 (cp 283); PFF 190; PFW 271; PMF 231; RUS 1:131, 2:185; RWA cp 151.

Pitcher-plant, California (Darlington californica) AFP 2:332; DEW 1:135; LWF 23 (cp 37); OOW cp 79; PFW 271; RUS 5:137; RWA cp 158; VPN 2:568.

Pitcher-plant, Hooded (Sarracenia minor) FNC 79; LWF 22 (cp 35); RUS 2:187; RWA cp 156.

Pitcher-plant, Purple Trumpet (Sarracenia drummondi) DEW 1:101 (cp 47); RWA cp 154. (S. leucophylla) EWF cp 158b.

Plaice, American (Hippoglossoides platessoides) GGF 77; NHE 158; OBV 49.

Plane-tree—See also **Sycamore, American** (Platanus), and **Maple, Sycamore** (Acer).

Plane-tree, London (Platanus acerifolia) BKT 105; DEW 1:155; EGT 133; MWF 236 (cp 769); OBT 192; TGS 183. (P. hispanica) MTB 257 (cp 24).

Plane-tree, Oriental (Platanus orientalis) BTN 161; DFP 218 (cp 1741); MTB 257 (cp 24).

Plantain, Common (Plantago major) AFP 4:16; BBF 3:245; NHE 187; OWF 61; PFF 300; PMF 63.

Plaintain, Hoary (Plantago media) BBF 3:246; EWF cp 15j; NHE 187; OWF 61.

Plaintain, Narrow-leaved (Plantago lanceolata) AFP 4:16; BBF 3:246; NHE 187; OWF 61; PFF 300; PMF 63; RUS 5:529.

Plantain, Sea (Plantago maritima) BBF 3:247; CWF 499; OWF 61; RUS 5:529.

Plantain, Woolly (Plantago purshii) AFP 4:21; BBF 3:248; PRP 146.

Platy (Xiphophorus maculatus) ALE 4:452, 460; PFF 515; WFW 364.

Pleurisy-root—See **Milkweed, Orange.**

Plover, Black-bellied (Squatarola squatarola) AAB 155; ABW 120; ALE 11:151; BBC 1:cp 46; CFG cp 7; GBC 137 (cp 24), 168 (pl 31); NGB 1:267; NGW 323; PEB 91 (pl 26), 102 (cp 29); PFF 594; PWB 102 (cp 25), 107 (pl 28); RBB 111; TBC 186 (cp 22a).

Plover, Collared (Charadrius collaris) AMB 34 (cp 2); DBM cp 1; PMB cp 10.

Plover, Golden (Pluvialis dominica) ABW 120; BBC 1:cp 46; BBE 113; CDB 82 (cp 266); CFG cp 7; GBC 137 (cp 24), 168 (pl 31); GFB 69; GGB 102; NGB 1:267; NGW 322-323; PBA 1:cp 39; PEB 91 (pl 26), 102 (cp 29); PFF 594; PWB 102 (cp 25), 107 (pl 28); RBB 111.

Plover, Kentish—See **Plover, Snowy.**

Plover, Piping (Charadrius melodus) AAB 149; BBC 1:cp 45; CFG cp 27; GBC 137 (cp 24); NGB 1:269; NGW 319; PEB 91 (pl 26), 102 (cp 29); PWB 102 (cp 25), 107 (pl 28); RBB 113.

Plover, Ruddy—See **Sanderling.**

Plover, Semipalmated (Charadrius semipalmatus) AAB 148; ABW 120; BBC 1:cp 45; CFG cp 7; GBC 137 (cp 24); GGS 148; NGB 1:269; NGW 319; PBA 1:cp 39; PEB 91 (pl 26), 102 (cp 29); PFF 593; PWB 102 (cp 25), 107 (pl 28); RBB 113; SAA 91.

Plover, Snowy (Charadrius alexandrinus) AAB 150; ALE 8:169, 187; BBC 1:cp 48; BBE 112; CDB 80 (cp 256); CFG cp 7; NGB 1:269; NGW 320; PEB 120 (cp 29); PWB 102 (cp 25), 107 (pl 28); RBB 113.

Plover, Upland (Bartramia longicauda) ALE 8:170; BBC 1:cp 50; BBE 125; CFG cp 8; GBC 161 (cp 30); GGB 103; NGB 1:271; NGW 334; PBA 1:cp 37; PEB 99 (pl 28), 103 (cp 30); PWB 115 (pl 30), 118 (cp 31); RBB 117; TBC 188 (cp 23b).

Plover, Wilson's (Charadrius wilsonia) AAB 153; CFG cp 27; NGB 1:269; NGW 321; PEB 102 (cp 29); RBB 113.

Poppy, Corn (Papaver rhoeas) AGF 196; BBF 2:137; DEW 1:137; DFP 45 (cp 355); EGA 141; MWF 221 (cp 718); NHE 214; OGF 83; OWF 105; PFW 220; RUS 2:203, 3:111, 4:155, 6:165; VPN 2:424.

Poppy, Gold (Eschscholtzia mexicana) LWF 68 (cp 110); RUS 3:109, 4:153, 6:165.

Poppy, Iceland (Papaver nudicaule) AGF 196; DEW 1:100 (cp 45); EGP 136; LFW 112 (cp 245); MWF 221 (cp 716); OGF 83; TGF 76.

Poppy, Matilija (Romneya coulteri) AFP 2:224; DFP 230 (cp 1837); EGP 143; EWF cp 154d; LWF 126 (cp 200); MEP 40; MWF 255 (cp 840); PFW 222; RUS 4:153. (R. trichocalyx) OOW cp 47.

Poppy, Mexican Tulip (Hunnemannia fumariaefolia) EGA 126; OGF 83; TGF 76.

Poppy, Opium (Papaver somniferum) BBF 2:137; FGF 216; LFW 108 (cp 237); MWF 221 (cp 719); NHE 214; PFW 220; VPN 2:424.

Poppy, Oriental (Papaver orientale) AGF 196; DFP 163 (cps 1300-1302); EGP 20, 137; EWF cp 46a; FGF 215; LFW 110 (cps 240-242, 244); MWF 221 (cp 717); PFF 180; PFW 221; TGF 76.

Poppy, Prickly (Argemone mexicana) BBF 2:139; DFP 30 (cp 240); EWF cp 154b; HYF cp 69; LWF 21 (cp 34); MEP 40; MWF 46 (cp 75); OGF 83; PFW 224; PMF 131, 179; RUS 2:181, 3:109. (A. albiflora) BBF 2:139; RUS 2:181, 3:111.

Poppy, Tree (Dendromecon rigida) AFP 2:229; DFP 195 (cp 1560); MWF 109 (cp 307); RWA cp 143.

Poppy, Welsh (Meconopsis cambrica) DFP 158 (cp 1264); EWF cp 11f; OWF 7; PFW 220; TGF 76.

Poppy, Yellow-horned (Glaucium flavum) DEW 1:140; DFP 38 (cp 299); EWF cp 30d; NHE 139; OWF 7; PMF 131; RUS 1:131.

Porbeagle—See **Shark, Mackerel.**

Porcupine (Erethizon dorsatum) ALE 11:409; BGM 196 (cp 19); BMC 230 (cp 23); CFG 304; FWA 49; GGM 67, 115; IWE 18:2455; JAW 83; LNA 166-167; NGA 286, 287, 293; OMW 73; PMG cp 26; SAA 122; SMW 148; WEA 297.

Porcupine Fish (Diodon holocanthus) ALE 5:240, 258; HFW 262 (cp 126), 279, 280; NGF 49. (D. hystrix) CFW 150; GGF 138; FWA 303; IWE 14:1823, 1824; LEA 257; WEA 296; WFW 177.

Porcupine-grass (Stipa spartea) BBF 1:177; HMG 451; PRP 68; VPN 1:718.

Porgy—See **Sheepshead.**

Porkfish (Anisotremus virginicus) CFW 109; GGF 114; HFW 169 (cp 77); LEA 241; NGF 147.

Porpoise, Bottle-nosed—See **Dolphin, Bottle-nosed.**

Porpoise, Common or Harbor (Phocoena phocoena) ALE 11:480; BGM 247; CFG 312; GGM 150; NHE 143; OBV 183; PFF 739; PMG 335; WMW 2:1129.

Porpoise, Dall's (Phocoena dalli) ALE 11:480; BGM 247; GGM 150; PMG 335; WMW 2:1130.

Portuguese Man-of-war (Physalia physalis) ALE 1:198, 271; CFG cp 47; GGS 47; IWE 14:1828, 1829; LEA 45; NHE 174; OIB 11; PFF 376; SOS 92.

Portulaca—See **Rose-moss.**

Possum—See **Opossum.**

Possumhaw (Ilex decidua) BBF 2:488; BTN 209; TSK 96, 124.

Potato, Duck or Swamp—See **Arrowhead, Broad-leaved.**

Potato, Irish (Solanum tuberosum) OFP 177; PFF 292; WYG 107.

Potato, Sweet (Ipomoea batatas) OFP 183; PFF 284; WYG 114.

Potato-vine, Wild (Ipomoea pandurata) BBF 3:43; FFK 118; FNC 156; HYF cp 153; PMF 13; RUS 1:345, 2:429, 3:327, 6:525.

Potoo, Common (Nyctibius griseus) ALE 8:425; AMB 16 (cp 1); CDB 119 (cp 457); DBM cp 11; GFB 96; GPB 196; IWE 14:1832; PMB cp 15; WAB 81.

Pout, Horned—See **Bullhead, Brown.**

Powder Puff (Calliandra inequalatera) EGE 115; FHP 109; LFW 4 (cp 8); MFW 67 (cp 151). (C. haematocephala) EWF cp 170d; MEP 53; PFW 159.

Prairie Chicken, Greater (Tympanuchus cupido) ABW 90; ALE 7:445; ANE 3:421, 423, 424; BBC 1:cp 37; CDB 67 (cp 190); CFG cp 27; GBC 128 (cp 21); GGB 124, 125; GPB 116; IWE 14:1836, 1837; LVS 211; NGB 1:240; NGW 274, 275; PEB 70 (cp 21); PFF 580; RBA 87; RBB 87; WAB 35, 55. (T. cupido attwateri) ANE 3:417.

Prairie Chicken, Lesser (Tympanuchus pallidicinctus) AAB 122; BBC 1:cp 37; GGB 126; NGB 1:240; NGW 275; PWB 90 (cp 21); RBB 87.

Prairie Dog, Black-tailed (Cynomys ludovicianus) ALE 11:239; AWW 27; BGM 101 (cp 10); CFG cp 30; GGM 77; IWE 14:1838, 1839; JAW 75; LMA 74; NGA 242; OMW 27; PMG cp 21; WMW 2:707, 708.

Prairie Dog, White-tailed (Cynomys gunnisoni or C. leucurus) BGM 101 (cp 10); GGM 76; NGA 243; PMG cp 21. (C. parvidens) LVS 70.

Prairie-clover, Purple (Petalostemum purpureus) BBF

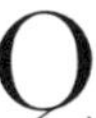

Q

R

Ragweed, Western (Ambrosia psilostachya) AFP 4:149; BBF 3:342; PRP 117; VPN 5:33.

Ragworm—See **Worm, Clam**.

Ragwort, Golden (Senecio aureus) FFK 250; HWF cp 263; HYF cp 224; LWF 51 (cp 85); PMF 109, 177; RUS 1:445, 2:551.

Ragwort, Tansy (Senecio jacobea) AFP 4:451; BBF 3:542; CWF 558; NHE 189; OWF 43; PMF 177; RUS 1:525, 5:537; VPN 5:295.

Rail, American Wood (Aramides cajanea) ALE 8:83; DBM cp 1; HBT 96 (cp 1); IWE 14:1904; PMB cp 10.

Rail, Black (Laterallus jamaicensis) AAB 141; BBC 1:cp 43; CFG cp 5; DBM cp 1; GGB 92; NGB 1:291; NGW 308; PBA 1:209, 210; PEB 71 (cp 22); PWB 99 (cp 24); RBB 103.

Rail, Clapper (Rallus longirostris) AAB 138; ANE 9:1643, 1645; CDB 75 (cp 236); CFG cp 5; GGB 93; HBT 96 (cp 1); NGB 1:291, 293; NGW 306; PBA 1:204; PEB 71 (cp 22); PFF 591; PWB 99 (cp 24); RBB 105.

Rail, Hawaiian (Pennula sandwichensis) BHB 95 (cp 30); MBH cp 4.

Rail, King (Rallus elegans) AAB 152; BWI 68; CFG cp 27; GBC 136 (cp 23); GGB 90; GPL 146; NGB 1:293; NGW 306; PBA 1:203; PEB 71 (cp 22); PFF 590; RBA 93; RBB 105.

Rail, Sora (Porzana carolina) AAB 139; ABW 110; ANE 10:1881; BBC 1:cp 43; CDB 75 (cp 233); GBC 136 (cp 23); GGB 94; HBT 96 (cp 1); NGB 1:291; NGW 308; PBA 1:cp 26; PEB 71 (cp 22); PFF 592; PWB 99 (cp 24); RBA 95; RBB 103; WAB 64.

Rail, Spotted (Pardirallus maculatus) BWI 69; DBM cp 1; PMB cp 10.

Rail, Uniform—See **Crake, Uniform**.

Rail, Virginia (Rallus limicola) AAB 139; ABW 110; ANE 9:1646; BBC 1:304, cp 43; CFG cp 5; GBC 136 (cp 23); GGB 91; NGB 1:291; NGW 307; PBA 1:206, 207; PEB 71 (cp 22); PFF 591; PWB 99 (cp 24); RBB 103.

Rail, Yellow (Coturnicops noveboracensis) ALE 8:84; BBC 1:cp 43; CFG cp 5; GBC 136 (cp 23); GGB 92; NGB 1:291; NGW 308; PEB 71 (cp 22); PFF 592; PWB 99 (cp 24); RBB 103.

Railroad Vine (Ipomaea pes-capraea) GGS 142; RUS 2:433.

Rampion, Clustered (Phyteuma comosum) DFP 18 (cp 137); EWF cp 15b; NHE 284.

Ranunculus (Ranunculus hybrids) AGF 201; DFP 22 (cp 176), 23 (cps 177-179), 168 (cp 1344), 169 (cp 1345); EGB 136; LFW 116 (cp 260), 117 (cp 261); MGB 276; MWF 250 (cps 821, 822); OGF 145; PFW 252.

Rape—See **Mustard, Field**.

Raspberry, Creeping (Rubus pedatus) AFP 2:460; CWF 270; RUS 5:147; RWA cp 182; VPN 3:181.

Raspberry, Purple-flowering (Rubus odoratus) FNC 89; HWF cp 101; HYF cp 89; LWF 131 (cp 209); PFF 202; PMF 219; RWA cp 180; TSK 52.

Raspberry, Red (Rubus idaeus) NHE 20; OFP 77; OWF 79; PFF 202; VPN 3:177; WYG 217.

Raspberry, Wild Black (Rubus occidentalis) HYF cp 82; TSK 50, 119, 241.

Rat, Black (Rattus rattus) ALE 11:371; BGM 181 (cp 18); CFG 291; GGM 113; IWE 16:2123; NHE 249; OBV 135; PMG cp 28; SMW 135 (cp 80); WMW 2:903.

Rat, Brown or Common—See **Rat, Norway**.

Rat, Cotton (Sigmodon hispidus) ANE 9:1649; BGM 180 (cp 17); CFG 291; GGM 102; PMG cp 33; WMW 2:802.

Rat, House—See **Rat, Black**.

Rat, Kangaroo (Dipodomys sp.) ANE 6:1010, 1011; ALE 11:297; BGM 149 (cp 14); BMC 134 (cp 15); CFG cp 31; GGM 92, 93; FWA 154; IWE 9:1215; LEA 531; NGA 285; PFF 709; PMF cp 29; SMW 96 (cp 69); WMW 2:744.

Rat, Norway (Rattus norvegicus) ALE 11:371; BGM 181 (cp 18); CFG 291; GGM 112; IWE 4:499-501; JAW 81; LEA 534; NGA 272, 273; NHE 249; OBV 135; PFF 712; PMG cp 28; SMW 135 (cp 81); WMW 2:903.

Rat, Pack—See **Rat, Wood**.

Rat, Pocket—See **Rat, Kangaroo**.

Rat, Rice (Oryzomys palustris) ALE 11:297; BGM 165 (cp 16); CFG 291; GGM 99; GPL 154; IWE 14:1953; PMG cp 33; WMW 2:759.

Rat, Ship—See **Rat, Black**.

Rat, Water—See **Water Rat**.

Rat, Wood (Neotoma sp.) ANE 9:1648; AWW 18, 28; BGM 181 (cp 18); BMC 135 (cp 16); CFG 291; IWE 12:1668, 1669; LEA 537; NGA 282; PFF 710; PMG cp 28; WMW 2:805.

Ratfish (Chimaera monstrosa and Siganus rivulatus) See **Rabbitfish**.

Ratfish (Hydrolagus colliei) ALE 4:128; GGF 29; HPF 66; NGF 216; WFW 216.

IWE 14:1932; NGB 2:254; NGS 341; PWB 274 (cp 55); RBB 299; SAA 139.

Redpoll, Common (Acanthis flammea) AAB 469; ABW 302; ALE 9:391; BBC 2:cp 114; BBE 283; CDB 207 (cp 916); CFG cp 28; GBC 317 (cp 64); GFB 192; GPB 316; NGB 2:254; NGS 340-341; PBA 3:cp 78; PEB 214 (cp 55); PFF 667; PWB 274 (cp 55); RBB 299.

Redstart, American (Setophaga ruticilla) AAB 432; BBC 2:cp 105; CDB 205 (cp 900); CFG cps 18, 19; GBC 285 (cp 60); GBI 101; HBT 241 (cp 14); NGB 2:198; NGS 289; PBA 3:cp 97; PEB 183 (cp 48); PFF 658; PWB 262 (cp 51); RBB 275; TBC 364 (cp 70a).

Redstart, Painted (Setophaga picta) ABW 285; ALE 9:371; BBC 2:cp 97; DBM cp 43; NGB 2:206; NGS 289; PMB cp 37; PWB 262 (cp 51); RBB 275.

Redstart, Slate-throated (Myioborus miniatus) AMB 89 (cp 7); CDB 205 (cp 897); DBM cp 43; PMB cp 37.

Redwood, Coast (Sequoia sempervirens) AFP 1:69; BTN 51; DFP 255 (cp 2038); MTB 84 (cp 5); OBT 101, 124; PFF 124; SFT 146.

Redwood, Dawn (Metasequoia glyptostroboides) BKT cp 8; BTN 51; DFP 254 (cp 2025); EGE 100; MTB 85 (cp 6); OBT 101, 125.

Redwood, Giant (Sequoia gigantea) AFP 1:69; BTN 51; DEW 1:37; DFP 255 (cps 2039, 2040); EGE 106; OBT 101, 124; PFF 123; TGS 38.

Reed, Common (Phragmites communis) BBF 1:232; GGS 145; GPL 53; HMG 191; NHE 106; PFF 358.

Reed, Giant (Arundo donax) AFP 1:183; HMG 188; MWF 47 (cp 80); NHE 109.

Reeve—See **Ruff**.

Reindeer—See **Caribou, Greenland**.

Remora (Echeneis naucrates) ALE 4:103, 5:138; CFG 509; GGF 140; IWE 14:1942-1943; MOL 93; WFW cp 290, 180.

Rheumatism-root—See **Twin-leaf**.

Rhododendron, California (Rhododendron macrophyllum) AFP 3:301; BTN 243; CWF 403; HFP 266, cp 14d; LWF 35 (cp 60); TGS 391; VPN 4:28.

Rhododendron, Carolina (Rhododendron carolinianum) EGE 143; TGS 391.

Rhododendron, Great—See **Laurel, Great**.

Rhododendron Hybrids (Rhododendron sp.) AGF 202-204; DEW 1:239; DFP 222 (cp 1773); EGE 35, 67, 143, 144; FGF 226, 227; HSC 98, 99, 102;

LFW 118 (cps 263-267), 218 (cps 491, 493); MWF 252 (cp 830), 253 (cps 831-834); PFW 109, 110, 111; TGS 390, 406.

Rhododendron, Purple (Rhododendron catawbiense) FNC 131; HYF cp 139; PMF 229; TSK 61.

Rhododendron, White-flowered (Rhododendron albiflorum) AFP 3:300; CWF 402; RWA cp 254; VPN 4:28.

Rhodora (Rhododendron canadensis) PMF 229; RWA cp 260; TGS 375.

Rhubarb (Rheum rhaponticum) OFP 163; PFF 155; WYG 142.

Rhubarb, Guatemala—See **Gout Plant**.

Ribwort—See **Plantain, Narrow-leaved**.

Riccia—See **Liverwort**.

Rice (Oryza sativa) OFP 9; PFF 350.

Rice Root—See **Mission Bells**.

Rice, Wild (Zizania aquatica) FNC 5; GPL 53; PFF 351.

Ricebird (Lonchura punctulata) ALE 9:439; BHB 228 (cp 59); IWE 11:1402; MBH cp 20; PWB 311 (cp 60).

Richweed—See **Horse-balm**.

Ringtail (Bassariscus astutus) ALE 12:94; AWW 19; BGM 100 (cp 9); IWE 3:345; NGA 168; PFF 682; PMG cp 35; WMW 2:1180.

Roadrunner (Geococcyx californianus) ABW 153; ALE 8:370; BBC 1:cp 64; BBW cp 35; CDB 112 (cp 427); CFG cp 21; FWA 156; GPB 184; IWE 15:1963; LBW 177 (cp 97); NGB 2:83; NGW 428-429; PFF 613; PMB cp 15; PWB 151 (cp 38); RBA 137; RBB 159.

Roadrunner, Lesser (Geococcyx velox or G. viaticus) DBM cp 12; PMB cp 15.

Robin, American (Turdus migratorius) AAB 350; ABW 253; ALE 9:290; ANE 9:1704-1705; BBC 2:cp 90; BBE 271; CDB 167 (cp 707); CFG cp 15; GBC 253 (cp 52); GBI 85; GFB 10, 161; GPB 269; IWE 1:32, 33; NGB 2:161; NGS 212, 213; PBA 3:cp 106; PEB 166 (cp 45); PFF 639; PWB 231 (cp 48); RBB 231.

Robin, Clay-colored (Turdus grayi) DBM cp 36; PMB cp 35.

Robin, Rufous-backed (Turdus rufopalliatus) AMB 77 (cp 6); DBM cp 36; PMB cp 35.

Robin's-plantain (Erigeron pulchellus) BBF 3:439; FFK 263; FNC 195; HYF cp 220; LWF 207 (cp 329); PFF 316; PMF 309, 363; RUS 1:481, 2:597, 3:473.

Rudderfish, Banded—See **Amberjack.**

Rue, Common (Ruta graveolens) DFP 237 (cp 1891); EWF cp 35b.

Rue-anemone (Anemonella thalictroides) ANE 1:58; BBF 2:102; FFK 109; HWF cp 68b; HYF cp 55; LWF 249 (cp 391); PFF 170; PMF 23; RUS 1:125, 2:179, 6:161; RWA cp 119.

Rue-anemone, False (Isopyrum biternatum) FFK 109; HYF cp 64; RUS 1:125, 2:179, 6:161.

Ruellia (Ruellia ciliosa) LWF 46 (cp 77); PRP 149; RUS 2:445. (R. humilis) HWF cp 188; RUS 1:351, 2:447, 3:343, 6:543. (R. macrantha) EWF cp 184b; FHP 141; MWF 259 (cp 857). (R. carolinensis) PMF 339; RUS 1:351, 2:445, 3:343. (R. strepens) FFK 137; RUS 2:445, 3:345, 6:539.

Ruff (Philomachus pugnax) ABW 122; ALE 7:255, 8:157, 170; BBE 122; CDB 87 (cp 292); GPB 146; IWE 15:1996-1999; LBW 92 (cp 54); PEB 118 (cp 31); RBB 123; SAA 91; WAB 23, 25, 125.

Rush, Common or Soft (Juncus effusus) AFP 1:353; BBF 1:467; FFK 87; NHE 104; PFF 370.

Rush, Flowering (Butomus umbellatus) DFP 126 (cp 1007); EWF cp 23d; NHE 102; OWF 109; PFW 56.

Rush, Rannoch (Scheuchzeria palustris) AFP 1:97; BBF 1:93; NHE 102; VPN 1:154.

Rush, Shore (Scirpus americanus) GGS 143; GPL 54; NHE 105.

Russula, Pungent (Russula emetica) GMC 49 (cps 95, 96); KMF 91 (cp 21b); LHM 203; NFP 74; NHE 48; ONP 137; PFF 84; SMG 249, cp 187.

Rust, Cedar Apple (Gymnosporangium sp.) NFP 44; PFF 76.

Rust, Grain or Wheat (Puccinia graminis) NFP 43; PFF 76.

Rutabaga (Brassica napobrassica) LPL 175; OFP 173; PFF 184; WYG 141.

Rye, Annual (Secale cereale) HMG 248; OFP 5; PFF 355; PRP 72.

Rye, Wild (Elymus canadensis) BBF 1:293; HMG 260; PFF 357; PRP 35.

Rye-grass (Lolium perenne) AFP 1:237; BBF 1:281; NHE 194; VPN 1:614.

S

Sable, American—See **Marten, American.**

Sabrewing, Violet (Campylopterus hemileucurus) ALE 8:454; DBM cp 14; PMB cp 19.

Sabrewing, Wedge-tailed (Campylopterus curvipennis) ALE 8:454; DBM cp 14; PMB cp 20.

Saddle-fungus—See **Fungus.**

Saffron (Crocus sativus) NHE 241; OFP 133; PFW 148; SGB 65 (cp 6).

Saffron, Meadow—See **Colchicum.**

Sage, Autumn (Salvia greggii) LWF 101 (cp 160); OOW cp 214; RUS 3:275.

Sage, Bladder (Salazaria mexicana) AFP 3:622; LWF 101 (cp 162); RUS 3:379, 4:559, 6:555.

Sage, Blue or Meadow (Salvia pratensis) BBF 3:129; LFW 220 (cp 494); NHE 186; OWF 177; RUS 2:473, 3:371; VPN 4:271. (S. azurea) RUS 6:551.

Sage, Common (Salvia officinalis) DFP 238 (cp 1897); OFP 141; OGF 105; PFF 289; PFW 154; TGF 189.

Sage, Hop (Grayia spinosa) AFP 2:92; PFF 157; VPN 2:204.

Sage, Jerusalem (Phlomis fruiticosa) DFP 217 (cp 1731); EWF cp 37b; HSC 87; MWF 230 (cp 750); OGF 105; TGS 342.

Sage, Lyre-leaved (Salvia lyrata) FFK 204; FNC 163; HYF cp 167; PMF 351; RUS 1:371, 2:473, 3:371, 6:551.

Sage, Pitcher (Salvia spathacea) AFP 3:640; OOW cp 189; RUS 4:551, 5:457.

Sage, Russian (Perovskia atriplicifolia) DFP 164 (cp 1309); HSC 87; OGF 153; TGF 204; TGS 342.

Sage, Scarlet (Salvia splendens) AGF 218; DFP 47 (cp 317); EGA 151; FGF 239; LFW 264 (cp 591); MWF 261 (cp 863); OGF 127; PFF 290; PFW 155; TGF 189. (S. elegans) EWF cp 163g.

Sagebrush (Artemisia tridentata) AFP 4:413; BBF 3:330; BTN 267; CWF 530; PFF 328; VPN 5:72.

Sagewort—See **Mugwort** and **Wormwood.**

Saguaro—See **Cactus, Saguaro.**

Sailfish (Istiophorus albicans or I. platypterus) ALE 5:192; GGF 89; IWE 15:2008-2009; NGF 314, 319-321; WFW 221.

Sainfoin (Psoralea onobrychis) BBF 2:365; HYF cp 101; PMF 353; RUS 1:519, 2:355.

St. Andrew's Cross (Ascyrum hypericoides) BBF 2:528; FFK 99; PMF 157; RUS 1:154, 2:209, 3:137, 6:201.

Sandpiper, Aleutian or Rock (Erolia ptilocnemis) NGB 1:276; NGW 337; PWB 102 (cp 25), 115 (pl 30), 119 (cp 32); RBB 121.

Sandpiper, Baird's (Calidris bairdii or Erolia bairdii) BBC 1:cp 52; BBE 131; CFG cp 9; GBC 156 (cp 27); NGB 1:278; NGW 339; PBA 1:cp 35; PEB 99 (pl 28), 119 (cp 32); PWB 115 (pl 30), 119 (cp 32); RBB 125.

Sandpiper, Buff-breasted (Tryngites subruficollis) ALE 8:170; BBC 1:cp 50; BBE 131; CDB 88 (cp 300); CFG cp 9; GBC 161 (cp 30); NGB 1:280; NGW 342; PBA 1:cp 37; PEB 99 (pl 28), 119 (cp 32); PWB 115 (pl 30), 119 (cp 32); RBB 117.

Sandpiper, Curlew (Calidris ferruginea or Erolia ferruginea) BBE 127; CDB 85 (cp 279); CFG cp 9; NGW 340; PEB 99 (pl 28), 118 (cp 31), 119 (cp 32); RBB 123.

Sandpiper, Least (Calidris minutilla or Erolia minutilla) AAB 172; ABW 121; ANE 9:1738-1739; BBC 1 1:cp 53; BBE 131; CFG cp 9; GBC 156 (cp 27), 168 (pl 31); GBI 39; NGB 1:278; NGW 339; PBA 1:cp 35; PEB 99 (pl 28), 119 (cp 32); PFF 599; PWB 115 (pl 30), 119 (cp 32); RBB 125; TBC 200 (cp 25b).

Sandpiper, Pectoral (Calidris melanotus or Erolia melanotus) AAB 171; BBC 1:cp 52; BBE 131; CFG cp 9; GBC 161 (cp 30); GGS 149; NGB 1:280; NGW 338; PBA 1:cp 35; PEB 99 (pl 28), 119 (cp 32); PFF 598; PWB 115 (pl 30), 119 (cp 32); RBB 123.

Sandpiper, Purple (Calidris maritima or Erolia maritima) AAB 169; BBE 125, 132; CDB 85 (cp 281); CFG 102; GBC 140 (cp 25); IWE 15:2022; NGB 1:276; NGW 337; PBA 1:cp 34; PEB 98 (pl 28), 119 (cp 32); PFF 598; RBB 121; SAA 91.

Sandpiper, Red-backed—See **Dunlin.**

Sandpiper, Rock—See **Sandpiper, Aleutian.**

Sandpiper, Rufous-necked (Erolia ruficollis) PWB 119 (cp 32); RBB 125.

Sandpiper, Semi-palmated (Calidris pusilla or Ereunetes pusillus) ANE 9:1738-1739; BBC 1:cp 53; BBE 131; CFG cp 9; GBC 156 (cp 27); NGB 1:282; NGW 341; PBA 1:cp 35; PEB 99 (pl 28), 119 (cp 32); PWB 119 (cp 32); RBB 125; TBC 200 (cp 25b).

Sandpiper, Sharp-tailed (Calidris acuminata or Erolia acuminata) BBE 131; GBC 160 (cp 29); NGB 1:280; NGW 338; PWB 119 (cp 32); RBB 123.

Sandpiper, Solitary (Tringa solitaria) AAB 164; BBC 1:cp 51; BBE 123; CFG cp 9; GBC 141 (cp 26), 168 (pl 31); GPL 148; NGB 1:274; NGW 335; PBA 1:cp 36; PEB 98 (pl 27), 118 (cp 31); PFF 596; PWB 114 (pl 29), 118 (cp 31); RBB 117.

Sandpiper, Spotted (Actitis macularia) AAB 164; ABW 121; ALE 7:385; BBC 1:cp 48; BBE 123; CFG cp 9; GBC 141 (cp 26), 168 (pl 31); GBI 38; GPL 149; NGB 1:274; NGW 334; PBA 1:cp 36; PEB 98 (pl 27), 119 (cp 32); PFF 596; PWB 114 (pl 29), 119 (cp 32); RBA 109; RBB 117; TBC 192 (cp 24a).

Sandpiper, Stilt (Micropalama himantopus) AAB 175; ALE 8:170; BBE 123; CDB 87 (cp 288); CFG cp 9; GBC 141 (cp 26); NGB 1:282; NGW 341; PBA 1:cps 33, 34; PEB 98 (pl 27), 118 (cp 31); PWB 114 (pl 29), 118 (cp 31); RBB 119.

Sandpiper, Upland—See **Plover, Upland.**

Sandpiper, Western (Ereunetes mauri) AAB 176; ANE 9:1738-1739; BBC 1:cp 53; CFG cp 9; GBC 156 (cp 27); GGS 149; NGB 1:282; NGW 341; PEB 119 (cp 32); PWB 115 (pl 30), 119 (cp 32); RBB 125.

Sandpiper, White-rumped (Calidris fuscicollis or Erolia fuscicollis) AAB 171; BBC 1:cp 52; BBE 131; CDB 85 (cp 280); CFG cp 9; GBC 156 (cp 27), 168 (pl 31); NGB 1:278; NGW 339; PBA 1:cp 35; PEB 99 (pl 28), 119 (cp 32); PWB 115 (pl 30), 119 (cp 32); RBB 125.

Sand-spurry (Spergularia macrotheca) AFP 2:157; RUS 4:253, 5:219; VPN 2:301.

Sand-spurry, Pink (Spergularia rubra) CWF 139; NHE 226; PMF 265, 311; RUS 4:253, 5:223, 6:269.

Sand-spurry, Sea (Spergularia marina) NHE 135; RUS 3:169, 4:253, 5:223, 6:267. (S. marginata) OWF 113.

Sand-verbena, Beach (Abronia umbellata) AFP 2:109; EGA 90; GGS 145; OOW cp 220; RUS 4:109, 5:103; VPN 2:223.

Sand-verbena, Desert (Abronia villosa) AFP 2:109; LWF 67 (cp 107); OOW cp 259; RUS 4:109; RWF 106, 109.

Sand-verbena, White (Abronia fragrans) BBF 2:33; HYF cp 46; RUS 3:85, 4:103, 6:119; VPN 2:221.

Sand-verbena, Yellow (Abronia latifolia) AFP 2:109; CWF 126; GGS 145; OOW cp 126; RUS 4:109, 5:103; VPN 2:223.

Sandworm—See **Worm, Clam.**

Sandwort, Capitate (Arenaria congesta) AFP 2:153; RUS 4:249, 5:221, 6:275; VPN 2:257.

Sandwort, Large-leaved (Arenaria macrophylla) CWF 127; RUS 5:221, 6:269; VPN 2:260.

Sandwort, Mountain (Arenaria groenlandica) BBF 2:57; PMF 37; RUS 1:195, 2:253.

Sanicle—See **Snakeroot, Western.**

Sapsucker, Red-breasted (Sphyrapicus ruber) NGB 2:61; PWB 167 (cp 40); TBC 284 (cp 40a).

Sapsucker, Williamson's (Sphyrapicus thyroideus) BBC 2:cp 72; BBW cp 49; GBC 205 (cp 42); IWE 15:2023; NGB 2:61; NGS 91; PWB 167 (cp 40); RBB 185; WAB 41.

Sapsucker, Yellow-bellied (Sphyrapicus varius) AAB 321; ABW 192; ALE 9:119; AWW 25; CDB 139 (cp 554); CFG cp 12; GBC 205 (cp 42); GBI 64; GPB 228; NGB 2:61; NGS 91; PBA 2:cp 62; PEB 154 (cp 41); PFF 622; PWB 167 (cp 40); RBA 166; RBB 185; TBC 282 (cp 39b).

Sardine, California (Sardinops caerulea) GGF 38; HPF 100.

Sargassum (Sargassum sp.) GGS 25; KSL 156; NFP 16; PFF 58.

Sargassum Fish—See **Frogfish.**

Sarsaparilla, Bristly (Aralia hispida) BBF 2:618; PMF 51; RUS 1:215.

Sarsaparilla, False (Hardenbergia violacea) EWF cp 130f; MEP 59; MWF 147 (cp 450).

Sarsaparilla, Wild (Aralia nudicaulis) AFP 3:215; BBF 2:618; CWF 338; HYF cp 124; LWF 138 (cp 219); PFF 263; RUS 1:215, 2:275, 6:301; VPN 3:507.

Sassafras (Sassafras albidum) BBF 2:134; BKT cp 112; BTN 157; DEW 1:60 (cps 28, 29); EGT 143; FNC 73; PFF 179; TGS 183; TSK 26, 108, 140, 480, 481.

Satin Flower—See **Godetia.**

Sauger (Stizostedion canadense) CFG 557; NGF 278.

Sausage Tree (Kigelia pinnata) DEW 2:177; MEP 136; PFW 44.

Savory, Winter (Satureia montana) DFP 171 (cp 1365); OFP 143; TGS 358.

Sawfish (Pristis pectinatus) ALE 4:118; GGF 28; HFW 56; IWE 15:2024-2025; NGF 330.

Sawfly, Curled Rose (Allantus cinctus) GBB cp 32; GIP 95; OBI 145.

Sawfly, Currant (Nematus ribesii) GBB cp 32; GIP 131; OBI 145; SCI 513.

Sawfly, Elm (Cimbex americanus) BIA cp 15; GIP 145; PFF 495; SCI 517.

Saw-grass (Cladium jamaicensis or Mariscus jamaicensis) BBF 1:348; GPL 55.

Saxicave, Arctic (Hiatella arctica) AAS 452; ALE 3:177; ASN 257; CFG 593; MGS pl 25; NHE 168; OIB 87.

Saxifrage, Early (Saxifraga virginensis) FFK 166; HWF cp 87a; HYF cp 75; LWF 256 (cp 405); PFF 191; PMF 69; RUS 1:205, 2:261.

Saxifrage, Merten's (Saxifraga mertensiana) AFP 2:364; CWF 222; HFP 142; RUS 5:247, 6:279; VPN 3:48.

Saxifrage, Purple (Saxifraga oppositifolia) AFP 2:356; CWF 226; DFP 25 (cp 197); EWF cp 2g; NHE 271; OGF 21; PFW 274; RUS 5:249, 6:279; RWA cp 162; VPN 3:57.

Saxifrage, Swamp (Saxifraga pensylvanica) HWF cp 86; PMF 69, 377; RUS 1:205, 2:259.

Scabiosa—See **Pincushion Flower.**

Scabious, Field (Knautia arvensis) BBF 3:290; CWF 507; NHE 235; OWF 157; PMF 301, 309; RUS 1:425, 6:615.

Scad (Trachurus trachurus) IWE 15:2030-2031; NHE 154; OBV 31; WEA 196. (Decapterus macarellus) CFG 487.

Scale, Black (Saissetia oleae) GIP 134; SCI 166.

Scale, Brown or Orange (Coccus hesperidum) GIP 87; PEI 144.

Scale, California Red (Aonidiella aurantii) GIP 133; SCI 161.

Scale, Cottony-cushion (Icerya purchasi) GGI 41; GIP 12, 135; IWE 15:2036; SCI 166; SIG cp 47b.

Scale, Cottony-maple (Pulvinaria innumerabilis) BIA 139; GBB cp 34; GIP 145.

Scale, Euonymus (Unaspis euonymi) GBB cp 33; SCI 163.

Scale, Juniper (Diaspis carueli) GBB cp 33. (Carulaspis juniperi) SCI 163.

Scale, Oystershell (Lepidosaphes ulmi) BIA 139; EGE 150; GBB cp 34; GGI 41; GIP 145; OBI 35; PFF 459; SCI 163; SIG cp 47c.

Scale, Pine-needle (Phenacaspis pinifolia) GBB cp 33; GIP 145; SCI 163.

Scale, San Jose (Aspidiotus perniciosus) BIA 139; GBB cp 34; GGI 40; GIP 134; OBI 35; SCI 161.

Scaleworm—See **Worm, Scale.**

Scallop, Atlantic Bay (Aequipecten irradians) AAS cp 33i; ASN 211; CFG cp 46; GGS 87; GSS 136; PFF 419.

Scallop, Atlantic Deep Sea (Placopecten magellanicus) AAS cp 33c; ASN 209; CFG 572; GGS 87; GSS 136.

Scallop, Calico (Aequipecten gibbus) AAS cp 33j; ASN 211; GGS 86; GSS 136.

Scallop, Hind's or Smooth (Pecten hindsii) ASN 209; GAS 200. (Chlamys rubidus) MGS pl 15.

Sea Bass, White (Cynoscion nobilis) GGF 119; HPF 295; NGF 125; WFW 171.

Sea Bat—See **Starfish, Sea Bat.**

Sea Biscuit—See **Sand Dollar.**

Sea Blush (Plectritis congesta) AFP 4:60; CWF 488, 498, 507; RUS 5:449; VPN 4:476.

Sea Colander (Agarum cribrosum) GGS 28; PFF 56. (A. fimbriatum) GUS 55.

Sea Cow (Trichechus manatus) See **Manatee.**

Sea Cow, Steller's (Hydrodamalis stelleri) ALE 12:510; LMA 40; PWC 241; WMW 2:1334.

Sea Cucumber, Burrowing or Worm-like (Leptosynapta inhaerens or L. clarki) ALE 3:302; CFG 636; GAS 174; GGS 66; JSS 245; KSL 217; OIB 187.

Sea Cucumber, Creeping Pedal (Psolus chitonoides) GAS 176; JSS 245; KSL cp 18; RCT 275 (pl 32).

Sea Cucumber, Large Red (Parastichopus californicus or Stichopus californicus) GAS 182; GGS 66; JSS 247; KSL cp 17; PFF 406; RCT 123 (pl 13).

Sea Cucumber, Red (Cucumaria miniata) ALE 3:312; BLA 270 (cp 140); GAS 178; JSS 245; KSL cps 17, 18. (Psolus phantapus) CFG 636.

Sea Cucumber, Tailed (Cucumaria frondosa) FWA 385; GGS 66; PFF 406.

Sea Cucumber, White (Eupentacta quinquesemita) BLA 270 (cp 140); GAS 180; KSL 99; RCT 277 (pl 33).

Sea Elephant—See **Seal, Elephant.**

Sea Fern (Bryopsis corticulans) GUS 17; PFF 52. (B. plumosa) GGS 23; NHE 140.

Sea Fir—See **Hydroid, Double-branching.**

Sea Gherkin—See **Sea Cucumber.**

Sea Grass (Enteromorpha sp.) DEW 3:53 (cp 9); GGS 22; GUS 3, 5, 7; KSL 108; NHE 140; ONP 27; PFF 51.

Sea Horse, American (Hippocampus hudsonius) CFG 480; FWA 388; HFW 81 (cp 33); LEA 211; LFI 114; MOL 10, 20, 89; NGF 303-311; SOS 43.

Sea Kale (Rhodymenia palmata) GUS 123; OFP 187; ONP 19; PFF 63.

Sea Lettuce (Ulva lactuca) GGS 22; GUS 9; NFP 16; NHE 140; ONP 9; PFF 53.

Sea Lily (Crinoid sp.) ALE 3:292; BAW 309; FWA 329; GAS 164; IWE 15:2068, 2069.

Sea Lion, California (Zalopus californianus) ALE 12:373, 400; BGM 90; FWA 419; GGM 64; JAW 142; LEA 578; NGA 352, 354-355; PMG cp 17; SMW 143 (cp 95); SOS 128, 142.

Sea Lion, Northern or Steller's (Eumetopias jubata) ALE 8:229, 12:373, 400; ANE 9:1764; BGM 90; BMC 327 (cp 35); FWA 318-319; IWE 15:2070-2071; NGA 342-343, 357; PFF 698; PMG cp 17; WMW 2:1288.

Sea Moss—See **Sea Fern.**

Sea Mouse (Aphrodite aculeata) ALE 1:373; AWW 100; GGS 57; IWE 15:2075; OIB 95. (A. hastata) CFG 638. (A. japonica) GAS 80.

Sea Nettle (Dactylometra quinquecirrha) BLA 79; CFG cp 47.

Sea Otter—See **Otter, Sea.**

Sea Palm—See **Kelp, Sea Palm.**

Sea Pen (Leioptilum quadrangularis) BLA 103; GAS 48. (Pennatula aculeata) GGS 52. (Stylatula elongata) JSS 91; SOS 59. (Veretillum cynomorium) ALE 1:263; BLA 38 (cp 10).

Sea Raven (Hemitripterus americanus) CFG 508; FWA 303; GGF 124.

Sea Rocket (Cakile edentula) AFP 2:273; BBF 2:196; CWF 183; HWF cp 82a; PMF 273; RUS 1:181, 183, 2:235, 237, 3:153, 4:231, 5:187; VPN 2:467.

Sea Slater (Ligia oceanica or L. pallasii) ALE 1:496; BLA 176 (cp 89); GAS 368; IWE 16:2167; JSS 292; KSL 123; RCT 178; WEA 395. (Nerocila bivittata) IWE 16:2168.

Sea Slug—See **Nudibranch.**

Sea Snail—See **Snailfish.**

Sea Spider (Nymphon sp.) FWA 380; IWE 15:2085; LEA 185; OIB 127; SOS 17, 115.

Sea Squirt, Broad-base (Cnemidocarpa joannae or C. finmarkiensis) GAS 424; KSL 198; RCT 278.

Sea Squirt, Hairy (Boltenia villosa) GAS 426; KSL 105.

Sea Squirt, Inflated (Corella inflata) GAS 420. (C. willmeriana) KSL 105.

Sea Squirt, Star (Botryllus schlosseri) ALE 3:428, 455; BLA 271 (cp 142); IWE 15:2086-2087; LEA 202; NHE 160; OIB 191.

Sea Squirt, Tube (Ciona intestinalis) ALE 3:428; BLA 288; CFG 658; FWA 385; GGS 40; IWE 15:2088; LEA 193; MOL 91; NHE 160; OIB 189.

Sea Squirt, Warty (Pyura haustor) GAS 428; KSL 104; RCT 275 (pl 32).

Sea Staghorn—See **Seaweed, Sponge.**

Sea Star—See **Starfish.**

Sea Urchin (Cidaris tribuloides or Eucidaris tribuloides) ALE 3:334; GGS 64.

Seedeater, White-collared (Sporophila torqueola) AMB 104 (cp 9); DBM cp 46; NGS 338; PMB cp 46; PWB 274 (cp 55); RBB 303.

Self-heal or Heal-all (Prunella laciniata) NHE 186; OWF 97. (P. grandiflora) NHE 186; OGF 81.

Self-heal or Heal-all, Common (Prunella vulgaris) AFP 3:629; BBF 3:115; CWF 459; FFK 205; HFP 311, cp 22a; HWF cp 187; HYF cp 172; LWF 198 (cp 312); NHE 186; OWF 145; PFF 289; PMF 351; RUS 1:375, 2:481, 3:377, 4:559, 5:465, 6:555; VPN 4:271.

Senna, Wild (Cassia marilandica) BBF 2:336; EGP 103; FFK 211; HWF cp 104; RUS 1:209, 2:319, 6:337.

Sensitive Plant (Mimosa pudica) DEW 1:283 (cp 175); EGA 136; LPL 88, 89. (M. strigillosa) RUS 2:317, 3:199.

Sensitive Plant, Wild (Cassia nicitans) HWF cp 105a; PMF 153; RUS 2:319, 3:209, 6:337.

Sensitive-brier (Schrankia microphylla) BBF 2:334; FFK 155; FNC 97; RUS 2:319, 3:205. (S. uncinata) BBF 2:333; PRP 100; RUS 3:205, 4:301, 6:333.

Sequoia—See **Redwood, Giant.**

Sergeant Major (Abudefduf saxatilis) GGF 132; NGF 205; SOS 82; WFW 384.

Serpent-star—See **Brittle-star.**

Serviceberry (Amelanchier sp.) AFP 2:472; BBF 2:292; BTN 173; CWF 231; DFP 181 (cps 1444, 1445); EGT 99; EWF cp 152c; FNC 96; MTB 289 (cp 26); PFF 198; PMF 3; RWA cp 190; TGS 246; TSK 44, 134; VPN 3:396.

Shad, American (Alosa sapidissima) CFG 521; CFW 43; GGF 37; HPF 95; NGF 267; PFF 505; WFW 107.

Shad, Gizzard (Dorosoma cepedianum) CFG 521; GGF 40; GPL 128.

Shad, Hickory (Pomolobus mediocris) CFG 521; NGF 268.

Shadbush—See **Serviceberry.**

Shadscale—See **Saltbush.**

Shaggy-name—See **Mushroom, Shaggy-mane.**

Shark, Basking (Cetorhinus maximus) ALE 4:93; CFG 465; CFW 29; HPF 34; NHE 159; OBV 5; WFW 149.

Shark, Blue (Prionace glauca or Carcharias glaucus) ALE 4:103; CFG 465; CFW 28; HPF 41; LFI 87; LSE 141; NGF 324; NHE 159; OBV 5; SOS 101; WFW 296.

Shark, Brown (Eulamia milberti) CFG 465; GGF 22.

Shark, Bull or Ground (Carcharhinus leucas) CFG 465; IWE 20:2671; LEA 231; NGF 327.

Shark, Greenland (Somniosus microcephalus) CFG 465; NHE 159; OBV 5; SOS 115; WFW 334.

Shark, Hammerhead (Sphyrna zygaena or S. mokarran) ALE 4:103; CFG 465; GGF 22; IWE 8:1014, 1015; LFI 22; LSE 139; NGF 322; OBV 9; SOS 84; WFW cp 6, 336.

Shark, Leopard (Triakis semifasciata) LFI 90; NGF 329.

Shark, Mackerel (Lamna nasus) ALE 4:104; CFG 465; HPF 36; IWE 14:1822; LFI 125; OBV 3; PFF 503.

Shark, Mako (Isurus oxyrinchus) AWW 147; CFG 465; HFW 20; LSE 140; NGF 326; OBV 3.

Shark, Man-eating—See **Shark, White.**

Shark, Nurse (Ginglymostoma cirratum) GGF 22; HFW 34 (cp 2); MOL 109; NGF 324; SOS 333.

Shark, Porbeagle—See **Shark, Mackerel.**

Shark, Sand (Carcharias taurus) CFG 465; HFW 18; IWE 14:1943; LEA 224; LFI 90; NGF 326.

Shark, Soupfin (Galeorhinus zyopterus) GGF 23; HPF 39; LFI 161; WFW 194.

Shark, Thresher (Alopias vulpinus) ALE 4:103; CFG 465; GGF 23; HPF 30; IWE 18:2404; NGF 329; OBV 5; SOS 100-101.

Shark, Tiger (Galeocerdo cuvieri) CFG 465; GGF 23; NGF 323; WFW 193.

Shark, Whale (Rhincodon typus) ALE 4:93; CFW 28; GGF 24; HFW 23; IWE 19:2598-2599; LFI 91; NGF 328; SOS 102; WFW 310.

Shark, White (Carcharodon carcharias) CFG 465; CFW 28; GGF 23; HPF 32; IWE 10:1395; NGF 324; SOS 100, 101; WFW 144.

Shark-eye—See **Moon Snail, Atlantic.**

Shaving Brush Tree (Pachira macrocarpa) LFW 256 (cp 570); PFW 47. (P. insignis) DEW 1:217 (cp 126).

Sheartail, Slender (Doricha enicura) DBM cp 15; PMB cps 19, 20. ·

Shearwater, Audubon's (Puffinus lherminieri) BWI 19; CFG 19; DBM cp 3; NGB 1:45; NGW 61; PEB 7 (pl 2); RBB 25.

Shearwater, Cory's (Puffinus diomedea) BBE 22; CFG 19; NGB 1:43; NGW 58; NHE 144; PEB 7 (pl 2); RBB 25.

Shearwater, Greater (Puffinus gravis) BBE 22; CDB

37 (cp 32); CFG 19; GBC 28 (pl 3); NGB 1:43;
NGW 59; NHE 144; PBA 1:81; PEB 7 (pl 2); RBB
25; WAB 23, 215.

Shearwater, Manx (Puffinus puffinus) AAB 18; ABW
34; ALE 7:147; BBE 21; CDB 38 (cp 34); CFG 19;
NGW 61; NHE 144; PWB 7 (pl 2); RBB 25; SAA 74.
(P. opisthomelas) DBM cp 3; NGB 1:47.

Shearwater, Pacific or Wedge-tailed (Puffinus pacificus)
AAB 14; BHB 51 (cp 3); CDB 38 (cp 33); DBM
cp 3; MBH 64 (cp 7).

Shearwater, Pale-footed (Puffinus carneipes) NGW 59;
PWB 7 (pl 2); RBB 27.

Shearwater, Pink-footed (Puffinus creatopus) NGB
1:47; NGW 58; PWB 7 (pl 2); RBB 25.

Shearwater, Slender-billed (Puffinus tenuirostris) AAB
17; ABW 35; AWW 147; CDB 38 (cp 35); GBC 28
(pl 3); NGB 1:47; NGW 61; PWB 7 (pl 2); RBB 27;
SAA 74; WAB 213.

Shearwater, Sooty (Puffinus griseus) ANE 10:1801;
BBE 23; CFG 19; GBC 28 (pl 3); GFB 25; GPB 47;
IWE 16:2106-2107; NGB 1:45; NGW 60; PEB 7 (pl
2); PWB 7 (pl 2); RBB 27; SAA 74; SOS 252.

Sheep, Big Horn—See **Sheep, Rocky Mountain**.

Sheep, Dall's Mountain (Ovis dallii) ALE 13:497;
BGM 225 (cp 24); BMC 391 (cp 46); FWA 246;
NGA 113; PMG cp 38; SAA 117; SLP 75; WMW
2:1477.

Sheep, Domestic (Ovis ammon or O. aries) ALE
13:498; IWE 16:2110-2113; LEA 608; PFF 729,
730; WEA 333.

Sheep Ked—See **Tick, Sheep**.

Sheep, Rocky Mountain (Ovis canadensis) ALE
13:497; ANE 10:1802; BGM 225 (cp 24); BMC 391
(cp 45); FWA 246; GGM 140; IWE 2:194-196; JAW
207; LEA 607; LNA 170-171; LVS 129; NGA 111;
PFF 730; PMG cp 38; SLP 86, 87; SMW 287 (cp
187); WMW 2:1477.

Sheep, Stone's Mountain (Ovis stonei) ALE 13:497;
NGF 112.

Sheep's-bit (Jasione montana) NHE 188; OWF 179;
RUS 1:347.

Sheepshead (Archosargus probatocephalus) CFG 494;
GGF 116; MOL 113; NGF 202.

Shell-flower, Mexican—See **Tiger Flower**.

Shepherd's Purse (Capsella bursa-pastoris) AFP 2:293;
BBF 2:158; DEW 1:142; NHE 217; OWF 71; PFF
182; PMF 83; RUS 1:181, 2:235, 3:161, 4:235,
5:183, 6:253; VPN 2:467.

Shield-fern—See **Fern, Shield**.

Shiner, Common (Notropis cornutus) CFG 539; NGF
268; PFF 511.

Shiner, Emerald (Notropis atherinoides) CFG 539;
GGF 59.

Shiner, Golden (Notemigonus chrysoleucus) CFG
539; GGF 58; GPL 123; NGF 269; PFF 511.

Shinleaf—See also **Wintergreen** (Pyrola).

Shinleaf (Pyrola elliptica) BBF 2:669; HWF cp 151b;
HYF cp 131; PMF 27; RUS 1:251, 4:339, 6:367;
VPN 4:25.

Shipworm (Teredo navalis or T. norvegica) ALE
3:177; CFG 594; GGS 110; GSS 155; IWE 16:2124;
NHE 168; OIB 87; (T. diegensis) MGS pl 26.
(Bankia setacea) GAS 244; KSL 95.

Shoeflower—See **Hibiscus**.

Shooting-star (Dodecatheon meadia) DFP 139 (cp
1112); FFK 116; FNC 143; HYF cp 142; LWF 194
(cp 305); OGF 45; PFW 243; PMF 221; RUS 1:297,
2:383, 3:279, 6:439; RWA cp 292; TGF 157.

Shooting-star, Alpine (Dodecatheon alpinum) AFP
3:339; DFP 7 (cp 56); RUS 4:419, 5:365, 6:439;
VPN 4:42.

Shooting-star, Few-flowered (Dodecatheon pauci-
florum or D. pulchellum) AFP 3:343; CWF 422;
EWF cp 156d; RUS 5:365, 6:439; RWA cp 293;
VPN 4:48.

Shooting-star, Jeffrey's (Dodecatheon jeffreyi) AFP
3:339; CWF 415; OOW cp 151; RUS 5:365, 6:439;
VPN 4:48.

Shoveler (Spatula clypeata) AAB 71; ALE 7:255;
ANE 3:570; BBC 1:cp 16, cp 18; CDB 50 (cp 96);
CFG cp 2, 41, 42; GBC 77 (cp 10); GGB 53; KWF
418 (cp 15), 422 (cp 17), 454 (cp 33); NGB 1:121;
NGW 170, 171; NHE 112; PBA 1:cp 14; PEB 22 (pl
7), 26 (pl 9), 39 (cp 14); PFF 568; PWB 34 (pl 7),
59 (cp 14); RBB 49; TBC 92 (cp 8b).

Shrew, Arctic (Sorex arcticus) BMC 6 (cp 1); BGM
20 (cp 1); CFG cp 31; GGM 22; PMG cp 5; SAA
136.

Shrew, Desert or Gray (Notiosorex crawfordi) ALE
10:189; GGM 23; PMG cp 5; WMW 1:151.

Shrew, Least or Little Short-tailed (Cryptotis parva)
ALE 10:189; BGM 20 (cp 1); CFG cp 31; GGM 22;
PMG cp 5; WMW 1:150.

Shrew, Masked (Sorex cinereus) BGM 20 (cp 1); BMC
6 (cp 1), 7 (cp 2); CFG cp 31; GGM 22; JAW 32;
NGA 324; PFF 680; PMG cp 5; SAA 136.

Shrew, Merriam (Sorex merriami) BGM 20 (cp 1); CFG 263.

Shrew, Pygmy (Microsorex hoyi) ALE 10:189; BMC 6 (cp 1); CFG 263; GGM 21; PMG cp 5; WMW 1:144.

Shrew, Short-tailed (Blarina brevicauda) ALE 10:189; ANE 10:1807; BGM 20 (cp 1); BMC 7 (cp 2); CFG cp 31; GGM 23; NGA 324; PFF 679; PMG cp 5; WMW 1:148.

Shrew, Water (Sorex palustris) ALE 10:189; BGM 20 (cp 1); BMC 6 (cp 1); CFG 263; GGM 23; GPL 154; PFF 680; PMG cp 5.

Shrew-mole (Neurotrichus gibbsi) ALE 10:190; BGM 20 (cp 1); GBI 19; PMG cp 4; WMW 1:172.

Shrike, Loggerhead or Migrant (Lanius ludovicianus) AAB 374; ANE 10:1810; BBC 2:cp 94; CFG cp 15; GBC 256 (cp 53); GBI 93; GFB 174; NGB 2:221; NGS 237; PEB 167 (cp 46); PFF 644; PWB 230 (cp 47); RBB 243.

Shrike, Northern (Lanius excubitor or L. borealis) AAB 373; ABW 268; ALE 9:195, 201, 202; ANE 10:1811; AWW 19; BBC 2:cp 94; BBE 208; CDB 157 (cp 651); GBC 256 (cp 53); GPB 259; IWE 3:334, 335, 16:2131; LBW 228 (cp 132); NGB 2:221; NGS 236; PBA 3:cp 90; PEB 167 (cp 46); PFF 644; PWB 230 (cp 47); RBB 243.

Shrike-tanager, Black-throated (Lanio aurantius) DBM cp 42; PMB cp 42.

Shrimp, Alaska or Gray (Crago alaskensis) GAS 372; KSL 208.

Shrimp, Edible (Penaeus astecus or P. setiferus) GGS 70; PAK 103.

Shrimp, Fairy (Branchinecta paludosa) GPL 89. (Eubranchipus sp.) BAW 274; GPL 89; PFF 427. (Chirocephalus sp.) IWE 6:729; OIB 135.

Shrimp, Ghost (Callianassa californiensis) JSS 328; KSL 230; NGF 186-187; RCT 293 (pl 41); SOS 270; (C. gigas) GAS 378.

Shrimp, Grass (Palaemonetes vulgaris) BAW 274-4; CFG 650. (P. paludosus) GPL 93.

Shrimp, Mantis (Squilla empusa) CFG cp 48; GGS 70. (Pseudosquilla bigelowi) BLA 210 (cp 91).

Shrimp, Opossum (Mysis or Neomysis sp.) IWE 12:1618, 1619; NHE 131; OIB 133. (Gnathophausia sp.) IWE 12:1619; MOL 79.

Shrimp, Phantom (Caprella kennerlyi) GAS 358; JSS 282; RCT 118.

Shrimp Plant (Beloperone guttata) DFP 54 (cp 431); EWF cp 184a; FHP 107; LFW 230 (cp 513, 515); MEP 144; MFW 56 (cp 113); PFW 14.

Shrimp, Sand (Crango septemspinosus) CFG cp 47; GGS 70; PFF 430.

Sicklepod (Arabis canadensis) BBF 2:182; PMF 87; RUS 1:173.

Sicklepod, Rushweed (Hoffmanseggia drepanocarpa) OOW cp 106; RUS 3:209, 4:305, 6:333.

Side-saddle Flower—See **Pitcher Plant** (Sarracenia purpurea).

Sidewinder (Crotalus cerastes) AWW 18; CGR 331; DRW pl 73; FWA 160, 161; GRA 113; IWE 16:2136; LFO 146; LRE 78, 91, 98; MAR 197 (pl 79), 198 (pl 80); PFF 548; PRW pl 135; SIR 253 (cp 136); SRA cp 38.

Silk Tassel (Garrya elliptica) AFP 3:285; DFP 203 (cp 1619); EWF cp 155e; HSC 55; MWF 139 (cp 417); OGF 1; PFW 120; VPN 3:591.

Silk Tree (Albizzia julibrissin) AGF 222; DEW 1:304; EGT 36, 97; LFW 4 (cp 8); MEP 49; TGS 134. (A. lophantha) MWF 35 (cp 36).

Silkweed—See **Milkweed, Common.**

Silverbell Tree (Halesia carolina) BBF 2:722; BTN 251; EGT 118; TGS 407; TSK 56, 289, 416, 417. (H. monticola) DFP 204 (cp 1628); TGS 407.

Silverberry (Elaeagnus commutata) CWF 318; RWA cps 237, 238. (E. argentea) BBF 2:576; VPN 3:462.

Silverfish (Lepisma saccharina) ALE 2:73; GGI 153; GIP 8, 34; IWE 3:284; KIA 20; KIW 33 (cp 1); OBI 1; PEI 30; PFF 442; SCI 58; SIG pl 1.

Silver-lace Vine (Polygonum auberti) AGF 223; MWF 239 (cp 780); TGS 71.

Silverleaf (Psoralea argophylla) BBF 2:363; HYF cp 100; PMF 353; RUS 1:519, 3:253, 4:371, 6:385; VPN 3:350.

Silverrod—See **Goldenrod, White.**

Silverside (Menidia menidia) CFG cp 41. (M. beryllina) GGF 81.

Silverside, Brook (Labidesthes sicculus) CFG 550; GGF 81.

Silverweed (Potentilla anserina) AFP 2:437; BBF 2:258; DEW 1:297; HWF cp 92b; NHE 211; OWF 17; PMF 135; RUS 4:163, 5:139, 6:173.

Siren, Greater (Siren lacertina) ALE 5:352; CRA 266 (pl 35); GPL 130; GRA 140; IWE 16:2148.

Siren, Lesser or Mud (Siren intermedia) ALE 5:352; BAR cp 1; CFG cp 1a; CRA 266 (pl 35). (Pseudobranchus striatus) GRA 140.

Snake, Green (Opheodrys sp.) BAR cp 46; CFG cp 36; CGR cp 13d; CRA 191 (cp 24); GPL 142; GRA 77; PFF 541; SIR 196-197 (cp 93), 198 (cp 95), 227; SRA cp 33; WWS 1:556, 563.

Snake, Ground (Sonora episcopa or S. semiannulata) CGR 301; CRA 174 (cp 21); GRA 78; SRA cp 32; WWS 2:675, 680, 685, 689.

Snake, Hognose—See **Hognose**.

Snake, Hook-nosed (Ficimia cana) CRA 143 (pl 18); SRA pl 34. (Gyalopion canum) GRA 82; WWS 1:287.

Snake, Indigo (Drymarchon corais) CGR cp 13f; CRA 158 (pl 19); GRA 94; LRE 138; PFF 543; SIR 202 (cp 102), 203 (cp 103); WWS 1:199.

Snake, King—See **Kingsnake**.

Snake, Lined (Tropidoclonion lineatum) CFG 384; CGR cp 12e; CRA 223 (cp 28); GRA 106; SRA cp 35; WWS 2:881.

Snake, Long-nosed (Rhinocheilus lecontei) CFG 404; CRA 174 (cp 21); GRA 101; SIR 204 (cp 106); SRA cp 31; WWS 2:631, 636, 641.

Snake, Lyre (Trimorphodon lambda) GRA 107; SRA cp 33; WWS 2:867. (T. vandenburghi) CGR cp 16a; WWS 2:877.

Snake, Milk (Lampropeltis doliata var.) BAR cp 53; BRW 113; CFG cp 35; CRA 174 (cp 21); IWE 9:1237; LEA opp 321; PFF 544; SIR 204 (cp 107), 241 (cp 116); WWS 1:352, 357, 363, 369.

Snake, Mud (Farancia abacura) BAR cp 44; CFG cp 36; CGR 275; CRA 191 (cp 24); GPL 141; GRA 75; MAR 160; PFF 540; WWS 1:271, 280.

Snake, Night (Hypsiglena torquata) AWW 28; CFG 404; CGR 311, cp 15e; CRA 143 (pl 18); GRA 107; SRA cp 33; WWS 1:318, 320, 322, 327.

Snake, Patch-nosed (Salvadora lineata or S. hexalepsis) CRA 190 (cp 23); GRA 88; SIR 229; SRA pl 34; WWS 2:652, 657.

Snake, Queen (Regina septemvittata or Natrix septemvittata) BAR cp 58; CFG 384; CRA 207 (cp 26); GPL 140; WWS 1:510.

Snake, Rainbow (Abastor erythrogrammus) CFG cp 36; CGR cp 13b; CRA 191 (cp 24); GPL 141; GRA 74; WWS 1:87.

Snake, Rat (Elaphe obsoleta var.) BAR cp 50; BRW 125; CFG cp 36; CGR 289; CRA 175 (cp 22); GRA 90, 91; IWE 14:1909, 1910; PRW pl 107; SIR 199 (cp 97), 200-201 (cps 98-100), 212; WWS 1:231, 239, 246, 252. (E. subocularis) PRW pl 108; SRA cp 32; WWS 1:259.

Snake, Red-bellied (Storeria occipitomaculata) BAR cp 57; CFG cp 36; CRA 222 (cp 27); GRA 106; LRE 142-143; SRA cp 35; WWS 2:720.

Snake, Ribbon (Thamnophis sauritus) ALE 6:406; BAR cp 55; CFG 384; CGR cp 12d; CRA 223 (cp 28); GPL 142; GRA 105; IWE 7:850; PFF 545; WWS 2:827, 831.

Snake, Ring-necked (Diadophis amabilis or D. punctatus) BAR cp 45; CFG cp 36; CGR cp 13a; CRA 191 (cp 24); GRA 76; MAR 160; PFF 541; SIR 195 (cp 90); SRA cp 31; WWS 1:160, 168, 173, 177, 183, 190.

Snake, Sand (Chilomeniscus cinctus) CGR cp 15d; GRA 79, 80; SIR 244 (cp 122); SRA cp 32; WWS 1:119.

Snake, Scarlet (Cemophora coccinea) BAR cp 54; CFG cp 35; CGR cp 14f; CRA 174 (cp 21), 238 (cp 29); LRE 144, 145; SIR 228; WWS 1:112. (C. doliata) GRA 100.

Snake, Sharp-tailed (Contia tenuis) CGR cp 15b; GRA 79; SRA cp 33; WWS 1:160.

Snake, Short-tailed (Stilosoma extenuatum) CGR 294; CRA 174 (cp 21); GRA 78; WWS 2:698.

Snake, Shovel-nosed (Chionactis occipitalis) CGR cp 15c; GRA 78; SRA cp 32; WWS 1:119, 127. (C. palarostris) CGR 311; SRA cp 32; WWS 1:131.

Snake, Striped Swamp (Liodytes alleni) CRA 222 (cp 27); GPL 141; GRA 79; WWS 1:420.

Snake, Water (Natrix sp.) ALE 6:420; BAR cps 58-61; CFG 384, 389, cp 36; CGR cps 11f, 12a; CRA 206 (cp 25), 207 (cp 26), GPL 140; GRA 102, 103; IWE 19:2572; PFF 544; SIR 191, 192; SRA cp 37; WWS 1:475, 481, 489, 510. (Regina sp.) CGR cps 12b, 12c.

Snake, Whip—See **Whipsnake**.

Snake, Worm—See **Boa, Rubber**.

Snake-bird—See **Anhinga**.

Snakehead—See **Turtlehead**.

Snake-mouth—See **Pogonia, Rose**.

Snakeroot, Black (Cimicifuga racemosa) AGF 223; DFP 132 (cp 1051); FFK 152; FNC 63; HWF cp 64; HYF cp 63; LFW 192 (cp 433); OGF 119; PFF 175; PMF 61; RUS 1:121, 2:171.

Snakeroot, Sampson's (Psoralea psoraliodes) FFK 184; HYF cp 90; PMF 353; RUS 2:355, 3:255, 6:387.

Snakeroot, Western (Sanicula crassicaulis) AFP 3:323; CWF 363; RUS 4:301, 5:263; VPN 3:583.

Snakeroot, White (Eupatorium rugosum) FFK 234;

1:454; CWF 63; OOW cp 9; PMF 67; RUS 1:37,
4:45, 5:37, 6:29; RWA cp 51.

Sora—See **Rail, Sora**.

Sorghum, Sweet (Sorghum vulgare var. saccharatum)
OFP 11; PFF 345.

Sorrel, Common (Rumex acetosa) BBF 1:654; NHE
183; OFP 191; OWF 59; PMF 381; VPN 2:170.

Sorrel, Mountain (Oxyria digyna) AFP 2:53; BBF
1:659; CWF 115; NHE 276; OWF 59; RUS 4:97,
5:97, 6:89; VPN 2:140.

Sorrel, Sheep's (Rumex acetosella) AFP 2:53; BBF
1:653; CWF 103; NHE 183; OWF 59; PFF 152;
PMF 311, 381; RUS 6:89; VPN 2:172. (R. hastatulus) FNC 54.

Sorrel Tree—See **Sourwood**.

Sorrel, Wood—See **Wood-sorrel**.

Sourgrass—See **Wood-sorrel, Large Yellow**.

Sourwood (Oxydendrum arboreum) BBF 2:692; BTN
241; DFP 215 (cp 1717); EGT 37, 68, 130; FNC
138; PFF 274; TGS 407; TSK 79, 420, 421.

Southernwood (Artemisia abrotanum) BBF 3:526;
HSC 14; OFP 145.

Sowbug (Armadillidium vulgare) ALE 1:496; BIA 51;
GIP 36; OIB 165; LEA 170. (Oniscus asellus) ALE
1:496; BLA 236; IWE 19:2642-2643; PFF 429.
(Platyarthrus hoffmanseggi) IWE 19:2644.

Sowbug, Water (Asellus sp.) GPL 91; NHE 131; OIB
133; PFF 429. (Idotea sp.) CFG 648; GAS 362,
364; KSL 134, 252; RCT 180, 272.

Sow-thistle, Common (Sonchus oleraceus) AFP 4:591;
BBF 3:317; NHE 240; OWF 35; PFF 333; PMF 111;
RUS 1:513, 2:639, 3:511, 4:747; VPN 5:517.

Sow-thistle, Field (Sonchus arvensis) AFP 4:589; BBF
3:316; CWF 559; NHE 240; OWF 35; PMF 111;
VPN 5:317.

Sow-thistle, Spiny-leaved (Sonchus asper) AFP 4:591;
BBF 3:317; FNC 187; NHE 240; PMF 111, 179;
RUS 1:509, 3:511, 4:747, 5:627, 6:731; VPN
5:517.

Soybean (Glycine max) OFP 25; PFF 219; WYG 168.

Spadebill, White-throated (Platyrinchus mystaceus)
DBM cp 29; HBT 209 (cp 12); PMB cp 29.

Spadefish, Atlantic (Chaetodipterus faber) ALE
5:102; GGF 132; NGF 212.

Spadefoot, Couch's (Scaphiopus couchii) ALE 5:399;
CAW cp 25; CGR 71; CRA 267 (pl 36); SRA cp 8;
WFA 110.

Spadefoot, Eastern (Scaphiopus holbrooki) BAR

cp 22; CAW 59, 60, 61; CFG cp 40; CGR cp 3c;
CRA 267 (pl 36); GPL 132; GRA 121; PFF 527;
WFA 15, 125, 128.

Spadefoot, Great Basin (Scaphiopus intermontanus)
IWE 16:2213; SRA cp 8.

Spadefoot, Plains (Scaphiopus bombifrons) BRW 19;
CFG cp 40; CRA 267 (pl 36); SRA cp 8.

Spadefoot, Western (Scaphiopus hammondi) CRA
267 (pl 36); GRA 121; SRA cp 8; WFA 117, 120.

Spanish Bayonet—See **Yucca, Spanish Bayonet**.

Sparrow, Bachman's or Pine-woods (Aimophila aestivalis) CFG cp 25; NGB 2:277; NGS 361; PEB 219
(cp 58); RBB 317; WAB 44.

Sparrow, Baird's (Ammodramus bairdii) BBC
2:cp 118; CFG cp 24; GBC 332 (cp 65); NGB
2:271; NGS 356; PEB 218 (cp 57); PWB 294 (cp
57); RBB 309.

Sparrow, Black-chested (Aimophila humeralis) DBM
cp 48; PMB cps 47, 48.

Sparrow, Black-chinned (Spizella atrogularis) NGB
2:286; NGS 367; PWB 295 (cp 58); RBB 319; WAB
47.

Sparrow, Black-throated or Desert (Amphispiza bilineata) AAB 485; BBC 2:cp 119; CFG cp 25; NGB
2:277; NGS 362; PBA 3:48; PWB 295 (cp 58); RBB
313.

Sparrow, Botteri's (Aimophila botterii) DBM cp 48;
NGS 361; PMB cp 48; PWB 294 (cp 57); RBB 317.

Sparrow, Brewer's (Spizella breweri) BBC 2:cp 121;
CFG cp 25; GBC 348 (cp 67); NGB 2:286; NGS
367; PWB 295 (cp 58); RBB 319.

Sparrow, Bridled (Aimophila mystacalis) DBM cp 48;
PMB cp 48.

Sparrow, Cape Sable (Ammospiza mirabilis) AAB
482; NGB 2:273; NGS 359; PEB 227 (cp 60); RBB
311; WID 333 (cp 29d).

Sparrow, Cassin's (Aimophila cassinii) BBC 2:cp 119;
CFG cp 25; NGB 2:277; NGS 361; PWB 294 (cp 57);
RBB 317.

Sparrow, Chipping (Spizella passerina) AAB 490;
ANE 10:1890; CFG cp 25; GBC 348 (cp 67); GBI
121, 125; NGB 2:284; NGS 365; PBA 3:cp 83; PEB
219 (cp 58); PFF 672; PWB 295 (cp 58); RBB 319;
TBC 400 (cp 83b).

Sparrow, Clay-colored (Spizella pallida) AAB 493;
BBC 2:cp 121; CFG cp 25; GBC 348 (cp 67); NGB
2:286; NGS 366; PEB 219 (cp 58); PWB 295 (cp
58); RBB 319; TBC 402 (cp 84a).

Sparrow, Dusky Seaside (Ammospiza nigrescens) NGB
2:273; NGS 358; PEB 227 (cp 60); RBB 311; WID
333 (cp 29e).

Sparrow, English or House (Passer domesticus) AAB
433; ABW 304; ALE 9:416; ANE 10:1895; BBE
275; BHB 208 (cp 55); CDB 214 (cp 954); CFG
cp 25; GBI 103; GPB 324; MBH cp 20; NGB 2:241;
NGS 290; NHE 256; PEB 215 (cp 56); PFF 658;
PWB 311 (cp 60); RBB 279.

Sparrow, Field (Spizella pusilla) AAB 494; ANE
10:1892; CFG cp 25; GBI 123; NGB 2:284; NGS
366; PBA 3:cp 83; PEB 219 (cp 58); PFF 673; PWB
295 (cp 58); RBB 319.

Sparrow, Fox (Passerella iliaca) AAB 499; ANE
10:1893; BBC 2:cp 123; CDB 197 (cp 862); CFG
cp 24; GBC 349 (cp 68); GBI 127; NGB 2:290; NGS
368; PBA 3:cp 83; PEB 218 (cp 57); PFF 674; PWB
294 (cp 57); RBB 323.

Sparrow, Golden-crowned (Zonotrichia atricapilla)
AAB 497; BBC 2:cp 122; GBC 349 (cp 68); NGB
2:286; NGS 368; PFF 674; PWB 295 (cp 58); RBB
321.

Sparrow, Grasshopper (Ammodramus savannarum)
AAB 479; CFG cp 25; GBC 332 (cp 65); NGB
2:271; NGS 355; PBA 3:cp 81; PEB 218 (cp 57);
PFF 670; PWB 294 (cp 57); RBB 309.

Sparrow, Green-backed (Arremonops chloronotus)
DBM cp 48; PMB cp 47.

Sparrow, Harris' (Zonotrichia querula) AAB 495; BBC
2:cp 122; CFG cp 25; GBC 333 (cp 66); NGB 2:288;
NGS 369; PBA 3:34; PEB 219 (cp 58); PFF 673;
PWB 295 (cp 58); RBB 321.

Sparrow, Henslow's (Passerherbulus henslowii) AAB
481; CFG cp 24; GBC 332 (cp 65); NGB 2:271;
NGS 355; PBA 3:cp 81; PEB 218 (cp 57); RBB 309.

Sparrow, Ipswich (Passerculus princeps) CFG cp 24;
GBC 333 (cp 66); NGB 2:269; NGS 355; PBA
3:cp 81; PEB 218 (cp 57); RBB 309; WID 333 (cp
29f).

Sparrow, Lark (Chondestes grammacus) AAB 483;
BBC 2:cp 119; CFG cp 25; GBC 333 (cp 66); GFB
190; NGB 2:275; NGS 359; PBA 3:32; PEB 219 (cp
58); PFF 671; PWB 295 (cp 58); RBB 313.

Sparrow, Le Conte's (Passerherbulus caudacutus) AAB
480; BBC 2:cp 118; CFG cp 25; GBC 332 (cp 65);
NGB 2:271; NGS 357; PEB 218 (cp 57); PWB 294
(cp 57); RBB 311.

Sparrow, Lincoln's (Melospiza lincolnii) AAB 499;
BBC 2:cp 123; CFG cp 24; GBC 349 (cp 68); NGB
2:294; NGS 372; PBA 3:cp 84; PEB 218 (cp 57);
PFF 675; PWB 294 (cp 57); RBB 323.

Sparrow, Olive or Texas (Arremonops rufivirgata)
DBM cp 48; NGB 2:265; NGS 353; PMB cp 47;
PWB 275 (cp 56); RBB 305.

Sparrow, Orange-billed (Arremon aurantirostris) ALE
9:342; DBM cp 47; PMB cp 47.

Sparrow, Rufous-crowned or Scott's (Aimophila ruficeps) BBC 2:cp 118; CFG cp 25; DBM cp 48; NGB
2:275; NGS 360; PMB cp 48; PWB 295 (cp 58);
RBB 317.

Sparrow, Rufous-winged (Aimophila carpalis) DBM
cp 48; NGB 2:275; NGS 360; PMB cp 48; PWB 294
(cp 57); RBB 317.

Sparrow, Rusty (Aimophila rufescens) AMB 105 (cp
9); DBM cp 48; PMB cp 48.

Sparrow, Sage (Amphispiza belli) BBC 2:cp 119; NGB
2:279; NGS 362; PWB 295 (cp 58); RBB 313; WAB
51.

Sparrow, Savannah (Passerculus sandwichensis) AAB
478; ANE 10:1896; CFG cp 24; DBM cp 48; NGB
2:269; NGS 355; PBA 3:cp 81; PEB 218 (cp 57);
PFF 670; PWB 294 (cp 57); RBB 309; TBC 392 (cp
81b).

Sparrow, Seaside (Ammospiza maritima) ALE 9:342;
CFG cp 24; LBW 367 (cp 215); NGB 2:273; NGS
357; PBA 3:cp 81; PEB 218 (cp 57); PFF 670; RBB
311; WAB 70.

Sparrow, Sharp-tailed (Ammospiza caudacuta) BBC
2:cp 118; CFG cp 24; GBC 332 (cp 65); NGB
2:273; NGS 355; PBA 3:cp 81; PEB 218 (cp 57);
PWB 294 (cp 57); RBB 311.

Sparrow, Song (Melospiza melodia) AAB 501; ALE
9:342; ANE 10:1898; BBC 2:cp 123; CDB 197 (cp
861); CFG cp 24; GBC 349 (cp 68); GBI 127; IWE
16:2209; NGB 2:292; NGS 370-371; PBA 3:cp 84;
PEB 218 (cp 57); PFF 676; PWB 294 (cp 57); RBB
323; TBC 406 (cp 85b).

Sparrow, Swamp (Melospiza georgiana) AAB 500;
ANE 10:1899; BBC 2:cp 123; CFG cp 25; GBC
349 (cp 68); GBI 127; GPL 151; NGB 2:294; NGS
372; PBA 3:cp 84; PEB 219 (cp 58); PFF 675; PWB
295 (cp 58); RBB 323.

Sparrow, Tree (Spizella arborea) AAB 492; ABW 298;
ALE 9:342; ANE 10:1900; CFG cp 25; GBC 348
(cp 67); GBI 123; NGB 2:284; NGS 365; PBA
3:cp 80; PEB 219 (cp 58); PFF 672; PWB 295 (cp
58); RBB 319; TBC 400 (cp 83a).

Sunapee (Salvelinus aureolus) GGF 2; NGF 233-237.
Sun-bittern—See **Bittern, Sun.**
Sundew, Great (Drosera anglica or D. longifolia) AFP
2:332; BBF 2:204; CWF 186; EWF cp 16f; NHE 73;
RUS 1:199, 6:293; VPN 2:568.
Sundew, Round-leaved (Drosera rotundifolia) AFP
2:332; BBF 2:203; CWF 195; EWF cp 16e; FNC 82;
GPL 65; HFP 132; HYF cp 74; NHE 73; OWF 83;
PFF 190; PFW 102; PMF 21, 233; RUS 1:199,
2:255, 6:293; VPN 2:568.
Sundew, Spatulate-leaved (Drosera intermedia) BBF
2:203; FNC 82; HWF cp 84; NHE 73; PMF 21; RUS
1:199, 2:255.
Sundrops (Oenothera fruticosa) DFP 161 (cp 1288);
HWF cp 147a; HYF cp 121; LWF 191 (cps 300, 301);
OGF 109; PFW 203; PMF 157; RUS 1:245, 2:309;
TGF 125. (O. tetragona) EGP 135; FFK 101; FNC
124; MWF 216 (cp 701).
Sunfish, Blue-gill (Lepomis macrochirus) CFG cp 44;
GGF 100; GPL 124; NGF 286; PFF 521; WFW
cp 278.
Sunfish, Green (Lepomis cyanellus) CFG 543; GGF
101; GPL 124; WFW 232.
Sunfish, Ocean (Mola mola) ALE 5:266; CFG 513;
CFW 150; GGF 139; HPF 640; IWE 12:1600, 1601;
MOL 96; NGF 215; NHE 158; OBV 43; WFW 251.
Sunfish, Pumpkinseed (Lepomis gibbosus) ALE 5:80;
CFG cp 44; GGF 101; GPL 124; NGF 286; PFF
519; WFW cp 277.
Sunfish, Warmouth (Chaenobryttus gulosus) ALE
5:80; CFG 543; GGF 103; GPL 124; NGF 286.
Sunflower, Common (Helianthus annus) AFP 4:113;
CWF 554; DFP 38 (cp 304); EGA 123; LFW 200 (cp
452); LWF 208 (cp 330); MWF 150 (cp 460); OFP
25; PFF 321; PMF 115, 181; RUS 1:453, 2:567,
3:439, 4:647, 5:551, 6:647; TGF 285; VPN 5:231.
Sunflower, False—See **Ox-eye.**
Sunflower, Hairy Wild (Helianthus mollis) HWF
cp 258; PMF 183; PRP 137.
Sunflower, Mexican (Tithonia rotundifolia) DFP 49
(cp 385); EGA 157; EWF cp 186b; LFW 269 (cp
603); MWF 285 (cp 942).
Sunflower, Narrow-leaved (Helianthus angustifolius)
FNC 201; HWF cp 249a; HYF 199; PMF 115; RUS
2:567, 3:441.
Sunflower, Pale-leaved Wood (Helianthus strumosus)
FFK 259; PMF 183; RUS 1:457, 2:571, 6:653;
RWA cp 369.

Sunflower, Thin-leaved (Helianthus decapetalus) EGP
121; FFK 260; LWF 210 (cp 333); MWF 150 (cp
461); PFF 321; PFW 82; PMF 183; RUS 1:455,
2:571.
Sunflower, Woolly (Eriophyllum lanatum) AFP
4:225; CWF 551; HFP 381; LWF 159 (cp 255);
RUS 4:665, 5:565, 6:655; VPN 5:200.
Sungrebe (Heliornis fulica) ALE 8:100; DBM cp 1;
PMB cp 10.
Sunrose (Helianthemum nummularium) DFP 11 (cps
84, 85); LFW 55 (cp 127); MWF 149 (cp 459); PFW
74; TGF 124.
Sun-star—See **Starfish, Sun.**
Surfbird (Aphriza virgata) AAB 156; BBW cp 25; GBC
160 (cp 29); NGB 1:265; NGW 324; PWB 115 (pl
30); 119 (cp 32); RBB 121.
Surgeonfish, Blue—See **Tang, Blue.**
Surgeonfish, Ocean (Acanthurus leucosternon) ALE
5:115; CFW 130; IWE 17:2311; LFI 139, 141; SOS
75; WFW cp 440. (A. bahianus) HFW 210 (cp 94),
214 (cp 98).
Surgeonfish, Yellow—See **Tang, Yellow.**
Swallow, Bank (Riparia riparia) AAB 303; ALE
7:255; ANE 10:1958; BBC 2:cp 80; BBE 193; CFG
cp 13; GBC 225 (cp 46); GPB 251; IWE 11:1439,
1440; NGB 2:174; NGS 120, 129; PBA 3:cp 88;
PEB 162 (cp 43); PFF 627; PWB 198 (cp 43); RBB
207; TBC 300 (cp 46a).
Swallow, Barn (Hirundo rustica) AAB 305; ABW 216;
ALE 7:255, 9:169, 170; ANE 10:1959, 1960; BBC
2:cp 80; CDB 150 (cp 617); CFG cp 13; GBC 225
(cp 46); GFB 137; GPB 250; IWE 17:2320; LBW
226 (cp 128), 296, 298; NGB 2:172; NGS 124; PBA
3:cp 88; PEB 162 (cp 43); PFF 628; PWB 198 (cp
43); RBB 205; TBC 300 (cp 46b); WEA 354.
Swallow, Cave (Petrochelidon fulva) BWI 161; NGS
125; PMB cp 17; PWB 198 (cp 43); RBB 205.
Swallow, Cliff (Petrochelidon pyrrhonota) AAB 322;
ABW 216; ALE 9:170; ANE 10:1962, 1963; BBC
2:cp 80; CFG cp 13; GBC 225 (cp 46); IWE
17:2321; NGB 2:172; NGS 126; PBA 3:cp 88; PEB
162 (cp 43); PFF 628; PWB 198 (cp 43); RBB 205;
TBC 302 (cp 47a); WAB 53.
Swallow, Mangrove (Tachycineta albilinea or
Iridoprocne albilinea) AMB 76 (cp 6); DBM cp 31;
PMB cp 17.
Swallow, Rough-winged (Stelgidopteryx ruficollis)
AAB 304; ABW 216; BBC 2:cp 80; CFG cp 13;

DBM cp 31; GBC 225 (cp 46); NGB 2:174; NGS 129; PBA 3:cp 88; PEB 162 (cp 43); PFF 627; PWB 198 (cp 43); RBB 207.

Swallow, Tree (Tachycineta bicolor or Iridoprocne bicolor) AAB 302; ABW 216; ANE 10:1964; BBC 2:cp 79; CDB 151 (cp 622); CFG cp 13; GBC 225 (cp 46); GFB 137; NGB 2:174; NGS 127; PBA 3:cp 88; PEB 162 (cp 43); PFF 627; PWB 198 (cp 43); RBB 207; TBC 298 (cp 45b).

Swallow, Violet-green (Tachycineta thalassina) AAB 301; BBC 2:cp 79; CFG cp 13; DBM cp 31; GBC 225 (cp 46); LBW 227 (cp 130); NGB 2:174; NGS 127; PFF 626; PWB 198 (cp 43); RBB 207; TBC 298 (cp 45a).

Swallower, Black or Great (Chiasmodon niger) AWW 166; CFW 16; SOS 111.

Swamp-candles (Lysimachia terrestris) ANE 6:1082; BBF 2:712; GPL 67; HWF cp 161b; HYF cp 144; NHE 97; OWF 27; PMF 107; RUS 1:303, 2:385, 5:371.

Swamp-pink—See **Arethusa.**

Swan, Mute (Cygnus olor) AAB 56; ABW 67; ALE 7:244, 255, 273, 11:257; BBC 1:128; BBE 42; GGB 153; GPB 88; IWE 17:2328-2332; KWF 390 (cp 1); LBW 78; NGW 145; PEB 18 (pl 5); PFF 560; RBB 39; WEA 357.

Swan, Trumpeter (Olor buccinator) ABW 67; ALE 7:273; ANE 10:1971-1974; BBC 1:cp 10; GBC 60 (cp 7); GGB 18; GPB 87; KWF 390 (cp 1); LVS 191; NGB 1:97; NGW 140-141, 142-143; PWB 26 (pl 5); RBA 43; RBB 39; SLP 95; WID 187.

Swan, Whistling (Olor columbianus) AAB 57; ALE 7:273; BBC 1:cp 10; GBC 60 (cp 7); GGB 20; KWF 390 (cp 1); NGB 1:97; NGW 144; PBA 1:cp 22; PEB 18 (pl 5), 19 (pl 6); PFF 560; PWB 26 (pl 5), 27 (pl 6); RBB 39; SAA 142.

Sweet Bay (Magnolia virginiana) BBF 2:82; BTN 151; EWF cp 150d; FNC 70; GGT 48; RWA cp 132.

Sweet Betsy—See **Allspice, Carolina.**

Sweet Gale (Myrica gale) AFP 1:508; BBF 1:584; CWF 103; GPL 72; NHE 69; OWF 191; VPN 2:75.

Sweet Sultan (Centaurea moschata) AGF 230; DFP 33 (cp 260); FGF 256; OGF 87.

Sweet William (Dianthus barbatus) DFP 36 (cp 283); EGA 114; EGP 112; FGF 257; LFW 44 (cps 100, 101); MWF 110 (cp 311); OGF 127; PFF 163; PFW 71; TGF 60.

Sweetbrier (Rosa rubiginosa or R. eglanteria) AFP 2:461; BBF 2:286; EWF cp 9a; OOW cp 178; OWF 117; PMF 257; VPN 3:168.

Sweetflag—See **Flag, Sweet.**

Sweet-fern (Comptonia peregrina) BBF 1:586; TGS 86; TSK 293.

Sweetleaf (Symploca tinctoria) BBF 2:721; BTN 249; FNC 144.

Swift, Black (Cypseloides niger) BBC 2:cp 69; BWI 132; GBC 204 (cp 41); NGB 2:42; NGW 457; RBB 171.

Swift, Chimney (Chaetura pelagica) AAB 258; ABW 165; ALE 8:426; ANE 10:1976; BBC 2:cp 69; GBC 204 (cp 41); GBI 57; GFB 99; IWE 16:2230, 2231; LBW 220; NGB 2:42; NGW 454, 457; PEB 162 (cp 43); PFF 618; RBB 171; TBC 268 (cp 35b).

Swift, Vaux's (Chaetura vauxi) AAB 259; GBC 204 (cp 41); NGB 2:42; NGW 457; RBB 171.

Swift, White-naped (Streptoprocne semicollaris) DBM cp 13; PMB cp 17.

Swift, White-throated (Aeronautes saxatilis) AAB 260; BBC 2:cp 69; BBW cp 41; GBC 204 (cp 41); NGB 2:42; NGW 457; PBA 2:178; RBB 171; WAB 52.

Sword-fern—See **Fern, Sword.**

Sword-fish (Xiphias gladius) ALE 5:192; ANE 4:677; CFG cp 42; GGF 90; HFW 235; IWE 17:2341; NGF 130; NHE 155; WFW 363.

Sword-tail (Xiphophorus helleri) ALE 4:51; IWE 17:2342; NGF 239; PFF 515; WEA 356; WFW cp 210.

Sycamore—See also **Maple, Sycamore.**

Sycamore, American (Platanus occidentalis) BBF 2:242; BTN 161; GGT 127; GPL 69; PFF 195.

Syringa—See **Mock Orange.**

T

Tamarack—See **Larch, American.**

Tamarisk (Tamarix parvifolia) BTN 270; MWF 279 (cp 925).

Tanager, Hepatic (Piranga flava) AAB 451; NGB 2:243; NGS 321; PWB 266 (cp 53); RBB 289.

Tanager, Scarlet (Piranga olivacea) AAB 450; ABW 293; ANE 10:1983, 1984; BBC 2:cp 109; CFG cp 27; IWE 17:2356; GBC 300 (cp 61); GBI 111; LBW 360 (cp 201); NGB 2:241; NGS 316-319; PBA 3:cp 87; PEB 199 (cp 54); PFF 662; PWB 266 (cp 53); RBB 289; TBC 378 (cp 76a); WAB 43.

Tanager, Shrike—See **Shrike-tanager.**

Tanager, Summer (Piranga rubra) AAB 451; ALE 9:361; ANE 10:1985; BBC 2:cp 109; CDB 201 (cp 877); CFG cp 22; GBC 300 (cp 61); NGB 2:241; NGS 320; PBA 3:cp 87; PEB 199 (cp 54); PFF 663; PWB 266 (cp 53); RBB 289.

Tanager, Western (Piranga ludoviciana) AAB 457; ANE 10:1986; BBC 2:cp 109; CFG cp 22; GBC 300 (cp 61); GFB 189; LBW 359 (cp 200); NGB 2:243; NGS 320; PEB 199 (cp 54); PFF 663; PWB 266 (cp 53); RBB 289; TBC 376 (cp 75b).

Tang, Blue (Acanthurus coeruleus) ALE 5:201; HFW 215 (cp 99); NGF 48, 49; WFW cp 437.

Tang, Orange-spot (Acanthurus olivaceus) NGF 340; WFW cp 443.

Tang, Yellow (Zebrasoma flavescens) HFW 212 (cp 96); IWE 17:2314; NGF 335. (Z. scopas) WFW cp 447.

Tangerine (Citrus reticulata) OFP 87; PFF 229; WYG 199.

Tansy, Common (Tanacetum vulgare) AFP 4:397; BBF 3:522; CWF 562; HYF cp 223; LWF 212 (cp 337); MWF 280 (cp 926); OFP 145; OWF 35; PFF 328; PMF 167; RUS 1:505, 2:633, 4:713, 6:727; TGF 237.

Tansy, Huron (Tanacetum huronense) PMF 167; RUS 1:505.

Tansy-mustard—See **Flixweed.**

Tapeworm (Echinococcus sp. or Taenia sp.) ALE 1:290; BLA 127; FWA 377; IWE 17:2361; LEA 61; OIB 27; PFF 399.

Tapioca—See **Cassava.**

Tapir, Baird's (Tapirus bairdii) ALE 13:22; ANE 10:1987; LEA 587; LVS 115; VWA cp 39; WID 109.

Tarantula—See **Spider, Bird.**

Tardigrade—See **Water Bear.**

Tare, Hairy—See **Vetch, Hairy.**

Tarpon, Atlantic (Megalops atlanticus or Tarpon atlanticus) ANE 10:1989; CFG 472; CFW 42; GGF 35; HFW 73; IWE 17:2369; NGF 97-100; OMW 280; PFF 505; WFW 346.

Tarweed (Madia elegans) AFP 167; HFP 376; OOW cp 131; RUS 3:463, 4:659, 5:559. (M. sativa) RUS 4:659, 5:561.

Tassel-rue—See **Bugbane, False.**

Tattler, Wandering (Heteroscelus incanus) GBC 160 (cp 29); NGB 1:276; NGW 337; PWB 114 (pl 29), 118 (cp 31); RBB 117.

Tautog (Tautoga onitis) CFG cp 41; GGF 130; NGF 206.

Tayra (Tayra barbara) ALE 12:66; AWW 43; FWA 224; JAW 115; SMW 204; WEA 363; WMW 2:1198.

Tea, California (Psoralea physodes) AFP 2:556; HFP 190; RUS 4:372, 5:335; VPN 3:350.

Tea, New Jersey (Ceanothus americanus) BBF 2:504; FNC 115; HWF cp 126; HYF cp 107; TSK 75, 283.

Tea Tree, Manuka (Leptospermum scoparium) DFP 13 (cp 99), 210 (cp 1674); HSC 74; MEP 98; MWF 181 (cp 571); OGF 103.

Teaberry, Western (Gaultheria ovatifolia) AFP 3:307; CWF 391; RUS 6:479; VPN 4:15.

Teal, Blue-winged (Anas discors) BBC 1:cp 15; CFG cp 2, 41, 42; GBC 77 (cp 10); GGB 49; KWF 414 (cp 13), 416 (cp 14), 454 (cp 33); NGB 1:121; NGW 166; PBA 1:cp 14; PEB 22 (pl 7), 26 (pl 9), 39 (cp 14); PFF 567; PWB 34 (pl 7), 42 (pl 9), 59 (cp 14); TBC 92 (cp 8a).

Teal, Cinnamon (Anas cyanoptera) AAB 83; BBC 1:cp 15; CFG cp 2, 41, 42; GBC 77 (cp 10); GGB 51; KWF 414 (cp 13), 416 (cp 14), 454 (cp 33); NGB 1:121; NGW 166; PEB 39 (cp 14); PFF 568; PWB 34 (pl 7), 42 (pl 9), 59 (cp 14); RBB 49;

Teal, Common or European (Anas crecca) ALE 7:305, 11:257; GBC 77 (cp 10); KWF 412 (cp 12); NGB 1:103; NHE 113; PEB 39 (cp 14); PWB 59 (cp 14); RBB 49; SAA 145.

Teal, Falcated (Anas falcata) ALE 7:304; BBE 54.

Teal, Green-winged (Anas carolinensis) AAB 70; ALE 11:257; BBC 1:cp 15; CFG cp 2, 41, 42; GBC 77 (cp 10); GGB 46, 47; GPL 144; KWF 412 (cp 12), 416 (cp 14), 454 (cp 33); NGB 1:103; NGW 166; PBA 1:cp 13; PEB 22 (pl 7), 26 (pl 9), 39 (cp 14); PFF 567; PWB 34 (pl 7), 42 (pl 9), 59 (cp 14); TBC 92 (cp 8).

Teal, Laysan—See **Duck, Laysan**.

Teasel, Common or Card (Dipsacus sylvestris) AFP 4:65; BBF 3:289; CWF 507; DEW 2:110 (cp 73); HWF cp 215a; PFF 306; PMF 301; RUS 1:425, 2:541, 5:529.

Teasel, Fuller's (Dipsacus fullonum) AFP 4:63; BBF 3:289; EWF cp 17b; NHE 235; OWF 157; PFW 101.

Tegula—See **Turban Shell**.

Tellin, Bodega (Tellina bodegensis) GGS 102; MGS pl 21; PFF 423.

Tellin, Northern Dwarf (Tellina agilis) AAS pl 30x; ASN 241; CFG 595.

Tellin, Speckled (Tellina interrupta or T. listeri) AAS cp 40L; ASN 241; GGS 102.

Tellin, Sunrise (Tellina radiata) AAS cp 40e; ASN 239; GGS 102; GSS 19, 149.

Tench, Golden (Tinca tinca) ALE 4:327, 336, 341; HFW 41 (cp 19); IWE 11:1470-1471; OBV 95; WFW cp 143.

Termite, Subterranean (Reticulitermes flavipes) BIA 89; GGI 30, 31; GIP 27; LPL 176; PFF 446; SCI 89; SIG cp 16.

Tern, Aleutian (Sterna aleutica) ALE 8:229; NGB 1:314; NGW 393; PWB 147 (pl 36); RBB 147.

Tern, Arctic (Sterna paradisaea) AAB 220; ABW 134; ALE 8:187, 212; BBC 1:cp 61; CDB 94 (cp 338); FWA 32; GBC 188 (cp 35); GBI 128; GPB 27; LBW 176; NGB 1:316; NGW 393; PBA 1:cp 7; PEB 130 (pl 35), 134 (cp 37); PFF 605; PWB 147 (pl 36), 150 (cp 37); RBB 143; SAA 31, 83, 103; SOS 139; WAB 14, 22.

Tern, Black (Chlidonias niger) AAB 210; ALE 8:211; BBC 1:cp 61; BBE 150; CDB 91 (cp 320); CFG cp 11; GBC 188 (cp 35); GPB 167; NGB 1:320; NGW 397; PBA 1:cp 8; PEB 131 (pl 36), 134 (cp 37); PFF 606; PWB 147 (pl 36), 150 (cp 37); RBB 147.

Tern, Bridled (Sterna anaethetus) BWI 96; RBB 147.

Tern, Caspian (Hydroprogne caspia) AAB 209; ALE 7:61; BBE 152; CDB 92 (cp 323); CFG cp 11; GBC 188 (cp 35); IWE 18:2390-2391; NGB 1:318; NGW 396; PBA 1:cp 8; PEB 130 (pl 35), 134 (cp 37); PFF 606; PWB 147 (pl 36), 150 (cp 37); RBB 145; WAB 71.

Tern, Common (Sterna hirundo) ABW 130; ALE 7:255, 385, 8:205; BBC 1:cp 61; BBE 153; CDB 94 (cp 337); CFG cp 11; GBI 41; GFB 81; GGS 151; GPB 166; LBW 175; NGB 1:316; NGW 392; PBA 1:cp 7; PEB 130 (pl 35), 134 (cp 37); PFF 605; PWB 147 (pl 36), 150 (cp 37); RBA 122; RBB 143.

Tern, Elegant (Thalasseus elegans) BBW cp 30; CDB 95 (cp 340); PWB 147 (pl 36), 150 (cp 37); RBB 145.

Tern, Fairy (Gygis alba) AAB 211; ABW 130; ALE 8:211; BHB 58 (cp 21); CDB 92 (cp 322); FWA 261; GPB 166; SOS 349.

Tern, Forster's (Sterna forsteri) AAB 203; BBC 1:cp 61; CFG cp 11; GBC 188 (cp 35); NGB 1:316; NGW 391; PBA 1:cp 7; PEB 130 (pl 35), 134 (cp 37); PWB 147 (pl 36), 150 (cp 37); RBB 143; TBC 230 (cp 28b).

Tern, Gull-billed (Gelochelidon nilotica) AAB 203; ALE 8:211; BBE 152; CFG cp 11; NGB 1:320; NGW 391; PBA 1:cp 7; PEB 130 (pl 35), 134 (cp 37); PWB 147 (pl 36), 150 (cp 37); RBB 145; WAB 71.

Tern, Least or Little (Sterna albifrons) ALE 8:187; ANE 11:1993; BBC 1:cp 61; BBE 154; CDB 94 (cp 334); CFG cp 11; LBW 176; LEA 416; NGB 1:320; NGW 394; PBA 1:cp 7; PEB 131 (pl 36), 134 (cp 37); PWB 147 (pl 36), 150 (cp 37); RBA 124; RBB 143; WAB 133.

Tern, Noddy (Anous stolidus) ABW 130; ALE 8:211; ANE 11:1995; BHB 57 (cp 19); CDB 91 (cp 318); GFB 81; GPB 166; IWE 12:1588; NGB 1:318; NGW 397; PEB 131 (pl 36); PFF 606; RBB 147. (A. minutus) IWE 12:1589. (A. tenuirostris) BHB 57 (cp 20); LBW 193; RBB 147.

Tern, Roseate (Sterna dougallii) ABW 134; BBE 154; CDB 94 (cp 335); CFG cp 11; GBC 188 (cp 35); NGB 1:316; NGW 392; PBA 1:cp 7; PEB 130 (pl 35), 134 (cp 37); RBB 143.

Tern, Royal (Sterna maximus or Thalasseus maximus) AAB 207; ABW 130; ANE 11:1992; CFG cp 11; GGS 151; GPB 168; NGB 1:318; NGW 394-395; PBA 1:cp 8; PEB 130 (pl 35), 134 (cp 37); PWB 147 (pl 36), 150 (cp 37); RBB 145; WAB 71.

Tern, Sandwich (Cabot's) (Sterna sandwichensis or Thalasseus sandvicensis) AAB 208; ALE 8:187; BBE 152; CFG cp 11; GPB 168; NGB 1:318; NGW 396; PEB 130 (pl 35), 134 (cp 37); RBB 145; SLP 33.

Tern, Sooty (Sterna fuscata) AAB 205; ABW 134; ANE 11:1995; BBE 151; BHB 54 (cp 16); CDB 94 (cp 336); IWE 18:2389; LBW 132 (cp 69); NGB

Thrasher, Oscellated (Toxostoma ocellatum) DBM cp 35; PMB cp 34.

Thrasher, Sage (Oreoscoptes montanus) AAB 348; BBC 2:cp 89; CFG cp 15; GBC 237 (cp 50); NGB 2:167; NGS 207; PWB 230 (cp 47); RBB 227; WAB 51.

Thrasher, Socorro (Mimodes graysoni) DBM cp 35; PMB cp 34.

Thresher—See **Shark, Thresher.**

Thrift—See **Sea-pink.**

Thrips, Banded Greenhouse (Hercinothrips femoralis) GIP 89; SCI 107.

Thrips, Citrus (Scirtothrips citri) GIP 137; SCI 107.

Thrips, Flower or Wheat (Frankliniella tritici) PFF 450; SCI 104; SIG cp 22.

Thrips, Gladiolus (Taeniothrips simplex) EGE 151; EGP 51; GBB cp 30; GIP 89; SCI 105.

Thrips, Greenhouse (Heliothrips haemorrhoidalis) GIP 89; SCI 104.

Thrips, Onion (Thrips tabaci) GIP 72; OBI 19; SCI 106.

Thrush, Aztec (Ridgwayia pinicola) DBM cp 36; PMB cp 35.

Thrush, Gray-cheeked (Hylocichla minima) AAB 353; BBE 268; CFG cp 15; GBC 252 (cp 51); NGB 2:163; NGS 217; PEB 166 (cp 45); PFF 640; PWB 231 (cp 48); RBB 233.

Thrush, Hawaiian (Phaeornis obscurus) BHB 118 (cp 40); MBH cp 8; PWB 310 (cp 59); WID 282 (cp 26).

Thrush, Hermit (Hylocichla guttata) AAB 351; ALE 9:221; ANE 11:2012; CFG cp 15; GBC 252 (cp 51); GBI 87; NGB 2:163; NGS 216; PBA 3:cp 105; PEB 166 (cp 45); PFF 639; PWB 231 (cp 48); RBB 233.

Thrush, Nightingale—See **Nightingale-thrush.**

Thrush, Olive-backed or Swainson's (Hylocichla ustulata) AAB 352; ANE 11:2013; BBE 268; CFG cp 15; GBC 252 (cp 51); NGB 2:163; NGS 216; PBA 3:cp 105; PEB 166 (cp 45); PWB 231 (cp 48); RBB 233.

Thrush, Varied (Ixoreus naevius) GBC 253 (cp 52); GBI 130; NGB 2:161; NGS 215; PFF 641; PWB 231 (cp 48); RBB 231.

Thrush, Water—See **Waterthrush.**

Thrush, Wilson's—See **Veery.**

Thrush, Wood (Hylocichla mustelina) AAB 351; ABW 252; ALE 9:221; ANE 11:2011, 2015; BBC 2:cp 90; CDB 164 (cp 684); CFG cp 27; GBC 252 (cp 51); GBI 86; GFB 160; NGB 2:163; NGS 208-209, 215;

PBA 3:cp 105; PEB 166 (cp 45); PFF 639; PWB 231 (cp 48); RBA 201; RBB 233.

Thyme (Thymus serpyllum) AGF 231; BBF 3:141; DFP 27 (cp 214); NHE 74; OGF 89; OFP 141; RUS 1:377, 2:481, 5:469; VPN 4:283.

Ti (Cordyline terminalis) DFP 61 (cp 481); MEP 16; MWF 93 (cp 249).

Tick, Cattle (Boophilus annulatus) GIP 49; PFF 439.

Tick, Sheep (Melophagus ovinus) GGI 151; GIP 60; OBI 141; SCI 641; SIG pl 174a.

Tick, Wood (Dermacentor sp.) BLA 253; GGI 153; GIP 46, 48; LFO 148; OIB 143; PFF 440.

Tickseed (Coreopsis tinctoria) AGF 80; DFP 35 (cp 274); EGA 110; PMF 189.

Tickseed, Lance-leaved (Coreopsis lanceolata) HWF cp 260a; HYF cp 222; LWF 211 (cp 335); MWF 93 (cp 250); RUS 1:449, 2:559, 561, 3:431.

Tickseed, Large-flowered (Coreopsis grandiflora) DFP 132 (cp 1055); EGP 109; LFW 193 (cp 436); RUS 2:561; TGF 284. (C. major) FFK 252; HYF cp 197.

Tickseed, Pink (Coreopsis rosea) HWF cp 261b; HYF cp 222; PMF 309; RUS 2:561.

Tick-trefoil, Prostrate (Desmodium rotundifolium) FFK 188; PMF 249; RUS 1:271, 2:349, 3:263, 6:395.

Tick-trefoil, Showy (Desmodium canadense) HYF cp 95; PMF 225, 249; RUS 1:271, 6:397.

Tidy Tips (Layia platyglossa) AFP 4:161; ANE 6:1042; LWF 54 (cp 90); OOW cp 122; RUS 4:655, 5:561. (L. glandulosa) AFP 4:161; RUS 4:655, 5:561, 6:689; VPN 5:255. (L. campestris) EGA 131. (L. elegans) DFP 41 (cp 323).

Tiger Flower (Tigridia pavonia) AGF 231; DFP 111 (cp 886); EGB 141; FGF 258; LFW 269 (cp 606); MEP 22; MGB 284; MWF 284 (cp 940); OGF 117; PFW 146; SGB cp 28; TGF 29.

Tilefish (Lopholatilus chamaeleonticeps) CFG cp 41; GGF 123; NGF 203.

Tillandsia (Tillandsia fasciculata) LWF 4 (cp 5); RUS 2:85; RWA cp 22. (T. cyanea) FHP 148; MEP 14; MWF 285 (cp 941); PFW 52.

Timothy (Phleum pratense) AFP 1:142; BBF 1:191; NHE 194; PFF 353; PRP 57; VPN 1:644.

Timothy, Mountain (Phleum alpinum) AFP 1:142; BBF 1:191; NHE 292; VPN 1:644.

Tinamou, Great (Tinamus major) DBM cp 1; PMB cp 7; WAB 82.

Tinamou, Little (Crypturellus soui) DBM cp 1; HBT 21; PMB cp 7.

Tinamou, Thicket (Crypturellus cinnamomeus) DBM cp 1; GFB 14; PMB cp 7.

Tinkerweed—See **Horse Gentian.**

Titmouse, Black-crested (Parus atricristatus) NGB 2:137; NGS 158; PWB 214 (cp 45); RBB 217; WAB 46.

Titmouse, Bridled (Parus wollweberi) NGB 2:137; NGS 159; PBA 3:209; PWB 214 (cp 45); RBB 217.

Titmouse, Plain (Parus inornatus) AAB 324; BBC 2:cp 84; NGB 2:137; NGS 47, 159; PWB 214 (cp 45); RBB 217. (Boeolophus inornatus) PFF 633.

Titmouse, Tufted (Parus bicolor) AAB 323; ALE 9:308; ANE 11:2023; CFG cp 14; GBC 233 (cp 48); GBI 79; GPB 291; GPL 151; LBW 344; NGB 2:137; NGS 40, 153, 158; PBA 3:cp 103; PEB 163 (cp 44); PFF 633; RBB 217.

Tityra, Masked (Tityra semifasciata) ABW 204; AMB 63 (cp 4); DBM cp 27; PMB cp 26.

Toad, American (Bufo americanus) ANE 4:736; BAR cp 27; CAW cp 38; CRA 267 (pl 36); CGR cp 4e; GPL 132; GRA 118, 122; LEA 280; PFF 528. (B. terrestis) CFG cp 39.

Toad, Bell (Ascaphus truei stejneger) ALE 5:361; CGR cp 3b; GRA 120; SRA cp 13.

Toad, Black (Bufo exsul) LVS 152; WFA 175; WID 351 (cp 31b).

Toad, Colorado River (Bufo alvarius) CAW 102, 103; CGR 91; SRA cp 9.

Toad, Dakota (Bufo hemiophrys) CRA 267 (pl 36); SRA pl 10.

Toad, Fowler's (Bufo fowleri) BAR cp 27; CAW cp 34; CRA 267 (pl 36); GRA 122; GPL 132.

Toad, Giant or Marine (Bufo marinus) ALE 5:439; BRW 26; CAW cp 30; CRA 267 (pl 36); IWE 11:1417, 1418; WFA 193.

Toad, Great Plains (Bufo cognatus) ALE 5:439; CFG cp 39; CGR 91; CRA 267 (pl 36); GRA 123; SRA cp 9; WFA 17, 168.

Toad, Green (Bufo debilis) CFG cp 39; CRA 271 (cp 38); SRA cp 8; WFA 175. (B. retiformis) LVS 153; SRA cp 8.

Toad, Horned—See **Lizard, Texas Horned.**

Toad, Narrow-mouthed (Gastrophryne olivacea) CRA 286 (cp 39); SRA cp 13. See also **Frog, Narrow-mouthed.**

Toad, Red Spotted (Bufo punctatus) CAW cp 36; CFG cp 39; CRA 267 (pl 36); SRA pl 10; WFA 193.

Toad, Spadefoot—See **Spadefoot.**

Toad, Texas (Bufo compactilis) CFG cp 39; CRA 267 (pl 36); WFA 168. (B. speciosus) SRA pl 10.

Toad, Western (Bufo boreas) CFG cp 39; GRA 123; SRA cp 9; WFA 147, 153.

Toad, Woodhouse's (Bufo woodhousei) BAR cp 27; CAW 104; CFG cp 39; CGR 96; CRA 267 (pl 36); SRA pl 10; WFA 205, 215.

Toadfish (Opsanus tau) CFG 513; CFW 153; HFW 282; IWE 18:2428; NGF 218; WFW 272. (O. beta) GGF 141.

Toadflax, Bastard (Comandra umbellata) AFP 1:527; BBF 1:640; CWF 110; HFP 80; HWF cp 28b; HYF cp 43; PFF 150; PMF 71; RUS 1:89, 2:141; VPN 2:105. (C. livida) AFP 1:528; BBF 1:640; CWF 110; RWA cp 97; VPN 2:105.

Toadflax, Blue (Linaria canadensis) AFP 3:785; BBF 3:177; FNC 170; HYF cp 178; PMF 345; RUS 1:395, 2:503, 3:393, 4:599, 5:515, 6:571; VPN 4:334.

Toadflax, Common—See **Butter-and-eggs.**

Toadflax, Ivy-leaved—See **Ivy, Kenilworth.**

Toadshade (Trillium sessile) BBF 1:523; DFP 112 (cp 889); FFK 76; OOW cp 169; PFW 298; PMF 241, 367; RUS 1:29, 2:33, 6:29; RWA cp 58.

Tobacco, Flowering (Nicotiana alata) AGF 108; DFP 44 (cp 351); EGA 139; FGF 198; FHP 135; LFW 256 (cp 571); OGF 129; PFW 285; TGF 205.

Tody, Cuban (Todus multicolor) BWI 176 (cp 7); GFB 102.

Tody, Jamaican (Todus todus) ABW 180; BWI 176 (cp 7); IWE 18:2429; SOS 209.

Tody, Puerto Rican (Todus mexicanus) BWI 176 (cp 7); CDB 127 (cp 494); GPB 210; WAB 99.

Tomato (Lycopersicon esculentum) OFP 125; PFF 293; WYG 112.

Tomato, Tree (Cyphomandra betacea) MWF 102 (cp 282); OFP 125.

Tomcod, Atlantic (Microgadus tomcod) CFG 508; GGF 72.

Tooth, Bleeding (Nerita pelorouta) GSS 19, 36; MOL 69.

Tooth Shell—See **Tusk Shell.**

Tooth-cup (Rotala ramosior) AFP 3:166; BBF 2:579; RUS 3:217, 4:319, 5:295, 6:347; VPN 3:467.

Toothwort—See also **Crinkleroot.**

Toothwort (Dentaria laciniata) FFK 113; FNC 77; HWF cp 81a; HYF cp 78; PFF 189; PMF 85, 273; RUS 1:167, 6:243; RWA cp 148. (D. tenella) CWF

183; RUS 5:193. (D. californica) RUS 4:229, 5:193.

Top Shell—See also **Turban Shell.**

Top Shell, Channeled (Calliostoma canaliculatum or
C. dolarium) AAS 114, cp 3q; ASN 71; GGS 113;
MGS pl 32.

Top Shell, Chocolate-lined (Calliostoma javanicum)
ASN 71; GSS 31. (C. zonamestum) AAS cp 3n.

Top Shell, Ribbed (Calliostoma ligatum) AAS 114;
ASN 71; GGS 113; KSL 183, 184; MGS pl 32; RCT
185 (pl 28).

Top Shell, Ringed (Calliostoma annulatum) AAS 114;
ALE 3:74; ASN 71; GAS 316; MGS pls 4, 32; PFF
409.

Topminnow, Black-stripe (Fundulus notatus) CFG
556; NGF 287.

Tortoise—See also **Terrapin** and **Turtle.**

Tortoise, Desert (Gopherus agassizi) AWW 19, 29;
FWA 159; LRE 21; PFF 534; PRW pl 45; SRA pl 15.

Tortoise, Gopher (Gopherus polyphemus) ALE 6:91,
115; CGR 158; CRA 78 (pl 9); GRA 27; SIR 28.

Tortoise, Texas Gopher (Gopherus berlandieri) CGR
cp 7c; CRA 78 (pl 9); IWE 18:2441; PRW pl 46; SIR
27.

Toucan, Keel-billed (Ramphastos sulphuratus) ABW
189; ALE 9:98; DBM cp 12; GPB 225; LBW 184 (cp
110); PMB cp 22; WAB 84.

Toucanet, Emerald (Aulacorhynchus prasinus) ABW
189; ALE 9:107; CDB 135 (cp 535); DBM cp 12;
PMB cp 22.

Touch-me-not—See **Jewelweed.**

Towhee, Abert's (Pipilo aberti) AAB 476; NGB 2:267;
NGS 351; PWB 275 (cp 56); RBB 305.

Towhee, Brown (Pipilo fuscus) ANE 11:2031, 2032;
BBC 2:cp 116; DBM cp 47; GBI 119; NGB 2:267;
NGS 352; PFF 669; PMB cp 48; PWB 275 (cp 56);
RBB 305.

Towhee, California or Canon—See **Towhee, Brown.**

Towhee, Collared (Pipilo ocai) DBM cp 47; PMB
cp 47.

Towhee, Green-tailed (Chlorura chlorura) AAB 474;
BBC 2:cp 116; CFG cp 23; LBW 366 (cp 213); NGB
2:267; NGS 353; PWB 275 (cp 56); RBB 305.

Towhee, Olive-backed—See **Towhee, Rufous-sided or
Spotted.**

Towhee, Rufous-sided or Spotted (Pipilo erythrophthalmus) AAB 475; ALE 9:342; ANE 11:2031;
BBC 2:cp 116; CDB 197 (cp 863); CFG cp 23; GBC
333 (cp 66); GBI 118; NGB 2:265; NGS 350, 351;

PBA 3:cp 84; PEB 215 (cp 56); PFF 668; PMB cp
cp 47; PWB 275 (cp 56); RBB 305.

Towhee, White-throated (Pipilo albicollis) DBM cp 47;
PMB cp 48.

Townhall Clock (Adoxa moschatellina) EWF cp 16a;
NHE 36; OWF 49; VPN 4:476.

Townsendia (Townsendia annua) RUS 3:475, 4:703,
6:687. (T. florifer) AFP 4:307; RUS 6:689; VPN
5:531. (T. incana) OOW cp 275; RUS 4:703; 6:687.

Trail Plant (Adenocaulon bicolor) AFP 4:417; BBF
3:457; RUS 5:615, 6:719; VPN 5:23.

Trailing-arbutus—See **Arbutus, Trailing.**

Treacle-mustard (Erysimum cheiranthoides) NHE 219;
OWF 9; RUS 2:225, 5:177; VPN 2:507. (E. repandum) NHE 219; RUS 6:223; VPN 2:510.

Tread Softly (Cnidoscolus stimulosus) FNC 106; LWF
28 (cp 49); RUS 2:153, 6:119.

Tree of Heaven (Ailanthus altissima) AFP 3:22; ANE
1:12; BBF 2:446; BKT cps 149, 151; BTN 199; EGT
97; MTB 325 (cp 30); MWF 34 (cp 33); OBT 185;
PFF 230; TGS 326; TSK 87, 117, 334, 335; VPN
3:397.

Treecreeper, Common—See **Creeper, Brown.**

Tree-duck, Black-bellied (Dendrocygna autumnalis)
ALE 7:268; GFB 43; GGB 19; KWF 450 (cp 31);
458 (cp 35); NGB 1:99; NGW 160; PWB 35 (pl 8),
58 (cp 13); RBA 45; RBB 51.

Tree-duck, Black-billed or West Indian (Dendrocygna
arborea) AAB 64; ALE 7:307; BWI 44; RBB 51.

Tree-duck, Fulvous (Dendrocygna bicolor) AAB 63;
ALE 7:268; GGB 33; GPB 78; KWF 450 (cp 31),
458 (cp 35); NGB 1:99; NGW 160; PEB 38 (cp 13);
PWB 35 (pl 8), 58 (cp 13); RBB 51.

Treefrog, Barking (Hyla gratiosa) CAW 113; CGR
cp 5a; CRA 286 (cp 39); WFA 15, 17, 325.

Treefrog, Bird-voiced or Whistling (Hyla avivoca) BAR
cp 31; CAW cp 60; CRA 286 (cp 39); GRA 127;
WFA 297.

Treefrog, Common or Gray (Hyla versicolor) ANE
11:2064; BAR cp 30; BRW 32; CAW 142, 179, 183,
cp 56; CGR 107; CRA 286 (cp 39); GPL 134; GRA
126; PFF 528; WFA 345, 348, 354.

Treefrog, Cuban (Hyla septentrionalis) ALE 5:440;
ANE 11:2061; CAW 120, 185, cp 48; CRA 286 (cp
39); WFA 337.

Treefrog, Green (Hyla cinerea) AWW 35; BAR cp 29;
CAW 111, cp 53; CGR cp 4f; CRA 286 (cp 39);
GPL 134; GRA 126; WFA 307.

Treefrog, Pacific (Hyla regilla) CAW 116, cp 52; GPL 134; GRA 127; SRA cp 13; WFA 337.

Treefrog, Pine-barrens (Hyla andersoni) ANE 11:2064; CRA 286 (cp 39); LVS 146; WFA 284; WID 351 (cp 31).

Treefrog, Southern or Squirrel (Hyla squirella) CGR 100; CRA 286 (cp 39); GRA 127; WFA 345.

Treefrog, Spring Peeper (Hyla crucifer) ANE 4:737, 11:2064; BAR cp 29; CAW 115, 179, cp 58; CGR 107; CRA 286 (cp 39); GPL 134; GRA 127; PFF 528; WFA 316.

Treehopper (Ceresa sp. or Stictocephala sp.) BIA 131; GGI 33; GIP 89; PFF 457; SCI 133; SIG cp 41.

Tree-huckleberry—See **Farkleberry.**

Trefoil (Lotus pinnatus) AFP 2:544; HFP cp 32a; RUS 5:355, 6:399; VPN 3:301. (L. oblongifolius) AFP 2:544; RUS 4:381, 5:355, 6:399.

Trefoil, Bird's-foot (Lotus corniculatus) AFP 2:556; BBF 2:359; CWF 290; DFP 156 (cp 1244); FFK 179; NHE 180; OWF 21; PMF 151; PRP 88; RUS 1:281, 3:271, 5:355, 6:399.

Trefoil, Tick—See **Tick-trefoil.**

Tremex, Pigeon (Tremex columba) BIA cp 15; GGI 136; IWE 15:2027; KIW 265 (cp 139); PFF 496; SCI 518; SIG cp 124.

Tricholoma, Narcissus (Tricholoma sulphureum) KMF 19 (cp 3a); LHM 85; ONP 127.

Tricholoma, Soap-scented (Tricholoma saponaceum) GMC 111 (cp 182); LHM 85; NFP 60; ONP 135.

Triggerfish, Gray (Balistes capriscus or B. carolinensis) GGF 134; OBV 43; WFW 126.

Triggerfish, Pacific—See **Humu-humu-nukunuku-a-pua'a.**

Triggerfish, Queen (Balistes vetula) HFW 259 (cp 122); GGF 2; IWE 18:2463; LSE 123; WFW cp 470.

Trillium, Dwarf White (Trillium nivale) BBF 1:524; FFK 76; HYF cp 12; PMF 11; RUS 1:29.

Trillium, Giant (Trillium chloropetalum) AFP 1:451; DFP 111 (cp 887); HFP 37, cp 10d; PFW 298; RUS 5:37; RWA cp 59; VPN 1:808.

Trillium, Large-flowered (Trillium grandiflorum) BBF 1:535; DFP 111 (cp 888); FFK 79; FNC 21; HWF cp 23b; HYF cp 25; LFW 224 (cp 505); LWF 224 (cp 355); PFF 381; PFW 297; PMF 11, 241; RUS 1:31, 2:29; RWA cp 56; TGF 28.

Trillium, Nodding (Trillium cernuum) BBF 1:526; FNC 18; HWF cp 24b; PMF 11; RUS 1:31, 2:29.

Trillium, Painted (Trillium undulatum) BBF 1:526; EWF cp 167c; FFK 78; FNC 20; HWF cp 24a; HYF cp 27; LWF 112 (cp 178); PMF 11, 213, 241; RUS 1:29, 2:29; RWA cp 57.

Trillium, Prairie (Trillium recurvatum) BBF 1:524; DEW 2:214 (cp 126); FFK 77; PMF 241; RUS 1:29, 2:33. (T. catesbaei) FNC 19; RUS 2:31.

Trillium, Red (Trillium erectum) BBF 1:525; EWF cp 167d; FFK 79; FNC 19; HWF cp 23a; HYF cp 26; LFW 224 (cp 503); LWF 222 (cp 350); PMF 213, 241; RUS 1:31, 2:29; RWA cps 54, 55.

Trillium, Sessile—See **Toadshade.**

Trillium, Western (Trillium ovatum) AFP 1:450; CWF 55, 62; HFP 38, cp 8; LWF 223 (cps 351, 352); OOW cp 167; RUS 5:37, 6:29; VPN 1:811.

Trillium, Yellow (Trillium viride var. luteum) FFK 77; FNC 17; LWF 224 (cp 354); RUS 1:29, 2:33.

Tripletail (Lobotes surinamensis) CFG 490; GGF 111.

Tritoma—See **Red Hot Poker.**

Triton, Dwarf (Ocenebra interfossa) AAS 217; ASN 127; GGS 127; PFF 411. (O. circumtexta) AAS 217; ASN 127; GGS 127.

Triton, Hairy (Cymatium pileare) ASN 119; GSS 69; MGS pl 69. (C. martinianum) AAS cp 9L.

Triton, Oregon (Fusitriton oregonensis or Argobuccinum oregonensis) AAS pl 24g; ASN 119; GAS 286; JSS 529; KSL 184; MGS pl 36; PFF 413.

Triton, Pacific—See **Triton's-trumpet.**

Triton's-trumpet (Charonia tritonis) AAS cp 5f; ALE 3:55; ASN 119; GSS 68; MGS pl 69.

Trogon, Collared or Bar-tailed (Trogon collaris) ABW 172; ALE 8:464; CDB 125 (cp 482); DBM cp 18; HBT 113 (cp 4); PMB cp 21.

Trogon, Coppery-tailed (Trogon elegans) AAB 267; BBW cp 45; DBM cp 18; NGB 2:85; NGS 77; PMB cp 21; PWB 151 (cp 38); RBB 179.

Trogon, Cuban (Priotelus temnurus) ALE 8:464; BWI 49 (cp 2).

Trogon, Gartered or Violaceous (Trogon violaceus or Chrysotrogon caligatus) ABW 172; DBM cp 18; HBT 113 (cp 4); PMB cp 21.

Trogon, Mexican or Mountain (Trogon mexicanus) DBM cp 18; PMB cp 21.

Trogon, Resplendent—See **Quetzal.**

Tropic-bird, Red-billed (Phaethon aethereus) AAB 15; ABW 39; ALE 7:157; BWI 21; FWA 260; GPB 50; NGW 67; RBB 31; SOS 161; WAB 215.

Tropic-bird, Red-tailed (Phaethon rubricauda) ABW 39; ALE 7:157; BHB 53 (cp 11); GFB 28; IWE 18:2467, 2468; MBH 64 (cp 7); NGB 1:56; NGW 66; PWB 319; SOS 348.

Tropic-bird, White-tailed (Yellow-billed) (Phaethon lepturus) AAB 25; ABW 39; ALE 7:157; BHB 53 (cp 10); BWI 22; CDB 38 (cp 38); IWE 18:2468; LBW 53; NGB 1:56; NGW 67; PEB 9; PWB 319; RBB 31.

Troupial (Icterus icterus) ABW 288; ALE 9:381; BWI 224 (cp 9); LBW 355 (cp 192).

Trout, Brook or Speckled (Salvelinus fontinalis) ALE 4:424; ANE 11:2068; CFG cp 43; CFW 51; GGF 47; GPL 121; HFW 34 (cp 4); IWE 18:2471; NGF 255; NHE 299; OBV 103; PFF 507; WFW cp 38.

Trout, Brown (Salmo trutta) ALE 4:224, 237, 11:105; ANE 11:2069; AWW 96; CFG cp 43; CFW 51; HPF 133; IWE 18:2471, 2472; NGF 253; NHE 299; PFF 507.

Trout, Cut-throat (Salmo clarkii) AWW 29; CFG 523; GGF 45; HPF 127; NGF 255; PFF 507.

Trout, Dolly Varden (Salvelinus malma) GGF 47; HPF 134; NGF 256.

Trout, Golden—See **Sunapee.**

Trout, Lake (Salvelinus namaycush) CFG cp 43; GGF 47; HFW 77; NGF 257; PFF 507. (Salmotrutta lacustris) ALE 4:224.

Trout, Rainbow (Salmo gairdneri) ALE 4:221, 222, 224, 237; ANE 11:2070; CFG cp 43; GGF 47; GPL 121; HPF 128; IWE 18:2471; NGF 255; NHE 299; OBV 103; PFF 507; WFW cp 37.

Trout-lily—See **Lily, Avalanche; Lily, Fawn; Lily, Glacier;** and **Violet, Dogtooth.**

Troutperch (Percopsis omiscomaycus) CFG 549; IWE 18:2473; NGF 290.

Truffle, Summer (Tuber aestivum) LHM 43; NFP 37; OFP 189; PFF 70.

Trumpet, Golden (Allamanda cathartica) AGF 20; DFP 51 (cp 406); FHP 104; LFW 228 (cp 510); MEP 108; PFW 29.

Trumpet Shell—See **Triton's-trumpet.**

Trumpet-creeper (Campsis radicans) AGF 234; EWF cp 162b; FNC 173; HSC 23; HYF cp 187; LFW 24 (cp 48); PFW 44; PMF 217; RWA 57 (cp 351); TGS 39; TSK 67, 178, 179.

Trumpets (Sarracenia flava) BBF 2:202; FNC 78; HYF cp 73; PMF 101; RUS 2:185; RWA cp 155.

Trumpet-vine—See **Trumpet-creeper.**

Trunkfish (Lactophrys trigonus) CFG 511; GGF 136; NGF 213; WFW 226.

Tuberose (Polianthes tuberosa) AGF 234; DFP 79 (cp 630); EGB 137; FGF 263; MEP 20; MGB 290; MWF 238 (cp 777); PFW 17.

Tubifex—See **Worm, Tubifex.**

Tuckahoe—See **Arum, Arrow.**

Tule—See **Bulrush, Great.**

Tulip Hybrids (Tulipa sp.) AGF 235-243; DFP 112-118 (cps 892-940); FGF 264-271; LFW 139-142 (cps 308-321); MGB 2-60; MWF 289 (cps 952-955); OGF 29, 31; PFF 374; PFW 173; RWF 46, 47; SGB cps 29-31; TGF 28.

Tulip, Star—See **Lily, Mariposa.**

Tulip Tree (Liriodendron tulipifera) BBF 2:83; BKT cps 113, 114; BTN 155; DEW 1:77, 78; DFP 210 (cp 1678); EGT 122; EWF cp 150e; FNC 70; MTB 257 (cp 24); MWF 187 (cp 594); OBT 145; PFF 176; PFW 181; RWA cp 137; TGS 183; TSK 41, 482, 483.

Tulip-tree, African (Spathodea campanulata) EWF cp 62b; LFW 176 (cp 398); MEP 138; MWF 271 (cps 899, 900); PFW 45.

Tumblegrass (Schedonnardus paniculatus) BBF 1:226; HMG 506; PRP 59.

Tumbleweed—See also **Thistle, Russian.**

Tumbleweed (Amaranthus graecizans) AFP 2:97; BBF 2:3; PMF 387; VPN 2:218.

Tun Shell, Giant (Tunna galea) ALE 3:55; ASN 121; GGS 123; GSS 70; NHE 164.

Tuna, Atlantic Blackfin or Bladefin (Thunnus atlanticus) CFG 500; IWE 18:2493.

Tuna, Bluefin (Thunnus thynnus) ALE 5:191; ANE 4:677; AWW 147; CFG cp 42; CFW 10, 134; GGF 87; HPF 379; IWE 18:2493; NGF 114; OBV 27; PFF 519; SOS 98; WFW 350.

Tuna, Little (Euthynnus alleteratus) CFG 492; GGF 86.

Tuna, Skipjack—See **Bonito, Oceanic.**

Tuna, Yellowfin (Thunnus albacores) CFG 492; GGF 87; IWE 18:2493; MOL 96; NGF 115; SOS 98; WFW 349.

Tunicate—See **Sea Squirt.**

Tunny—See **Tuna, Bluefin.**

Tunny, Longfin—See **Albacore.**

Tupelo, Black (Nyssa sylvatica) BBF 2:665; BTN 239; DFP 214 (cp 1712); EGT 129; GGT 41; TGS 246; TSK 140, 364, 365. (N. aquatica) BBF 2:239; BTN 239; GPL 69.

Turban Shell, Black (Tegula funebralis) ASN 75; GAS 312; GGS 114; MGS pl 32; PFF 409.

Turban Shell, Chestnut (Turbo castaneus) AAS cp 3g; ASN 77; GGS 113; GSS 32. (Turbonilla castanea) MGS pl 33.

138; CRA 47 (cp 6), 78 (pl 9); GPL 137; GRA 22; IWE 11:1529; PFF 531; SIR 16, 50 (cp 3).

Turtle, Ornate (Western) Box (Terrapene ornata) BRW 54; CFG 354; CRA 62 (cp 7); GRA 39; OMW 29; PRW pl 27; SIR 49 (cp 2); SRA pl 14.

Turtle, Pacific or Western Pond (Clemmys marmorata) GPL 139; GRA 41; PFF 532; SRA pl 14.

Turtle, Painted (Chrysemys picta) ALE 6:105; ANE 11:2077; AWW 32; BAR cp 37; CFG cp 33; CRA 46 (cp 5), 110 (cp 13); GPL 138; GRA 32, 33; IWE 12:1674, 1675; PFF 533; PRW pl 32; SIR 52 (cp 8); SRA pl 15.

Turtle, Pond Slider (Pseudemys scripta) CFG cp 33; GPL 138; IWE 16:1676; SRA pl 15.

Turtle, Red-bellied (Pseudemys rubriventris) ANE 11:2077; CFG cp 33; CRA 110 (cp 13); GPL 138; PRW pl 34.

Turtle, Red-eared (Pseudemys scripta elegans or Chrysemys scripta elegans) ALE 6:105; BAR cp 37; BRW 60; CGR cp 7b; CRA 47 (cp 5), 110 (cp 13); GRA 28, 29; LEA 293; MAR 66 (pl 26); SIR 22, 53 (cp 10).

Turtle, Ridley (Lepidochelys kempi) ANE 11:2077; CFG 361; CGR 163; CRA 79 (pl 10); OMW 32, 33; PRW pl 50; WID 329. (L. olivacea) LVS 159; SRA pl 16.

Turtle, Ringed Sawback (Graptemys oculifera) ALE 6:105; CRA 63 (cp 8).

Turtle, Smooth Soft-shell (Trionyx muticus) BAR cp 39; CRA 46 (cp 5), 94 (pl 11); CFG 361.

Turtle, Snapping (Chelydra serpentina) ALE 6:70; ANE 11:2076; BAR cp 33; BRW 50-51; CFG 361; CGR cp 5f; CRA 47 (cp 6), 79 (pl 10); FWA 392; GPL 137; GRA 24; IWE 16:2187-2189; PFF 531; PRW pls 22, 23; SIR 12, 14, 15; SRA pl 14.

Turtle, Spiny Soft-shell (Trionyx spinifer) ALE 6:116; ANE 11:2076; BAR cp 39; CRA 46 (cp 5), 94 (pl 11); FWA 392; IWE 16:2200, 2201; SIR 56 (cps 16, 17); SRA pl 15.

Turtle, Spotted (Clemmys guttata) ALE 6:105; ANE 11:2076; BRW 49; CRA 47 (cp 6), 62 (cp 7); GPL 139; GRA 40; MAR 69 (cp 5); PFF 532; PRW pl 37; SIR 51 (cp 6).

Turtle, Wood (Clemmys insculpta) ANE 11:2076; CFG 353; CGR cp 6b; CRA 47 (cp 6), 62 (cp 7); GRA 43; PFF 532; PRW pl 36; SIR 50 (cp 5).

Turtle, Yellow Mud (Kinosternon flavescens) CFG cp 33; CRA 78 (pl 9); GRA 23; LEA 294.

Turtlehead (Chelone glabra) FFK 196; FNC 169; HWF cp 197; HYF cp 181; PMF 59; RUS 1:409, 2:513; RWA cp 330. (C. obliqua) DFP 128 (cp 1024); HYF cp 181; LWF 46 (cp 76); RUS 2:513.

Turtlehead, Red (Chelone lyoni) EGP 106; PMF 227; RUS 1:409, 2:513.

Tusk Shell, Indian Money (Dentalium pretiosum) ASN 187; GAS 248; GGS 140; GSS 7; MGS pl 41; PFF 407.

Tusk Shell, Stimpson's (Dentalium entale stimpsoni) ASN 187; GGS 140.

Twayblade, Bog (Liparis loeselii) BBF 1:572; COA 275; HWF cp 42b; NHE 79; PMF 373; RUS 1:87, 2:117, 6:81; VPN 1:853.

Twayblade, Broad-lipped (Listera convallarioides) AFP 1:480; BBF 1:567; COA 125; PMF 119; RUS 2:101, 4:73, 5:73, 6:73; VPN 1:856.

Twayblade, Heart-leaved (Listera cordata) AFP 1:480; BBF 1:568; COA 125; CWF 91; HFP 68; NHE 79; OWF 45; PMF 243; RUS 1:71, 2:101, 4:73, 5:73, 6:69; RWA cp 79; VPN 1:856.

Twayblade, Kidney-leaf (Listera smallii) BBF 1:567; COA 122; FNC 44; RUS 2:101.

Twayblade, Lily-leaved (Liparis lilifolia) BBF 1:572; COA 275; FFK 64; FNC 49; HWF 84; HYF cp 43; PMF 243; RUS 1:87, 2:117; RWA cp 88.

Twinberry, Black (Lonicera involucrata) AFP 4:53; BBF 3:282; CWF 503; HFP 350; RWA cp 360; VPN 4:461.

Twinberry, Red (Lonicera utahensis) AFP 4:53; CWF 499; VPN 4:466.

Twinflower (Linnaea borealis) AFP 4:49; BBF 3:276; CWF 502; HFP 342; HWF cp 213a; HYF cp 191; LWF 271 (cp 433); NHE 25; PFF 304; PMF 237; RUS 5:451, 6:539; RWA cp 362; TGF 188; VPN 4:457.

Twin-leaf (Jeffersonia diphylla) BBF 2:129; FFK 112; HWF 115; PMF 23; RUS 1:157, 2:217; RWA cp 140. (J. dubia) DFP 13 (cp 97); PFW 233.

Twinspur (Diascia barberae) DFP 36 (cp 287); EGA 114; TGF 220.

Twisted-stalk, Pink (Streptopus roseus) BBF 1:520; CWF 54; FNC 24; HWF 58; PFF 381; PMF 255, 293; RUS 1:35, 2:35, 5:37; VPN 1:805.

Twisted-stalk, White (Streptopus amplexcaulis) AFP 1:457; BBF 1:520; CWF 42; HFP 46; NHE 38; PMF 371; RUS 1:35, 2:35, 4:41, 5:37, 6:37; RWA cp 52; VPN 1:805.

Tyrranulet, Beardless—See **Flycatcher, Beardless.**

Tyrannulet, Paltry (Tyranniscus vilissimus) DBM cp 30; PMB cp 29.

Tyrannulet, Yellow-bellied (Ornithion semiflavum) DBM cp 30; PMB cp 29.

Tyrant, Cattle or Fire-crowned (Machetornis rixosus) ALE 9:143; LBW 192 (cp 126); WAB 89.

U

Umbrella Plant (Peltiphyllum peltatum) DEW 1:281 (cp 167); DFP 163 (cp 1303); HFP 154; LWF 257 (cp 407); PFW 272; RUS 5:251.

Umbrella Tree (Schefflera actinophylla or Brassaia actinophylla) MEP 102; MWF 61 (cp 135).

Umbrella-leaf (Diphylleia cymosa) BBF 2:129; FNC 68; RUS 2:217.

Umbrella-wort—See **Four O'Clock, Wild.**

Unicorn Fish (Naso lituratus) ALE 5:182, 201; NGF 333; WFW cp 445. (Bregmaceros macclellandi) SOS 333; WFW 139.

Unicorn Plant (Proboscidea louisianica) AFP 4:4; DFP 43 (cp 338); EGA 148; EWF cp 162c; RUS 1:411, 2:523, 3:405, 5:517.

Urchin—See **Sea Urchin.**

Ursinia (Ursinia anethoides) DFP 49 (cp 389); EGA 159; TGF 268.

V

Valerian, Common (Valeriana officinalis) AFP 4:57; AGF 245; BBF 3:286; EGP 149; NHE 100; OWF 123; PMF 297; RUS 1:517, 6:535; TGF 188.

Valerian, Greek—See also **Jacob's Ladder.**

Valerian, Greek (Polemonium reptens) BBF 3:63; FFK 135; HYF cp 160; LWF 268 (cp 426); PMF 323; RUS 1:327, 2:413, 6:463; RWA cp 309.

Valerian, Mountain (Valeriana stichensis) AFP 4:57; CWF 506; HFP 354; RUS 5:449, 6:535; RWA cp 363.

Valerian, Red (Centranthus or Kentranthus ruber) AFP 4:63; EGP 105; EWF cp 17a; LFW 22 (cp 42); OWF 123; PFW 303; RUS 5:451; TGF 188.

Vanilla (Vanilla planifloia) COA 162; OFP 131; RUS 2:119. (V. fragrens) PFF 391.

Vanilla-leaf (Achlys triphylla) AFP 2:222; CWF 174; HFP 118; LWF 253 (cp 398); OOW cp 34; RUS 5:207, 6:211; VPN 2:416.

Varnish Tree—See **Golden Rain Tree.**

Vase Shell (Vasum muricatum) AAS pl 23L; ASN 149; GSS 90. (V. caestus) MGS pl 60.

Veery (Hylocichla fuscescens) ANE 11:2105; BBC 2:cp 91; CFG cp 15; GBC 252 (cp 51); NGB 2:163; NGS 217; PBA 3:cp 105; PWB 231 (cp 48); RBB 233.

Velvet-leaf (Abutilon theophrasti) AFP 3:85; PFF 250; PMF 143; RUS 1:149, 2:204, 3:125, 4:177, 6:191.

Venus, Cross-barred (Chione cancellata) AAS cp 39h; ASN 233; PFF 423.

Venus' Fly-trap (Dionaea muscipula) DEW 1:247, 284 (cp 177); EWF cp 158a; FNC 83; HYF cp 74; PFW 103; RWA cp 159.

Venus' Girdle (Folia parallela) GGS 53. (Cestus veneris) ALE 1:271; OIB 17.

Venus, King (Chione paphia) AAS cp 39a; ASN 233; GSS 147.

Venus' Looking-glass (Specularia perfoliata) AFP 4:79; BBF 3:298; FFK 139; FNC 184; HFP 360; HWF cp 219b; HYF cp 186; PMF 341; (S. speculum) DFP 48 (cp 377). (Legousia speculum-veneris) NHE 236.

Verbena—See also **Vervain.**

Verbena Hybrids (Verbena hybrida) AGF 245; DFP 49 (cp 392); EGA 160; FGF 272; LFW 268 (cps 599-602), 269 (cp 604); MWF 292 (cp 961); PFF 286; PFW 303; TGF 189.

Verdigris (Stropharia aeruginosa) DEW 3:137 (cp 67); GMC 275; KMF 103 (cp 24b); LHM 145; NFP 83; ONP 31.

Verdin (Auriparus flaviceps) AAB 325; ALE 9:308; ANE 11:2106; NGB 2:141; NGS 160; PWB 214 (cp 45); RBB 219.

Vernal-grass, Sweet (Anthozanthum odoratum) AFP 1:123; BBF 1:171; NHE 243; VPN 1:490.

Vervain, Blue (Verbena hastata) AFP 3:608; BBF 3:95; HWF cp 183b; HYF cp 166; PMF 317; RUS 1:363, 2:465, 3:367, 4:543, 5:455, 6:545; VPN 4:246.·

(cp 54); NGB 2:223; NGS 244, 249; PBA 3:cp 91;
PEB 182 (cp 47), 194 (cp 50); PFF 645; RBB 247;
WAB 43.

Virginia Creeper (Parthenocissus tricuspidata) DFP
249 (cp 1985); HSC 86; MWF 222 (cp 723). (P.
quinquefolia) BBF 2:511; FNC 110; PFF 246; TSK
135, 188.

Vole, Alaska or Singing (Microtus miurus) BMC 166
(cp 18). (M. abbreviatus) SAA 119.

Vole, Boreal Red-backed (Clethrionomys gapperi)
BGM 180 (cp 17); BMC 166 (cp 18); CFG cp 31;
GGM 104; NGA 277. (C. rutilus) SAA 119.

Vole, Heather (Phenacomys intermedius) BGM 180
(cp 17); BMC 134 (cp 15); CFG 296.

Vole, Long-tailed (Microtus longicaudus) BMC 134 (cp
15); GGM 105.

Vole, Meadow—See **Mouse, Field or Meadow.**

Vole, Pine—See **Mouse, Pine.**

Vole, Prairie (Microtus ochrogaster) BGM 180 (cp 17);
BMC 134 (cp 15); GGM 105.

Vole, Sagebrush (Lagurus curtatus) BGM 180 (cp 17);
BMC 134 (cp 15); CFG 296; GGM 105.

Volute, Junonia (Scaphella junonia) AAS cp 13f; ASN
152, 153; GSS 99.

Volvaria, Showy (Volvariella speciosa) GMC 216; LHM
121; MSM 111; NFP 77.

Vulture, Black (Coragyps atratus) ABW 72; ALE
7:334; BBC 1:cp 24; CDB 54 (cp 131); CFG cp 4;
GBI 44; NGB 1:147; NGW 211, 213; PEB 58 (pl 17);
PWB 75 (pl 18); RBB 65.

Vulture, California—See **Condor, California.**

Vulture, King (Sarcoramphus papa) ABW 72; ALE
7:334; CDB 55 (cp 132); DBM cp 4; GPB 91; LBW
100; PMB cp 4.

Vulture, Turkey (Cathartes aura) AAB 90; ABW 72;
ALE 7:334; ANE 11:2119, 2120; BBC 1:cp 24;
CDB 54 (cp 130); CFG cp 4; GBC 104 (cp 15), 125
(pl 20); GBI 44; GPB 90; IWE 18:2502-2504; LDE
88; NGB 1:147; NGW 212; PBA 2:cp 43; PEB 58
(pl 17); PFF 573; PWB 75 (pl 18); RBA 61; RBB 65.

W

Wagtail, Pied or White (Motacilla alba) ABW 264; ALE
9:184, 189; BBE 200, 206; CDB 153 (cp 632); GFB
169; IWE 19:2543; RBB 239.

Wagtail, Yellow (Motacilla flava) AAB 367; ALE
8:187, 9:184, 189; BBE 204; CDB 154 (cp 634);
GBC 364 (cp 69); GFB 169; NGS 228-229; RBB
239.

Wahoo (fish) (Acanthocybium solanderi) CFW 135;
GGF 85; MOL 95; NGF 116.

Wahoo, Eastern (plant) (Euonymous atropurpurea)
BBF 2:491; BTN 209; PFF 239; TSK 97, 126.

Wahoo, Western (plant) (Euonymous occidentalis)
AFP 3:57; BTN 209; VPN 3:413.

Wake-robin—See **Trillium.**

Walkingstick (Diapheromera femorata) ANE 11:2122;
BIA 87; GGI 17; KIA 31; KIW 36 (cp 5); PFF 444;
SCI 71; SIG pl 5.

Walleye (Stizostedion vitreum) GGF 97; HFW 182;
IWE 13:1731; NGF 278; PFF 521; WFW 340.

Wallflower (Cheiranthus cheiri) DFP 5 (cp 34), 33 (cp
262), 128 (cps 1021-1023); EGA 105; EGP 105;
LFW 24 (cp 47); MWF 82 (cp 205); NHE 219; OGF
33; PFW 97; TGF 77.

Wallflower, Western (Erysimum asperum) CWF 187;
HFP 130; HYF cp 81; OOW cp 135; RUS 1:167,
3:155, 4:207, 6:223; TGF 92; VPN 2:507.

Wallpepper—See **Stonecrop, Mossy.**

Wall-rue (Asplenium ruta-muraria) FFK 31; NFP 136;
NHE 245; ONP 73.

Walnut, Black (Juglans nigra) BBF 1:579; BTN 93;
EGT 119; GGT 136; MTB 192 (cp 17); OFP 29;
PFF 133; TSK 338.

Walnut, California (Juglans californica) AFP 1:509;
BTN 95.

Walnut, English (Juglans regia) BTN 95; MTB 192 (cp
17), 195; NHE 294; OBT 193; OFP 29; PFF 133;
TGS 86.

Walnut, White—See **Butternut.**

Walrus (Odobenus rosmarus) ALE 8:229, 12:26, 374,
399, 400; AWW 37; BGM 90; CFG 333; FWA 25,
419; IWE 19:2549-2552; JAW 144; LEA 578; LMA
27; NGA 346-347, 353, 362; OBV 181; PFF 700;
PMG cp 16; PWC 240; SLP 80, 81; SOS 166; VWA
cp 18; WEA 383; WID 90.

Wandering Jew (Zebrina pendula) EWF cp 187d; PFF
369; PFW 77; RUS 2:63.

Wapato—See **Arrowleaf.**

Wapiti—See **Elk, American.**

Warbler, Hooded (Wilsonia citrina) AAB 429; ABW 285; ALE 9:371; BBC 2:cp 105; CFG cps 18, 20; GBC 284 (cp 59); NGB 2:187; NGS 287; PBA 3:cp 98; PEB 187 (cp 50), 195 (cp 52); PFF 657; RBB 208.

Warbler, Kentucky (Oporornis formosus) AAB 425; AWW 25; CFG cp 18; GBC 285 (cp 60); NGB 2:189; NGS 284; PBA 3:cp 98; PEB 187 (cp 50); PFF 655; RBB 273.

Warbler, Kirtland's (Dendroica kirtlandii) AAB 419; CFG cp 16; FWA 54; GBC 265 (cp 56); NGB 2:202; NGS 280; OMW 175; PEB 186 (cp 49); RBB 269; SLS 75; WAB 39; WID 333 (cp 29c).

Warbler, Lawrence's (Vermivora lawrencei) CFG cp 17; PEB 187 (cp 50); RBB 255.

Warbler, Lucy's (Vermivora luciae) AAB 405; BBC 2:cp 99; NGB 2:204; NGS 265; PWB 262 (cp 51); RBB 259.

Warbler, MacGillivray's (Oporornis tolmiei) AAB 427; ANE 11:2130; BBC 2:cp 104; CFG cp 18; GBC 285 (cp 60); LBW 288 (cp 187); NGB 2:187; NGS 285; PWB 262 (cp 51); RBB 273; TBC 360 (cp 68b).

Warbler, Magnolia (Dendroica magnolia) AAB 408; ABW 286; ALE 9:371; BBC 2:cp 100; CDB 204 (cp 892); CFG cps 16, 19; GBC 265 (cp 56); NGB 2:193; NGS 268; PBA 3:cp 97; PEB 186 (cp 49), 194 (cp 51); PFF 650; PWB 247 (cp 50); RBB 261; TBC 352 (cp 65a); WAB 61.

Warbler, Mangrove (Dendroica erithachorides) DBM cp 43; PMB cp 38.

Warbler, Mourning (Oporornis philadelphia) AAB 426; CFG cps 18, 20; GBC 285 (cp 60); NGB 2:187; NGS 285; PBA 3:cp 100; PEB 187 (cp 50); PFF 656; PWB 262 (cp 51); RBB 273.

Warbler, Myrtle (Dendroica coronata) AAB 411; ANE 11:2137; BBC 2:cp 100; CFG cps 16, 19; GBC 268 (cp 57); GBI 101; NGB 2:202; NGS 269; PBA 3:cp 94; PEB 186 (cp 49), 194 (cp 51); PFF 651; PWB 247 (cp 50); RBB 261; TBC 352 (cp 65b).

Warbler, Nashville (Vermivora ruficapilla) AAB 404; BBC 2:cp 99; CFG cps 17, 20; GBC 265 (cp 56); NGB 2:195; NGS 264; PBA 3:cp 93; PEB 187 (cp 50), 195 (cp 52); PWB 262 (cp 51); RBB 255.

Warbler, Olive (Peucedramus taeniatus) NGS 267; PBA 3:123; PWB 262 (cp 51); RBB 257.

Warbler, Olive-backed (Parula pitiayuma) HBT 241 (cp 14); PMB cp 38; PWB 262 (cp 51); RBB 259.

Warbler, Orange-crowned (Vermivora celata) AAB 403; BBC 2:cp 98; CDB 205 (cp 901); CFG cps 17, 20; GBC 265 (cp 56); NGB 2:200; NGS 264; PBA 3:cp 93; PEB 183 (cp 48), 195 (cp 52); PWB 262 (cp 51); RBB 257; TBC 350 (cp 64a).

Warbler, Palm (Dendroica palmarum) CFG cps 16, 19; GBC 284 (cp 59); NGB 2:189; NGS 281; PBA 3:cp 95; PEB 186 (cp 49), 194 (cp 51); PFF 654; PWB 247 (cp 50); RBB 269.

Warbler, Parula (Parula americana) AAB 406; ANE 11:2138; BBC 2:cp 99; CFG cps 17, 19; GBC 264 (cp 55); NGB 2:195; NGS 266; PBA 3:cp 94; PEB 183 (cp 48), 194 (cp 51); PFF 649; RBB 259.

Warbler, Pine (Dendroica pinus) AAB 418; ANE 11:2139; BBC 2:694; CFG cps 16, 19; GBC 269 (cp 58); NGB 2:191; NGS 280; PBA 3:cp 95; PEB 186 (cp 49), 194 (cp 51); PFF 653; RBB 269.

Warbler, Prairie (Dendroica discolor) AAB 420; CFG cps 16, 19; GBC 284 (cp 59); NGB 2:189; NGS 281; PBA 3:cp 95; PEB 186 (cp 49), 194 (cp 51); PFF 654; RBA 219; RBB 269; WAB 61.

Warbler, Prothonotary (Protonatoria citrea) AAB 398; ABW 285; ALE 9:371; ANE 11:2140; BBC 2:cp 97; CFG cps 17, 20; GBC 264 (cp 55); NGB 2:204; NGS 260; PBA 3:cp 92; PEB 187 (cp 50), 195 (cp 52); PFF 647; RBA 213; RBB 253;

Warbler, Red (Ergaticus ruber) ALE 9:371; AMB 89 (cp 7); DBM cp 43; PMB cp 37.

Warbler, Red-faced (Cardellina rubrifrons) AAB 428; NGB 2:185; NGS 254-255; PMB cp 37; PWB 262 (cp 51).

Warbler, Rufous-capped (Basileuterus rufifrons) AMB 89 (cp 7); CDB 203 (cp 890); DBM cp 44; PMB cp 38.

Warbler, Semper's (Leucopeza semperi) BWI 201; WID 315.

Warbler, Swainson's (Lymnothlypis swainsoni) AAB 399; BBC 2:cp 97; CFG cp 17; NGB 2:204; NGS 261; PBA 3:114; PEB 183 (cp 48); RBB 253.

Warbler, Tennessee (Vermivora peregrina) AAB 402; BBC 2:cp 98; CFG cps 17, 20; GBC 265 (cp 56); NGB 2:195; NGS 262; PBA 3:cp 93; PEB 183 (cp 48), 195 (cp 52); PFF 649; PWB 262 (cp 51); RBB 257.

Warbler, Townsend's (Dendroica townsendi) AAB 412; BBC 2:cp 101; CFG cp 16; GBC 268 (cp 57); NGB 2:206; NGS 272; PBA 3:145; PWB 247 (cp 50); RBB 263; TBC 354 (cp 66b); WAB 61.

Warbler, Virginia's (Vermivora virginiae) BBC 2:cp 99;

Waterleaf, Broad-leaved (Hydrophyllum canadense) FFK 119; PMF 55; RUS 2:415.

Waterleaf, Dwarf (Hydrophyllum capitatum) AFP 3:483; CWF 438; RUS 5:405, 6:485; VPN 4:149.

Waterleaf, Large-leaved (Hydrophyllum macrophyllum) FFK 119; PMF 55; RUS 2:415.

Waterleaf, Pacific or Slender (Hydrophyllum tenuipes) AFP 3:478; CWF 434; VPN 4:152.

Waterleaf, Virginia (Hydrophyllum virginianum) FNC 158; HWF cp 180; HYF cp 161; PMF 55, 323; RUS 1:327, 2:413, 6:485.

Water-lily, Fragrant (Nymphaea odorata) DEW 1:127; DFP 161 (cp 1284); FFK 107; FNC 60; GPL 61; HWF cp 57; HYF cp 52; LFW 172 (cp 385); LWF 19 (cp 30); PFF 167; PMF 7; RUS 1:105, 2:157, 3:99, 5:105, 6:127; RWA cp 106; VPN 2:317.

Water-lily, Fringed—See **Floating-heart.**

Water-lily, Royal (Victoria amazonica) EWF cp 169a; MEP 38; RWF 45.

Water-lily, Western (Nymphaea polysepola or Nuphar polysepola) AFP 2:172; CWF 146; EWF cp 151a; GPL 61; HFP 94; RUS 4:123, 5:105, 6:127; VPN 2:315.

Water-lily, White (Nymphaea tuberosa) GPL 61; HWF cp 58; PFW 196; RUS 1:105, 2:157. (N. alba) MWF 215 (cp 693); NHE 91; OWF 67.

Water-lily, Yellow (Nuphar advena) FFK 106; GPL 61; HWF cp 56; HYF cp 54; PFF 167; RUS 1:105, 2:161, 3:99; RWA cp 107. (N. lutea) DEW 1:62 (cp 32); FNC 60; OOW cp 130; OWF 7. (N. variegatum) PMF 101; RUS 1:105, 6:127.

Watermeal (Wolffia sp.) AFP 1:736; BBF 1:449; FNC 12; GPL 57; PFF 367.

Watermelon (Citrullus vulgaris) OFP 121; PFF 308; WYG 144.

Water-milfoil (Myriophyllum sp.) GPL 65; NHE 93; OWF 53; PFF 263.

Water-parsnip (Sium suave) CWF 362; GPL 67; HYF cp 127; PMF 53; RUS 4:291, 5:271. (S. cicutae-folium) HWF cp 149. (S. latifolium) NHE 95.

Water-pepper (Polygonum hydropiper) NHE 183; OWF 59; PMF 381. (P. hydropiperoides) PMF 277; RUS 3:77, 4:99, 5:97, 6:93.

Water-plantain (Alisma subcordatum) BBF 1:93; FFK 82; PFF 339; RUS 1:55, 2:55, 3:37, 4:53. (A. triviale) PMF 9; RUS 1:55, 3:37, 4:53, 5:65, 6:55.

Water-plantain, Common (Alisma plantago-aquatica) AFP 1:98; GPL 51; NHE 102; OWF 109; VPN 1:144.

Water-scorpion (Ranatra sp.) BIA 115; GPL 103; PEI 112; PFF 455; SCI 111; SIG cp 35. (Nepa sp.) BIA 115; IWE 19:2569; NHE 129; OBI 31; PEI 112; SCI 111.

Water-shield (Brasenia schreberi) AFP 2:173; BBF 2:76; CWF 139; GPL 61; PFF 168; PMF 231; RUS 1:109, 2:161, 3:99, 4:123, 5:105, 6:131; VPN 2:313.

Water-shield, Carolina—See **Fanwort.**

Water-stick Insect—See **Water-scorpion.**

Waterthrush, Louisiana (Seiurus motacilla) ANE 11:2182; BWI 202; CFG cp 18; GBC 284 (cp 59); NGB 2:189; NGS 283; PBA 3:cp 92; PEB 183 (cp 48); PFF 655; RBB 271.

Waterthrush, Northern (Seiurus noveboracensis) AAB 422; BBC 2:cp 103; CFG cp 18; GBC 284 (cp 59); GBI 99; HBT 241 (cp 14); NGB 2:189; NGS 283; PBA 3:cp 92; PEB 183 (cp 48); PFF 655; PWB 247 (cp 50); RBB 271.

Waterweed (Elodea canadensis or Anacharis canaden-sis) GPL 59; NHE 102; OWF 53; PFF 339; RUS 1:523, 2:157, 3:39, 4:59, 6:67; VPN 1:150.

Water-willow—See also **Loosestrife, Swamp.**

Water-willow (Justica americana) FFK 210; HWF cp 207; PFF 299; PMF 325; RUS 1:351, 2:447, 3:343, 6:543.

Waxbell, Yellow (Kirengeshoma palmata) DFP 153 (cp 1223); OGF 111; PFW 141.

Wax-plant (Hoya carnosa) FHP 125; LFW 168 (cps 375, 376); MWF 157 (cp 489); PFW 38.

Waxwing, Bohemian (Bombycilla garrulus) AAB 389; ALE 9:196; BBE 210; CDB 159 (cp 660); CFG cp 28; GBC 256 (cp 53); GPB 262; NGB 2:221; NGS 234; PBA 3:cp 89; PEB 167 (cp 46); PFF 643; PWB 238; RBB 241; TBC 336 (cp 61a).

Waxwing, Cedar (Bombycilla cedrorum) AAB 370; ANE 11:2184; BBC 2:cp 94; CDB 158 (cp 659); CFG cp 15; GBC 256 (cp 53); GBI 92; IWE 19:2581; LBW 235 (cp 147); NGB 2:221; NGS 232; PBA 3:cp 89; PEB 167 (cp 46); PFF 643; PWB 238; RBB 241; TBC 336 (cp 61a).

Weakfish—See **Squeteague, Gray.**

Weasel, Least (Mustela rixosa) ALE 11:257, 12:55, 56; BGM 53 (cp 5); BMC 325; CFG 326; GGM 41; PFF 685; PMG cp 10; WEA 389; WMW 2:1192.

Weasel, Long-tailed (Mustela frenata) ALE 12:55; BGM 53 (cp 6); CFG cp 32; GGM 41; PFF 685; PMG cp 10; WMW 2:1191.

Weasel, Short-tailed (Mustela erminea) ALE 11:105, 12:40, 55; BGM 53 (cp 6); BMC 320; CFG 326; FWA 28; GGM 40; IWE 17:2280-2283; JAW 111; NGA 182; OBV 171; PFF 686; PMG cp 10; SAA 134, 135; WMW 2:1192.

Weather-glass, Poor Man's—See **Pimpernel, Scarlet.**

Webworm (Various species) GBB cp 18; GGI 97; GIP 82, 115; SCI 304.

Weevil—See also **Curculio.**

Weevil, Acorn—See **Weevil, Nut.**

Weevil, Alfalfa (Hypera postica) GIP 105; LPL 177; SCI 484.

Weevil, Bean (Acanthoscelides obtectus) GBB cp 35; GIP 150; SCI 475.

Weevil, Black Vine (Brachyrhinus sulcatus) GBB cp 35; GIP 97; SCI 481.

Weevil, Boll (Anthonomus grandis) BIA 203; GGI 135; GIP 107; LPL 176; PAK 191; SCI 489.

Weevil, Clover-leaf (Hypera punctata) GIP 106; OBI 191; SCI 482; (H. nigrirostris) GIP 107; SCI 482.

Weevil, Cowpea (Callosobruchus maculatus) GIP 150; SCI 475; SIG cp 119.

Weevil, Granary (Sitophilus granarius or Calendra granarius) GIP 146; OBI 191; SCI 498.

Weevil, Nut (Curculio sp.) AWW 90; KIA 133; KIW 129; NHE 66; OBI 189; PEI 250; SCI 490, 492. (Balaninus sp.) GGI 135; LIN 49.

Weevil, Pea (Bruchus pisorum) GIP 150; OBI 189; SCI 474.

Weevil, Pine (Hylobius abietis) FWA 50; NHE 66; OBI 191; PEI 251. (H. congener) SCI 486.

Weevil, Rice (Sitophilus oryzae) GIP 146; LPL 177; SCI 498.

Weevil, Strawberry Root (Brachyrhinus ovatus) GIP 79; SCI 482.

Weevil, Sweet-potato (Cylas formicarius elegantulus) GIP 78; LPL 177; SCI 478; SIG cp 120b.

Weigela Hybrids (Weigela sp.) AGF 250; DFP 245 (cps 1952-1954); FGF 282; HSC 122; LFW 151 (cp 335); MWF 297 (cp 980); OGF 59; PFW 68; TGS 342.

Wentletrap, Angled (Epitonium angulatum) AAS pl 22b; ASN 97; CFG 574; PFF 409.

Wentletrap, Brown-banded (Epitonium rupicolum) AAS pl 22e; ASN 97; CFG 574; GGS 116.

Wentletrap, Greenland (Epitonium greenlandicum) ASN 97; GGS 116; MGS pl 33.

Wentletrap, Noble (Sthenorytis pernobilis) AAS 161; ASN 95; GSS 40.

Wentletrap, Wroblewski's (Opalia wroblewskii) AAS pl 20j; ASN 95; GGS 116; MGS pl 33.

Whale—See also **Narwhal** and **Rorqual.**

Whale, Beaked (Cuvier's) (Ziphius cavirostris) ALE 11:479; BGM 247; CFG 308; GGM 149; NGA 389; OBV 189; PMG 337.

Whale, Beaked (Sowerby's) (Mesoplodon bidens) ALE 11:480; NHE 142; OBV 189.

Whale, Beluga—See **Whale, White.**

Whale, Blue (Balaenoptera musculus or Sibbaldus musculus) ALE 11:465; BGM 259; CFG 315; GGM 146-147; IWE 2:248-249; JAW 91; LEA 540; NGA 384-385; OBV 191; PFF 741; PMG 333; SAA 60; SOS 172-173; VWA 96 (cp 42); WMW 2:1139.

Whale, Bottle-nose (Hyperoodon ampullatus or H. rostratus) ALE 11:480; BGM 247; CFG 308; GGM 149; IWE 2:169; LEA 540; OBV 189; PMG 337; SAA 61; SOS 177.

Whale, Bowhead (Balaena mysticetus) ALE 11:463; BGM 259; CFG 315; LEA 540; NGA 383; PFF 740; PMG 333; WMW 2:1142.

Whale, False Killer (Pseudorca crassidens) ALE 11:480; BGM 247; IWE 6:734, 735; OBV 187; PMG 337; SOS 183.

Whale, Finback (Balaenoptera physalus) ALE 11:464; ANE 12:2201; BGM 259; CFG 315; FWA 314; GGM 147; LEA 543; NGA 384; OBV 191; PMG 333; SAA 60; WMW 2:1136.

Whale, Goosebeak—See **Whale, Beaked (Cuvier's).**

Whale, Gray (Eschrichtius glaucus or Rhachianectes glaucus) ALE 11:464; BGM 259; GGM 147; IWE 7:961; NGA 387; OMW 49; PMG 333; SAA 61; SOS 171, 174, 175; WMW 2:1132.

Whale, Humpback (Megaptera novaeangliae) ALE 11:465; BGM 259; CFG 315; FWA 315; GGM 146; JAW 90; LEA 540, 545; LVS 102-103; NGA 386; PMG 333; SAA 61; SOS 172-173; WMW 2:1138. (M. nodosa) IWE 9:1140-1141.

Whale, Killer (Orcinus orca or Grampus orca) ALE 11:480; BGM 253; CFG 312; FWA 316; IWE 9:1225-1227; JAW 89; LEA 545; NGA 390; OBV 187; PMG 337; SAA 61; SOS 177.

Whale, Piked or Minke (Balaenoptera acutorostrata) ALE 11:464; BGM 259; CFG 315; IWE 15:1987, 1988; NHE 143; OBV 191; SOS 172; WMW 2:1136.

Whale, Pilot (Globicephala melaena) ALE 11:480; BGM 247; CFG 312; FWA 316; IWE 13:1765; NGA 380; NGF 167; OBV 187; PMG 337; SOS 177. (G. scammoni) GGM 151; IWE 13:1766.

Whale, Pygmy Sperm (Kogia breviceps) ALE 11:474; BGM 253; CFG 308; PMG 335.

Whale, Right (Eubalaena glacialis) ALE 11:463; CFG 315; GGM 146; IWE 14:1956-1958; NGA 382; OMW 46-47, 48; PMG 333; SOS 172-173; WMW 2:1143. (E. sieboldi) BGM 259; LEA 542; SAA 61.

Whale, Sei—See **Rorqual.**

Whale, Sperm (Physeter catodon) ALE 11:474; BGM 253; CFG 308; GGM 148; IWE 16:2223; JAW 87; LEA 540; NGA 388; OBV 189; PFF 740; PMG 333; SAA 61; SOS 176-177; WMW 2:1100.

Whale, Sulphur-bottom—See **Whale, Blue.**

Whale, White (Delphinapterus leucas) ALE 11:480; BGM 247; CFG 308; FWA 314; IWE 2:190, 191; NGF 172, 173; NHE 143; PMG 337; SAA 61; SOS 168; WEA 392.

Wheat (Triticum aestivum) HMG 244; OFP 3; PFF 355; PRP 72.

Wheatear (Oenanthe oenanthe) AAB 358; ABW 254; ALE 9:270, 280; BBC 2:cp 91; BBE 257; CDB 165 (cp 697); GBC 252 (cp 51); LBW 277 (cp 165); NGS 221; NHE 202; PEB 226 (cp 59); PWB 308; RBB 231; SAA 148.

Whelk, Channeled (Busycon canaliculatum) AAS pl 23n; ASN 139; CFG 572; GGS 130; GSS 87; PFF 413; SOS 21.

Whelk, Common Northern (Waved) (Buccinum undatum) ALE 3:56, 71; ASN 133; CFG cp 45; GGS 131; GSS 81; LEA 88; NHE 163; OIB 43; PFF 413.

Whelk, Dog—See **Basket Shell.**

Whelk, Glacial (Buccinum glaciale) AAS pl 24t; ASN 133; CFG cp 45; MGS pl 38.

Whelk, Knobbed (Busycon carica) AAS pl 23i; ASN 139; CFG 572; GGS 130; GSS 87. (Busycoptypus aruanum) PFF 413.

Whelk, Lightning (Busycon contrarium) AAS pl 23o; ASN 137; GGS 131; GSS 87; MOL 69.

Whelk, Spitzbergen (Colus spitzbergensis) AAS 228; CFG cp 45; MGS pl 38.

Whelk, Stimpson's (Colus stimpsoni) AAS pl 23x; ASN 133; CFG cp 45; PFF 413.

Whelk, Tabled (Neptunea tabulatus) AAS 228; GAS 272; GGS 130; MGS pl 39; PFF 413.

Whelk, Ten-ridged—See **Neptune, New England.**

Whimbrel (Numenius phaeopus or N. hudsonicus) AAB 162; ALE 8:170; AWW 93; BBC 1:cp 49; BBE 116; CDB 87 (cp 290); CFG cp 8; GBC 157 (cp 28); GPB 146; NGB 1:272; NGW 333; NHE 84; PBA 1:cp 38;

PEB 90 (pl 25), 103 (cp 30); PFF 595; PWB 103 (cp 26), 106 (pl 27); RBB 115; SAA 91.

Whip-poor-will, Eastern (Caprimulgus vociferus) ABW 164; ALE 8:425; BBC 1:cp 68; CDB 120 (cp 461); GBC 204 (cp 41); IWE 14:1821; NGB 2:44; NGW 450; PBA 2:168; PEB 135 (cp 38); PFF 617; PWB 151 (cp 38); RBB 169.

Whip-poor-will, Ridgway's (Caprimulgus ridgwayi) DBM cp 13; PMB cp 15; RBB 169.

Whip-scorpion (Mastigoproctus giganteus) BLA 218 (cps 105, 106); FWA 381; GSP 116; LEA 180.

Whipsnake (Masticophis taeniatus) CGR 281; GRA 87; SRA cp 30; WWS 1:457, 463.

Whispering Bells (Emmenanthe penduliflora) AFP 3:520; RUS 4:483, 5:415, 6:493.

Whistler—See **Golden-eye.**

White Sails (Spathiphyllum wallisii) DFP 82 (cp 650); PFW 35. (S. blandum) MWF 271 (cp 898). (S. clevelandii) FHP 145.

Whitefish, Lake (Coregonus clupaeformis) CFG 525; CFW 52; GGF 48; NGF 265; PFF 505.

Whitefish, Round (Prosopium cylindraceum) CFG 525; GGF 49.

Whitefly—See **Fly, White.**

Whiting—See **Kingfish.**

Whitlow-grass, Carolina (Draba reptans) AFP 2:293; PMF 83; VPN 2:501.

Whitlow-grass, Common (Draba verna) AFP 2:293; BBF 2:148; OGF 21; OWF 71; PMF 83; RUS 1:177, 2:231, 5:169, 6:213; VPN 2:501.

Whitlow-grass, Yellow (Draba aizoides) EWF cp 11e; NHE 274; OGF 21; TGF 92. (D. incerta) CWF 183; RUS 5:169, 6:213.

Wicky—See **Laurel, Sheep.**

Widgeon, American (Mareca americana) AAB 73; ALE 7:307; BBC 1:cp 16; BBE 53; CFG cp 2, 41, 42; GBC 76 (cp 9); GGB 43; NGB 1:101; NGW 169; PBA 1:cp 13; PEB 22 (pl 7), 26 (pl 9), 39 (cp 14); PFF 566; PWB 34 (pl 7), 42 (pl 9), 59 (cp 14); RBB 47; TBC 90 (cp 7a).

Widgeon, European (Mareca penelope) AAB 72; ALE 7:303, 385; BBE 52; CFG cp 2; GBC 76 (cp 9); GGB 43; NGB 1:101; NGW 168; NHE 113; PBA 1:cp 13; PEB 39 (cp 14); PWB 59 (cp 14); RBB 47; SAA 145.

Widow's Cross—See **Stonecrop, Pink.**

Wild Bean—See **Groundnut.**

Wild Calla (Calla palustris) BBF 1:444; DEW 2:286 (cp 169); HWF cp 4; HYF cp 3; NHE 107; PFF 365; PFW 33; PMF 7; RUS 1:88; RWA cp 17.

337); MWF 297 (cps 982-985); OGF 63; PFF 216; PFW 162; TGS 71.

Wisteria, Wild (Wisteria frutescens) RWA cp 203. (W. macrostachya) TSK 59, 190.

Witch (Glyptocephalus cynoglossus) ALE 5:234; CFG 508; NHE 158; OBV 47.

Witch Hazel (Hamamelis virginiana) BBF 2:235; BTN 159; FNC 87; LWF 258 (cp 408); RWA cp 167; TSK 44, 275. (H. intermedia) PFW 136. (H. vernalis) EWF cp 155f; TGS 199.

Witch Hazel, Chinese (Hamamelis mollis) DEW 1:152; DFP 240 (cp 1632), 205 (cps 1633, 1634); EWF cp 94a; HSC 59; MWF 147 (cp 449); OBT 148; OGF 3; PFW 136.

Witch Hazel, Japanese (Hamamelis japonica) DEW 1:100 (cp 46); DFP 204 (cps 1630, 1631); HSC 59.

Witch-alder (Fothergilla major) FNC 87; HSC 54. (F. gardenii) BBF 2:234; DFP 202 (cp 1613). (F. monticola) DEW 1:153; DFP 202 (cp 1614); PFW 136; TG TGS 199.

Witchgrass (Panicum capillare) AFP 1:113; BBF 1:139; HMG 688; PFF 348; PRP 48; VPN 1:636.

Witherod—See **Haw, Black.**

Woad (Isatis tinctoria) NHE 216; OWF 11; RUS 6:219; VPN 2:515.

Wolf, Brush or Prairie—See **Coyote.**

Wolf, Gray or Timber (Canis lupus) ALE 12:205, 13:163; ANE 12:2275, 2276; AWW 22; BGM 68 (cp 7); BMC 231 (cp 24); CFG cp 32; FWA 30; GGM 57; IWE 19:2622; JAW 94; LEA 553; LVS 95; NGA 120, 128-129; NHE 51; PFF 689; PMG cp 12; SAA 126, 127; WMW 2:1150.

Wolf, Red (Canis niger) ALE 12:205; BGM 68 (cp 7); CFG cp 32; LVS 98; NGA 130; PMG cp 12.

Wolf-eel (Anarrhichthys ocellatus) HFW 240; HPF 351; NGF 214; WFW 111.

Wolf-fish, Atlantic (Anarhichas lupus) ALE 5:162, 181; CFG 496; GGF 146; HFW 216 (cp 103); MOL 106; NHE 156.

Wolverine (Gulo luscus or G. gulo) ALE 12:41, 83; ANE 12:2278; AWW 93; BGM 52 (cp 5); BMC 295 (cp 32); CFG 326; FWA 59; GGM 45; IWE 19:2625, 2626; LEA 562; NGA 185; PFF 688; PMG cp 8; SAA 131; SMW 205; WMW 2:1204.

Wood-betony—See **Lousewort, Common.**

Woodbine—See **Virginia Creeper.**

Woodchuck (Marmota monax) ALE 11:239; BGM 100 (cp 9); BMC 38 (cp 11); CFG cp 30; FWA 53; GGM

68, 69; IWE 19:2633-2635; NGA 236, 238; PFF 705; PMG cp 27; WMW 2:706.

Woodcock, American (Philohela minor) AAB 159; ALE 8:170; ANE 12:2287; BBC 1:cp 48; CDB 87 (cp 291); CFG cp 27; GBC 140 (cp 25), 168 (pl 31); GGB 100, 101; NGB 1:271; NGW 331; PBA 1:cp 31; PEB 98 (pl 27), 118 (cp 31); PFF 595; RBB 127; TBC 186 (cp 22b).

Wood-fern—See **Fern, Wood.**

Woodland-star (Lithophragma heterophyllum) AFP 2:372; OOW cp 35; RUS 4:263, 5:245. (L. parviflorum) AFP 2:373; CWF 206; RUS 4:265, 5:245, 6:283; VPN 3:23.

Wood-lily, Speckled—See **Clintonia, White.**

Woodlouse—See **Sowbug, Water.**

Wood-nymph (Thalurania furcata) ALE 8:453; CDB 123 (cp 477); PMB cp 18; WAB 91. (T. townsendi) DBM cp 14.

Woodpecker, Acorn or California (Melanerpes formicivorus) AAB 274; ANE 12:2289; AWW 25; BBW cp 47; FWA 68; NGB 2:66; NGS 90; PFF 621; PWB 167 (cp 40), 179; RBB 185.

Woodpecker, Arizona (Dendrocopas arizonae) AAB 278; NBG 2:59; NGS 94; PMB cp 23; PWB 167 (cp 40); RBB 187; WAB 45.

Woodpecker, Black-backed Three-toed (Picoides arcticus) AAB 279; CFG cp 28; GBC 220 (cp 43); NGB 2:63; NGS 95; PBA 2:cp 60; PEB 154 (cp 41); PFF 623; PWB 167 (cp 40); RBB 187; TBC 286 (cp 41b).

Woodpecker, Black-cheeked (Centurus pucherami) CDB 138 (cp 550); PMB cp 23.

Woodpecker, Chestnut-colored (Celeus castaneus) DBM cp 20; PMB cp 23.

Woodpecker, Downy (Dendrocopos pubescens) AAB 276; ANE 12:2290; AWW 25; CFG cp 12; GBC 220 (cp 43); GBI 16, 65; NGB 2:57; NGS 78, 92; PBA 2:cp 59; PEB 154 (cp 41); PFF 622; PWB 167 (cp 40); RBB 187; TBC 286 (cp 41a).

Woodpecker, Gila (Centurus uropygialis) ANE 1:5; AWW 18, 28; CDB 136 (cp 541); LBW 187 (cp 116); NGB 2:70; NGS 89; PBA 2:163; PMB cp 23; PWB 167 (cp 40); RBB 183; WAB 49.

Woodpecker, Golden-cheeked (Centurus chrysogenys) AMB 53 (cp 3); DBM cp 20; PMB cp 23.

Woodpecker, Golden-fronted (Centurus aurifrons) ABW 193; NGB 2:70; NGS 88; PMB cp 23; PWB 167 (cp 40); RBB 183.

X-Y

Yerba Mansa (Anemopsis californica) AFP 1:485; ANE 6:1072; RUS 3:67, 4:79, 5:83, 6:85; VPN 1:864.

Yesterday, Today and Tomorrow (Brunfelsia calycina) DEW 2:162 (cp 80); DFP 55 (cp 436); EGE 114; FHP 108; MWF 63 (cp 140); PFW 286. (B. latifolia) MEP 126.

Yew, Eastern (Taxus canadensis) BBF 1:67; NFP 152; PFF 114; TSK 122, 160.

Yew, European (Taxus baccata) DFP 256 (cps 2042, 2043); MTB 48 (cp 1), 51; NHE 18; OBT 21, 25, 57, 68; OWF 185; PFF 114; TGS 22.

Yew, Podocarpus (Podocarpus andinus) MTB 49 (cp 2); OBT 105. (P. macrophylla) NFP 152.

Yew, Western (Taxus brevifolia) AFP 1:51; BTN 21.

Ylang-ylang (Cananga odorata) DEW 1:58 (cp 24); EWF cp 110c; MEP 39.

Yoldia, Broad (Yoldia thraciaeformis) AAS pl 27e; ASN 191; CFG 593; MGS pl 9.

Yoldia, File (Yoldia limatula) AAS 337; ASN 191; CFG 594; MGS pl 9.

Yoldia, Labrador or Oval (Yoldia myalis) AAS pl 27d; CFG 594; MGS pl 9.

Youth-and-old-age—See **Zinnia Hybrids.**

Youth-on-age (Tolmiea menziesii) AFP 2:376; CWF 219; RUS 5:239; VPN 2:68.

Yucca—See also **Joshua Tree, Our Lord's Candle, Soaptree,** and **Soapweed.**

Yucca, Fleshy-fruited (Yucca baccata) AFP 1:447; BBF 1:512; RUS 3:35, 4:49, 6:35.

Yucca, Giant Dagger (Yucca carnerosana) LWF 61 (cp 99); RUS 3:35.

Yucca, Mohave (Yucca mohavensis or Y. schidigera) AFP 1:447; DEW 2:215 (cp 128); RUS 4:49.

Yucca, Spanish Bayonet (Yucca filamentosa) AGF 17; BBF 1:513; DFP 245 (cp 1955); FNC 26; MWF 299 (cp 988); PFF 382; PMF 5; RUS 2:51; TGF 46. (Y. torreyi) LWF 60 (cp 98); RUS 3:31, 4:49.

Z

Zauschneria (Zauschneria californica) PFW 202; RUS 4:331, 5:305. (Z. septentrionalis) RUS 5:305.

Zebra Plant (Aphelandra squarrosa) FHP 105; MWF 43 (cp 67); PFW 13. (A. sinclairiana) MEP 142.

Zebu—See **Cattle, Brahman.**

Zenobia (Zenobia pulverulenta) EWF cp 161a; FNC 136; HSC 123. (Z. cassinefolia) RWA cp 267.

Zinnia, Creeping (Sanvitalia procumbens) DFP 47 (cp 372); EGA 152; LFW 271 (cp 614); TGF 284.

Zinnia, Desert (Zinnia pumila) LWF 105 (cp 169). (Z. grandiflora) BBF 3:466; RUS 3:463, 4:687, 6:669.

Zinnia Hybrids (Zinnia elegans) AGF 253-256; DFP 50 (cps 397, 398); EGA 163; FGF 285, 286; LFW 270 (cps 608-612), 271 (cp 613); MWF 302 (cps 996-998); OGF 137; PFF 322; TGF 284.

Scientific Name Index

Acmaea persona — Limpet, Mask
Aconitum columbianum — Monkshood, Columbia
Aconitum napellus — Monkshood, Common
Aconitum uncinatum — Monkshood, Wild
Acorus calamus — Flag, Sweet
Acris crepitans — Frog, Cricket
Acris gryllus — Frog, Cricket
Actaea alba — Baneberry, White
Actaea arguta — Baneberry, Red
Actaea pachypoda — Baneberry, White
Actaea rubra — Baneberry, Red
Actaca spicata — Baneberry, Common
Actias luna — Moth, Luna
Actitis macularia — Sandpiper, Spotted
Acyrthosiphon pisum — Aphid, Pea
Adalia sp. — Beetle, Ladybird
Adenocaulon bicolor — Trail Plant
Adiantum capillus-veneris — Fern, Venus-hair
Adiantum pedatum — Fern, Maidenhair
Adlumia fungosa — Alleghany-vine
Adonis vernalis — Adonis, Spring
Adoxa moschatellina — Townhall Clock
Adula californiensis — Clam, Rock-boring
Aechmolophus mexicanus — Flycatcher, Pileated
Aechmophorus occidentalis — Grebe, Western
Aedes aegypti — Mosquito, Yellow-fever
Aegolius acadicus — Owl, Saw-whet
Aegolius funereus — Owl, Boreal
Aegolius ridgwayi — Owl, Unspotted Saw-whet
Aeolis papillosa — Nudibranch, Brown or Plumed
Aequipecten circularis — Scallop, Pacific
Aequipecten gibbus — Scallop, Calico
Aequipecten irradians — Scallop, Atlantic Bay
Aequorea sp. — Jellyfish, Water
Aeronautes saxatilis — Swift, White-throated
Aesculus californica — Buckeye, California
Aesculus carnea — Horse-chestnut
Aesculus glabra — Buckeye, Ohio
Aesculus hippocastaneum — Horse-chestnut
Aesculus octandra — Buckeye, Yellow
Aesculus pavia — Buckeye, Red
Aethia cristatella — Auklet, Crested
Aethia pusilla — Auklet, Least
Aethia pygmaea — Auklet, Whiskered
Agalinus purpurea — Gerardia, Purple
Agalinus tenuifolia — Gerardia, Slender
Agapanthus africanus — Lily, African
Agaricus campestris — Mushroom, Field or Meadow

Agarum cribrosum — Sea Colander
Agarum fimbriatum — Sea Colander
Agastache nepetoides — Giant-hyssop, Yellow
Agastache scrophulariaefolia — Giant-hyssop
Agastache urticifolia — Horsemint, Nettle-leaved
Agave americana — Agave
Agave deserti — Agave
Agelaius icterocephalus — Blackbird, Yellow-headed
Agelaius phoeniceus — Blackbird, Red-winged
Agelaius tricolor — Blackbird, Tricolored
Ageratum houstonianum — Floss Flower
Agkistrodon bilineatus — Mocassin, Mexican
Agkistrodon contortrix — Copperhead
Agkistrodon piscivorus — Mocassin, Water
Aglaophenia latirostris — Hydroid, Ostrich-plume
Aglaophenia struthionides — Hydroid, Ostrich-plume
Agoseris aurantiaca — Mountain-dandelion
Agoseris glauca — Mountain-dandelion, Pale
Agoseris villosa — Mountain-dandelion
Agrimonia eupatoria — Agrimony
Agrimonia gryposepala — Agrimony, Tall Hairy
Agriocharis ocellata — Turkey, Ocellated
Agriotes mancus — Wireworm, Wheat
Agriotes obscurus — Wireworm, Wheat
Agropyron repens — Quackgrass
Agrostemma githago — Corn Cockle
Agrostis sp. — Bent-grass
Ahnfeltia plicata — Seaweed, Ahnfelt's
Ailanthus altissima — Tree of Heaven
Aimophila aestivalis — Sparrow, Bachman's or Pine-
  woods
Aimophila botterii — Sparrow, Botteri's
Aimophila carpalis — Sparrow, Rufous-winged
Aimophila cassinii — Sparrow, Cassin's
Aimophila humeralis — Sparrow, Black-chested
Aimophila mystacalis — Sparrow, Bridled
Aimophila rufescens — Sparrow, Rusty
Aimophila ruficeps — Sparrow, Rufous-crowned or
  Scott's
Aira caryophylla — Hairgrass, Silver
Aira praecox — Hairgrass, Early
Aix sponsa — Duck, Wood
Ajaia ajaja — Spoonbill, Roseate
Ajuga pyramidalis — Bugle, Pyramid
Ajuga reptans — Bugle
Akebia quinata — Akebia
Alabama argillacea — Leaf-worm, Cotton
Alaris esculenta — Henware

Alaria sp. — Kelp, Wing
Alauda arvensis — Skylark
Albizzia julibrissin — Silk Tree
Albizzia lophantha — Silk Tree
Albula vulpes — Bonefish
Alburnus alburnus — Bleak
Alca torda — Auk, Razor-bill
Alces alces — Moose
Alchemilla major — Lady's-mantle
Alchemilla mollis — Lady's-mantle
Alchemilla vulgaris — Lady's-mantle
Alcyonium sp. — Dead Men's Fingers (coral)
Alectoris chukar — Chukar
Alectoris graeca — Chukar
Alectoris rufa — Partridge, Red-legged
Aletris aurea — Colic-root
Aletris farinosa — Colic-root
Aleuria aurantia — Fungus, Orange Cup
Alisma plantago-aquatica — Water-plantain, Common
Alisma subcordatum — Water-plantain
Alisma triviale — Water-plantain
Allamanda cathartica — Trumpet, Golden
Allantus cinctus — Sawfly, Curled Rose
Alle alle — Dovekie
Alliaria officinalis — Mustard, Garlic
Alligator mississippiensis — Alligator, American
Allionia incarnata — Windmills
Allium acuminatum — Onion, Hooker's
Allium ampeloprasum var. porrum — Leek
Allium amplestens — Onion, Narrow-leaved
Allium canadense — Onion, Wild
Allium cepa — Onion, Common
Allium cernuum — Onion, Nodding
Allium crenulatum — Onion, Hooker's
Allium falcifolium — Onion, Narrow-leaved
Allium moly — Garlic, Golden
Allium sativum — Garlic
Allium schoenopraesum — Chives
Allium sibiricum — Chives, Wild
Allium stellatum — Onion, Wild
Allium tricoccum — Leek, Wild
Allium vineale — Garlic, Field or Crow
Allotropa virgata — Barber's-pole
Alnus cordata — Alder, Italian
Alnus glutinosa — Alder, European
Alnus incana — Alder, Gray or Speckled
Alnus oregona — Alder, Red or Oregon
Alnus rhombifolia — Alder, White

Alnus rubra — Alder, Red or Oregon
Alnus rugosa — Alder, Smooth or Hazel
Alnus serrulata — Alder, Smooth or Hazel
Alnus sinuata — Alder, Sitka
Alnus sitchensis — Alder, Sitka
Alnus tenuifolia — Alder, Mountain or Thinleaf
Alnus viridus — Alder, Green
Alobates pennsylvanica — Beetle, Tenebrionid or
    Darkling
Alopecurus aequalis — Grass, Short-awned Foxtail
Alopecurus pratensis — Grass, Meadow Foxtail
Alopex lagopus — Fox, Arctic or White
Alopias vulpinus — Shark, Thresher
Alosa pseudoharengus — Alewife
Alosa sapidissima — Shad, American
Alsophila pometaria — Cankerworm, Fall
Alstroemeria aurantiaca — Lily, Peruvian
Althaea officinalis — Mallow, Marsh
Althaea rosea — Hollyhock
Alyssum alyssoides — Alyssum, Sweet
Alyssum maritima — Alyssum, Sweet
Alyssum saxatile — Basket-of-gold
Amanita caesarea — Mushroom, Caesar's or Orange
Amanita calyptroderma — Mushroom, Caesar's or
    Orange
Amanita citrina — Mushroom, Lemon-yellow
Amanita muscaria — Mushroom, Fly
Amanita pantherina — Mushroom, Panther
Amanita phalloides — Death Cap
Amanita verna — Destroying Angel
Amanita virosa — Destroying Angel
Amaranthus caudatus — Love-lies-bleeding
Amaranthus graecizans — Tumbleweed
Amaranthus retroflexus — Pigweed, Common
Amaranthus tricolor — Joseph's Coat
Amaryllis belladonna — Lily, Belladonna
Amaurolimas concolor — Crake, Uniform
Amauropsis islandica — Moon Snail, Iceland
Amazilia beryllina — Hummingbird, Berylline
Amazilia candida — Emerald, White-bellied
Amazilia chionopectus — Emerald, White-bellied
Amazilia cyanocephala — Hummingbird, Azure-
    crowned
Amazilia cyanura — Hummingbird, Blue-tailed
Amazilia rutila — Hummingbird, Cinnamon
Amazilia tzacatl — Hummingbird, Rieffer's or Rufous-
    tailed
Amazona albifrons — Parrot, White-fronted

Amazona collaria — Parrot, Yellow-billed
Amazona finschi — Parrot, Lilac-crowned
Amazona guildingii — Parrot, St. Vincent
Amazona ochrocephala — Parrot, Yellow-headed
    Amazon
Amazona versicolor — Parrot, St. Lucia
Amazona viridigenalis — Parrot, Red-crowned or Green-
    cheeked
Amazona vittata — Parrot, Puerto Rican
Ambloplites rupestris — Bass, Rock
Amblycheila cylindriformis — Beetle, Tiger
Ambrosia artemisiaefolia — Ragweed, Common
Ambrosia psilostachya — Ragweed, Western
Ambystoma annulatum — Salamander, Ringed
Ambystoma jeffersonianum — Salamander, Jefferson's
Ambystoma macrodactylum — Salamander, Long-toed
Ambystoma maculatum — Salamander, Spotted
Ambystoma mexicanum — Axolotl
Ambystoma opacum — Salamander, Marbled
Ambystoma talpoideum — Salamander, Mole
Ambystoma texanum — Salamander, Small-mouthed
Ambystoma tigrinum — Salamander, Tiger
Ameiurus nebulosus — Bullhead, Brown
Amelanchier sp. — Serviceberry
Amia calva — Bowfin
Amianthemum muscaetoxicum — Fly-poison
Ammodramus bairdii — Sparrow, Baird's
Ammodramus savannarum — Sparrow, Grasshopper
Ammospermophilus harrisi — Squirrel, Antelope
    Ground
Ammospermophilus leucurus — Squirrel, Antelope
    Ground
Ammospiza caudacuta — Sparrow, Sharp-tailed
Ammospiza mirabilis — Sparrow, Cape Sable
Ammospiza maritima — Sparrow, Seaside
Ammospiza nigrescens — Sparrow, Dusky Seaside
Amorpha canescens — Leadplant
Amorpha fruiticosa — Indigo, False
Ampelopsis brevipedunculata — Grape, Ornamental
Amphicarpa bracteata — Hog-peanut
Amphimallon majalis — Beetle, Summer Chafer
Amphimallon solstitialis — Beetle, Summer Chafer
Amphiopholis squamata — Brittle-star, Scaly
Amphisbaena alba — Lizard, Red Worm
Amphispiza belli — Sparrow, Sage
Amphispiza bilineata — Sparrow, Black-throated or
    Desert
Amphissa columbiana — Snail, Wrinkled

Amphiuma means — Eel, Congo
Amsinckia intermedia — Fiddle-neck
Amsonia ciliata — Dogbane, Blue
Amsonia tabernaemontana — Dogbane, Blue
Amyda ferox — Turtle, Florida Soft-shell
Anableps sp. — Four-eyed Fish
Anabrus simplex — Cricket, Mormon
Anacardium occidentale — Cashew
Anacharis canadensis — Waterweed
Anadara notabilis — Ark Shell, Eared
Anadara ovalis — Ark Shell, Blood
Anadara transversa — Ark Shell, Transverse
Anagallus arvensis — Pimpernel, Scarlet
Ananas comosus — Pineapple
Anaphalis margaritacea — Everlasting, Pearly
Anarhichas lupus — Wolf-fish, Atlantic
Anarrhichthys ocellatus — Wolf-eel
Anas acuta — Pintail, American
Anas bahamensis — Duck, Bahama
Anas carolinensis — Teal, Green-winged
Anas crecca — Teal, Common or European
Anas cyanoptera — Teal, Cinnamon
Anas diazi — Duck, Mexican
Anas discors — Teal, Blue-winged
Anas falcata — Teal, Falcated
Anas fulvigula maculosa — Duck, Mottled
Anas laysanensis — Duck, Laysan
Anas platyrhynchos — Mallard
Anas rubripes — Duck, Black
Anas strepera — Gadwall
Anas wyvilliana — Duck, Hawaiian
Anasa tristis — Bug, Squash
Anax junius — Dragonfly, Green Darner
Anchoa mitchilli — Anchovy, Bay or Common
Anchusa azurea italica — Alkanet, Large Blue
Anchusa officinalis — Alkanet, True
Ancistrodon bilineatus — Mocassin, Mexican
Ancistrodon contortrix — Copperhead
Ancistrodon piscivorus — Mocassin, Water
Andrena sp. — Bee, Mining
Andromeda glaucophylla — Rosemary, Bog
Andromeda polifolia — Rosemary, Bog
Andropogon gerardi — Grass, Big Bluestem
Androsace septentrionalis — Rock-jasmine, Northern
Androsace villosa — Rock-jasmine, Woolly
Aneides aeneus — Salamander, Green
Aneides flavipunctatus — Salamander, Black
Aneides lugubris — Salamander, Arboreal

Anemone alpina — Anemone, Alpine
Anemone blanda — Anemone, Greek
Anemone canadensis — Anemone, Canada
Anemone coronaria — Anemone, Poppy
Anemone drummondii — Anemone, Drummond's
Anemone japonica — Anemone, Japanese
Anemone narcissiflora — Anemone, Daffodil
Anemone nemorosa — Anemone, Wood
Anemone occidentalis — Anemone, Western
Anemone oregana — Anemone, Blue
Anemone patens — Pasque Flower
Anemone pulsatilla — Pasque Flower
Anemone quinquefolia — Anemone, Wood
Anemonella thalictroides — Rue-anemone
Anemopsis californica — Yerba Mansa
Anethum graveolens — Dill
Angelichthys ciliaris — Angelfish, Queen
Anguilla bostoniensis — Eel, American
Anguilla rostrata — Eel, American
Anhinga anhinga — Anhinga
Anisostichus capreolata — Cross-vine
Anisotremus virginicus — Porkfish
Anniella pulchra — Lizard, Legless
Annona cherimolia — Custard-apple
Anolis carolinensis — Anole, Green
Anomia peruviana — Jingle Shell
Anomia simplex — Jingle Shell
Anopheles quadrimaculatus — Mosquito, Malaria
Anoplarchus insignis — Cockscomb
Anoplarchus purpurescens — Cockscomb
Anotopterus pharao — Daggerfish
Anous minutus — Tern, Noddy
Anous stolidus — Tern, Noddy
Anous tenuirostris — Tern, Noddy
Anser albifrons — Goose, White-fronted
Anser fabalis — Goose, Bean
Antennaria alpina — Pussy-toes
Antennaria neglecta — Pussy-toes, Field
Antennaria plantaginifolia — Everlasting, Plantain-
  leaved
Antennaria rosea — Everlasting, Rosy
Antennaria solitaria — Pussy-toes, Solitary
Antennaria umbrinella — Everlasting, Brown or
  Isabella
Anthemis arvensis — Chamomile, Corn or Field
Anthemis cotula — Chamomile, Yellow
Anthemis tinctoria — Chamomile, Yellow
Antheraea polyphemus — Moth, Polyphemus

Anthericum liliago — Lily, St. Bernard's
Anthocharis cardamines — Butterfly, Orange-tip
Anthophora acervorum — Bee, Hairy Flower
Anthophora occidentalis — Bee, Hairy Flower
Anthophora retusa — Bee, Hairy Flower
Anthonomus grandis — Weevil, Boll
Anthopleura elegantissima — Sea Anemone, Aggregated
Anthopleura xanthogrammica — Sea Anemone, Green
Anthozanthum odoratum — Vernal-grass, Sweet
Anthracothorax nigricollis — Mango, Black-throated
  (bird)
Anthrenus scrophulariae — Beetle, Carpet
Anthurium andreanum — Lily, Flamingo
Anthurium scherzeranum — Flamingo Flower
Anthus spinoletta — Pipit, American or Water
Anthus spraguei — Pipit, Sprague's
Anthyllis vulneraria — Vetch, Kidney
Antigonon leptopus — Coral Vine
Antilocapra americana — Antelope
Antiplanes sp. — Turrid Shell
Antirrhinum majus — Snapdragon
Antrozous pallidus — Bat, Pallid
Anuraphis maidiradicis — Aphid, Corn Root
Anuraphis roseus — Aphid, Rosy Apple
Aonidiella aurantii — Scale, California Red
Apatura ilia — Butterfly, Purple Emperor
Apatura iris — Butterfly, Purple Emperor
Aphanostephus skirrobasis — Daisy, White
Aphelandra sinclairiana — Zebra Plant
Aphelandra squarrosa — Zebra Plant
Aphelocoma coerulescens — Jay, Scrub or Florida
Aphelocoma coerulescens woodhousei — Jay,
  Woodhouse's
Aphelocoma unicolor — Jay, Unicolored
Aphelocoma ultramarina — Jay, Mexican or Arizona
Aphis gossypii — Aphid, Cotton or Melon
Aphis fabae — Aphid, Bean
Aphis pomi — Aphid, Apple
Aphonopelma sp. — Spider, Bird
Aphredoderus sayanus — Perch, Pirate
Aphriza virgata — Surfbird
Aphrodite aculeata — Sea Mouse
Aphrodite hastata — Sea Mouse
Aphrodite japonica — Sea Mouse
Aphrophora quadrinotata — Spittlebug
Apios americana — Groundnut
Apis mellifera — Bee, Honey
Apium graveolens — Celery

Aplectrum hyemale — Puttyroot
Aplodinotus grunniens — Drum, Freshwater
Aplodontia rufa — Beaver, Mountain
Apocynum androsaemifolium — Dogbane, Spreading
Apocynum cannabinum — Dogbane, Common or Hemp
Apogon sp. — Cardinalfish
Apolymetis intastriata — Macoma Shell
Aponogeton distachys — Pondweed, Cape
Aporrhais occidentalis — Pelican's Foot, American
Aquila chrysaetos — Eagle, Golden
Aquilegia canadensis — Columbine, Eastern
Aquilegia chrysantha — Columbine, Yellow or Golden
Aquilegia coerulea — Columbine, Blue
Aquilegia flavescens — Columbine, Yellow or Golden
Aquilegia formosa — Columbine, Western
Aquilegia vulgaris — Columbine, Common
Ara ararauna — Macaw, Blue-and-yellow
Ara chloroptera — Macaw, Red-and-blue
Ara macao — Macaw, Scarlet
Ara militaris — Macaw, Military
Arabidopsis thaliana — Cress, Thale
Arabis albida — Snow-in-summer
Arabis canadensis — Sicklepod
Arabis hirsuta — Cress, Rock
Arabis laevigata — Cress, Smooth Rock
Arabis lyrata — Cress, Rock
Arachis hypogaea — Peanut
Aralia californica — Spikenard, American
Aralia hispida — Sarsaparilla, Bristly
Aralia japonica — Fatsia
Aralia nudicaulis — Sarsaparilla, Wild
Aralia racemosa — Spikenard, American
Aralia spinosa — Hercules'-club
Aramides cajanea — Rail, American Wood
Aramus guarauna — Limpkin
Araneus diadematus — Spider, Garden
Aratinga astec — Parakeet, Aztec or Olive-throated
Aratinga canicularis — Parakeet, Orange-fronted
Aratinga holochlora — Parakeet, Green
Arbacia punctulata — Sea Urchin, Purple
Arbutus unedo — Strawberry Tree
Arca zebra — Turkey Wing
Arcaucaria imbricata — Monkey Puzzle Tree
Arceuthobium campylopodium — Mistletoe, Western
   Dwarf
Archilochus alexandri — Hummingbird, Black-chinned
Archilochus colubris — Hummingbird, Ruby-throated
Archips fumiferana — Moth, Spruce Budworm

Architeuthis harveyi — Squid, Giant
Architeuthis princeps — Squid, Giant
Archoplites interruptus — Perch, Sacramento
Archosargus probatocephalus — Sheepshead
Arctica islandica — Clam, Quahog
Arctium lappa — Burdock, Great
Arctium minus — Burdock, Lesser
Arctium tomentosum — Burdock, Downy or Woolly
Arctostaphylos alpina — Ptarmigan-berry
Arctostaphylos columbiana — Manzanita, Bristly
Arctostaphylos manzanita — Manzanita
Arctostaphylos uva-ursi — Bearberry
Arctotis sp. — Daisy, African
Ardea herodias — Heron, Great Blue
Ardea occidentalis — Heron, Great White
Ardeola ibis — Egret, Cattle
Arenaria congesta — Sandwort, Capitate
Arenaria groenlandica — Sandwort, Mountain
Arenaria interpres — Turnstone, Ruddy
Arenaria macrophylla — Sandwort, Large-leaved
Arenaria melanocephala — Turnstone, Black
Arenicola claperedii — Lugworm
Arenicola cristata — Lugworm
Arethusa bulbosa — Arethusa
Argemone albiflora — Poppy, Prickly
Argemone mexicana — Poppy, Prickly
Argemone platyceras — Chicalote
Argiope aurantia — Spider, Black-and-yellow Garden
Argiope trifasciata — Spider, Black-and-yellow Garden
Argobuccinum oregonensis — Triton, Oregon
Argonauta argo — Paper Nautilus, Common
Argonauta hians — Paper Nautilus, Brown
Argulus foliaceus — Louse, Fish
Argynnis euphrosyne — Butterfly, Pearl-bordered
   Fritillary
Argynnis selene — Butterfly, Pearl-bordered Fritillary
Argyroneta aquatica — Spider, Water
Argyropelecus hemigymnus — Hatchetfish
Argyrotaenia velutinano — Leaf-roller, Red-banded
Arion sp. — Slug, Garden
Arisaema atrubens — Jack-in-the-pulpit
Arisaema dracontium — Dragonroot or Green
   Dragon
Arisaema triphyllum — Jack-in-the-pulpit
Aristolochia californica — Dutchman's-pipe
Aristolochia clematitis — Birthwort
Aristolochia durior — Dutchman's-pipe
Aristolochia elegans — Calico Plant

Aristolochia grandiflora — Pelican-flower
Arizona elegans — Snake, Glossy
Armadillidium vulgare — Sowbug
Armeria maritima — Sea-pink
Armeria plantaginea — Sea-pink
Armoracia rusticana — Horseradish
Arnica amplexicaulis — Arnica, Clasping-leaved
Arnica cordifolia — Arnica, Heart-leaved
Aronia arbutifolia — Chokeberry, Red
Aronia melanocarpa — Chokeberry, Black
Arremon aurantirostris — Sparrow, Orange-billed
Arremonops chloronotus — Sparrow, Green-backed
Arremonops rufivirgata — Sparrow, Olive or Texas
Arrhenatherum elatius — Oat-grass, Tall
Artedius sp. — Sculpin
Artemisia abrotanum — Southernwood
Artemisia absinthium — Wormwood, Absinthe
Artemisia annua — Wormwood, Annual
Artemisia biennis — Wormwood, Annual
Artemisia campestris — Mugwort, Breckland
Artemisia lactiflora — Mugwort, Breckland
Artemisia maritima — Wormwood, Sea
Artemisia stelleriana — Dusty Miller
Artemisia suksdorfi — Mugwort, Breckland
Artemisia tridentata — Sagebrush
Artemisia vulgaris — Mugwort, Common
Artocarpus altilis — Breadfruit
Artocarpus communis — Breadfruit
Arum italicum — Arum, Italian
Aruncus dioicus — Goatsbeard
Aruncus sylvester — Goatsbeard
Arundinaria gigantea — Cane, Giant or Southern
Arundinaria japonica — Bamboo, Japanese
Arundo donax — Reed, Giant
Asarum arifolium — Little Brown Jug
Asarum canadense — Ginger, Wild
Asarum caudatum — Ginger, Western Wild
Asarum hartwegi — Ginger, Hartweg's Wild
Asarum lemmoni — Ginger, Lemmon's Wild
Ascaphus truei — Frog, Tailed
Ascaphus truei stejneger — Toad, Bell
Asclepias amplexicaulis — Milkweed, Blunt-leaved
Asclepias curvassavica — Blood Flower
Asclepias incarnata — Milkweed, Swamp
Asclepias purpuracens — Milkweed, Purple
Asclepias quadrifolia — Milkweed, Four-leaved
Asclepias speciosa — Milkweed, Showy
Asclepias syriaca — Milkweed, Common

Asclepias tuberosa — Milkweed, Orange
Asclepias variegata — Milkweed, White
Asclepias verticillata — Milkweed, Whorled
Ascophyllum nodosum — Wrack, Knotted
Ascyrum hypericoides — St. Andrew's Cross
Ascyrum stans — St.-Peter's-wort
Asellus sp. — Sowbug, Water
Asilus sp. — Fly, Robber
Asimina triloba — Papaw
Asio flammeus — Owl, Short-eared
Asio flammeus sandwichensis — Owl, Short-eared
Asio otus — Owl, Long-eared
Asparagus officinalis — Asparagus
Asparagus plumosus — Asparagus-fern
Asparagus sprengeri — Asparagus-fern
Aspatha gularis — Motmot, Blue-throated
Asperula odorata — Woodruff, Sweet
Asphodelus luteus — Asphodel, Yellow
Aspidiotus perniciosus — Scale, San Jose
Asplenium nidus-avis — Fern, Bird's-nest
Asplenium ruta-muraria — Wall-rue
Asplenium trichomanes — Spleenwort, Maidenhair
Aspris caryophylla — Hairgrass, Silver
Aspris praecox — Hairgrass, Early
Aster ericoides — Aster, Heath
Aster laevis — Aster, Smooth
Aster lateriflorus — Aster, Calico
Aster macrophyllus — Aster, Large-leaved
Aster nova-angliae — Aster, New England
Aster novaebelgii — Daisy, Michaelmas
Aster patens — Aster, Late Purple
Aster prenanthoides — Aster, Crooked-stem
Aster puniceus — Aster, Red-stalked or Purple-stemmed
Aster sericeus — Aster, Western Silvery
Aster simplex — Aster, Panicled
Aster spectabilis — Aster, Seaside or Showy
Aster umbellatus — Aster, Tall Flat-top White
Aster undulatus — Aster, Wavy-leaf
Asterias forbesi — Starfish, Common
Asterias rubens — Starfish, Common
Asterina miniata — Starfish, Sea Bat
Astilbe japonica — Astilbe
Astraea undosa — Turban Shell, Wavy
Astragalus alpinus — Milk-vetch, Alpine
Astragalus canadensis — Milk-vetch
Astragalus coccineus — Locoweed, Scarlet
Astragalus distortus — Milk-vetch
Astragalus lentiginosus — Milk-vetch

Astrangia danae — Coral, Star
Astrantia major or maxima — Masterwort
Asyndesmus lewis — Woodpecker, Lewis'
Ateles sp. — Monkey, Spider
Athyrium filix-femina — Fern, Lady
Athyrium thelypteroides — Spleenwort, Silvery
Atlapetes pileatus — Finch, Rufous-capped
Atriplex confertifolia — Saltbush
Atriplex hastata — Orache, Halberd-leaved
Atriplex hortensis — Orache, Common
Atriplex littoralis — Orache, Halberd-leaved
Atriplex patula — Orache, Common
Atropa belladonna — Nightshade, Deadly
Atthis heloisa — Hummingbird, Bumblebee or Heloise
Attila spadiceus — Attila, Bright-rumped
Aubrieta deltoides — Cress, False Rock
Aucuba japonica — Laurel, Spotted
Aulacorhynchus prasinus — Toucanet, Emerald
Aulicus terrestricus — Beetle, Checkered
Aurelia aurita — Jellyfish, Moon
Auriparus flaviceps — Verdin
Automeris io — Moth, Io
Automeris memusae — Butterfly, Peacock
Autoserica castanea — Beetle, Asiatic Garden
Avena fatua — Oat, Wild
Avena sativa — Oat
Avicularia sp. — Spider, Bird
Aythya affinis — Scaup, Lesser
Aythya americana — Duck, Redhead
Aythya collaris — Duck, Ring-necked
Aythya fuligula — Duck, Tufted
Aythya marila — Scaup, Greater
Aythya valisneria — Canvasback
Azolla caroliniana — Fern, Mosquito or Water
Azolla filiculoides — Fern, Mosquito or Water

B

Baccharis halimifolia — Groundsel-tree
Baileya multiradiata — Marigold, Desert
Baiomys taylori — Mouse, Pygmy
Balaena mysticetus — Whale, Bowhead
Balaenoptera acutorostrata — Whale, Piked or Minke
Balaenoptera borealis — Rorqual
Balaenoptera musculus — Whale, Blue
Balaenoptera physalus — Whale, Finback
Balaninus sp. — Weevil, Nut
Balanophyllia elegans — Coral, Orange-red or Cup

Balanus sp. — Barnacle, Rock or Acorn
Balistes capriscus — Triggerfish, Gray
Balistes carolinensis — Triggerfish, Gray
Balistes vetula — Triggerfish, Queen
Balsamorhiza deltoidea — Balsamroot
Bankia setacea — Shipworm
Baptisia australis — Indigo, Blue False
Baptisia leucantha — Indigo, White False
Baptisia leucophaea — Indigo, Nodding False
Baptisia tinctoria — Indigo, Wild False
Barbarea americana — Cress, Winter
Barbarea orthoceras — Cress, Winter
Barbarea vulgaris — Cress, Winter
Barnea costata — Angel Wing, Common
Bartonia virginica — Bartonia
Bartramia longicauda — Plover, Upland
Basileuterus bellii — Warbler, Golden-browed
Basileuterus culicivorus — Warbler, Golden-crowned
Basileuterus rufifrons — Warbler, Rufous-capped
Basiliscus vittatus — Basilisk, Banded
Bassariscus astutus — Ringtail
Batodendron arboreum — Farkleberry
Batrachoseps attenuatus — Salamander, Slender or Worm
Batrachoseps pacificus — Salamander, Slender or Worm
Batrachoseps wrighti — Salamander, Slender or Worm
Bauhinia sp. — Orchid Tree
Begonia rex — Begonia
Begonia semperflorens — Begonia
Begonia tuberhybrida — Begonia
Bellis perennis — Daisy, English or Lawn
Beloperone californica — Chuparosa or Chuperosa
Beloperone guttata — Shrimp Plant
Bembix spinolae — Wasp, Sand
Benzoin aestivale — Spicebush
Berberis aquifolium — Oregon Grape
Berberis nervosa — Oregon Grape
Berberis repens — Oregon Grape or Barberry, Creeping
Berberis thunbergii — Barberry, Japanese
Berberis vulgaris — Barberry, European
Bergenia cordifolia — Bergenia
Bergenia purpuracens — Bergenia
Beta vulgaris — Beet, Sugar
Beta vulgaris var. — Beet
Beta vulgaris var. cicla — Chard, Swiss
Betula alleghaniensis — Birch, Yellow
Betula lenta — Birch, Black or Sweet or Cherry
Betula lutea — Birch, Yellow

Betula nigra — Birch, Red or River
Betula occidentalis — Birch, Western or Water
Betula papyrifera — Birch, Paper
Betula pendula — Birch, Silver or White
Betula populifolia — Birch, Gray
Betula pubescens — Birch, Common
Bidens cernua — Bur-marigold, Nodding
Bidens comosa — Beggar-ticks, Leafy-bracted
Bidens frondosa — Beggar-ticks, Sticktight
Bignonia capreolata — Cross-vine
Biorhiza pallida — Gall, Oak-apple
Bison bison — Bison, American
Bittium alternatum — Snail, Screw
Bittium eschrichtii — Snail, Screw
Blandfordia nobilis — Christmas Bells
Blarina brevicauda — Shrew, Short-tailed
Blatta orientalis — Cockroach, Common or Oriental
Blattella germanica — Cockroach, German
Blechum spicant — Fern, Deer
Blissus leucopterus — Bug, Chinch
Bloomera crocea — Golden-stars
Boehmeria cylindrica — Nettle, False
Boeolophus inornatus — Titmouse, Plain
Boisduvalia densiflora — Boisduvalia, Dense-flowered
Bolborhynchus lineata — Parakeet, Barred
Bolborhynchus lineola — Parakeet, Barred
Boletus badius — Boletus, Sweet Chestnut
Boletus edulis — Boletus, Edible
Boletus elegans — Boletus, Elegant
Boletus luridus — Boletus, Lurid
Boletus luteus — Boletus, Brown-yellow
Boletus scaber — Boletus, Rough-stemmed
Boletus subtomentosus — Boletus, Yellow-cracked
Boltenia villosa — Sea Squirt, Hairy
Boltonia asteroides — Boltonia, Aster-like
Bombus sp. — Bee, Bumble
Bombycilla cedrorum — Waxwing, Cedar
Bombycilla garrulus — Waxwing, Bohemian
Bombyliopsis abrupta — Fly, Tachina
Bonasa umbellus — Grouse, Ruffed
Boophilus annulatus — Tick, Cattle
Borago officinalis — Borage
Boriomyia fidelis — Lacewing, Brown
Bos indicus — Cattle, Brahman
Bos taurus — Cattle, Domestic
Boschniakia hookeri — Ground-cone, Vancouver
Botaurus lentiginosus — Bittern, American
Botaurus pinnatus — Bittern, Pinnated

Bothriocyrtum californicum — Spider, Trap-door
Bothrops atrox — Fer-de-lance
Botrychium sp. — Fern, Grape
Botrychium lunaria — Moonwort
Botryllus schlosseri — Sea Squirt, Star
Botula californiensis — Clam, Rock-boring
Bougainvillea glabra — Bougainvillea
Bougainvillea spectabilis — Bougainvillea
Bourletiella hortensis — Springtail, Garden
Bouteloua curtipendula — Grama, Sideoats
Bouteloua gracilis — Grama, Blue
Bouteloua hirsuta — Grama, Hairy
Bouvardia glaberrima — Bouvardia
Bovicola ovis — Louse, Sheep-biting
Brachidontes recurvus — Mussel, Hooked
Brachycome iberidifolia — Daisy, Swan River
Brachyistius frenatus — Perch, Kelp
Brachyramphus brevirostre — Murrelet, Kittlitz's
Brachyramphus marmoratum — Murrelet, Marbled
Brachyrhinus ovatus — Weevil, Strawberry Root
Brachyrhinus sulcatus — Weevil, Black Vine
Branchinecta paludosa — Shrimp, Fairy
Branchiostoma caribaeum — Amphioxus
Branchiostoma virginiae — Amphioxus
Branta bernicla — Brant, American
Branta canadensis — Goose, Canada
Branta leucopsis — Goose, Barnacle
Branta nigricans — Brant, Black
Branta sandivicensis — Goose, Hawaiian
Brasenia schreberi — Water-shield
Brassaia actinophylla — Umbrella Tree
Brassia caudata — Orchid, Spider
Brassica alba — Mustard, White
Brassica arvensis — Mustard, Field
Brassica campestris — Cabbage, Field
Brassica caulorapa — Kohlrabi
Brassica hirta — Mustard, White
Brassica kaber — Mustard, Field
Brassica napobrassica — Rutabaga
Brassica nigra — Mustard, Black
Brassica oleracea — Kale, Curly (Collards)
Brassica oleracea var. botrytis — Broccoli
Brassica oleracea var. capitata — Cabbage
Brassica oleracea var. gemmifera — Brussel Sprouts
Brassica pekinensis or B. chinensis — Cabbage, Chinese
Brassica rapa — Turnip
Bregmaceros macclellandi — Unicorn Fish
Brevoortia tyrannus — Menhaden

Breynia nivosa — Jacob's Coat
Briza maxima — Grass, Large Quaking
Briza media — Grass, Quaking
Brodiaea ida-maia — Firecracker Flower
Brodiaea sp. — Brodiaea
Bromus erectus — Brome, Upright
Bromus inermis — Brome, Awnless or Smooth
Bromus japonicus — Brome, Japanese
Bromus secalinus — Brome, Rye
Bromus sterilis — Brome, Barren
Bromus tectorum — Brome, Downy or Drooping
Brosme brosme — Cusk
Brotogeris jugularis — Parakeet, Orange-chinned
Broussonetia papyrifera — Mulberry, Paper
Browallia speciosa major — Browallia
Brownea grandiceps — Rose of Venezuela
Bruchus pisorum — Weevil, Pea
Brunfelsia calycina — Yesterday, Today and Tomorrow
Brunfelsia latifolia — Yesterday, Today and Tomorrow
Bryonia dioica — Bryony
Bryopsis corticulans — Sea Fern
Bryopsis plumosa — Sea Fern
Bubo virginianus — Owl, Great Horned
Bubulcus ibis — Egret, Cattle
Buccinum glaciale — Whelk, Glacial
Buccinum undatum — Whelk, Common Northern
   (Waved)
Bucephala albeola — Bufflehead
Bucephala clangula — Golden-eye, American
Bucephala islandica — Golden-eye, Barrow's
Buchloe dactyloides — Buffalograss
Buddleia davidii — Butterfly Bush
Bufo alvarius — Toad, Colorado River
Bufo americanus — Toad, American
Bufo boreas — Toad, Western
Bufo cognatus — Toad, Great Plains
Bufo compactilis — Toad, Texas
Bufo debilis — Toad, Green
Bufo exsul — Toad, Black
Bufo fowleri — Toad, Fowler's
Bufo hemiophrys — Toad, Dakota
Bufo marinus — Toad, Giant or Marine
Bufo punctatus — Toad, Red Spotted
Bufo retiformis — Toad, Green
Bufo speciosus — Toad, Texas
Bufo terrestis — Toad, American
Bufo woodhousei — Toad, Woodhouse's
Bugula sp. — Bryozoan

Bulbilis dactyloides — Buffalograss
Bulla striata — Bubble Shell
Bulweria bulweri — Petrel, Bulwer's
Bumelia lycioides — Bumelia, Buckthorn
Bureo swainsoni — Hawk, Swainson's
Burhinus bistriatus — Thick-knee, Double-striped
Busarellus nigricollis — Hawk, Black-collared
Busycon canaliculatum — Whelk, Channeled
Busycon carica — Whelk, Knobbed
Busycon contrarium — Whelk, Lightning
Busycoptypus aruanum — Whelk, Knobbed
Butea frondosa — Butea's Blossom
Buteo albicaudatus — Hawk, White-tailed
Buteo albonotatus — Hawk, Zone-tailed
Buteo brachyurus — Hawk, Short-tailed
Buteo harlani — Hawk, Harlan's
Buteo jamaicensis — Hawk, Red-tailed
Buteo lagopus — Hawk, Rough-legged
Buteo lineatus — Hawk, Red-shouldered
Buteo nitidus — Hawk, Gray
Buteo platypterus — Hawk, Broad-winged
Buteo regalis — Hawk, Ferruginous
Buteo solitarius — Hawk, Hawaiian
Buteogallus anthracinus — Hawk, Black or Crab
Butomus umbellatus — Rush, Flowering
Butorides virescens — Heron, Green
Buxbaumia aphylla — Moss, Elf-cap
Buxus sempervirens — Box

C

Cabomba caroliniana — Fanwort
Cabomba piauhiensis — Fanwort
Cacalia atriplicifolia — Indian-plantain, Pale
Cacalia tuberosa — Indian-plantain, Pale
Cacicus cela — Cacique, Yellow-rumped
Cadlina marginata — Nudibranch, Yellow
Caesalpinia pulcherrima — Barbados Pride
Cairina moschata — Duck, Muscovy
Cakile edentula — Sea Rocket
Caladium bicolor — Caladium, Fancy-leaved
Calamavilfa longifolia — Hack
Calamintha ascendens — Calamint
Calamospiza melanocorys — Bunting, Lark
Calandrinia ciliata — Red Maids
Calandrinia umbellata — Purslane, Rock
Calcarius ornatus — Longspur, Chestnut-collared
Calcarius lapponicus — Bunting, Lapland

Calcarius lapponicus lapponicus — Longspur, Lapland
Calcarius pictus — Longspur, Smith's
Calceolaria crenatiflora — Pocketbook Flower
Calendra callosa — Billbug
Calendra granarius — Weevil, Granary
Calendra setiger — Billbug
Calendula officinalis — Marigold, Pot
Calidris acuminata — Sandpiper, Sharp-tailed
Calidris alba — Sanderling
Calidris alpina — Dunlin
Calidris bairdii — Sandpiper, Baird's
Calidris canutus — Knot
Calidris ferruginea — Sandpiper, Curlew
Calidris fuscicollis — Sandpiper, White-rumped
Calidris leucophaea — Sanderling
Calidris maritima — Sandpiper, Purple
Calidris melanotus — Sandpiper, Pectoral
Calidris minutilla — Sandpiper, Least
Calidris pusilla — Sandpiper, Semi-palmated
Caliroa cerasi — Pear-slug
Calla palustris — Wild calla
Calliactis parasitica — Sea Anemone, Hermit Crab
Callianassa californiensis — Shrimp, Ghost
Callianassa gigas — Shrimp, Ghost
Calliandra inequalatera — Powder Puff
Callicarpa sp. — Beauty Berry
Callinectes sapidus — Crab, Blue
Callionymus lyra — Dragonet
Callionymus maculatus — Dragonet
Calliostoma annulatum — Top Shell, Ringed
Calliostoma canaliculatum — Top Shell, Channeled
Calliostoma dolarium — Top Shell, Channeled
Calliostoma javanicum — Top Shell, Chocolate-lined
Calliostoma zonamestum — Top Shell, Chocolate-lined
Callipepla squamata — Quail, Scaled
Calliphora sp. — Fly, Blow or Bluebottle
Callirhoe involucrata — Mallow, Poppy
Calliostoma ligatum — Top Shell, Ribbed
Callisaurus draconoides — Lizard, Zebra-tailed
Callistemon citrinus — Bottlebrush
Callistemon speciosus — Bottlebrush
Callistemon viminalis — Bottlebrush
Callistephus chinensis — Aster, China
Callitroga hominivorax — Fly, Screw-worm
Callorhinus ursinus — Seal, Alaska Fur
Callosamia promethea — Moth, Promethea
Callosobruchus maculatus — Weevil, Cowpea
Calluna vulgaris — Heather, Scotch or Ling

Calocera viscosa — Fungus, Calocera
Calochortus sp. — Lily, Mariposa
Calochortus albus — Fairy Lantern
Calochortus nuttallii — Lily, Sego
Calochortus pulchellus — Fairy Lantern
Calocitta formosa — Jay, Magpie
Calodendron capense — Chestnut, Cape
Calonyction aculeatum — Moonflower
Calopogon pulchellus — Grass-pink
Calopteron reticulatum — Beetle, Banded Net-winged
Calopteron terminale — Beetle, Banded Net-winged
Calopteryx sp. — Dragonfly
Calosaturnia mendocino — Moth, Silk
Calosoma scrutator — Beetle, Fiery Searcher or Hunter
Calosoma sycophanta — Beetle, Fiery Searcher or
    Hunter
Calothorax lucifer — Hummingbird, Lucifer
Caltha asarifolia — Marsh-marigold, White
Caltha biflora — Marsh-marigold, White
Caltha leptosepala — Marsh-marigold, Western
Caltha palustris — Marsh-marigold, Common
Calvatia gigantea — Puffball, Giant
Calvatia maxima — Puffball, Giant
Calycanthus fertilis — Allspice, Carolina
Calycanthus floridus — Allspice, Carolina
Calycanthus occidentalis — Allspice, Carolina
Calypso bulbosa — Fairy-slipper
Calypte anna — Hummingbird, Anna's
Calypte costae — Hummingbird, Costa's
Calypte helenae — Hummingbird, Bee
Calyptraea chinensis — Snail, Chinese Hat
Calyptraea fastigiata — Snail, Chinese Hat
Calyptraea mammillaris — Snail, Chinese Hat
Calytridium umbellatum — Pussy Paws
Camassia leichtlinii — Camas, Great
Camassia quamash — Camas
Camassia scilloides — Hyacinth, Wild
Cambarus bartoni — Crayfish, Eastern
Camellia japonica — Camellia
Camnula pellucida — Grasshopper, Clear-winged
Campanula americana — Bellflower, Tall
Campanula carpatica — Bellflower, Tussock
Campanula isophylla — Bellflower, Italian
Campanula lasiocarpa — Harebell, Alpine
Campanula medium — Canterbury Bells
Campanula persicifolia — Bellflower, Peach-leaved or
    Willow
Campanula rapunculoides — Bellflower, Creeping

Campanula rotundifolia — Harebell
Campanula scouleri — Harebell, Alpine
Campephilus imperialis — Woodpecker, Imperial
Campephilus principalis — Woodpecker, Ivory-billed
Camponotus herculeanus — Ant, Black Carpenter
Camponotus pennsylvanicus — Ant, Black Carpenter
Campsis radicans — Trumpet-creeper
Camptosorus rhizophyllus — Fern, Walking
Camptostoma imberbe — Flycatcher, Beardless
Campylopterus curvipennis — Sabrewing, Wedge-tailed
Campylopterus hemileucurus — Sabrewing, Violet
Campylorhynchus brunneicapillus — Wren, Cactus
Canachites canadensis — Grouse, Spruce
Cananga odorata — Ylang-ylang
Cancellaria cassidiformis — Nutmeg, Helmet-shaped
    (mollusk)
Cancellaria reticulata — Nutmeg, Common (mollusk)
Cancer irroratus — Crab, Rock
Cancer magister — Crab, Dungeness
Cancer oregonensis — Crab, Hairy
Cancer pagurus — Crab, Rock
Cancer productus — Crab, Red
Canis familiaris — Dog
Canis latrans — Coyote
Canis lupus — Wolf, Gray or Timber
Canis niger — Wolf, Red
Canna generalis — Canna
Canna indica — Canna
Cannabis sativa — Hemp, Soft (Marijuana)
Cantharellus cibarius — Chanterelle, Yellow
Cantharellus cinnabarinus — Chanterelle, Vermilion
Canthigaster sp. — Puffer-fish, Sharp-nose
Capella gallinago — Snipe, Common or Wilson's
Capparis spinosa — Caper Bush
Capra aegagrus hircus — Goat, Domestic
Capra angorensis — Goat, Domestic
Caprella kennerlyi — Shrimp, Phantom
Caprimulgus caroliniensis — Chuck-will's-widow
Caprimulgus ridgwayi — Whip-poor-will, Ridgway's
Caprimulgus vociferus — Whip-poor-will, Eastern
Capsella bursa-pastoris — Shepherd's Purse
C apsicum annum — Pepper (cultivated)
Capsicum frutescens — Pepper (cultivated)
Caracara cheriway — Caracara, Audubon's or Common
Caranx bartholomaei — Jack, Yellow
Carassius auratus — Goldfish
Carcharhinus leucas — Shark, Bull or Ground
Carcharias taurus — Shark, Sans

Carcharius glaucus — Shark, Blue
Carcharodon carcharias — Shark, White
Carcinus maenas — Crab, Green or Shore
Cardamine bulbosa — Cress, Spring
Cardamine douglasii — Cress, Bitter
Cardamine hirsuta — Cress, Bitter
Cardamine pensylvanica — Cress, Bitter
Cardamine pratensis — Cuckoo-flower
Cardellina rubrifrons — Warbler, Red-faced
Cardiospermum halicacabum — Balloon Vine
Carduus nutans — Thistle, Musk or Nodding
Caretta caretta — Turtle, Loggerhead
Carica papaya — Papaya
Caristius macropus — Manefish
Carnegiea gigantea — Cactus, Saguaro or Giant
Carpenteria californica — Carpenteria
Carpinus betulus — Hornbeam
Carpinus caroliniana — Hornbeam
Carpocapsa pomonella — Moth, Coddling
Carpodacus cassinii — Finch, Cassin's
Carpodacus mexicanus — Finch, House
Carpodacus purpureus — Finch, Purple (Eastern)
Carpophilus hemipterus — Beetle, Dried Fruit
Carulaspis juniperi — Scale, Juniper
Carum carvi — Caraway
Carya aquatica — Hickory, Water
Carya cordiformis — Hickory, Bitternut
Carya glabra — Hickory, Pignut
Carya illinoensis — Pecan
Carya laciniosa — Hickory, Shellbark
Carya leiodermis — Hickory, Bitternut
Carya ovata — Hickory, Shagbark
Carya tomentosa — Hickory, Mockernut
Caryopteris sp. — Spirea, Blue
Casmerodius albus — Egret, Common or Great
Cassia alata — Candlebush
Cassia fasciculata — Partridge-pea
Cassia fistula — Golden Shower
Cassia marilandica — Senna, Wild
Cassia nicitans — Sensitive Plant, Wild
Cassidix mexicanus — Grackle, Boat-tailed
Cassiope mertensiana — Heather, White
Cassiopeia sp. — Jellyfish
Cassis cornuta — Helmet, Horned or Large
Cassis flammea — Helmet, Flame
Cassis tuberosa — Helmet, King
Castanea dentata — Chestnut, American
Castanea pumila — Chinquapin, Allegheny

Castanea sativa — Chestnut, Sweet or Spanish
Castanopsis chrysophylla — Chinquapin, Golden-leaved
Castilleja coccinea — Indian Paintbrush or Painted Cup
Castilleja levisecta — Indian Paintbrush, Golden
Castilleja miniata — Indian Paintbrush, Common Red
Castilleja sessiliflora — Indian Paintbrush, Golden
Castor canadensis — Beaver
Catalpa bignonioides — Catalpa, Southern
Catalpa speciosa — Catalpa, Northern or Western
Catananche coerulea — Cupid's Dart
Catharacta skua — Skua
Catharanthus rosea — Periwinkle, Madagascar (plant)
Cathartes aura — Vulture, Turkey
Catharus mexicanus — Nightingale-thrush, Black-headed
Catharus occidentalis — Nightingale-thrush, Russet
Catherpes mexicanus — Wren, Canyon
Catoptrophorus semipalmatus — Willet
Catostomus occidentalis — Sucker, White
Cattleya sp. — Orchid
Cattleya sp. — Orchid
Caulanthus inflatus — Desert Candle
Caulophyllum thalictroides — Cohosh, Blue
Cavia porcellus — Guinea-pig
Ceanothus americanus — Tea, New Jersey
Ceanothus cuneatus — Buckbrush
Ceanothus integerrimus — Deer-brush
Ceanothus sanguineus — Buckbrush
Ceanothus thyrsiflorus — Lilac, California or Blue-
   blossom
Ceanothus velutinus — Laurel, Sticky
Cebus capucinus — Capuchin, White-throated
Cedrus atlantica — Cedar, Atlantic or Atlas
Cedrus deodara — Cedar, Deodar
Cedrus libani — Cedar, Lebanon
Celandine majus — Celandine
Celastrus scandens — Bittersweet, American
Celeus castaneus — Woodpecker, Chestnut-colored
Celosia argentea — Cockscomb
Celosia cristata — Cockscomb
Celtis laevigata — Hackberry
Celtis occidentalis — Hackberry
Celtis tenuifolia — Hackberry
Cemophora coccinea — Snake, Scarlet
Cemophora doliata — Snake, Scarlet
Cenchrus pauciflorus — Sandbur
Cenchurs tribuloides — Sandbur
Centaurea americana — Knapweed, American
Centaurea calcitrapa — Star-thistle

Centaurea cyanus — Cornflower
Centaurea jacea — Knapweed, Brown
Centaurea maculosa — Knapweed, Spotted
Centaurea melitensis — Star-thistle
Centaurea montana — Bluet, Mountain
Centaurea moschata — Sweet Sultan
Centaurea rutifolia — Dusty Miller
Centaurea solstitialis — Thistle, Barnaby's
Centaurium umbellatum — Centaury
Centranthus ruber — Valerian, Red
Centrocercus urophasianus — Grouse, Sage (Sage Hen)
Centropomus undecimalis — Snook
Centropristes striatus — Sea Bass, Black
Centrurus sp. — Scorpion
Centurus aurifrons — Woodpecker, Golden-fronted
Centurus carolinus — Woodpecker, Red-bellied
Centurus chrysogenys — Woodpecker, Golden-cheeked
Centurus pucherami — Woodpecker, Black-cheeked
Centurus uropygialis — Woodpecker, Gila
Cephalanthera austinae — Orchid, Phantom
Cephalanthus occidentalis — Buttonbush
Cephalocereus senilis — Cactus, Old Man
Cepphus columba — Guillemot, Pigeon
Cepphus grylle — Guillemot, Black
Ceramium fastigiatum — Ceramium
Ceramium pacificum — Ceramium
Ceramium rubrum — Ceramium
Cerastium arvense — Chickweed, Field
Cerastium tomentosum — Snow-in-summer
Cerastium vulgatum — Chickweed, Mouse-ear
Cerastoderma corbis — Cockle, Heart or Nuttall's
Cerastoderma pinnulatum — Cockle, Dwarf or Little
Ceratina dupla — Bee, Carpenter
Ceratitis capitata — Fly, Fruit (Mediterranean)
Ceratophyllum demersum — Hornwort, Common
Cercidium floridum — Palo Verde, Blue
Cercidium microphyllum — Palo Verde, Blue
Cercis canadensis — Judas Tree
Cercis occidentalis — Redbud, California or Western
Cercis siliquastrum — Judas Tree
Cerebratulus lacteus — Worm, Ribbon
Ceresa sp. — Treehopper
Cereus pedunculatus — Sea Anemone, Daisy
Cerithidea californica — Hornshell, California
Cerithium sp. — Cerith
Cerorhinca monocerata — Auklet, Rhinoceros
Certhia familiaris — Creeper, Brown
Cervus canadensis — Elk, American

Cervus elaphus — Elk, American
Ceryle torquata — Kingfisher, Ringed
Cestrum aurantiacum — Cestrum, Orange
Cestrum fasciculatum — Cestrum, Orange
Cestrum nocturnum — Jasmine, Night-blooming
Cestrum parqui — Cestrum, Orange
Cestus veneris — Venus' Girdle
Cetorhinus maximus — Shark, Basking
Cettia diphone — Warbler, Bush
Ceuthophilus gracilipes — Cricket, Cave
Chaenactis douglasii — Chaenactis
Chaenactis thompsoni — Chaenactis
Chaenobryttus gulosus — Sunfish, Warmouth
Chaenomeles japonica — Quince, Flowering
Chaenomeles lagenaria — Quince, Flowering
Chaenomeles speciosa — Quince, Flowering
Chaetodipterus faber — Spadefish, Atlantic
Chaetodon fremblii — Butterflyfish, Blue-stripe
Chaetopleura apiculata — Chiton, Eastern
Chaetopterus pergamentaceus — Worm, Parchment-tube
Chaetopterus variopedatus — Worm, Parchment-tube
Chaetura pelagica — Swift, Chimney
Chaetura vauxi — Swift, Vaux's
Chalybion caeruleum — Wasp, Blue Mud-dauber
Chalybion californicum — Wasp, Blue Mud-dauber
Chamaea fasciata — Wrentit
Chamaecrista fasciculata — Partridge-pea
Chamaecyparis lawsoniana — Cedar, Port Orford
Chamaecyparis nootkatensis — Cedar, Alaska Yellow
Chamaecyparis pisifera — Cypress, Sawara
Chamaecyparis thyoides — Cedar, White
Chamaedaphne calyculata — Leatherleaf (Cassandra)
Chamaelirium luteum — Devil's-bit
Chamaethlypis poliocephala — Ground-chat
Chanda ranga — Glassfish
Chanda wolfii — Glassfish
Chanos chanos — Milkfish
Chaoborus albipes — Midge, Phantom
Chaoborus astictopus — Midge, Phantom
Chaos diffugens — Amoeba Proteus
Chara sp. — Stonewort
Charadrius alexandrinus — Plover, Snowy
Charadrius collaris — Plover, Collared
Charadrius melodus — Plover, Piping
Charadrius semipalmatus — Plover, Semipalmated
Charadrius wilsonia — Plover, Wilson's
Charadrius vociferus — Killdeer
Charina bottae — Boa, Rubber

Charonia tritonis — Triton's-trumpet
Chasmodes bosquianus — Blenny, Striped
Chauliodus danae — Viperfish
Chauliodus macouni — Viperfish
Chauliodus sloanei — Viperfish
Chauliognathus pennsylvanicus — Beetle, Soldier
Cheilanthes lanosa — Lip-fern, Hairy
Cheiranthus cheiri — Wallflower
Chelone glabra — Turtlehead
Chelone lyoni — Turtlehead, Red
Chelone obliqua — Turtlehead
Chelonia mydas — Turtle, Green
Chelydra serpentina — Turtle, Snapping
Chen caerulescens — Goose, Blue
Chen hyperborea — Goose, Snow
Chen rossii — Goose, Ross
Chenopodium album — Goosefoot, White or Pigweed
Chenopodium bonus-henricus — Good King Henry
Chenopodium botrys — Goosefoot, Sticky or Feather
  Geranium
Chenopodium capitatum — Strawberry-blite
Chenopodium glaucum — Goosefoot, Oak-leaved
Chenopodium hybridum — Goosefoot, Maple-leaved or
  Sowbane
Chenopodium murale — Goosefoot, Nettle-leaved
Chenopodium polyspermum — Goosefoot, Many-seeded
Chenopodium rubrum — Goosefoot, Red
Chenopodium vulvaria — Goosefoot, Stinking
Chermes abietis — Aphid, Spruce Gall
Chiasmodon niger — Swallower, Black or Great
Chilomeniscus cinctus — Snake, Sand
Chilomycterus schoepfi — Burrfish
Chilopsis linearis — Desert-willow
Chimaera affinis — Chimera
Chimaera monstrosa — Rabbitfish
Chimaphila maculata — Wintergreen, Spotted
Chimaphila umbellata — Pipsissewa
Chimonanthus praecox — Winter Sweet
Chionactis occipitalis — Snake, Shovel-nosed
Chionactis palarostris — Snake, Shovel-nosed
Chionanthus retusa — Fringe Tree
Chionanthus virginica — Fringe Tree
Chione cancellata — Venus, Cross-barred
Chione paphia — Venus, King
Chionodoxa luciliae — Glory of the Snow
Chiranthodendron pentadactylon — Hand-flower Tree
Chirocephalus sp. — Shrimp, Fairy
Chironectes minimus — Opossum, Water

Chironomus sp. — Midge
Chiroxiphia linearis — Manakin, Long-tailed
Chlamys hericius — Scallop, Pacific Pink
Chlamys rubidus — Scallop, Hind's or Smooth
Chlidonias niger — Tern, Black
Chlorella sp. — Alga, Green
Chloris verticillata — Grass, Windmill
Chloroceryle aenea — Kingfisher, Pygmy
Chloroceryle americana — Kingfisher, Green or Texas
Chlorohydra viridissima — Hydra
Chlorophanes spiza — Honeycreeper, Green
Chlorostilbon canivetii — Emerald, Fork-tailed
Chlorostilbon maugaeus — Emerald, Puerto Rican
Chlorura chlorura — Towhee, Green-tailed
Choisya ternata — Mexican Orange Blossom
Chondestes grammacus — Sparrow, Lark
Chondrohierax uncinatus — Kite, Hook-billed
Chondrus cripsus — Irish Moss
Chordeiles acutipennis — Nighthawk, Lesser or Texas
Chordeiles minor — Nighthawk, Common
Chordeiles virginianus — Nighthawk, Common
Chromis caeruleus — Damselfish, Blue-green
Chromis chromis — Damselfish, Blue-green
Chromis cyanea — Damselfish, Blue-green
Chrosomus erythrogaster — Dace, Southern Redbelly
Chrysanthemum var. — Chrysanthemum
Chrysanthemum coccineum — Daisy, Painted
Chrysanthemum coronarium — Daisy, Crown
Chrysanthemum frutescens — Marguerite, Golden
Chrysanthemum leucanthemum — Daisy, Ox-eye
Chrysanthemum maximum — Daisy, Shasta
Chrysanthemum parthenium — Feverfew
Chrysanthemum segetum — Marigold, Corn
Chrysanthemum shastense — Daisy, Shasta
Chrysemys concinna — Turtle, Cooter or Slider
Chrysemys floridana — Turtle, Cooter or Slider
Chrysemys picta — Turtle, Painted
Chrysemys scripta elegans — Turtle, Red-eared
Chrysis nitidula — Wasp, Cuckoo
Chrysis smaragdula — Wasp, Cuckoo
Chrysobothris femorata — Borer, Apple Tree (Flat-
  headed)
Chrysogonum virginianum — Goldstar
Chrysopa sp. — Lacewing, Golden-eye or Green
Chrysops caecutiens — Fly, Deer
Chrysops callidas — Fly, Deer
Chrysops vittatus — Fly, Deer
Chrysopsis mariana — Aster, Maryland Golden

Chrysopsis villosa — Aster, Golden
Chrysothamnus nauseosus — Rabbit Brush
Chrysotrogon caligatus — Trogon, Gartered or
  Violaceous
Ciccaba nigrolineata — Owl, Black-and-white
Ciccaba virgata — Owl, Mottled Wood
Cichlasoma biocellatus — Jack Dempsey
Cichorium endiva — Endive
Cichorium intybus — Chicory
Cicidela sp. — Beetle, Tiger
Cicuta bulbifera — Water Hemlock
Cicuta douglasii — Water Hemlock
Cicuta maculata — Water Hemlock
Cidaris tribuloides — Sea Urchin
Ciliata mustelus — Rockling, Five-bearded
Cimicifuga elata — Bugbane
Cimbex americanus — Sawfly, Elm
Cimex lectularius — Bedbug
Cimicifuga racemosa — Snakeroot, Black
Cinclus mexicanus — Dipper
Cineraria maritima — Dusty Miller
Ciona intestinalis — Sea Squirt, Tube
Circaea alpina — Nightshade, Alpine Enchanter's
Circaea lutetiana — Nightshade, Common Enchanter's
Circaea quadrisulcata — Nightshade, Common
  Enchanter's
Circulifer tenellus — Leaf-hopper, Beet
Circus cyaneus — Hawk, Marsh
Circus hudsonius — Hawk, Marsh
Cirsium arvense — Thistle, Canada or Creeping
Cirsium discolor — Thistle, Field
Cirsium edule — Thistle, Edible
Cirsium horridulum — Thistle, Yellow
Cirsium muticum — Thistle, Swamp
Cirsium undulatum — Thistle, Wavy-leaf
Cirsium vulgare — Thistle, Bull
Cissilopha beechei — Jay, Purplish-backed (Beechey's)
Cissilopha san-blasiana — Jay, San Blas
Cistothorus platensis — Wren, Short-billed Marsh
Cistus sp. — Rockrose
Citellus beecheyi — Squirrel, California Ground
Citellus columbianus — Squirrel, Columbian Ground
Citellus franklini — Squirrel, Franklin Ground
Citellus lateralis — Squirrel, Golden-mantled Ground
Citellus leucurus — Squirrel, Antelope Ground
Citellus parryi — Squirrel, Arctic Ground
Citellus richardsoni — Squirrel, Richardson's Ground
Citellus tridecemlineatus — Squirrel, Thirteen-lined
  Ground

Citellus undulatus — Squirrel, Arctic Ground
Citharichthys sordidus — Sanddab
Citrullus vulgaris — Watermelon
Citrus aurantifolia — Lime
Citrus aurantium — Orange, Seville or Sour
Citrus limonia — Lemon
Citrus paradisi — Grapefruit
Citrus reticulata — Tangerine
Citrus sinensis — Orange, Sweet
Cladium jamaicensis — Saw-grass
Cladius isomerus — Rose-slug, Bristly
Cladonia bellidiflora — Lichen
Cladonia coccifera — Lichen
Cladonia cristatella — Lichen
Cladonia gracilis — Lichen
Cladothamnus pyrolaeflorus — Copper Bush
Cladrastris lutea — Yellow-wood
Clangula hyemalis — Old-squaw
Claravis pretiosa — Dove, Ground (Blue)
Clarkia amoena — Clarkia
Clarkia elegans — Clarkia
Clarkia pulchella — Clarkia
Clarkia rubicunda — Clarkia
Clavaria botrytis — Fungus, Coral
Clavaria stricta — Fungus, Coral
Claviceps purpurea — Ergot
Claytonia caroliniana — Spring Beauty, Carolina
Claytonia lanceolata — Spring Beauty, Western
Claytonia virginica — Spring Beauty, Virginia
Cleistes divaricata — Pogonia, Spreading
Clematis columbiana — Clematis, Blue
Clematis crispa — Jasmine, Blue
Clematis hirsutissima — Sugar Bowl
Clematis jackmanii — Clematis, Showy
Clematis ligusticifolia — Clematis, Virgin's Bower
Clematis verticillaris — Clematis, Virgin's Bower
Clematis viorna — Clematis, Leather-flower
Clematis virginiana — Clematis, Virgin's Bower
Clemmys guttata — Turtle, Spotted
Clemmys insculpta — Turtle, Wood
Clemmys marmorata — Turtle, Pacific or Western Pond
Clemmys muhlenbergi — Turtle, Bog
Cleome serrulata — Bee Plant, Rocky Mountain
Cleome spinosa — Spider Flower
Clerodendron thomsonae — Glory Bower
Clerodendron trichotomum — Glory Bower
Clethra acuminata — Pepperbush, Sweet
Clethra alnifolia — Pepperbush, Sweet

Clethrionomys gapperi — Vole, Boreal Red-backed
Clethrionomys rutilus — Vole, Boreal Red-backed
Clevelandia ios — Goby, Arrow
Clinocardium ciliatum — Cockle, Iceland
Clinocardium nuttalli — Cockle, Heart or Nuttall's
Clinocottus sp. — Sculpin
Clinopodium vulgare — Basil, Wild
Clinostomus elongatus — Dace, Redside
Clintonia andrewsiana — Clintonia, Red
Clintonia borealis — Clintonia, Yellow
Clintonia umbellatum — Clintonia, White
Clintonia uniflora — Queen's Cup
Cliona celate — Sponge, Boring or Sulphur
Clione kincaide — Sea Angel or Sea Butterfly
Clione limacina — Sea Angel or Sea Butterfly
Clitocybe odora — Clitocybe, Sweet-scented
Clitoria mariana — Pea, Butterfly
Clivia miniata — Lily, Kaffir
Clossiana selene — Butterfly, Pearl-bordered Fritillary
Clupea harengus — Herring, Sea
Clypeaster rosaceus — Sand Dollar
Cnemidocarpa finmarkiensis — Sea Squirt, Broad-base
Cnemidocarpa joannae — Sea Squirt, Broad-base
Cnemidophorus sp. — Lizard, Whiptail
Cnicus benedictus — Thistle, Blessed
Cnidoscolus stimulosus — Tread Softly
Cobaea hookerana — Ivy, Violet
Cobaea scandens — Cup-and-saucer-Vine or Ivy, Violet
Coccinella sp. — Beetle, Ladybird
Coccothraustes coccothraustes — Hawfinch
Cocculus carolinus — Coral Beads
Coccus hesperidum — Scale, Brown or Orange
Coccyzus americanus — Cuckoo, Yellow-billed
Coccyzus erythropthalmus — Cuckoo, Black-billed
Coccyzus minor — Cuckoo, Mangrove
Cochlearius cochlearius — Heron, Boat-billed
Cochlearia officinalis — Scurvy-grass, Common
Cochliomyia hominivorax — Fly, Screw-worm
Cocos nucifera — Palm, Coconut
Codakia orbicularis — Lucina, Tiger
Codiaeum variegatum — Croton
Codium fragile — Seaweed, Sponge
Coereba bahamensis — Bananaquit
Coereba flaveola — Bananaquit
Coffee arabica — Coffee
Colaptes auratus — Flicker, Yellow-shafted
Colaptes cafer — Flicker, Red-shafted
Colaptes chrysoides — Flicker, Gilded

Colchicum autumnale — Colchicum
Colchicum speciosum — Colchicum
Coleonyx variegatus — Gecko, Banded
Coleus blumei — Coleus
Coleus frederici — Coleus
Coleus thyrsoideus — Coleus
Colias croceus — Butterfly, Clouded Yellow
Colias eurytheme — Butterfly, Alfalfa or Orange
   Sulphur
Colias hyale — Butterfly, Clouded Yellow
Colibri thalassinus — Violet-ear, Green
Colinus ridgwayi — Bobwhite, Masked
Colinus virginianus — Bobwhite
Collinsia bicolor — Chinese Houses
Collinsia grandiflora — Blue-eyed-Mary
Collinsia hetrophylla — Chinese Houses
Collinsia verna — Blue-eyed-Mary
Collinsonia canadensis — Horse-balm
Collomia grandiflora — Collomia, Large-flowered
Collybia butyracea — Collybia, Buttery
Collybia dryophila — Collybia, Oak-loving
Collybia maculata — Collybia, Spotted
Collybia radicata — Collybia, Rooting
Coluber constrictor var. — Racer
Columba cayennensis — Pigeon, Rufous
Columba fasciata — Pigeon, Band-tailed
Columba flavirostris — Pigeon, Red-billed
Columba leucocephala — Pigeon, White-crowned
Columba livia — Pigeon, Common (Rock Dove)
Columba speciosa — Pigeon, Scaled
Columbicola columbae — Louse, Pigeon
Columbina minuta — Dove, Ground
Columbina passerina — Dove, Ground
Colus spitzbergensis — Whelk, Spitzbergen
Colus stimpsoni — Whelk, Stimpson's
Colymbus articus — Loon, Pacific
Comandra livida — Toadflax, Bastard
Comandra umbellata — Toadflax, Bastard
Commelia communis — Dayflower
Commelia erecta — Dayflower
Compsilura concinnata — Fly, Tachina
Comptonia peregrina — Sweet-fern
Concephalum conicum — Liverwort, Great Scented
Condylura cristata — Mole, Star-nosed
Conepatus leuconotus — Skunk, Hog-nosed
Conepatus mesoleucus — Skunk, Hog-nosed
Conger conger — Eel, Conger
Conger oceanicus — Eel, Conger

Coniophanes imperialis — Snake, Black-striped
Conium maculatum — Poison Hemlock
Conopholis americana — Cancer-root
Conophytum sp. — Living Stones
Conotrachelus nenuphar — Curculio, Plum
Conringia orientalis — Mustard, Hare's-ear
Constrictor constrictor — Boa Constrictor
Contia tenuis — Snake, Sharp-tailed
Contopus cinereus — Pewee, Tropical (Caribbean)
Contopus pertinax — Flycatcher, Coues'
Contopus sordidulus — Pewee, Western Wood
Contopus virens — Pewee, Eastern Wood
Conuropsis carolinensis — Parakeet, Carolina
Conus sp. — Cone Shell
Convallaria majallis — Lily-of-the-valley
Convallaria montana — Lily-of-the-valley
Convolvulus althaeoides — Bindweed, Mallow-leaved
Convolvulus arvensis — Bindweed, Field or Small
Convolvulus cyclostegius — Morning Glory, Western
Convolvulus occidentalis — Morning Glory, Western
Convolvulus sepium — Bindweed, Great or Hedge
Convolvulus soldanella — Bindweed, Sea
Convolvulus spithamaeus — Bindweed, Upright or Low
Convolvulus tricolor — Morning Glory, Dwarf
Conyza canadensis — Horse-weed
Coprinus atramentarius — Mushroom, Inky-cap
Coprinus comatus — Mushroom, Shaggy-mane
Coprinus micaceus — Mushroom, Glistening Inky-cap
Coptis groenlandica — Goldthread
Coptis trifoliata — Goldthread
Coragyps atratus — Vulture, Black
Corallina sp. — Coralline
Coralliophila abbreviata — Snail, Coral
Coralliophila caribaea — Snail, Coral
Coralliophila costata — Snail, Coral
Corallium rubrum — Coral, Red or Precious
Corallorhiza maculata — Coral-root, Spotted
Corallorhiza striata — Coral-root, Striped
Corallorhiza trifida — Coral-root, Northern
Corallhoriza wisteriana — Coral-root, Spring or Wister's
Corbula contracta — Clam, Basket
Corbula luteola — Clam, Basket
Cordia sebestena — Geiger Tree
Cordyline australis — Cabbage Tree
Cordyline terminalis — Ti
Coregonus artedii — Cisco
Coregonus clupaeformis — Whitefish, Lake
Corella inflata — Sea Squirt, Inflated

Corella willmeriana — Sea Squirt, Inflated
Coreopsis grandiflora — Tickseed, Large-flowered
Coreopsis lanceolata — Tickseed, Lance-leaved
Coreopsis major — Tickseed, Large-flowered
Coreopsis rosea — Tickseed, Pink
Coreopsis tinctoria — Tickseed
Corixa interrupta — Backswimmer
Corixa punctata — Backswimmer
Cornus alternifolia — Dogwood, Alternate-leaf
Cornus canadensis — Bunchberry
Cornus florida var. — Dogwood, Flowering
Cornus kousa — Dogwood, Kousa or Oriental
Cornus mas — Cherry, Cornelian
Cornus nuttallii — Dogwood, Mountain or Pacific
Cornus stolonifera — Dogwood, Western
Cornus suecica — Bunchberry
Coronilla varia — Crown-vetch
Cortaderia atacamensis — Grass, Pampas
Cortaderia selloana — Grass, Pampas
Cortinarius albo-violaceus — Cortinarius, Violet
Cortinarius violaceus — Cotinarius, Violet
Corvus brachyrhynchos — Crow, American or Common
Corvus caurinus — Crow, Northwestern
Corvus ossifragus — Crow, Fish
Corvus corax — Raven, Common
Corvus cryptoleucus — Raven, White-necked
Corvus tropicus — Crow, Hawaiian
Corydalis aurea — Corydalis, Golden or Yellow
Corydalis flavula — Corydalis, Golden or Yellow
Corydalis scouleri — Corydalis, Western
Corydalis sempervirens — Corydalis, Pale or Pink
Corydalis cornutus — Fly, Dobson
Corydalis solida — Corydalis, Purple
Corylopsis sp. — Winter-hazel
Corylus americana — Filbert, Western
Corylus avellana — Filbert
Corylus californica — Filbert, Western
Corylus cornuta — Filbert, Western
Corylus maxima — Filbert, Giant
Coryphaena equiselis — Dolphin (fish)
Coryphaena hippurus — Dolphin (fish)
Corythucha sp. — Bug, Lace
Cosmos bipinnatus — Cosmos
Costaria costata — Kelp, Seersucker
Cotinga amabilis — Cotinga, Lovely
Cotinis nitida — Beetle, Figeater or Green June
Cotinus coggygria — Smoke Tree
Cotinus obovatus — Smoke Tree

Cotoneaster sp. — Cotoneaster
Cottus sp. — Sculpin
Cotula coronopifolia — Brass Buttons
Coturnicops noveboracensis — Rail, Yellow
Couroupita guianensis — Cannon-ball Tree
Cowania mexicana — Cliffrose
Cowania stansburiana — Cliffrose
Crago alaskensis — Shrimp, Alaska or Gray
Crango septemspinosus — Shrimp, Sand
Craspedacusta sowerbyi — Jellyfish, Freshwater
Crassinella mactracea — Crassinella, Lindsley's
Crassoftrea gigas — Oyster, Japanese or Giant Pacific
Crataegus crus-galli — Hawthorn, Cockspur
Crataegus douglasii — Hawthorn, Black
Crataegus flabellata — Hawthorn, Downy
Crataegus mollis — Hawthorn, Downy
Crataegus monogyna — Hawthorn, Common
Crataegus oxyacantha — Hawthorn, English
Craterellus cornucopioides — Horn of Plenty
Craterolophus tethys — Jellyfish, Stalked
Cratogeomys castanops — Gopher, Mexican or Plateau Pocket
Crax rubra — Curassow, Great
Crepidula adunca — Slipper Shell, Hooked
Crepidula convexa — Slipper Shell, Convex
Crepidula fornicata — Slipper Shell, Common
Crepis acuminata — Hawk's-beard, Long-leaved
Crepis atrabarba — Hawk's-beard, Slender
Crepis capillaris — Hawk's-beard, Smooth
Crepis occidentalis — Hawk's-beard, Large-flowered
Crex crex — Crake, Corn
Cribina xanthogrammica — Sea Anemone, Green
Crinoid sp. — Sea Lily
Crinum americanum — Lily, Swamp
Crinum bulbispermum — Lily, Bengal
Crinum powelii — Lily, Bengal
Crioceris asparagi — Beetle, Asparagus
Crioceris duodecimpunctata — Beetle, Asparagus
Crocethia alba — Sanderling
Crocidium multicaule — Goldstars
Crocodylus acutus — Crocodile, American
Crocus sativus — Saffron
Crocus vernus — Crocus, Spring
Crossandra infundibuliformis — Crossandra
Crossaster papposus — Starfish, Rose or Sun
Crossostrea virginica — Oyster, Eastern or Virginia
Crotalaria sagittalis — Rattlebox
Crotalus adamanteus — Rattlesnake, Diamond-back (East.)

Crotalus atrox — Rattlesnake, Diamond-back (Western)
Crotalus cerastes — Sidewinder
Crotalus horridus — Rattlesnake, Timber
Crotalus horridus atricaudatus — Rattlesnake, Cane-
    brake
Crotalus lepidus — Rattlesnake, Rock
Crotalus molossus — Rattlesnake, Black-tailed
Crotalus ruber — Rattlesnake, Diamond-back (Red)
Crotalus scutulatus — Rattlesnake, Mojave
Crotalus tigris — Rattlesnake, Tiger
Crotalus viridus — Rattlesnake, Prairie
Crotalus willardi — Rattlesnake, Ridge-nosed
Crotaphytus collaris — Lizard, Collared
Crotaphytus wislizenii — Lizard, Leopard
Crotophaga ani — Ani, Smooth-billed
Crotophaga sulcirostris — Ani, Groove-billed
Crucibulum levis — Fungus, Bird's-nest
Crucibulum vulgare — Fungus, Bird's-nest
Cryptobranchus alleganiensis — Hellbender
Cryptochiton stelleri — Chiton, Giant
Cryptolithodes sitchensis — Crab, Butterfly or Sitka
Cryptomeria japonica — Cedar, Japanese
Cryptotis parva — Shrew, Least or Little Short-tailed
Crypturellus cinnamomeus — Tinamou, Thicket
Crypturellus soui — Tinamou, Little
Ctenocephalides canis — Flea, Dog
Ctenocephalides felis — Flea, Cat
Ctenodiscus crispatus — Starfish, Mud
Ctenosauria acanthura — Iguana, Spiny-tailed
Ctenosauria pectinata — Iguana, Spiny-tailed
Cuclotogaster heterographus — Louse, Chicken or Shaft
Cucujus cinnaberinus — Beetle, Flat-bark
Cucujus clavipes — Beetle, Flat-bark
Cucumaria frondosa — Sea Cucumber, Tailed
Cucumaria miniata — Sea Cucumber, Red
Cucumis anguria — Cucumber
Cucumis melo — Muskmelon or Cantaloupe
Cucumis sativus — Cucumber
Cucurbita foetidissima — Gourd, Wild
Cucurbita maxima — Squash, Winter
Cucurbita pepo — Pumpkin or Gourd
Cucurbita pepo ovifera — Gourd
Culex pipiens — Mosquito, House
Culicoides guttipennis — Fly, Sand
Cumingia californicus — Cumingia
Cumingia tellinoides — Cumingia
Cunila origanoides — Dittany
Cuphea sp. — Cigar Flower or Plant

Cupressus arizonica — Cypress, Arizona
Cupressus glabra — Cypress, Arizona
Cupressus goveniana — Cypress, Gowen
Cupressus macrocarpa — Cypress, Monterey
Curculio sp. — Weevil, Nut
Cuscuta epithymum — Dodder, Thyme
Cuscuta gronovii — Dodder
Cuscuta rostrata — Dodder
Cuscuta salina — Dodder, Salt-marsh
Cyanea capillata — Jellyfish, Pink or Sun or Sea
    Blubber
Cyanocitta cristata — Jay, Blue
Cyanocitta stelleri — Jay, Stellar's
Cyanocompsa cyanoides — Grosbeak, Blue-black
Cyanocorax dickeyi — Jay, Tufted
Cyanocorax yncas — Jay, Green
Cyanolyea cucullata — Jay, Azure-headed
Cyanolyea nana — Jay, Dwarf
Cyas revoluta — Palm, Sago
Cyclamen europaeum — Cyclamen
Cyclamen neapolitanum — Cyclamen
Cyclamen persicum — Cyclamen
Cyclarhis gujanensis — Peppershrike, Rufous-browed
Cyclopterus lumpus — Lumpsucker, Atlantic
Cyclorrhynchus psittacula — Auklet, Parakeet
Cyclura cornuta — Iguana, Rhinocerus
Cydonia oblonga — Quince
Cygnus olor — Swan, Mute
Cylas formicarius elegantulus — Weevil, Sweet-potato
Cymatium martinianum — Triton, Hairy
Cymatium pileare — Triton, Hairy
Cymbalaria muralis — Ivy, Kenilworth
Cymbidium hybrids — Orchid, Cymbidium
Cynanthus latirostris — Hummingbird, Broad-billed
Cynanthus sordidus — Hummingbird, Dusky
Cynara scolymus — Artichoke, Globe
Cynips sp. — Wasp, Gall
Cynodon dactylon — Grass, Bermuda
Cynoglossum sp. — Forget-me-not, Chinese
Cynoglossum grande — Hound's-tongue, Western
Cynoglossum officinale — Hound's-tongue
Cynoglossum virginianum — Comfrey, Wild
Cynomys gunnisoni — Prairie Dog, White-tailed
Cynomys leucurus — Prairie Dog, White-tailed
Cynomys ludovicianus — Prairie Dog, Black-tailed
Cynomys parvidens — Prairie Dog, White-tailed
Cynoscion nebulosus — Squeteague, Spotted
Cynoscion nobilis — Sea Bass, White

Cynoscion regalis — Squeteague, Gray
Cyperus papyrus — Egyptian Paper Plant
Cyphomandra betacea — Tomato, Tree
Cypraea carneola — Cowry, Carnelian or Orange-banded
Cypraea cinerea — Cowry, Atlantic
Cypraea isabella — Cowry, Isabel's
Cypraea mauritiana — Cowry, Hump-backed or
  Mourning
Cypraea moneta — Cowry, Money
Cypraea spadicea — Cowry, Chestnut
Cypraea spurca — Cowry, Atlantic
Cypraea tigris — Cowry, Tiger
Cypraea zebra — Cowry, Measled
Cyprinodon sp. — Pupfish
Cyprinus carpio — Carp
Cypriodon variegatus — Minnow, Sheepshead or
  Variegated
Cypripedium acaule — Lady's-slipper, Pink
Cypripedium arietinum — Lady's-slipper, Ram's-head
Cypripedium calceolus var. pubescens — Lady's-slipper,
  Yellow
Cypripedium californicum — Lady's-slipper, California
Cypripedium candidum — Lady's-slipper, Small White
Cypripedium fasciculatum — Lady's-slipper, Clustered
Cypripedium montanum — Lady's-slipper, Mountain
Cypripedium passerinum — Lady's-slipper, Sparrow's-
  egg
Cypripedium reginae — Lady's-slipper, Showy
Cypseloides niger — Swift, Black
Cypselurus sp. — Flying-fish
Cyrtonyx montezumae — Quail, Harlequin or Mearns'
Cyrtonyx ocellatus — Quail, Ocellated
Cyrtopleura costata — Angel Wing, Common
Cystophora cristata — Seal, Hooded
Cystopteris fragilis — Fern, Bladder or Brittle
Cystopteris montana — Fern, Bladder or Brittle
Cytisus scoparius — Broom, Scotch

D

Daboecia cantabrica — Heath, Irish
Dactylis glomerata — Orchard-grass
Dactylometra quinquecirrha — Sea Nettle
Dactylopterus volitans — Gurnard, Flying
Dactylortyx thoracicus — Quail, Singing (Long-toed)
Dahlia hybrids — Dahlia
Daldinia concentrica — Fungus, Carbon
Dalea spinosa — Smoketree, Desert

Dalibardia repens — Dewdrop
Dallia pectoralis — Blackfish, Alaska
Dama dama — Deer, Fallow
Danaus aglea — Butterfly, Monarch
Danaus plexippus — Butterfly, Monarch
Daphne cneorum — Garland Flower
Daphne laureola — Spurge-laurel
Daphne mezereum — Daphne
Daphne odora — Daphne, Sweet
Daphnia sp. — Water-flea
Daptrius americanus — Caracara, Red-throated
Darlington californica — Pitcher-plant, California
Dascyllus aruanus — Damselfish, Three-striped or
  Black and White
Dasistoma macrophylla — Foxglove, Mullein
Dasya sp. — Alga, Red
Dasyatis centroura — Stingray
Dasyatis pastinaca — Stingray
Dasyatis sayi — Stingray
Dasyatis violacea — Stingray
Dasymutilla nigripes — Wasp, Velvet-ant
Dasymutilla occidentalis — Wasp, Velvet-ant
Dasyneura rhodophaca — Midge, Rose
Dasypus novemcinctus — Armadillo, Nine-banded
Datana ministra — Caterpillar, Yellow-necked
Datura sp. — Angel's Trumpet
Datura meteloides — Jimsonweed
Datura stramonium var. tatula — Jimsonweed
Datura wrightii — Indian Apple
Daucus carota — Queen Anne's Lace
Daucus carota var. sativa — Carrot
Davidia involucrata — Dove Tree
Decapterus macarellus — Scad
Decodon verticillatus — Loosestrife, Swamp
Deirochelys reticularia — Turtle, Chicken
Delonix regia — Poinciana, Royal
Delphinapterus leucas — Whale, White
Delphinium sp. — Larkspur Hybrids
Delphinium ajacis — Larkspur, Rocket
Delphinium carolinianum — Larkspur, Blue
Delphinium elatum — Larkspur, Candle
Delphinium exaltatum — Larkspur, Tall
Delphinium glaucous — Larkspur, Tall or Rocky
  Mountain
Delphinium menziesii — Larkspur, Menzies'
Delphinium nudicaule — Larkspur, Red
Delphinium parryi — Larkspur, Parry's
Delphinium tricorne — Larkspur, Dwarf

Delphinium trolliifolium — Larkspur, Tall
Delphinium virescens — Larkspur, Plains
Delphinus delphis — Dolphin, Common
Demodex sp. — Mite, Follicle
Dendragapus obscurus — Grouse, Blue or Sooty
Dendraster excentricus — Sand Dollar
Dendrobeania lichenoides — Bryozoan
Dendrocopos albolarvatus — Woodpecker, White-headed
Dendrocopos arizonae — Woodpecker, Arizona
Dendrocopos borealis — Woodpecker, Red-cockaded
Dendrocopos nuttallii — Woodpecker, Nuttall's
Dendrocopos pubescens — Woodpecker, Downy
Dendrocopus scalaris — Woodpecker, Ladder-backed
Dendrocopos villosus — Woodpecker, Hairy
Dendrocygna arborea — Tree-duck, Black-billed or West Indian
Dendrocygna autumnalis — Tree-duck, Black-bellied
Dendrocygna bicolor — Tree-duck, Fulvous
Dendroica auduboni — Warbler, Audubon's
Dendroica caerulescens — Warbler, Black-throated Blue
Dendroica castanea — Warbler, Bay-breasted
Dendroica cerulea — Warbler, Cerulean
Dendroica chrysoparia — Warbler, Golden-cheeked
Dendroica coronata — Warbler, Myrtle
Dendroica discolor — Warbler, Prairie
Dendroica dominica — Warbler, Yellow-throated
Dendroica erithachorides — Warbler, Mangrove
Dendroica fusca — Warbler, Blackburnian
Dendroica graciae — Warbler, Grace's
Dendroica kirtlandii — Warbler, Kirtland's
Dendroica magnolia — Warbler, Magnolia
Dendroica nigrescens — Warbler, Black-throated Gray
Dendroica occidentalis — Warbler, Hermit
Dendroica palmarum — Warbler, Palm
Dendroica pensylvanica — Warbler, Chestnut-sided
Dendroica petechia — Warbler, Yellow
Dendroica pinus — Warbler, Pine
Dendroica striata — Warbler, Blackpoll
Dendroica tigrina — Warbler, Cape May
Dendroica townsendi — Warbler, Townsend's
Dendroica virens — Warbler, Black-throated Green
Dendromecon rigida — Poppy, Tree
Dendronotus frondosus — Nudibranch, Bushy-backed
Dendronotus giganteus — Nudibranch, Giant
Dendrotyx barbatus — Partridge, Bearded
Dendrotyx leucophrys — Partridge, Highland or Ruby-crowned
Dendrotyx macroura — Quail, Tree (Long-tailed)

Dennstaedtia punctilobula — Fern, Hay-scented
Dentalium entale stimpsoni — Tusk Shell, Stimpson's
Dentalium pretiosum — Tusk Shell, Indian Money
Dentaria californica — Toothwort
Dentaria diphylla — Crinkleroot
Dentaria laciniata — Toothwort
Dentaria tenella — Toothwort
Dermacentor sp. — Tick, Wood
Dermanyssus gallinae — Mite, Chicken
Dermasterias imbricata — Starfish, Leather
Dermestes lardarius — Beetle, Larder
Dermestes maculatus — Beetle, Hide
Dermochelys coriacea — Turtle, Leatherback
Descurainia sophia — Flixweed
Desmanthus illinoensis — Mimosa, Prairie
Desmarestia sp. — Alga, Brown
Desmodium canadense — Tick-trefoil, Showy
Desmodium rotundifolium — Tick-trefoil, Prostrate
Desmodus rotundus — Bat, Vampire
Desmognathus fuscus — Salamander, Dusky
Desmognathus monticola — Salamander, Seal
Desmognathus ochrophaeus — Salamander, Mountain
Desmognathus quadramaculatus — Salamander, Black-bellied
Desmognathus welteri — Salamander, Dusky
Desmognathus wrighti — Salamander, Pygmy
Deutzia sp. — Deutzia
Diabrotica sp. — Beetle, Cucumber
Diadophis amabilis — Snake, Ring-necked
Diadophis punctatus — Snake, Ring-necked
Dianthus alpinus — Pink, Alpine
Dianthus armeria — Pink, Deptford
Dianthus barbatus — Sweet William
Dianthus carthusianorum — Pink, Alpine
Dianthus caryophyllus — Carnation
Dianthus chinensis — Pink, Chinese
Dianthus deltoides — Pink, Maiden
Diaphania hyalinata — Melonworm
Diapensia lupponica — Pincushion Plant
Diapheromera femorata — Walkingstick
Diarthronomyia chrysanthemi — Midge, Chrysanthemum Gall
Diascia barberae — Twinspur
Diaspis carueli — Scale, Juniper
Diatraea saccharalis — Borer, Sugar-cane
Diaulula sandiegensis — Nudibranch, Ringed
Dicamptodon ensatus — Salamander, Pacific Giant
Dicentra canadensis — Squirrel-corn

Dicentra cucullatia — Dutchman's-breeches
Dicentra eximia — Bleeding-heart, Fringed
Dicentra formosa — Bleeding-heart, Western
Dicentra spectabilis — Bleeding-heart, Garden
Dichromanassa rufescens — Egret, Reddish
Dicrostonyx groenlandicus — Lemming, Collared or Varying
Dicrostonyx hudsonius — Lemming, Collared or Varying
Dictamnus alba — Burning Bush
Dictyophora duplicata — Stinkhorn, Collared
Didelphis marsupialis — Opossum
Didelphis virginiana — Opossum
Didiscus trachymene caeruleus — Laceflower, Blue
Diemictylus viridescens — Newt, Red-spotted
Diervilla diervilla — Honeysuckle, Bush
Diervilla lonicera — Honeysuckle, Bush
Diervilla sessilifolia — Honeysuckle, Bush
Digitalis purpurea — Foxglove
Digitaria sanguinalis — Grass, Crab
Dimorphotheca aurantiaca — Marigold, Cape
Dineutes americanus — Beetle, Whirligig
Dinocardium robustum — Cockle, Great Heart or Giant Atlantic
Diodia virginiana — Buttonweed
Diodon holocanthus — Porcupine Fish
Diodora aspera — Limpet, Rough Keyhole
Diomedea exulans — Albatross, Wandering
Diomedea immutabilis — Albatross, Laysan
Diomedea nigripes — Albatross, Black-footed
Dionaea muscipula — Venus' Fly-trap
Diopatra cuprea — Worm, Plume
Dioscorea quaternata — Yam, Wild
Diospyros kaki — Persimmon, Common
Diospyros virginiana — Persimmon, Common
Diphylleia cymosa — Umbrella-leaf
Diplolepis sp. — Wasp, Gall
Diplora labyrithiformis — Coral, Brain
Dipodomys sp. — Rat, Kangaroo
Dipsacus fullonum — Teasel, Fuller's
Dipsacus sylvestris — Teasel, Common or Card
Dipsosaurus dorsalis — Iguana, Desert
Dirca palustris — Leatherwood
Disporum hookeri — Fairy Bell, Hooker's
Disporum lanuginosum — Mandarin, Yellow
Disporum maculatum — Mandarin, Nodding or Spotted
Disporum smithii — Fairy Bell, Large-flowered

Dissosteira carolina — Locust, Carolina (insect)
Divaricella quadrisulcata — Lucina, Cross-hatched
Dives dives — Blackbird, Melodious or Sumichrast's
Dodecatheon alpinum — Shooting-star, Alpine
Dodecatheon jeffreyi — Shooting-star, Jeffrey's
Dodecatheon meadia — Shooting-star
Dodecatheon pauciflorum — Shooting-star, Few-flowered
Dodecatheon pulchellum — Shooting-star, Few-flowered
Dolichonys oryzivorus — Bobolink
Dolichos lablab — Bean, Hyacinth
Dolichos lignosus — Bean, Hyacinth
Dolichovespula maculata — Hornet, Bald-faced or White-faced
Dolomedes triton — Spider, Fishing
Donax fossor — Coquina
Donax variabilis — Coquina
Doricha enicura — Sheartail, Slender
Dormitator maculatus — Sleeper
Doronicum caucasian — Leopard's-bane
Doronicum paradalianches — Leopard's-bane
Doronicum plantagineum — Leopard's-bane
Dorosoma cepedianum — Shad, Gizzard
Dorotheanthus bellidiformis — Daisy, Livingstone
Dosinia discus — Dosinia
Dosinia elegans — Dosinia
Dosinia ponderosa — Dosinia
Douglasia laevigata — Douglasia
Douglasia nivalis — Douglasia
Draba aizoides — Whitlow-grass, Yellow
Draba incerta — Whitlow-grass, Yellow
Draba reptans — Whitlow-grass, Carolina
Draba verna — Whitlow-grass, Common
Dracocephalum virginianum — Dragonhead, False
Dracunculus vulgaris — Dragon-plant
Dromococcyx phasianellus — Cuckoo, Pheasant
Drosera anglica — Sundew, Great
Drosera intermedia — Sundew, Spatulate-leaved
Drosera longifolia — Sundew, Great
Drosera rotundifolia — Sundew, Round-leaved
Drosophila melanogaster — Fly, Fruit (Vinegar)
Dryas drummondii — Avens, Mountain
Dryas octopetala — Avens, Mountain
Drymarchon corais — Snake, Indigo
Dryocopus lineatus — Woodpecker, Lineated
Dryocopus pileatus — Woodpecker, Pileated
Dryopteris cristata — Fern, Shield (Crested)

Dryopteris dilatata — Fern, Wood (Spreading)
Dryopteris dryopteris — Fern, Oak
Dryopteris filix-mas — Fern, Male
Dryopteris intermedia — Fern, Shield (Crested)
Dryopteris marginalis — Fern, Wood (Marginal)
Dryopteris noveboracensis — Fern, New York
Dryopteris phegopteris — Fern, Beech
Dryopteris spinulosa — Fern, Wood (Spinulose)
Duchesnea indica — Strawberry, Indian or Mock
Dudleya farinosa — Live-forever
Dugesiella californicum — Spider, Bird
Dulus dominicus — Palm Chat
Dumetella carolinensis — Catbird
Dynastes tityus — Beetle, Rhinocerus
Dysithamnus mentalis — Antvireo, Plain
Dysticus marginalis — Beetle, Predacious Diving

E

Eacles imperialis — Moth, Imperial
Echeneis naucrates — Remora
Echinacea purpurea — Cone-flower, Purple
Echinarachnius excentricus — Sand Dollar
Echinarachnius parma — Sand Dollar
Echinocactus grusonii — Cactus, Barrel
Echinocereus coccineus — Cactus, Hedgehog
Echinocereus fenderi — Cactus, Hedgehog
Echinocereus triglochidiatus — Cactus, Claret-cup
Echinocereus viridescens — Cactus, Calico
Echinocereus viridiflorus — Cactus, Calico
Echinochloa crusgalli — Grass, Barnyard
Echinococcus sp. — Tapeworm
Echinops exaltatus — Thistle, Globe
Echinops ritro — Thistle, Globe
Echium vulgare — Bugloss, Viper's
Echinocystis oreganus — Cucumber, Wild
Eciton hamatum — Ant, Army or Legionary
Evasterias trochelli — Starfish, Mottled
Edwardsiana rosae — Leaf-hopper, Rose
Egretta alba — Egret, Common or Great
Eichhornia crassipes — Water-hyacinth
Elacatinus oceanops — Goby, Cleaner or Neon
Elaeagnus angustifolia — Olive, Russian
Elaeagnus argentea — Silverberry
Eleagnus commutata — Silverberry
Eleagnus pungens — Oleaster
Elaenia flavogaster — Elaenia, Yellow-bellied
Elaenia martinica — Elaenia, Caribbean

Elanoides forficatus — Kite, Swallow-tailed
Elanus leucurus — Kite, White-tailed
Elaphe guttata — Snake, Corn
Elaphe obsoleta var. — Snake, Rat
Elaphe subocularis — Snake, Rat
Elaphe vulpina — Snake, Fox
Electron carinatum — Motmot, Keel-billed
Eleodes opaca — Wireworm, Plains False
Eleutherodactylus angusti — Frog, Barking or Robber
Eleutherodactylus ricordi planirostris — Frog, Green-
   house
Elodea canadensis — Waterweed
Elsholtzia stauntonii — Elsholtzia
Elymus canadensis — Rye, Wild
Embiotoca jacksoni — Perch, Black
Embiotoca lateralis — Seaperch, Striped
Embothrium coccineum — Firebush
Emerita analoga — Crab, Mole or Sand
Emerita talpoida — Crab, Mole or Sand, or Sand-bug
Emmenanthe penduliflora — Whispering Bells
Empetrum nigrum — Crowberry
Empidonax difficilis — Flycatcher, Western
Empidonax flavirostris — Flycatcher, Yellow-bellied
Empidonax flaviventris — Flycatcher, Yellow-bellied
Empidonax fulvifrons — Flycatcher, Buff-breasted
Empidonax hammondi — Flycatcher, Hammond's
Empidonax mexicanus — Flycatcher, Pileated
Empidonax minimus — Flycatcher, Least
Empidonax oberholseri — Flycatcher, Dusky
Empidonax traillii — Flycatcher, Traill's
Empidonax virescens — Flycatcher, Acadian
Empoa rosae — Leaf-hopper, Rose
Empoasca fabae — Leaf-hopper, Potato
Emys blandingi — Turtle, Blanding's
Enallagma sp. — Damselfly
Encelia farinosa — Brittle-bush
Enceliopsis argophylla — Daisy, Panamint
Enceliopsis covillei — Daisy, Panamint
Endomychura hypoleuca — Murrelet, Xanthus'
Endymion non-scriptus — Bluebell
Engraulis encrasicolus — Anchovy, Pacific or Northern
Engraulis mordax — Anchovy, Pacific or Northern
Enhydra lutris — Otter, Sea
Enhydra lutris nereis — Otter, Sea
Enhydrus sulcatus — Beetle, Whirligig
Enkianthus campanulatus — Enkianthus
Enoclerus sphegeus — Beetle, Checkered
Ensatina eschscholtzii — Salamander, Eschscholtz's

Ervatamia coronaria — Jasmine, Crape
Erysimum asperum — Wallflower, Western
Erysimum capitatum — Rocket, Prairie
Erysimum cheiranthoides — Treacle-mustard
Erysimum repandum — Treacle-mustard
Erythrina crista-galli — Cockscomb (tree)
Erythrina herbacea — Coral-bean
Erythrina indica — Coral-bean
Erythronium albidum — Violet, Dogtooth (White)
Erythronium americanum — Violet, Dogtooth (Yellow)
Erythronium dens-canis — Violet, Dogtooth
Erythronium grandiflorum — Lily, Glacier
Erythronium montanum — Lily, Avalanche
Erythronium oregonum — Lily, Fawn
Erythronium revolutum — Lily, Coast Fawn
Eschrichtius glaucus — Whale, Gray
Eschscholtzia californica — Poppy, California
Eschscholtzia mexicana — Poppy, Gold
Esox americanus vermiculatus — Pickerel, Grass
Esox lucius — Pike, Northern
Esox masquinongy — Muskellunge
Esox niger — Pickerel, Chain
Etheostoma nigrum — Darter, Johnny
Euarctos americana — Bear, Black or Cinnamon
Eubalaena glacialis — Whale, Right
Eubalaena sieboldi — Whale, Right
Eubranchipus sp. — Shrimp, Fairy
Eucalia inconstans — Stickleback, Brook
Eucalyptus globulus — Gum, Blue
Eucharis grandiflora — Lily, Amazon
Eucidaris tribuloides — Sea Urchin
Eucomis bicolor — Lily, Pineapple
Eucomis comosa — Lily, Pineapple
Euderma maculatum — Bat, Spotted
Eudistylia vancouveri — Worm, Plume
Eudocimus albus — Ibis, White
Eudocimus ruber — Ibis, Scarlet
Eudromius morinellus — Dotterel
Eugenes fulgens — Hummingbird, Rivoli's
Euglena sp. — Euglenoid
Eulamia milberti — Shark, Brown
Eumeces fasciatus — Skink, Five-lined
Eumeces inexpectatus — Skink, Five-lined
Eumeces laticeps — Skink, Broad-headed or
  Greater Five-lined
Eumeces multivirgatus — Skink, Many-lined
Eumeces obsoletus — Skink, Great Plains or Sonoran
Eumeces septentrionalis — Skink, Prairie

Eumeces skiltonianus — Skink, Western
Eumenes fraternus — Wasp, Potter
Eumetopias jubata — Sea Lion, Northern or Steller's
Eumicrotemus orbis — Lumpsucker, Pacific Spiny
Euonymous alatus — Spindle Tree
Euonymous atropurpurea — Wahoo, East
Euonymous europaeus — Spindle Tree
Euonymous occidentalis — Wahoo, Western (plant)
Euonymus americanus — Strawberry Bush
Euonymus obovatus — Strawberry Bush, Running
Eupatorium cannabinum — Agrimony, Hemp
Eupatorium coelestinum — Mist Flower
Eupatorium fistulosum — Joe-pye-weed, Hollow
Eupatorium hyssopifolium — Thoroughwort, Hyssop-
  leaved
Eupatorium maculatum — Joe-pye-weed, Spotted
Eupatorium perfoliatum — Boneset, Purple
Eupatorium purpureum — Joe-pye-weed, Sweet
Eupatorium rugosum — Snakeroot, White
Eupatorium serotinum — Thoroughwort, Late-flowering
Eupentacta quinquesemita — Sea Cucumber, White
Euphagus carolinus — Blackbird, Rusty
Euphagus cyanocephalus — Blackbird, Brewer's
Euphorbia cyparissias — Spurge, Cypress
Euphorbia helioscopia — Spurge, Sun or Wart
Euphorbia heterophylla — Poinsettia, Wild
Euphorbia ipecacuanhae — Ipecac, Carolina
Euphorbia marginata — Snow-on-the-mountain
Euphorbia milii — Crown of Thorns
Euphorbia pulcherrima — Poinsettia
Euphorbia splendens — Crown of Thorns
Eupleura caudata — Drill, Thick-lipped Oyster
Eurycea bislineata — Salamander, Two-lined
Eurycea longicauda — Salamander, Long-tailed
Eurycea lucifuga — Salamander, Cave
Eurycea multiplicata — Salamander, Many-ribbed
Eurycea tynerensis — Salamander, Oklahoma
Eurymus philodice — Butterfly, Clouded Sulphur
Eurypelma spinicrus — Spider, Bird
Eurypyga helias — Bittern, Sun
Euspongia sp. — Sponge, Bath or Commercial
Euspongilla sp. — Sponge, Fresh-water
Eustoma exaltatum — Gentian, Catchfly
Eustoma grandiflorum — Gentian, Prairie
Eutamias merriami — Chipmunk, Merriam's
Eutamias minimus — Chipmunk, Least
Eutamias townsendi — Chipmunk, Oregon or Town-
  send's

Euthlypis lachrymosa — Warbler, Fan-tailed
Euthynnus alleteratus — Tuna, Little
Exoglossum maxillingua — Chub, Cutlip

F

Fagopyrum esculentum — Buckwheat
Fagopyrum sagittatum — Buckwheat
Fagus grandifolia — Beech, American
Fagus sylvatica — Beech, Common or European
Falcata comosa — Hog-peanut
Falco columbarius — Hawk, Pigeon
Falco deiroleucus — Falcon, Orange-breasted
Falco femoralis — Falcon, Aplomado
Falco mexicanus — Falcon, Prairie
Falco peregrinus — Falcon, Peregrine
Falco rusticolus — Gyrfalcon
Falco sparverius — Hawk, Sparrow
Fallugia paradoxa — Apache Plume
Fannia canicularis — Fly, Little House
Farancia abacura — Snake, Mud
Fasciola hepatica — Fluke, Liver
Fasciolaria tulipa — Band Shell, Tulip
Fatshedera lizei — Ivy, Japanese
Fatsia japonica — Fatsia
Favia fragum — Coral, Star
Felicia amelloides — Daisy, Blue
Felicia angustifolia — Daisy, Blue
Felis concolor — Cougar
Felis cougar — Cougar
Felis domestica — Cat, Domestic
Felis onca — Jaguar
Felis pardalis — Ocelot
Felis wiedi — Cat, Margay
Felis yagouaroundi — Cat, Jaguarundi
Ferocactus acanthodes — Cactus, Barrel
Ferocactus wizlizeni — Cactus, Barrel
Festuca arundinacea — Fescue, Tall
Festuca elatior — Fescue, Meadow
Festuca ovina — Fescue, Sheep
Festuca pratensis — Fescue, Meadow
Ficimia cana — Snake, Hook-nosed
Ficus benjamina — Fig, Weeping
Ficus carica — Fig, Common
Ficus communis — Fig Shell
Ficus elastica — India Rubber Plant
Filipendula hexapetala — Dropwort
Filipendula rubra — Queen-of-the-Prairie

Filipendula ulmaria — Queen-of-the-meadow
Filipendula vulgaris — Dropwort
Filix fragilis — Fern, Bladder or Brittle
Fistulina hepatica — Fungus, Beefsteak
Fittonia verschaffeltii — Nerve Plant
Florida caerulea — Heron, Little Blue
Foeniculum vulgare — Fennel
Folia parallela — Venus' Girdle
Fomes fomentarius — Rot, Yellowish Sapwood
Forcipiger longirostris — Butterflyfish, Long-nose
Forficula auricularia — Earwig
Formica rufa — Ant, Wood
Formicarius analis — Antthrush, Black-faced
Forsythia suspensa — Forsythia
Fortunella margarita — Kumquat
Fothergilla gardenii — Witch-alder
Fothergilla major — Witch-alder
Fothergilla monticola — Witch-alder
Fouquieria splendens — Ocotilla
Fragaria ananassa — Strawberry (cultivated)
Fragaria chiloensis — Strawberry, Beach
Fragaria vesca — Strawberry, Wood
Fragaria virginiana — Strawberry, Wild
Franklinia alatamaha — Franklinia
Frankliniella tritici — Thrips, Flower or Wheat
Frasera speciosa — Deer's-tongue
Fratercula artica — Puffin, Atlantic or Common
Fratercula corniculata — Puffin, Horned
Fraxinus americana — Ash, White
Fraxinus nigra — Ash, Black
Fraxinus ornus — Ash, Flowering or Manna
Fraxinus pennsylvanica — Ash, Green or Red
Fraxinus quadrangulata — Ash, Blue
Fregata ariel — Frigatebird, Lesser
Fregata magnificens — Frigatebird, Magnificent
Fregata minor — Frigatebird, Great
Fremontia californica — Fremontia
Fremontia mexicana — Fremontia
Fringilla coelebs — Chaffinch
Fringilla montifringilla — Brambling
Fritillaria atropurpurea — Fritillary, Purple
Fritillaria camtschatcensis — Fritillary, Kamchatka
Fritillaria imperialis — Crown Imperial
Fritillaria lanceolata — Mission Bells
Fritillaria meleagris — Fritillary, Snake's Head
Fritillaria pudica — Yellow Bells
Fuschsia sp. — Fuchsia Hybrids
Fucus vesiculosus — Wrack, Bladder

Fulica americana — Coot, American
Fulmarus glacialis — Fulmar
Fumaria officinalis — Fumitory, Common
Fundulus diaphanus — Killifish, Banded
Fundulus heteroclitus — Mummichog
Fundulus notatus — Topminnow, Black-stripe
Fusitriton oregonensis — Triton, Oregon

G

Gadus callarias — Codfish
Gadus macrocephalus — Codfish
Gadus morhua — Codfish
Gadus virens — Coalfish
Gaillardia aristata — Gaillardia or Indian Blanket
Gaillardia pulchella — Gaillardia or Indian Blanket
Galanthus nivalis — Snowdrop
Galax aphylla — Galax
Galega officinalis — Goat's-rue
Galeichthys felis — Catfish, Sea
Galeocerdo cuvieri — Shark, Tiger
Galeopsis tetrabit — Hemp-nettle, Common
Galeorhinus zyopterus — Shark, Soupfin
Galerucella xanthomelaena — Beetle, Elm Leaf
Galium aparine — Cleavers
Galium boreale — Bedstraw, Northern
Galium circaezans, — Licorice, White Wild
Galium mollugo — Bedstraw, Hedge
Galium triflorum — Bedstraw, Fragrant
Galium verum — Bedstraw, Yellow
Gallinula chloropus — Gallinule, Common
Gallus domesticus — Chicken
Gallus gallus — Fowl, Jungle
Gambusia affinis — Mosquito-fish
Gambusia affinis holbrooki — Mosquito-fish
Gammarus locusta — Hopper, Seaweed
Ganoderma applanatum — Fungus, Artist's or Shelf
Gardenia jasminoides — Gardenia
Gardenia spatulifolia — Gardenia
Garrya elliptica — Silk Tassel
Gasterophilus intestinalis — Botfly, Horse
Gasterosteus aculeatus — Stickleback, Three-spined
Gastrophryne carolinensis — Frog, Narrow-mouthed
Gastrophryne olivacea — Toad, Narrow-mouthed
Gaultheria hispidula — Snowberry, Creeping
Gaultheria ovatifolia — Teaberry, Western
Gaultheria procumbens — Wintergreen, Creeping
Gaultheria shallon — Salal

Gaura biennis — Gaura, Biennial
Gaura coccinea — Gaura, Biennial
Gavia adamsi — Loon, Yellow-billed
Gavia arctica — Loon, Arctic or Black-throated
Gavia arctica pacifica — Loon, Pacific
Gavia immer — Loon, Common
Gavia stellata — Loon, Red-throated
Gaylussacia brachycera — Huckleberry, Box
Gaylussacia dumosa — Huckleberry, Box
Gazania hybrids — Gazania
Geastrum rufescens — Earthstar
Geastrum triplex — Earthstar
Gelastocoris oculatus — Bug, Toad
Gelochelidon nilotica — Tern, Gull-billed
Gelsemium rankinii — Jessamine, Caroline
Gelsemium sempervirens — Jessamine, Carolina
  or Yellow
Gemma gemma — Clam, Amethyst Gem
Genista tinctoria — Greenweed, Dyers
Gentiana amarella — Gentian, Rose
Gentiana andrewsii — Gentian, Closed
Gentiana asclepiadea — Gentian, Willow
Gentiana calycosa — Gentian, Blue
Gentiana crinata — Gentian, Fringed
Gentiana lutea — Gentian, Yellow
Gentiana pneumonthe — Gentian, Marsh
Gentiana quinquefolia — Gentian, Stiff
Gentiana saponaria — Gentian, Soapwort
Gentiana thermalis — Gentian, Western Fringed
Gentiana verna — Gentian, Spring
Geococcyx californianus — Roadrunner
Geococcyx velox — Roadrunner, Lesser
Geococcyx viaticus — Roadrunner, Lesser
Geomys sp. — Gopher, Eastern or Plains Pocket
Geopelia striata — Dove, Barred
Geothlypis beldingi — Yellowthroat, Belding's
Geothlypis speciosa — Yellowthroat, Black-polled
Geothlypis trichas — Yellowthroat, Maryland
Geotrygon sp. — Dove, Quail
Geranium bicknellii — Geranium, Bicknell's
Geranium carolinianum — Cranesbill, Carolina
Geranium dissectum — Cranesbill, Cut-leaved
Geranium maculatum — Cranesbill, Spotted or Wild
Geranium molle — Cranesbill, Dove's-foot
Geranium oreganum — Cranesbill, Oregon
Geranium pratense — Cranesbill, Meadow
Geranium pusillum — Cranesbill, Small-flowered
Geranium robertianum — Herb Robert

Geranium sanguineum — Cranesbill, Bloody
Geranium sylvaticum — Cranesbill, Wood
Geranium viscosissimum — Geranium, Sticky
Gerardia purpurea — Gerardia, Purple
Gerbera jamesonii — Daisy, Transvaal
Geronospiza nigra — Hawk, Black Crane
Gerrhonotus sp. — Lizard, Alligator
Gerris sp. — Water Strider, Common
Geukensia demissa — Mussel, Ribbed
Geum aleppicum var. strictum — Avens, Yellow
Geum macrophyllum — Avens, Large-leaved
Geum rivale — Avens, Purple or Water
Geum triflorum — Avens, Purple or Water
Gigartina exasperata — Batters
Gigartina stellata — Batters
Gilia aggregator — Gilia, Scarlet
Gilia capitata — Gilia, Blue
Gilia matthewsii — Cactus, Desert Calico
Gillenia stipulata — Indian Physic
Gillenia trifoliata — Bowman's-root or Indian Physic
Ginglymostoma cirratum — Shark, Nurse
Ginkgo bilboa — Maidenhair Tree
Girella nigricans — Opaleye
Glaucidium brasilianum — Owl, Ferruginous Pygmy
Glaucidium gnoma — Owl, Pygmy
Glaucium flavum — Poppy, Yellow-horned
Glaucomys sabrinus — Squirrel, Flying
Glaucomys volans — Squirrel, Flying
Glaux maritima — Milkwort, Sea
Glecoma hederacea — Ground Ivy
Gleditsia aquatica — Locust, Water (tree)
Gleditsia triacantha — Locust, Honey (tree)
Globicephala melaena — Whale, Pilot
Globicephala scammoni — Whale, Pilot
Gloriosa rothschildiana — Lily, Glory
Glycera americana — Worm, Corrugated
Glyceria striata — Grass, Manna
Glycine max — Soybean
Glycyrrhiza glabra — Licorice
Glycyrrhiza lepidota — Licorice
Glyptocephalus cynoglossus — Witch
Glyptopleura setulosa — Carved-seed
Gnaphalium obtusifolium — Everlasting, Sweet
Gnaphalium uliginosum — Cudweed
Gnathodon speciosus — Jack, Yellow
Gnathophausia sp. — Shrimp, Opossum
Gobiesox meandricus — Clingfish
Gobiosoim ocearrops — Goby, Cleaner or Neon

Godetia amoena — Godetia
Godetia grandiflora — Godetia
Gomphrena globosa — Amaranth, Globe
Gonepteryx rhamni — Butterfly, Brimstone
Gonorhynchus gonorhynchus — Sandfish
Goodyera oblongifolia — Rattlesnake-plantain
Goodyera pubescens — Rattlesnake-plantain, Downy
Goodyera repens — Rattlesnake-plantain, Creeping
Goodyera tessellata — Rattlesnake-plantain, Loddiges
Gopherus agassizi — Tortoise, Desert
Gopherus berlandieri — Tortoise, Texas Gopher
Gopherus polyphemus — Tortoise, Gopher
Gordius sp. — Worm, Horsehair
Gordonia alatamaha — Franklinia
Gordonia lasianthus — Bay, Loblolly
Gorgonocephalus sp. — Basket-star
Gossypium herbaceum — Cotton
Gossypium hirsutum — Cotton
Gramphidelphis griseus — Dolphin, Risso's
Grampus griseus — Dolphin, Risso's
Grampus orca — Whale, Killer
Granatellus sallaei — Chat, Gray-throated
Granatellus venustus — Chat, Red-breasted
Graphocephala coccinea — Leaf-hopper, Red-banded
Graptemys geographica — Turtle, Map
Graptemys kohni — Turtle, Mississippi Map
Graptemys oculifera — Turtle, Ringed Sawback
Graptemys pseudogeographica — Turtle, False Map
Gratiola aurea — Hedge-hyssop, Golden
Gratiola neglecta — Hedge-hyssop
Grayia spinosa — Sage, Hop
Grindelia integrifolia — Gumweed
Grindelia lanceolata — Gumweed
Grindelia squarrosa — Gumweed
Grindelia stricta — Gumweed
Grus americana — Crane, Whooping
Grus canadensis — Crane, Sandhill
Grus grus — Crane, Common
Gryllotalpa gryllotalpa — Cricket, Mole
Gryllotalpa hexadactyla — Cricket, Mole
Gryllus assimilis — Cricket, Field
Gryllus campestris — Cricket, Field
Gryllus domesticus — Cricket, House
Guaiacum officinale — Lignum Vitae
Guiraca caerulea — Grosbeak, Blue
Gulo gulo — Wolverine
Gulo luscus — Wolverine
Gutierrezia dracunculoides — Broomweed

Gutierrezia lucida — Broomweed
Gutierrezia microcephala — Broomweed
Gyalopion canum — Snake, Hook-nosed
Gygis alba — Tern, Fairy
Gymnachirus nudus — Sole, Naked
Gymnachirus williamsoni — Sole, Naked
Gymnocarpium dryopteris — Fern, Oak
Gymnocladus dioica — Coffee-tree, Kentucky
Gymnodinium breve — Red Tide
Gymnogyps californianus — Condor, California
Gymnorhinus cyanocephalus — Jay, Pinon (Pinyon)
Gymnosporangium sp. — Rust, Cedar Apple
Gymnostinops montezuma — Oropendola, Montezuma
Gymnothorax mordax — Eel, California Moray
Gypsophila elegans — Baby's-breath
Gypsophila paniculata — Baby's-breath
Gyrinophilus palleucus — Salamander, Tennessee Cave
Gyrinophilus porphyriticus — Salamander, Spring or
    Purple

H

Habenaria blephariglottis — Orchid, White-fringed
Habenaria ciliaris — Orchid, Orange- or Yellow-fringed
Habenaria clavellata — Orchid, Small Green
Habenaria dilatata — Orchid, Tall White Bog
Habenaria fimbriata — Orchid, Purple-fringed
Habenaria lacera — Orchid, Ragged Fringed
Habenaria leucostachys — Orchid, Tall White Bog
Habenaria orbiculata — Orchid, Large Round-leaved
Habenaria psycodes — Orchid, Purple-fringed
Hackelia floribunda — Stickseed
Hackelia jessicae — Stickseed
Hackelia longituba — Stickseed
Haemanthus sp. — Lily, Blood
Haematopinus adventicius — Louse, Hog
Haematopus bachmani — Oyster-catcher, Black
Haematopus palliatus — Oyster-catcher, American
Haemopis sanguisuga — Leech, Horse
Haemulon plumieri — Grunt, White
Haemulon sciurus — Grunt, Blue-striped
Haideotriton wallacei — Salamander, Georgia Blind
Halesia carolina — Silverbell Tree
Halesia monticola — Silverbell Tree
Haliaeetus albicilla — Eagle, White-tailed or Gray Sea
Haliaeetus leucocephalus — Eagle, Bald
Halichoerus grypus — Seal, Gray
Haliclona oculata — Dead Men's Fingers (Sponge)

Haliclystus sp. — Jellyfish, Stalked
Haliotis corrugata — Abalone, Pink
Haliotus cracherodi — Abalone, Black
Haliotis fulgens — Abalone, Green or Splendid
Haliotis kamtschatkana — Abalone, Northern or Pinto
Haliotis rufescens — Abalone, Red
Halisidota sp. — Moth, Tussock
Halocyptena microsoma — Petrel, Least
Halosaccion sp. — Alga, Red
Halosydna brevisetosa — Worm, Scale
Halosydna gelatinosa — Worm, Scale
Halticus bracteatus — Fleahopper, Garden
Hamamelis intermedia — Witch Hazel
Hamamelis japonica — Witch Hazel, Japanese
Hamamelis mollis — Witch Hazel, Chinese
Hamamelis vernalis — Witch Hazel
Hamamelis virginiana — Witch Hazel
Haplopappus greenei — Haplopappus
Haplopappus spinulosus — Haplopappus
Hardenbergia violacea — Sarsaparilla, False
Harmolita tritici — Wasp, Wheat Jointworm
Harpia harpyja — Eagle, Harpy
Hebe speciosa — Hebe, Showy
Hedeoma pulegioides — Pennyroyal, American
Hedera canariensis — Ivy, English
Hedera helix — Ivy, English
Hedysarum occidentale — Hedysarum, Western
Hedysarum sulphurescens — Hedysarum, Yellow
Helenium autumnale — Sneezeweed
Helenium pinnatifidum — Sneezeweed
Helenium tenuifolium — Sneezeweed
Helianthella quinquenervis — Helianthella
Helianthemum canadense — Frostweed
Helianthemum nummularium — Sunrose
Helianthus angustifolius — Sunflower, Narrow-leaved
Helianthus annus — Sunflower, Common
Helianthus decapetalus — Sunflower, Thin-leaved
Helianthus mollis — Sunflower, Hairy Wild
Helianthus strumosus — Sunflower, Pale-leaved Wood
Helianthus tuberosa — Artichoke, Jerusalem
Helichrysum bracteatum — Strawflower
Heliopsis helianthoides — Ox-eye
Heliornis fulica — Sungrebe
Heliothis zea — Earworm, Corn
Heliothrips haemorrhoidalis — Thrips, Greenhouse
Heliotropium arborescens — Heliotrope, Common
Heliotropium curassivicum — Heliotrope, Seaside
Heliotropium peruvianum — Heliotrope, Common

Helix aspersa — Snail, Garden
Helleborus atrorubens — Lenten or Winter Rose
Helleborus niger — Christmas Rose
Helleborus orientalis — Lenten or Winter Rose
Helmitheros vermivorus — Warbler, Worm-eating
Helobdella stagnalis — Leech, Pond
Heloderma suspectum — Gila Monster
Helostoma temmincki — Gourami, Kissing
Helvella crispa — Helvella, White
Helvella lacunosa — Helvella
Hemerobius sp. — Lacewing, Brown
Hemerocallis sp. — Daylily
Hemerocallis flava — Lily, Day
Hemerocallis fulva — Lily, Day
Hemerocampa leucostigma — Moth, Tussock
Hemerocampa leucostigma — Moth, Tussock
Hemichromis bimaculatus — Jewel Fish
Hemigrapsus nudus — Crab, Shore
Hemigrapsus oregonensis — Crab, Shore
Hemilepidotus hemilepidotus — Irishlord, Red
Hemipodus borealis — Worm, Iridescent
Hemitomes congestum — Cone-plant
Hemitripterus americanus — Sea Raven
Henricia leviuscula — Starfish, Blood or Red
Henricia sanguinolenta — Starfish, Blood or Red
Hepatica acutiloba — Hepatica, Sharp-lobed
Hepatica americana — Hepatica, Round-lobed
Hepatica triloba — Hepatica, Sharp-lobed
Heracleum lanatum — Cow-parsnip
Heracleum maximum — Cow-parsnip
Heracleum sphondylium — Hogweed
Hercinothrips femoralis — Thrips, Banded Greenhouse
Hermissenda crassicornis — Nudibranch, Opalescent
Herpailurus yagouaroundi — Cat, Jaguarundi
Herpetotheres cachinnans — Falcon, Laughing
Hesperiphona vespertina — Grosbeak, Evening
Hesperis matronalis — Rocket, Dame's
Hesperochiron pumilus — Hesperochiron
Hesperocallis undulata — Lily, Desert
Hetaerina americana — Damselfly, Ruby-spot
Heterodon nasicus — Hognose, Western
Heterodon platyrhinos — Hognose, Eastern
Heteroscelus incanus — Tattler, Wandering
Heterospizias meridionalis — Hawk, Savannah
Heterotheca subaxillaris — Camphorweed
Heuchera sanguinea — Coral Bells
Heuchua americana — Alumroot
Heuchua micrantha — Alumroot

Hexagenia bilineata — Fly, May
Hexagenia limbata — Fly, May
Hexagrammos decagrammus — Greenling
Hexagrammos octogrammus — Greenling
Hexalectris spicata — Coral-root, Crested
Hexastylis shuttleworthii — Ginger, Shuttleworth's Wild
Hexastylis virginianum — Ginger, Virginia Wild
Hiatella arctica — Saxicave, Arctic
Hibiscus coccineus — Mallow, Rose
Hibiscus esculentus — Okra
Hibiscus moscheutos — Mallow, Swamp
Hibiscus palustris — Mallow, Rose
Hibiscus rosa-sinensis — Hibiscus
Hibiscus schizopetolus — Hibiscus, Fringed
Hibiscus syriacus — Rose of Sharon
Hibiscus tiliaceus — Hibiscus Tree
Hibiscus trionum — Flower-of-an-hour
Hieracium albiflorum — Hawkweed, White-flowered
Hieracium aurantiacum — Hawkweed, Orange
Hieracium florentium — King Devil
Hieracium gracile — Hawkweed, Alpine
Hieracium pratense — King Devil
Hieracium scouleri — Hawkweed, Scouler's
Hieracium venosum — Rattlesnake Weed
Hieracium villosum — Hawkweed, Woolly or Shaggy
Hierochloe odorata — Grass, Vanilla
Himantopus himantopus knudseni — Stilt, Hawaiian
Himantopus mexicanus — Stilt, Black-necked
Hinnites multirugosus — Scallop, Rock
Hiodon tergisus — Mooneye
Hippeastrum hybrids — Amaryllis
Hippiospongia sp. — Sponge, Bath or Commercial
Hippocampus hudsonius — Sea Horse, American
Hippodamia convergens — Beetle, Ladybird
Hippoglossoides platessoides — Plaice, American
Hippoglossus hippoglossus — Halibut
Hippoglossus stenolepis — Halibut
Hippuris vulgaris — Mare's-tail
Hirudo medicinalis — Leech, Medicinal
Hirundo rustica — Swallow, Barn
Hister abbreviatus — Beetle, Hister
Historio historio — Frogfish
Histrionicus histrionicus — Duck, Harlequin
Hoffmanseggia densiflora — Hog-potato
Hoffmanseggia drepanocarpa — Sicklepod, Rushweed
Hoffmanseggia jamesii — Hog-potato
Holacanthus ciliaris — Angelfish, Queen

Holbrookia sp. — Lizard, Earless
Holcus lanatus — Grass, Velvet
Holcus mollis — Grass, Velvet
Holmskioldia sanguinea — Chinese Hat Plant
Holocentrus ascensionis — Squirrel-fish
Holocentrus diadema — Squirrel-fish
Holocentrus xantherythrus — Squirrel-fish
Holodiscus discolor — Ocean Spray
Homarus americanus — Lobster
Hordeum jubatum — Barley, Foxtail or Wild
Hordeum pusillum — Barley, Little
Hordeum vulgare — Barley
Hosta crispula — Lily, Plantain
Hosta fortunei — Lily, Plantain
Hosta plantaginea — Lily, Plantain
Hoya carnosa — Wax-plant
Houstonia caerulea — Bluets
Hudsonia ericoides — Heather, Golden
Hudsonia montanum — Heather, False
Hudsonia tomentosa — Heather, False
Humulus lupulus — Hop
Hunnemannia fumariaefolia — Poppy, Mexican Tulip
Hyacinthus orientalis — Hyacinth, Common
Hyalophora cecropia — Moth, Cecropia
Hydnum repandum — Mushroom, Hedgehog
Hydra americana — Hydra
Hydra littoralis — Hydra
Hydra oligactis — Hydra
Hydranassa tricolor — Heron, Louisiana
Hydrangea arborescens — Hydrangea, Wild
Hydrangea hybrids — Hydrangea
Hydrastis canadensis — Goldenseal
Hydrocharis morsus-ranae — Frogbit
Hydrobates pelagicus — Petrel, Storm
Hydrocotyle americana — Pennywort, Marsh
Hydrocotyle umbellata — Pennywort, Marsh or Water
Hydrocotyle vulgaris — Pennywort, Marsh
Hydrodamalis stelleri — Sea Cow, Steller's
Hydrolagus colliei — Ratfish
Hydromantes brunus — Salamander, Limestone
Hydromantes platycephalus — Salamander, Mount Lyell
Hydrophilus triangularis — Beetle, Water Scavenger
Hydrophyllum canadense — Waterleaf, Broad-leaved
Hydrophyllum capitatum — Waterleaf, Dwarf
Hydrophyllum macrophyllum — Waterleaf, Large-leaved
Hydrophyllum tenuipes — Waterleaf, Pacific or Slender
Hydrophyllum virginianum — Waterleaf, Virginia
Hydroprogne caspia — Tern, Caspian

Hyla andersoni — Treefrog, Pine-barrens
Hyla avivoca — Treefrog, Bird-voiced or Whistling
Hyla cinerea — Treefrog, Green
Hyla crucifer — Treefrog, Spring Peeper
Hyla gratiosa — Treefrog, Barking
Hyla regilla — Treefrog, Pacific
Hyla septentrionalis — Treefrog, Cuban
Hyla squirella — Treefrog, Southern or Squirrel
Hyla versicolor — Treefrog, Common or Gray
Hylemya sp. — Maggot, Fly
Hylobius abietis — Weevil, Pine
Hylobius congener — Weevil, Pine
Hylocereus undatus — Cactus, Night-flowering Cereus
Hylocharis eliciae — Goldentail, Blue-throated
Hylocharis leucotis — Hummingbird, White-eared
Hylocharis xantusi — Hummingbird, Xantus'
Hylocichla fuscescens — Veery
Hylocichla guttata — Thrush, Hermit
Hylocichla minima — Thrush, Gray-cheeked
Hylocichla mustelina — Thrush, Wood
Hylocichla ustulata — Thrush, Olive-backed or
    Swainson's
Hylomanes momotula — Motmot, Tody
Hymenocallis sp. — Spider-lily
Hymenocallis calathina — Ismene
Hymenophyllum tunbridgense — Fern, Filmy
Hyoscyamus niger — Henbane
Hypentelium nigricans — Hogsucker, Northern
Hypera nigrirostris — Weevil, Clover-leaf
Hypera postica — Weevil, Alfalfa
Hypera punctata — Weevil, Clover-leaf
Hypericum anagalloides — St.-John's-wort, Creeping
Hypericum buckleyi — St.-John's-wort, Shrubby
Hypericum ellipticum — St.-John's-wort, Pale
Hypericum moserianum — Gold Flower
Hypericum patulum — Golden Cup
Hypericum perforatum — St.-John's-wort, Common
Hypericum prolificum — St.-John's-wort, Shrubby
Hypericum pyramidatum — St.-John's-wort, Great
Hypericum scouleri — St.-John's-wort, Scouler's
Hypericum spathulatum — St.-John's-wort, Shrubby
Hyperoodon ampullatus — Whale, Bottlenose
Hyperoodon rostratus — Whale, Bottlenose
Hypholoma sublateritium — Brick-tuft
Hypochoeris radicata — Cat's-ear
Hypoderma bovis — Fly, Warble
Hypoderma lineatum — Fly, Warble
Hypoxis hirsuta — Stargrass, Yellow

Hypsiglena torquata — Snake, Night
Hypsypops rubicunda — Garibaldi
Hysibius sp. — Water Bear
Hyssopus officinalis — Hyssop
Hystrix patula — Grass, Bottle-brush

I

Iberis sempervirens — Candytuft
Iberis umbellata — Candytuft
Iboza riparis — Nutmeg Bush
Icerya purchasi — Scale, Cottony-cushion
Icichthys lockingtoni — Medusafish
Icosteus aenigmaticus — Ragfish
Ictalurus furcatus — Catfish, Blue
Ictalurus melas — Bullhead, Black
Ictalurus natalis — Bullhead, Yellow
Ictalurus nebulosus — Bullhead, Brown
Ictalurus punctatus — Catfish, Channel
Icteria virens — Chat, Yellow-breasted
Icterus auratus — Oriole, Orange
Icterus bullockii — Oriole, Bullock's
Icterus chrysater — Oriole, Yellow-backed
Icterus cucullatus — Oriole, Hooded
Icterus galbula — Oriole, Baltimore
Icterus graduacauda — Oriole, Black-headed
Icterus gularis — Oriole, Lichtenstein's
Icterus icterus — Troupial
Icterus mesomelas — Oriole, Yellow-tailed
Icterus parisorum — Oriole, Scott's
Icterus pectoralis — Oriole, Spot-breasted
Icterus spurious — Oriole, Orchard
Ictinia mississippiensis — Kite, Mississippi
Ictinia plumbea — Kite, Plumbeous
Ictiobus bubalus — Buffalofish, Small-mouth
Ictiobus cyprinellus — Buffalofish, Big-mouth
Idotea sp. — Sowbug, Water
Idria columnaris — Boojum Tree
Iguana iguana — Iguana, Common or Green
Ilex aquifolium — Holly, English
Ilex cassine — Dahoon
Ilex crenata — Holly, Japanese
Ilex decidua — Possumhaw
Ilex montana — Winterberry, Mountain
Ilex opaca — Holly, American
Ilex verticellata — Winterberry
Ilex vomitoria — Yaupon
Iliamna rivularis — Globe-mallow, Stream

Illex illecebrosus — Squid, Short-finned
Impatiens balsamina — Balsam, Garden
Impatiens biflora — Jewelweed, Spotted
Impatiens capensis — Jewelweed, Spotted
Impatiens pallida — Jewelweed, Pale
Impatiens sultanii — Patience Plant or Patient Lucy
Impatiens walleriana — Busy Lizzie
Incarvillea delavayi — Gloxinia, Hardy
Indigofera sp. — Indigo
Inula helenium — Elecampane
Ipheion uniflorum — Star Flower, Spring
Ipomoea batatas — Potato, Sweet
Ipomoea hederacea — Morning Glory, Ivy-leaved
Ipomoea lacunosa — Morning Glory, Small White
Ipomoea pandurata — Potato-vine, Wild
Ipomoea pes-caprae — Railroad Vine
Ipomoea purpurea — Morning Glory, Common
Ipomoea tricolor — Morning Glory, Heavenly Blue
Ipomopsis aggregator — Gilia, Scarlet
Iresine herbstii — Bloodleaf
Iridaceae — Gladiolus Hybrids
Iridomyrmex humilis — Ant, Argentine
Iridoprocne albilinea — Swallow, Mangrove
Iridoprocne bicolor — Swallow, Tree
Iris bracteata — Iris, Siskiyou
Iris cristata — Iris, Crested
Iris fulva — Iris, Copper or Red
Iris germanica — Iris, Bearded (cultivated)
Iris hartwegi — Iris
Iris hexagona — Iris
Iris innominata — Iris, Golden
Iris japonica — Iris, Japanese
Iris kaempferi — Iris, Japanese
Iris macrosiphon — Iris, Ground
Iris missouriensis — Iris, Western
Iris pseudacorus — Flag, Yellow
Iris reticulata — Iris
Iris sibirica — Iris, Siberian
Iris tectorum — Iris, Roof
Iris tenax — Iris, Oregon
Iris tenuis — Iris, Clackamas
Iris verna — Iris, Dwarf
Iris versicolor — Flag, Blue (Wild Iris)
Iris virginica — Flag, Southern Blue
Iris xiphium — Iris, Dutch Bulbous, or
   Iris, Spanish
Iris xiphioides — Iris, Spanish
Isanthus brachiatus — Pennyroyal, False

Isatis tinctoria — Woad
Isia isabella — Caterpillar, Woolly Bear or Moth, Tiger
Isoetes braunii — Quillwort
Isoetes engelmanni — Quillwort
Isoetes lacustris — Quillwort
Isognomon alatus — Oyster, Flat Tree
Isomeris arboreus — Bladder-pod
Isopyrum biternatum — Rue-anemone, False
Isotria verticullata — Pogonia, Whorled
Istiophorus albicans — Sailfish
Istiophorus platypterus — Sailfish
Isurus oxyrinchus — Shark, Mako
Ixia hybrids — Lily, Corn
Ixobrychus exilis — Bittern, Least
Ixora coccinea — Ixora, Scarlet
Ixora macrothyrsa — Ixora, Scarlet
Ixoreus naevius — Thrush, Varied

J

Jacana spinosa — Jacana, American or Northern
Jacaranda acutifolia — Jacaranda
Jacaranda mimosaefolia — Jacaranda
Jasione montana — Sheep's-bit
Jasminum mesnyi — Jasmine, Primrose
Jasminum officinale — Jasmine, Common
Jatropha multifida — Coral Plant
Jatropha podagrica — Gout Plant or Guatemala Rhubarb
    Rhubarb
Jeffersonia diphylla — Twin-leaf
Jeffersonia dubia — Twin-leaf
Juglans californica — Walnut, California
Juglans cinerea — Butternut
Juglans nigra — Walnut, Black
Juglans regia — Walnut, English
Junco aikeni — Junco, White-winged
Junco caniceps — Junco, Gray-headed
Junco hyemalis — Junco, Slate-colored
Junco oreganus — Junco, Oregon
Junco oreganus mearnsii — Junco, Oregon
Junco phaeonotus — Junco, Mexican or Yellow-eyed
Junco phaeonotus palliatus — Junco, Mexican or
    Yellow-eyed
Juncus effusus — Rush, Common or Soft
Juniperus chinensis — Juniper, Chinese
Juniperus communis — Juniper, Common
Juniperus horizontalis — Juniper, Creeping
Juniperus occidentalis — Juniper, Western

Juniperus osteosperma — Juniper, Utah
Juniperus sibirica — Juniper, Mountain
Juniperus virginiana — Cedar, Pencil or Red
Jussiaea decurrens — Primrose-willow
Jussiaea repens — Primrose-willow
Justica americana — Water-willow

K

Kalanchoe blossfeldiana — Kalanchoe
Kalmia angustifolia — Laurel, Sheep
Kalmia latifolia — Laurel, Mountain
Kalmia polifolia — Laurel, Pale or Swamp
Katherina tunicata — Chiton, Black or Leather
Katsuwonus pelamis — Bonito, Oceanic (Skipjack)
Kentranthus ruber — Valerian, Red
Kerria japonica — Mallow, Jew's
Kigelia pinnata — Sausage Tree
Kinosternon flavescens — Turtle, Yellow Mud
Kinosternon subrubrum — Turtle, Mud
Kirengeshoma palmata — Waxbell, Yellow
Klauberina riversiana — Lizard, Island Night
Knautia arvensis — Scabious, Field
Kniphofia uvaria — Red Hot Poker
Kochia scoparia — Cypress, Summer
Koelreuteria paniculata — Golden Rain Tree
Kogia breviceps — Whale, Pygmy Sperm
Kohleria bogotensis — Devil's-breeches
Kolkwitzia amabilis — Beauty Bush
Krigia biflora — Dandelion, Goat or Dwarf
Krigia montana — Dandelion, Goat or Dwarf
Krigia virginica — Dandelion, Goat or Dwarf
Kuhnia eupatorioides — Boneset, False
Kyphosus sectatrix — Chub, Bermuda

L

Labidesthes sicculus — Silverside, Brook
Labidus coecus — Ant, Army or Legionary
Laburnum sp. — Golden Chain Tree
Lachenalia aloides — Cape Cowslip
Lachnolaimus maximus — Hogfish
Lactarius deliciosus — Milky Cap, Delicious
Lactarius scrobiculatus — Milky Cap, Pitted
Lactarius vellereus — Milky Cap, Velvet
Lactophrys quadricornis — Cowfish
Lactophrys trigonus — Trunkfish
Lactuca biennis — Lettuce, Blue

Lactuca pulchella — Lettuce, Blue
Lactuca sativa — Lettuce, Garden
Lactuca scariola — Lettuce, Prickly or Wild
Lactuca serriola — Lettuce, Prickly or Wild
Laevicardium mortoni — Cockle, Morton's
Lagenorhynchus acutus — Dolphin, White-sided (Atlantic)
Lagenorhynchus albirostris — Dolphin, White-beaked
Lagenorhynchus obliquidens — Dolphin, White-sided or Striped (Pacific)
Lagerstroemia indica — Crape Myrtle
Lagopus lagopus — Ptarmigan, Willow
Lagopus leucurus — Ptarmigan, White-tailed
Lagopus mutus rupestris — Ptarmigan, Rock
Lagurus curtatus — Vole, Sagebrush
Laminaria digitata — Kelp, Fan
Laminaria saccharina — Wrack, Sugar
Lamium album — Dead-nettle, White
Lamium amplexicaule — Dead-nettle, Henbit
Lamium maculatum — Dead-nettle, Spotted
Lamium purpureum — Dead-nettle, Purple or Red
Lamna nasus — Shark, Mackerel
Lampetia equestris — Fly, Narcissus Bulb
Lampris guttata — Opah
Lampris regius — Opah
Lampronetta fischeri — Eider, Spectacled
Lampropeltis doliata var. — Snake, Milk
Lampropeltis getula var. — Kingsnake, Common
Lampropeltis zonata — Kingsnake, California Mountain
Langloisia matthewsii — Desert Calico
Languria mozardi — Borer, Clover Stem
Lanio aurantius — Shrike-tanager, Black-throated
Lanius borealis — Shrike, Northern
Lanius excubitor — Shrike, Northern
Lanius ludovicianus — Shrike, Loggerhead or Migrant
Lantana camara — Lantana
Lapageria rosea — Chile Bells
Laphygma frugiperda — Armyworm, Fall
Lappula diffusa — Stickseed
Lappula redowskii — Stickseed
Lapsana communis — Nipplewort
Larix laricina — Larch, American
Larix occidentalis — Larch, Western
Larrea divaricata — Creosote Bush
Larrea glutinosa — Creosote Bush
Larus argentatus — Gull, Herring
Larus atricilla — Gull, Laughing
Larus californicus — Gull, California

Larus canus — Gull, Mew
Larus delawarensis — Gull, Ring-billed
Larus glaucescens — Gull, Glaucous-winged
Larus glaucoides — Gull, Iceland
Larus heermanni — Gull, Heermann's
Larus hyperboreus — Gull, Glaucous
Larus marinus — Gull, Great Black-headed
Larus minutus — Gull, Little
Larus occidentalis — Gull, Western
Larus pacificus — Gull, Pacific
Larus philadelphia — Gull, Bonaparte's
Larus pipixcan — Gull, Franklin's
Larus ridibundus — Gull, Black-headed
Lasionycteris noctivagans — Bat, Silver-haired
Lasiurus borealis — Bat, Red
Lasiurus cinereus — Bat, Hoary
Lasius alienus — Ant, Cornfield
Lasius niger — Ant, Cornfield
Lateiporus sulphureus — Mushroom, Chicken
Laterallus jamaicensis — Rail, Black
Lathyrus hirsutus — Vetchling, Hairy
Lathyrus japonicus — Pea, Beach
Lathyrus latifolius — Pea, Everlasting
Lathyrus maritimus — Pea, Beach
Lathyrus nevadensis — Pea, Purple
Lathyrus odorata — Pea, Sweet
Lathyrus palustris — Vetchling, Marsh
Lathyrus pratensis — Vetchling, Meadow
Latrodectus mactans — Spider, Black Widw
Laurencia pinnatifida — Dulse, Pepper
Laurocerasus officinalis — Laurel, Cherry
Laurus nobilis — Bay, Sweet
Lavatera arborea — Mallow Tree
Lavatera assurgentiflora — Mallow Tree
Lavatera trimestris — Mallow Tree
Lavendula officinalis — Lavender, Common
Lavendula spica — Lavender, Common (Old English)
Layia campestris — Tidy Tips
Layia elegans — Tidy Tips
Layia glandulosa — Tidy Tips
Layia platyglossa — Tidy Tips
Leander serratus — Prawn, Common
Leathesia difformis — Alga, Brown
Lebistes reticulatus — Guppy
Ledum grandulosum — Labrador Tea
Ledum groenlandicum — Labrador Tea
Legatus leucophaius — Flycatcher, Piratic or Striped
Legousia speculum-veneris — Venus' Looking-glass

Leiophyllum buxifolium — Sand-myrtle
Leioptilum quadrangularis — Sea Pen
Lemaireocereus marginatus — Cactus, Organ-pipe
Lemaireocereus thurberi — Cactus, Organ-pipe
Lemmus lemmus — Lemming, Norwegian
Lemmus sibiricus — Lemming, Brown
Lemmus trimucronatus — Lemming, Brown
Lemna sp. — Duckweed
Lens culinaris — Lentil
Leonitis leonurus — Lion's Ear
Leontodon autumnalis — Dandelion, Tall
Leontodon nudicaulis — Dandelion, Tall
Leontopodium alpinum — Edelweiss
Leonurus cardiaca — Motherwort, Common
Leopardus wiedi — Cat, Margay
Lepas anatifera — Barnacle, Deep-sea or Goose
Lepas fascicularis — Barnacle, Northern Goose
Lepas hillii — Barnacle, Deep-sea or Goose
Lepidium campestre — Pepperwort, Common
Lepidium montanum — Peppergrass, Mountain
Lepidium ruderale — Peppergrass, Narrow-leaved
  (Pepperwort)
Lepidium sativum — Cress, Garden
Lepidium virginicum — Pepper, Poor Man's (Pepper-
  grass)
Lepidochelys kempi — Turtle, Ridley
Lepidochelys olivacea — Turtle, Ridley
Lepidochitona lineata — Chiton, Lined
Lepidosaphes ulmi — Scale, Oystershell
Lepiota procera — Mushroom, Parasol
Lepiota rhacodes — Mushroom, Parasol
Lepisma saccharina — Silverfish
Lepisosteus osseus — Gar, Long-nosed
Lepisosteus productus — Gar, Spotted
Lepisosteus spatula — Gar, Alligator
Lepista nuda — Blewits
Lepista saeva — Blewits
Leplopecten latiauratus — Scallop, Kelp-weed
Lepomis cyanellus — Sunfish, Green
Lepomis gibbosus — Sunfish, Pumpkinseed
Lepomis macrochirus — Sunfish, Blue-gill
Leptamnian virginianum — Beech-drops
Leptasterias hexactis — Starfish, Six-rayed
Leptinotarsa decemlineata — Beetle, Colorado Potato
Leptocoris trivittatus — Bug, Boxelder
Leptodeira annulata — Snake, Cat-eyed
Leptodeira septentrionalis — Snake, Cat-eyed
Leptospermum scoparium — Tea Tree, Manuka

Leptosynapta clarki — Sea Cucumber, Burrowing or
  Worm-like
Leptosynapta inhaerens — Sea Cucumber, Burrowing
  or Worm-like
Leptotila fulviventris — Dove, White-fronted
Leptotila verveauxi — Dove, White-fronted
Leptotyphlops dulcis — Snake, Blind
Leptotyphlops humilis — Snake, Blind
Lepus alleni — Jack-rabbit, Antelope
Lepus americanus — Rabbit, Snowshoe
Lepus articus — Hare, Arctic
Lepus californicus — Jack-rabbit, Black-tailed
Lepus capensis — Hare, European or Brown
Lepus cuniculus — Rabbit, Domestic
Lepus europaeus — Hare, European or Brown
Lepus timidus — Hare, Blue or Mountain
Lepus townsendii — Jack-rabbit, White-tailed
Lepyronia quadrangularis — Spittlebug
Lespedeza capitata — Bush-clover, Round-headed
Lespedeza hirta — Bush-clover, Hairy
Lespedeza intermedia — Bush-clover, Wand-like
Lespedeza procumbens — Bush-clover, Creeping
Lespedeza repens — Bush-clover, Creeping
Lespedeza stipulacea — Clover, Japanese
Lespedeza striata — Clover, Japanese
Lespedeza violacea — Bush-clover
Lespedeza virginica — Bush-clover, Slender
Lesquerella ludoviciana — Bladder-pod
Lethocerus americanus — Bug, Electric Light or Giant
  Water
Leucobryum glaucum — Moss, White Cushion
Leucocoryne ixiodes — Glory of the Sun
Leucocrinum montanum — Lily, Sand
Leucojum aestivum — Snowflake
Leucojum autumnale — Snowflake
Leucojum vernum — Snowflake
Leucopeza semperi — Warbler, Semper's
Leucophoyx thula — Egret, Snowy
Leucosolenia botryoides — Sponge, Purse
Leucosticte atrata — Finch, Black Rosy
Leucosticte australis — Finch, Brown-capped Rosy
Leucosticte tephrocotis — Finch, Gray-crowned Rosy
Leucothoe axillaris — Fetterbush
Leucothoe catesbaei — Fetterbush
Leuresthes sardina — Grunion
Leuresthes tenuis — Grunion
Leutkea pectinata — Partridge-foot
Lewisia columbiana — Bitterroot, Columbia

Lewisia cotyledon — Bitterroot, Imperial
Lewisia kelloggii — Lewisia, Kellogg's
Lewisia leana — Lewisia, Opposite-leaved
Lewisia nevadensis — Lewisia, Nevada
Lewisia oppositifolia — Lewisia, Opposite-leaved
Lewisia pygmaea — Lewisia, Alpine or Dwarf
Lewisia rediviva — Bitterroot
Lewisia triphylla — Lewisia, Three-leaved
Lewisia tweedyi — Bitterroot, Tweedy's
Liatris sp. — Blazing Star
Libellula luctuosa — Dragonfly
Libellula pulchella — Dragonfly
Libellula quadrimaculata — Dragonfly
Libinia emarginata — Crab, Spider
Libocedrus decurrens — Cedar, Incense
Ligia oceanica — Sea Slater
Ligia pallasii — Sea Slater
Ligustrum japonicum — Privet
Ligustrum ovafolium — Privet
Ligustrum vulgare — Privet
Lilium auratum — Lily, Japanese Gold-band
Lilium canadense — Lily, Canada
Lilium candidum — Lily, Madonna
Lilium columbianum — Lily, Columbia
Lilium dauricum — Lily, Candlestick
Lilium humboldtii — Lily, Humboldt
Lilium martagon — Lily, Turk's-cap
Lilium pardilinum — Lily, Leopard
Lilium philadelphicum — Lily, Wood
Lilium pyrenaicum — Lily, Turk's-cap
Lilium regale — Lily, Regal
Lilium speciosum — Lily, Showy
Lilium superbum — Lily, Turk's-cap
Lilium tigrinum — Lily, Tiger
Lilium umbellatum — Lily, Candlestick
Lilium washingtonianum — Lily, Washington
Lima scabra — Clam, Rough File
Limax maximus — Slug, Spotted
Limenitis archippus — Butterfly, Viceroy
Limenitis arthemis — Butterfly, White Admiral
Limenitis camilla — Butterfly, White Admiral
Limnanthus douglasii — Meadow-foam
Limnanthus gracilis — Meadow-foam
Limnodromus griseus — Dowitcher, Short-billed
Limnodromus scolopaceus — Dowitcher, Long-billed
Limnoria lignorum — Gribble
Limonium carolinianum — Sea-lavender
Limonium nashii — Sea-lavender

Limonium sinuatum — Sea-lavender
Limonius agonus — Wireworm, Eastern Field
Limosa fedoa — Godwit, Marbled
Limosa haemastica — Godwit, Hudsonian
Limosa lapponica — Godwit, Bar-tailed
Limulus polyphemus — Crab, Horseshoe or King
Linaria canadensis — Toadflax, Blue
Linaria vulgaris — Butter-and-eggs
Lindera benzoin — Spicebush
Linnaea borealis — Twinflower
Linognathus setosus — Louse, Dog
Linum flavum — Flax, Yellow
Linum grandiflorum — Flax, Scarlet
Linum lewisii — Flax, Blue
Linum perenne — Flax, Blue
Linum usitatissimum — Flax, Common
Linum virginianum — Flax, Yellow
Liobunum vittatum — Daddy-long-legs
Liodytes alleni — Snake, Striped Swamp
Liomys irroratus — Mouse, Pocket
Liparis atlanticus — Snailfish
Liparis cyclops — Snailfish
Liparis lilifolia — Twayblade, Lily-leaved
Liparis loeselii — Twayblade, Bog
Liposcelis divinatorius — Louse, Book
Lippia lanceolata — Fog-fruit
Liquidambar styraciflua — Gum, Sweet or Red
Liriodendron tulipifera — Tulip Tree
Liriomyza pusilla — Fly, Leaf-miner
Lironeca ovalis — Louse, Fish
Lissodelphis borealis — Dolphin, Right Whale
Listera convallarioides — Twayblade, Broad-lipped
Listera cordata — Twayblade, Heart-leaved
Listera smallii — Twayblade, Kidney-leaf
Lithophragma bulbifera — Rock-star
Lithophragma heterophyllum — Woodland-star
Lithophragma parviflorum — Woodland-star
Lithops sp. — Living Stones
Lithospermum arvense — Gromwell, Corn
Lithospermum californicum — Puccoon, Shasta
Lithospermum canescens — Puccoon, Yellow
Lithospermum caroliniense — Puccoon, Yellow
Lithospermum diffusum — Gromwell, Scrambling
Lithospermum incisum — Puccoon, Shasta
Lithospermum officinale — Gromwell, Common
Lithospermum ruderale — Gromwell, Western
Littorina irrorata — Periwinkle, Salt Marsh (mollusk)
Littorina littorea — Periwinkle, Common (mollusk)

Littorina obtusata — Periwinkle, Smooth (mollusk)
Littorina sitkana — Periwinkle, Sitka (mollusk)
Lloydia serotina — Lily, Alp
Lobaria oregana — Lungwort, Tree
Lobaria pulmonaria — Lungwort, Tree
Lobelia cardinalis — Cardinal-flower
Lobelia dortmanna — Lobelia, Water
Lobelia erinus — Lobelia, Common (cultivated)
Lobelia fulgens — Cardinal-flower
Lobelia inflata — Indian Tobacco
Lobelia kalmii — Lobelia, Brook
Lobelia puberula — Lobelia, Downy
Lobelia siphilitica — Lobelia, Great Blue
Lobelia spicata — Lobelia, Pale-spiked
Lobipes lobatus — Phalarope, Northern or Red-necked
Lobotes surinamensis — Tripletail
Lobularia maritima — Alyssum, Sweet
Loiseleuria procumbens — Azalea, Alpine
Loligo opalescens — Squid, Opalescent
Loligo pealii — Squid, American or Common
Lolium perenne — Rye-grass
Lomatium dissectum — Chocolate Tips
Lomatium macrocarpum — Hog-fennel
Lomatium martindalei — Hog-fennel
Lomatium nudicaule — Indian Consumption Plant
Lomatium utriculatum — Spring Gold
Lonchura punctulata — Ricebird
Lonicera ciliosa — Honeysuckle, Orange
Lonicera dioica — Honeysuckle, Smooth-leaved
Lonicera hispidula — Honeysuckle, Purple
Lonicera involucrata — Twinberry, Black
Lonicera japonica — Honeysuckle, Japanese
Lonicera periclymenum — Honeysuckle, Common
Lonicera sempervirens — Honeysuckle, Trumpet or
  Coral
Lonicera utahensis — Twinberry, Red
Loomelania melania — Petrel, Black
Lophius americanus — Angler Fish
Lophius piscatorius — Angler Fish
Lophodytes cucullatus — Merganser, Hooded
Lopholatilus chamaeleonticeps — Tilefish
Lopholithodes foraminatus — Crab, Box
Lophopanopeus bellus — Crab, Black-clawed
Lophophora williamsii — Peyote
Lophornis ornata — Coquette, Tufted
Lophortyx californicus — Quail, California
Lophortyx douglasii — Quail, Douglas or Elegant
Lophortyx gambelii — Quail, Gambel's

Lota lota — Burbot
Lotus corniculatus — Trefoil, Bird's-foot
Lotus oblongifolius — Trefoil
Lotus pinnatus — Trefoil
Loxia curvirostia — Crossbill, Common or Red
Loxia leucoptera — Crossbill, White-winged
Loxops coccinea — Akepa
Loxops maculata — Creeper, Hawaiian
Lucanus cervus — Beetle, Stag
Ludwigia alternifolia — Seedbox
Ludwigia palustris — Loosestrife, False
Luina hypoleuca — Luina
Luina nordosima — Luina
Luina stricta — Luina
Lumbricus sp. — Earthworm
Lunaria annua — Honesty
Lunaria biennis — Honesty
Lunatia heros — Moon Snail, Common Northern
Lunatia triseriata — Moon Snail, Spotted
Lunda cirrhata — Puffin, Tufted
Lupinus sp. — Lupine Hybrids
Lupinus arboreus — Lupine, Tree
Lupinus argentus — Lupine, Silvery
Lupinus caudatus — Lupine
Lupinus densiflorus — Lupine
Lupinus latifolius — Lupine
Lupinus nanus — Lupine, Dwarf
Lupinus perennis — Lupine, Wild or Common
Lupinus polyphyllus — Lupine, Large-leaved
Lupinus pusillus — Lupine
Lupinus sericeus — Lupine, Pursh's
Lupinus subcarnosa — Texas Bluebonnet
Lupinus subcarnosus — Bluebonnet
Lupinus texensis — Bluebonnet
Luscinia svecica — Bluethroat
Lutjanus analis — Snapper, Mutton
Lutjanus apodus — Schoolmaster
Lutjanus griseus — Snapper, Gray or Mangrove
Lutra canadensis — Otter, River
Lycaena phlaeas — Butterfly, American Copper
Lychnis alba — Campion, White
Lychnis chalcedonica — Maltese Cross
Lychnis coronaria — Campion, Rose
Lychnis flos-cuculi — Ragged-robin
Lychnis viscaria — Catchfly, Red German
Lycium chinense — Matrimony Vine
Lycopersicon esculentum — Tomato
Lycopodium sp. — Clubmoss

Lycoris squamigera — Amaryllis, Hardy
Lycoperdon gemmatum — Puffball, Gemmed
Lycoperdon perlatum — Puffball, Common
Lycoperdon pyriforme — Puffball, Pear-shaped
Lycosa sp. — Spider, Wolf
Lycoteuthis diadema — Squid, Deep-sea
Lyctus opaculus — Beetle, Powder-post
Lygaeus reclivatus — Bug, Milkweed
Lygodium palmatum — Fern, Climbing
Lygosoma laterale — Skink, Ground
Lygus hesperus — Bug, Tarnished Plant
Lygus lineolaris — Bug, Tarnished Plant
Lymantria dispar — Moth, Gypsy
Lymeon orbum — Wasp, Ichneumon
Lymnaea auricularis — Snail, Pond
Lymnaea stagnalis — Snail, Pond
Lymnothlypis swainsoni — Warbler, Swainson's
Lyngbya majuscula — Mermaid's Hair
Lynx canadensis — Lynx
Lynx rufus — Bobcat
Lyonia lucida — Fetterbush
Lyonia mariana — Staggerbush
Lyonsia arenosa — Lyonsia, Sanded
Lyonsia hyalina — Lyonsia, Glassy
Lyropecten nodosus — Scallop, Lion's Paw
Lysichitum americanum — Skunk Cabbage, Western
Lysimachia ciliatum — Loosestrife, Fringed
Lysimachia lanceolatum — Loosestrife, Lance-leaved
Lysimachia nummularia — Moneywort
Lysimachia punctata — Loosestrife, Large Yellow
Lysimachia quadrifolia — Loosestrife, Whorled
Lysimachia terrestris — Swamp-candles
Lysimachia thrysiflora — Loosestrife, Tufted
Lysimachia vulgaris — Loosestrife, Garden
Lythrum alatum — Loosestrife, Wing-angled
Lythrum hyssopifolia — Loosestrife, Hyssop-leaved
Lythrum lanceolatum — Loosestrife, Purple or Spiked
Lythrum salicaria — Loosestrife, Purple or Spiked
Lythrum virgatum — Loosestrife, Slender
Lythrypnus dalli — Goby, Blue-banded

M

Machaeranthera tanacetifolia — Daisy, Tahoka
Machaeranthera tortifolia — Aster, Desert or Mojave
Machetornis rixosus — Tyrant, Cattle or Fire-crowned
Macoma nasuta — Clam, Bent-nose
Macoma secta — Clam, White Sand

Macrobiotus sp. — Water Bear
Macrochelys temmincki — Turtle, Alligator Snapping
Macrocystis sp. — Kelp, Perennial
Macrodactylus subspinosus — Beetle, Rose Chafer
Macronoctua onusta — Borer, Iris
Macrosiphum pisum — Aphid, Pea
Macrosteles fascifrons — Leaf-hopper, Six-spotted
Madia elegans — Tarweed
Madia sativa — Tarweed
Magicicada septemdecim — Locust, Seventeen-year
   (insect)
Magnolia acuminata — Cucumber Tree
Magnolia denudata — Lily Tree
Magnolia fraseri — Magnolia, Fraser's
Magnolia grandiflora — Magnolia, Southern
Magnolia macrophylla — Magnolia, Big-leaf
Magnolia soulangeana — Magnolia, Saucer
Magnolia stellata — Magnolia, Star
Magnolia tripetala — Magnolia, Umbrella
Magnolia virginiana — Bay, Sweet, or Sweet Bay
Mahonia aquifolium — Oregon Grape
Mahonia repens — Barberry, Creeping
Maianthemum bifolium — Lily-of-the-valley, Wild
Maianthemum canadense — Mayflower, Canada
Maianthemum dilatatum — Lily-of-the-valley, Wild
Makaira albidus — Marlin, White
Makaira ampla — Marlin, Blue
Makaira audax - Marlin, Striped
Makaira nigricans — Marlin, Blue
Malacanthus hoedtii — Sandfish
Malaclemys terrapin — Terrapin, Diamond-back
Malacosoma americana — Caterpillar, Tent
Malacosoma disstria — Caterpillar, Tent
Malapterus electricus — Catfish, Electric
Malacothrix sonchoides — Malacothrix, Sow-thistle
Malaxis brachypoda — Adder's-mouth, White
Malaxis monophylla — Adder's-mouth, White
Malaxis uniflora — Adder's-mouth, Green
Malclura pomifera — Orange, Osage
Malcolmia maritima — Stock, Virginia
Malus angustifolia — Apple, Southern Crab
Malus coronaria — Apple, Sweet Crab
Malus sylvestris — Apple, Crab
Malva moschata — Mallow, Musk
Malva neglecta — Mallow, Common, or Cheeses
Malva sylvestris — Mallow, Common
Malvastrum rotundifolium — Mallow, Five-spot
Malviviscus arboreus — Turk's Cap

Mammillaria dioca — Cactus, Pincushion
Mammillaria longimamma — Cactus, Pincushion
Mammillaria microcarpa — Cactus, Fishhook
Mammillaria tetracistra — Cactus, Fishhook
Mammillaria vivipara — Cactus, Pincushion
Manculus quadridigitatus — Salamander, Dwarf
Manettia bicolor — Firecracker Vine
Manettia inflata — Firecracker Vine
Mangifera indica — Mango (plant)
Manihot angustiloba — Cassava
Manihot utilissima — Cassava
Manta birostris — Manta, Atlantic
Mantis religiosa — Mantis, Praying
Marah oreganus — Cucumber, Wild
Maranta leuconeura — Prayer Plant
Marasmius androsaceus — Mushroom, Black-stemmed
Marasmius oreades — Fairy Ring or Mushroom, Fairy
   Ring
Marchantia polymorpha — Liverwort, Common
Mareca americana — Widgeon, American
Mareca penelope — Widgeon, European
Margarites pupillus — Margarite, Puppet
Mariscus jamaicensis — Saw-grass
Marmota caligata — Marmot, Hoary or Whistling
Marmota flaviventris — Marmot, Yellow-bellied
Marmota monax — Woodchuck
Marrubium vulgare — Horehound
Marshallia graminifolia — Barbara's Buttons
Marshallia grandiflora — Barbara's Buttons
Marsilea quadrifolia — Fern, Water-clover
Martes americana — Marten, American
Martes pennanti — Fisher
Masticophis flagellum — Coachwhip
Masticophis taeniatus — Whipsnake
Mastigoproctus giganteus — Whip-scorpion
Matelea carolinensis — Milkweed, Climbing
Matricaria chamomilla — Chamomile, German
Matricaria eximia — Feverfew
Matricaria matricariodes — Pineapple Weed
Matteuccia pensylvanica — Fern, Ostrich
Matteuccia struthiopteris — Fern, Ostrich
Matthiola incana — Stock
Mazama americana — Deer, Brocker
Meandrina meandrites — Coral, Brain
Meconella oregana — Meconella
Meconopsis cambrica — Poppy, Welsh
Medeola virginiana — Cucumber-root, Indian
Medicago lupulina — Medick, Black

Medicago sativa — Alfalfa
Megaceryle alcyon — Kingfisher, Belted
Megaceryle torquata — Kingfisher, Ringed
Megachile centuncularis — Bee, Leaf-cutting
Megachile latimanus — Bee, Leaf-cutting
Megalops atlanticus — Tarpon, Atlantic
Megaptera nodosa — Whale, Humpbacck
Megaptera novaeangliae — Whale, Humpback
Megarhyssa macrurus — Wasp, Ichneumon
Megathura crenulata — Limpet, Great Keyhole
Melaleuca quinquenervia — Cajeput-tree
Melampodium leucanthemum — Daisy, Desert
Melampyrum lineare — Cow-wheat
Melanerpes erythrocephalus — Woodpecker, Red-
   headed
Melanerpes formicivorus — Woodpecker, Acorn or
   California
Melanitta deglandi — Scoter, White-winged or Velvet
Melanitta fusca — Scoter, White-winged or Velvet
Melanitta nigra — Scoter, Common or American
Melanitta perspicillata — Scoter, Surf
Melanogrammus aeglefinus — Haddock
Melanthium virginicum — Bunchflower
Meleagris gallopavo — Turkey, Common or Wild
Melia azedarach — Chinaberry
Melilotus alba — Clover, White Sweet
Melilotus indicus — Clover, Yellow Sweet
Melilotus officinalis — Clover, Yellow Sweet
Melittia cucurbitae — Borer, Squash Vine
Melolontha melolontha — Beetle, Cockchafer
Melongena corona — Conch, Crown
Melongena melongena — Conch, Crown
Melongena patula — Conch, Crown
Melophagus ovinus — Tick, Sheep
Melopsittacus undulatus — Parakeet, Budgerigar
Melospiza georgiana — Sparrow, Swamp
Melospiza lincolnii — Sparrow, Lincoln's
Melospiza melodia — Sparrow, Song
Membranipora sp. — Bryozoan
Menaloplus sp. — Grasshopper, Short-horned
Menidia beryllina — Silverside
Menidia menidia — Silverside
Menispermum canadense — Moonseed, Canada
Menopon gallinae — Louse, Chicken or Shaft
Mentha aquatica — Mint, Water
Mentha arvensis — Mint, Field or Wild
Mentha canadensis — Mint, Field or Wild
Mentha longifolia — Horsemint, European

Mentha piperita — Peppermint
Mentha pulegium — Pennyroyal
Mentha rotundifolia — Mint, Apple-scented
Mentha spicata — Spearmint
Menticirrhus americanus — Kingfish
Menticirrhus saxatilis — Kingfish
Mentzelia decapetala — Evening-star
Mentzelia laevicaulis — Blazing Star
Mentzelia lindleyi — Blazing Star
Menyanthes trifoliata — Buckbean
Menziesia ferruginea — Huckleberry, False
Menziesia glabella — Huckleberry, False
Mephitis macroura — Skunk, Hooded
Mephitis mephitis — Skunk, Striped
Mercenaria campechiensis — Clam, Quahog
Mercenaria mercenaria — Clam, Quahog
Mergus merganser — Merganser, Common
Mergus serrator — Merganser, Red-breasted
Merluccius bilinearis — Hake, Silver
Merluccius productus — Hake, Pacific
Merodon equestris — Fly, Narcissus Bulb
Meromyza americana — Maggot, Fly
Mertensia alpina — Lungwort, Alpine
Mertensia bella — Lungwort, Oregon
Mertensia ciliata — Bluebell, Mountain
Mertensia maritima — Lungwort, Sea
Mertensia paniculata — Lungwort, Tall
Mertensia virginiana — Bluebell, Virginia
Mesembryanthemum chilense — Fig Marigold
Mesembryanthemum chrystallinum — Ice Plant
Mesembryanthemum criniflorum — Daisy, Livingstone
Mesembryanthemum edule — Fig Marigold or
    Hottentot-fig
Mesocricetus auratus — Hamster, Golden
Mesoplodon bidens — Whale, Beaked (Sowerby's)
Metasequoia glyptostroboides — Redwood, Dawn
Metopocerus cornutus — Iguana, Rhinocerus
Metridium dianthus — Sea Anemone, Plumrose
Metridium senile — Sea Anemone, Senile
Micrathene whitneyi — Owl, Elf
Micrampelis lobata — Cucumber, Wild
Microcentrum rhomboideum — Grasshopper, Meadow
Microciona prolifera — Sponge, Red
Microgadus tomcod — Tomcod, Atlantic
Micropalama himantopus — Sandpiper, Stilt
Micropogon undulatus — Croaker, Atlantic
Micropterus dolomieu — Bass, Small-mouthed Black
Micropterus punctulatus — Bass, Spotted

Micropterus salmoides — Bass, Large-mouthed Black
Microsorex hoyi — Shrew, Pygmy
Microspathodon chrysurus — Damselfish, Yellow-tail
Microsphaeria alni — Mildew, Powdery Lilac
Microstomus kitt — Sole, Lemon
Microstomus pacificus — Sole, Dover
Microtus abbreviatus — Vole, Alaska or Singing
Microtus longicaudus — Vole, Long-tailed
Microtus miurus — Vole, Alaska or Singing
Microtus ochrogaster — Vole, Prairie
Microtus pennsylvanicus — Mouse, Field or Meadow
Microtus pinetorum — Mouse, Pine
Micruroides euryxanthus — Snake, Arizona Coral
Micrurus fulvius — Snake, Coral
Mikania scandens — Hempweed, Climbing
Milla biflora — Lily, Star
Miltonia hybrids — Orchid, Pansy
Mimetus notius — Spider, Pirate
Mimodes graysoni — Thrasher, Socorro
Mimosa pudica — Sensitive Plant
Mimosa strigillosa — Sensitive Plant
Mimulus alsinoides — Monkey-flower, Little
Mimulus aurantiacus — Monkey-flower, Bush
Mimulus guttatus — Monkey-flower, Common
Mimulus lewisii — Monkey-flower, Pink
Mimulus moschatus — Monkey-flower, Musk
Mimulus primuloides — Monkey-flower, Primrose
Mimulus ringens — Monkey-flower, Square-stemmed
Mimus polyglottos — Mockingbird
Mimus polyglottos leucopterus — Mockingbird
Mirabilis jalapa — Four O'Clock
Mirabilis multiflora — Four O'Clock, Giant
Mirabilis nytaginea — Four O'Clock, Wild
Miranda aurantia — Spider, Black-and-yellow Garden
Mirounga angustirostris — Seal, Elephant (Northern)
Misumena vatia — Spider, Crab or Flower
Mitchella repens — Partridge-berry
Mitella calescens — Mitrewort
Mitella diphylla — Mitrewort
Mitella polymerus — Barnacle, Goose
Mitella trifida — Mitrewort
Mitra sp. — Miter Shell
Mnemiopsis sp. — Comb-jelly
Mniotilla varia — Warbler, Black-and-white
Mnium cuspidatum — Moss, Star
Modiola caroliniana — Mallow, Carolina
Modiolus capax — Mussel, Horse
Modiolus demissus — Mussel, Ribbed (Atlantic)

Modiolus modiolus — Mussel, Horse
Modiolus rectus — Mussel, Horse
Moho braccatus — Oo, Kauai
Mola mola — Sunfish, Ocean
Mollugo verticillata — Carpet Weed
Molothrus ater — Cowbird, Brown-headed
Molothrus bonariensis — Cowbird, Glossy or Shiny
Moluccella laevis — Bells of Ireland
Momotus mexicanus — Motmot, Russet-crowned
Momotus momota — Motmot, Blue-crowned
Monachus schauinslandi — Seal, Hawaiian Monk
Monarda didyma — Bee-balm
Monarda fistulosa — Bergamot, Wild
Monarda media — Bergamot, Purple
Monarda punctata — Horsemint
Monardella odoratissima — Monardella, Mountain
Monardella villosa — Coyote-mint
Moneses uniflora — Wintergreen, One-flowered
Monodon monceros — Narwhal
Monomorium minimum — Ant, Little Black
Monomorium pharaonis — Ant, Pharaoh
Monoptilon bellioides — Desert Star
Monotropa hypopitys — Pinesap
Monotropa lanuginosa — Pinesap
Monotropa uniflora — Indian Pipe
Monstera deliciosa — Ceriman
Montia cordifolia — Miner's-lettuce
Montia parvifolia — Miner's-lettuce
Montia perfoliata — Miner's-lettuce
Montia sibirica — Miner's-lettuce
Mopalia ciliata — Chiton, Hairy
Mopalia muscosa — Chiton, Mossy
Morchella esculenta — Morel, Common
Morone americanus — Perch, White
Morowe saxatilis — Bass, Striped
Morpho sp. — Butterfly, Morpho
Morus alba — Mulberry, White
Morus nigra — Mulberry, Black
Morus rubra — Mulberry, Red
Motacilla alba — Wagtail, Pied or White
Motacilla flava — Wagtail, Yellow
Mugil cephalus — Mullet, Striped
Muhlenbergia schreberi — Nimblewill
Mulinia lateralis — Clam, Dwarf Surf
Muraena sp. — Eel, Moray
Murex sp. — Murex Shell
Murgantia histrionica — Bug, Stink (Harlequin)
Mus musculus — Mouse, House

Musa paradisiaca — Banana
Musa sapientum — Banana
Musa textilis — Hemp, Manila
Musca domestica — Fly, House
Muscaria botryoides — Grape Hyacinth
Muscivora forficata — Flycatcher, Scissor-tailed
Muscivora tyrannus — Flycatcher, Fork-tailed or
   Swallow-tailed
Mustela erminea — Weasel, Short-tailed
Mustela frenata — Weasel, Long-tailed
Mustela nigripes — Ferret, Black-footed
Mustela rixosa — Weasel, Least
Mustela vison — Mink
Mutinus caninus — Stinkhorn, Dog
Mya arenaria — Clam, Soft-shell
Mya truncata — Clam, Horse or Gaper
Myadestes townsendi — Solitaire, Townsend's
Mycena epipterygia — Mycena, Capped or Helmet
Mycena galericulata — Mycena, Capped or Helmet
Mycteria americana — Ibis, Wood
Mycteroperca bonaci — Grouper, Black
Mycteroperca venenosa — Grouper, Yellow-fin
Myctophum affine — Lanternfish
Myiarchus cinerascens — Flycatcher, Ash-throated
Myiarchus crinitus — Flycatcher, Great Crested
Myiarchus tuberculifer — Flycatcher, Olivaceous
Myiarchus tyrannulus — Flycatcher, Wied's Crested
Myiarchus yucatenensis — Flycatcher, Yucatan
Myioborus miniatus — Redstart, Slate-throated
Myiodynastes luteiventris — Flycatcher, Sulphur-bellied
Myiodynastes maculatus — Flycatcher, Streaked
Myiopagis viridicata — Elaenia, Greenish
Myiozetetes similis — Flycatcher, Social or Vermillion-
   crowned
Myliobatis aquila — Ray, Eagle
Myliobatis freminvilli — Ray, Eagle
Myocastor coypus — Nutria
Myosotis alpestris — Forget-me-not, Alpine
Myosotis arvensis — Forget-me-not, Common or Field
Myosotis laxa — Forget-me-not, Smaller
Myosotis scorpioides — Forget-me-not, True (Water)
Myosotis sylvatica — Forget-me-not, Woodland
Myosotis verna — Forget-me-not, Spring
Myosurus minimus — Mousetail
Myotis lucifugus — Bat, Little Brown
Myoxocephalus sp. — Sculpin
Myrica californica — Bayberry
Myrica cerifera — Bayberry

Myrica gale — Sweet Gale
Myrica inodora — Bayberry
Myrica pensylvanica — Bayberry
Myriophyllum sp. — Water-milfoil
Myrmecocystus sp. — Ant, Honey
Myrmeleon sp. — Ant-lion
Myrmotherula axillaris — Antwren, White-flanked
Myrmotherula schisticolor — Antwren, Slaty
Mysis sp. — Shrimp, Opossum
Mytilus californianus — Mussel, California or Surf
Mytilus edulis — Mussel, Blue or Edible
Myrtus communis — Myrtle, Common
Myxine glutinosa — Hagfish, Atlantic
Myzus persicae — Aphid, Green Peach
Myzinum quinquecinctum — Wasp, Tiphiid

N

Nabis ferus — Bug, Damsel
Naematoloma capnoides — Mushroom, Brick-top
Naematoloma sublateritium — Mushroom, Brick-top
Nama demissum — Purple Mat
Nama hispidum — Nama
Nandina domestica — Bamboo, Heavenly or Sacred
Napaeozapus insignis — Mouse, Jumping
Narcissus sp. — Narcissus
Narthecium alternifolium — Asphodel, Bog
Narthecium californicum — Asphodel, Bog
Narthecium ossifragum — Asphodel, Bog
Naso lituratus — Unicorn Fish
Nassarius fossatus — Basket Shell
Nassarius mendicus — Basket Shell
Nassarius obsoletus — Basket Shell
Nassarius vibex — Basket Shell
Nasturtium officinale — Cress, Water
Nasua narica — Coati, White-nosed
Natica canrena — Natica, Atlantic
Natica clausa — Natica, Arctic
Natica pusilla — Natica, Miniature
Natrix sp. — Snake, Water
Natrix septemvittata — Snake, Queen
Naucrates ductor — Pilotfish
Naumburgia thrysiflora — Loosestrife, Tufted
Nautichthys sp. — Sculpin
Necator americanus — Hookworm
Necrophorus marginatus — Beetle, Sexton
Necrophorus vespillo — Beetle, Sexton
Nectaria cinnabarina — Coral Spot

Necturus maculosus — Mudpuppy
Nelumbo lutea — Lotus, American
Nelumbo nucifera — Lotus, Sacred
Nematus ribesii — Sawfly, Currant
Nemesia strumosa — Nemesia
Nemichthys scolopaceus — Eel, Snipe
Nemobius sylvestris — Cricket, Wood
Nemophila maculata — Five-spot
Nemophila menziesii — Baby Blue-eyes
Neofiber alleni — Water Rat, Florida
Neolamprima adolphinae — Beetle, Stag
Neomysis sp. — Shrimp, Opossum
Neophasganophora capitata — Fly, Stone
Neopieris mariana — Staggerbush
Neoseps reynoldsi — Skink, Sand
Neotoma sp. — Rat, Wood
Nepa sp. — Water-scorpion
Nepeta cataria — Catnip or Catmint
Nepeta mussinii — Catnip or Catmint
Nephrolepis exaltata — Fern, Boston
Nephrotoma crocata — Daddy-long-legs
Neptunea decemcostata — Neptune, New England
Neptunea tabulatus — Whelk, Tabled
Nereis procera — Worm, Clam
Nereis succinea — Worm, Clam
Nereis virens — Worm, Clam
Nereocystis leutkeana — Kelp, Bladder or Ribbon
Nerine bowdenii — Lily, Guernsey
Nerine seriensis — Lily, Guernsey
Nerita pelorouta — Tooth, Bleeding
Nerium oleander — Oleander
Nerocila bivittata — Sea Slater
Neurotrichus gibbsi — Shrew-mole
Nezara viridula — Bug, Stink (Southern Green)
Nicotiana alata — Tobacco, Flowering
Nierembergia sp. — Cup Flower
Nigella damascena — Love-in-a-mist
Noctilio leporinus — Bat, Fish-eating or Fisherman
Noctiluca miliaris — Night-light
Noctiluca scintillans — Night-light
Noetia ponderosa — Ark Shell, Heavy or Ponderous
Nolina parryi — Bear-grass
Nomeus gronovii — Man-o'-war Fish
Nostoc sp. — Alga, Blue-green
Notemigonus chrysoleucus — Shiner, Golden
Nothoscordum bivalve — Garlic, False
Notiosorex crawfordi — Shrew, Desert or Gray
Notonecta glauca — Backswimmer

Notonecta undulata — Backswimmer
Notophthalmus viridescens — Newt, Red-spotted
Notropis atherinoides — Shiner, Emerald
Notropis cornutus — Shiner, Common
Noturus sp. — Madtom
Nucella lamellosa — Dogwinkle, Frilled
Nucella lapillus — Dogwinkle, Atlantic
Nucifraga columbiana — Nutcracker, Clark's
Nucula sp. — Clam, Nut
Numenius americanus — Curlew, Long-billed
Numenius borealis — Curlew, Eskimo
Numenius hudsonicus — Whimbrel
Numenius phaeopus — Whimbrel
Numenius tahitiensis — Curlew, Bristle-thighed
Numida meleagris — Guinea-fowl, Common or Helmeted
Nuphar advena — Water-lily, Yellow
Nuphar lutea — Water-lily, Yellow
Nuphar polysepola — Water-lily, Western
Nuphar variegatum — Water-lily, Yellow
Nuttallornis borealis — Flycatcher, Olive-sided
Nyctanassa violacea — Heron, Yellow-crowned Night
Nyctea scandiaca — Owl, Snowy
Nyctibius griseus — Potoo, Common
Nycticorax nycticorax — Heron, Black-crowned Night
Nyctidromus albicollis — Pauraque
Nygmia phaeorrhoea — Moth, Brown-tail
Nymphaea alba — Water-lily, White
Nymphaea odorata — Water-lily, Fragrant
Nymphaea polysepola — Water-lily, Western
Nymphaea tuberosa — Water-lily, White
Nymphalis io — Butterfly, Peacock
Nymphoides peltata — Floating-heart
Nymphon sp. — Sea Spider
Nyssa aquatica — Tupelo, Black
Nyssa sylvatica — Tupelo, Black

O

Obelia sp. — Hydroid, Double-branching
Obolaria virginica — Pennywort
Oceanites oceanicus — Petrel, Wilson's Storm
Oceanodroma castro — Petrel, Harcourt's Storm
Oceanodroma furcata — Petrel, Fork-tailed
Oceanodroma homochroa — Petrel, Ashy
Oceanodroma leucorhoa — Petrel, Leach's
Oceanodroma markhami — Petrel, Sooty Storm
Oceanodroma melania — Petrel, Black
Oceanodroma socorrensis — Petrel, Socorro Storm

Oceanodroma tristrami — Petrel, Sooty Storm
Ocenebra circumtexta — Triton, Dwarf
Ocenebra interfossa — Triton, Dwarf
Ochotona princeps — Pika
Ocimum basilicum — Basil, Sweet
Octopus bairdii — Octopus, Common
Octopus bimaculatus — Octopus, Two-spotted
Octopus vulgaris — Octopus, Common
Ocypode arenaria — Crab, Ghost or Sand
Ocypode quadratus — Crab, Ghost or Sand
Ocyurus chrysurus — Snapper, Yellow-tail
Odobenus rosmarus — Walrus
Odocoileus hemionus — Deer, Mule
Odocoileus hemionus columbianus — Deer, Black-tailed
Odocoileus virginianus — Deer, White-tailed or Virginia
Odocoileus virginianus clavium — Deer, Florida Key
Odontites lutea — Bartsia, Yellow
Odontophorus guttatus — Quail, Spotted Wood
Odostomia sp. — Odostome
Oecanthus niveus — Cricket, Tree
Oenanthe oenanthe — Wheatear
Oenanthe sarmentosa — Parsley, Water
Oenothera albicaulis — Evening-primrose
Oenothera biennis — Evening-primrose, Common
Oenothera caespitosa — Evening-primrose, Desert
Oenothera deltoides — Evening-primrose, Desert
Oenothera fruticosa — Sundrops
Oenothera hookeri — Evening-primrose, Yellow
Oenothera laciniata — Evening-primrose, Cut-leaved
Oenothera missouriensis — Evening-primrose, Missouri
Oenothera ovata — Sun Cups
Oenothera pallida — Evening-primrose
Oenothera serrulata — Evening-primrose
Oenothera speciosa — Evening-primrose, Mexican
Oenothera tetragona — Sundrops
Oestrus ovis — Botfly, Sheep
Oidemia americana — Scoter, Common or American
Oidemia nigra — Scoter, Common or American
Olea europaea — Olive
Olearia sp. — Daisy-bush
Oligocottus maculosus — Sculpin, Tide-pool
Oliva porphyria — Olive Shell, Tent
Oliva sayana — Olive Shell, Lettered
Olivella baetica — Olive Shell, Beatic Dwarf
Olivella biplicata — Olive Shell, Purple Dwarf
Olor buccinator — Swan, Trumpeter
Olor columbianus — Swan, Whistling
Omphalodes verna — Blue-eyed-Mary

Oncorhynchus gorbuscha — Salmon, Pink or Humpback
Oncorhynchus keta — Salmon, Chum or Dog
Oncorhynchus kisutch — Salmon, Coho or Silver
Oncorhynchus nerka — Salmon, Sockeye or Red
Oncorhynchus tshawytscha — Salmon, Chinook
Oncostoma cinereigulare — Bentbill, Northern or Gray-throated
Ondatra zibethica — Muskrat
Oniscus asellus — Sowbug
Onoclea sensibilis — Fern, Sensitive
Onocopeltus fasciatus — Bug, Milkweed
Onopordum acanthium — Thistle, Scotch or Cotton
Onos mustelus — Rockling, Five-bearded
Onychomys leucogaster — Mouse, Grasshopper
Opalia wroblewskii — Wentletrap, Wroblewski's
Opheodrys sp. — Snake, Green
Ophioblennius atlanticus — Blenny, Red-lip
Ophioderma brevispinum — Brittle-star, Green
Ophiodon elongatus — Lingcod
Ophioglossum engelmannii — Adder's-tongue, Lime-stone
Ophioglossum vulgatum — Adder's-tongue, Common
Ophiopholis aculeata — Brittle-star, Daisy
Ophiothrix fragilis — Brittle-star, Common
Ophisaurus attenuatus — Lizard, Slender Glass
Ophisaurus ventralis — Lizard, Eastern Glass
Ophiura lutkenii — Brittle-star
Opisthognathus aurifrons — Jawfish
Opisthognathus macrognathus — Jawfish
Oplopanax horridum — Devil's-club
Oporornis agilis — Warbler, Connecticut
Oporornis formosus — Warbler, Kentucky
Oporornis philadelphia — Warbler, Mourning
Oporornis tolmiei — Warbler, MacGillivray's
Opsanus beta — Toadfish
Opsanus tau — Toadfish
Opuntia basilaris — Cactus, Beavertail
Opuntia bigelovii — Cholla, Jumping
Opuntia compressa — Prickly-pear
Opuntia echinocarpa — Cactus, Staghorn or Thorny-fruited
Opuntia engelmannii — Prickly-pear, Engelmann's
Opuntia erinacea — Cactus, Hedgehog
Opuntia fragilis — Prickly-pear, Brittle or Fragile
Opuntia lindheimeri — Prickly-pear, Lindheimer's
Opuntia linguiformis — Cactus, Cow Tongue
Opuntia occidentalis — Prickly-pear
Opuntia phaecantha — Prickly-pear, Engelmann's

Opuntia polyacantha — Prickly-pear, Many-spined or Yellow
Opuntia rufida — Prickly-pear, Blind
Opuntia spinosior — Cholla, Yellow
Opuntia versicolor — Cholla, Purple
Orantium aquaticum — Golden Club
Orchelium vulgare — Grasshopper, Meadow
Orchestia traskiana — Flea, Sand (Beach Hopper)
Orchis rotundifolia — Orchis, Round-leaved
Orchis spectabilis — Orchis, Showy
Orcinus orca — Whale, Killer
Oreamnos americanus — Goat, Rocky Mountain
Orectochilus villosus — Beetle, Whirligig
Oregonia gracilis — Crab, Spider
Oreophasis derbianus — Guan, Horned
Oreortyx pictus — Quail, Mountain
Oreoscoptes montanus — Thrasher, Sage
Origanum vulgare — Marjoram
Ornithion semiflavum — Tyrannulet, Yellow-bellied
Ornithogalum umbellatum — Star of Bethlehem
Orobanche fasciculata — Broomrape
Orobanche ludoviciana — Broomrape
Orobanche minor — Broomrape, Lesser
Orobanche ramosa — Broomrape, Branched
Orobanche uniflora — Broomrape, Naked or One-flowered
Ortalis leucogaster — Chachalaca, White-bellied
Ortalis poliocephala — Chachalaca
Ortalis ruficauda — Chachalaca, Rufous-vented
Ortalis vetula — Chachalaca
Ortalis wagleri — Chachalaca, Rufous-bellied or Wagler
Orthezia insignis — Bug, Mealy
Orthocarpus purpurascens — Clover, Owl's
Orthocarpus tenuifolius — Clover, Owl's
Oryza sativa — Rice
Oryzaephilus surinamensis — Beetle, Saw-toothed Grain
Oryzomys palustris — Rat, Rice
Oscillatoria sp. — Alga, Blue-green
Osmanthus fragrans — Olive, Sweet
Osmaronia cerasiformis — Oso-berry
Osmerus mordax — Smelt, American
Osmorhiza chilensis — Cicely, Sweet
Osmorhiza claytonia — Cicely, Sweet
Osmorhiza longistylis — Cicely, Sweet
Osmunda cinnamomea — Fern, Cinnamon
Osmunda claytoniana — Fern, Interrupted
Osmunda regalis — Fern, Royal
Ostrea frons — Oyster, Coon

Ostrea gigas — Oyster, Japanese or Giant Pacific
Ostrea lurida — Oyster, Native Pacific (Olympia)
Ostrya virginiana — Hornbeam, Hop
Otus asio — Owl, Screech
Otus barbarus — Owl, Bearded Screech
Otus cooperi — Owl, Cooper Screech
Otus flammeolus — Owl, Flammulated Screech
Ovalipes ocellatus — Crab, Lady
Ovibus moschatus — Muskox
Ovis ammon — Sheep, Domestic
Ovis aries — Sheep, Domestic
Ovis canadensis — Sheep, Rocky Mountain
Ovis dallii — Sheep, Dall's Mountain
Ovis stonei — Sheep, Stone's Mountain
Oxalis acetosella — Wood-sorrel, Common
Oxalis corniculata — Wood-sorrel, Creeping
Oxalis grandis — Wood-sorrel, Large Yellow
Oxalis montana — Wood-sorrel, Common
Oxalis oregana — Wood-sorrel, Redwood
Oxalis rubra — Wood-sorrel, Garden
Oxalis stricta — Wood-sorrel, Yellow
Oxalis violacea — Wood-sorrel, Violet
Oxycoccus palustris — Cranberry, Bog or Small
Oxydendrum arboreum — Sourwood
Oxypolis rigidior — Cowbane
Oxyria digyna — Sorrel, Mountain
Oxytropis besseyi — Locoweed
Oxytropis lambertii — Crazyweed, Lambert's
Oxytropis splendens — Locoweed
Oxyura dominica — Duck, Masked
Oxyura jamaicensis — Duck, Ruddy

P

Pachira insignis — Shaving Brush Tree
Pachira macrocarpa — Shaving Brush Tree
Pachycereus pringlei — Cactus, Cordon
Pachyramphus cinnamomeus — Becard, Cinnamon
Pachyramphus major — Becard, Gray-collared or
    Mexican
Paeonia sp. — Peony
Paeonia brownii — Peony, Wild
Paeonia suffruticosa — Peony, Tree
Pagophila alba — Gull, Ivory
Pagophila eburnea — Gull, Ivory
Pagophilus groenlandica — Seal, Harp
Pagurus sp. — Crab, Hermit
Palaecrita vernata — Cankerworm, Spring

Palaemon serratus — Prawn, Common
Palaemonetes paludosus — Shrimp, Grass
Palaemonetes vulgaris — Shrimp, Grass
Palinurus interruptus — Lobster, Spiny
Panax quinquefolium — Ginseng
Panax trifolium — Ginseng, Dwarf
Pandion halietus — Osprey
Pandora bilirata — Pandora Shell
Pandora gouldiana — Pandora Shell
Panera aquatica — Elm, Water
Panicum capillare — Witchgrass
Panope generosa — Geoduck
Panorpa communis — Fly, Scorpion
Panorpa nebulosa — Fly, Scorpion
Panthera onca — Jaguar
Panthera pardalis — Ocelot
Panulirus argus — Lobster, Spiny
Panulirus interruptus — Lobster, Spiny
Panus stipticus — Mushroom, Panus
Papaver nudicaule — Poppy, Iceland
Papaver orientale — Poppy, Oriental
Papaver rhoeas — Poppy, Corn
Papaver somniferum — Poppy, Opium
Papilio sp. — Butterfly, Swallow-tail
Papilio polyxenes — Celeryworm
Parabuteo unicinctus — Hawk, Harris'
Paralichthys dentatus — Flounder, Summer
Paramecium sp. — Paramecium
Paranemertes peregrina — Worm, Restless
Paranemertes plana — Worm, Restless
Parapholas californica — Piddock, California
Parascalops breweri — Mole, Hairy-tailed
Parastichopus californicus — Sea Cucumber, Large Red
Pardirallus maculatus — Rail, Spotted
Parentucellia viscosa — Bartsia, Yellow
Parkinsonia aculeata — Jerusalem-thorn
Parnassia fimbriata — Grass-of-parnassus, Fringed
Parnassia glauca — Grass-of-parnassus
Parnassia palustris — Grass-of-parnassus or Grass-of-
    parnassus, Marsh
Parnassius apollo — Butterfly, Apollo
Parnassius phoebus — Butterfly, Apollo
Paroaria coronata — Cardinal, Red-crested
Paroaria cristata — Cardinal, Red-crested
Paroctopus apolloyon — Octopus, Common
Parophrys velutus — Sole, Lemon
Parrotia persica — Iron Tree
Parthenocissus tricuspidata — Virginia Creeper

Parula americana — Warbler, Parula
Parula pitiayuma — Warbler, Olive-backed
Parupeneus multifasciatus — Goatfish
Parupeneus pleurostigma — Goatfish
Parus atricapillus — Chickadee, Black-capped
Parus atricristatus — Titmouse, Black-crested
Parus bicolor — Titmouse, Tufted
Parus carolinensis — Chickadee, Carolina
Parus cinctus — Chickadee, Gray-headed
Parus gambeli — Chickadee, Mountain
Parus hudsonicus — Chickadee, Boreal or Brown-capped
Parus inornatus — Titmouse, Plain
Parus rufescens — Chickadee, Chestnut-backed
Parus sclateri — Chickadee, Mexican
Parus wollweberi — Titmouse, Bridled
Paspalum dilatatum — Grass, Dallis
Passer domesticus — Sparrow, English or House
Passerculus princeps — Sparrow, Ipswich
Passerculus sandwichensis — Sparrow, Savannah
Passerella iliaca — Sparrow, Fox
Passerherbulus caudacutus — Sparrow, Le Conte's
Passerherbulus henslowii — Sparrow, Henslow's
Passerina amoena — Bunting, Lazuli
Passerina ciris — Bunting, Painted
Passerina cyanea — Bunting, Indigo
Passerina versicolor — Bunting, Varied
Passiflora alato-caerula — Passion Flower
Passiflora caerulea — Passion Flower
Passiflora incarnata — Maypops
Pastinaca sativa — Parsnip
Patiria miniata — Starfish, Sea Bat
Paulownia tomentosa — Paulownia, Royal
Pavo cristatus — Peafowl
Pecari angulatus — Peccary, Collared
Pecten hericius — Scallop, Pink
Pecten hindsii — Scallop, Hind's or Smooth
Pectinophora gossypiella — Bollworm, Pink
Pedicularis bracteosa — Lousewort, Bracted or
   Fern-leaved
Pedicularis canadensis — Lousewort, Common
Pedicularis densiflora — Indian Warrior
Pedicularis groenlandica — Elephant-head
Pedicularis lanceolata — Lousewort, Swamp
Pedicularis racemosa — Lousewort, Swamp
Pediculus humanus var. — Louse, Head or Body
Pediocactus simpsonii — Cactus, Simpson's
Pedioecetes phasianellus — Grouse, Sharp-tailed
Pegomya hyascyami — Fly, Leaf-miner

Pelagia sp. — Jellyfish, Luminous
Pelagodroma marina — Petrel, White-faced Storm
Pelargonium domesticum — Geranium, Martha
   Washington
Pelargonium hortorum — Geranium, Common
Pelargonium peltatum — Geranium, Ivy-leaved
Pelargonium zonale — Geranium, Zonal
Pelecanus erythrorhynchos — Pelican, White
Pelecanus occidentalis — Pelican, Brown
Pelecinus polyturator — Wasp, Pelecinid
Pellaea sp. — Fern, Cliff-brake
Peltandra virginica — Arum, Arrow
Peltiphyllum peltatum — Umbrella Plant
Penaeus aztecus — Shrimp, Edible
Penaeus setiferus — Shrimp, Edible
Penelope purpurescens — Guan, Crested
Penicillium digitatum — Mold, Green
Pennatula aculeata — Sea Pen
Pennisetum ruppellii — Grass, Fountain
Pennula sandwichensis — Rail, Hawaiian
Penstemon barbatus — Penstemon
Penstemon cobaea — Penstemon
Penstemon digitalis — Beardtongue, Foxglove
Penstemon fruiticosus var. scouleri — Penstemon,
   Shrubby
Penstemon gairdneri — Beardtongue, Gairdner's
Penstemon grandiflorus — Beardtongue, Large-
   flowered
Penstemon gloxinioides — Beardtongue
Penstemon hirsutus — Beardtongue, Hairy
Penstemon menziesii — Beardtongue, Menzie's
Penstemon newberryi — Mountain Pride
Penstemon parryi — Beardtongue, Parry's
Penstemon procerus — Beardtongue, Small Purple
Penstemon rupicola — Penstemon, Rock
Penstemon tenuiflorus — Beardtongue, Slender-
   flowered
Peperomia obtusifolia — Pepper-elder
Pepis formosa — Wasp, Tarantula-hawk
Pepis mildei — Wasp, Tarantula-hawk
Perca flavescens — Perch, Yellow
Percopsis omiscomaycus — Troutperch
Perdix perdix — Partridge, Gray or Hungarian
Perilla frutescens — Beefsteak Plant
Periplaneta americana — Cockroach, American
Periploma sp. — Clam, Spoon
Perisoreus canadensis — Jay, Canada or Gray
Perognathus sp. — Mouse, Pocket

Peromyscus boylei — Mouse, Brush
Peromyscus eremicus — Mouse, Cactus
Peromyscus leucopus — Mouse, White-footed
Peromyscus maniculatus — Mouse, Deer
Peromyscus polionotus — Mouse, Beach or Oldfield
Peromyscus truei — Mouse, Pinon or Pinyon
Perovskia atriplicifolia — Sage, Russian
Persea americana — Avocado (Avocado Pear)
Petalostemum candidum — Prairie-clover, White
Petalostemum purpureus — Prairie-clover, Purple
Petasites palmatus — Coltsfoot, Sweet
Petasites sagittata — Coltsfoot, Sweet
Petasites speciosa — Coltsfoot, Sweet
Petrea kohautiana — Sandpaper Vine
Petrea volubilis — Sandpaper Vine
Petricola pholadiformis — Angel Wing, False
Petrochelidon fulva — Swallow, Cave
Petrochelidon pyrrhonota — Swallow, Cliff
Petrolisthes eriomerus — Crab, Porcelain
Petromyzon marinus — Lamprey, Sea
Petroselinum crispum — Parsley
Petroselinum sativum — Parsley
Petunia hybrids — Petunia
Peucedramus taeniatus — Warbler, Olive
Peziza aurantia — Fungus, Orange Cup
Peziza coccinea — Fungus, Scarlet Cup
Peziza repanda — Fungus, Scarlet Cup
Peziza vesiculosa — Fungus, Early Cup
Phacelia sp. — Phacelia
Phacelia campanularia — Bluebell, California or
    Canterbury Bells
Phacelia purshii — Miami-mist
Phacus acuminatus — Euglenoid
Phaeornis obscurus — Thrush, Hawaiian
Phaethon aethereus — Tropic-bird, Red-billed
Phaethon lepturus — Tropic-bird, White-tailed
Phaethon rubricauda — Tropic-bird, Red-tailed
Phaethornis superciliosus — Hermit, Long-tailed
Phainopepla nitens — Phainopepla
Phalaemoptilus nuttallii — Poor-will, Nuttall's
Phalaris arundinacea — Canary-grass, Reed
Phalaris canariensis — Canary-grass
Phalacrocorax auritus — Cormorant, Double-crested
Phalacrocorax carbo — Cormorant, Great
Phalacrocorax olivaceus — Cormorant, Mexican
    or Olivaceous
Phalacrocorax pelagicus — Cormorant, Pelagic
Phalacrocorax penicillatus — Cormorant, Brandt's

Phalacrocorax urile — Cormorant, Red-faced
Phalaropus fulicarius — Phalarope, Red or Gray
Phalaropus lobatus — Phalarope, Northern or
    Red-necked
Phallus impudicus — Stinkhorn, Common
Pharomachrus mocinno — Quetzal
Phascolosoma sp. — Worm, Peanut
Phaseolus coccineus — Bean, Scarlet Runner
Phaseolus limensis — Bean, Lima or Butter
Phaseolus lunatus — Bean, Lima or Butter
Phaseolus polystachios — Bean, Wild
Phaseolus vulgaris — Bean, Garden or Kidney
Phasianus colchicus — Pheasant, Ring-necked
Phegopteris hexagonoptera — Fern, Beech
Phenacaspis pinifolia — Scale, Pine-needle
Phenacoccus gossypii — Bug, Mealy
Phenacomys intermedius — Vole, Heather
Phenacomys longicaudus — Mouse, Red Tree
Pheucticus chrysopeplus — Grosbeak, Yellow
Pheucticus ludovicianus — Grosbeak, Rose-breasted
Pheucticus melanocephalus — Grosbeak, Black-headed
Phidippus sp. — Spider, Jumping
Phidolopora pacifica — Bryozoan
Philacte canagica — Goose, Emperor
Philadelphus lewisii — Mock Orange
Philaenus leucophthalmus — Spittlebug
Phillyrea decora — Privet, Mock
Philohela minor — Woodcock, American
Philosamia cynthia — Moth, Silk
Phleum alpinum — Timothy, Mountain
Phleum pratense — Timothy
Philomachus pugnax — Ruff
Phlogiotus helvelloides — Mushroom, Apricot Jelly
Phlomis fruiticosa — Sage, Jerusalem
Phlox austromontana — Phlox, Western Mountain
Phlox diffusa — Phlox, Spreading
Phlox divaricata — Phlox, Wild Blue
Phlox drummondii — Phlox, Annual
Phlox longifolia — Phlox, Long-leaved
Phlox maculata — Phlox, Wild Sweet-william
Phlox paniculata — Phlox, Garden
Phlox pilosa — Phlox, Downy
Phlox sublata — Phlox, Moss
Phoca fasciata — Seal, Ribbon
Phoca groenlandica — Seal, Harp
Phoca hispida — Seal, Ringed
Phoca vitulina — Seal, Hair or Harbor
Phocoena dalli — Porpoise, Dall's

Phocoena phocoena — Porpoise, Common or Harbor
Phoenicaulis cheiranthoides — Dagger-pod
Phoenicopterus ruber — Flamingo, American
Phoenix dactylifera — Palm, Date
Pholcus phalangioides — Spider, Long-legged
Pholiota caperata — Mushroom, Gypsy
Pholis gunnellus — Gunnel
Pholis ornata — Gunnel
Phoradendron californicum — Mistletoe
Phoradendron flavescens — Mistletoe
Phoradendron villosum — Mistletoe
Photina fraseri — Hawthorn, Chinese
Photina serrulata — Hawthorn, Chinese
Photinus pyralis — Firefly
Phyciodes tharos — Butterfly, Pearl Crescent
Phygelius capensis — Figwort, Cape
Phyllitis scolopendrium — Fern, Hart's-tongue
Phyllodactylus tuberculatus — Gecko, Leaf-toed
Phyllodactylus xanti — Gecko, Leaf-toed
Phyllodoce empetriformis — Heather, Red or Mountain
Phyllodoce granduliflora — Heather, Yellow
Phyllophaga fusca — Beetle, May (or June)
Phyllophaga rugosa — Beetle, May (or June)
Phylloscopus borealis — Warbler, Arctic
Physalia physalis — Portugese Man-of-war
Phragmites communis — Reed, Common
Phryma leptostachya — Lopseed
Phrynosoma cornutum — Lizard, Texas Horned
Phrynosoma coronatum — Lizard, Coast Horned
Phrynosoma coronatum blainvillei — Lizard, Coast
    Horned
Phrynosoma douglasii — Lizard, Short-horned
Phrynosoma modestum — Lizard, Round-tailed Horned
Phrynosoma platyrhinus — Lizard, Desert Horned
Phtherius pubis — Louse, Crab
Phymata crassipes — Bug, Ambush
Phymata pennsylvanica — Bug, Ambush
Physalis alkekengi — Chinese Lantern
Physalis crassifolia — Cherry, Ground
Physalis francheti — Chinese Lantern
Physalis heterophylla — Ground-cherry, Clammy
Physaria didymocarpa — Bladder-pod
Physeter catodon — Whale, Sperm
Physocarpus capitatus — Ninebark
Physocarpus opulifolius — Ninebark
Physostegia virginiana — Dragonhead, False
Phyteuma comosum — Rampion, Clustered
Phytolacca americana — Pokeweed or Pokeberry

Phytomyza sp. — Fly, Leaf-miner
Phytophaga destructor — Fly, Hessian
Piaya cayana var. — Cuckoo, Squirrel or Chestnut
Pica nuttallii — Magpie, Yellow-billed
Pica pica — Magpie, Black-billed
Picea abies — Spruce, Norway
Picea engelmannii — Spruce, Engelmann's
Picea pungens — Spruce, Colorado Blue
Picea sitchensis — Spruce, Sitka
Picoides arcticus — Woodpecker, Black-backed Three-
    toed
Picoides tridactylus — Woodpecker, Three-toed
Piculus auricularis — Woodpecker, Gray-crowned
Piculus rubiginosus — Woodpecker, Golden-olive or
    Green
Pieris brassicae — Butterfly, Cabbage White
Pieris japonica — Andromeda, Japanese
Pieris rapae — Butterfly, Cabbage White or Cabbage-
    worm, Imported
Pilea cadieri — Aluminum Plant
Pimephales notatus — Minnow, Blunt-nosed
Pimpinella anisum — Anise or Aniseed
Pinctada mertensi — Oyster, Pearl
Pinctada radiata — Oyster, Pearl
Pinguicula vulgaris — Butterwort
Pinicola enucleator — Grosbeak, Pine
Pinnotheres pisum — Crab, Pea
Pinus albicaulis — Pine, White-barked
Pinus cembroides — Pine, Pinon or Nut
Pinus contorta — Pine, Lodge-pole
Pinus flexilis — Pine, Limber
Pinus lambertiana — Pine, Sugar
Pinus monophylla — Pine, Pinon or Nut
Pinus monticola — Pine, White
Pinus palustris — Pine, Long-leaf
Pinus ponderosa — Pine, Western Yellow
Pinus radiata — Pine, Monterey
Pinus resinosa — Pine, Red or Norway
Pinus rigida — Pine, Pitch
Pinus strobus — Pine, White
Pinus sylvestris — Pine, Scotch
Pionus senilis — Parrot, White-crowned
Piophila casei — Skipper, Cheese
Pipile cujubi — Guan, Piping
Pipile pipile — Guan, Piping
Pipilo aberti — Towhee, Abert's
Pipilo albicollis — Towhee, White-throated
Pipilo erythrophthalmus — Towhee, Rufous-sided

Pipilo fuscus — Towhee, Brown
Pipilo ocai — Towhee, Collared
Pipistrellus subflavus — Bat, Pipistrelle
Pipra mentalis — Manakin, Red-capped or Yellow-thighed
Piranga flava — Tanager, Hepatic
Piranga ludoviciana — Tanager, Western
Piranga olivacea — Tanager, Scarlet
Piranga rubra — Tanager, Summer
Pirata piraticus — Spider, Pirate
Pisaster brevispinus — Starfish, Short-spined
Pisaster ochraceus — Starfish, Ochre
Pisaura mirabilis — Spider, Wolf
Piscicola geometra — Leech, Fish
Pisum arvense — Pea, Garden
Pisum sativum — Pea, Garden
Pitangus sulphuratus — Flycatcher, Derby or Kiskadee
Pituophis catenifer var. — Snake, Bull
Pituophis melanoleucus — Snake, Bull
Pitymys pinetorum — Mouse, Pine
Placopecten magellanicus — Scallop, Atlantic Deep Sea
Plantago lanceolata — Plantain, Narrow-leaved
Plantago major — Plantain, Common
Plantago maritima — Plantain, Sea
Plantago media — Plantain, Hoary
Plantago purshii — Plantain, Woolly
Platanus acerifolia — Plane Tree, London
Platanus hispanica — Plane Tree, London
Platanus occidentalis — Sycamore, American
Platanus orientalis — Plane Tree, Oriental
Platichthys stellatus — Flounder, Starry
Platyarthrus hoffmanseggi — Sowbug
Platycerium bifurcatum — Fern, Staghorn
Platycodon grandiflorum — Balloon Flower
Platypsaris aglaiae — Becard, Rose-throated
Platyrinchus mystaceus — Spadebill, White-throated
Platystemon californicus — Cream Cups
Plautus alle — Dovekie
Plectania coccinea — Fungus, Scarlet Cup
Plectritis congesta — Sea Blush
Plectrophenax hyberboreus — Bunting, McKay's Snow
Plectrophenax nivalis — Bunting, Snow (Eastern)
Plegadis chihi — Ibis, White-faced Glossy
Plegadis falcinellus — Ibis, Glossy
Plegadis mexicana — Ibis, White-faced Glossy
Plethodon cinereus — Salamander, Red-backed
Plethodon dorsalis — Salamander, Zigzag
Plethodon glutinosus — Salamander, Slimy

Plethodon jordani — Salamander, Red-cheeked
Plethodon richmondi — Salamander, Ravine
Plethodon vandykei — Salamander, Van Dyke's
Plethodon vehiculum — Salamander, Western Red-backed
Plethodon yonahlossee — Salamander, Yonahlossee
Pleurobrachia sp. — Comb-jelly
Pleurotus ostreatus — Mushroom, Oyster
Pleurotus serotinus — Mushroom, Oyster
Plodia interpunctella — Moth, Indian-meal
Pluchea camphorata — Fleabane, Salt Marsh
Pluchea purpurascens — Fleabane, Salt Marsh
Plumatella sp. — Bryozoan
Plumbago capensis — Leadwort, Cape
Plumbago scandens — Leadwort, Cape
Plumeria acutifolia — Frangipani
Plumeria rubra — Frangipani, Red
Pluvialis dominica — Plover, Golden
Poa alpina — Bluegrass, Alpine
Poa annua — Bluegrass, Annual
Poa palustris — Bluegrass, Fowl
Poa pratensis — Bluegrass, Kentucky
Podiceps auritus — Grebe, Horned
Podiceps caspicus — Grebe, Eared
Podiceps dominicus — Grebe, Least or Mexican
Podiceps grisegena — Grebe, Red-necked or Holboell's
Podilymbus podiceps — Grebe, Pied-billed
Podocarpus andinus — Yew, Podocarpus
Podocarpus macrophylla — Yew, Podocarpus
Pododesmus macroschisma — Oyster, Rock
Podophyllum peltatum — Mayapple
Podura aquatica — Springtail, Water
Pogonia ophioglossoides — Pogonia, Rose
Pogonias cromis — Drum, Black
Pogonomyrmex badius — Ant, Harvester
Pogonomyrmex occidentalis — Ant, Harvester
Polemonium caeruleum — Jacob's Ladder, Blue
Polemonium elegans — Jacob's Ladder, Alpine
Polemonium foliosissimum — Polemonium, Skunk
Polemonium pulcherrimum — Jacob's Ladder, Showy
Polemonium reptens — Valerian, Greek
Polemonium van bruntiae — Jacob's Ladder, American
Polemonium viscosum — Polemonium, Skunk
Polianthes tuberosa — Tuberose
Polinices draconis — Moon Snail, Lewis'
Polinices duplicatus — Moon Snail, Atlantic or Shark-eye
Polinices lewisii — Moon Snail, Lewis'

Polioptila caerulea — Gnatcatcher, Blue-gray
Polioptila melanura — Gnatcatcher, Black-tailed
Polioptila nigriceps — Gnatcatcher, Black-capped
Polioptila plumbea — Gnatcatcher, Black-tailed
Polistes sp. — Wasp, Paper
Pollachius virens — Pollack or Pollock
Pollicipes polymerus — Barnacle, Goose
Polyborus cheriway — Caracara, Audubon's or Common
Polyborus plancus — Caracara, Crested
Polygala brevifolia — Milkwort, Short-leaved
Polygala cruciata — Milkwort, Cross-leaved or Marsh
Polygala lutea — Milkwort, Yellow
Polygala pauciflora — Milkwort, Fringed
Polygala sanguinea — Milkwort, Field
Polygala verticillata — Milkwort, Whorled
Polygonatum biflorum — Solomon's Seal
Polygonatum canoliculatum — Solomon's Seal
Polygonatum multiflorum — Solomon's Seal
Polygonella articulata — Jointweed
Polygonia interrogationis — Butterfly, Question Mark
Polygonum amphibium — Bistort, Amphibious
Polygonum auberti — Silver-lace Vine
Polygonum aviculare — Knotweed, Prostrate
Polygonum bistorta — Bistort
Polygonum bistortoides — Knotweed, Mountain
  Meadow
Polygonum convolvulus — Bindweed, Black
Polygonum hydropiper — Water-pepper
Polygonum lapathifolium — Smartweed, Pale
Polygonum orientale — Prince's-feather
Polygonum paronychia — Knotweed, Beach
Polygonum pensylvanicum — Pinkweed
Polygonum persicaria — Lady's-thumb
Polygonum punctatum — Smartweed, Water
Polygonum scandens — Buckwheat, Climbing False
Polygonum virginianum — Knotweed, Virginia
Polygonum viviparum — Bistort, Alpine
Polyodon spathula — Paddle-fish
Polyorchis penicillatus — Jellyfish, Red-eyed
Polypodium polypodioides — Fern, Resurrection
Polypodium virginianum — Fern, Rockcap
Polyporus squamosus — Fungus, Dryad's Saddle
Polyporus sulphureus — Mushroom, Chicken
Polypus bimaculatus — Octopus, Two-spotted
Polystichum acrostichoides — Fern, Christmas
Polystichum aculeatum — Fern, Shield (Prickly)
Polystichum andersonii — Fern, Sword
Polystichum braunii — Fern, Shield (Prickly)

Polystichum lonchitis — Fern, Holly
Polystichum munitum — Fern, Sword
Polystichum scopulinum — Fern, Shield (Prickly)
Polysticta stelleri — Eider, Steller's
Polytrichum commune — Moss, Hair-cap
Polytrichum juniperinum — Moss, Hair-cap
Pomaceus paludas — Snail, Apple
Pomatomus saltatrix — Bluefish
Pomolobus mediocris — Shad, Hickory
Pomoxis annularis — Crappie, White
Pomoxis nigromaculata — Crappie, Black
Poncirus trifoliata — Orange, Chinese or Japanese
Pontederia cordata — Pickerel Weed
Pooecetes gramincus — Sparrow, Vesper
Popilla japonica — Beetle, Japanese
Populus alba — Poplar, White
Populus balsamifera — Poplar, Balsam
Populus deltoides — Cottonwood, Eastern
Populus heterophylla — Cottonwood, Swamp
Populus nigra italica — Poplar, Lombardy
Populus tremula — Aspen, Quaking
Populus tremuloides — Aspen, Quaking
Populus trichocarpa — Cottonwood, Black
Poronotus triacanthus — Butterfish
Porphyrula martinica — Gallinule, Purple
Porthetria periscelidactyla — Moth, Gypsy
Portulaca grandiflora — Rose-moss
Portulaca oleracea — Purslane
Porzana carolina — Rail, Sora
Porzana flaviventer — Crake, Spotted
Porzana porzana — Crake, Spotted
Postelsia palmaeformis — Kelp, Sea Palm
Potamogeton crispus — Pondweed, Crisp or Curly
Potamogeton natans — Pondweed, Floating
Potentilla anserina — Silverweed
Potentilla argentea — Cinquefoil, Hoary or Silvery
Potentilla arguta — Cinquefoil, Tall
Potentilla canadensis — Cinquefoil, Dwarf or Common
Potentilla comarum — Cinquefoil, Marsh
Potentilla diversifolia — Cinquefoil, Mountain Meadow
Potentilla flabellifolia — Cinquefoil, Fringe-leaf
Potentilla fruticosa — Cinquefoil, Shrubby
Potentilla glandulosa — Cinquefoil, Sticky
Potentilla gracilis — Cinquefoil, Graceful
Potentilla norvegica — Cinquefoil, Norwegian
Potentilla palustris — Cinquefoil, Marsh
Potentilla recta — Cinquefoil, Rough-fruited or Sulphur
Potentilla simplex — Cinquefoil, Common

Potentilla tridentata — Cinquefoil, Three-toothed
Prenanthes alba — Rattlesnake-root
Prenanthes altissima — Lettuce, Tall White
Prenanthes racemosa — Lettuce, Smooth White
Prenanthes serpentaria — Lion's-foot
Prenanthes trifoliata — Gall-of-the-earth
Primula auricula — Bear's Ear
Primula denticulata — Primrose, Himalayan
Primula farinosa — Primrose, Bird's-eye
Primula japonica — Primrose, Japanese
Primula malacoides — Primrose, Fairy
Primula mistassinica — Primrose, Bird's-eye
Primula obconica — Primrose, Poison
Primula officinalis — Cowslip
Primula parryi — Primrose, Parry's
Primula polyanthus — Primrose, Polyanthus
Primula veris — Cowslip
Primula vulgaris — Primrose, Common
Prionace glauca — Shark, Blue
Prionotus carolinus — Searobin
Prionotus scitulus — Searobin
Priotelus temnurus — Trogon, Cuban
Pristis pectinatus — Sawfish
Proboscidea louisianica — Unicorn Plant
Procambarus blandingii acutus — Crayfish, Swamp
Procambarus clarki — Crayfish, Swamp
Procyon lotor — Raccoon
Progne chalybea — Martin, Gray-breasted
Progne subis — Martin, Purple
Prognichthys rondeleti — Flying-fish
Prosopium cylindraceum — Whitefish, Round
Prosopis grandulosa — Mesquite
Prosopis juliflora — Mesquite
Protea cynaroides — King Protea
Proteides clarus — Skipper, Silver-spotted
Protomyctophum thompsoni — Lanternfish
Protonotaria citrea — Warbler, Prothonotary
Protoparce quinquemaculata — Hornworm, Tomato or
    Moth, Sphinx or Hawk
Protoparce sexta — Hornworm, Tobacco
Protothaca staminea — Clam, Littleneck
Prunella grandiflora — Self-heal or Heal-all
Prunella laciniata — Self-heal or Heal-all
Prunella vulgaris — Self-heal or Heal-all, Common
Prunus sp. — Almond
Prunus americana — Plum, American Wild
Prunus angustifolia — Plum, Chickaw
Prunus armeniaca — Apricot

Prunus avium — Cherry, Sweet
Prunus cerasifer — Plum, Cherry
Prunus cerasus — Cherry, Sour
Prunus demissa — Cherry, Choke
Prunus domestica — Plum, Common
Prunus emarginata — Cherry, Bitter
Prunus hortulana — Plum, Wildgoose
Prunus laurocerasus — Laurel, Cherry
Prunus maritima — Plum, Cherry
Prunus mume — Apricot
Prunus munsoniana — Plum, Wildgoose
Prunus padus — Cherry, Bird or Pin
Prunus pennsylvanica — Cherry, Bird or Pin
Prunus persica — Peach
Prunus persica nectarina — Nectarine
Prunus sargentii — Cherry, Sargent's
Prunus serotina — Cherry, Black (Wild)
Prunus serrulata — Cherry, Flowering
Prunus spinosa — Blackthorn or Sloe
Prunus subhirtella — Cherry, Spring
Prunus virginiana — Cherry, Choke
Psaltriparus melanotis — Bushtit, Black-eared or Lloyd's
Psaltriparus minimus — Bushtit, Common
Pseudacris sp. — Frog, Chorus
Pseudaletia unipuncta — Armyworm
Pseudemys concinna — Turtle, Cooter or Slider
Pseudemys floridana — Turtle, Cooter or Slider
Pseudemys rubriventris — Turtle, Red-bellied
Pseudemys scripta — Turtle, Pond Slider
Pseudemys scripta elegans — Turtle, Red-eared
Pseudobranchus striatus — Siren, Lesser or Mud
Pseudococcus sp. — Bug, Mealy
Pseudohydnum gelatinosum — Mushroom, White Jelly
Pseudolarix amabilis — Larch, Golden
Pseudolucanus capreolus — Beetle, Stag
Pseudopleuronectes americanus — Flounder, Winter
Pseudorca crassidens — Whale, False Killer
Pseudosquilla bigelowi — Shrimp, Mantis
Pseudotriton montanus — Salamander, Mud
Pseudotriton ruber — Salamander, Red
Pseudotsuga menziesii — Fir, Douglas
Pseudotsuga taxifolia — Fir, Douglas
Pseudupeneus maculatus — Goatfish, Spotted
Psila rosae — Fly, Carrot Rust
Psilotum nudum — Fern, Whiskbroom
Psittirostra cantans — Finch, Laysan
Psolus chitonoides — Sea Cucumber, Creeping Pedal
Psolus phantapus — Sea Cucumber, Red

Psoralea argophylla — Silverleaf
Psoralea esculenta — Turnip, Prairie
Psoralea onobrychis — Sainfoin
Psoralea physodes — Tea, California
Psoralea psoraliodes — Snakeroot, Sampson's
Psoralea tenuiflora — Wild-alfalfa
Psylla pyricola — Psylla, Pear
Psylliodes affinis — Beetle, Flea
Ptelea trifolia — Hop-tree
Pteria nebulosa — Oyster, Pacific Pearl
Pteridium aquilinum — Fern, Brake or Bracken
Pteridium latiusculum — Fern, Brake or Bracken
Pteris pensylvanica — Fern, Ostrich
Pterocarya flaxinifolia — Wing-nut
Pterodroma cahow — Petrel, Bermuda
Pterodroma hasitata — Petrel, Black-capped
Pterodroma hypoleuca — Petrel, Bonin Island
Pteroglossus torquatus — Aracari, Collared
Pterois volitans — Lionfish
Pterophylla camellifolia — Katydid, Common True
Pterorytis foliata — Snail, Leafy Hornmouth
Pterospora andromeda — Pine Drops
Pterygophora californica — Kelp, Pompon
Ptilichthys goodei — Quillfish
Ptilimnium capillaceum — Bishop's-weed, Mock
Ptinus fur — Beetle, Spider
Ptychodera bahamensis — Worm, Acorn
Ptychoramphus aleuticus — Auklet, Cassin's
Puccinia graminis — Rust, Grain or Wheat
Pueraria lobata — Kudzu Vine
Pueraria thunbergiana — Kudzu Vine
Puffinus carneipes — Shearwater, Pale-footed
Puffinus creatopus — Shearwater, Pink-footed
Puffinus diomedea — Shearwater, Cory's
Puffinus gravis — Shearwater, Greater
Puffinus griseus — Shearwater, Sooty
Puffinus lherminieri — Shearwater, Audubon's
Puffinus opisthomelas — Shearwater, Manx
Puffinus pacificus — Shearwater, Pacific or Wedge-tailed
Puffinus puffinus — Shearwater, Manx
Puffinus tenuirostris — Shearwater, Slender-billed
Pugettia gracilis — Crab, Kelp
Pugettia productus — Crab, Kelp
Pulex irritans — Flea, Human
Pulsatrix perspicillata — Owl, Spectacled
Pulvinaria innumerabilis — Scale, Cottony-maple
Puncturella noachina — Limpet, Linnaeus' Keyhole
Punica granatum — Pomegranate

Purpura foliata — Snail, Leafy Hornmouth
Purpura patula — Purpura, Wide-mouthed
Purshia tridentata — Antelope Brush
Pycnanthemum flexuosum — Mountain-mint, Hairy
Pycnanthemum incanum — Mountain-mint, Hoary
Pycnanthemum muticum — Mountain-mint, Hairy
Pycnanthemum pilosum — Mountain-mint, Hairy
Pycnanthemum pycnanthemoides — Mountain-mint, Hoary
Pycnopodia helianthoides — Starfish, Sunflower
Pygosteus pungitius — Stickleback, Nine- or Ten-spined
Pylodictis olivaris — Catfish, Flathead
Pyracantha sp. — Firethorn
Pyrausta nubilalis — Borer, European Corn
Pyrocephalus rubinus — Flycatcher, Vermilion
Pyrola aphylla — Wintergreen, Leafless
Pyrola asarifolia — Wintergreen, Large
Pyrola chlorantha var. virens — Wintergreen, Greenish-flowered
Pyrola elliptica — Shinleaf
Pyrola minor — Wintergreen, Common
Pyrola rotundifolia — Wintergreen, Round-leaf
Pyrostegia ignea — Flame Vine
Pyrostegia venusta — Flame Vine
Pyrrhula pyrrhula — Bullfinch
Pyrrhuloxia cardinalis — Cardinal
Pyrrhuloxia sinuata — Pyrrhuloxia
Pyrus arbutifolia — Chokeberry, Red
Pyrus communis — Pear
Pyrus coronaria — Apple, Wild Crab
Pyrus diversifolia — Apple, Wild Crab
Pyrus fusca — Apple, Wild Crab
Pyrus malus — Apple
Pyrus melanocarpa — Chokeberry, Black
Pyura haustor — Sea Squirt, Warty
Pyxidanthera barbulata — Moss, Pixie

Q

Quamoclit coccinea — Morning Glory, Red
Quamoclit pennata — Cypress Vine
Quamoclit sloteri — Morning Glory, Red
Quercus agrifolia — Oak, Live (California)
Quercus alba — Oak, White
Quercus castaneifolia — Oak, Chestnut-leaved
Quercus coccinea — Oak, Scarlet
Quercus gambelii — Oak, Gambel's
Quercus garryana — Oak, Garry's

Quercus imbricaria — Oak, Shingle
Quercus kelloggi — Oak, Kellogg's
Quercus macrocarpa — Oak, Bur
Quercus nigra — Oak, Water
Quercus palustris — Oak, Pin
Quercus phellos — Oak, Willow
Quercus rubra — Oak, Red
Quercus suber — Oak, Cork
Quercus velutina — Oak, Black
Quercus virginiana — Oak, Live (Eastern)
Quincula lobata — Cherry, Ground
Quiscalus quiscula — Grackle, Common

R

Rachycentron canadum — Cobia
Rafinesquia neomexicana — Chicory, Desert
Raja binoculata — Skate, Big
Raja eglanteria — Skate, Brier or Clearnose
Raja erinacea — Skate, Little
Raja laevis — Skate, Barn-door
Raja ocellata — Skate, Big
Rallus elegans — Rail, King
Rallus limicola — Rail, Virginia
Rallus longirostris — Rail, Clapper
Ramphastos sulphuratus — Toucan, Keel-billed
Ramphocaenus melanurus — Gnatwren, Long-billed
Ramphocaenus rufiventris — Gnatwren, Long-billed
Rana areolata var. — Frog, Crawfish or Gopher
Rana aurora — Frog, Red-legged
Rana catesbiana — Bullfrog
Rana clamitans — Frog, Green or Bronze
Rana palustris — Frog, Pickerel
Rana pipiens — Frog, Leopard or Meadow
Rana pretiosa — Frog, Spotted
Rana septentrionalis — Frog, Mink
Rana sylvatica — Frog, Wood
Ranatra sp. — Water-scorpion
Rangifer arcticus — Caribou, Barren Ground
Rangifer caribou — Caribou, Woodland
Rangifer tarandus — Caribou, Greenland
Ranunculus acris — Buttercup, Common or Meadow
Ranunculus alismaefolius — Buttercup, Marsh or Swamp
Ranunculus aquaticus — Buttercup, Water
Ranunculus bulbosus — Buttercup, Bulbous
Ranunculus circinatus — Buttercup, Rigid-leaved
Ranunculus eschscholtzii — Buttercup, Alpine or
    Sub-alpine

Ranunculus fascicularis — Buttercup, Early
Ranunculus ficaria — Buttercup, Lesser Celandine
Ranunculus flammula — Buttercup, Lesser Spearwort
Ranunculus glaberrimus — Buttercup, Sagebrush
Ranunculus glacialis — Buttercup, Glacier
Ranunculus hispidus — Buttercup, Hairy or Hispid
Ranunculus hybrids — Ranunculus
Ranunculus longirostris — Buttercup, White-water
Ranunculus occidentalis — Buttercup, Western
Ranunculus recurvatus — Buttercup, Hooked
Ranunculus repens — Buttercup, Creeping
Ranunculus sceleratus — Buttercup, Cursed
Ranunculus septentrionalis — Buttercup, Marsh or
    Swamp
Raphanus raphanistrum — Radish, Wild
Raphanus sativus — Radish, Garden
Rasbora heteromorpha — Harlequinfish, Red
Ratibida columnaris — Cone-flower, Prairie
Ratibida pinnata — Cone-flower, Prairie
Rattus norvegicus — Rat, Norway
Rattus rattus — Rat, Black
Recurvirostra americana — Avocet, American
Regalecus glesne — Oar-fish
Regina sp. — Snake, Water
Regina septemvittata — Snake, Queen
Regulus calendula — Kinglet, Ruby-crowned
Regulus satrapa — Kinglet, Golden-crowned
Reithrodontomys sp. — Mouse, Harvest
Reseda odorata — Mignonette
Reticulitermes flavipes — Termite, Subterranean
Rhachianectes glaucus — Whale, Gray
Rhagoletis cingulata — Fly, Fruit (Cherry)
Rhagoletis pomonella — Maggot, Fly
Rhagovelia obesa — Water Strider, Small
Rhamnus caroliniana — Buckthorn, Carolina
Rhamnus purshiana — Buckthorn, Cascara
Rhamphocottus richardsoni — Sculpin, Grunt
Rheum rhaponticum — Rhubarb
Rhexia mariana — Meadow-beauty, Maryland
Rhexia virginica — Meadow-beauty, Virginia
Rhinanthus crista-galli — Yellow-rattle
Rhinanthus minor — Yellow-rattle
Rhincodon typus — Shark, Whale
Rhinecanthus aculeatus — Humuhumu-nukunuku-a-
    pua'a
Rhineura floridana — Lizard, Worm
Rhinobatos lentiginosus — Guitar-fish
Rhinobatos productus — Guitar-fish

Rhinobatos rhinobatus — Guitar-fish
Rhinocheilus lecontei — Snake, Long-nosed
Rhinoptynx clamator — Owl, Striped
Rhizopus stolonifer — Mold, Bread
Rhododendron sp. — Azalea Hybrids
Rhododendron sp. — Rhododendron Hybrids
Rhododendron albiflorum — Rhododendron, White-flowered
Rhododendron calendarlaceum — Azalea, Flame
Rhododendron canadensis — Rhodora
Rhododendron carolinianum — Rhododendron, Carolina
Rhododendron catawbiense — Rhododendron, Purple
Rhododendron lapponicum — Rosebay, Lapland
Rhododendron macrophyllum — Rhododendron, California
Rhododendron maximum — Laurel, Great
Rhododendron nudiflorum — Azalea, Pink
Rhododendron occidentale — Azalea, Western
Rhododendron roseum — Azalea, Mountain or Early
Rhododendron viscosa — Azalea, White
Rhododendron viscosum — Honeysuckle, Swamp
Rhodostethia rosea — Gull, Ross'
Rhodymenia palmata — Sea Kale
Rhus diversiloba — Poison Oak
Rhus glabra — Sumac, Smooth
Rhus radicans — Poison Ivy
Rhus typhina — Sumac, Staghorn
Rhus vernix — Sumac, Poison
Rhyacotriton olympicus — Salamander, Olympia
Rhynchites bicolor — Curculio, Rose
Rhynchophanes mccownii — Longspur, McCown's
Rhynchopsitta pachyrhyncha — Parrot, Thick-billed
Rhytipterna holerythra — Mourner, Rufous
Ribes aureum — Currant, Golden
Ribes divaricatum — Gooseberry, American
Ribes sanguineum — Currant, Red Flowering
Ribes viscosissimum — Currant, Sticky
Ribes sativum — Currant, Common or Garden
Riccia fluitans — Liverwort or Slender Riccia
Riccinus communis — Bean, Castor
Ricciocarpus natans — Liverwort or Purple-fringed Riccia
Richmondena cardinalis — Cardinal
Ridgwayia pinicola — Thrush, Aztec
Riparia riparia — Swallow, Bank
Rissa brevirostris — Kittiwake, Red-legged
Rissa tridactyla — Kittiwake, Black-legged

Robinia hispida — Locust, Bristly (tree)
Robinia pseudo-acacia — Locust, Black (tree)
Roccus americanus — Perch, White
Roccus chrysops — Bass, White
Roccus mississippiensis — Bass, Yellow
Roccus saxatilis — Bass, Striped
Romanzoffia stichensis — Mistmaidens
Romanzoffia suksdorfii — Mistmaidens
Romanzoffia unalaschcensis — Mistmaidens
Romerolagus diazi — Rabbit, Volcano
Romneya coulteri — Poppy, Matilija
Romneya trichocalyx — Poppy, Matilija
Rorippa islandica — Cress, Yellow
Rosa sp. — Rose Hybrids
Rosa carolina — Rose, Carolina
Rosa eglanteria — Sweetbrier
Rosa gymnocarpa — Rose, Dwarf
Rosa laevigata — Rose, Dwarf
Rosa moyesii — Rose, Moyes
Rosa nutkana — Rose, Nootka
Rosa palustris — Rose, Swamp
Rosa rubiginosa — Sweetbrier
Rosa setigera — Rose, Prairie
Rosmarinus officinalis — Rosemary
Rostanga pulchra — Nudibranch, Red
Rostrhamus sociabilis — Kite, Everglades or Snail
Rotala ramosior — Tooth-cup
Rozites caperata — Mushroom, Gypsy
Rubus allegheniensis — Blackberry
Rubus argutus — Blackberry, Highbush
Rubus caesuis — Dewberry
Rubus fruticosus — Blackberry
Rubus idaeus — Raspberry, Red
Rubus occidentalis — Raspberry, Wild Black
Rubus odoratus — Raspberry, Purple-flowering
Rubus parviflorus — Thimbleberry
Rubus pedatus — Raspberry, Creeping
Rubus spectabilis — Salmonberry
Rubus ulmifolius — Blackberry
Rubus ursinus — Blackberry
Rudbeckia amplexicaulis — Cone-flower, Clasping-leaf
Rudbeckia fulgida — Cone-flower, Orange
Rudbeckia hirta — Cone-flower
Rudbeckia laciniata — Cone-flower, Green-headed
Rudbeckia triloba — Cone-flower, Thin-leaved
Ruellia carolinensis — Ruellia
Ruellia ciliosa — Ruellia
Ruellia humilis — Ruellia

Ruellia macrantha — Ruellia
Ruellia strepens — Ruellia
Rumex acetosa — Sorrel, Common
Rumex acetosella — Sorrell, Sheep's
Rumex aquaticus — Dock, Water
Rumex crispus — Dock, Curly
Rumex hastatulus — Sorrel, Sheep's
Rumex maritimus — Dock, Golden
Rumex obtusifolius — Dock, Broad or Bitter
Rumex orbiculatus — Dock, Water
Rumex verticillatus — Dock, Water
Ruscus aculeatus — Broom, Butcher's
Russelia equisetiformis — Coral Plant
Russelia juncea — Coral Plant
Russula emetica — Russula, Pungent
Ruta graveolens — Rue, Common
Rynchops nigra — Skimmer, Black

S

Sabal palmetto — Palmetto, Cabbage
Sabatia angularis — Rose-pink
Sabatia campestris — Marsh-pink, Slender
Sabatia dodecandra — Marsh-pink, Large
Sabatia stellaris — Marsh-pink
Sabella pavonina — Worm, Peacock
Saccharomyces cervisiae — Yeast
Saccharum officinarum — Cane, Sugar
Saccoglossus sp. — Worm, Acorn
Sagina apetala — Pearlwort, Mossy
Sagina procumbens — Pearlwort, Mossy or Procumbent
Sagitta sp. — Worm, Arrow
Sagittaria cuneata — Arrowleaf
Sagittaria engelmanniana — Arrowhead, Engelmann's
Sagittaria falcata — Arrowhead, Scythe-fruited
Sagittaria graminea — Arrowhead, Grass-leaved
Sagittaria latifolia — Arrowhead, Broad-leaved
Saintpaulia ionantha — Violet, African
Saissetia oleae — Scale, Black
Salazaria mexicana — Sage, Bladder
Salicornia ambigua — Glasswort, Woody
Salicornia bigelovii — Glasswort, Dwarf
Salicornia fruiticosa — Glasswort, Red
Salicornia pacifica — Glasswort, Woody
Salicornia rubra — Glasswort, Red
Salicornia virginica — Glasswort, Woody
Salipiglossus sinuata — Painted Tongue
Salix alba — Willow, White

Salix arctica — Willow, Arctic
Salix babylonica — Willow, Weeping
Salix caprea — Willow, Pussy
Salix discolor — Willow, Pussy
Salix fragilis — Willow, Crack or Yellow
Salix interior — Willow, Sandbar
Salix nigra — Willow, Black
Salix nivalis — Willow, Snow
Salix viminalis — Willow, Basket or Osier
Salmo clarkii — Trout, Cut-throat
Salmo gairdneri — Trout, Rainbow
Salmo salar — Salmon, Atlantic
Salmo trutta — Trout, Brown
Salmo trutta lacustris — Trout, Lake
Salpinctes obsoletus — Wren, Rock
Salsola kali — Thistle, Russian
Salticus scenicus — Spider, Zebra
Salvadora hexalepsis — Snake, Patch-nosed
Salvadora lineata — Snake, Patch-nosed
Salvelinus aureolus — Sunapee
Salvelinus fontinalis — Trout, Brook or Speckled
Salvelinus malma — Trout, Dolly Varden
Salvelinus namaycush — Trout, Lake
Salvia azurea — Sage, Blue or Meadow
Salvia columbariae — Chia
Salvia elegans — Sage, Scarlet
Salvia greggii — Sage, Autumn
Salvia lyrata — Sage, Lyre-leaved
Salvia officinalis — Sage, Common
Salvia pratensis — Sage, Blue or Meadow
Salvia spathacea — Sage, Pitcher
Salvia splendens — Sage, Scarlet
Salvinia natans — Fern, Water
Sambucus canadensis — Elder, American or Black-
  berried
Sambucus cerulea — Elder, Blue
Sambucus glauca — Elder, Blue
Sambucus pubens — Elder, Red-berried
Sambucus racemosa — Elder, Red-berried
Samia cecropia — Moth, Cecropia
Sanguinaria canadensis — Bloodroot
Sanguisorba canadensis — Burnet, Canadian
Sanguisorba officinalis — Burnet, Great
Sanguisorba sitchensis — Burnet, Sitka
Sanicula arctopoides — Footsteps of Spring
Sanicula crassicaulis — Snakeroot, Western
Sanninoidea exitiosa — Borer, Peach Tree
Sansevieria trifasciata — Mother-in-law's Tongue

Santolina chamaecyparis — Lavender Cotton
Sanvitalia procumbens — Zinnia, Creeping
Saperda candida — Borer, Apple Tree (Round-headed)
Sapindus drummondi — Soapberry
Saponaria officinalis — Bouncing Bet
Saprolegnia sp. — Mold, Water
Sarcobatus vermiculatus — Greasewood
Sarcodes sanguines — Snowplant
Sarcophaga sp. — Fly, Flesh
Sarcoptes scabiei — Mite, Itch
Sarcoramphus papa — Vulture, King
Sarcoscypha coccinea — Fungus, Scarlet Cup
Sarda chiliensis — Bonito, Common
Sarda sarda — Bonito, Common
Sardinops caerulea — Sardine, California
Sargassum sp. — Sargassum
Sarracenia drummondi — Pitcher-plant, Purple Trumpet
Sarracenia flava — Trumpets
Sarracenia leucophylla — Pitcher-plant, Purple Trumpet
Sarracenia minor — Pitcher-plant, Hooded
Sarracenia purpurea — Pitcher-plant
Sassafras albidum — Sassafras
Satureia montana — Savory, Winter
Satureja douglassii — Yerba Buena
Satureja vulgaris — Basil, Wild
Sauromalus obesus — Chuckwalla
Saururus cernuus — Lizard's-tail
Saxidomus giganteus — Clam, Butter or Washington
Saxidomus nuttalli — Clam, Butter or Washington
Saxifraga mertensiana — Saxifrage, Merten's
Saxifraga oppositifolia — Saxifrage, Purple
Saxifraga pensylvanica — Saxifrage, Swamp
Saxifraga sarmentosa — Geranium, Strawberry
Saxifraga stolonifera — Geranium, Strawberry
Saxifraga umbrosa primuloides — London Pride
Saxifraga virginensis — Saxifrage, Early
Sayornis nigricans — Phoebe, Black
Sayornis phoebe — Phoebe, Eastern
Sayornis saya — Phoebe, Say's
Scabiosa atropurpurea — Pincushion Flower (annual)
Scabiosa caucasica — Pincushion Flower (perennial)
Scalopus aquaticus — Mole, Eastern
Scalopus latimanus — Mole, Eastern
Scapanus townsendii — Mole, Oregon or Townsend's
Scaphella junonia — Volute, Junonia
Scaphidura oryzivora — Cowbird, Giant
Scaphiopus bombifrons — Spadefoot, Plains
Scaphiopus couchii — Spadefoot, Couch's

Scaphiopus hammondi — Spadefoot, Western
Scaphiopus holbrooki — Spadefoot, Eastern
Scaphiopus intermontanus — Spadefoot, Great Basin
Scaphirhynchus platorhynchus — Sturgeon, Shovel-nose
Scardafella inca — Dove, Inca
Sceliphron cementarium — Wasp, Mud-dauber
Sceloporus clarkii — Lizard, Clark's Spiny
Sceloporus magister — Lizard, Desert Spiny
Sceloporus occidentalis — Lizard, Fence
Sceloporus olivaceus — Lizard, Texas Spiny
Sceloporus poinsetti — Lizard, Crevice Spiny
Sceloporus undulatus — Lizard, Fence
Schedonnardus paniculatus — Tumblegrass
Schefflera actinophylla — Umbrella Tree
Scheuchzeria palustris — Rush, Rannoch
Schiffornis turdinus — Manakin, Thrush-like
Schilbeodes sp. — Madtom
Schinus molle — Pepper-tree
Schistosoma mansoni — Fluke, Blood
Schistostega pennata — Moss, Luminous
Schizanthus hybrids — Butterfly Flower
Schizostylis coccinea — Lily, Kaffir
Schizothaerus nuttalli — Clam, Horse or Gaper
Schizura concinna — Caterpillar, Red-humped
Schrankia microphylla — Sensitive-brier
Schrankia uncinata — Sensitive-brier
Sciadopitys verticillata — Pine, Umbrella
Sciaenops ocellata — Bass, Channel or Red Drum
Scilla campanulata — Bluebell, Spanish
Scilla peruviana — Lily, Cuban
Scilla siberica — Squill, Siberian
Scirpus acutus — Bulrush, Great
Scirpus validus — Bulrush, Great
Scirtothrips citri — Thrips, Citrus
Sciurus aberti — Squirrel, Abert's
Sciurus carolinensis — Squirrel, Gray
Sciurus griseus — Squirrel, Gray
Sciurus kaibabensis — Squirrel, Kaibab
Sciurus niger — Squirrel, Fox
Scleroderma sp. — Puffball, Thick-skinned
Scoliopus bigelovii — Adder's-tongue, Fetid
Scoliopus hallii — Adder's-tongue, Fetid
Scolopendra morsitans — Centipede, Giant
Scolytus rugulosus — Borer, Shot-hole
Scomber colias — Mackerel, Chub
Scomber japonicus — Mackerel, Pacific
Scomber scombrus — Mackerel, Atlantic or Common
Scomberomorus cavalla — Mackerel, King

Scomberomorus maculatus — Mackerel, Spanish
Scomberomorus regalis — Cero
Scophthalmus maximus — Turbot
Scorpaena grandicornis — Scorpionfish
Scorpaena plumieri — Scorpionfish
Scorpaenichthys marmoratus — Cabezon
Scripus americanus — Rush, Shore
Scudderia sp. — Katydid, Fork-tailed Bush
Scutellaria antirrhinoides — Skullcap
Scutellaria epilobiifolia — Skullcap, Marsh
Scutellaria integrifolia — Skullcap, Larger
Scutellaria lateriflora — Skullcap, Mad-dog
Scutellaria serrata — Skullcap, Showy
Scutellaria tuberosa — Skullcap
Scutigera coleoptrata — Centipede, House
Scypha coronata — Sponge, Tufted
Scypha lingua — Sponge, Tufted
Scytosiphon lomentaria — Seaweed, Whip-tube
Sebastes alutus — Perch, Ocean
Sebastes caurinus — Rockfish, Copper
Sebastes marinus — Perch, Ocean
Sebastes melanops — Rockfish, Black
Sebastes miniatus — Rockfish, Vermilion
Sebastes mystinus — Rockfish, Blue
Sebastes nigrocinctus — Rockfish, Tiger
Sebastodes caurinus — Rockfish, Copper
Sebastodes melanops — Rockfish, Black
Sebastodes miniatus — Rockfish, Vermilion
Sebastodes mystinus — Rockfish, Blue
Sebastodes nigrocinctus — Rockfish, Tiger
Secale cereale — Rye, Annual
Sedum acre — Stonecrop, Mossy
Sedum oreganum — Stonecrop, Oregon
Sedum pulchellum — Stonecrop, Pink
Sedum purpureum — Live-forever
Sedum rhodanthum — Rose Crown
Sedum rosea — Roseroot
Sedum spathulifolium — Stonecrop, Broad-leaved
Sedum spectabile — Stonecrop, Showy
Sedum stenopetalum — Stonecrop, Narrow-petaled
Sedum telephioides — Live-forever
Sedum telephium — Live-forever
Sedum ternatum — Stonecrop, Wild
Seiurus aurocapillus — Ovenbird
Seiurus motacilla — Waterthrush, Louisiana
Seiurus noveboracensis — Waterthrush, Northern
Selaginella sp. — Clubmoss, Little
Selasphorus platycercus — Hummingbird, Broad-tailed

Selasphorus rufus — Hummingbird, Rufous
Selasphorus sasin — Hummingbird, Allen's
Selene vomer — Lookdown
Selenicereus grandiflorus — Cactus, Night-flowering
  Cereus
Semotilus atromaculatus — Chub, Creek
Sempervivum tectorum — Houseleek
Senecio aureus — Ragwort, Golden
Senecio cineraria — Dusty Miller
Senecio confusus — Flame Vine, Mexican
Senecio glabellus — Butterweed
Senecio jacobea — Ragwort, Tansy
Senecio neowebsteri — Butterweed
Senecio vulgaris — Groundsel, Common
Senecio websteri — Butterweed
Sequoia gigantea — Redwood, Giant
Sequoia sempervirens — Redwood, Coast
Serinus canarius — Canary, Yellow
Serinus flaviventris — Canary, Yellow
Seriola dorsalis — Amberjack
Seriola dumerili — Amberjack, Greater
Seriola zonata — Amberjack
Sesuvium maritimum — Sea-purslane
Sesuvium verrucosum — Sea-purslane
Setaria sp. — Brittle-grass
Setophaga picta — Redstart, Painted
Setophaga ruticilla — Redstart, American
Shepherdia canadensis — Buffalo Berry
Sherardia arvensis — Field-madder, Blue
Shortia galacifolia — Oconee Bells
Sialia currocoides — Bluebird, Mountain
Sialia mexicana — Bluebird, Western
Sialia sialis — Bluebird, Eastern
Sibbaldia procumbens — Cinquefoil, Least
Sibbaldus musculus — Whale, Blue
Sicalis luteola — Yellow-finch, Grassland
Sicyos angulatus — Cucumber Bur
Sida spinosa — Mallow, Prickly
Sidalcea campestris — Hollyhock, Wild
Sidalcea hendersoni — Hollyhock, Wild
Sidalcea malvaeflora — Checkerbloom
Sidalcea oregona — Hollyhock, Wild
Sidalcea virgata — Hollyhock, Wild
Siganus rivulatus — Rabbitfish
Sigmodon hispidus — Rat, Cotton
Silene acaulis — Campion, Moss
Silene antirrhinum — Catchfly, Sleepy
Silene armeria — Catchfly, Sweet William

Silene californica — Pink, Indian
Silene caroliniana — Pink, Wild
Silene cucubalus — Campion, Bladder
Silene gallica — Catchfly, French or Small-flowered
Silene laciniata — Pink, Indian
Silene latifolia — Campion, Bladder
Silene maritima — Campion, Sea
Silene noctiflora — Campion, Night-scented
Silene rotundifolia — Catchfly, Round-leaved
Silene stellata — Campion, Starry
Silene virginica — Pink, Fire
Silene vulgaris — Campion, Bladder
Siliqua costata — Clam, Atlantic Razor
Siliqua patula — Clam, Pacific Razor
Silphium laciniatum — Compass-plant
Silphium perfoliatum — Cup-plant
Silybum marinum — Thistle, Milk
Simulium sp. — Fly, Black
Sinapis alba — Mustard, White
Sinningia speciosa — Gloxinia
Sipunculus nudus — Worm, Peanut
Siredon mexicanum — Axolotl
Siren intermedia — Siren, Lesser or Mud
Siren lacertina — Siren, Greater
Sistrurus catenatus — Rattlesnake, Massasauga
Sistrurus miliarius — Rattlesnake, Pygmy
Sisymbrium altissimum — Mustard, Tumble
Sisymbrium irio — Rocket, London
Sisymbrium officinale — Mustard, Hedge
Sisyrinchium angustifolium — Blue-eyed Grass, Narrow-
leaved
Sisyrinchium californicum — Yellow-eyed Grass (or
Golden-eyed)
Sisyrinchium campestre — Blue-eyed Grass
Sisyrinchium douglasii — Grass Widows
Sisyrinchium idahoense — Blue-eyed Grass
Sitona hispidula — Curculio, Clover Root
Sitophilus granarius — Weevil, Granary
Sitophilus oryzae — Weevil, Rice
Sitta canadensis — Nuthatch, Red-breasted
Sitta carolinensis — Nuthatch, White-breasted
Sitta pusilla — Nuthatch, Brown-headed
Sitta pygmaea — Nuthatch, Pygmy
Sium cicutaefolium — Water-parsnip
Sium latifolium — Water-parsnip
Sium suave — Water-parsnip
Skimmia japonica — Skimmia
Smilacina racemosa — Solomon's Seal, False

Smilacina stellata — Solomon's Seal, Starry False
Smilax herbacea — Carrion Flower
Smilax hispida — Greenbrier
Smilax laurifolia — Greenbrier
Smilax rotundifolia — Greenbrier
Solandra sp. — Cup-of-gold
Solanum carolinense — Horse-nettle
Solanum dulcamara — Nightshade, Bitter
Solanum melongena — Eggplant
Solanum nigrum — Nightshade, Black
Solanum pseudocapsicum — Cherry, Jerusalem
Solanum rostratum — Buffalo Berry
Solanum tuberosum — Potato, Irish
Solanum verbascifolium — Nightshade, Black
Solaster sp. — Starfish, Sun
Solen sicarius — Clam, Pacific Jackknife
Solen viridis — Clam, Green Razor
Solenodon paradoxus — Solenodon, Haitian or
Hispaniolan
Solenopsis sp. — Ant, Fire
Solidago altissima — Goldenrod, Tall
Solidago arguta — Goldenrod, Sharp or Cut-leaved
Solidago bicolor — Goldenrod, White or Silverrod
Solidago caesia — Goldenrod, Blue-stemmed
Solidago californica — Goldenrod, California
Solidago canadensis — Goldenrod, Canada
Solidago cutleri — Goldenrod, Alpine
Solidago decumbens — Goldenrod, Dwarf
Solidago erecta — Goldenrod, Erect or Slender
Solidago fistulosa — Goldenrod, Pine-barren
Solidago flexicaulis — Goldenrod, Broad-leaved or
Zigzag
Solidago gigantea — Goldenrod, Late
Solidago graminifolia — Goldenrod, Fragrant or Grass-
leaved
Solidago hispida — Goldenrod, Hairy
Solidago juncea — Goldenrod, Early
Solidago macrophylla — Goldenrod, Large-leaved
Solidago nemoralis — Goldenrod, Gray
Solidago odora — Goldenrod, Sweet
Solidago patula — Goldenrod, Rough-leaved
Solidago puberula — Goldenrod, Downy
Solidago rigida — Goldenrod, Hard-leaved or Stiff
Solidago rugosa — Goldenrod, Rough-stemmed
Solidago sempervirens — Goldenrod, Seaside
Solidago speciosa — Goldenrod, Showy
Solidago squarrosa — Goldenrod, Stout
Solidago stricta — Goldenrod, Wandlike

Solidago tenuifolia — Goldenrod, Slender Fragrant
Solidago uliginosa — Goldenrod, Bog
Solidago ulmifolia — Goldenrod, Elm-leaved
Somateria mollissima — Eider, Common or American
Somateria spectabilis — Eider, King
Somniosus microcephalus — Shark, Greenland
Sonchus arvensis — Sow-thistle, Field
Sonchus asper — Sow-thistle, Spiny-leaved
Sonchus oleraceus — Sow-thistle, Common
Sonora episcopa — Snake, Ground
Sonora semiannulata — Snake, Ground
Sophora japonica — Pagoda Tree
Sorbus americana — Mountain-ash, American
Sorbus arbutifolia — Chokeberry, Red
Sorbus aucuparia — Mountain-ash, European
Sorbus scopulina — Mountain-ash, Western
Sorbus sitchensis — Mountain-ash, Sitka
Sorex arcticus — Shrew, Arctic
Sorex cinereus — Shrew, Masked (Common)
Sorex merriami — Shrew, Merriam
Sorex palustris — Shrew, Water
Sorghastrum nutans — Indiangrass
Sorghum halepensis — Grass, Johnson
Sorghum sudanense — Sudangrass
Sorghum vulgare var. saccharatum — Sorghum, Sweet
Sparassis crispa — Mushroom, Cauliflower
Sparassis radicata — Mushroom, Cauliflower
Sparganium sp. — Bur-reed
Spartina pectinata — Grass, Cord
Spartium junceum — Broom, Spanish
Spathiphyllum blandum — White Sails
Spathiphyllum clevelandii — White Sails
Spathiphyllum wallisii — White Sails
Spathodea campanulata — Tulip-tree, African
Spatula clypeata — Shoveler
Specularia perfoliata — Venus' Looking-glass
Specularia speculum — Venus' Looking-glass
Speotyto cunicularia — Owl, Burrowing
Spergula arvensis — Spurry, Corn
Spergularia marginata — Sand-spurry, Sea
Spergularia macrotheca — Sand-spurry
Spergularia marina — Sand-spurry, Sea
Spergularia rubra — Sand-spurry, Pink
Spermophilus columbianus — Squirrel, Columbian Ground
Spermophilus lateralis — Squirrel, Golden-mantled Ground
Spermophilus richardsoni — Squirrel, Richardson's Ground

Sphaeralcea ambigua — Mallow, Desert
Sphaeralcea coccinea — Mallow, Globe
Sphaeralcea davidsonii — Mallow, Globe
Sphaeroides sp. — Puffer-fish
Sphagnum palustre — Sphagnum, Boat-leaved
Sphecius speciosus — Wasp, Cicada-killer
Sphenophorus maidis — Billbug
Sphyraena argentea — Barracuda, Pacific
Sphyraena barracuda — Barracuda, Great
Sphyrapicus ruber — Sapsucker, Red-breasted
Sphyrapicus throideus — Sapsucker, Williamson's
Sphyrapicus varius — Sapsucker, Yellow-bellied
Sphyrna mokarran — Shark, Hammerhead
Sphyrna zygaena — Shark, Hammerhead
Spigelia marilandica — Pink, Indian
Spilogale putorius — Skunk, Spotted
Spinacia oleracea — Spinach
Spinus laurencei — Goldfinch, Lawrence's
Spinus pinus — Siskin, Northern or Pine
Spinus psaltria — Goldfinch, Arkansas or Lesser
Spinus tristis — Goldfinch, American
Spiraea sp. — Spiraea Hybrids
Spiraea densiflora — Spiraea, Mountain
Spiraea douglasii — Hardhack
Spiraea latifolia — Meadowsweet
Spiraea pyramidata — Hardhack
Spiraea tomentosa — Hardhack
Spiranthes cernua — Ladies'-tresses, Nodding
Spiranthes gracilis — Ladies'-tresses, Slender
Spiranthes lucida — Ladies'-tresses, Wide-leaved
Spiranthes romanzoffiana — Ladies'-tresses, Hooded
Spiranthes vernalis — Ladies'-tresses, Spring or Early
Spirobis borealis — Worm, Coiled
Spirula spirula — Squid, Ram's-horn
Spisula solidissima — Clam, Atlantic Surf
Spiza americana — Dickcissel
Spizaetus ornatus — Hawk-eagle, Ornate
Spizella arborea — Sparrow, Tree
Spizella atrogularis — Sparrow, Black-chinned
Spizella breweri — Sparrow, Brewer's
Spizella pallida — Sparrow, Clay-colored
Spizella passerina — Sparrow, Chipping
Spizella pusilla — Sparrow, Field
Spizella wortheni — Sparrow, Worthen's
Spondylus americanus — Oyster, Atlantic Thorny
Spongilla sp. — Sponge, Fresh-water
Sporophila americana — Seedeater, Variable
Sporophila minuta — Seedeater, Minute

Sporophila surita — Seedeater, Variable
Sporophila torqueola — Seedeater, White-collared
Spraguea umbellatum — Pussy Paws
Sprekelia formosissima — Lily, Aztec
Squalus acanthias — Dogfish, Spiny
Squatarola squatarola — Plover, Black-bellied
Squilla empusa — Shrimp, Mantis
Stachys arvensis — Woundwort, Field
Stachys bullata — Hedge-nettle
Stachys colleyae — Hedge-nettle
Stachys germanica — Woundwort, Field
Stachys palustris — Hedge-nettle, Marsh
Stachys tenuifolia — Hedge-nettle, Smooth
Stagmomantis carolina — Mantid, Carolina
Stanleya pinnata — Prince's Plume
Staphylea colchica — Bladder-nut
Staphylea pinnata — Bladder-nut
Staphylea trifolia — Bladder-nut
Steatornis caripensis — Oilbird
Steganopus tricolor — Phalarope, Wilson's
Steironema ciliatum — Loosestrife, Fringed
Steironema lanceolatum — Loosestrife, Lance-leaved
Steironema quadrifolia — Loosestrife, Whorled
Stelgidopteryx ruficollis — Swallow, Rough-winged
Stellaria graminea — Stitchwort
Stellaria longifolia — Chickweed, Long-leaved
Stellaria media — Chickweed, Common
Stellaria pubera — Chickweed, Star
Stenanthium gramineum — Featherbells
Steneotarsonemus pallidus — Mite, Cyclamen
Steno bredanensis — Dolphin, Rough-toothed
Stenocara eburnea — Beetle, Tenebrionid or Darkling
Stenocarpus sinuatus — Firewheel Tree
Stenorhynchus seticornus — Crab, Spider
Stenotomus chrysops — Scup
Stepelia gigantea — Carrion Flower
Stephanitis rhododendri — Bug, Lace
Stephanitis pyrioides — Bug, Lace
Stephanotis floribunda — Stephanotis
Stercorarius longicaudus — Jaeger, Long-tailed
Stercorarius parasiticus — Jaeger, Parasitic
Stercorarius pomarinus — Jaeger, Pomarine
Stercorarius skua — Skua
Stereochilus marginatus — Salamander, Many-lined
Stereolepis gigas — Sea Bass, Giant
Sterna albifrons — Tern, Least or Little
Sterna aleutica — Tern, Aleutian
Sterna anaethetus — Tern, Bridled

Sterna dougallii — Tern, Roseate
Sterna forsteri — Tern, Forster's
Sterna fuscata — Tern, Sooty
Sterna hirundo — Tern, Common
Sterna maximus — Tern, Royal
Sterna paradisaea — Tern, Arctic
Sterna sandwichensis — Tern, Sandwich (Cabot's)
Sternbergia lutea — Crocus, Autumn
Sternotherus odoratus — Turtle, Musk (Stinkpot)
Stewartia ovata — Camellia, Mountain
Stewartia pseudo-camellia — Camellia, Mountain
Sthenorytis pernobilis — Wentletrap, Noble
Stichopus californicus — Sea Cucumber, Large Red
Stictocephala sp. — Treehopper
Stilosoma extenuatum — Snake, Short-tailed
Stipa pennata — Grass, Feather
Stipa spartea — Porcupine-grass
Stizostedion canadense — Sauger
Stizostedion vitreum — Walleye
Stokesia laevis — Aster, Stokes
Stomoxys calcitrans — Fly, Stable (Biting)
Storeria dekayi var. — Snake, Brown (De Kay's)
Storeria occipitomaculata — Snake, Red-bellied
Stratiomys sp. — Fly, Soldier
Strelitzia reginae — Bird-of-paradise Flower
Streptanthus inflatus — Desert Candle
Streptocarpus hybrids — Primrose, Cape
Streptopelia chinensis — Dove, Spotted or Lace-necked
Streptoprocne semicollaris — Swift, White-naped
Streptopus amplexcaulis — Twisted-stalk, White
Streptopus roseus — Twisted-stalk, Pink
Streptosolen jamesonii — Browallia, Orange
Strix nebulosa — Owl, Great Gray
Strix occidentalis — Owl, Spotted
Strix varia — Owl, Barred
Strobilomyces floccopus — Fungus, Cone-like or Pine-cone
Strobilomyces strobilaceus — Fungus, Cone-like or Pine-cone
Strombus alatus — Conch, Fighting (Florida)
Strombus gigas — Conch, Queen
Strombus pugilis — Conch, Fighting (West Indian)
Strongylocentrotus drobachiensis — Sea Urchin, Green
Strongylocentrotus franciscanus — Sea Urchin, Giant Red
Strongylocentrotus purpuratus — Sea Urchin, Purple
Stropharia aeruginosa — Verdigris
Struthiopteris spicant — Fern, Deer

Strymon melinus — Butterfly, Gray Hairstreak
Sturnella magna — Meadowlark, Eastern
Sturnella neglecta — Meadowlark, Western
Sturnus vulgaris — Starling, Common
Stylatula elongata — Sea Pen
Stylosanthes biflora — Pencil-flower
Styrax americana — Snowbell
Styrax japonica — Snowbell
Suaeda maritima — Sea-blite
Subularia aquatica — Awlwort
Suillus grevillei — Boletus, Elegant
Sula bassana — Gannet
Sula dactylatra — Booby, Masked
Sula leucogaster — Booby, Brown
Sula nebouxi — Booby, Blue-footed
Sula sula — Booby, Red-footed
Surnia ulula — Owl, Hawk
Surnia ulula caparoch — Owl, Hawk
Sus scrofa — Boar, Wild
Sus scrofa domestica — Hog, Domestic
Swainsonia galegifolia — Pea, Darling
Swertia perennis — Felwort, Marsh
Swertia radiata — Deer's-tongue
Sylvilagus aquaticus — Rabbit, Swamp
Sylvilagus auduboni — Rabbit, Cottontail
Sylvilagus backmani — Rabbit, Brush
Sylvilagus floridanus — Rabbit, Cottontail
Sylvilagus palustris — Rabbit, Marsh
Sylvilagus transitionalis — Rabbit, Cottontail
Symphoricarpos albus — Snowberry
Symphoricarpos orbiculatus — Coralberry
Symphoricarpos rivularis — Snowberry
Symphytum officinale — Comfrey, Common
Symphytum peregrinum — Comfrey, Common
Symploca tinctoria — Sweetleaf
Symplocarpus foetidus — Skunk Cabbage, Eastern
Synaptomys borealis — Lemming, Bog
Synaptomys cooperi — Lemming, Bog
Syngnathus sp. — Pipefish
Synthliboramphus antiquum — Murrelet, Ancient
Synthyris reniformis — Grouse Flower
Synthyris rotundifolia — Grouse Flower
Syringa vulgaris — Lilac, Common
Syrphus sp. — Fly, Flower or Hover
Systena blanda — Beetle, Flea

T

Tabanus atratus — Fly, Horse

Tabanus bovinus — Fly, Horse
Tabanus bromius — Fly, Horse
Tachycineta albilinea — Swallow, Mangrove
Tachycineta bicolor — Swallow, Tree
Tachycineta thalassina — Swallow, Violet-green
Tachyterellus quadrigibbus — Curculio, Apple
Tadarida brasiliensis — Bat, Mexican Free-tailed
Tadarida mexicana — Bat, Mexican Free-tailed
Taenia sp. — Tapeworm
Taeniothrips simplex — Thrips, Gladiolus
Tagelus divisus — Clam, Purplish Razor
Tagelus gibbus — Clam, Atlantic Jackknife or Razor
Tagelus plebeius — Clam, Stout Razor
Tagetes erecta — Marigold, African
Tagetes patula — Marigold, French
Talinum teretifolium — Fameflower
Talorchestia longicornis — Flea, Sand (Long-horned)
Tamarix parvifolia — Tamarisk (or Flowering Cypress)
Tamias striatus — Chipmunk, Eastern
Tamiasciurus douglasii — Squirrel, Douglas
Tamiasciurus hudsonicus — Squirrel, Red
Tanacetum huronense — Tansy, Huron
Tanacetum vulgare — Tansy, Common
Tangavius aeneus — Cowbird, Bronzed
Tantilla gracilis — Snake, Flat-headed
Tantilla nigriceps — Snake, Black-headed
Tapinoma sessile — Ant, House
Tapirus bairdii — Tapir, Baird's
Taraba major — Antshrike, Great
Taraxacum officinale — Dandelion, Common
Taricha rivularis — Newt, Red-bellied
Taricha torosa — Newt, California
Tarpon atlanticus — Tarpon, Atlantic
Tautoga onitis — Tautog
Taxidea taxus — Badger
Taxodium distichum — Cypress, Bald or Swamp
Taxus baccata — Yew, European
Taxus brevifolia — Yew, Western
Taxus canadensis — Yew, Eastern
Tayassu albirostris — Peccary, White-lipped
Tayassu pecari — Peccary, White-lipped
Tayassu tajucu — Peccary, Collared
Tayra barbara — Tayra
Tecoma stans — Elder, Yellow
Teesdalia nudicaulis — Cress, Shepherd's
Tegenaria derhami — Spider, Sheetweb
Tegenaria domestica — Spider, Sheetweb
Tegeticula alba — Moth, Yucca
Tegeticula yuccasella — Moth, Yucca

Tegula funebralis — Turban Shell, Black
Telea polyphemus — Moth, Polyphemus
Telia crassicornis — Sea Anemone, Dahlia
Telia felina — Sea Anemone, Dahlia
Tellima grandiflora — Fringe Cup
Tellina agilis — Tellin, Northern Dwarf
Tellina bodegensis — Tellin, Bodega
Tellina interrupta — Tellin, Speckled
Tellina listeri — Tellin, Speckled
Tellina radiata — Tellin, Sunrise
Telmatodytes palustris — Wren, Long-billed Marsh
Tendipes decorus — Midge
Tenebrio molitor — Beetle, Mealworm, or Mealworm
Tenebrio obscurus — Mealworm
Tephrosia virginiana — Goat's-rue
Terebra dislocata — Auger, Atlantic
Terebra strigata — Auger, Zebra
Terebratalia transversa — Lampshell
Terebratulina sp. — Lampshell
Teredo navalis — Shipworm
Teredo norvegica — Shipworm
Terrapene carolina — Turtle, Box (Eastern)
Terrapene ornata — Turtle, Ornate (Western) Box
Tetranychus telarius — Mite, Spider
Tetrapturus albidus — Marlin, White
Teucrium canadense — Germander
Teucrium chamaedrys — Germander
Thais emarginata — Dogwinkle, Emarginate
Thais lamellosa — Dogwinkle, Frilled
Thais lapillus — Dogwinkle, Atlantic
Thalarctos maritimus — Bear, Polar
Thalasseus elegans — Tern, Elegant
Thalasseus maximus — Tern, Royal
Thalasseus sandvicensis — Tern, Sandwich (Cabot's)
Thalassoma bifasciatum — Wrasse, Bluehead
Thalassoma duperreyi — Wrasse, Saddle
Thaleichthys pacificus — Eulachon
Thalictrum alpinum — Meadow-rue, Western
Thalictrum aquilegifolium — Meadow-rue, Great
Thalictrum dasycarpum — Meadow-rue, Purple
Thalictrum dioicum — Meadow-rue, Early
Thalictrum dipterocarpum — Meadow-rue, Lavender
Thalictrum lucidum — Meadow-rue, Great
Thalictrum occidentales — Meadow-rue, Western
Thalictrum polygamum — Meadow-rue, Tall
Thalurania furcata — Wood-nymph
Thalurania townsendi — Wood-nymph
Thamnistes anabatinus — Antshrike, Russet or Tawny

Thamnophis sp. — Snake, Garter
Thamnophis sauritus — Snake, Ribbon
Thelepus crispus — Worm, Shell-binder
Thelypodium laciniatum — Thelypodium
Thelypteris hexagonoptera — Fern, Beech
Thelypteris noveboracensis — Fern, New York
Thelypteris palustris — Fern, Marsh
Thelypteris phegopteris — Fern, Beech
Theobroma cacao — Cacao
Theragra chalcogramma — Pollack or Pollock
Theridion tepidariorum — Spider, House
Thermopsis caroliniana — Pea, Bush
Thermopsis divaricarpa — Pea, Golden
Thermopsis macrophylla — Lupine, False
Thermopsis mollis — Pea, Bush
Thermopsis pinetorum — Pea, Golden
Thermopsis rhombifolia — Pea, Golden
Thermopsis villosa — Pea, Bush
Theromyzon tesselatum — Leech, Duck
Thlaspi arvense — Pennycress, Field
Thlaspi rotundifolium — Pennycress, Field
Thomomys sp. — Gopher, Western Pocket
Thrips tabaci — Thrips, Onion
Thryomanes bewicki — Wren, Bewick's
Thryothorus felix — Wren, Happy
Thryothorus ludovicianus — Wren, Carolina
Thryothorus pleurostictus — Wren, Banded
Thryothorus sinaloa — Wren, Bar-vented
Thuidium delicatulum — Moss, Common Delicate Fern
Thuja occidentalis — Cedar, Northern White
Thuja orientalis — Arborvitae, Chinese
Thuja plicata — Cedar, Western Red or Giant
Thunnus alalunga — Albacore
Thunnus albacores — Tuna, Yellowfin
Thunnus atlanticus — Tuna, Atlantic Blackfin or Blade-
fin
Thunnus thynnus — Tuna, Bluefin
Thunbergia alata — Black-eyed Susan
Thunbergia erecta — Black-eyed Susan
Thunbergia grandiflora — Black-eyed Susan
Thymallus arcticus — Grayling
Thymallus montanus — Grayling
Thymus serpyllum — Thyme
Thyridopteryx ephemeraeformis — Bagworm
Thysanocarpus curvipes — Lacepod
Tiarella cordifolia — Foamflower
Tiarella laciniata — Mitrewort, False
Tiarella unifoliata — Mitrewort, False

Tibouchina urvilleana — Glory Bush
Tigridia pavonia — Tiger Flower
Tilia sp. — Lime
Tilia americana — Basswood, American
Tillandsia cyanea — Tillandsia
Tillandsia fasciculata — Tillandsia
Tillandsia usneoides — Moss, Spanish
Tinamus major — Tinamou, Great
Tinca tinca — Tench, Golden
Tinea pellionella — Moth, Clothes (casemaking)
Tineola bisselliella — Moth, Clothes (webbing)
Tiphia sp. — Wasp, Tiphiid
Tipula sp. — Fly, Crane
Tipula maxima — Daddy-long-legs
Tipula oleracea — Daddy-long-legs
Tithonia rotundifolia — Sunflower, Mexican
Tityra semifasciata — Tityra, Masked
Tivela stultorum — Clam, Pismo
Todus mexicanus — Tody, Puerto Rican
Todus multicolor — Tody, Cuban
Todus todus — Tody, Jamaican
Tofieldia glutinosa — Asphodel, False
Tofieldia racemosa — Asphodel, False
Tonicella lineata — Chiton, Lined
Toredo diegensis — Shipworm
Torenia fournieri — Wishbone Flower
Torilis japonica — Hedge-parsley, Upright
Torpedo californica — Ray, Electric
Torpedo marmoratus — Ray, Electric
Torpedo nobiliana — Ray, Electric or Torpedo
Torpedo torpedo — Ray, Electric or Torpedo
Torreya californica — Nutmeg, California (tree)
Totanus flavipes — Yellowlegs, Lesser
Totanus melanoleucus — Yellowlegs, Greater
Tolmiea menziesii — Youth-on-age
Tolomerus notatus — Fly, Robber
Townsendia annua — Townsendia
Townsendia exscapa — Easter-daisy
Townsendia florifer — Townsendia
Townsendia incana — Townsendia
Toxicondendron vernix — Sumac, Poison
Toxostoma bendirei — Thrasher, Bendire's
Toxostoma cinereum — Thrasher, Gray
Toxostoma curvirostre — Thrasher, Curve-billed
Toxostoma dorsale — Thrasher, Crissal
Toxostoma lecontei — Thrasher, Le Conte's
Toxostoma longirostre — Thrasher, Long-billed
Toxostoma ocellatum — Thrasher, Oscellated

Toxostoma redivivum — Thrasher, California
Toxostoma rufum — Thrasher, Brown
Toxotes jaculatrix — Archer Fish
Trachelospermum jasmanoides — Jasmine, Confederate
Trachinotus falcatus — Pompano, Round
Trachinotus carolinus — Pompano, Common
Trachurus symmetricus — Jack Mackerel, Pacific
Trachurus trachurus — Scad
Tragopogon dubius — Salsify, Yellow
Tragopogon porrifolius — Salsify, Purple
Tragopogon pratensis — Goat's-beard, Yellow
Trapa natans — Water-chestnut
Trautvetteria caroliniensis — Bugbane, False
Trautvetteria grandis — Bugbane, False
Tremex columba — Tremex, Pigeon
Tresus nuttalli — Clam, Horse or Gaper
Triakis semifasciata — Shark, Leopard
Triatoma sanguisuga — Bug, Blood-sucking Conenose
Tribolium confusum — Beetle, Confused Flour
Tribulus terrestris — Caltrops, Land
Trichechus manatus — Manatee
Trichiurus lepturus — Cutlass-fish
Trichocereus candicans — Cactus, Quisco
Trichocereus chiloensis — Cactus, Quisco
Trichodectes canis — Louse, Dog
Trichodes apivorus — Beetle, Checkered
Trichodon trichodon — Sandfish
Trichogramma minutum — Wasp, Trichogrammid
Tricholoma saponaceum — Tricholoma, Soap-scented
Tricholoma sulphureum — Tricholoma, Narcissus
Trichomanes boschianum — Fern, Filmy
Trichomanes krausii — Fern, Filmy
Trichomanes radicans — Fern, Filmy
Trichotropis cancellata — Snail, Checkered Hairy
Trichostema dichotomum — Bluecurls
Trientalis borealis — Star Flower
Trientalis europaea — Star Flower
Trientalis latifolia — Star Flower
Trifolium agrarium — Clover, Hop
Trifolium arvense — Clover, Hare's-foot or Rabbit's-foot
Trifolium campestre — Clover, Hop
Trifolium dubium — Clover, Lesser Yellow
Trifolium fragiferum — Clover, Strawberry
Trifolium hybridum — Clover, Alsike
Trifolium incarnatum — Clover, Crimson
Trifolium medium — Clover, Zigzag
Trifolium pratense — Clover, Red
Trifolium procumbens — Clover, Hop

Trifolium repens — Clover, White
Trifolium thompsoni — Clover, Thompson's
Triglochin palustris — Arrow-grass, Marsh
Triglochin maritima — Arrow-grass, Seaside
Trillium catesbaei — Trillium, Prairie
Trillium cernuum — Trillium, Nodding
Trillium chloropetalum — Trillium, Giant
Trillium erectum — Trillium, Red
Trillium grandiflorum — Trillium, Large-flowered
Trillium nivale — Trillium, Dwarf White
Trillium ovatum — Trillium, Western
Trillium recurvatum — Trillium, Prairie
Trillium sessile — Toadshade
Trillium undulatum — Trillium, Painted
Trillium viride var. luteum — Trillium, Yellow
Trimorphodon lambda — Snake, Lyre
Trimorphodon vandenburghi — Snake, Lyre
Tringa flavipes — Yellowlegs, Lesser
Tringa melanoleucus — Yellowlegs, Greater
Tringa solitaria — Sandpiper, Solitary
Trionys ferox — Turtle, Florida (Spiny) Soft-shell
Trionyx muticus — Turtle, Smooth Soft-shell
Trionyx spinifer — Turtle, Spiny Soft-shell
Triopha carpenteri — Nudibranch, Carpenter's
Triosteum aurantiacum — Horse Gentian, Yellow
Triosteum perfoliatum — Horse Gentian
Triphora trianthophora — Pogonia, Nodding
Tripoxylon clavatum — Wasp, Pipe-organ Mud-dauber
Tripoxylon politum — Wasp, Pipe-organ Mud-dauber
Tripsacum dactyloides — Gamagrass, Eastern
Trisetum flavescens — Oat-grass, Yellow
Triticum aestivum — Wheat
Tritonia crocata — Montbretia
Tritonia crocosmaefolia — Montbretia
Trivia sp. — Coffee Bean
Trogium pulsatorium — Louse, Book
Troglodytes aedon — Wren, House
Troglodytes brunneicollis — Wren, Brown-throated
Troglodytes troglodytes — Wren, Winter
Trogon collaris — Trogon, Collared or Bar-tailed
Trogon elegans — Trogon, Coppery-tailed
Trogon mexicanus — Trogon, Mexican or Mountain
Trogon violaceus — Trogon, Gartered or Violaceous
Trollius laxus — Globe-flower, American
Trombicula sp. — Chigger
Tropaea luna — Moth, Luna
Tropaeolum majus — Nasturtium
Tropidoclonion lineatum — Snake, Lined

Tryngites subruficollis — Sandpiper, Buff-breasted
Tuber aestivum — Truffle, Summer
Tubifera tenax — Fly, Drone
Tubifex tubifex — Worm, Tubifex
Tubulanus annulatus — Worm, Ribbon
Tubulanus polymorphus — Worm, Ribbon
Tubulanus punctatus — Worm, Ribbon
Tulipa sp. — Tulip Hybrids
Tunga penetrans — Flea, Chigoe
Tunna galea — Tun Shell, Giant
Turbo castaneus — Turban Shell, Chestnut
Turbonilla castanea — Turban Shell, Chestnut
Turdus grayi — Robin, Clay-colored
Turdus migratorius — Robin, American
Turdus pilaris — Fieldfare
Turdus rufopalliatus — Robin, Rufous-backed
Tursiops gilli — Dolphin, Bottle-nosed
Tursiops truncatus — Dolphin, Bottle-nosed
Tussilago farfara — Coltsfoot
Tsuga canadensis — Hemlock, Eastern or Canadian
Tsuga caroliniana — Hemlock, Eastern
Tsuga heterophylla — Hemlock, Western
Tsuga mertensiana — Hemlock, Mountain
Tympanuchus cupido — Prairie Chicken, Greater
Tympanuchus pallidicinctus — Prairie Chicken, Lesser
Typha angustifolia — Cat-tail, Narrow-leaved
Typha latifolia — Cat-tail, Broad-leaved
Typhlichthys subterraneus — Cavefish, Southern
Typhlomolge rathbuni — Salamander, Texas Blind
Typhlotriton spelaeus — Salamander, Grotto
Tyrannus crassirostris — Kingbird, Thick-billed
Tyrannus dominicensis — Kingbird, Gray
Tyrannus melancholicus — Kingbird, Tropical or Olive-
    backed
Tyrannus melancholicus couchi — Kingbird, Tropical or
    Olive-backed
Tyrannus tyrannus — Kingbird, Eastern
Tyrannus verticalis — Kingbird, Western or Arkansas
Tyrannus vociferans — Kingbird, Cassin's
Tyranniscus vilissimus — Tyrannulet, Paltry
Tyto alba — Owl, Barn

U

Uca sp. — Crab, Fiddler
Ulex europaeus — Gorse
Ulmus alata — Elm, Winged
Ulmus americana — Elm, American

Ulmus campestris — Elm, English
Ulmus carpinifolia — Elm, Smooth-leaved
Ulmus fulva — Elm, Red or Slippery
Ulmus glabra — Elm, Wych
Ulmus procera — Elm, English
Ulmus rubra — Elm, Red or Slippery
Ulmus thomasii — Elm, Rock
Ulva lactuca — Sea Lettuce
Uma inorata — Lizard, Fringe-toed
Uma notata — Lizard, Fringe-toed
Uma scoparia — Lizard, Fringe-toed
Umbellularia californica — Laurel, California
Unaspis euonymi — Scale, Euonymus
Uniola paniculata — Sea-oats
Upogebia pugettensis — Crayfish, Marine
Uria aalge — Murre, Common
Uria lomvia — Murre, Thick-billed
Urocyon cinereoargentatus — Fox, Gray
Urophycis chuss — Hake, Squirrel
Urophycis floridanus — Hake, Southern
Uropsila leucogaster — Wren, White-bellied
Urosalpinx cinerea — Drill, Oyster
Urosaurus ornatus — Lizard, Tree
Ursinia anethoides — Ursinia
Ursus americana — Bear, Black or Cinnamon
Ursus arctos — Bear, Alaskan Brown
Ursus arctos nelsoni — Bear, Mexican Grizzly
Ursus gyas — Bear, Alaskan Brown
Ursus horribilis — Bear, Grizzly
Ursus maritimus — Bear, Polar
Ursus middendorfii — Bear, Kodiak or Big Brown
Urtica dioica — Nettle, Stinging
Urtica gracilis — Nettle, Stinging
Urtica lyalli — Nettle, Stinging
Usnea barbata — Lichen, Beard
Usnea strigosa — Lichen, Beard
Ustilago sp. — Smut
Uta stansburiana — Lizard, Side-blotched
Utricularia gibba — Bladderwort, Humped
Utricularia inflata — Bladderwort, Swollen
Utricularia purpurea — Bladderwort, Purple
Utricularia vulgaris — Bladderwort, Common or Greater
Uvularia grandiflora — Bellwort, Large-flowered
Uvularia perfoliata — Bellwort, Perfoliate
Uvularia sessilifolia — Bellwort, Sessile-leaved

V

Vaccinium sp. — Blueberry

Vaccinium arboreum — Farkleberry
Vaccinium macrocarpon — Cranberry, American
Vaccinium membranaceum — Huckleberry, Blue or
  Mountain
Vaccinium ovatum — Huckleberry, Evergreen
Vaccinium oxycoccux — Cranberry, Bog or Small
Vaccinium parvifolium — Huckleberry, Red
Vaccinium scoparium — Grouseberry
Vaccinium stamineum — Deerberry
Vaccinium vitis-idaea — Cranberry, Mountain
Valeriana officinalis — Valerian, Common
Valeriana stichensis — Valerian, Mountain
Valerianella dentata — Corn-salad
Valerianella intermedia — Corn-salad
Valerianella locusta — Corn-salad
Valerianella olitoria — Corn-salad
Vallisneria americana — Celery, Wild
Vallota speciosa — Lily, Scarborough
Vancouveria hexandra — Inside-out Flower
Vancouveria chrysantha — Inside-out Flower
Vanessa cardui — Butterfly, Painted Lady
Vanessa atalanta — Butterfly, Red Admiral
Vanilla fragrens — Vanilla
Vanilla planifolia — Vanilla
Vasum caestus — Vase Shell
Vasum muricatum — Vase Shell
Velella lata — By-the-wind-sailor
Velella mutica — By-the-wind-sailor
Venidium fatuosum — Monarch-of-the-veldt
Veniliornis fumigatus — Woodpecker, Smoky-brown
Veratrum californicum — Hellebore, White False
Veratrum viride — Hellebore, False
Verbascum blattaria — Mullein, Moth
Verbascum lychnitis — Mullein, White
Verbascum nigrum — Mullein, White
Verbascum thapsiforme — Mullein, White
Verbascum thapsus — Mullein, Common
Verbena hastata — Vervain, Blue
Verbena hybrida — Verbena Hybrids
Verbena simplex — Vervain, Narrow-leaved
Verbena stricta — Vervain, Hoary
Verbesina encelioides — Crownbeard
Verbesina helianthoides — Crownbeard
Verbesina occidentalis — Crownbeard
Veretillum cynomorium — Sea Pen
Vermicularia fargoi — Worm-shell, Fargo's
Vermicularia knorri — Worm-shell, Florida
Vermivora bachmanii — Warbler, Bachman's
Vermivora celata — Warbler, Orange-crowned

Vermivora chrysoptera — Warbler, Golden-winged
Vermivora crissalis — Warbler, Colima
Vermivora lawrencei — Warbler, Lawrence's
Vermivora leucobronchialis — Warbler, Brewster's
Vermivora luciae — Warbler, Lucy's
Vermivora peregrina — Warbler, Tennessee
Vermivora pinus — Warbler, Blue-winged
Vermivora ruficapilla — Warbler, Nashville
Vermivora virginiae — Warbler, Virginia's
Vernonia altissima — Ironweed, Tall
Vernonia missurica — Ironweed, New York
Vernonia noveboracensis — Ironweed, New York
Veronica americana — Speedwell, American
Veronica chamaedrys — Speedwell, Bird's-eye or
  Germander
Veronica cusickii — Speedwell, Cusick's
Veronica latifolia — Speedwell, Bird's-eye or Germander
Veronica officinalis — Speedwell, Common
Veronica persica — Speedwell, Large Field
Veronica scutellata — Speedwell, Marsh
Veronica serpyllifolia — Speedwell, Thyme-leaved
Veronicastrum virginicum — Culver's-root
Verpa bohemica — Morel, Early
Vespa crabro — Hornet, European or Giant
Vespula diabolica — Yellow-jacket
Vespula maculata — Hornet, Bald-faced or White-faced
Vespula maculifrons — Yellow-jacket
Vespula pennsylvanica — Yellow-jacket
Vestiaria coccinea — Honeycreeper, Hawaiian
Viburnum acerifolium — Viburnum, Maple-leaved
Viburnum alnifolium — Hobblebush
Viburnum burkwoodii — Viburnum, Burkwood's
Viburnum cassinoides — Haw, Black
Viburnum davidii — Viburnum, Burkwood's
Viburnum dentatum — Arrowwood
Viburnum edule — Cranberry, High-bush
Viburnum lentago — Nannyberry
Viburnum opulus — Snowball
Viburnum pauciflorum — Cranberry, High-bush
Viburnum prunifolium — Haw, Black
Viburnum tinus — Laurustinus
Vicia americana — Vetch, American
Vicia cracca — Vetch, Tufted
Vicia gigantea — Vetch, Giant
Vicia hirsuta — Vetch, Hairy
Vicia sativa — Vetch, Common
Vicia villosa — Vetch, Woolly or Hairy
Victoria amazonica — Water-lily, Royal

Vigna luteola — Cowpea
Vigna sinensis — Cowpea
Vigna unguiculata — Cowpea
Vinca major — Periwinkle, Greater (plant)
Vinca minor — Periwinkle, Lesser or Myrtle (plant)
Vinca rosea — Periwinkle, Madagascar (plant)
Viola adunca — Violet, Hooked-spur or Western Long-
  spur
Viola affinis — Violet, Le Conte's
Viola blanda — Violet, Sweet White
Viola canadensis — Violet, Canada
Viola conspersa — Violet, Dog (American)
Viola cucullata — Violet, Marsh Blue
Viola emarginata — Violet, Triangle-leaved
Viola eriocarpa — Violet, Smooth Yellow
Viola fimbriatula — Violet, Northern Downy
Viola glabella — Violet, Brook or Stream
Viola hallii — Violet, Hall's
Viola hastata — Violet, Halberd-leaved Yellow
Viola hirta — Violet, Hairy
Viola incognita — Violet, Large-leaved White
Viola lanceolata — Violet, Lance-leaved
Viola nephrophylla — Violet, Northern Bog
Viola nuttallii — Violet, Nuttall's
Viola odorata — Violet, Sweet
Viola palmata — Violet, Wood
Viola palustris — Violet, Marsh
Viola papilionacea — Violet, Blue
Viola pedata — Violet, Bird's-foot
Viola pedatifida — Violet, Prairie
Viola peduculata — Violet, California Golden
Viola pensylvanica — Violet, Smooth Yellow
Viola primulifolia — Violet, Primrose-leaved
Viola purpurea — Violet, Mountain
Viola rafinesquii — Pansy, Field
Viola rostrata — Violet, Long-spurred
Viola rotundifolia — Violet, Early Yellow
Viola sagittata — Violet, Arrow-leaved
Viola selkirkii — Violet, Great-spurred
Viola sempervirens — Violet, Evergreen
Viola sororia — Violet, Woolly Blue
Viola villosa — Violet, Hairy
Vireo altilquus — Vireo, Black-whiskered
Vireo atricapilla — Vireo, Black-capped
Vireo bairdi — Vireo, Cozumel
Vireo bellii — Vireo, Bell's (Least)
Vireo flavifrons — Vireo, Yellow-throated
Vireo flavoviridis — Vireo, Yellow-green

Vireo gilvus — Vireo, Warbling
Vireo griseus — Vireo, White-eyed
Vireo huttoni — Vireo, Hutton's
Vireo hypochryseus — Vireo, Golden
Vireo magister — Vireo, Yucatan
Vireo olivaceus — Vireo, Red-eyed
Vireo pallens — Vireo, Mangrove
Vireo philadelphicus — Vireo, Philadelphia
Vireo solitarius — Vireo, Solitary
Vireo vincinior — Vireo, Gray
Vitex agnus castus — Chaste Tree
Vitis sp. — Grape
Vitis coignetiae — Glory Vine
Volatinia jacarina — Grassquit
Volvariella speciosa — Volvaria, Showy
Vomer setapinnis — Moonfish
Vulpes fulva — Fox, Red
Vulpes macrotis — Fox, Kit or Swift
Vulpes velox — Fox, Kit or Swift
Vulpes vulpes — Fox, Red

W

Waldsteinia fragarioides — Strawberry, Barren
Washingtonia filifera — Palm, Desert
Weigela sp. — Weigela Hybrids
Wilsonia canadensis — Warbler, Canada
Wilsonia citrina — Warbler, Hooded
Wilsonia pusilla — Warbler, Wilson's
Wisteria sp. — Wisteria Hybrids
Wisteria frutescens — Wisteria, Wild
Wisteria macrostachya — Wisteria, Wild
Wolffia sp. — Watermeal
Woodsia obtusa — Woodsia
Woodsia scopulina — Woodsia
Woodwardia virginica — Fern, Chain
Wyethia glabra — Mule-ears
Wyethia helanthiodes — Mule-ears
Wyethia mollis — Mule-ears

X

Xanthisma texanum — Star of Texas
Xanthium echinatum — Clotbur
Xanthium strumorium — Clotbur
Xanthocephala xanthocephala — Blackbird, Yellow-
  headed
Xanthoriza simplicissima — Yellowroot

Xantusia arizonae — Lizard, Arizona Night
Xantusia henshawi — Lizard, Granite Night
Xantusia riversiana — Lizard, Island Night
Xantusia vigilis — Lizard, Desert Night
Xema sabini — Gull, Sabine's
Xenops minutus — Xenops, Plain (Little)
Xenopsylla cheopsis — Flea, Rat
Xeranthemum annum — Immortelle
Xerophyllum asphodelioides — Turkey Beard
Xerophyllum tenax — Bear-grass
Xiphias gladius — Sword-fish
Xiphophorus helleri — Sword-tail
Xiphophorus maculatus — Platy
Xylaria sp. — Dead Man's Finger
Xylocopa virginica — Bee, Carpenter
Xyloryctes satyrus — Beetle, Rhinocerus
Xyris sp. — Yellow-eyed Grass

Y

Yoldia limatula — Yoldia, File
Yoldia myalis — Yoldia, Labrador or Oval
Yoldia thraciaeformis — Yoldia, Broad
Yucca baccata — Yucca, Fleshy-fruited
Yucca brevifolia — Joshua Tree
Yucca carnerosana — Yucca, Giant Dagger
Yucca elata — Soaptree
Yucca filamentosa — Yucca, Spanish Bayonet
Yucca glauca — Soapweed
Yucca mohavensis — Yucca, Mohave
Yucca schidigera — Yucca, Mohave
Yucca schottii — Yucca, Schott's
Yucca torreyi — Yucca, Spanish Bayonet
Yucca whipplei — Our Lord's Candle

Z

Zalopus californianus — Sea Lion, California
Zamia floridana — Coontie
Zaniolepis latipinnis — Combfish
Zannichellia palustris — Pondweed, Horned
Zantedeschia aethiopia — Calla Lily
Zantedeschia elliottiana — Calla Lily, Yellow
Zantedeschia palustris — Calla Lily
Zantedeschia rehmanii — Calla Lily, Pink
Zanthoxylum clava-herculis — Hercules'-club
Zapus hudsonius — Mouse, Jumping
Zapus princeps — Mouse, Jumping

Zarhynchus wagleri — Oropendola, Chestnut-headed
Zauschneria california — Zauschneria
Zauschneria septentrionalis — Zauschneria
Zea mays var. — Corn
Zebra scopas — Tang, Yellow
Zebra soma flavescens — Tang, Yellow
Zebrina pendula — Wandering Jew
Zenaida asiatica — Dove, White-winged
Zenaida auriculata — Dove, Eared
Zenaida aurita — Dove, Zenaida or Yucatan
Zenaida macroura — Dove, Mourning
Zenobia cassinefolia — Zenobia
Zenobia pulverulenta — Zenobia
Zenopsis ocellata — Dory, American John
Zephranthes atamasco — Lily, Atamasco
Zephyranthes candida — Lily, Storm
Zephyranthes grandiflora — Lily, Zephyr
Zephyranthes rosea — Lily, Zephyr
Zephyranthes treatiae — Lily, Zephyr
Zeus faber — Dory, John
Zingiber officinale — Ginger
Zinnia elegans — Zinnia Hybrids

Zinnia grandiflora — Zinnia, Desert
Zinnia pumila — Zinnia, Desert
Ziphius cavirostris — Whale, Beaked (Cuvier's)
Zirfaea crispata — Piddock, Great or Northern
Zirfaea gabbi — Piddock, Rough
Zirfaea pilsbryi — Piddock, Rough or Pilsbry's
Zizania aquatica — Rice, Wild
Zizia aptera — Alexanders, Golden
Zizia aurea — Alexanders, Golden
Zizia trifoliata — Alexanders, Golden
Zonotrichia albicollis — Sparrow, White-throated
Zonotrichia atricapilla — Sparrow, Golden-crowned
Zonotrichia leucophrys — Sparrow, White-crowned
Zonotrichia querula — Sparrow, Harris'
Zostera marina — Eelgrass
Zygadenus elegans — Camas, Mountain Death
Zygadenus fremontii — Lily, Star
Zygadenus glaucus — Camas, Poison
Zygadenus leimanthoides — Camas, Poison
Zygadenus paniculatus — Sand-corn
Zygadenus venenosus — Camas, Death
Zygocactus truncatus — Cactus, Christmas

Bibliography by Title

American Seashells. R. Tucker Abbott. Photos by
Frederick M. Bayer. Princeton, N. J., D. Van
Nostrand, 1960 (c1954). (AAS)

Amphibians and Reptiles of Kentucky. Roger W. Barbour. (Kentucky Nature Studies : 2.) Lexington,
University Press of Kentucky, 1971. (BAR)

Animal Atlas of the World. E. L. Jordan. Maplewood,
N. J., Hammond, 1969. (JAW)

Animals of the Arctic: The Ecology of the Far North.
Bernard Stonehouse. New York, Holt, Rinehart
and Winston, 1971. (SAA)

Animals of the Seashore. Muriel Lewin Guberlet. 3d
ed., rev. Portland, Ore., Binfords and Mort, 1962.
(GAS)

Animals without Backbones. Ralph Buchsbaum. Rev.
ed. University of Chicago Press, 1948. (BAW)

Annuals. James Underwood Crockett. (Time-Life Encyclopedia of Gardening. New York, Time-Life
Books, 1971. (EGA)

The Audubon Illustrated Handbook of American Birds.
Edgar M. Reilly, Jr. Drawings by Albert Earl Gilbert. New York, McGraw-Hill, 1968. (AAB)

Audubon Nature Encyclopedia. 12 vols. Philadelphia,
Curtis Publishing, 1964. (ANE)

Between Pacific Tides. Edward F. Ricketts and Jack
Calvin. 3d ed., rev. Stanford, Calif., Stanford
University Press, 1962. (RCT)

The Birds. Roger Tory Peterson and editors of Life.
(Life Nature Library.) New York, Time, Inc.,
1963. (LBI)

Birds: A Guide to the Most Familiar American Birds.
Herbert S. Zim and Ira N. Gabrielson. (Golden
Nature Guide Series.) New York, Golden Press,
1956. (GBI)

Birds of America. T. Gilbert Pearson, editor-in-chief.
3 vols in 1. Garden City, N. Y., Garden City
Books, 1936. (PBA)

The Birds of Canada. W. Earl Godfrey. Ottawa, Ontario, National Museum of Canada (Bulletin 203),
1966. (GBC)

Birds of Canada. P. A. Taverner. Ottawa, Ontario, National Museum of Canada (Bulletin 72), 1934.
(TBC)

Birds of Colorado. Alfred M. Bailey and Robert J. Niedrach. 2 vols. Denver Museum of Natural History,
1965. (BBC)

Birds of Europe. Bertel Bruun. Paintings by Arthur
Singer. New York, Golden Press, 1971. (BBE)

Birds of Hawaii. George C. Munro. Rutland, Vt.,
Charles E. Tuttle, 1960. (MBH)

Birds of North America. Austin L. Rand. (Animal Life
of North America series.) New York, Doubleday,
n.d. (RBA)

Birds of North America. Chandler S. Robbins, Bertel
Bruun and Herbert S. Zim. (Golden Field Guide
series.) New York, Golden Press, 1966. (RBB)

Birds of the West Indies. James Bond. 2d ed. Boston,
Houghton Mifflin, 1971. (BWI)

Birds of the World. Oliver L. Austin, Jr. New York,
Golden Press, 1961. (ABW)

Birds of Trinidad and Tobago. G. A. C. Herklots. London, Collins, 1961. (HBT)

Birds of Western North America. Laurence C. Binford.

Paintings by Kenneth L. Carlson. New York, Macmillan, 1974. (BBW)

The Book of Birds. Gilbert Grosvenor and Alexander Wetmore, editors. 2 vols. Washington, D.C., The National Geographic Society, 1937. (NGB)

Bulbs. James Underwood Crockett. (Time-Life Encyclopedia of Gardening.) New York, Time-Life Books, 1971. (EGB)

Cacti of the Southwest (Texas, New Mexico, Oklahoma, Arkansas and Louisiana). Del Weniger. Austin, University of Texas Press, n.d. (WCS)

Collins Guide to Mushrooms and Toadstools. Morten Lange and F. Bayard Hora. London, Collins, 1963. (LHM)

Color Dictionary of Flowers and Plants for Home and Garden. Roy Hay and Patrick M. Synge. New York, Crown Publishers, 1969. (DFP)

Common Insects of North America. Lester A. Swan and Charles S. Papp. New York, Harper and Row, 1972. (SCI)

Complete Field Guide to American Wildlife (east, central and north). Henry Hill Collins, Jr. New York, Harper, 1959. (CFG)

Complete Guide to Bulbs. Patrick M. Synge. New York, E. P. Dutton, 1961. (SGB)

The Complete Guide to Garden Flowers. Herbert Askwith, editor. New York, A. S. Barnes, 1961. (AGF)

The Desert. A. Starker Leopold and editors of Life. (Life Nature Library.) New York, Time, Inc., 1961. (LDE)

Dictionary of Birds in Color. Bruce Campbell. New York, Viking Press, 1974. (CDB)

The Ducks, Geese and Swans of North America. Francis H. Kortright. Washington, D. C., American Wildlife Institute, 1943. (KWF)

Edible and Poisonous Mushrooms of Canada. J. Walton Groves. Ottawa, Ontario, Research Branch, Canada Department of Agriculture, 1962. (GMC)

Evergreens. James Underwood Crockett. (Time-Life Encyclopedia of Gardening.) New York, Time-Life Books, 1971. (EGE)

Exotic Plants. Julia F. Morton. Illustrated by Richard E. Younger. (Golden Nature Guide series.) New York, Golden Press, 1971. (MEP)

Families of Birds. Oliver L. Austin, Jr. (Golden Science Guide series.) New York, Golden Press, 1971. (GFB)

Fascinating World of Animals. Pleasantville, N. Y., Reader's Digest Association, 1971. (FWA)

Field Guide to Mexican Birds (and Adjacent Central America). Roger Tory Peterson and Edward L. Chalif. Boston, Houghton Mifflin, 1973. (PMB)

Field Guide to Reptiles and Amphibians of the Eastern United States and Canada. Roger Conant. (Peterson Field Guide series.) Boston, Houghton Mifflin, 1958. (CRA)

Field Guide to Shells of the Pacific Coast and Hawaii. Percy A. Morris. 2d ed. (Peterson Field Guide series.) Boston, Houghton Mifflin, 1966. (MGS)

Field Guide to the Birds (east of the Rockies). Roger Tory Peterson. 2d ed. Boston, Houghton Mifflin, 1947. (PEB)

Field Guide to the Birds of Mexico and Central America. L. Irby Davis. Illustrated by F. P. Bennett, Jr. Austin, University of Texas Press, 1972. (DBM)

A Field Guide to the Butterflies of North America, East of the Great Plains. Alexander B. Klots. (Peterson Field Guide series.) Boston, Houghton Mifflin, 1951. (KGB)

A Field Guide to the Ferns and Their Related Families. Boughton Cobb. (Peterson Field Guide series.) Boston, Houghton Mifflin, 1963. (CGF)

A Field Guide to the Insects of America north of Mexico. Donald J. Borror and Richard E. White. (Peterson Field Guide series.) Boston, Houghton Mifflin, 1970. (BIA)

Field Guide to the Mammals. William Henry Burt. Illustrated by Richard Philip Grossenheider. 2d ed., rev. (Peterson Field Guide series.) Boston, Houghton Mifflin, 1964. (BGM)

Field Guide to the Trees of Britain and Northern Europe. Alan Mitchell. Boston, Houghton Mifflin, 1974. (MTB)

Field Guide to Western Birds. Roger Tory Peterson. 2d ed. Boston, Houghton Mifflin, 1961. (PWB)

Field Guide to Western Reptiles and Amphibians. Robert C. Stebbins. (Peterson Field Guide series.) Boston, Houghton Mifflin, 1966. (SRA)

Field Guide to Wildflowers (northeastern and North-central North America). Roger Tory Peterson and Margaret McKenny. (Peterson Field Guide series.) Boston, Houghton Mifflin, 1968. (PMF)

Fieldbook of Natural History. E. Laurence Palmer and H. Seymour Fowler. 2d ed. New York, McGraw-Hill, 1975. (PFF)

Finding the Birds in Western Mexico. Peter Alden. Tucson, University of Arizona Press, 1969. (AMB)

The Fishes. F. D. Ommanney and editors of Life. (Life Nature Library.) New York, Time, Inc., 1964. (LFI)

Fishes: A Guide to Familiar American Species. Herbert S. Zim and Hurst H. Shoemaker. (Golden Nature Guide series.) New York, Golden Press, 1956. (GGF)

Fishes of the World. Allan Cooper. (Grosset All-Color Guide.) New York, Grosset and Dunlap, 1971. (CFW)

Fishes of the World: An Illustrated Dictionary. Alwyne Wheeler. New York, Macmillan, 1975. (WFW)

Flowering House Plants. James Underwood Crockett. (Time-Life Encyclopedia of Gardening.) New York, Time-Life Books, 1971. (FHP)

Flowers of the World. Frances Perry. New York, Crown Publishers. 1972. (PFW)

Flowers of the World (in Full Color). Robert S. Lemmon and Charles L. Sherman. Garden City, N.Y., Hanover House, 1958. (LFW)

The Forest. Peter Farb and editors of Life. (Life Nature Library.) New York, Time, Inc., 1961. (LFO)

Forest Trees of the Pacific Slope. George B. Sudworth. Washington, D.C., Government Printing Office, 1908. (SFT)

Gamebirds: A Guide to North American Species and Their Habits. Alexander Sprunt IV and Herbert S. Zim. (Golden Nature Guide series.) New York, Golden Press, 1961. (GGB)

Garden Flowers in Color. Daniel J. Foley. New York, Macmillan, 1959 (c1943). (FGF)

The Gardener's Bug Book. Cynthia Westcott. 3d ed. Garden City, N. Y., Doubleday, 1964. (GBB)

The Glory of the Tree. B. K. Boom and H. Kleijn. Garden City, N. Y., Doubleday, 1966. (BKT)

The Great Book of Birds. John Gooders. New York, Dial Press, 1975. (GPB)

Grzimek's Animal Life Encyclopedia. Bernhard Grzimek, editor-in-chief. 13 vols. New York, Van Nostrand Reinhold, 1974. (ALE)

Guide to Garden Flowers. Norman Taylor. Boston, Houghton Mifflin, 1958. (TGF)

Guide to Garden Shrubs and Trees. Norman Taylor. Boston, Houghton Mifflin, 1965. (TGS)

Guide to the Wildflowers and Ferns of Kentucky. Mary E. Wharton and Roger W. Barbour. (Kentucky Nature Studies: 1.) Lexington, University Press of Kentucky, 1971. (FFK)

Handbook of Frogs and Toads of the United States and Canada. Albert Hazen Wright and Anna Allen Wright. 3d ed. Ithaca, N. Y., Comstock Publishing., 1949. (WFA)

Handbook of Snakes. Albert Hazen Wright and Anna Allen Wright. 2 vols. Ithaca, N. Y., Comstock Publishing, 1957. (WWS)

Hawaiian Birdlife. Andrew J. Berger. Honolulu, University Press of Hawaii, 1972. (BHB)

An Illustrated Flora of the Northern United States, Canada and the British Possessions. Nathaniel Lord Britton and Addison Brown. 2d ed. 3 vols. New York Botanical Garden, 1936. (BBF)

Illustrated Flora of the Pacific States: Washington, Oregon and California. Leroy Abrams and Roxana Stinchfield Ferris. 4 vols. Stanford, Calif., Stanford University Press, 1960. (AFP)

The Insect Guide. Ralph B. Swain. Garden City, N.Y., Doubleday, 1948. (SIG)

Insect Pests: A Guide to More Than 350 Pests of Home, Garden, Field and Forest. George S. Fichter. (Golden Nature Guide series.) New York, Golden Press, 1966. (GIP)

The Insects. Peter Farb and editors of Life. (Life Nature Library.) New York, Time, Inc., 1962. (LIN)

Insects: A Guide to Familiar American Insects. Herbert S. Zim and Clarence Cottam. (Golden Nature Guide series.) New York, Golden Press, 1951. (GGI)

Insects of North America. Alexander B. Klots and Elsie B. Klots. (Animal Life of North America series.) New York, Doubleday, n.d. (KIA)

International Wildlife Encyclopedia. Maurice Burton and Robert Burton, editors. 20 vols. New York, Marshall Cavendish, 1969. (IWE)

The Land and Wildlife of North America. Peter Farb and editors of Life. (Life Nature Library.) New York, Time, Inc., 1964. (LNA)

Larousse Encyclopedia of Animal Life. New York, McGraw-Hill, 1967. (LEA)

The Last Paradises: On the Track of Rare Animals. Eugen Schuhmacher. Garden City, N. Y., Doubleday, 1967. (SLP)

Last Survivors. Noel Simon and Paul Geroudet. New York, World Publishing, 1970. (SLS)

Living Amphibians of the World. Doris M. Cochran. (World of Nature series.) Garden City, N.Y., Doubleday, 1961. (CAW)

Living Birds of the World. E. Thomas Gilliard. Garden City, N. Y., Doubleday, 1958. (LBW)

Living Fishes of the World. Earl S. Herald. Garden City, N. Y., Doubleday, 1961. (HFW)

Living Insects of the World. Alexander B. Klots and Elsie B. Klots. Garden City, N.Y., 1965(?). (KIW)

Living Mammals of the World. Ivan T. Sanderson. (World of Nature series.) Garden City, N. Y., Doubleday, 1961. (SMW)

Living Reptiles of the World. Karl P. Schmidt and Robert F. Inger. Garden City, N.Y., Doubleday, 1957. (SIR)

The Lower Animals: Living Invertebrates of the World. Ralph Buchsbaum and Lorus J. Milne, with Mildred Buchsbaum and Margery Milne. (World of Nature series.) Garden City, N. Y., Doubleday, 1962. (BLA)

The Mammal Guide: Mammals of North America north of Mexico. Ralph S. Palmer, Garden City, N. Y., Doubleday, 1954. (PMG)

The Mammals. Richard Carrington and editors of Life. (Life Nature Library.) New York, Time, Inc., 1963. (LMA)

Mammals: A Guide to Familiar American Species. Herbert S. Zim and Donald F. Hoffmeister. (Golden Nature Guide series.) New York, Golden Press, 1955. (GGM)

Mammals of Canada. A. W. F. Banfield. Toronto, Ontario, University of Toronto Press, 1974. (BMC)

Mammals of the World. Ernest P. Walker et al. 2 vols. Baltimore, Johns Hopkins Press, 1964. (WMW)

Manual of the Grasses of the United States. A. S. Hitchcock. 2d ed. Washington, D. C., Government Printing Office, 1950. (HMG)

The Mountains. Lorus J. Milne and Margery Milne and editors of Life. (Life Nature Library.) New York, Time, Inc., 1962. (LMT)

The Mushroom Hunter's Field Guide. Alexander H. Smith. Rev. ed. Ann Arbor, University of Michigan Press, 1963. (SMG)

Mushrooms and Other Fungi. H. Kleijn. Garden City, N. Y., Doubleday, 1962. (KMF)

Native Orchids of North America (north of Mexico). Donovan Stewart Correll. Waltham, Mass., Chronica Botanica, 1950. (COA)

Natural History of Europe. Harry Garms. London, Paul Hamlyn, 1967. (NHE)

The New Field Book of Reptiles and Amphibians. Doris M. Cochran and Coleman J. Goin. New York, G. P. Putnam's Sons, 1970. (CGR)

Non-Flowering Plants. Floyd S. Shuttleworth and Herbert S. Zim. (Golden Nature Guide series.) New York, Golden Press, 1967. (NFP)

Ocean Life. Norman Marshall and Olga Marshall. (Macmillan Color series.) New York, Macmillan, 1971. (MOL)

Our Magnificent Wildlife: How to Enjoy and Preserve It. Pleasantville, N. Y., Reader's Digest Association, 1975. (OMW)

Owls of the World. John A. Burton, editor. New York, E. P. Dutton, 1973. (BOW)

Oxford Book of Flowerless Plants. Frank H. Brightman. Illustrated by B. E. Nicholson. Oxford (England) University Press, 1966. (ONP)

Oxford Book of Food Plants. S. G. Harrison, G. B. Masefield, Michael Wallis. Illustrated by B. E. Nicholson. Oxford (England) University Press, 1969. (OFP)

Oxford Book of Garden Flowers. E. B. Anderson et al. Illustrated by B. E. Nicholson. Oxford (England) University Press, 1963. (OGF)

Oxford Book of Insects. John Burton et al. Illustrated by Joyce Bee, Derek Whiteley and Peter Parks. Oxford (England) University Press, 1968. (OBI)

Oxford Book of Invertebrates. David Nichols, with John A. L. Cooke. Illustrated by Derek Whiteley. Oxford (England) University Press, 1971. (OIB)

Oxford Book of Trees. A. R. Clapham. Illustrated by B. E. Nicholson. London, Oxford University Press, 1975. (OBT)

Oxford Book of Vertebrates. Marion Nixon. Illustrated by Derek Whiteley. Oxford (England) University Press, 1972. (OBV)

Oxford Book of Wild Flowers. S. Ary and M. Gregory. Illustrated by B. E. Nicholson. Oxford (England) University Press, 1960. (OWF)

Pacific Fishes of Canada. J. L. Hart. Ottawa, Ontario, Fisheries Research Board of Canada (Bulletin 180), 1973. (HPF)

Parade of the Animal Kingdom. Robert Hegner, with Jane Z. Hegner. New York, Macmillan, 1937. (PAK)

Pasture and Range Plants. Bartlesville, Okla., Phillips Petroleum Co., 1963. (PRP)

Perennials. James Underwood Crockett. (Time-Life Encyclopedia of Gardening.) New York, Time-Life Books, 1972. (EGP)

Pheasants of the World. Jean Delacour. Illustrated by

J. C. Harrison. London, Country Life, 1965
(C1951, 1957). (DPW)

Pictorial Encyclopedia of Insects. V. J. Stanek. London,
Paul Hamlyn, 1969. (PEI)

The Plants. Frits W. Went and editors of Life. (Life Nature Library.) New York, Time, Inc.,1963. (LPL)

Plants of the World. H. C. D. deWit. 3 vols. New York,
E. P. Dutton, 1966-1969. (DEW)

**Pocket Encyclopedia of Cacti and Other Succulents in
Color.** Edgar Lamb and Brian Lamb. New York,
Macmillan, 1970. (LCS)

**Pond Life: A Guide to Common Plants and Animals of
North American Ponds and Lakes.** George K.Reid.
(Golden Nature Guide series.) New York, Golden
Press, 1967. (GPL)

Rand McNally Atlas of World Wildlife. Foreword by
Sir Julian Huxley. New York, Rand McNally,
1973. (AWW)

The Reptile World. Clifford H. Pope. New York, Alfred A. Knopf, 1956. (PRW)

The Reptiles. Archie Carr and editors of Life. (Life Nature Library.) New York, Time,Inc.,1963. (LRE)

**Reptiles and Amphibians: A Guide to Familiar Ameri-
can Species.** Herbert S. Zim and Hobart M. Smith.
(Golden Nature Guide series.) New York, Golden
Press, 1956. (GRA)

Reptiles of the World. Raymond L. Ditmars. Rev. ed.
New York, Macmillan, 1941(c1933). (DRW)

The Savory Wild Mushroom. Margaret McKenny; revised and enlarged by Daniel E. Stuntz. Seattle,
University of Washington Press, 1971. (MSM)

The Sea. Leonard Engel and editors of Life. (Life Nature Library.) New York, Time,Inc.,1961. (LSE)

Sea Shells of the World. R. Tucker Abbott. (Golden Nature Guide series.) New York, Golden Press, 1962.
(GSS)

Seashells of North America. R. Tucker Abbott. (Gold-
en Field Guide series.) New York, Golden Press,
1968. (ASN)

Seashore Animals of the Pacific Coast. Myrtle Elizabeth
Johnson and Harry James Snook. New York,
Macmillan, 1935. (JSS)

**Seashore Life of Puget Sound, the Strait of Georgia and
the San Juan Archipelago.** Eugene N. Kozloff. Seattle, University of Washington Press,1973. (KSL)

**Seashores: A Guide to Animals and Plants along the
Beaches.** Herbert S. Zim and Lester Ingle. (Gold-
en Nature Guide series.) New York, Golden Press,
1955. (GGS)

Seaweeds at Ebb Tide. Muriel Lewin Guberlet. Illustrated by Elizabeth L. Curtis. Seattle, University
of Washington Press, 1956. (GUS)

Secrets of the Seas. Pleasantville, N. Y., Reader's Digest Association, 1972. (SOS)

Shrubs in Colour. A. G. L. Hellyer. Garden City, N. Y.,
Doubleday, 1966. (HSC)

Song and Garden Birds of North America. Washington,
D. C., The National Geographic Society, 1964.
(NGS)

The Spider Book. John Henry Comstock. Garden City,
N. Y., Doubleday, Page, 1920. (CSB)

Spiders and Their Kin. Herbert W. Levi and Lorna R.
Levi. (Golden Nature Guide series.) New York,
Golden Press, 1968. (GSP)

Trees. James Underwood Crockett. (Time-Life Encyclopedia of Gardening.) New York, Time-Life Books,
1972. (EGT)

Trees: A Guide to Familiar American Trees. Herbert S.
Zim and Alexander C. Martin. (Golden Nature
Guide series.) New York,Golden Press,1956. (GGT)

Trees and Shrubs of Kentucky and Surrounding Areas.
Mary E. Wharton and Roger W. Barbour. Lexington, University Press of Kentucky, 1973. (TSK)

Trees of North America. C. Frank Brockman. (Golden Field Guide series.) New York, Golden Press, 1968. (BTN)

Vanishing Species. Introduction by Romain Gary. New York, Time-Life Books, 1974. (LVS)

Vanishing Wild Animals of the World. Richard Fitter. Paintings by John Leigh-Pemberton. London, Midland Bank, 1968. (VWA)

Vascular Plants of the Pacific Northwest. C. Leo Hitchcock et al. 5 vols. Seattle, University of Washington Press, 1969. (VPN)

Water, Prey, and Game Birds of North America. Washington, D.C., The National Geographic Society, 1965. (NGW)

What Flower is That? Stirling Macoboy. New York, Crown Publishers, 1971. (MWF)

Wild Animals of North America. Washington, D. C., The National Geographic Society, 1960. (NGA)

Wild Flower Book Clarence J. Hylander. Illustrated by Edith Farrington Johnston. New York, Macmillan, 1954. (HYF)

Wild Flowers. Homer D. House. New York, Macmillan, 1961. (HWF)

Wild Flowers of America. H. W. Rickett. New York, Crown Publishers, 1953. (RWA)

Wild Flowers of British Columbia. Lewis J. Clark. Sidney, B. C., Grays Publishing, 1973. (CWF)

Wild Flowers of North Carolina. William S. Justice and C. Ritchie Bell. Chapel Hill, University of North Carolina Press, 1968. (FNC)

Wild Flowers of the Pacific Coast. Leslie L. Haskin. 2d ed. Portland, Ore., Binfords and Mort, 1967.(HFP)

Wild Flowers of the United States. Harold William Rickett. 6 vols in 14 parts. New York, McGraw-Hill, 1966. (RUS)

Wild Flowers of the World. Barbara Everard and Brian D. Morley. New York, G. P. Putnam's Sons, 1970. (EWF)

Wildflowers of North America (in Full Color). Robert S. Lemmon and Charles C. Johnson. Garden City, N. Y., Hanover House, 1961. (LWF)

Wildflowers of Western America. Robert T. Orr and Margaret C. Orr. New York, Alfred A. Knopf, 1974. (OOW)

Wildlife Crisis. H.R.H. Prince Philip, Duke of Edinburgh, and James Fisher. New York, Cowles, 1970. (PWC)

Wildlife in Danger. James Fisher, Noel Simon, Jack Vincent. New York, Viking Press, 1969. (WID)

Wondrous World of Fishes. Washington, D. C., The National Geographic Society, 1965. (NGF)

World Atlas of Birds. London, Mitchell Beazley Publishers, 1974. (WAB)

World Encyclopedia of Animals. Maurice Burton, editor. New York, World Publishing,1972. (WEA)

The World in Your Garden. Wendell H. Camp, Victor R. Boswell and John R. Magness. Illustrated by Else Bostelmann. Washington, D. C., The National Geographic Society, 1957. (WYG)

The World of Amphibians and Reptiles. Robert Mertens. New York, McGraw-Hill, 1960. (MAR)

The World of Flowers. Herbert Reisigl, editor. New York, Viking Press, 1964. (RWF)

The World of Reptiles and Amphibians. Maurice Burton. New York, Crown Publishers, 1973. (BRW)